HISTORY OF ANTHROPOLOGICAL THOUGHT

ABOUT THE AUTHORS

DR. V.S. UPADHYAY (*b.* 20 January, 1942) is presently University Professor in the Post-graduate Department of Anthropology, Ranchi University, Ranchi, Bihar. He is serving this institution for the past 30 years. He has been an author of 30 research papers which have been published in the journal of national and international repute. He has been an author and co-author of five books, namely, *Kharia: Then and Now, Development of Researchers in Anthropology in India, Changing Dietary Pattern and Habits, Socio-cultural Implications of Leprosy* and *Bharat Men Janjatiya Sanskriti* (in Hindi). He has wide field experience in the field of anthropology, ranging from Andaman and Nicobar Islands to Himalayan region. A widely travelled man, he has attended several international conferences in India and abroad. He is a member of IUAES, and Chairman of S.E. Asian Regional Centre of Urgent Anthropological Research. He is an authority on anthropology of development. His recent work in the field of Medical Anthropology, specially on Leprosy, is first of its kind in India. He has guided more than a dozen of Ph.D. Scholars and directed 5 large scale research projects, mostly funded by the Government of India.

DR. GAYA PANDEY (*b.* 3rd February, 1954) is presently a Research Associate in Centre of Advanced Study, Department of Anthropology, Ranchi University, Ranchi, Bihar. He passed his Master of Science examination in anthropology in April 1979. He was awarded Doctoral Research fellowship of U.G.C. at A.N. Sinha Institute of Social Studies, Patna. As Doctoral fellow, he wrote doctoral thesis on Bonded Labour of Palamau, which was awarded by the University of Ranchi in December 1983. During 1983-84, he got opportunity to supervise a large scale research project as Research Officer in the same institution. From February 1985, he is serving as Research Associate. During his a decade long career as anthropologist, he has contributed half dozen paper in the journals and edited books of national repute. He is also co-author of the book, *Sun-worship in India*, which has been released. Bonded Labour, exploitation and oppression of Scheduled Castes and Scheduled Tribes, Sun worship and folkloric traditions of Maghi Cultural areas are his special field of research interest.

HISTORY OF ANTHROPOLOGICAL THOUGHT

V.S. UPADHYAY
GAYA PANDEY

CONCEPT PUBLISHING COMPANY, NEW DELHI 110059

ISBN: 81-7022-492-6 (HB)
ISBN: 81-7022-677-5 (PB)

First Published 1993
Reprinted 1997, 2016

Published and Printed by
Ashok Kumar Mittal
Concept Publishing Company
A/15-16, Commercial Block, Mohan Garden
New Delhi-110059 (INDIA)
Phones : 25351460, 25351794
Fax : 091-11-25357109
Email : publishing@conceptpub.com

PREFACE

Book writing is a constant phenomenon since the birth of civilization. However, the purpose might differ from one to another contribution. The field of Anthropology, though quite developed in the western countries, is still in its adolescence in India. It is unfortunate that the society and the administration have not realised its importance in academic as well as applied field. This is clear from the fact that hardly 32 universities (out of 170) have independent departments of Anthropology in India.

This has also hindered the growth of book writing in various fields of Anthropology, and the anthropological theory is the worst sufferer. There are books (see bibliography), but the matter is either dealt in very detail or in a form not conducive to Indian process of thinking and expression, as most of them are written by foreigners.

The purpose of writing the book is purely contextual. The authors do not claim to have contributed something new which cannot be found in others writings. Sometimes others expressions have also been followed as it is, word by word *in toto*. All this have been done with the sole aim to bring maximum materials under one cover for the benefits of the students of Anthropology. The simple language of the book may help them to understand the contributions of the Great Masters of Anthropology. One cannot claim to be perfect in expression, therefore the readers might excuse us for the mistakes, which might still be there in spite of our best efforts.

Makar Sankranti
14th January, 1993

V.S. UPADHYAY
GAYA PANDEY
Department of Anthropology
Ranchi University
Ranchi-834008 India

CONTENTS

INTRODUCTION

'Anthropological Thought' deals with theories developed and contributions made by different anthropologists. Literature available suggests that the man, his culture and society, have been subject of study right from the time of Herodotus, a Greek traveller and philosopher (c. 484 B.C.-425 B.C.). It has been calculated that his travel covered some seventeen hundred miles east to west, and sixteen hundred miles from north to south. In his various writings, he wrote about more than fifty different cultural groups. He made observations about the spoken languages, material culture, marriage and divorce rules, laws, government, war pattern and religion. He was the first to report couvade, the custom in which father goes to bed, as if for child bearing, when his wife is having a baby. His descriptions of marriage pattern cover the whole Tylorian range, from promiscuity to patrilineal monogamy. However, there is general consensus among the scholars that the establishment of evolutionary theory in the field of cultural anthropology marked the theoretical beginning of the subject of anthropology. T.K. Peniman, in his book *Hundred Years of Anthropology* (1935), has treated the origin of the discipline of anthropology as only hundred years old. Malinowski, in his book *Scientific Theory of Culture* (1944), has opined that the theoretical beginning and teaching of anthropology appeared too late in comparison to other social sciences. The subject was taught under different social sciences, because in the beginning, it was difficult to decide the subject-matter of anthropology. But now anthropology has emerged as a full-fledged discipline of teaching and research.

Anthropological thinkers, whose theories and contributions are discussed under anthropological thought, can be grouped together under the following schools for the purpose of analysis:

1. Evolutionary School
2. Diffusional School
3. Functional School
4. Structural School
5. Culture and Personality School
6. Civilizational School
7. Neo-anthropological School.

Evolutionary School, on the basis of old and new doctrines put forth by its followers, can be divided into two: Classical Evolutionary School and Neo-evoluntionary School. Classical evolutionary school again can be divided, on the basis of nationality, into three sub-schools: British classical evolutionary school, German classical evolutionary school and American classical evolutionary school. Maine, McLennan, Tylor and Frazer are the followers of British classical evolutionary school. Bachofen and Bastian are supporters of German or continental classical evolutionary school. L.H. Morgan is the only pioneer of American classical evolutionary school.

These classical evolutionists, from fifties onward of 19th century, began to publish their findings in book form, in which they attempted to show evolutionary stages of culture and cultural institutions. They were convinced that culture and cultural institutions had undergone progressive and development-oriented changes, but always in a sequence from simple to complex, homogeneity to heterogeneity, and uncertainty to certainty. They were more interested in similarities than differences. They explained similarities in culture and cultural institutions of the world in terms of psychic unity and parallel evolution or cultural parallelism. They evolved historical method to establish stages of development in a sequence. They selected tribal societies as representing the early condition of mankind, and among them, compared their early stages with developed ones. They took the concept of survival as the major tool of evolutionary reconstruction. With these basic assumptions, they postulated the theory of evolutionism in the field of cultural anthropology.

When evolutionary theory emerged in anthropology, many schools came into being, which began to claim themselves as anti-evolutionary schemes. The major critics were diffusionists. They were not convinced by progress, concept of psychic unity, and parallel development of culture or cultural parallelism. They were of view that culture not only developed, but it also degenerated. Again, they were convinced that man was basically uninventive, and important inventions were made only once at a particular place from where it was diffused, migrated, borrowed, and imitated, to the other parts of the world. Thus, according to the assumption of diffusionists, cultural development and growth were due to diffusion and were historically related. School of diffusion can be divided into three sub-schools, on the basis of nationality of the followers and some minor variations in their ideas. They are: British School of Diffusion, German School of Diffusion and American School of Diffusion. Smith, W.J. Perry and Rivers are the followers of British school of diffusion. Ratzel, Graebner and Father Schmidt are the pioneers of German diffusional school, whereas FranzBoas; Clark Wissler, Kroeber etc. are the supporters of American diffusional school. British diffusionists are known as Egytologists or British School of diffusion is known as Pan-Egyptian School. Because according to them, cultural growth in the world took place from Egypt. It was the only cultural cradle from where culture diffused in other parts of the universe. German School of diffusion is known as culture historic school or Kulture Kreis (district) School. According to them, cultural growth was product of migration taken place in course of history. They were of view that culture had diffused in terms of districts or circles, formed in different periods. In a district or circle, there were many layers of culture, developed in course of time. They were again of view that in a circle or district, there were primary and secondary cultural diffusions.

American diffusionists were interested in the study of a particular area in historical perspective with a view to understand the diffusion of culture from one area to another area, or from a cultural centre to entire culture area. They are known as historical particularist, cultural relativist and culture areaist. These three schools of diffusion were historically-oriented. They possessed some similar ideas of diffusion of culture. However, there were also some differences among these schools, about which a detail description is available in second chapter.

Both schools of evolution and diffusion were historically-oriented. They explained cultural growth which had taken place in past, but could not explain why and how development took place. Malinowski, a British anthropologist, criticised both evolutionists and diffusionists. According to him, no cultural traits were functionless. They consisted of a body of institutions related to the current adaptative needs of man. It is the study of these institutions — economic, political, educational, law, religious, family organisation and individual relationship to them, that must take precedence over historical reconstruction of evolutionists and diffusionists.

Malinowski developed the theory of functionalism to explain social phenomenon. He was more interested in the study of present and now, than past and then. His functional view of culture lays down the principle that in every type of civilization, every customs, material object, idea and belief fulfills some vital function. Each has some task to accomplish and represents an indispensable part within the working whole. Culture exists to satisfy human needs. In other words, the function of culture as a whole, or different cultural traits within an institution, is satisfaction of human needs — primary, instrumental and integrative. By primary needs, he means biological needs such as sex and feeding. By secondary or instrumental needs, he means those institutions, such as economic, legal and educational, which help to achieve primary needs. By integrative or tertiary needs, he means those that help the society to cohere, such as religion, magic and play.

Radcliffe-Brown, another British anthropologist and contemporary of Malinowski, developed the concept of social structure to explain forms. According to him, social structure deals with the study of status and role of person within an institution. In other words, it deals with network of social relations within an institutional framework. As Radcliffe-Brown added the concept of function to structure, he is also known as structural-functionalist. To him, function means the contribution, which is a partial activity to the total activity, of which it is part. His concept of function was different from Malinowski's concept of function, according to which culture operates to satisfy universally applicable needs of man. Radcliffe-Brown's concept of function is based on analogy with an organism. When he talks of social morphology, he is referring to social structure. Social physiology means how social structure functions. Social evolution means how social structure changes. Social condition refers to the health of society. However, Radcliffe-Brown, like Malinowski, believes in synchronic as well as diachronic studies of society. Other followers of structure-functional school were Leach, Fortes, Firth, etc., about whom appreciations have been made under the structural school.

Malinowski and Radcliffe-Brown were influenced to a great extent by French Sociologist; Emile Durkheim. Another French anthropologist, Levi-Strauss, developed the concept of structuralism in-different ways than British Structural-functionalists. He took his tool of structural reconstruction from the linguists like Spair and Troubetzkoy and attempted to study human thought process. He attempted to know as to how structure of thought is formed in human mind. He made detail study of myth, legend, kinship terminology and religion to make a structural analysis of human thought process. According to him, the study of language and formation of words was essential to know the social structure. He does not treat social structure as empirical reality. According to him, social relation consists of raw materials, out of which models, making up the social structure, are built. It is a method applied to the study of social relations but not a model.

While British scholars were stressing upon the structural-functionalism, some pupils of Franz Boas in America began to study the influence of culture on personality and *vice versa*. They ultimately formed a school in anthropology known as culture and personality school. The pioneers of this school are Ruth Benedict, Margaret Mead, Linton, Kardiner and KoraDu-Bois. Ruth Benedict is known as patternists. She attempts to explain as to how cultural pattern or cultural design is formed due to the psychological process of personality formation. She, on the basis of her study, demonstrated that personality played significant role in formation of pattern or design of a cultural group, according to which all members behave and interact in the same manner. Mead, on the basis of her study, attempted to show the impact of culture on personality formation. She is of opinion that it is culture, according to which the personality of a cultural group is shaped. The three tribes of Newguinea, namely Mundugumor, Tschambuli and Arapes, though living in same geographical region, represented different personality types, because their cultures are different. In different cultures, their socialization processes differ, and that's why differences in their ways of interacting and behaving come into existence. Linton and Kardiner attempted to study the influence of both culture and personality on each other. They developed the concept of 'basic personality type'. According to this concept, each culture or society has a basic personality type, according to which its members interact and behave. The basic personality type differs from one group to another. KoraDu-Bois developed the concept of 'Modal personality', because it was established after psychological test.

Another important contribution of culture and personality school is the use multidisciplinary approach to study man and his personality and culture. Equally significant contribution of his school is study of 'National Character' on the basis of study of few respondents. This approach was very useful to study culture at a distance.

While anthropologist of Columbia University were interested in the study of culture, personality and national character in twenties, some scholars of Chicago University became interested in the study of civilization, the leader of which was Robert Redfield. Redfield and Redfieldians coined several concepts useful for the purpose of studying civilization and its various dimensions. Redfield developed the concepts of folk-urban continuum and great and little traditions, which were very useful concepts for studying a civilization and its various dimensions such as, tribal, folk, semi-urban and urban. He also introduced the study of communities such as folk-communities, having little traditions, urban communities which have great traditions, and peasant communities, having some characteristics of folk and some urban. Thus, village, town and city studies were introduced with a view to focus attention on interaction among various dimensions of civilization. Moriss E. Opler, Milton Singer, McKim Marriot, Mandel Baum, etc., all of Chicago School, came to India and developed several useful concepts for the study of Indian civilization and her dimensions. Opler, with R.D. Singh, developed the concept of 'Unity and Extension', which was very much useful for studying intra-village and inter-village unity and its extension of other places and regions. Marriot developed the concept of 'Universalization' and Parochiali- zation', in order to know the process of acceptance of great traditions in little traditions, and little traditions in great traditions. Thus, study of simple and complex societies were initiated by the scholars of civilizational school.

After World War II, a movement arose among the scholars of anthropology to evaluate the methods of its different sub-fields such as physical anthropology, archaeology, linguistics and cultural anthropology. This effort led towards co-operation among four-field approaches. Archaeologists began to view their findings as representative of cultural system. Physical anthropologists turned towards the study of human evolution in the light of culture and ecology. Linguists now began to concern themselves with cultural and psychological elements of language, while cultural anthropologists took linguistic methodology as a model for their own studies. These attempts were to discover units of explanation that can be used cross-culturally in an objective and unbiased manner. Interest in cross-cultural analysis motivated scholars to study universals in culture. The study of community was first conscious attempt to extent the insights gained from the study of homogeneous societies to more complex ones. Searching for a wider framework, one in which the findings of archaeology, linguistics and physical anthropology could also be encompassed, anthropologists rediscovered evolution.

The evolutionary concerns that had marked the beginning of anthropology as an independent discipline were never lost from sight. V. Gordon Childe of England, and Lesile White and Julian Steward of America, kept this tradition alive. They are known as neo-evolutionists. Childe and White are universal evolutionists, whereas Steward is multilinear evolutionist. Childe described evolution in terms of three major events: the invention of food production, urbanization and industrialization. Analysing the transitions that took place under the impact of these revolutions, Childe presented an over all view of the evolutionary process and delineated its common factors.

Lesile White went a step further. Although he was a student of Boas, he was a greater admirer of Tylor and Morgan. Like them, he believed in progressive course of evolution, but he tried to explain what caused progress itself and how it worked. Searching for a universal principle of explanation, he found it in energy. According to him, culture is basically a survival mechanism and energy is required to provide man with the necessities for his continued existence. Thus, culture evolves as energy harnessed per capita and the efficiency of technology increases. Thus,

White talks about over-all view of evolution or general evolution. He has dealt with advance, not with divergence, and with general process, not with adaptation. He has taken the position that evolution does occur on a planetary scale. He regards the amount of energy, available to human group at a given period in cultural development, a convenient macrocosmic framework for the discussion of a long-term evolutionary history. White's views of over all evolution, which obscure particular events, were subjected to a great deal of criticism, because of its inability to account for short-time development.

Julian Steward pleaded for multilinear evolutionism, which establishes sequences of parallel developments that could be investigated in empirical reality. It was Steward's thesis that societies, with similar technology existing in similar environment, would parallel one another in their forms of social and political organisation. Steward's multilinear approach differs from earlier one, but does not necessarily discredit them. White stressed upon general evolution, while Steward upon particular evolution, and the debate between the evolutionists, with different predictions, were nothing more than semantic squabbles.

White's followers tend to stress material factors and technology as determinants of social organisation, but their is often a functional rather than an evolutionary approach. Multilinear evolutionists have generally acknowledged the interrelationships between environment and technology, so that the latter became viewed as variable, rather than ultimate, cause of evolution.

Various new approaches to the study of evolution called attention to the question, how to combine particulars with generals, or how the study of individual cultures could yield meaningful information about culture writ large. The issue became sharpened by the writings of Marvin Harris, who emphasised upon Radcliffe-Brown's earlier distinction between nomothetic and ideographic approaches to the study of culture. Nomothetic researches attempt to discover general social law. Ideographic researches attempt to discover in particular terms and are not necessarily analytic. Harris favours nomothetic researches over the ideographic ones.

Harris has dealt with contrast between 'etic' and 'emic' approaches in his book, *Rise of Anthropological Theory* (1968). These terms were coined by the linguist Kenneth Pike, utilising the last part of the words 'phonetic' and 'phonemic'. In linguistics, phonetics is description of all speech sounds as produced by human speech organs, while phonemics is the sorting out of these sounds in order to arrive at their distinctive differences. Phonetic systems can be universally applied because the human organ of speech are similar everywhere, but phonemic systems differ from language to language, because sound combination and distinctive differences are unique for every linguistic group. In terms of cultural behaviour, etics provide a set of criteria capable of classifying all data into a single system, while emics attempts to discover the meaningful structure of specific cultures. Etics is classificatory and non-structural, emics reflects the internal structural relationships found in specific cultural system. Harris favours etics over emics.

Now-a-days several anthropological sub-fields have developed, stressing a separate and specific cultural aspects, and all using the prefix 'ethno' to indicate their alliance with culture, such as ethno-science, ethno-musicology, ethno-botany, ethno-zoology, ethno-medicine, ethno-psychology, ethno-ecology, ethno-folklore and so forth. Ethno-science, thus accounts for cultural relationships in terms of the information used by members of a culture in their linguistic categories.

Thus, the present book is an enthusiastic attempt to critically explain and evaluate the contributions and theories of different anthropological schools and theirs scholars. The book is not only useful for understanding anthropological thought, but it also supplies significant informations on 'Social Anthropology' and 'Research Methodology'. If one goes through the contents of different schools and contributions of different anthropologists, it appears clearly that the notions of 'Anthropological Thought', 'Social Anthropology' and 'Research Methodology' are interdependent and interrelated. A clear-cut understanding of each idea is not possible in isolation. For instance, social anthropology, in which culture, social structure, economic system, political institutions, magic, science and religion, family, marriage, kinship etc. are taught, covers the contributions and view of different scholars, belonging to different schools, on the topic concerned. Research Methodology, in which origin, use, advantages, and disadvantages of different research methods and techniques of field data collection are taught, covers the methods and techniques used by different scholars, belonging to different schools of anthropological thought. Methods of social anthropology are: Historical method, Comparative method, Structural-functional method and archaeological method. Techniques of data collection are: observation, interview, questionnaire, case study, life history, sampling etc. The origin and use of these techniques can be seen clearly while going through the contribution of different anthropologists. For instance, questionnaire and interview technique of data collection was introduced by the evolutionists, Morgan and Tylor. Tylor introduced use of statistical method in anthropology. G.T. Method was introduced by Morgan and elaborated by W.H.R. Rivers. Malinowski introduced the use of participant observation method of data collection. Scholars of culture personality school used life history and case study technique of data collection. Redfield used a methodology of folk-urban continuum and of 'great and little tradition' to study dimensions of civilization.

It is not possible to over look the contributions of anthropologists of Indian origin, while dealing with the history of anthropological thought. The present book also attempts to reveal the contribution of six eminent Indian anthropologists; namely, S.C. Roy, N.K. Bose, D.N. Majumdar, M.N. Srinivas, S.C. Dube and L.P. Vidyarthi.

At the end, the book covers literature on 'fieldwork and fieldwork traditions in anthropology' and also in Indian context. In almost all chapters attempts have been made to Indianise the examples of different theories suggested by the anthropologists. The book will be of great value for the post-graduate students of anthropology.

1

EVOLUTIONARY SCHOOL

Evolutionary school of anthropological thought came into being at a time when Charles Darwin's theory of origin of species was attaining renowned popularity. Simultaneously, cultural evolutionists also propounded the theory of cultural evolutionism in the second half of 19th century. This has created confusion among the scholars so far as the question of influence of Darwinism on cultural evolutionism is concerned. However, there is no unanimity among the scholars on this very point. Some believe that as the minimum condition for cultural evolutionism is Hominidae, therefore, cultural evolution was like biological evolution of Darwinism. Taggart has strongly pointed out that Darwin's book *Origin of Species*, which appeared in 1859, was too late to have hardly an effect upon the evolutionary schemes of cultural evolutionism. The pioneers of cultural evolutionism like Tylor, Morgan, Maine, McLennan, Bachofen and Bastian had published their major writings in period between 1861 to 1865. This means that they were being planned and written about the same time when Darwin was carrying out his researches and organising and writing down his conclusions. However, the similarities and differences between cultural evolution and biological evolution will be dealt with, later on, in this chapter. Let us confine our discussion here on evolutionary school of anthropological thought.

Evolutionary theory in the field of cultural anthropology developed simultaneously in Britain, America and Germany in the second half of 19th century, when pioneers, like E.B. Tylor, H.J.S. Maine and J.F. McLennan in Britain, L.H. Morgan in America and J.J. Bachofen and Adolf Bastian in Germany used evolutionary scheme as a methodology to reconstruct the cultural history of social institutions and culture of mankind as a whole. These great personalities of their time popularised the assumption that the history of social institutions and culture was witness of successive development in sequences. The present developed stage of mankind had undergone progressive changes in course of which the direction of evolution occurred from simple to complex, homogeneity to heterogeneity and indefinite to definite. These scholars believed in unilinear sequence of cultural evolution in which similarities in cultures of the world, without known historical connections, were regarded as the cause of Mental Unity or Psychic Unity of mankind. Similar mentality to think and react with similar environmental condition caused mankind of the universe to develop independently their material and non-material aspects of cultural life. Each cultural groups started leading a life of hunters and gathers at different places without knowing each other. Thus, though they were genetically unrelated but yet passed through the same sequences of historical developments such as savegery, barbarism and civilization. Not only mankind as a whole, but socio-cultural institutions like marriage, family, kinship property, law, etc. had also followed the same sequence of evolution in unilinear direction i.e. from simple to complex forms.

These great pioneers were not basically trained anthropologists, but on the basis of their critical mind and data gathered from secondary sources, i.e., data supplied by travellers, business men, missionaries, they compared the present developed or civilized stage of man with early stages. When they did not find sufficient informations, they took into considerations those uncommon cultural survivals, which were functionally less important, but were of great significant for representing the early stages of cultural development. Thus,on the basis of comparing present situations with past they were successful in their ambitions of establishing evolutionary stages in historical perspective.

E.B. Tylor is regarded as the greatest pioneer of evolutionary school of anthropological thought, because it was he who established anthropology as a separate discipline in 1884 at Oxford University. He led a number of scholars to conduct researches using evolutionary schemes to trace the genesis and development of cultural institutions. L.H. Morgan in America, a great contemporary of E.B. Tylor, enthusiastically contributed sufficient informations on origin and development of family, marriage and kinship systems of the societies. Similar was the case with other cultural evolutionists.

But the unilinear sequence of evolutionary schemes of 19th century evolutionists was criticised by diffusionists and 20th century cultural relativists so far as the question of psychic unity and unilinear pattern of cultural evolution was concerned. On the basis of historical and empirical data, they disfavoured evolutionary approach and emphasised upon the cultural diversities caused by local areas or sub areas. Thus, according to them, the course of cultural development was divergent and related. They attacked on both psychic unity and unilinear theory of evolution in cultures or culture of human beings.

Evolutionary schemes of cultural evolutionism was revived by Leslie White and Julian Steward in America and V. Gordon Childe in Britain, keeping in view the criticism labelled against classical evolutionists. White and Childe together postulated universal evolutionary scheme in which the frame of reference was shifted from particular to general. In other words, universal evolution was concerned with culture rather than with cultures. Julian Steward propounded a multilinear approach to study the evolution of culture which emphasised upon the search for parallels of limited occurrence. Marshal D. Sahlins and Elman Service, students as well as colleague of White and Steward proposed to place evolutionary data in two broad categories — general and specific evolution in culture. These 20th century evolutionists are termed as Neo or modern evolutionists.

Thus, from the above discussions, it is evident that evolutionary school of anthropological thought may be divided into two groups on the basis of old and new doctrines of cultural evolution proposed by them. These are: classical evolutionary school and neo-evolutionary school. Classical evolutionary school may be subdivided into three categories on the basis of nationality, viz. British evolutionary school, American evolutionary school and German evolutionary school. Similarly, Neo-evolutionary school may be subdivided into two groups on the basis of nationality, which are: American Neo-evolutionary school and British Neo-evolutionary school.

E.B. Tylor, H.J.S. Maine J.F. McLennan, and Frazer belonged to British evolutionary school, while Morgan was the only leaders of American school of evolution, whereas, J.J. Bachofen and Bastian were pioneers of German school of evolution. Likewise, Leslie White and Julian Steward were supporters of American Neo-evolutionary school, while V. Gordon Childe was pioneer of British Neo-evolutionary school.

This classification and sub-classification of evolutionary school can be understood better by putting a glance at the chart given below:

Evolutionary School

- Classical Evolutionary School
  - British Evolutionary School
    1. E.B.Tylor,
    2. H.J.S. Maine
    3. J.F. McLennan
    4. S.J.G.Frazer
  - American Evolutionary School
    1. L.H. Morgan
  - German Evolutionary School
    1. J.J. Bachofen
    2. A. Bastian
- Neo-Evolutionary School
  - British School
    1. V.G. Childe
  - American School
    1. Leslie A. White
    2. Julian H. Steward

Before dealing with the contribution of individual schools and their contributors, it will be fitness of the thing to present here, some basic things related to cultural evolution such as what is evolution ? How cultural evolution differs from biological evolution? What are the typologies suggested for cultural evolution? What were the methodological approaches of evolutionists? and so on.

WHAT IS EVOLUTION?

Evolution may be defined as a process in which different forms are produced or developed orderly in a system. It is concerned with the continuous progress in a system that brings complexity in simplicity, heterogeneity in homogeneity and certainty in uncertainty. In other words, evolution reveals changes in a system in course of time, which can be shown stage after stage or period after period in continuous sequence from past to present. It never deals with change of system, as revolution attempts to do, but it discusses changes in a system. The direction of evolution is always from simple to complex, similarity to dissimilarity and indefinite to definite. This can be shown by establishing stages of development in which simple thing developed into a complex one.

Evolutionists have used evolution as a methodology to reconstruct the history of mankind from past to present. Thus, it can also be defined as a methodology or approach which compares the present to past and establishes sequences of development.

Herbert Spencer, a British sociologist and anthropologist, who was a follower of evolutionary approach, has defined evolution as follows:

> Evolution is integration of matter and concomitant dissipation of motion during which matter passes from an indefinite incoherent homogeneity to definite coherent heterogeneity (Spencer, 1906:396).

The principle of evolution is applicable to both biological and cultural spheres.

Cultural Evolution

Cultural evolution may be defined as a process by which different successive forms in socio-cultural institutions or culture of mankind as a whole are developed and accumulated to constitute the growth of culture over different periods of time, but in a continuity. Cultural evolutionists have used it as a methodological approach to show the history of mankind from past to present by establishing sequence through stages. The methodology of cultural evolution contains two vitally important assumptions. First, it postulates that genuine cultural parallels or cultural similarities, developed independently in all cultures in historical sequences. Second, it assumes that parallels or similarities developed independently due to psychic unity of mankind. Thus, cultural evolution as a methodology is avowedly scientific and generalising rather than historical and particularising. It is less concerned with unique and divergent or convergent patterns and features of culture; although it does not necessarily deny such divergence than with parallels or similarities or regularities that recur crossculturally. Further, it endeavours to determine recurrent patterns and processes and to formulate interrelationships between phenomena in terms of law. The 19th century cultural evolutionists are important to contemporary studies more because of their scientific objective and pre occupation than because of their particular substantive historical reconstruction.

Thus, cultural evolution may be defined as a quest for cultural similarities or cultural parallels or cultural regularities.

Cultural and Biological Evolution

It is necessary here to clear the meaning of cultural evolution in relation to biological evolution. Because, there is tendency to consider the former as an extension of and analogous to the latter. It is no denying the fact that there is relationship between cultural and biological evolution, because the minimum development of Hominidae was a precondition of culture. But cultural development is extension of or analogy to biological development only in a chronological sense. The nature of evolutionary scheme and of developmental process differ profoundly in biology and culture.

In biological evolution, it is assumed that all forms are genetically related and their development is essentially divergent or convergent. Parallels such as swimming, flying, walking etc. are superficial and fairly uncommon. They are genetically considered to be instances of convergent evolution rather than true parallels.

In cultural evolution, on the other hand, it is assumed that cultural patterns in different parts of the world are genetically unrelated yet pass through parallel sequences. The divergent trends, which do not follow the postulated universal sequences, such as those caused by local environment or areas or sub areas, are attributed to only secondary importance. This was the basic assumption of not only 19th century classical evolutionists but modern or Neo-evolutionists like White and Childe also escaped from the awkward facts of cultural divergence and local variations to deal with culture as a whole, rather than particular cultures.

V.G. Childe, a Neo-evolutionist of Britain, has attempted to make a distinction between biological and cultural evolution by stressing the divergent nature of the former and operation of diffusion and frequency of convergence in the latter. It is interesting that such history as implied in cultural relativism or historical particularism is similar to biological evolution. In cultural relativism, variations or unique patterns of different areas or subareas are clearly conceived as to represent divergent development and presumably an ultimate genetic relationship. It is only complementary concept of diffusion, which tends to level differences, a phenomena unknown in biology, that prevents cultural relativism from having an exclusively genetic significance like that of biological evolution.

Analogies between cultural and biological evolution are also represented by two attributes of each (i) a tendency towards increasing complexity of forms and (ii) the development of superior forms i.e. improvement or progress. It is, of course, quite possible to define complexity and progress so as to make them characteristics of evolution. But they are not attributes exclusively of evolution. They may also be considered characteristics of culture change or development as conceived from any non-evolutionary point of view. The assumption that culture change normally involves increasing complexity is found virtually in all historical interpretations of cultural data, but complexity in biological and cultural evotion differs.

According to Kroeber, an American anthropologist, the process of cultural evolution is an additive and therefore, accumulative one, whereas the process of organic evolution is substitutive one. It is on the question not of complexity but divergent that relativists and evolutionists differ.

Typology of Cultural Evolution

Julian Steward, an American anthropologists, who revived evolutionary theory of culture growth in 20th century, has attempted to provide us typology of cultural evolution, in which the data related to cultural evolution can be placed. These are:

(i) Unilinear Cultural Evolution
(ii) Universal Cultural Evolution
(iii) Multilineal Cultural Evolution

(i) *Unilinear Cultural Evolution*

The basic assumptions of 19th century classical evolutionists such as unilinear sequences, parallel inventions and psychic unity of mankind deal with unilinear cultural evolution. In this evolutionary scheme it is postulated that culture or cultures of world pass through different, successive developmental stages in continuity. As a result of which simple forms change into complex ones, homogeneity moves towards heterogeneity and the state of uncertainty goes towards certainty. A detailed description about unilinear cultural evolution will be given later on, while describing the contribution of each school.

(ii) *Universal Cultural Evolution*

It is rather arbitrary label to designate the modern revamping of unilinear evolution. It is concerned with the evolution of culture of mankind as a whole, rather than with particular cultures. Thus, universal evolution which is represented to-day by Leslie White of America and V. Gordon Childe of Britain, who are also known as neo-evolutionists, is the heritage of 19th century classical or unilinear evolutionists. It is so only in the scope of its generalisations but not in its treatment of particulars. White and Childe endeavour to keep evolutionary concept of cultural stages alive by relating those stages to the culture of mankind as a whole. In this scheme, distinctive cultural traditions and local variations are excluded as irrelevant. The details about universal cultural evolution will be presented, while dealing with the contributions of Lesile White and V.G. Childe under sub-heading Neo-evolutionary school.

(iii) *Multilinear Cultural Evolution*

It is somewhat less ambitious approach than the others two i.e. unilinear and universal evolution. It is like unilinear evolutionary scheme, in dealing with development sequences, but it is distinctive in searching for independent discoveries or parallels of limited occurrence instead of universals. Methodological approach of multilinear evolution is based on the assumption that significant regularities or similarities due to parallel discoveries occur in cultural change, which is concerned with the determination of cultural laws. Its method is empirical rather than deductive. It is inevitably concerned also with historical reconstructions, but it does not expect that historical data can be classified in universal stages. The kinds of parallels or similarities with which multilinear evolution deals are distinguished by their limited occurrence and their specificity. For this reason outstanding methodological problem of multilinear evolution is an appropriate taxonomy of cultural phenomena. Multilinear evolution will be discussed in detail while explaining the contributions of

Julian Steward.

Specific and General Evolution

Marshal D. Sahlins and Elman Service, students and colleagues of Julian Steward and White, have developed the concept of specific and General evolution to reconcile White's and Steward's views by presenting evolutionary schemes in two broad categories as mentioned above.

According to them evolution in both biological and cultural spheres moves simultaneously in two directions. On one side, it creates diversity through adaptative modifications as a result new forms differentiate from old. On the other hand, evolution generates progress, because of which higher forms arise and surpass lower ones. The former is specific evolution and the latter is general evolution. They opine that specific and general evolution are not different reality, rather they are aspects of the same total process. Thus, specific and general evolution are two context in which evolutionary things and events can be placed. We may view any given change in a form of life of culture either in the perspective of adaptatiôn or from the point of overall progress. However, the context is very important. A difference in taxonomy is required in examining these two aspects of evolution. The study of specific evolution employs phylogenetic classification concerned with lines of descent. In general evolution emphasis shifts to the character of progress itself and forms are classed in stages or levels of development, without reference to phylogeny. According to them, the failure to keep in mind the dual character of evolution, a concept well expressed by Tylor as "the evolution of culture can be studied both stage by stage as well as along its many lines" and upheld by the biologist Julian Huxley, has created confusion and polemical controversy about such terms as 'unilinear', 'multilinear' and 'universal' as well as about the differences between 'history' and 'evolution'.

The general cultural evolution is the study of successive forms such as hunting and gathering bands, agriculturists, industrial revolution, atomic age etc. through long periods of time. The specific cultural evolution, on the other hand, is the development of local cultures or groups of cultures through relatively short period of time. The key note of specific evolution is cultural diversity brought about by localized factors such as environment, diffusion, invention and the like. In general evolutionary perspectives, all the diversities become merged in to larger patterns that unfold in progressive fashion. Progress as objectively measured is the key note of general evolution. Specific cultures arise, diffuse proliterate, or become extinct, leaving a complex entanglement of evolutionary path.

The same sort of general specific distinction can be applied to the study of cultural sub-units as well as cultures. One could trace general evolution of religion or kinship structure or focus on specific diversity of kinship or religion.

Classical Evolutionary Theory

Basic Postulates of Classical Evolutionary Scheme

Although, classical evolutionists have been criticised by relativists, particularists, diffusionists and migrationists, who have discredited the fundamental postulates of evolutionists on the basis of empirical findings, but it is beyond doubt that they were first and foremost thinkers who opined that the concept of racial superiority is a psychological and myth. For them, the primitives or tribal societies of mankind were ancestors of modern civilized societies of the universe. The former represented the earlier stage of humanity through which the civilized mankind as a whole had evolved out. Their such thinking reflects clearly that they had critical mind and analytical brain to understand the cultural history of mankind in the dynamic dimensions of time. Although their evolutionary schemes were to a great extent de-educative and speculative but they were certainly aware of facts and explanation of processes of change. They seriously aimed at showing that mankind was a unity not diversity. The lower developmental stages of mankind were directly related to latter ones. In absence of written records, it was a difficult task for them to show the evolution of mankind. But their critical mind devised a method to fill in the gap by the concepts of survivals. Survivals were uncommon customs, which had lost their significance in present state, but had valuable meaning in past. Thus, survivals were indicators of conditions of culture of mankind in earlier periods.

They were of the opinion that historical explanations were sufficient to the understanding of cultural varieties. They did not confuse history with evolution, but they took help of historical explanations to show that human culture had undergone progressive and cumulative change in 19th century. Their this method of reconstruction was also known as historical method.

They compared the early stage of primitive people with civilized ones and assumed that formers were the reflection of early condition of the latters. They also compared survivals, both material and non-material, to establish sequence of development from simple to the complex, from homogeneity to heterogeneity and from uncertainty to certainty. This method of comparing cultures or cultural institutions of the world, became known as comparative method of cultural evolutionists.

Evolutionists were very much puzzled, while dealing with the evolutionary schemes, on the question of similarities in culture traits, culture complex and culture patterns of the people of the world without known historical connection. Was it due to independent invention or because of diffusion? The theory of diffusion could not seem convincing to them and they postulated that similarities in traits, complex and patterns of cultures existing all over the world were not due to diffusion, but they revealed certainly that parallel inventions or discoveries were made in different parts of the world by human beings, who were genetically unrelated, yet passed through the same developmental sequences. Independent inventions or parallel discoveries of culture traits, culture complex and culture patterns are designated as cultural parallels. The ideologies of evolutionists related to the formation of cultural parallels are termed as cultural parallelism, which is synonymic to cultural similarism.

The evolutionists assumed that cultural parallels or cultural similarities came into existence due to *Psychic unity of mankind.* Psychic unity of mankind refers to similar mentality of human beings to react and think similarly with like environmental situation at a particular period of time. It was because of psychic unity of mankind that human beings residing at different places of the world passed through the similar stages of savagery, barbarism and civilization. The invention of agriculture took place simultaneous in South-east Asia, South-west Asia and America. The use of zero was invented at the same time in Hind, Babylonia and Maya cultures. The invention of paper and printing came in to being independently at the same time in East and West. Writing also came into being simultaneously in many countries of the world. Such examples of cultural similarities or cultural parallels bear testimony that human beings possess psychic unity. Differences in environments and situations create diversities in traits, complexes and patterns, which occupy secondary significance in evolution of culture.

Thus, classical evolutionists postulated that in the beginning all cultures possessed similar and simple culture traits, but they gradually developed into complex forms or patterns due to cultural developments.

Salient Features of Unilinear Evolutionism

1. Human culture as a whole or socio-cultural institutions, evolve in unilinear sequence, stage after stage.
2. The direction of cultural evolution is from simple to complex, from similarity to dissimilarity, and from indefinite to definite.
3. Different stages of evolution can be established by speculating

historical explanations and using comparative method.
4. Similarities in culture traits, culture complex, culture patterns of the world are caused by psychic unity of mankind and parallel inventions.
5. Cultural diversities do not occupy significant place in unilinear evolutionary scheme.
6. In the higher stage of culture, some residues of primitive stages can be seen, which are termed as survivals, and which remind us about the earlier stages of the culture.

GENERAL CONTRIBUTION OF CLASSICAL EVOLUTIONISTS

Classical evolutionists used evolutionary schemes as a methodology or approach to reconstruct the developmental stages of culture of mankind as a whole as well as to establish developmental sequences of cultural institutions like marriage, family, kinship etc. In this approach they applied comparative method to reconstruct cultural history of mankind as a whole or cultural institutions.

Considering the primitive people as reflecting the early condition of men and comparing their early culture with developed ones, Tylor and Morgan postulated that man kind as a whole has passed through the stages of savagery, barbarism and civilization. Tylor did not place specific cultures into different stages of cultural development of human beings, but Morgan subdivided the stags of savagery and barbarism each in to three groups, namely lower, middle and upper. He was of opinion that lower savagery began with development of language and gathering of fruits and nuts as subsistence. This stage ended with development of fishing subsistence and use of fire. No living example can be cited to this stratum.

In middle status of savagery, fishing subsistence and use of fire continued, but ended with invention of bow and arrow. During this period, mankind expanded to cover the greater part of earth's surface. He placed Australians and Polynesians at the time of first contact with European.

In upper status of savagery, invention of bow and arrow continued, but ended with the invention of pottery. Examples of this stage are American Indians of the Western sub-arctic, columbia River valley tribes and certain tribes of North and South America at the time of first contact with Europeans.

Lower status of barbarism witnessed continuation of pottery inventions, either by original or by adoption and ended with invention of animal domestication in eastern hemisphere, but invention of plant cultivation by irrigation and use of adobe brick and stone in house construction. He cited examples of American Indian tribes east of Missori river, and tribes of Europe and Asia, who had pottery, but no domesticated animals.

Middle status of barbarism witnessed animal domestication in old world and use of plant cultivation, adobe brick and stone in New world and invention of iron ore smelting in both worlds. Examples are pueblo Indians of America, village dwelling Indians of Mexico, Central America and Tribes in eastern hemisphere.

In upper status of barbarism, smelting of iron continued and ended with the invention of phonetic alphabet and use of written literature. Examples are Gracian tribes of Homericage, Italian tribes before foundation of Rome and Germanic tribes of Julius Caesar's time.

The stage of civilization began with phonetic alphabet and literary writing. Morgan's classification of stages of development of humankind in terms of ethnic period such as savagery, barbarism and civilization, are what anthropologists generally call hunting and food gathering societies, horticultural tribals, and pre or proto state societies.

Thus, Morgan compared the tools and levels of subsistence and attempted to trace development stages of mankind as a whole. Tylor and Morgan's offensive words like savagery and barbarism have been dropped by present day anthropologists, but all have accepted historical sequence from hunting and gathering to domestication of plants and animals and most single item, writing, as the beginning of civilization.

These evolutionists also tried to establish the historical sequence of marriage, family and kinship. According to Tylor, Morgan, McLennan, J.J. Bachofen and Adolf Bastian, Sexual promiscuity was the early stage of marriage in historical sequence, from which present day monogamy evolved out, through group marriage and polyandry.

They all have postulated that societies in early stage was matriarchal and residence was matrilocal from which patriarchal family and patrilocal residence evolved out in historical period. Thus, matrilineality proceeded the patrilineality. In kinship organisation, descent was traced through female in early societies from which the present patrilineal descent developed in course of time.

Morgan was of the opinion that family system has passed through fifteen successive stages of development, the early stage of family was consangninal family and monogamous family was the developed stage. In kinship terminology, classificatory system was the early stage, which proceeded the descriptive system.

Maine was exception, whose sequence of family organisation revealed that patriarchy was the early stage of family organisation which proceeded matriarchy, which was not acceptable to other evolutionists.

But his historical sequences of kinship organisation to territorial organization, from status to contract, from civil law to criminal was accepted by all.

It was Tylor, who took enthusiastic interest in establishing historical sequences of religion. He was of opinion that animism, i.e., belief in soul, was the early stage of religion, from which present stage of monotheism has developed through polytheism.

Unilinear evolutionary approaches were applied to show the historical sequences of economic organisation, technology and art, etc. In the field of economic organisation developmental stages are: hunting and gathering, domestication of plant and animal, industrial labour, etc. In the field of technology, three stages of successive development are: stone age, bronze age, and iron age. A.C. Haddon, in his book *Development of Art*, has established three successive stages of development, which are realistic, symbolic and geometric. According to Frazer, society has passed through three successive stages of development, i.e. magic, religion, and science.

BRITISH EVOLUTIONARY SCHOOL

Edward Burnett Tylor (1832-1917)

E.B. Tylor was born at Camberwell, England, on 2nd October, 1832. He was the third son of parents Joseph Tylor and Harrite Skipper. His father ran a prosperous brass foundary, which belonged to the family. Both parents were Quakers and E.B. Tylor was to make to most of his inheritance of freedom from religious formality. This independence lost him a classical education, because he could not pass the tests of religious orthodoxy, which were then required for admission to the universities. Instead, he received a brief and formal education at a school maintained by the Society of Friends.

When he was sixteen years old, he entered the family business and worked there for seven years. In 1855, at the age of 23, his health showed signs of breaking down. He was advised by parents to quit work and indulge his health by leisurely travel. He spent a year travelling in United States, and in the spring of 1856, was in Cuba. Here, his Quaker affiliations provided the chance opportunity that so often gives direction to a man's life. While on a Havana bus, he heard a passenger using 'thou', which at that time identified the speaker as a Quaker. Tylor approached the stranger and introduced himself as a fellow Quaker. The Stranger Quaker was Henry Christy, a prosperous businessman, who had become an archaeologist and ethnologist of considerable reputation. Henry Christy was one of the archaeologists, who later made the important confirmation of the validity of Boucher de Perthes' discoveries concerning the antiquity of man. Henry Christy and Tylor took an immediate linking to each other. Christy persuaded Tylor to accompany him on an archaeological expedition to Mexico. Under Scholarly expertise and mature guidance of Christy, Tylor developed curiosity and insight for careful observation and balanced judgement, which helped him much in reconstructing the prehistory of Mexico. He was specially interested in the development of Mexico. He took in to consideration the material remains of culture discovered by the two travellers as well as antiquities of popular rites, custom, beliefs and legends which were to be observed among the contemporary people of Mexico. His observations revealed that many extant customs were similar to the customs of ancient people. He observed that the practice of Mexican penitents, scourging themselves at church under the fierce exhortations of moth, was reminded of the identical rite at the Egyptian festival of Isis. This observation played significant role in formulation of the theory of cultural survivals, which were regarded as the most important achievements in anthropology by Tylor.

Another problems that interested Tylor on Mexican expedition was that of independent origin or diffusion of cultural institution. This question was to become a crucial one in anthropology with important implications for social, political and religious thought. In order to solve this question, Tylor employed a caution which characterised much of his subsequent works: "Set the difficulties on one side of the question against those on the other, and they will nearly balance".

Though Tylor stayed at Mexico for six month only, but this shorter expedition shaped once and for all the course of his life's work. His stay at Mexico made him devoted to the founding of a science of culture. The theory of cultural evolution or cultural reconstruction, developed by him, attracted wider recognition among the leading anthropological evolutionists of 19th century. His achievement in the field of cultural evolution led the way to establish anthropology as an independent and scientific field of study in Europe. He championed anthropology so strongly that many of his contemporaries half jokingly referred to it as 'Mr. Tylor's Science'. His science, anthropology, did not remain without academic recognition. He occupied Britain's first recognised University post, as the keeper of the university museum of Oxford, and a year later, in 1884, as reader in anthropology in the same University.

Tylor was a commanding benevolent figure. He wall tall, well-built and extremely handsome. His simplicity, patience, and quiet humour made him popular and organiser. His writings were always free from jargon or pretension of any kind, a sequence of the fact that he was taken from school at sixteen and never again became a student in academic science.

He was married to Anna in 1858. The relationship between Tylor and Anna was regarded as a model of marital life. They lived together quietly and happily for 59 years, until Tylor's death in 1917. It is said that Lady Tylor always encouraged and cooperated her husband in academic activities. She used to attend certain series of her husband's lectures. On one occasion, Tylor turned towards his wife after a lengthy exposition and said absent mindedly, "and so my dear Anna we observe.......".

Contributions of Tylor on Cultural Evolution

Tylor published his first book entitled, *Anahuac*: also known as *Mexico-Mexican, Ancient and Modern*, in 1861 from London. In his book, Tylor discusses the evolution or reconstruction of cultural history of Mexico. On the basis of observing and comparing the material remains of culture and antiquities of popular rites, customs, beliefs, myths, legends, folklore etc., he came to the conclusion that culture of Mexico-mexican has developed from primitive to civilized stage. He used a number of different techniques for such reconstructions. One of those was assignment of conditions opposite to present one to early stage of development, another was his concept of 'survivals, which he used in a manner similar to Maine and McLennan's concept of *Survivals*. According to him, survivals are processes, customs and opinions that persist by force of habit, even when they loose their utility. Thus, survivals remain proof of earlier condition. He found such survivals in both material and non-material aspects of culture. He cited an examples of saying 'God bless you' to some one who sneezed. This custom was existing even in civilized society indicating an earlier belief that sneezing was an attempt of the soul to leave the body. This danger was encountered by saying, "God bless you". Such belief is also existing among Indians, because sneezing is regarded as a bad omen. When anyone sneezes, it is a custom to say that May God grant a long life.

Tylor's second book entitled *Researches into the Early History of Mankind and Development of Civilization*, was published in 1865. This book deals with progressive theory of cultural development on the basis of similarity of human mind. When he thought about development of civilization, the basic question which perplexed him was whether the differences between civilized and savage life was to be explained by the progress of the former, or the degeneration of the latter. Following the same approach of collecting material and non-material aspects of cultural survivals and comparing them in time sequence, the conclusion of the book revealed that differences in primitive and civilized people were due to progress which took place in culture as a whole. He was of opinion that culture as a whole had progressed rather than degenerated, and in the reconstruction of cultural history of civilization, the progress of culture must be taken into consideration. On the basis of evaluating the progress of culture, his researches into early history of mankind and development indicated that the present civilization has evolved from savagery (early stage of human kind) through barbarism. Thus, there were three successive stages of cultural development through which the present form of civilization has emerged.

Another question, which puzzled Tylor in reconstructing the history of mankind and development of civilization, was similarity in cultural traits and cultural complexes in existing cultures of the world. Why all cultures have language, religion, family, marriage, arts, crafts, etc. without any known contact in past ? It was due to independent development or diffusion of cultural institutions ? He solved this question on the basis of *Psychic Unity of Mankind* and rejected the idea of diffusion. Psychic unity of mankind reveals that under similar environmental condition mankind of the world progress in similar way. It means that mankind were equally capable of progress. The differences between cultures were "those of development rather than of origin, rather of degree than of kind" (Tylor, 1865 : 232). Tylor believed in independence inventions or discoveries of cultural institutions in similar unilinear sequence, i.e., from simple form to complex form. He gave examples of similar culture traits between people without known historical connections. For instance, he observed Australian aborigines raising scars on their bodies like African tribes, circumcising like Jews and Arabs, baring marriage in female line like the Iroquois, dropping out language, names of plants and animals, which were used as personal names of dead men, and making new words to serve instead, like the Abipones of South America.

Such observations made by him helped him much in reconstructing the history of mankind and developmental processes of civilizations. He was of opinion that history of culture and civilization was a witness of *parallel or independent evolution* of cultural institutions. Like environmental condition compelled prehistoric men of the universe to develop stone tools, invent potteries, domesticate animals, and to do agriculture. Such inventions of prehistoric men did not originated at a particular place from where they diffused in other cultural setting, but parallel or independent or free inventions took place at several places at the same time. Above explanation clearly revealed that prehistoric culture and civilization of men has passed through three successive developmental stages, viz. stone age, bronze age and iron age.

Tylor's most recognised book, *Primitive Culture* was published in 1871. This book was regarded as anthropological classic which marks the beginning of the scientific study of culture. Two major contributions to cultural anthropology emerged from this book. The 'doctrine of survivals' and 'theory of animism'.

In this book, it was Tylor, who gave a scientific definition of culture. According to him, "culture is that complex whole which includes knowledge, belief, art, morals, law, custom and any other capabilities and habit acquired by man as a member of society" (Tylor, 1871:1).

In this definition of culture, the term 'Acquired' is the key word, because it meant that culture was the product of social learning, rather than of biological heredity, and that the differences in cultural development were not the result of degeneration, but of progress in cultural knowledge. Tylor's insistence that culture was a 'complex whole' implied that it included all socially learned behaviour, no matter if it seemed trivial or not. Thus, every facet of social life was worthy of study, because it contributed to the understanding of mankind.

In his book, *Primitive Culture*, Tylor has discussed the origin of culture and religion in primitive culture. Tylor considered two methods of revolutionary reconstruction, which also suggested the method of survivals to him. One was reconstruction of material culture by the archaeologists and geologists on the basis of the discoveries of material relics (artifacts) in geological strata. The archaeologist working with geologists could establish from a few surviving artifacts such a fragments of weapons, implements, pottery, etc. a general picture of material culture of an ancient society and its approximate place in chronological series. On the basis of surviving material relics and correlating them with chronological sequence, Tylor observed that the evolution of material culture has passed through three successive stages of development, viz. stone, bronze and iron.

The doctrine of survivals added utility and prestige to the comparative method as the key to ethnological study. It is because of this fact that Tylor is often referred to as the founder of comparative ethnology. On the basis of comparing the survivals (material and non-material) in his study, Tylor was able to conclude that contemporary savage people represented the earlier stages of cultural development, which had been traversed by civilized people. Thus, the three successive developments of societies were — savagery, barbarism and civilization. However, Tylor did not attempt to force specific cultures into savagery or barbarism, as done by L.H. Morgan, a contemporary American evolutionist.

Although Tylor reconstructed possible sequence of many cultural institutions, but his most comprehensive treatment was in the field of *primitive religion.* In his book *Primitive Culture*, Tylor defined religion as belief in spiritual beings. He stated that religion was a cultural universal, because no known cultures were without such beliefs. According to him, religion originated as belief in soul, which is also designated by the term 'animism' (*anima* means soul). Therefore, animism was the ancient form of religion. As souls were numerous, who were worshipped on different occasions in the form of ancestral worship, this created belief in polytheism, which following the processes of cultural evolution, reached at a stage of monotheism, the great belief of civilized people. Thus, the evolution of religion has passed through the development processes of animism, polytheism and monotheism.

In order to trace the origin and development of primitive religion, Tylor studied the myths and legends associated with the origin of religion. Analysing different myths and legends, he came to the conclusion that primitive religion came into existence as belief in spirits or soul (animism). Primitive man observed soul as making a man alive or dead. They viewed that there was some unseen spirit in man, which made him to speak, walk, breath, eat, etc. But as soon as the unseen spirit, left the body, a man was declared as dead. Man would have met such experience as a result of which, a belief in soul came into existence, though he did not possess necessary knowledge to reason scientifically. On this rationale, Tylor called primitive men as 'Savage philosopher'.

Primitive men gradually developed a belief that every man possessed not only a material body but also a life and a phantomic (evil spirit). Life enabled the body to think and perform acts, but the phantom was its image or second self. Both were inseparable from the body. Life went permanently after death from the body, but phantom could appear to people at a distance as in dream. In this way, savages began to consider two identical idea of soul — (i) Body Soul and (ii) Ghost Soul. Body-soul left the body permanently but Ghost soul appeared before them on many occasions. This belief grew up that souls continued even after death. In another stage of development, this belief was extended to include all other living and non-living objects, because animals, plants, weapons, boats, mountain, rivers, seas, wells, etc., all used to appear in dream as spirits. In this way, savages began to realise that every thing possessed life and soul or spirit, and this early stage of religion was called as *animism* by the great evolutionist E.B. Tylor.

Three general beliefs concerning the existence of ghost-souls after death are derived from these early stages of animism: (i) the conviction that ghost-souls hover round the earth and take an interest in living, sometimes visit their former homes as well, (2) the belief in metempsychosis-the transmigration of souls in to other human beings or animals, plants and things, and (3) the idea of special residence in another world, such as western Islands, the under world, the mountains, heavens etc. The last kind of belief falls in to one of two categories, which Tylor calls as 'continuance theory' and 'retribution' theory. In case of former, a life similar to earthly life is carried out, but in latter, the Ghost-souls are rewarded or punished according to the deeds of earthly life. The second theory commanded a special effect on the social behaviour of the people who adopted the belief.

The general idea of primitive Ghost-soul animating men, animals, plants, and things naturally leads to belief in another order of spiritual beings which are on a higher level. They are called *'Manes'*, which are souls in origin but which acquire a special quality raising them to the level of demons or deities. They might be a parent, hence ancestor worship came into existance. They might also be the soul or spirit of a tribal chief, a tribal hero, or any other powerful person. They might be a power for good or evil. Thus, the concept of *benevolent* and *malevolent* spirit came into existence and an active practice of offering worship was witnessed.

Another feature in the development of primitive religion was the general idea of embodiment or incarnation of spirits. As a result of this, the concept of *spirit possession* developed in primitive mind. This also led to the development of the practice of exorcism as the therapeutic device for dealing with invading demon spirits. The exorcists remove the spirits by cajolery, bribes, threats, persuading or driving it to another abode.

Related to the theory of 'spirit possession', is the next important application of incarnation or embodiment idea, known as fetishism. Though the term fetishism was used by August Comte, but Tylor used this term to indicate a subordinate department of animism. He restricted its use only to spirits embodied in or related to material objects, living or non-living. Fetishism merges in to idolatory, when a fetish object is altered in some material way by worshipper so as to indicate its special function as the abode for a spirit. According to Tylor, idolatory embodied soul and spirit in idol, in the same way as they were embodied in human body.

The next stage in development of animism took place, when primitive mind drew analogy between human behaviour and the behaviour of nature at large. As the human body functions by virtue of its inhabiting-Ghost-soul, so does nature appear in general to be animated by analogous agents. Thus, animism, beginning as a philosophy of human life, became a comprehensive philosophy of all nature. The causes of all natural phenomena were regarded as natural spirits. They caused the wind to blow, the sky to rain, rivers to move, volcanoes to erupt.

Beginning, most likely, from very particular spirits for particular events, the idea of nature spirits became generalised and, there arose specific deities, Gods of heaven, earth, sky, water, river, forest, sea, diseases, agriculture, war, peace etc. This is the great stage of polytheism.

Finally the concept of one supreme deity came into existence. In Hindu society, *Pram Brahma Parmeshwar*, is regarded as the Supreme Being, Who commands nature, man and Gods. Thus, monotheism, the great belief of civilized people has evolved from the primitive past belief, i.e., animism.

Tylor's analysis of primitive religion has been appreciated as well as criticised both. He has been appreciated for collecting abundant ethnographic materials and illustrating each point with suitable examples, His definition of religion and views on religion as cultural universal was accepted by all. He was criticised for using meaningless ethnographic data. The critiques alleged that Tylor did not take into consideration the religious system as a whole, rather tried to reconstruct the origin and development of belief in supernatural powers, souls, offering, sacrifice, and various other selected aspects. To him, religion was mainly an attempt to understand the events of human experience and the primitive logician, rationally analysing the world in same matter as western scientists. In this rational exercise, Tylor sought the difference between earlier and later forms of religion in content and degree of knowledge, but social character of religion remained untreated and unexplained.

His fourth book entitled, *Anthropology: An Introduction to the Study of Man and Civilization* was published in 1881. In this book, Tylor dealt with the continuity of phenomena of cultural history. Taking into consideration, the survivals and correlating them with historical development, he was able to reconstruct the history of mankind and civilization. In his study, on the basis of comparative methods, he has convinced that the mankind as a whole has reached up to the stage of civilization from earlier stages of savagery and barbarism. While discussing the three stages of development of mankind, Tylor did not consider them as law governing the cultural historical processes, but he emphasised upon empirical generalizations, which enabled ethnographer to comprehend the continuity of culture. In fact, he was concerned with the study of human thought and action in wider historical perspective. He was of opinion that culture is a historical process subject to the development in time perspective.

In this book, the holistic four-field approach, which is particularly strong in America, was also present. This book included chapters on antiquity of man, his relationship to other animals, races of mankind and on language. He also referred to archaeology. His examination of communication among deaf-mutes provides a model for the study of exotic system of communication. His insights into the nature of symbolization and its importance to human life are crucial for an understanding of the nature of culture and of man.

In 1889, Tylor wrote an essay, on A Method of Investigating the Development of Institutions: Applied to the Laws of Marriage and Descent, which was published in *Journal of Royal Anthropological Institute of Great Britain and Ireland*. In order to trace the development of marriage as an institution, he used statistics. He prepared a questionnaire and took data from 282 societies from savage hordes to cultural nations. He correlated post-marital residence pattern with the custom of in-law avoidance and came to the conclusion that matrilineality and matrilocality had proceeded patrilineality and patrilocality. His observation on custom of *couvade* pointed out in this direction revealed that matrilineal societies did not practise it at all because women's position was dominant. Most societies in intermediate patri-matrilineality stage adopted this custom, because men needed to establish their authority over women, thus limited their habit. Going into child bed like women, they symbolically started their paternity. In pure patrilineal society, some still practised *couvade* as survival, other had already dropped the customs because it had lost its function. Thus, matrilineality have been the earlier form of the society.

On the whole, Tylor's evolutionary reconstructions were more closely related to Lamarkian transformationism than to Darwinian natural selection. In the preface of the book *Primitive Culture*, Tylor acknowledged the importance of Darwin and Spencer, but added that his work was arranged on its own lines and not directly influenced by their writings. In fact, Tylor rarely recognised any of his predecessors, although many 19th century trends converge in his theories. His treatment of anthropology as history, his interest in exotic phenomena, his belief in progress, development stages, concept of survival, emphasis on empirical data and on the scientific nature of anthropology, all are adumbrated. But the synthesis of all these trends in to one coherent whole was Tylor's great achievement. He established anthropology as an independent and scientific field of study in Europe.

Tylor sent his students in different places to collect ethnographic materials. Since then, data collecting became the hall mark of anthropology. He is often called as an arm-chair anthropologist, one who relies upon the data from secondary sources and does not visit field. His criticism as arm-chair anthropologist comes into existence because he was not basically a field worker, though he had spent a year in United States, six months in Mexico and a shorter period in Cuba. Therefore, he relied upon the materials collected by travellers, missionaries etc. for his own reconstructions of cultural history and civilization. But he was not uncritical of these data and attempted to test their accuracy by comparative method. It was he who recognised the need for scientifically-oriented fieldwork and he was instrumental in founding the organisations fostering the practice of fieldwork.

Tylor breathed his last in the year 1917, but his contributions in the field of anthropology in general and cultural anthropology in particular, are the witness that he is immortal. Such titles, used for him by us as 'father of anthropology, founder of cultural anthropology or culture, founder of comparative ethnology, and founder of modern anthropology', reveal clearly statuses, which he enjoyed during his life time on account of contributions in the field of discipline of anthropology. So long as the discipline of anthropology exists over world, he will be remembered for his great contributions.

R.R. Marett (1866-1943)

R.R. Marett was born at London in 1866. He was a student of E.B. Tylor. In 1936, he published Tylor's bibliography in which he presented Tylor's major contributions in the field of anthropology in general and cultural anthropology in particular. He reviewed Tylor's theoretical contributions such as concept of survivals, animism, inclusive definitions of culture and religion, his use of comparative method, attempts at statistical reconstructions and so forth. Perhaps none of these was entirely original, but he attempted to bring them in a coherent whole. In his hands, anthropology became 'the science of culture'.

Influenced by the ideas and concept of primitive religion under the inspiring guidance of a teacher like E.B. Tylor, he was also interested in the study of primitive religion. He wrote a book entitled, *The Threshold of Religion*, which was published from London in 1909. In this book, he transformed the Tylor's concept of animism, i.e., belief in soul. He critically concluded that the primitive mankind's destiny was guided and controlled by the natural phenomenon. Therefore, primitive religion could be understood in terms of *animatism,* i.e., belief in some impersonal power behind every material objects besides living beings.

Henry James Summer Maine (1822-1888)

Sir Henry Maine was born in 1822 in Scotland. By training and education, he belonged to law discipline. He was founder of Comparative Jurisprudence in England. For some time, he was also Professor of Jurisprudence in Cambridge and Oxford. He came to India in connection with the study of primitive law in Primitive Societies. In 1869, he became the Vice-Chancellor of Calcutta University.

Henry Maine published a number of books on *Ancient Laws and Customs,* which are as follows:

1. *Ancient Law*, Henry Holt and Company, New York, 1861.
2. *Early Law and Custom*, London, 1883.
3. *Village Communities in East and West*, London, 1871.
4. *Lectures on Early History of Institutions*, New York, 1875.
5. *Popular Government*, London, 1890.

Maine's Contribution in Evolutionary Theory

The major contribution of Maine in the field of cultural evolutionary theory is the development of family system. He was of opinion that the family, in original form, was Patrilineal and Patriarchal. This idea of Maine was unlike those of Bachofen, Morgan, McLennan and Tylor, whose observations and conclusions revealed that family system in early stage of development was matrilineal and matriarchal. The present form of patriarchal and patrilineal family evolved from matrilineal and matriarchal family.

Maine declared in the preface of his book *Ancient Law* that he wanted to examine some of the earliest ideas of mankind as they are reflected in ancient law and to point out the relationship of those ideas to modern thought. It meant, Maine was interested in the evolution of law in western world. But the difficulty involved was that nothing much could be known about the laws of people before the invention of writing. Main attempted to solve this question by devising a method of reconstruction. Being specialist in Roman Law, he observed that changes in law were not made manifest in condition. Older form continued to exist as "legal fictions" and these, thus, were survivals to earlier times, when they were real functioning laws. In this way, he chose legal fiction as survivals to serve the purpose of reconstruction.

By this method, Maine found a number of sequences of development particularly from kinship organisation to territorial organisation, status to contract, civil law to criminal law, and decree to case law to true legislation. Of those, the first, i.e., the evolution of kinship organisation to territorial organisation is often discussed by the anthropologists, because it deals with the early forms of family organisation.

In the support of his hypothesis that family in earlier stage was patriarchal and patrilineal, Maine cited an example which is as follows:

> In Roman Law, the legal fiction prevailed that a father was a *Patria Potestas,* which meant that father had absolute power over wife, children, servant and even life and death. In the period for which documentation existed, fathers did not possess such powers, but this legal fiction must have existed at earlier times. Thus, patriarchal was the earliest form of family organisation. As true government and legislation were absent in those days, it must have been the early forms of early political organisations as well in early societies. In course of time, when group began to unite around common land-holdings, the territorial notions developed by the necessity of time. But patrilineal kinship reckoning remained kinship based until the time nations developed, which were determined by territoriality exclusively.

Maine's most important contribution lies in his suggestion that the kinship had provided the basic principle of organisation of primitive societies. The primeval groups are families in which a dispotic father exercises absolute power over his wives and children. These families aggregated through legal fictions to form larger groups without surrendering their autonomy. Hence, the unit of ancient society was a family and of modern society an individual. Therefore, movement of progressive societies has been uniform with respect to gradual dissolution of family dependency and growth of individual obligation in its place. This movement is examined by Maine with respect to a number of related transitions expressed in terms of useful dichotomies. Family organised society is fixed status society, individual society is free contact society. The movement is from status to contract. Family organised societies own property in common, individual organised societies embody the growth of private ownership. In the most primitive stage of law, all injuries may be compensated by agreement of families involved, thus civil and criminal law are confounded. Later on, certain injuries involve only individuals, while others are crime against the whole society.

Weakness of Maine's Scheme

Evolutionary theory of Maine has been criticised by contemporary anthropologists. Critiques levelled charges that he had no knowledge of ethnography, though he published books on ancient law. In absence of deep knowledge of races of mankind, his scheme of evolution cannot be treated as universally valid scheme. He had gone through books and reports in Europe and India, but made it sound as if he were referring to all human kind. McLennan (1865:115) attacked on Maine as one "who has been unable to convince how human beings could be grouped on any principle more primitive than that of patriarchal system".

John Fergusan McLennan (1827-1881)

McLennan, like Maine, was also born in Scotland in the year 1827. Like Maine, he was also a lawyer by profession. Being a lawyer, he became interested in the evolution of the institution of marriage and his contribution in the field of evolution of marriage is still regarded as unparallel.

He published two important books which are as follows:

(i) *Primitive Marriage: An Enquiry into the Origin of form of Capture in Marriage Ceremonies*, Adam and Charles Black, Edingburg, 1865.
(ii) *Studies in Ancient History*, Macmillan, 1876.

His first book is regarded as the most famous book so far as the theory of cultural evolution is concerned. For him, it is often said that no one before him had attempted to reconstruct the social conditions of primitive people. He was much better acquainted with ethnographic literature than Maine and was convinced that the survival of 'rude' contemporary people were good example of early socio-cultural conditions.

His major item of reconstruction was bride capture, which was still carried out in mock battle in some contemporary societies. He observed that among Kalmuks, there was a custom to pay bride price and to carry away the girl on a horse amidst the struggling scenes or mock resistance. His another observation revealed that among the Welsh, the grooms and his friends, were engaged in a mock battle with friends of bride, until the latter inevitably lost. Postulating that these customs were survivals of former actual situations of bride price, McLennan set out to explain why women should have been taken in this manner. He arrived at logical conclusion that there must have been a stage of shortage of bride. This was so because primitive people practice female infanticide, neglecting or sometimes outright killing their new born daughters. McLennan called this practice of female infanticide not mere cruelty, but rather a functional necessity. The primal human population lived under harsh conditions. The groups were small and subjected to intense struggle for existence both within and between groups. Immature women were burden upon the meager subsistence economy. The foremost effect of this struggle for food and security was an alleged prevalence of female infanticide. Female infanticide necessarily resulted in an unfavourable male-female ratio, as a result of which capture became the common rule. The shortage of women led to *polyandry,* in which a number of men took women as their common wife.

However, this was not the earliest stage of the society. In the beginning, marriage and kinship did not exist at all and mating was fairly random. Such sexual promiscuity made it impossible to recognise paternity. Thus, kinship was reckoned through female only. It means that in reckoning descent, matrilineality was a stage of development in rude promiscuity. The next stage of development was of a more regulated and less rude form of promiscuity, namely *polyandry,* where several men had a common wife. Polyandry were of two types: (i) Tibetan or fraternal polyandry and (ii) Nair polyandry or non-fraternal polyandry. In case of former, husbands were brothers but in case of latter, husbands were unrelated. In case of polyandry, women had to live in the camp of brothers, as a result of which patrilineal descent came into existence in place of matrilineal descent. Fraternal polyandry was no longer actually practised, but its former existence was attested by the occurrence of the institution of *levirate,* a custom that a younger brother is obliged to marry the wife or wives of his deceased older brother.

In latter version, McLennan (1876: 57) shifted his ground and postulated that female descent or matrilineal descent originated before wife capture. When kinship through females became strengthened, captured wives or women were recognised as full member of the group into which they had married. McLennan used the terms *endogamy* and *exogamy* to indicate the rules of marriage with women from inside the group or outside the group. But his arguments about the evolution of these institutions were not clear. Marriage by capture, of course, indicated exogamy, but when captured women or foreign women became recognised as member of the group, their offsprings or descendants were considered as marriage partners and exogamy was thus practised under the guise of endogamy.

Eventually, kinship became reckoned through males. For instance, in Tibetan polyandry, this development was most clear. The oldest brother assumed responsibility for all children, and thus became the legal father. Children inherited from him rather than from mother.

When agriculture came to replace hunting and gathering, subsistence became less precarious and female infanticide could be abandoned, so that sex ratio evened out. At that time, property became more important and inheritance was, thus, a focus of concern. The best solution was monogamy, because it clearly solved the relationship of children to their parents. Thus, according to McLennan, the present form of monogamous marriage has evolved from sexual promiscuity or from the state of sexual communism through the stages of polyandry and polygyny. The early form of family was matriarchal, in which descent was traced through mother and inheritance of property was from mother to daughter. Patriarchal family has evolved out of matriarchal family stage after stage in course of time.

Like Maine and Morgan, the evolutionary scheme of McLennan also briefly discussed the origin of state. Like Maine and Morgan, he held that the continued growth of importance of private property brought about a reduction of kinship relations outside of nuclear family. Hence, the rise of state was accompanied by the decay of tribe and other kinship grouping.

McLennan-Morgan as Critique of Each Other

In spite of their agreement reached independently on the stage of promiscuity and priority of matrilineal over patrilineal descent. McLennan and Morgan were bitter critiques of each other. McLennan tried to destroy Mogan's theory of kinship terminology. He denied the significance of classificatory and descriptive terminologies in societies. He asserted that they had no baring on family and descent but were mere modes of addressing persons. McLennan displayed remarkable "code for a man like Morgan, who had never seen an Indian".

Morgan, on the other hand, successfully exposed McLennan confusion concerning the nature of the exogamous groupings, which were supposed to have taken wives from each other. Morgan pointed out that exogamy and endogamy were very well existing side by side. The *clan* was exogamous, but tribe as a whole was endogamous.

One of the most interesting points made by Morgan was that McLennan had erroneously constructed matrilineal descent, a mode of reckoning clan affiliation, as the entire realm of kinship. Morgan correctly insisted that his system of consanguinity and affinity, proved the existence of *bilateral* reckoning of kinship regardless of the nature of descent rule employed.

Sir James George Frazer (1854-1941)

Frazer was born on January 1, 1854 at Glasgow, Scotland. He was one of four children born to Daniel Frazer and the former Katherine Brown. The father was the leading partner of a prosperous drug and chemical firm in Glassgow and the mother was the daughter of a prosperous merchant.

He began his schooling with a red-faced domini of the old school and recollected nothing of the experience. He attended Springfield Academy, where he spent his happiest school days and received the foundation and inspiration for much of his later work. It was here that he learned the rudiments of Latin and Greek, which were to play such a large part in his later studies. In 1869, at the age of fifteen, he matriculated at Glasgow University, where the foundation for subsequent career was firmly laid.

While at Glasgow, Frazer thought of competing for a scholarship at Oxford, but his father, mistrusting the High Church tendencies of Oxford, decided that Frazer should go to Cambridge instead. Thus, Frazer entered Trinity College at Cambridge on a scholarship in 1873. There he remained the rest of his life, his fellowship being renewed three times and finally for the whole life.

At Cambridge, Frazer continued his work in classical literature and philosophy and also studied law. The philosopher James Ward soon directed Frazer's attention towards Tylor's *Primitive Culture*. This book of Tylor stimulated Frazer's interest in anthropology. It was William Robertson Smith, however, who fired Frazer with a lasting enthusiasm for anthropology. Smith was a minister, who had been expelled from his teaching position at Free Church College, on the ground of heresy connected with his work in comparative religion. He was welcomed at Cambridge, where he favoured Frazer with his interest and friendship. Smith being engaged as editor of the ninth edition of *Encyclopaedia Britannica* and knowing Frazer's interest in anthropology, assigned to Frazer the writing of the article on 'Taboo and Totemism', which appeared in 1888. In 1883, Frazer read one of his anthropological papers on 'Certain Burial Customs as Illustrative of the Primitive Theory of Soul'.

The first edition of *The Golden Bough* was published in two volumes in 1890, the second edition of *Golden Bough* was published in three volumes in 1900, and the third edition of *Golden Bough* in twelve volumes appeared inbetween 1911 and 1915.

Frazer's most important classical study came out in 1898, after nine years of study. It was a translation of and commentary on 'Pausanias' Description of Greece and its six volumes constituted a great summary of the knowledge of classical Greece.

His *Psyche's Task* was published in 1909 and again in 1928 with the addition of one more paper as 'The Devil's Advocate'. Here Frazer argued that although superstitions has often been an evil, it has also had a positive value for mankind in promoting respect for authority and abstention from many forms of violence. It is *Psyche's Task* to separate the true from the false, but this may not always be a gain from the point of view of accepted ethical standards and social behaviour.

His four volumes of *Totemism and Exogamy* was published in 1910. Here the idea was advanced that after totem had become hereditary, exogamy developed as a means for preventing inbreeding.

His book, *The Belief Immortality and the Worship of Dead* was published in three volumes between 1913 and 1924. This work employed Tylor's idea of polytheism as originating in personified causes or nature spirits. According to Frazer, scientific theories eventually replace nature spirits as explanations for a given class of events, but the idea of deity is retained as the one great cause.

His book, *Folklore in the Old Testament*, was published in three volumes in 1918. In this work, Frazer treated the old testament as a body of folklore, which he defined as 'the whole body of people's traditionary beliefs and customs, so far as thing appears to be due to collective action of the multitude and cannot be traced to the individual influence of greatmen'.

His book entitled, *The Worship of Nature* was published in 1926 and presented the now familiar thesis that religion is based on the human personification of nature.

Frazer's remaining works included the *Gorgon's Head* (1927), containing literary essays, articles, and translations, in prose and verse, *The Fasti of Ovid* (1929), which started out to be a translation, but developed characteristically into a five-volume treatise on roman history and *Mythology and Aftermath* (1937), a supplement to *Golden Bough*.

Frazer's one venture outside the libraries was in a teaching position at Liver Pool University, where he was appointed as the Professor of Social Anthropology. He resigned after one year, convinced that he should never have left the library. Unwelcome respite from his work occurred on those occasions, when he journeyed to accept the many academic honours and awards that were bestowed upon him. He was an original fellow of British Academy, was knighted in 1914, elected a member of order of Merit (1924), elected to the Royal Society (1920), and received high recognition from France, being made an associate member of the Institute de France and a Commander of the Legion of Honour. In 1921, the Frazer lectureship in social anthropology was founded in his honour at the Universities of Oxford, Cambridge, Glasgow and Liverpool.

Frazer was an arm-chair anthropologist. He never conducted field studies. In other words, he was a man of monumental learning, but had no first hand acquaintance with the life of primitive people about whom he wrote. He hoped to discover the fundamental truth about the nature of human psychology by comparing the details of human culture on a world-wide scale, on the basis of secondary sources.

Frazer's Approaches

Frazer is the representative of an epoch in anthropology, which ends with his death. He was the last survivor of British classical anthropology. He represented better than any of our contemporaries that trend in humanism which sought inspiration from the comparative study of man for the understanding of the Greek, Latin and Oriental cultures of antiquity. In all his directly theoretical contributions, he is an evolutionist interested in primitive, whether he refers to mankind at large, or to specific beliefs, customs and practices of contemporary savages. He worked by the comparative method, collecting and examined evidence from all parts of the world, at all levels of development and in all cultures. The comparative method, combined with evolutionary, implies certain general assumptions. Men are substantially similar. They develop gradually from a primitive level and pass through various stages of evolution. The common measure in their actions and thoughts can be discovered by induction based on a vast survey of collected data. In this the concept of survival is essential to the evolutionist. It serves as the key for the understanding of continuity within transformation and as a link between the various stages. What was a strong and flourishing belief at one level, becomes a superstition in next higher one. Forms of marriage and kinship may become ossified into terminologies and survive as linguistic usage, long after the practices of group marriage or promiscuity have ceased. As we move down the various levels of development, we find the most primitive stage accessible, i.e., the origin of human institutions, customs and ideas.

Frazer never developed any full theoretical statement of evolutionary principles. We can not find in his work any precise definition of such concepts as origin, stage, survival, nor yet any scheme of explanation, which would allow us to assess how he imagined that evolution had proceeded, or what were the driving forces of progress. But he worked with all these concepts and constantly utilised the evolutionary as well as comparative scheme of explanation.

Frazer was essentially addicted to psychological interpretations of human belief and practice. His theory of magic, as the result of association of ideas, his three consecutive hypothesis about the origin of totemism in terms of belief in external soul, magical inducement of fertility, and in animal incarnation, are essentially conceived in terms of individual psychology. His treatment of taboos, or various aspects of totemism, of development of magic, religion and science, clearly reveal that the he in his explicit theories is little aware of the problem of social psychology. He is fundamentally hostile to psychoanalysis, while behaviourism never enters his universe of discourse.

Frazer's Evolutionary Principle

As referred to earlier, Frazer's convenient pegs were evolution, the principle of psychic unity of mankind, but he never clearly defined these ideas, nor did he develop full theoretical statements about them. His evolution was primarily one of the mental progresses of mankind. He described the meaning of *Golden Bough* as follows:

> The cycle of the Golden Bough depicts, in its sinuous outline, in its play of alternative light and shadow, the long evolution by which the thoughts and efforts of man have passed through the successive stages of Magic, Religion and Science. It is in some measure, an epic of humanity, which starting from magic, attaints to science in its ripe age.......

Thus, according to Frazer, the society or culture of mankind has passed through three successive development stages, namely, religion, and science.

Frazer's Views on Totem and Taboo

As referred to earlier, Frazer wrote articles on totem and taboo, for *Encyclopaedia Britannica*, the 9th edition, which appeared in 1888. For Frazer, these articles were the beginning of a systematic application to anthropology and especially to a study of backward races of men, whom we call savages and barbarians. Frazer gave his reason for concentrating on savagery than on civilization as follows:

> Civilization is extremely complex, savagery is comparatively simple. Savagery is undoubtedly the source from which all civilization has been ultimately derived by a slow process of evolution. It seemed to me, therefore, that if we are to understand the complex product, we must begin by studying the simple elements out of which it has been gradually compounded. In other words, we must try to understand savagery before we can hopefully to comprehend civilization.

In his article on totemism and taboo, Frazer has given a general idea about social origins, which became the guiding principle for much of his work, namely that from irrational beginning, system of great adaptative value for society are evolved. In taboo, Frazer remarks, we shall scarcely err in believing that even in advanced society the moral sentiments, in so far as they are merely sentiments are not based on an induction from experience, desire much of their force from an original system of taboo. Thus, on the taboo were grafted the golden fruits of law and morality.

According to Frazer, a totem is a class of material objects, which a savage regards superstitions with respect believing that there exists between him and every member of clan an intimate all together a special relation.

In his four volumes book entitled, *Totemism and Exogamy* (1910), Frazer gave a theory of soul for the origin of totem. He opined that totem originated as belief in soul. Savages believed that souls of human beings, after death, resided in plant, tree, animals, birds etc. The plant, tree, animal or bird, which was possessed by the soul of dead persons, the savages began to pay respect towards them. Eating and killing of those objects were strictly tabooed. In this way totemism came in to being. He cited example from Arunta tribe of Australia, in whose belief system, totems were regarded as responsible for causing pregnancy among women. Thus, totemism came into being from female side rather than male side. When in course of time, totems had become hereditary, exogamy developed as a means for preventing in breeding.

Frazer's views on Magic, Religion and Science

In his book, *Golden Bough*, Frazer explained that early man knew nothing of science. In this way, they possessed completely wrong idea of natural causes. He lived primarily by two erroneous principles on which all his magic was based. These two erroneous principles of magic were, namely (i) law of similarity and (ii) the law of contact. The first law presumed that like produces like. The magic associated with this law or principle of similarity is designated as Homeopathic magic or imitative magic. In this, magicians were, thus, convinced that they could control nature by imitating it. Thus, if rain was needed, water was poured out, and to harm an enemy, a doll was fashioned in his image and needles run through its head and heart.

The second principle of magic, i.e., law of contact, presumed that once in contact was always in contact. The magic associated with this law was known as contagious magic. This law posited that connections remained en force even after separation. Thus, one could get hold of one's hair or nail, or clippings or clothes, he had worn, and burn or otherwise mutilate such items in the conviction that the same would happen to their former owner.

But when the human mind progressed, people began to realise that they were fairly helpless, that their laws did not always work, and that they could not control nature by their own effort. The conviction then arose that higher, superhuman or supernatural powers governed the universe. With these insight, religion was born. Magicians became religious specialists and their supposed ability to contact and persuade supernatural spirits to act on their behalf gave them prestige and authority over people. Gradually, they became divine kings, whose departed souls were revered as Gods. The scientific stage was the highest development of human mind. Science was closely related to magic in as far as man once more began to manipulate nature by his own skills, but now he was equipped with correct laws. Frazer calls magic as 'bastard sister' of science or 'psuedo-science'.

Thus, Frazer depicted early men and contemporary primitives as rather irrational beings, although he would not deny that they had some capabilities as modern men. While it is true that science in a modern sense is of late appearance, in the history of mankind, it does not follow that non-literate people are wholy ignorant of natural causation. As Malinowski showed later on, that Trobriand islanders employed magic to increase their crops, but they also carried out all other rational tasks necessary for production. Moreover, Frazer's stages cannot be found in ethnographic reality, and both magic and religion are certainly co-existent with science.

Frazer's evolutionary framework offered him ample opportunity to display his data, which he collected from many sources. Such as classic literature, existing ethnographies, folklore, and so forth. He also carried on an extensive correspondence with field workers, missionaries, and other foreign travellers. For their guidance, he wrote a pamphlet called "Questions on Manners, Customs, Religions, Superstitions, etc. of uncivilized or semi-civilized people. In this way, he collected an immense quantity of date using them to illustrate and demonstrate his stages of magic and religion in to meaningful and coherent whole, presenting a fascinating epic of the development of mankind, i.e. *The Golden Bough* in twelve volumes. Malinowski called the *Golden Bough* as the greatest scientific odyssey in modern humanism.

AMERICAN EVOLUTIONARY SCHOOL

Lewis Henry Morgan (1818-1881)

L.H. Morgan was born in Aurora, New York in 1818. He studied law in Albany and settled as a lawyer in Rochester. Here, he was in close contact with Iroquois Indians. Like many contemporary Americans, he was attracted by clubs, lodge and similar fraternal societies. During his career as student, he formed the Order of the Gordian Knot, which purpose was to study ancient Greek myth and to imitate Greek customs. But when he became interested in the Iroquois, the lodge was remodeled and named as Grand Order of the Iroquois. He himself was elected as the chief under the lodge name of Skenenancloah. The members of this society called themselves as warriors. They discussed Iroquois Customs at their meetings and carried little to mahawks. Morgan along with other became interested in the study of Indian customs. Fortunately, Morgan met a young Seneca Indian in a book store, whose non-Indian name was Ely Parker. Parker was also a student in law and spoke english fluently. With the help of Parker, Morgan got opportunities to meet Indian chiefs and members of several Indian communities. Once Parker was invited to deliver a lecture at a meeting of Grand Order on songs, myths and ancient lore of his time, but instead he explained the miserable conditions of their Indian brotheren, who were poor, unhappy, desperate and victims of exploitation. His speech melted the heart of the members of society and Morgan made up his mind to take up the issue seriously. Not only that he assisted Seneca or Parker in their legal struggle with the government over land rights, in this connection, Morgan became aware that Indian cultures were rapidly changing and their customs should be recorded as early as possible. Visiting and interviewing many Iroquois Indians, he gathered informations related to dances, games, religion, language, material culture, form of government and family organisations. He analysed these research data systematically and published them in the form of a book entitled, *League of the Iroquois* in 1851. The book was considered as the first account of an Indian tribe ever given to the world and the best general book on this classic people.

While studying Iroquors Indian, he was keenly interested in government and family organisation of these classic people. For this purposes, he probed deeply into Indian marriage rules and system of matrilineal descent, but he was particularly struck by their system of naming relatives. He observed that an Iroquois child called his mother's sisters as mother, father's brothers as father, grandmother's sisters as grandmother and so on. Children of two or more sisters called each other brother and sister, and same was also true for children of two or more brothers. Morgan called this a *classificatory* kinship system, contrasting with the *descriptive kinship* system of civilized societies. First believing that it was a system of their own making, he soon discovered that Ojibwa Indians possessed a very similar system. Both must be derived from a common source. Because it seemed unlikely to Morgan that such a strange system could have been invented twice. It followed that if this system was prevalent or universal among all American Indians, the unity of their origin would be proved. Furthermore, if the same system could also be found to exist in Asia, it would prove that American Indians were Asiatic in origin, a question that was by no means firmly settled in Morgan's time.

In order to test this hypothesis, Morgan took the help of questionnaire technique for data collection. He constructed a seven-page questionnaire,containing more than 200 questions for this purpose. The questionnaires were mailed to foreign missions and diplomatic representatives in United States and all over the world with the financial assistance of Smithsonian Institution. Set of questionnaires was also sent in India to collect informations from Tamil. Although many questionnaires were not returned dully filled in, because everyone had no time and energy to complete the complex questionnaire. But informations received revealed that other American Indians used a similar kinship terminology. Informations received from Tamils in India indicated that they also used a classificatory system of kinship terminology. Morgan was happily convinced that his hypothesis that American Indian Tribes were Asiatic in origin, was true and obtained its definite proof. The details of questionnaires and analysis of data were published in the form of book entitled, *System of Consanquinity and Affinity of Human Family* (1870). The publication of the book received appreciation as well as severe criticism. Mayer Fortes (1969:19) reviewed the book as golden vein of kinship and social organisation for scientific mining in the history of the human sciences. McLennan, a British classical evolutionist, whose theory was that patrilineality came first, while Morgan felt that matrilineality proceeded patrilineality, argued that Morgan misunderstood kinship terms altogether and had overestimated their importance. Lord Avebury observed that Morgan's own data revealed that classificatory kinship systems were present in Australia and Polynesia, then why did American Indians originate in Asia, rather than in other parts of the world.

Morgan was very much influenced by a minister and Sanskrit Scholar named Joshua McIlvaine, who pointed out to him that a wide spread occurrence of classificatory system did not merely indicate American Indians relationship to Asia, but would prove that all primitive groups, who used it, were related and that classificatory system might classify an earlier stage of human development. McIlavaine's remarks compelled Morgan to purchase a copy of Darwin's *Origin of Species*. Before reading this book, he believed in divine creation of man. It is not well known, at what precise moment, Morgan felt to change his mind and to adopt the conclusion that man commenced at the bottom of scale from which he worked himself up to his present status. Later on, Morgan explained the evolution of marriage from '*endogamy*' to '*exogamy*' in terms of deleterious biological consequences of in breeding.

Morgan's paper entitled, "A Conjectural Solution to the Origin of the Classificatory System of Relationship" was published by the American Academy of Arts and Sciences in 1868. Thereafter, he emerged as a full-fledged evolutionist. In this paper, he traced the history of human family from primitive sexual promiscuity through fifteen stages of evolution to modern monogamy. In this reconstruction of history of marriage, he used a vast array of different types of kinship nomenclature. From this time onward, he began to work on the reconstruction of world history rather than that of American Indians alone. His thinking and researches in this direction produced monumental book *Ancient Society: Researches in Lines of Human Progress from Savagery through Barbarism to Civilization* in 1877.

In this book Morgan envisioned human history as consisting three major "ethnical periods" - Savagery, Barbarism and Civilization. The first two periods were divided into sub-periods denoted Lower, Middle and Upper. These ethnical periods and their subdivisions were defined by the following sequence of technological innovations:

Ethnic Periods	:	Technological Development.
Lower Savagery	:	Invention of speech, subsistence on fruits and nuts.
Middle Savagery	:	Fish subsistence and the use of fire.
Upper Savagery	:	Bow and arrow.
Lower Barbarism	:	Pottery
Middle Barbarism	:	Domestication of animals in the old world, Cultivation of maize by irrigation, adobe and stone brick buildings in New World.
Upper Barbarism	:	Iron-smelting and Iron tools.
Civilization	:	Phonetic alphabet and writing.

He was of opinion that each of these periods had a distinct culture and exhibits a mode of life more or less special and peculiar to itself. This specialization of ethnical periods rendered it possible to treat a particular society according to its condition of relative advancement and to make it a subject of independent study and discussion (1877: 9-18).

Edward B. Tylor had also talked about the evolution of ethnical periods as savagery, barbarism and civilization but he never placed a particular groups of cultures and technological inventions into any categories as Morgan did. His assumption was that survivals of materials and non-material cultures were sufficient evidence to indicate that the mankind has reached into complex form of civilization from simple form of savagery through barbarism. Thus, unlike Tylor, Morgan assigned specific known cultures to the various stages of development. He was of opinion that lower savagery had passed out of existence. Australians and most polynesians were in middle savagery. Indian tribes east of Missouri river were in the stage of lower barbarism. Village Indians in Mexico, Central America and Peru were in middle barbarism, while Homeric Greeks, Germanic tribes of Caesar's time, and ancient Italians were in the stage of upper barbarism.

Except for civilization, Morgan used criteria of subsistence and material culture for the recognition of his periods of human history. He also established sequences of family organisation, kinship terminology, descent pattern, socio-political organisation and rules of inheritance of property. At every point, he asked himself how far and why institutions changed from one form to next. His observations revealed that kinship based society proceeded the state formation, concept of property was not developed in early stage and inheritance pattern in those days was also absent. Therefore, he came to the conclusion that descriptive kinship terminology and monogamy were relatively late in their emergence.

His correlations, sequence and conclusions were also criticised. His analysis was also of a functionalist nature, particularly when he talked about the aspects of socio-political organisations interrelated with one another and tied to technological developments and economic persuits.

The major weakness of Morgan's system rests in the confusion between *synchronic* and *diachronic* reconstructions. Extrapolating from living culture, he felt that past society could be fully recovered not by archaeological evidence but by simple accepting the Idea that contemporary non-literate societies in their totality were accurate reflections of the past. Tylor and McLennan were careful in explanations of the comparative method. They reconstructed the sequences of specific institutions or of discrete cultural elements, but not of whole cultures.

Morgan's last book entitled *Houses and House Life of American Aborigines* was published in 1881. This book was an another land mark in the field of Anthropology. He was the first anthropologist to recognise that products of material culture do not occur in isolation from other social developments. He showed that the patterns of architecture interrelate with forms of family organisations and social life.

Weaknesses of Morgan's Scheme

The major weakness of Morgan's scheme was confusion between synchronic and diachronic approaches to the study of historical reconstructions. Clear-cut application of comparative method did not appear in his study. His characterisation of contemporary cultures in terms of historical stages was also faulty. His correlations did not fit in and can be disproven even by a cursory glance at the ethnographic data. For instance, Hawaiiyans with a kinship system was early in Morgan's scheme, developed agriculture, were highly stratified and possessed a complex form of government. In the old world, civilization existed long before the use of iron. The Aztecs worked with native metals and had no knowledge of iron smelting, but nevertheless had a state government and developed a system of writing.

Enduring Aspects of Morgan's Scheme

In spite of severe criticism, Morgan made substantial contributions in the field of anthropology. His kinship terminology attracted many scholars to study the kinship organisation as a result of which nearly thousands of studies on kinship system were published after his death. His example of fieldwork, and first hand data collection were followed energetically even by Baasian, who were critical of him. His evolutionary schemes raised all problems basic to explanations of social change, and conclusive answers for all these have not been found. Implicitly, he recognised cultures as a functional whole, because all institutions were seen interrelated.

The present-day anthropologists have dropped the offensive words savagery and barbarism, but accept a historical sequence from hunting and gathering to domestication of plant and animals, and writing as the beginning of civilization. His observation that kinship based societies were the early form of government which proceeded state formation was accepted by all.

He is often criticised that he did not study deeply into the role of religion. But it is often over looked. He devoted on Iroquois religion in his book League of Iroquois. In his book *Ancient Society* he dealt with the problem of interrelationship between totemism and kinship.

Morgan and Tylor on Evolutionary Theory

For Morgan and Tylor, there were two logical explanations for the development of cultures along similar line, either the major patterns were independently reinvented time after time or the patterns had diffused from group to group as a result of intercultural communication. But what could cause the similarity in two patterns that had been independently invented? Their answer in essence was that there existed a basic 'psychic unity' among all man-kind. Morgan reasoned that all men possessed certain 'germ ideas' that served as the basis of parallel development of socio-cultural patterns. These 'germ idea' had been part of man kind's mental equipment from the lowest period of savagery.

Morgan pointed out (1877: 255) "human mind, specially the same in all individuals and in all the tribes and nations of mankind, limited in range of power works and must work, in the same uniform channels, and within narrow limits of variations. Its result in disconnected region of space, and in widely separated ages of time articulates in a logically connected chain of common experiences. In the grand aggregate may still be recognised the few primary germs of thought, working upon primary human necessities, which through the natural process of development have produced such vast result".

Tylor agreed, nothing that the mental processes of man everywhere were essentially similar and that there were basic similarities of life-ways among saves that were not due to diffusion (1871). In abstract, both explanations — psychic unity and independent invention — were allowable. The rub came, when trying to decide which of the two adequately explained the specific similarities between diverse groups. When it was discovered that a given culture trait — such as a specific family from, a game such as the Indian Pachise, or metallurgy, was found among widely separated people, could the co-occurrence be due to wide-spread transmission from a single origin or was it the result of a series of independent inventions time after time in each of the groups?

There were profound implications riding on which of the two alternatives was finally to be selected and again the issue of progress versus degeneration was involved. Some anthropologists observed that degenerated savage group could progress only under the influence of more advanced people, i.e., due to diffusion. But if Tylor were to combat this issue, he would have to push the independent invention as alternative, i.e., evolution. This he did in *Primitive Culture* (1871) to the limits his empirical-oriented conceive would allow. On the other hand, diffusion could have made the evidence for the universality of certain mental processes much more questionable, because there would have been the dilemma of whether the similarities were not actually due to wide-spread transmission of traits.

As a matter of fact, neither Tylor nor Morgan, ever argued exclusively for one of the two alternatives. There were many instances of diffusion to be ignored for the sake of 'psychic unity'. Their conclusion about which of the two, explanations, accounted for a given similarity, were drawn on the basis of evidence as they saw to fit to use it. Tylor was perhaps the more cautious of the two, often presenting the dilemma and then withdrawing to wait for more evidence to accumulate. Morgan, in a logical contradiction to his germ idea concept, suggested a world wide diffusion of a given type of kinship group from a single origin and suggested other world wide dispersals of specific family forms, based only on the argument that forms were too complex to have been invented more than once (1877: 379-386).

There was still a sticky issue to be resolved. However, if 'Psychic unity' and 'diffusion' were both operative, how could the simultaneous, 19th century existence of both civilized and savage groups be explained? Why had some groups evolved faster or more rapidly than others? On this issue, Morgan and Tylor became tangled in confusion of racial and socio-cultural factors as causes of evolutionary process. The relative clarity of psychic unity/diffusion alternative became frustratingly muddled.

Morgan and Tylor on Biological and Cultural Processes

Morgan and Tylor resorted at time to racist explanations for the unsynchronised evolutionary development along the mankind of the world. For instance, Morgan while describing the widespread dispersion of Gonowanian family type, went beyond mere diffusion as an explanation and argued that this form was transmitted with the blood (1870: 274). The mind of American Indian never experienced, what could be called as 'Profit motive'. This was the great reason for his continuance in hunter stage. Tylor (1881) compared civilised morality with that of savages and barbarians. His observations revealed that there were differences in high and low races of men and dull-minded barbarians had no power of thought enough to come up at civilized man's best moral standard.

But how can these explanations be fitted with notion of Psychic unity? The anthropologist, Marvin Harris (1968:139-140) offered his interpretation of Morgan's ideas:

> As the races evolve, they pass through similar bio cultural stages. At any particular stage, the innate mental condition of the descendants of any branch of human species tends to be essentially similar. They, thus, tend to react to similar conditions in similar ways and to move in parallel fashion from savagery to civilization.

Thus, there were superior and inferior races as indicted by the level of cultural evolution. Of all racial groups, only white man had achieved the arbitrary standards of civilization by mid 19th century.

However, Harris interpretation does not resolve the apparent contradiction of evolution of human kind due to biological factor or cultural factor. Even Tylor and Morgan either did not see the problem or simply ignored them. To make the confusion more profound, both writers seemed at times to use the term races and cultures interchangeably. As they did not stick solely either to psychic unity or diffusion for cultural similarities, in the same way they did not resort strictly to racial explanations for the differences between savages and civilized men. Tylor (1881) for example, cited savage's lack of the 'large experience' of civilized cultures — a difference that is not clearly the result of savage genes. But whether this meant that savages lacked a large experience because they were inherently stupid or they did not have access to the scholarly knowledge accumulated and stored in thousands of years of other human literacy.

In fact, neither Tylor nor Morgan used biological analogies as extensively as Herbert Spencer. Morgan reported that emergence of consanguine family among savages afforded a good illustrations of the principle of natural selection, although he did not pursue the principle very actively (1877: 425). Tylor (1871) wrote, 'History .... and ethnography.... combine to show that institutions, which can best hold their own in world, gradually supersede the less fit ones, which determines the general resultant course of culture. However, when such pronouncements are separated from analysis, it becomes apparent that Tylor was not particularly interested in demonstrating the biological analogies, nor was he willingly to acknowledge a great intellectual debt to Darwin.

Yet Tylor and Morgan both shared a degree in the 'Social Darwinist' notions prevalent in their time. This was implicit in their assigning victorian England and America to the highest known stages of cultural evolution. The bearers of civilization were 'better and happier than those at lower stages of evolution. The application of the 'survival of the fittest' dogma imposed on much of their analysis a moralistic bias that was contrary to modern caynons of objective social science. The racial explanation for differences in evolutionary progress hindered scholarly inquiry in to the roles of psychic unity and diffusion in change process.

Influence of Morgan's Scheme on Marx and Engles

It is often quoted that Marx bought a copy of Morgan's Ancient Society' and found in it a confirmation of his own materialistic conception of history. When Marx died, he left instructions for Engles to present Morgan's finding to a wider audience and a year later, Engles published, *The Origin of the Family, Private Property and the State, in the Light of Researches of Lewis Henry Morgan* (1884). The book contains a summary of Morgan's arguments and evolutionary theory.

Why was Morgan's theory so important for Marx and Engles ? Morgan himself was certainly more of bourgeois than a revolutionary, and he was inclined to consider his own American civilization as an epitome of safety and happiness. Yet his over all theory could be interpreted as evolution of economic production (fruits and nuts, fishing, agriculture, domestications of animal) and on the tools assisting these modes of subsistence (fire, bow, pottery, iron) was in the line with Marxian concept that production and the tools necessary for production are the basic factors determining the course of history. Since Morgan had made these criteria diagnostic for stages of cultural evolution and he had made all other aspects of society subordinate to that base, it was not surprising that Marx was impressed. Marx could present a total picture of social evolution in the materialistic manner. As neither he nor Engles possessed much knowledge of Primitive or Prehistoric cultures, Morgan with his first-hand knowledge was obviously a specialist in this area. Engles called Morgan as the first man who with expert knowledge had attempted to introduce a definite order into history of primitive man.

GERMAN OR CONTINENTAL EVOLUTIONARY SCHOOL

Johnn Jacob Bachofen (1815-1877)

J.J. Bachofen was a classical continental evolutionist. Like Morgan, Maine, McLennan, he was also a lawyer by training. Like Morgan and McLennan, he believed that matrilineality was the early form of reckoning kinship, where as patrilineality was a developed form of kinship descent. In this way, the hypothesis of Maine that Patrilineality came earlier than matrilineality was not accepted by other evolutionists of his era.

Bachofen, a Swiss lawyer by profession, got opportunities to survey Greek classical writings and ethnographic literatures, in which he observed that in early societies children were named after their mothers. Literature further confirmed that it was still the case in some nonliterate societies. On the basis of such observations in literatures, he arrived at a conclusion that *'matriarchy'* must have proceeded the *patriarchy*.

Bachofen observed that matriarchy was the second stage of development. Before reaching the stage of matriarchy, there existed a stage of *heterism* or sexual promiscuity or sexual communism. This stage, he deduced from the survivals of temple prostitution, a custom where priestesses gave themselves freely to male worshippers. Thus, his conclusion was that this practice must have been a survival of earlier promiscuous condition. In this way, the arguments of Bachofen were more speculation and mystical than those of Morgan and Maine.

Such observations made Bachofen interested in collecting more and more informations on matrilineal societies. The data gathered were analysed and published in book form under the title, *Das Mutterrecht* or *Mother Right* in 1861. In this book Bachofen developed the following sequences of development of patriarchy:

In the early period of sexual promiscuity, women were merely treated as sex objects. Kinship lines or descents were traced through mother i.e. female, because in random mating it was quite impossible to know the real father of the child. This submissiveness was taken an ill and ancient women liberation movement revolted against it. As a result of this, they were successful in managing the chance to get upper hand in social affairs, ushering in the period of Amazonian assertiveness, where Gynocracy (mother-right) prevailed. In this stage female began to rule the world. Females deities were worshipped, female left was raised in dignity over male right side, the moon (because it regulated menstruation) was as more important than Sun. The earth began to rule over ocean, sorrow over joy, death over life, darkness over light and the youngest born was preferred over the oldest.

Eventually, women got tired of whole business and wanted husband to care for them. Simultaneously, male strove to over throw the female reign. First men pretended that they, too, could give birth and invented the couvade, a custom where a father goes to bed as if for child-bearing, when his wife is giving birth, so as to make believe that he has delivered a child and is thus equal to women. But even without such concepts men succeeded in their dominance. They rose to a new and higher principle of religion that of spirit. This highest principles of life is based on fatherhood as opposed to motherhood. The essertation of patriarchy and patrilineality reserved all former symbolism, the sun ruled the moon, the heavenly light prevailed over the darkness of the earth etc.

Taking Bachofen, Maine and McLennan together they have in common, first and foremost, an interest in history of social institutions and the dynamic dimensions of time. Although their evolutionary theories were to a great extent deductive and speculative, but is it beyond doubt that they were aware of proof and explanation of processes of change. They seriously examined the classical writings and ethnographic literatures to show that mankind was a unity and lower stages of development were directly related to later ones. When written documentation was lacking, they deviced means to fill the gap by survivals' concept, which also came to play an important role in Tylor's reconstruction of primitive culture. According to them, the concept of survivals meant that items of culture that were no longer active or functional but must have had meaning before, and were thus indication of conditions of earlier periods.

On the whole, they focused attention on the importance of development of social institutions. Not only they, thus contributed to the analysis of culture, but they clearly understood that Law, kinship, marriage etc. were to be understood in relationship to each other and to social conditions in general.

In their views, historical explanations were sufficient to the understanding of varieties of culture. Their method became known as 'historical method', which meant the attempt to show that human culture had undergone progressive and acumulative growth. Thus, it was necessary to reconstruct total panorama of human history. They relied also upon the 'comparative method' which postulated that primitive cultures or societies reflect the early conditions of mankind. Evolutionary sequences could thus be established by comparing and analysing certain aspects or institutions to complex ones. The equation of primitive with early was justified by the idea that primitive populations were conservative to an extreme degree.

Although, they intended to give an over all picture of evolution of specific social institutions, and were rather convinced that progress had taken place in an orderly way so that higher forms of organisation followed lower one by necessity of time. They were, however, not strict unilinear evolutionist. They recognised that environmental or social conditions sometimes embedded change, some times accelerated it. McLennan pointed out two types of development of polyandry — Tibetan and Nair. Maine was of opinion that societies advanced at different rates of progress.

As a whole, the aim of these evolutionists, was to present an over all view of cultural history, but they did not attempt to reconstruct unequivocal stages to total cultural development. Instead, they focused attention upon separate but related phenomena of law, family, marriage and kinship.

Adolf Bastian (1826-1905)

Adolf Bastian, was an another German ethnographer, who strongly championed the psychic unity principle in reconstructing culture history. Being empiricist, he criticised and rejected both Lamanck's and Darwin's theories of evolution on the ground that no one had seen species changing into another. He wrote two books in German language, which have not been translated into English. These are as follows:

(i) *Der Menschy in der Geschichut*, O'Wigand, Leipzig, 1860
(ii) *Ethnische Elementargedanken in der Lahrevom Manschem*, Berlin, 1895.

These books revealed that he was interested in the study of history of culture in terms of social evolution. His emphasis was more on similarities of culture between different types of people rather than their differences. He was of opinion that similarities were caused due to psychic unity of man kind. His opinion revealed that there was a restricted number of basic ideas common to all mankind, a theory presently examined by Le'vi-Strauss. Bastian called these basic ideas as Elementargedankengo, which means, elementary thought pattern. Since these ideas develop in various environments, they always find their specific expression as 'Volkergedanken' (folk idea). Those ideas with similar 'folk ideas' constituted 'Geographical provinces', a concept foreshadowing later American culture areas concept. Bastian gladly admitted that these provinces had not remained pure, because migration and diffusion had introduced different culture traits. In this way, he was better aware of complexity of cultural evolution that than many other 19th century evolutionists.

Bastian's writing are virtually unknown to present day anthropologists and perhaps with good reason because his style was confused, obscure, ornate, bombastic, and untranslatable, but he clearly realised that simple stages of development could not exist because too many different factors had intervened. As he was well travelled, he also collected various objects of material culture, which eventually found their way into the Museum fur volkerkunde in Berlin, which he helped to establish. Along with Rudolf Virchow, he founded the German Society for Anthropology. He also founded the German African Society by which his scientific journal of anthropological fields entitled "Zeitschrift fur Ethnolgie" was published.

CRITICISM OF CLASSICAL EVOLUTIONARY THEORY

There is no denying the fact that classical evolutionists tried their best to explore, analyse and understand cultural processes on the basis of their postulates and theories of evolution of cultures or culture as a whole. It is also true that they surveyed ample existing literatures, left by travellers, missionaries, ethnographers to reconstruct the history of cultural institutions and mankind as a whole. Where the written account was not available, they took help of cultural survivals, which played significant role in their analysis of reconstruction. Historical and comparative approach, used by them as method of viewing research, is still accepted as important tool for understanding the present cultural phenomena in relation to past. In this way, they have preserved a vast material on development of human culture and civilization of further inquiry and explorations for the coming generations. But inspite of all such valuable contributions made in the field of anthropology in general and cultural and social anthropology in particular, their theories of cultural evolution have been subjected to many criticism. Major criticism levelled against them are as follows:

I. These evolutionists mostly tried to show independent evolution of culture stage after stage or period after period in a sequence. Thus, their explanation was one sided. This one sided analysis was their greatest weakness for which they were frequently criticised by other anthropologists in general and diffusionists in particular.

II. These evolutionists have accepted that origin of similar cultural traits was due to similar cause. This assumption of evolutionist is also a subject to criticism because human history is a witness that different cultures have originated in same geographical environment. If these scholars would have gone through more historical and archaeological evidences, they might have accepted their such mistake. It is true that each society has dissimilar geographical and other environmental conditions, which naturally influences the processes of cultural development. Then how it is possible that in ununiform environmental situations, the process of evolution was similar. Critiques believe that in different environmental condition, the processes of evolution also follow different ways and direction. For instance, the institution of polygeneous marriage originated due to plenty of women at a place, while on another place, it existed on account of social prestige and wealth.

III. The claim of these evolutionists, that mankind of world has passed through different stages or period of cultural development in a sequence, also does not stand true for all cultural or social groups. It can not be said safely that the evolutionary sequences of economic development such as food gathering and hunting, domestication of plant and animal, introduction of agriculture, and setting of industry, were similar, for all societies. Later anthropological researches do not support this conclusion. For instance, practice of hunting and food gathering indicates the early stage of economic development, historically and archaeologically, but this stage of hunting and gathering is still existing among the societies belonging to other stages of economic development. Again we do not have sufficient evidence to refer to that in history of mankind there was a time, when men survived only on hunting. The survey of primitive world reveals that there are many tribes of America and

Africa, which carry on agriculture but they have not passed through the stage of domestication of animal. It means that among them, the stage of agriculture developed from hunting and gathering without following the evolutionary sequence of pastoralism. This indicates that the sequence of evolution can get broken by other existing situation. For example, in India the setting up of industries have made many tribals industrial labour, who led a life like hunter, gatherer and pastoral. In this way, they did not reach into a stage of agriculture, before reaching the stage of industrial labour.

In the same way, the sequence of technological developments — stone age, bronze age and iron age — do not appear true as for all societies of mankind. Though the evidences of technological developments in European countries throw sufficient light to believe that culture of mankind as a whole has passed through the successive periods of stone age, bronze age and iron age, but evidences gathered from African countries indicate that Africa witnessed the development of iron age after stone age. Uptill now, there is no proof available to refer to existence of copper age there. Such examples reveal clearly that evolutionary theory of cultural processes can not be limited in boundary of certain definite sequence.

IV. The evolutionists are also criticised for adopting weak method of study. They all were arm-chair anthropologists, who never visited the field for actual observation of the phenomena, rather they were disinterested in fieldwork. They relied upon the data gathered by travellers and missionaries and never showed interest in testing the reliability of data before arriving at a conclusion. They had become so extremist in establishing their theory of cultural evolutionism that wherever they observed similarities in culture traits, they tried to place them in a sequence.

V. Evolutionists were so biased with their preconceptions that they forgot the theory of diffusion or migration of culture traits. In other words, they overlooked that culture traits diffuse or migrate from one place to another. Culture is dynamic not static, which is an important characteristic of culture. Diffusionists have tried to show that culture growth is also caused by the process of diffusion. As culture is imitated, when groups having different cultures come in contact with each other, they imitate culture traits of each other. As a result of this, the diffusion of culture takes place at distant places.

VI. Golden-wieser, an American diffusionist, criticised evolutionists not only because they ignored the significance of diffusion in cultural development, but, at the same time, the classical evolutionists also neglected the importance of discovery or invention. According to him, culture is an invention or discovery of human beings through social needs. Historical evidences make it clear that evolution in culture does not take place in that sense in which the evolutionists have used. It is tradition of society which makes a culture living. Many generations join their hands and shoulder in its continuation. Each generation adds new knowledge etc. in the developmental process of culture. Whether this processes of cultural development would be termed as evolution ? If it is, it cannot be denied that evolution means only change in form, but also in quality. Qualitative change is possible through creative processes, whose expression can be found in social invention or discovery. For qualitative change in cultural form, he does not believe in psychic unity, but it was possible by way of diffusion of invented traits.

In spite of these severe criticism, evolutionism is now no longer unfashionable. Though much modern theories differ from earlier ones, but the relevance of their over all approach is generally recognised.

POSITIVE CONTRIBUTIONS OF CLASSICAL EVOLUTIONISTS

Although on the basis of empirical researches of 20th century, classical evolutionary scheme has been criticised, but their following contributions cannot be forgotten:

1. Anthropology as a 'science of culture' and separate discipline of study was established by the greatest pioneer E.B. Tylor in 1884 at Oxford university, London.
2. They developed the concept of culture and advanced the principle that culture and race must not be confused in studying the lifeways of human society.
3. They distinguished those subdivisions of culture, which we a call today, as aspects and showed their usefulness in studying culture.
4. They established the principle of continuity and orderly development of culture, a principle, that must underly any realistic approach to the analysis of cultural dynamics.
5. By analysing and comparing the cultures of the universe, they have provided rich material to cultural anthropology for the study and further explorations.

Neo-Evolutionary School

Classical or unilinear evolutionists had to face rough criticism by 20th century diffusionists and relativists, on the ground of empirical data. Diffusionists emphasised upon the need of cultural diffusion which brought about similarities in cultures of the world. They disfavoured the idea of 'psychic unity' and 'parallel inventions' on the argument that basically men were uninventive, but they had limitless capacity to adapt and imitate, which is possible either by diffusion or by migration. Historical particularists or cultural relativists emphasised upon divergent trends in culture of a area or sub-area. They were not ready to accept unilinear sequences of cultural evolution, in which cultural diversities were not denied, but they were of mere secondary importance.

In order to remove those shortcomings, Neo-evolutionary scheme was proposed by Neo-evolutionists. Among Neo-evolutionists, Leslie White and Julian Steward of America and V. Gordon Childe of Britain, occupy most significant place in reviving evolutionary theory. Neo-evolutionists believe that all weaknesses of classical evolutionary theory can be solved, if it is accepted that culture develops not in unilinear sequence but in the form of *Parabolic curve.* According to parabolic curve theory of cultural evolution, a social institutions is born in specific form in the early stage. It, then, gradually develops in entirely different form in different direction. It again moves towards original form but in a new developed form. For instance: the institution of property was born in the form of communal ownership or communism. In Medieval time, the common ownership took the form of private ownership. Today, again the concept of common ownership through state has developed. Similarly, in the beginning there was lack of clothes and men used to remain naked. Invention of clothes made it possible to cover the entire body. But in present time, the adoption of fashion is compelling to remain half-naked. This sequence can also be observed in the field of sex-relation. In early stage, there was sexual promiscuity, in course of time monogamy came into existence, and again in present time, arguments are made in favour of sex-freedom. There examples can be shown by graph as follow:

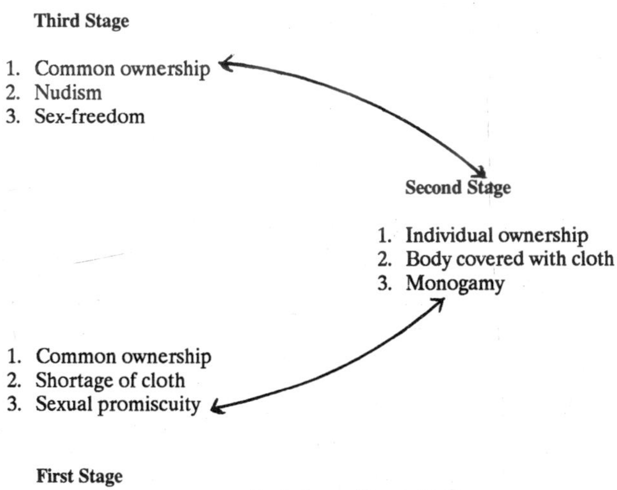

Evolution in Parabolic Curve

This is particularly true for the western countries. But societies in east will also follow it.

British Neo-Evolutionary School

V. Gordon Childe (1892-1957)

The only pioneer, of British School of Neo-evolutionism, was V. Gordon Childe, V. Gordon Childe was a trained archaeologists and on the basis of collection of materials remains from East and Europe, and comparing them, he attempted to make evolutionary scheme alive. Before dealing with his evolutionary theory, it would be worthy to mention here the list of publications made by him. These are so follows:

1. *The Dawn of Western Civilization*, New York 1925
2. *New Light on most Ancient East*, New York, 1934
3. *What happened in History*, New York, 1946
4. *Social Evolution*, New York, 1951
5. *Man Makes Himself*, New York 1951
6. *What is History*, New York, 1953

His most famous book, which describes evolution of culture, is *Social Evolution*. He described evolution of culture in terms of three major events: (i) invention of food production, (ii) urbanisation and (iii) industrialization. Analysing the transitions that took place under the impact of these major events, he presented an overall view of evolutionary process and delineated its common factors.

According to him, the evolution of archaeological periods and cultural developments are as follows:

Sl. No.	*Archaeological period*	*Cultural development*
1.	Palaeolithic period	Savagery
2.	Neolithic period	Barbarism
3.	Copper age	Higher Barbarism
4.	Early Bronze age	Civilization

His above scheme of evolutionary sequence clearly reveals that he was very much influenced by Tylor's and Morgan's evolutionary schemes of cultural development, i.e., Savagery, Barbarism and Civilization. Thus, he was a devout follower of unilinear evolution of classical evolutionists. He did not place particular cultural groups into savagery, barbarism and civilization as L.H. Morgan had done. But he was more close to E.B. Tylor, who had talked that mankind as a whole had passed through the successive cultural development stages of savagery, barbarism and civilization. As V.G. Childe discussed evolution of culture of mankind as a whole, Julian Steward called him as universal evolutionist, because he had placed general stages of evolution applicable to mankind as a whole not of specific or particular cultures which were the creation of local environmental factors. In establishing universal sequence of cultural development. Childe opined that all societies had lived in different historical environments and had passed through different ups and downs due to which their traditions had diverged. As a result of which multiplicity had emerged in cultural ethnography. Childe further stressed that the considerations of multiplicity or particular or specific culture would be our handicap, if objective was to establish general stages in evolution of culture. He was of opinion that in establishing general stages of evolution, diffusion must also be discounted, because any society must be in a position to accept diffused technological and social features.

The universal evolutionary scheme of Childe was similar to Leslie White, a contemporary evolutionist of America, who also believed in universal sequence of evolution. Therefore, the names of V.G. Childe and Leslie White; are frequently uttered together as pioneers, who revived evolutionary theory in 20th century in the same unilinear sequence as proposed by 19th century classical evolutionist. Their universal sequence was similar to unilinear sequence of 19th century evolutionists in scope of its generalization; but not in its treatment to particulars. Their emphasis was more on culture, i.e., general evolution of mankind or/and culture as a whole. But they never, took in to consideration, the local environmental factors in their universal evolutionary scheme.

Childe postulated different order of evolution from those of 19th century evolutionists. His cultural sequences were so general that they were neither very arguable like classical evolutionists, nor very useful. No one can dispute that hunting and gathering, which is Childe's diagnostic of savagery, proceeded plant and animal domestication, which is his criterion of barbarism. Domestication of plant and animal was the precondition of large populations, cities, internal social differentiation and specialization, and the development of writing and mathematics, are his characteristics of civilization. Childe opined that a drastic change in the life pattern of mankind appeared in civilizational stage, in which an aggressive attitude towards environment developed among mankind. Forest-dwellers or cave-dwellers became house-dwellers. Hunters and gatherers became food producer by adopting agriculture. Writing made them capable of preserving their tradition and mathematics came into being for counting things. The development of cities made them urbanised and technological advancement of smelting copper, bronze, iron etc. made them capable of producing durable utensils and implements. Thus, according to him, at each stage of cultural development, mankind developed their technological skill to exploit natural resources. In the early stage, less advanced technological skill, had made them less aggressive towards environment, but as knowledge went on increasing, they became more and more aggressive.

While correlating cultural development with technological materials, V. Gordon Childe; a key figure in English archaeology, was a marxist and devout follower of Morgan's stages of savagery, barbarism and civilization. As Marx was very much influenced by Morgan's evolutionary scheme, and Childe also supported Morgan's scheme, therefore, he was regarded as a Marxist. Marx believed that production and the tools necessary for production were the basic factors determining the course of history.

When V. Gordon Childe discusses specific sequence of middle East and Europe, he seems more closer to historical particularism than to historical materials. Childe's working model of evolution was like Darwinian tree of life. He treated variations as invention, heredity as learning and diffusion and selection as cultural adaptation and choice. It was certainly a worthy objective to seek universal laws of cultural change. It must be stressed, however, that universal laws postulated are concerned with the fact that culture changes and, thus, can not explain particular features of particular cultures. Thus, the laws of cultural and biological evolution are similar.

Despite his explicit Marxist learning, Childe was unsuccessful in achieving reconciliation between the abstract over all transition from savagery to civilization, and his super knowledge of specific development sequences in Middle-East and Europe. He did recognise certain parallels in the end product, but he saw there as resulting more from diffusion than from parallel evolution.

The interesting steps in development did not exhibit even abstract parallelism.

> "the observed developments in rural economy do not run parallel. They cannot be defined stages common to all the sequences examined..... In fine, the development of barbarians rural economics in the regions surveyed exhibits not parallelism but divergence and convergence" (Childe 1951:116).

Childe was unfamiliar with the importance of irrigation in Mesoputania and Egypt both from the perspective of productivity and organisational exigencies and controls as appears from the following quotation:

> Conditions of life in a river valley or other oasis place in the hands of society exhibit an exceptional power for coercing its members. The community can refuse a recalcitrant access to water and can close the channels that irrigate his fields. Rain falleth upon the just and unjust alike, but irrigating waters reach the field by channels that community has constructed. And what society has provided, society can also withdraw from the unjust and confine to the just one. The social solidarity needed by irrigators can, thus, be imposed due to the very circumstances that demand it. And young man cannot escape the restraint of their elders by founding fresh villages, when all beyond the oasis is waterless desert. So, when the social wills come to be expressed through a chief or a king, he is invested not merely with moral authority, but with coercive force, too. He can apply sanctions against the disobedient (Childe 1946: 90).

Weaknesses of Childe's Scheme

1. Childe's most serious short comings was lack of interest in the civilizational sequence outside of the middle east and Europe. At one hand, he correctly concluded that there was little resemblance between the specific steps involved in the development of civilization in Europe, but he was unprepared to look for parallels in Mexico or Peru, on the other hand.
2. He relied too much on archaeological data to explain cultural evolution, but he could not be able to differentiate the old hunters and gatherers from today, because they differ significantly in possession of hunting implements.
3. He could not take into consideration the universal existing institutions of matriarchy, sexual promiscuity, etc. without giving any argument.

Despite of such criticism, it was V. Gordon Childe, who made alive the evolutionary theory even after serious criticism by 20th century relativists, particularists, diffusionists etc. Being a man of archaeology, he was successful in presenting universal scheme of cultural evolution in terms of archaeological sequences.

Julian H. Steward (1902-1972)

Julian H. Steward was one of the students of A.L. Kroeber at the University of California and had contributed data to "the Culture-

Element-Distribution Study". He was trained at Berkeley, where he received Ph.D. in 1931. His earlier work was dominated by particularist influences emancipating from Kroeber and Lowie. Steward's own interest in environmental factors was first consolidated by fieldwork among the Eastern Mono and pailute of Owens Valley, California in 1927 and 1928. Up to the publication of his, *The Economic and Social Basis of Primitive Bands*, Steward's position corresponded essentially to those anthropolo- gists, who regarded the natural environment as a vauguely limiting or enabling factor in culture history. But later on, he selected to focus his attention on "Cultural Ecology" and "Multilinear Evolution".

His most famous book entitled, *Theory of Culture Change* was published in 1955 from University of Illinois Press, Urbana. Besides this book, he contributed a good number of papers in reputed journals, which are as follows:

1. 1929: "Diffusion and Independent Invention: A Critique of Logic", *American Anthropologist*, 31:491-95.
2. 1936: "Economic and Social Basis of Primitive Bands" R. Lowie ed., *Essays in Anthropology* presented to A.L. Kroeber, University of California Press, Berkeley, 133-45.
3. 1937: "Ecological Aspects of South Western Society", *Anthropos,* 32:87-104.
4. 1938: *Basin-Plateau Aboriginal Socio-Political Groups*, Washington, 104.
5. 1946: "Hand Book of South American Indian", *Washington, Bureau of American Ethnology Bull*, 120.
6. 1948: "A Functional Developmental Classification of American High Culture". W. Bennet ed. *A Repraisal of Peruvian Archaeology*, Memories of the Society for American Archaeology, 103-104.
7. 1949: "Cultural Casualty and Law: A Trial Formulation of Early Civilization", *American Anthropologist*, 51: 1-27.
8. 1956: "Cultural Evolution", Scientific American, 194:69:80.
9. 1960: "Review of White's The Evolution of Culture", *American Anthropologist*, 62: 144-48.

Steward's Three-fold Classification of Evolution

In his book *Theory of Culture Change*, Julian Steward has suggested a three-fold classification of evolutionary approaches. These are: Unilinear, Universal and Multilinear evolution. The Unilinear, says Steward, was characteristic of classical evolutionist, of the emergence of a distinctively European culture area. In actual practice. Childe is more inclined towards multi-linear evolution than Steward. Unilinear and universal evolution have been described earlier. Let us discuss here Steward's multilinear evolution.

Steward's Multilinear Evolution

Steward was of opinion that all cultures of the world have not passed through the same developmental stage, rather their stages were different in different areas or sub-areas. For example, the sequences of cultural developments, in ice-area, deserted area, forested area and plain area, are different due to varied environmental situations. Cultural evolution of these areas can be studied by choosing the limited parallels of evolution and comparing them with each other. Thus, cross-cultrual examinations of regularities or parallels will yield successful result of evolution. Steward studied the cultures of Mexico, Mesopotania, Egypt and China cross-culturally, and arrived at a conclusion that these cultures have evolved in the same developed stage beginning from pre-agriculture stage, but in different areas and in different period following the multilinear course of evolution.

Thus, multilinear evolution is a methodology based on assumption that significant regularities or parallels occur in cultural change, and it is concerned with the determination of cultural laws. Its method is empirical rather than deductive. It is inevitably concerned with historical reconstruction but it does not expect that historical data can be classified into universal stages. It is concerned with local variations and diversified facts which force the frame of reference from particular to general. Thus, what is lost in universality, will be gained in concreteness and specificity. Multilinear evolution, therefore, has no priori schemes or law. It puts question simply whether any genuine parallels or similarities occur between certain cultures. These similarities may involve salient feature of the whole culture or they may involve only special features, such as a clan, societies, classes, priesthood, military pattern and the like.

Steward's Method of Multilinear Evolution: Parallelism and Casuality

Parallelism and casuality are always present in the study of cultures. The methodological approach of multilinear evolution is to establish sequences of parallel development that could be investigated in empirical reality. It was Steward's thesis that society with a similar technology, existing in similar environment, would parallel one another also in their forms of social and political organisation. Thus, it appeared to him that hunter-gatherers tended to form patrilineal band, and that widely scattered Indian societies, that had accepted the worse after its introduction into America, were comparable in their socio-political organisations. His argument was strengthened by the researches of Karl Wittfogel, who showed that societies located in war undulating river, which carried out irrigation agriculture, originated state organizations, demonstrating the interaction between environment, technology and political organisations. Thus, multilinear evolutionists have generally acknowledge the interrelationships between environment and technology, so that latter can be viewed as a variable rather than ultimate cause of evolution. It called upon the attention to the question as to how to combine the particular with general or how the study of individual culture could yield meaningful information about culture writ at large.

Steward's Concept of Man-Habitat Interaction: Cultural Ecology

Steward suggested a systematic way to study the dynamics of man-habitat interaction so as to get a process and at the same time to provide cross-cultural generalisations. His method was based on a simple assumption that not all features of a given habitat, ecology, are relevant to a given socio-cultural system, nor all systemic elements, i.e., religion, politics, technology and kinship etc. are equally affected by man-habitate interaction. The analyst task is to determine what features of the habitat bear upon the productive patterns of the system by focusing on those systematic features, which empirical analysis shows to be most closely involved in the utilization of habitat in culturally prescribed ways. The idea is to strip those who dealt with particular cultures placing them in a stages of universal sequences. Thus, he called Tylor, Morgan, Maine, McLennan, Bachofen and Bastian as unilinear evolutionists. But every one of classical evolutionists also fits in Steward's Second category, the Universal evolution, which is arbitrary label to designate White's revamping of unilinear evolution, and which is connected with culture rather than with cultures. He called specially White and V. Gordon Childe as universal evolutionist. Steward's third brand of evolutionism is multilinear evolution, which is defined as follows:

> . . . it is interested in particular cultures, but instead of finding local variations and diversities which force the frame of reference from the particular to general. Thus, it deals with only those limited parallels of form, function and sequence, which have empirical validity (1955: 14-19).

The inadequacy of this classification is shown by the fact that the two anthropologists, whom Steward nominates for universal evolutionism, namely White and Childe, are equally good contenders for at least one of the other categories. White as much as classical evolutionists, has attempted to locate specific cultures in relation to universal schemes. In his book, *The Evolution of Culture* (1956), White not only attempted to trace the whole course of cultural development, from the transition of anthropoid to human society, to the beginning of iron age, but he also reconstructed specific culture sequences in the light of the general trends manifested in universal sequence. White's practice to interpret the significance of various institutions in particular societies is based on the assumption that the culture has reached certain stage of evolution.

As for evolutionism of V. Gordon Childe, there must be taken into consideration not only Childe's adherence to Morgan's universal stages of savagery, barbarism and civilization in the presentation of Middle Eastern archaeological sequences, but his highly particularistic treatment to do away all irrelevant aspects of both environment and socio-cultural system so as to clarify the ecological relationship and its change through time. This stripping away of all but those features most directly involved with exploiting the habitat, leave only the evolutionary important portion of socio-cultural system, which Steward called the *Culture Core.* The system's technology is the basic component of the core, but technology must always be analysed in terms of the conditions of the local habit. He defined such cores as the constellation of features which are most closely related to subsistence activities and economic arrangements. He states that there were three fundamental procedure of cultural ecology:

1. Interrelationship between technology and environment must be analysed.
2. The behaviour patterns involved in exploitation of a particular area by means of a particular technology must be analysed.
3. To ascertain the extent, to which the behaviour pattern entailed in exploiting the environment, affects other aspects of culture (Steward 1955: 40-41).

Calling diffusionist interpretation of South American culture, as unsatisfactory, he states that the acceptance or rejection of diffused traits was always contingent upon local potentiality. These potentialities are a function of local ecology, i.e. interaction of environment, exploitative devices and socio-economic habit.

Steward's Concept of Cultural Taxonomy in Relation to Cultural Evolution

According to Steward, all science must have precise means of identifying and classifying the recurrent phenomena with which they deal with. It is sumptomatic of historical rather than scientific orientation of cultural studies that few terms have been used to designate whole culture or component of cultures, which may be employed cross-culturally as well. Such taxonomic terms as hill culture, plain culture, forest culture, Indian culture, Tribal culture, Muslim culture, Hindu culture, European culture, American culture etc. appear frequently, which also suggest parallels of form. These statuses of cultural taxonomy reveal a preoccupations with relativism or historical particularism. Such taxonomic terms reveal that they are fundamentally derived from culture area concept.

Culture can also be classified in terms of value system or ethos. It has also the same basis as that of culture-areas. Such classification reveals a common core of shared culture traits which causes all members of society to have the same outlook and psychological characteristics. Thus, Benedict's concept of pattern, Mead's concept of national character. Opler's concept of themes are derived from a taxonomic approach, which is basically like that of Wissler, Kroeber etc.

If a taxonomic system is to be devised for the purpose of determining cross-cultural parallels and regularities rather than of stressing upon contrasts and differences, there is need of a concept *Culture Types.* Culture type differs from culture-area in several respects. It is characterised by selected features. The selection of diagnostic features must be determined by the problem and frame of reference. The selected features are presumed to have the same functional interrelationship with one another in each case. The taxonomic schemes to determine parallels and regularities in terms of development processes will have to distinguish in many cultural types. The universal methodology as proposed by White will not serve our purpose. Thus, cultural taxonomy is related to cultural evolution in determining cross-cultural regularities or similarities in different cultural types, which ultimately yield multilinear trends of evolution.

Weaknesses of Steward's Scheme

1. Marvin Harris (1969:655) has not accepted multilinear evolutionism as a methodology. To him, link between cultural ecology and cultural materialism appears spurious issue of evolutionism.

2. The question as to how many is multilinear is not solved in Steward's Scheme.
3. His concept of cultural core seems confusing and analogous to base of Marx.
4. White, a contemporary of Steward, has criticised him for confusing history with evolution, because history is concerned with particulars, while evolution seeks to generalise.

Leslie A. White (1900-1975)

White had acquired a strong Boasian outlook during his graduate studies. At the New School in New York, he was taught by Alexander Golden Wiezer and at the University of Chicago, he was influenced by Boasians, where he obtained Ph.D. degree in 1927. His first anthropological article was published in 1925, which was a typical Boasians plea for the importance of cultural factors in the determination of personality. This was in many ways parallel to the programme upon which Margaret Mead was about to embark.

The beginning of White's anti-Boasian position took place during the two years that he taught at the University of Buffalo. At it was an Iroquois territory, he was obliged to read Morgan for the first time. He was shocked on those who had accepted Morgan as a worthless example of speculative philosophy on the basis of second-hand opinion. It was at this point that he observed Morgan as remarkable scholar. The step from Morgan to Marx via Engles was inevitable. By 1929, he was deeply involved in Marxist matter to take time out for a trip to Soviet Union. White returned from Soviet Union to take up teaching position at the University of Michigan. He ultimately succeeded in establishing one of the major centres of anthropology. White was uncompromisingly and out spokenly hostile to historical particularism of Boasians and others, psychological reductionism, to doctrine of free will and theological teleology. He managed to avoid placing his critique within the arena of Marxist disputation.

White over and over again has insisted in defence of 19th century evolutionists that they never proposed that all cultures necessarily passed through the same set of stages, e.g., Savagery, Barbarism and Civilization. It also becomes clear from the observations of Sahlins and Service (1960:12) that Tylor laid down that study of cultural evolution deals with stage by stage as well as along its many lines. The only issue worth discussing is the frequency of convergence and parallelism, not whether they are exceptions to the regularities of the history, but rather how frequently they occur.

He was of opinion that in perspective of Tylor and Morgan, there is no doubt, that the parallelism and convergence were often assumed to be far more frequent than the facts have subsequently justified. It was his faith, in the uniformity in historical experiences which led him to suppose that his fragmentary data on archaic Greece was adequate for identifying matrilineal stage.

When Tylor spoke of tendency of experiences of mankind to move through uniform channels, it was not to say that mankind in general as distinguished from mankind in particular shared these channels. Such a distinction is a refinement for which White's heroes had no need. Tylor meant that most (not all) cultures unfolded along similar lines. The exceptions recognised by both Tylor and Morgan, were explicable in terms of race, diffusion and environmental specialities. Thus, to speak the position of Tylor and Morgan in terms of impoverished antinomy is misleading.

It clearly appears that White was very much influenced by L.H. Morgan and E.B. Tylor, although his writings were also incorporated a good deal from Spencer, Marx, Engles and Durkhiem. His own evolutionary theory was what there men had in 19th century, but was also benefited from additional anthropological data that accumulated since.

White (1945: 335) labelled a severe criticism against Boas and his followers, historical particularists. He called them as premature and scientifically suspect in their rejection of evolutionism. He called them premature, because they never really gave evolutionary approaches a chance to accomplish their intended result, and scientifically suspect because they distorted what Morgan and Tylor had talked about such issues as universal stages and importance of diffusion as a dynamic process.

Repeatedly attacking on the cautious empiricism of Boas groups, White writes,

> In addition to being anti-materialist, they are anti-philosophic and anti-intellectualist and anti-evolutionist. In fact, they are opposed to so many things that someone has characterised their philosophy as eclectic negativism. It has been their mission to demonstrate that there are no laws of significance in cultural phenomena, that civilization is the foremost exponent of this philosophy (White 1949:368).

White made a good number of contributions in making the evolutionary scheme alive by publishing books and articles, which are as follows:

1. 1925 : "Personality and Culture". *The Open Court*, 39: 145-49.
2. 1939 : "A Problem in Kinship Terminology", *American Anthro-*

pologist, 41: 566-73.

3. 1940 : *Pioneers in American Anthropology: The Bandelier-Morgan letters 1873-1883.* Albuquerque: University of New Mexico Press.
4. 1942 : *The Pueblo of Santa Ana,* New Mexico, American Anthropological Association, Memoir, 60.
5. 1943 : "Energy and Evolution of Culture", *American Anthropologist,* 45: 335-56.
6. 1945 : "Diffusion versus Evolution of Culture: An anti-evolutionist Fallacy". *American Anthropologist,* 45: 335-56.
7. 1947(a): The Expansion of Scope of Science". *Journal of the Washington Academy of Sciences,* 37: 181: 210.
8. 1947(b): "Evolutionism in Cultural Anthropology: A Rejoinder". *American Anthropologist,* 49: 400-11.
9. 1949(a): "The Science of Culture", New York, Grove Press.
10. 1949(b): "Ethnological Theory", R.W. Sales ed. *Philosophy for Future: The Quert of Modern Materialism.* New York, Macmillan 357: 84.
11. 1957 : "Review of Steward's Theory of Culture Change", *American Anthropologist,* 59: 540-42.
12. 1958 : "What is classificatory kinship Terms", *South-Western Journal of Anthropology,* 14: 375-85.
13. 1959(a): "The concept of Evolution in Cultural Anthropology", B. Meggars ed., *Evolution and Anthropology.* Washington: The Anthropological Society of Washington, 106-25.
14. 1959(b): *The Evolution of Culture,* New York: McGraw-Hill.
15. 19663 : The Ethnology and Ethnography of Franz Boas, Austin: *Bulletin of the Texas Memorial Museum.*
16. 1966 : *The Social Organisation of Ethnological Theory,* Rice Universities Studies, 52: 1-66.

White's Approach to Evolutionary Theory

Out of these publications, his two famous books *The Science of Culture* (1949) and *The Evolution of Culture* (1959), deal with the theoretical issues related to his approaches of neo-evolutionism. The basic strategy of White's evolutionism is cultural materialism phrased in energy terms. For White, processes related to socio-cultural system consists of three parts: (i) Techno-economic, (ii) Social and (iii) Ideological. Thus, culture becomes primarily a mechanism for harnessing energy and of putting it to work in service of man. Secondarily, of challenging and regulating his behaviour not directly concerned with subsistence and offence and defence. Social Systems are therefore, determined by technological systems. Philosophies and arts express experience as it is defined by technology and refracted by social system.

For White culture is an extrasomatic temporal continuum of things and events dependent upon symbolism. Specifically and concretely, culture consists of tools, implements, utensils, clothing, ornaments, customs, institutions, beliefs, rituals, games, works of art, language etc.

This definition of culture by White is like of Tylor's definition of culture. But he has placed emphasis on *extrasomatic temporal continuum*, which is key concept in White's Scheme. This approach of White can be understood in following series of logical steps:

1. Culture depends upon man for its existence, but can be analysed as a system in and of itself. Man need not be considered a variable in the system, so long as it is understood that the level of analysis is the totality of culture throughout time, not specific cultures at specific times.
2. All life can be understood as a process of capturing and utilizing free energy as trees convert so large energy in to protoplasm, and man converts food energy in to new cells. Thus, culture is fundamentally a means for capturing and utilising energy that is its primary function. When culture is considered as a system in and of itself, its dynamics are analogous to those operating at the organic level i.e. culture system captures and utilizes energy. In organic evolution energy captured and used by the system increases, the system itself becomes more complex and highly organised.
3. The cultural system can be divided into three sub-systems. The most basic one is technology, tools, weapons and knowledge of their use. Here lies the means for capturing and utilising energy as well as for meeting two other important requirements for cultural survival, protection from elements and defence against enemies. The two other subsystems are social structural and ideological or philosophical (for example marriage, kinship and family, and belief moral, totem, taboo etc.). All three are in a mutually influencing interrelationship, but technology dominates by operating through social structure on ideology. Thus, both social structure and prevalent ideology are shaped mostly by the technology, even though they occasionally operate to limit the extent of technological development.
4. Technological subsystem controls the amount of energy captured and utilized by the cultural system. As the technology becomes more efficient more energy is captured and utilized, which leads to

development in the culture as a whole. He stated this formally as the law of cultural development, which is as follow:

> Culture advances as the amount of energy harnessed per capita per year increases or as the efficiency or economy of the means of controlling energy is increased or both (White 1959: 56).

This law of cultural development can be expressed as a formula which is as follows:

$$E \times T = C$$

Where E is energy, T is technology and C is cultural development.

Energy is more important than technology, however, technology can conceivably become extremely efficient without leading to development, if the amount of captured energy is not, thereby, increased. Technology is vehicle, means, scaffolding and the skeleton, whereas energy is the dynamic and living force that animates cultural system and develops them to higher levels and forms.

The operation of this law is potent in the history of mankind. Hunting and gathering subsistence produced a somewhat low level of usable energy in the portion to the amount expanded by the hunters. Neither fire nor wind were significant as sources of energy in this earliest and longest stage of cultural evolution (White 1959: 43-44).

Energy captured was limited to what man's own muscle could provide as a means. White estimated that in such hunting and gathering societies, the amount of energy captured was limited to about 1/20 horse power per capita per year (Ibid: 45).

As soon as agriculture and animal husbandry were discovered, a new quantum jump in cultural evolution took place. Now man could control his sources of energy, which meant greater yields in usable energy with less energy expenditure by man himself. This was the agricultural revolution as a result of which labour specialization, large population, ever more sophisticated technology in short civilization like ancient Mesoputania, Egypt, Greece and Rome etc., came into existence.

Energy exploitation by capture then hit plateau, forced by monosophistic controls by elite, until the next break through, the fuel revolution. This corresponded to growth of industrial production which used coal as a major source of energy, much greater than the potential of farming and herding. The amount of energy per capita per year went another quantum jump upward. But this time, the development was more spectacular than what occurred as a result of agriculture.

Goaded by war and search for larger shares of economic market, men developed their industrial technology to the point at which they could not profitably continue the full production in their factories. Thus, there was another plateau, but a brief one, until the next and most recent one break through in the harnessing of energy, the atomic revolution. Thus, White's stages of development were savagery, barbarism, civilization and energy revolution. He added one more stage in stages suggested by Tylor and Morgan.

Throwing light on social organisation, he opined that it is combination of three processes i.e. nutrition, protection and reproduction. He formulated social organisation as:

$$N \times P \times R = S$$

Where N is nutrition, P is Protection, R is Reproduction and S is social organisation.

He formulated property as follows:

$$T \times L = P$$

Where T is things, L is labour and P is property.

White's Concept of Evolution and History

White made a clear-cut distinction between evolution and history. According to him, history is concerned with particular events unique in time and place, whereas evolution is concerned with classes of things and events regardless of particular time and place. The evolutionists process always takes place somewhere and in a temporal continuum, but the particular time and particular place are not significant. It is temporal sequence of forms that count. Thus, historical studies are particularising, evolutionary studies are generalizing.

From this it appears that White was interested in general evolution of mankind. It is because of this fact that Steward called him as universal evolutionist, who dealt with culture as a whole not particular cultures or specific cultures. He believed in progressive course of evolution, but he tried to explain what caused progress itself and how it worked. Searching for a universal principle of explanation, he found it in energy. He reasoned that culture is basically a survival mechanism and energy is required to provide man with necessities for his continued existence. His overall view of evolution did not account divergence and with general process not with adaptation. Thus, according to Sahlins and Service, he was a general evolutionist, while Steward was a specific evolutionist.

Examples of Evolutionary Theory in Indian Context

Classical evolutionist have proposed that the mankind as a whole has passed through three successive developments viz. savagery, barbarism and civilization. If this is taken as true, the mankind of India would also have passed through these stages of development. Previously it was thought that civilization stage in India came into existence after the arrival of Aryan. But recent discoveries of Indus Valley revealed that the inhabitants of Indus Valley had attained the stage of civilization much earlier than Aryans.

Like prehistoric Europe, Northern India experienced ice-ages, and it was after second of these, in second interglacial period, more than 1000,000 years before Christ, that man first left surviving traces in India. These are the Palaeolithic pebble tools of Soan culture, so called from the little river in Punjab, where they have been found in large number. In type they resemble tools widely distributed all over the old world, from England to Africa and China. In India, no human remains have been found in association with the tools, but elsewhere such industries have been shown to be the work of primitive anthropoid types such as Pithicanthropus of Java and China.

In South there existed an another prehistoric stone industry, which is not conclusively dated, but which may have been approximately contemporary to that of Soan valley. The men of this culture made core tools, specially fine hand, axes, formed by striking of flakes from a large pebble and they evidently had such better command over their material than the Soan men. This Madras Industry, as it is called by archaeologists, has affinities with similar core tool industries in Africa, Western Europe and Southern England, where it has been found in association with a more advanced type of man a true homosapiens

The Ganga Valley is one of the newest parts of earth surface, and geologists believe that much of it was still a shallow Sea at the time when these two stone age industries were flourishing but there may have been contact between them by way of Rajasthan, for the tools of one culture have been found sporadically in the region of the other. The men who have used these palaeoliths must have lived in India for many millennia. Who they were and what became of them, we do not know? Their blood may still flow in the inhabitants of modern India, but if the pebble industry of Soan was the work of proto-human anthropoids, they must have vanished long ago, like the Neanderthal men in Europe and Pithicanthropi of Far-East. Homosapiens continued in India, and his skill and technical equipment imperceptibly improving down the ages. He learnt to fashion microliths, tiny and delicate stone scrappers and other implements, which have been found in many parts of India, from N-W Frontier to the extreme South. Similar microlithic industries occur in many parts of the Near East and Africa, but their chronological relationship with the microlithic industries of India is not clear. In parts of Deccan, microliths are often found together with polished stone axes, and it would seem that in remote parts of the Peninsula their use was only fully replaced by that of iron tools around the beginning of Christian age.

Palaeolithic man was a hunter and gatherer and lived in very small communities, which were usually nomadic. In course of time, he learnt to kindle fire, to protect his body from the weather with skin, bark or leaves and to tame wild dogs which lurked round his camp fire. In India as all over the world, people, thus, lived for many thousand of years.

Then, very recently in geological time, great changes took place in man's way of living. Certainly not earlier than 10,000 B.C., and perhaps as late as 6000 B.C., man developed what Professor V. Gordon Childe calls, "an aggressive attitude to his environment". He learnt how to grow food crops, to tame domestic animals, to make pots and to weave garments. Before, discovering the use of metal, he taught himself to make well polished stone implements far in advance of those of palaeolithic age. Such implements have been found all over India, but mostly in the North-West and in Deccan, and usually on or near the surface. In much of the country neolithic culture survived long and many of the wilder hill tribes of the present day have only recently emerged from this stage.

Developed agriculture and permanent villages probably began in the middle-east in the 7th millennium. In India the earliest remains of settled cultures are of little agricultural villages in Baluchistan and lower Sindh, perhaps dating from the end of 4th millennium B.C.

Classical writers show that when in 326 B.C., Alexander of Macedon crossed the Indus, the climate of North-West India was much as it today, though perhaps a little moister. The river valleys were fertile and well wooded, though the coastal strip to the west of the Indus, now called the Makran, and much of Baluchistan, were already dry and desolate. But in 3000 B.C., the climate was rather different. The whole region was well forested, providing fuel to burn bricks and food for wild elephant and rhynoceros, and Baluchistan, now almost a waterless desert, was rich in rivers. This region supported many villages of agriculturists, who had settled in upland valleys of Baluchistan and they fertile plains of Makran and lower Indus.

In early part of 3rd millennium, civilization, in the sense of an organised system of government over a comparatively large area, developed in the river valleys of Nile, Euphrates, and Indus. We know a great deal about the civilizations of Egypt and Mesoputania, for they have left us written material, which have been satisfactorily deciphered. The Indus people, on the other hand, did not engrave long inscriptions on stone or place papyrus scrolls in tombs of their dead. whatever we know of their writing, it is derived from brief inscriptions of their seals and their is no Indian counter part of Rosetta stone. Several brilliant efforts have been made to read the indus seals, but none so far has succeeded. Hence, our knowledge of Indus civilization is inadequate in many respects and it must be classed as prehistoric, for it has no history in strict sense of the term.

The civilization of Indus, also known to archaeologists as Harappa culture, was extended for some 950 miles from north to south and the pattern of civilization was so uniform that even the bricks were usually of same size and shape from one end of it to the other. Outside this area, the village cultures of Baluchistan seem to have continued much as before.

Indus valley civilization was a combination of stone-age and metalage. Many material remains of copper and bronze have been discovered, which suggest that Indus valley civilization was a copper age and bronze age civilization, which is also termed as chalcolithic age.

The arrival of iron age throws significant light on economic development of mankind as well as technological advancement. Archaeological evidences of iron remains have been found in Baluchistan, North-West India, land situated between Ganges and Yamuna, and in South India. According to prehistoric evidences, use of iron implements came into being in 1100 B.C., but literary evidences support the origin of iron age in 700 B.C.

From the above accounts, it is clear that India has passed through the stages of stone age (further divided into Eolithic age, Palaeolithic age, Mesolithic age and Neolithic age), copper age, bronze age and iron age in the field of technological advancements.

Stages of Economic Development

Classical evolutionists have opined that mankind as a whole has passed through the economic stages of hunting and gathering, domesticating animals, carrying out agriculture and working as labour in industries. These stages of economic developments are also existing in Indian contexts. Anthropologists have tried to classify the stages of economic developments of tribal India. These stages are:

1. Hunting and gathering stage
2. Pastoral stage
3. Agricultural stage
4. Industrial stage.

Hunting and Gathering Stage

This was the early stage of economic development of man. In India, nearly all tribes who have reached at the stage of civilization, practised hunting and gathering in one way or other, but there are some tribal groups, who are, even to-day, dependent on hunting and gathering for their livelihood and survival. For example, the Rajis of Uttar Pradesh, Birhor, Hill-Kharia, Parahiyas, Birjias, and Korwas in Bihar, Juang in Orissa, Hill Maria Gonds of Bastar in Madhya Pradesh, Chenchus and Yanadis in Andhra Pradesh, Kadars, Male-Pantarams, the Arandans, and Kkurumbas of Malabar in Kerala, the Paliyans of Madurai in Tamil Nadu, Onges, Jarawas, Sentinales, Shompen and Nicobarese in Andaman and Nicobar Islands.

Vedas of Sri Lanka, Pigmy of Philippine and Malaya Islands, and Bushmen of Africa are also examples of hunting and gathering economy.

Pastoral Stage

The classic locus of pastoral tribes in India is Nilgiri, in Tamil Nadu, where the Pastoral people, the Todas live, and the Gujars, Bakarwala, Gaddis, and Jodhs live in Champa in Himachal Pradesh in North-Western Himalayas. Pastoralism proper involves full commitment to herding and this is true especially with Todas. They are purely pastoral tribe and inspite of efforts to make them agriculturists even to present time, they still cling on pastoralism. In central India, the Kisans or Nagesias of Bihar and Madhya Pradesh are also considered to some extent to pastoral. The Bharward or Maldhari and Rai Sipotra of Gujarat and the Rabaris of Gujarat and Rajasthan are the cattle herders of Western India. The Gollars, Kurubas and Lambadis are the herders in South India. The Sansis of Punjab and the Choupans of Jammu and Kashmir in Himalayan region also come under herder type. The Bhots of Almora district depend on cattle rearing.

Agricultural Stage

The agricultural stage of primitive people may be divided into two: Hill cultivation type and Plain agricultural type.

The practice of hill cultivation is wide-spread in our country. The tribal people inhabiting, the hill forest of Assam, Meghalaya, Manipur, Tripura, i.e., in North-East Himalayan region, Bihar, Madhya Pradesh and Orissa in Middle India and Andhra Pradesh in South India are dependent on hill cultivation for their livelihood. The hill cultivator tribes in India are represented by Garoas, Tripuris, Noatias, a few Halalus and Riangs, Chakmas, Moga and Naga tribes in North-East Himalaya, Malars and Sauria Paharia of Santhal Pargana, a few Hill Khariyas, Korwas, Parahiyas and Birjias in Chota Nagpur, Saoras and Kuttiakhond in Orissa, Kamars, Baigas, Maria Gonds in Madhya Pradesh, Dhoras, Muka Dhoras, Smanthus, and few Bagatas in Andhra Pradesh and Mala Kudias in Mysore in South India.

The hill cultivation is known as *Jhum* in North-East Himalayan region, Kurawa or Khallu in Santhal Pargana, Bewar in Chota Nagpur, Podu, Rema, Dahi, Kamau, Bringa, Gudia, Dongar Chas in Orissa, Penda Dahiya, Bewar, Guharsh, Farhha, Dippa, Marhan or Erka in Madhya Pradesh, and Konda Paddy in Andhra Pradesh.

Plain agriculture type is represented by the Khasis and Jaintias of Assam and Meghalaya, Khasas and Tharus of Tarai area of Uttar Pradesh, Kiunauras, Pangawalas, Swangalas in Himachal Pradesh, Bhumij, Korawas, Bhuiyas, Santhals, Mundas, Oraons, Hos, Kharwars, Gonds in middle India, Bhils, Minas, Garasias, Damarias, Koli Maldadevis, Varlis, Thakurs, Korkles, Dubla in Western India.

Industrial Stage

Examples of this type of separate economic organization is very few and recent development in primitive societies. This goes on side by side along with hunting, gathering, pastoralism and agricultural activities. But there are some examples in which some tribes subsist on crafts and cottage industries like basket making, tool making (iron and wooden), spinning, weaving, metal work and iron-smithy, etc. Only few tribes come under this category with poor individual population strength. They live in tribal villages as a part of it, and have no exclusive village of their own tribesmen. These people are tied to major tribes by a chord or more or less jajmani relation as is the system prevailing in Hindu villages. They visit the periodical markets with their finished goods and dispose them of by barter or on cash in tradition to jajmani exchange.

The craft and cottage industries are peculiar features of the tribal people as a whole and most of them know matting, basketry, rope-making, pottery-making, spinning and weaving. This work is subsidiary occupation for them.

The Gujjars of Kashmir and Kinnauris of Himachal Pradesh produce wood products. The Kanjars of Uttar Pradesh are engaged in basketry and rope-making. In middle India, Loharas, Karmalis, Chik-Baraiks and Mahalis (from Chota Nagpur, Bihar) are the artisan tribes. Loharas and Karmalis fulfil the needs of agricultural tribes or other people by making and repairing their agricultural implements and other tools. The Chik-Baraiks supply hand-woven clothes to other tribes like Munda, Oraon etc. The Mahalis make baskets and other bamboo-products and earn their livelihood. Asurs of Bihar and Agerias of Madhya Pradesh are traditionally iron-smiths. In Western India, the Godulia Lohars of Rajasthan are iron-smiths and have work shops in their traditionally mobile homes in bullock-cart. The Kolams of Maharashtra were formerly engaged in baskets and mats making. The Vitolias of Maharashtra are also engaged making bamboo mats, baskets, winnowing fans. In South India-Irulas of Tamil Nadu and Thotis of Andhra Pradesh make baskets, mats, ropes and winnowing trays etc. The Kotas of Nilgiri depend on carpentry, pottery and tool making.

Some individuals or tribal communities of the country are working for their livelihood in different offices, hospitals, factories, mines, business enterprises etc. Some of them are engaged in commercial trade of their own. Apart from their imitiation, the seat reservation in different services, as laid down in our democratic constitution, has helped a lot in creating this type of economic development among the tribals. In the skilled and white collar jobs no particular Indian tribe can be placed. It is observed that mostly educated and converted christian tribals are engaged in offices, hospitals, administrative jobs etc. They are scattered throughout India in different capacities.

From the above accounts, it seems probable that the economic life of tribals has passed through the developmental stages in different periods of time, as a result of which, the present complex form of economic organisation came into existence.

Evolution of Marriage

Classical evolutionists have attempted to show the development of institution of marriage in sequences. Tylor, Morgan, Maine, McLennan etc. have shown that the institution of marriage has passed through the stages of sexual promiscuity, group marriage, polyandrous marriage, polygenous marriage and monogamous marriage. According to Morgan, group marriage was the first stage of the institution of marriage, in which all males of a group marry all females of another group. In Indian context, group marriage as an institution is not prevalent in present time.

But among the tribes of Australia, group marriage is still existing.

Polyandry is a marriage between one female and more than one males. It was McLennan who pointed out the custom of polyandry. This type of marriage is found among Bantu and Wahuma of Africa, and Alaska and Eskimos in America. In India, polyandry is prevalent among Khas of Dehradun, Uttar Pradesh, Toda of Nilgiri in extreme south, Khasis and Garos of North-East India, and Nayar of Kerala.

Polyandry is of two types: (i) Fraternal Polyandry or Adelphic polyandry and (ii) non-fraternal or non-adelphic polyandry. In case of former, husbands married to a woman are brothers. On the other hand, in latter case husbands of a woman are not brothers. Khas, Toda, Kota are example of fraternal polyandry. McLennan had observed this tradition among tribes of Tibet, therefore, he called fraternal polyandry as Tibetan polyandry. Nayar of Malabar of Kerala is an example of non-fraternal polyandry. McLennan called it as Nayar polyandry.

The example of polyandry is also found in Hindu Epics, *Mahabharata*. Five Pandavas were married to same Drapuadi.

Levirate marriage: This marriage is known as *Devar Vivah*. In this marriage, the widow marries the younger brother of the husband after his death. The example of levirate marriage is also found in *Ramayana*. Vibhishan was married to Ravana's wife, Mandodari, Sugriva was married to his brother Bali's wife, Tara. This marriage is also found among Khas and Toda tribes of India. Backward and lower caste Hindus also practise this marriage.

Polygyny is a kind of marriage in which one man marries more than one woman. This marriage is found among the tribes of Africa, Osceania and Malenesia. Baganda of Uganda also practice this kind of marriage. Though at present time, monogamy is a rule, but polygyny is also found among all societies of India, i.e., tribal, Hindu, Muslim etc.

Sororate marriage, is a kind of marriage, in which a man marries his wife's younger sister either after her death or being barren. This marriage is also prevalent among many Indian societies.

Exogamous marriage: It was McLennan who observed exogamy and Endogamy. In tribal societies, clan is exogamous and tribe is endogamous. In Hindu society, caste is endogamous and Gotra is exogamous. Village exogamy is also prevalent.

Monogamy is present form of marriage in which one man marries one woman.

Evolution of Family and Societies

According to Morgan the institution of family has passed through fifteen stages of development. Among them five main stages are as follows:

1. *Consanguine family*: This was the early stage of family when there was sexual promiscuity and marriage between blood relation was not forbidden.
2. *Punaluant family*: This was the second stage of family when group marriage was prevalent and all brothers of a group marry all sisters of another group.
3. *Syndasmian family*: In this stage one man married one woman, but he was also free to establish sex relations with other women married in the family.
4. *Patriarchal family*: In this stage man's ascendancy and dominance in the family had fully achieved. He could marry many women and had sex relations with them.
5. *Monogamous family*: This is the present stage of family in which one man can marry one woman and *vice versa*.

Tylor, McLennan and Bachofen were of opinion that matrilineal form of society was the early form in which mothers were regarded as supreme authority. The residence was matrilocal. Kinship descent was traced through mother and inheritance of property was from mother to daughter. Partilineal form of society evolved out of matrilineal form. In patriarchal society, the residence became patrilocal, descent began to be traced through father and inheritance of property went from father to son. They cited example of couvade as a survival of early stage, in which father attempted to take power of mothers by playing roles like them on the occasion of child birth.

In India, the Hindu societies are mostly patrilocal, patriarchal patrilineal, and patrinymic. The families of tribal societies in India are also mostly of patrilocal, patrilineal, patriarchal and patrinymic nature. Some of them are also matrilocal, matriarchal, matrilineal and matrinymic. In few cases, both patriarchal and matriarchal form exist together.

In North-Western Himalaya region, the families of Gujjars, Goddis and Pangawals, of Jammu and Kashmir and Himachal Pradesh, are patrilineal. The Khas of Uttar Pradesh practise polyandry but are of patrilineal type. The Tharus follow the rule of patriliny, but the position of woman is primary with them. In North-Eastern Himalaya, the Garos and Khasis are matrilineal people. All members get motherhood and claim descent from a common ancestress or mother. In Mikirs, children belong to father clan and inherit the property. The Mizos are patriarchal. The Kachharis follow the rule of double descent, i.e., sons descend on father line and daughters on mother line. In middle India, all tribes of Bihar such as Santal, Munda, Oraon, Ho, Gond, Bhil, Kol, Kharia, are all patrilocal, patrilineal, patriarchal and patrinymic. Similar is the case with Orissa and Madhya Pradesh.

In Western India, Bhil, Minas, Mahadeu Kolis, Varlis, Koknes, Thakurs, Kothodis, Koli Malhars, Kili Dhors, Dublas, Gamits etc. are patrilineal and patriarchal.

In South India, the tribes of Kerala like Nayar, Kurichchians, Kundu vadians, Malayaurs are matrilineal. Tribes of Tamil Nadu are also matrilineal. Toda of Nilgiri area are also matriarchal.

Kinship Terminology

Morgan was of opinion that kinship terminology in early stage was classificatory from which present descriptive form came into existence. In classificatory kinship terminology, the same term is used to designate more than one individual. Thus, in it various kins are classified in one category and all are referred to by the same term. In Hindu society, the term uncle is a classificatory term. It is used for *chacha, mama, mausa, foofa, taoot* etc. Similarly, nephew, cousin and in-laws are classificatory term. *Samadhi* and *Samadhin* are also classificatory terms. The former refers to bride's and groom's fathers, whereas latter refers to bride's and groom's mothers.

The tribals of India also used classificatory terms. The Sema Naga of Assam use *Aja* for mother, father's brother's wife, and mother's sister. Among Kuki, *hepu* is used for father's father, mother's father, mother's brother, wife's father, mother's brother's son; wife's brother and wife's brother's son. Among Angami Naga, the same term is used for member of opposite sexes. The word she stands for elder brother, wife's elder sister, husband's elder brother elder sister's husband, elder brother's wife, mother's brother's wife, father's brother's wife.

Under descriptive system one term refers to only one relation. It describes exact relation of a person towards another. For instance, terms like father, mother, son, daughter, grand-son, grand-daughter etc. are descriptive term. In Hindi we have mostly descriptive terms.

Kinship Usages

Classical evolutionists not only studied kinship terminologies and kinship descent, but they also included the study of behaviour patterns of different kins. They observed that every relationship involved a particular type of behaviour. The behaviour of a son towards his father was of respect, while behaviour of husband towards wife was of love. The behaviour of a brother towards sister was of affection. These were some of usages, which regulated behaviour of different kins. These usages were termed by evolutionists as kinship usages. Their observations on kinship usages are as follows:

1. *Avoidance*: It was Tylor who observed the custom of avoidance among Mexicans. He was of opinion that the early form of family was matriarchal, in which son-in-law (*Damad*) had to come to stay with wife's family members. As a result of which son-in-law and mother-in-law avoidance came to existence. Tylor observed adverse situation among patriarchal society in which avoidance between daughter-in-law and father-in-law was prevalent. This hypothesis of Tylor was criticised by many anthropologists on the basis of empirical researches carried out in different areas. Among Luni, though the family is matriarchal, but avoidance between son-in-law and mother-in-law is not maintained. Tribes of Australia, who are patrilocal, they maintain avoidance with son-in-law, but not with daughter-in-law.

   Whatever the origin may be, but in societies usages of avoidance is observed in one form or the other. According to this, two kins should avoid each other. They should not only avoid sexual relations but even avoid seeing the face. In Hindu societies, Sasur (father-in-law) avoids *Putoh* (daughter-in-law), *Bhainsur* (husband's elder brother) avoids *Bhawah* (younger brother's wife). Similar instances appear in case of tribal societies who are patriarchal. In matriarchal tribal societies, *Sas* (mother-in-law) avoids *Damad* (son-in-law) as in case of Toda, Khasis etc., who practise this kinship usage of avoidance.
2. *Joking Relationship*: It is reverse of avoidance relationship. In it, two kins are permitted to tease or to make fun with each other. In India in all societies, joking relations between *Jija-Sali, Dever-bhabhi, Sala-bahnoi, Nanad-bhabi, Samadhi-Samadhi*, etc. are found.
3. *Teknonymy*: The word teknonymy has been taken from Greek word '*teknon*' and was used in Anthropology for the first time by Tylor. On the basis of statistical method, Tylor compared the data of 282 societies and correlated post-marital residence with the custom of in-law avoidance. He came to the conclusion that matrilineality and matrilocality had proceeded patrilineality and patrilocality. According to him, teknonymy was related to matriarchal family. In this family, women were the main authority and husbands were

regarded as outsiders. Husbands were not included in primary kin groups but accepted as secondary kins. It was because of this fact, husbands were called through the names of children. Thus, a kin became the reference of two kins. For instance, among Hindus, a wife is tabooed to take the name of husband, *Sasur* (father-in-law), *Bhaisur* (husband's elder brother). She used the term like Ram's father, Ram's grandfather, Ram's uncle in order to refer to husband, *Sasur* and *Bhaisur* respectively.

The custom of teknonymy is prevalent among the tribal societies of South Africa, West Canada, India, Australia, Andaman, Sri Lanka, Phizidwip, Newguinea, Malaya, China, North Syberia, British Columbia, Malenesia etc.

Tylor's correlation of teknonymy with matriarchal societies has not been accepted by R.H. Lowie. He argued that usage of teknonymy is existing not only in matriarchal societies, but also in patriarchal societies. He was of opinion that in some societies, the custom of teknonymy originated on account of low status of women, and in some due to lack of nouns in their languages.

4. *Avunculate*: This peculiar usage is observed among matriarchal societies. This gives to maternal uncle (*mama*) a prominent place in life of his nephew and nieces. He has special obligations towards them which exceed those of father. He has a prior right over their loyalties. He comes first among all relatives. The avunculate usage is observed in India among all matriarchal societies, about which a description has already been given.

   It is true that avunculate is a peculiar feature of matriarchal societies, but some patriarchal societies are also no exception. For example, the Thonga of South Africa are patriarchal, but the usage of avunculate is observed.
5. *Amitate*: This is a kinship usage, in which father's sister *(phua)* is given a special role. She gets more respect than mothers. W.H.R. Rivers observed this usage among Baxdwip. Among Toda tribe of India, *Bua* or *Phua* (father's sister) plays significant role in name giving ceremony of the child.
6. *Couvade*: This custom was observed by Tylor and McLennan. They observed that matrilineal societies did not practise it at all, because women's position was dominant. Most societies in the intermediate patri-matrilineality stage, adopted this custom, because men needed to establish their authority over women and, thus, imitated their habits. According to Tylor, couvade was a custom, in which fathers had to play the role like mothers particularly at the time of delivery of child. Tylors opined that some practised this cus-

tom in pure patrilineal societies as survival, others had already dropped the custom because it had lost its function. Thus, matrilineality had been the earlier form.

This is a queer usage which is found among many primitive tribes like Khasis and Toda. Under this, the husband is made to lead the life of an invalid along with his wife, whenever she gives birth to a child. He refrains from active work, and takes sick diet. He observes the same taboos, which are observed by his wife. This kinship, usage, thus, involves husband and wife.

Evolution of Religion

It was Tylor who provided for the first time a minimum definition of religion as belief in spiritual beings. He treated religion as cultural universal. He also explained as to how belief could have arisen. According to him, animism was the early form of religion. As souls were numerous, it gave rise to polytheism (belief in many spirits), but at a latter stage, it was believed that all spirits are manifestation of the same. As a result of which, monotheism came in to existence. Thus, according to him, religion has passed through three successive stages of development namely, animism, polytheism and monotheism.

In Indian context, the concept of animism, polytheism and monotheism can be observed prevailing together in almost all societies. All societies practise ancestral worship, which is an example of animism. They have faith in many deities, which throws light on the concept of polytheism. For instances, Hindus believe in 33 crores of Gods and Goddesses. Tribals practise animatism, naturalism etc. which reveals the prevalent concept of polytheism. Both tribals and Hindus have deep faith in one supreme being, who is regarded as God of deities as well as human being. Tribals regard Sun-God (*Singbonga*) as the Supreme being and the responsibility of all events caused in their life and surrounding is placed upon his shoulder. Hindus call *Param-Brahma-Parmeshwar* as the supreme God. He is God of Gods, earth, sky and heaven. Thus, the concept of monotheism is also prevalent among Indians.

2

DIFFUSIONAL SCHOOL

Nineteenth century evolutionists were well aware that a full understanding of culture required explanations of both their similarities and differences. Although not all their interpretations were alike, it was held in general that differences existed because of unequal pace of march of progress, but degree of outside influence and adaptation to environment were not neglected. They were of views that similarities emerged because of mental uniformity caused mankind to react roughly in the same way to uniform environment, added, however, by the development of progress of mind. Cultures in the same stage of development were not related, because a greater or lesser part of the cultural inventory was discovered freely. When uniform traits appeared in the area far apart and without historical contact, it was accepted that they had evolved separately. Thus, similar parallel inventions were the strongest proof of 'psychic unity'.

Though they recognised that diffusion was an undeniable fact, but none of the evolutionists even maintained that culture traits were more often invented than imitated. Diffusion does not necessarily deny evolution, but it certainly interferes in the neatness of evolutionary schemes.

During 20th century, several schools of thought appeared in Britain, America and Germany that claimed to be anti-evolutionist, but in fact they were more critical of 'psychic unity'. They emphasised upon the idea that man was basically uninventive and thus, important inventions were made only once at a particular place, from where they spread through rest of the world by diffusion or migration. The difference between these two ideas is not always appreciated, but in fact they represent two different processes of cultural change. Diffusion is taking over of traits by imitation, while migration implies that culture carrier broke away from their original settlements and moved to other parts of the world taking their cultural inventory with them, but adapting it to new environmental conditions.

Thus, cultural diffusion is the process by which culture traits, discovered or invented at one place or society, are spread directly or indirectly to other societies or places. Although, the exact origin of specific cultural traits is difficult to trace, but diffusion of a trait can fairly be traced. Historically, more is known about diffusion than origin of culture.

In history, certain societies or places have served as centres from where cultural traits have spread to other parts of the world. These centres of cultural diffusion were more progressive societies and had developed rapidly by invention and discovery. Egypt was, for many centuries a cultural centre from where culture traits in the field of arts and political organisation spread to north-west in Europe and to east as far India. Subsequently, Rome was a great cultural centre, from where Roman law spread in most countries of Europe. In Asia, Chinese middle kingdom was, from early times, a dominant cultural centre, from where culture traits spread throughout the Asiatic main land. From India, Buddhist Religion diffused in other Asiatic countries. About 4th century B.C., Western Europe became the dominant cultural centre. At present, United States and other developed counries are exporting its culture to other countries. Indian decimal system crossed to Arabia and Europe.

It may not, however, be supposed that the centres of cultural diffusion have always been the places of cultural development. In some cases, they have been mere a trader in culture than originator of culture. It deals with cultural migration. Thus, early Greeks were more trader in culture than originator of culture. In ancient time, when territory of India was extended up to Afghan, Kabul was an important centre of trade, where merchants of different countries used to meet and exchange their goods as well as ideas. The following factors are influential in process of diffusion:

(i) Relation and communication
(ii) Need for and desire for new traits
(iii) Competition with old traits and their opposition
(iv) Respect and recognition of those who bring new traits.

CONDITIONS RELATED TO CULTURAL DIFFUSION

Diffusionists have explained some conditions and characteristics of cultural diffusion which are as follows:

1. Any cultural group will adopt a culture trait of other cultural group, only when it would be meaningful and useful either economically or socially or both.
2. In course of diffusion, culture trait may not remain in original

form, but changes in it can take place due to different environmental situations.

3. Process of diffusion of culture traits always follow from high culture to low culture or developed culture to underdeveloped culture.
4. Process of diffusion may create culture change in groups adopting culture of other groups. Sometimes, borrowed culture traits get assimitated easily, but sometimes, they are responsible for many changes.
5. There are some obstacles in cultural diffusion, such as lack of transport and communication facilities, ocean, river, mountain, desert etc.

SCHOOLS OF DIFFUSION

Diffusionists have not shown unanimity on the question as to which was the place from where culture traits reached in other parts of the world. As a result of differences in their opinions, on this point, the diffusionists are divided into three schools, namely, British School of diffusion, German School of diffusion and American School of diffusion. This division also indicates the nationality of diffusionists. The division of school of diffusion and their followers can be understood better by presenting in chart as below:

School of Diffusion

British School of Diffusion	German School of Diffusion	American School of Diffusion
1. G.E. Smith (1871-1937)	1. F. Ratzel (1884-1904)	1. Franz Boas (1858-1942)
2. W.J. Perry (1887-1949)	2. F. Graebner (1887-1934)	2. Clark Wissler (1870-1947)
3. W.H.R. Rivers (1864-1922)	3. F.W. Schmidt (1868-1954)	3. A.L. Kroeber (1876-1960)

British School of Diffusion

British school of diffusion is also known as Pan-Egyptian School. This school came into being too late in the history of anthropology, but was first to disappear. Elliot Smith was the founder of this school and W.J. Perry was his true follower. They are designated as extreme diffusionists and Egyptogist, because for them, Egypt was the only centre of culture, from where culture traits diffused or migrated to rest parts of the world. They did not pay any attention towards their German counterpart. They went on popularising blindly that Egypt was the only culture cradle. They used both explanations, diffusion as well migration, in context of Egypt as a centre of culture. For their narrow views, the extreme diffusionists or Egyptologists have been criticised very much. Before dealing with criticism, let us discuss follower's contribution one by one.

Grafton Elliot Smith (1871-1937)

Elliot Smith was basically an anatomist by profession, and his scientific accomplishments were appreciated well, by his colleagues. At one state, in his carrier as an anatomist, he got a chance to pay a visit at Egypt. He became a great admirer of Egypt's ancient civilization. Upon his return to Cambridge, he was surprised to see similarities between Egyptian complex of large stone monuments in association with Sun worship, and that of English Megalith such as stone henge. These similarities in monuments of Egypt and Megalith of England, compelled him to think that the rude and primitive Drueds would not have invented this complex temple structure. It means that they were borrowed from ancient Egypt. He ultimately arrived at a conclusion that English monuments were Crude imitations of Egyptian pyramids and mastabas. He published his such findings in 1911, but continued further investigations. More and more explorations in this direction revealed to him that Megaliths were present not only in Europe, but other pyramidal complex structures were existing in other parts of the world as well. He studied Mayapyramids, Japanese Pagodas, Cambodian and Balenese temples and American Indian burial mounds. They all were displaying the same basic form and, in this way, they were related to Egyptian prototypes. As Egypt was an ancient centre of civilization, he concluded his findings that culture traits of monuments and Megaliths spread to other spheres of world from Egypt from about 400 B.C. onward.

His first famous book entitled *The Origin of Civilization* was published in 1928, from New York. In this book he emphasised upon Egypt as the origin of civilization. It was the place where agriculture through irrigation channel came into existence. Thus, ancient Egypt began to plant more and more seeds by controlling river's inundations, and inventing a full-fledged system of hydraulic agriculture. Stimulated by their successes, they invented such necessary items as pottery, weaving, the wheel, plough and writing. They began to build cities, and established the institutions of law, government, religion worshipping sun-God as their major deity. Their kings became deities because they were personifications of Sun. They knew to mummify dead bodies and to built graves in the name of deads. Egyptians discovered navigation and travelled far and wide in search of precious stones and metal, bringing the benefit of their civilizational developments to many areas of the world. The recipients were, however, weak immitators and nowhere in the world, civilization attained the same height as Egypt. Thus, he attempted his best to indicate origin of civilization, for the first time, in Egypt.

Smith was well aware that man was more older than civilization. Many primitive or nonliterate societies were without pyramids or monuments indicating no influence of Egypt. He called all people outside the civilization as natural man. He described their cultures or collection of negative traits, because there was no clothing, housing, ornaments, government, burrials etc. He was rather unique in his attempt to deprive natural man even of magic.

A revolution in life of natural man came into existence, when they borrowed civilizational traits from Egypt or civilized traits were diffused or migrated to their environment. He popularised this idea on the ground that man was basically uninventive. Inventions or discoveries began first in Egypt, therefore; discovered or invented traits appeared in their cultures because of contact, communication and migration. Thus, multiple origin, independent invention, multiple origin, psychic unity, progress and survivals were all abolished in one mighty stroke of Smith. It is because of this very fact that he was popularly designated as extreme diffusionist or pan Egyptologist. He explained diffusion of cultural traits from Egypt to rest spheres of world also in his second book entitled *Diffusion of Culture*, London, 1933.

Willium James Perry (1877-1949)

W.J. Perry was a devout supporter of Elliot Smith's scheme of diffusion of culture. He did not made any specific theoretical contribution, but he blindly supported Smith's theory that Egypt was the only cultural cradle in the world. It is because of this facts, the names of Smith and Perry are uttered in one breath as Egyptologist.

Perry, once visited, Cairo to take part in archaeological excavations. He, thus got opportunity to see remains of Sun-temples at Cairo. He was so encouraged and impressed that he made his mind to publish a book on Sun-God. He collected informations on beliefs and attitudes related to sun-worship among the people of Cairo. He analysed data and published them in the form of a book under the title *The Children of the Sun*. This book was published in 1923 from London for the first time, but attracted attention of a good number of readers because of which, it was reprinted several time. In this book he called Egyptians as children of Sun, because only Sun-God was regarded as a universal deity. Such idea related to Sun-God diffused in other parts of the word, from Egypt. Among Egyptians, it was believed that Sun-God incarnated as rulers. Thus, Sun-God not only commanded natural happenings, but as a ruler He used to command His children on the earth. In this way, Sun-worship was the ancient form of worship, which originated at Egypt and such ideas diffused all over world. He was of opinion that pyramid structures, temple building, use of gold and silver ornaments, etc. were all the creations of Egypt's civilization. Thus, whatever the civilizational traits or complex the world is possessing today, are the boons of ancient Egyptian civilization. In this way, he extended full co-operation to Smith in establishing British School of diffusion and Egypt as the ancient-centre of civilization.

He was against the Psychic unity and independent inventions of evolutionists. He was of opinion that similarities were caused due to diffusion of culture traits, and Egypt was the ancient centre of civilization.

William H.R. Rivers (1864-1922)

By profession, W.H.R. Rivers was a medical doctor of Britain. He was also a member of the famous Torres Strait Expedition (1898). This was the first interdisciplinary anthropological expedition meant to cover all sides of primitive life by trained investigations. Rivers along with his students, C.S. Meyers and William McDougal, examined the psychological abilities of natives, more specifically their sensory capacities. In course of his study, he arrived at a conclusion that there were no racial difference in pure sense acuity.

His famous article entitled "A Genealogical Method of Collecting Social and Vital Statistics", was published in *Royal Anthropological Institute of Great Britain and Ireland* in 1900. This paper was outcome of his trip made for studying psychological abilities of primitive life. He recorded Genealogies and kinship terms, observing specific behaviour patterns associated with them, including rights, duties, privileges, status and roles. He followed such schemes like Morgan for analysing data in meaningful contexts. Since then Genealogical Method became a scientific method for collecting data in kinship organisation.

In 1904, W.H.R. Rivers came to India to study the polyandrous Toda of Nilgiri hill. *Monograph on Toda* was published from New York in 1906. This was regarded as a classic monograph ever presented to world on the study of Indian Tribe. In this book Rivers brought into light the interrelatedness of Toda culture with the buffalo complex. Till the time of publication of this monograph one does not find the influence of diffusionism upon the writing and ideas of Rivers. If it would have been so, he could have discussed the diffusion of Hinduism among the Toda of Nilgiri hill. But he never did so, though by the time of his study Todas were strongly influenced by culture traits of Hinduism. He never claimed himself as diffusionist till 1910.

In 1907, he wrote an important paper entitled, "Origin of the Classificatory Kinship of Relationship" in honour of E.B. Tylor. This paper was, later on, incorporated in his own book *Social Organisation* published in 1914.

In 1911, Rivers in his presidential address to section H of British Association for the Advancement of Science, presented a paper entitled, "Ethnological Analysis of Culture", in which he suddenly announced that he had been led independently to the same general position as diffusionists and migrationists.

In 1912, he published a degeneration-oriented article entitled "Disappearance of Useful Arts". In this paper he dealt with degeneration together with uninventiveness of human mind. He was of opinion that culture traits not only progressed but degenerated as well.

The theory of degeneration and uninventiveness became major tool of explanation in his book, *The History of Melanesian Society* published in 1914 from Cambridge University Press, Cambridge. He explained that some of the Melanesian islands people had no canoes, but they once must have known these items like any small island population, because without them they could never even think for home and reached their present habitat. The canoe craft guilds had died out, but this was a clear example that culture traits frequently disappeared. However, there were some other phenomena that could not be explained so easily. For instance, in Australia, he noted the presence of five different burial rituals in an otherwise homogeneous population within a fair small geographical region. These simple and uninventive aboriginals could not have developed so many variations just by themselves. Thus, he arrived at conclusions that small successive migrations had occurred among them. Physical similarities between the people were explained by the conjecture that only males arrived in the canoes, and since then they married local women, their offsprings soon lost the racial characteristics of their forefathers. Forced to learn language of their wives so that original language disappeared without a trace, the men became, thus, almost completely assimilated with their host culture. Now, they had no objections to abandoning all their original habits, except one, namely, burial rites. They had such strong emotional attachment to those practices that they refused to give them up and the puzzling variations were, thus, explained away. It remained, of course, unexplained how the rites had arisen in the first place and why the original Australian groups so readily gave up their own burial rites to which they must have been equally emotionally attached.

Thus, W.H.R. Rivers opined the similarities in cultures could be explained in better way by taking into consideration the imitation and migration. In this way he strongly supported the theory of uninventiveness put forward by his contemporaries Smith and Perry. He believed in migration as well diffusion of cultural traits.

The other famous books of Rivers are as follows:

1. 1914: *Kinship and Social Organisation*, London, Constable.
2. 1920: *Instinct and Unconsciousness*, Cambridge, Cambridge University Press.
3. 1922: *History and Ethnology*, New York: Macmillan.
4. 1923: *Conflict and Dream*, New York: Harcourt, Brace.

Rivers was also associated with Cambridge University, for sometime and used to teach Social Anthropology. A.R. Radcliffe Brown was one of his students. Under his guidance Brown came to India to study the 'Onge' tribe of Andaman Island.

There was a time, when Rivers appeared as a big shining stars in British anthropology and it was believed that he would lead British anthropology instead of E.B. Tylor, but he did not achieve this success and he soon disappeared from the scene of British anthropology. The work of River was also criticised for the following short comings:

1. Lowie was of opinion that Rivers never did intensive study of language, art, religion, history of culture, technology etc. How he considered himself as a competitor of E.B. Tylor and Boas.
2. Rivers was so overwhelmed by his study that he considered his finding as an invention.
3. He was also not well red and was like a modern marringer, shouting with glee over the discovery of America.

Weakness of British School of Diffusion

British diffusionists were clearly anti evolutionists and unanimous in their convictions that inventiveness was rare and similarities in cultures could be explained by imitation only. It is true that every cultural group borrows more than it invents. But this does not mean that inventions are made only once and at a particular place. This was a great weakness of this scheme due to which they are labelled as extreme diffusionists.

Another shortcoming of these extreme diffusionists was that they used the hypothetical un-inventiveness of man as an explanatory principle of everything they wanted to prove, without taking into account, the entirely different functions and cultural meanings of their diagnostic culture traits.

They were so biased in their scheme that they did not consider places other than Egypt as the centre of culture traits from where rest parts of the world borrowed. If they would have been in India, they could have accepted India as a centre of civilization from where other countries borrowed cultural traits. Thus, according to them, world's civilizations were gift of Egypt. But this is not true. There were many contemporary civilizations in the world.

They took into account only simple form of diffusion, i.e., diffusion of cultural traits, but they never emphasized upon the diffusion of culture complex.

Their emphasis, while explaining diffusion, was upon material culture only. Thus, they ignored the non-material aspects of culture, while explaining cultural diffusions.

It is because of their narrow scope of diffusion, i.e., extremism and Egyptism, they were last to come, but first to disappear, from the scene of British anthropology.

German School of Diffusion

German or Australian continental diffusionists are considered superior to British counterparts in their outlook, methodological approaches and ideologies. They were not extreme diffusionists like British contemporaries, who talked about diffusion of culture traits to the other spheres of earth only from Egypt. They ignored completely the idea of independent inventions as put forward by classical evolutionists. Believing in theory of cultural diffusion, German diffusionists also touched the evolutionary schemes. According to them; development of culture takes place not only at a particular place like Egypt, but it occurs at several different places at several times. This means that different cultural traits and cultural complexes originated independently or freely, at several parts of earth, from where they are imitated or migrated to other places. They were of view that discoveries of all things were not possible at the same time and at the same place, rather they were discovered at several places by several generations i.e. not at a particular place by same generation. Invention and discoveries were continuous process. They held opinion that cultural traits or complexes developed at different places and reached into places of other parts by migration. Thus, they accepted the theory of diffusion as well as evolution both for the cultural development and growth.

German diffusionists opined that if different layers of cultural traits were examined and analysed scientifically, migrations of different traits from different places could be identified easily. They, further, opined that different circles or districts developed at different places in different phases. Thus, each culture trait and complex had a circle or a district from where they migrated to other places, but it was not necessary that all traits or complexes might migrate all over the world. Migration of traits could be explained with the help of historical data. As they talk about spread of culture traits from one circle to another or from one district to another, their school is also known as *Kulture Kreise School* or 'Culture Circle' school, or 'Culture District' school. As they talk about diffusion of culture traits from one circle to another, which can be examined on the basis of historical facts, their school is also known as *Culture historic school*. Let us now discuss the contributions of each German diffusionists one by one. The greatest weakness of this school is that it talks about what is diffusion, but never explains how the diffusion takes place.

Friedrich Ratzel (1844-1904)

Ratzel was basically a zoologist, but he soon turned towards geography at the University of Leipzig, Germany. Again from Geography, his interest developed into Anthropology. He wrote many volumes on Anthropo-geography, and, therefore, he is regarded as founder of anthropology discipline at Germany in general, and German school of diffusion in particular. Diffusionists like Graebner and Schmidt owe great debt to Ratzel, from whom they learnt many things which helped them in developing theoretical and methodological approaches.

Ratzel's famous book entitled *Anthropo-Geography* was published in 1882. In this book, he not only emphasised upon the relation between anthropology and geography, but also made a clear-cut distinction between territorial and social geography. It was his interest in latter branch of science that held his interest and he called it *Anthropo-Geography*. He considered it mainly as the study of people's relationships to neighbouring countries. Particularly in terms of trait distributions. Considering that environment played significant adaptive role, he was nevertheless convinced that people were more influenced by one another than by factors of climate and terrain.

His another famous book entitled *Volkur Kunda* also known as *His-*

tory of Mankind was published in three volumes in-between the years 1885-88. This book was later on, published in two volumes between 1894-96.

His views on Psychic Unity was neither clearly pro nor anti. At one hand he appears as believing in it, on the other hand, his writings reveal that he was against the principle of psychic unity. For example, he observed that Athabaskan Indians were "poorly endowed", the Negro childish and imaginative, and the Chinese highly imaginative.

In any case, Ratzel did not use psychic unity as an explanatory principle, but he tended to deny multiple independent inventions. Like diffusionist, he shared the views that man is much more given to imitation than to creativity. He specifically attacked on Bastian, an evolutionist of the same country, who maintained that similar inventions came into existence due to people's Geist of material objects, but developed their own form of it. Ratzel stoutly declared that arrows and axes, had no souls and it was useless to search for them.

According to him, the most important consideration was to discover from where cultural traits came and where they went. He was of opinion that there were no spatial limits to the pathways they might take single cultural items usually diffused, but whole cultural complexes were transplanted by migration. Yet, in every case, adaptation to environment would cause variations in culture traits to take on somewhat different outward shapes. How then could their relationship be recognised. Ratzel warned that not every similarities could be taken as a proof of historical connection because objects of material culture, in order to have any utility at all, must possess certain features. For example, a canoe paddle needs a blade, and an arrow head or a spear must have a point. If, however, there were other similar qualities, unrelated to use, they must evidence historical relationship. So if paddles have similar incised ornamentations, or spears have feathers attached to their shafts, this cannot be accidental, must certainly imply borrowing or migration, even though respective cultures may be widely separated in time and space. Ratzel called this principle as *Formengedanke* or 'Criterion of form'. Applying this principle to African bow and arrow, he observed that cross section of bow shaft, the fasterings of bow strings and the feathering of the arrows were quite like those in Indonesia. Thus, he assumed that borrowing must have taken place.

Ratzel was not an extreme degenerationist. He felt that culture traits may become simplified or elaborated in their course of diffusion or migration, depending upon the local conditions and relative sophistication of local technology. It seems probable that he was influenced by the biological concept of adaptive radiation, which indicates that a common ancestry and relationships between varieties of species can be discovered, but they need not be identical because in species as well elements of culture there will be local adjustments.

Leo Frobenius (1873-1938)

Leo Frobenius, a student and colleague of Ratzel, took this idea of diffusion several steps further. He observed that historical connections usually implied much more than transmission of single culture traits, because often enough whole culture complexes were involved. He, thus, concluded that migration was more important factor of explanation than diffusion in explanation of cultural similarities. Finding that not only the forms of bow and arrows were similar in West Africa and Indonesia, but areas also resembled each other in form of house, shields, masks and drums, which indicate that migration had taken place. He, thus, added an another criterion of form other than Ratzel's Formengedanke. He called it as *Geographical Statistics*. His geographical statistics meant that one should count the number of similarities. Further he developed an another criterion namely, biological criterion or developmental criterion. By this he meant that internal changes have to be taken into account. Because, when people migrate into a different environment, their cultures would have to be adjusted. Some traits would change and some would disappear becoming useless. In this way, not only similarities but significant differences related to ecological adaptation could become indicators of historical connections.

He did not confine his research to only material culture like Ratzel, he also took into consideration, the study of mythology. Comparing similarities between traditional stories in Africa and Indonesia, he observed that in latter area myths were all related and formed an epic, while in Africa, the stories appeared singly. Indonesia, thus, must have been the homeland. He was also of opinion that higher cultures were always the originators and lower ones the imitators.

Ratzel's criterion of forms and Leo Frobenius geographical statistics, were vigorously combined in the strategy of Kulture Kreise School. Whose main figures were Graebner and Father Wilhelm Schmidt.

Frietz Graebner (1877-1934)

Graebner was a museum curator at Germany, but he emerged as main leader of Kulture Kreise School. Graebner applied the culture circle and culture strata idea on a world basis. He spelled out the methodological principles of this culture circle movement in his famous book *Methodder*

Ethnology published in 1911 from Heildberg. In this book, he attempted to elaborate the criteria for identifying affinities and chronologies or similarities and historical relationships. The two basic rules, simple enough and accepted by both Graebner and Schmidt in connection to culture circle or culture district and culture strata, were as follows:

(i) *Criterion of Form* as called by Graebner or *Criterion of Quality* as termed by Schmidt. It states that similarities between two culture elements which do not automatically arise out of nature, material purpose of the traits or objects, should be interpreted as resulting from diffusion, regardless of the distance which separates the two instances.

(ii) *Criterion of Quantity* (as called by both) – It states that the probability of historical relationship between two items increases as the number of additional items showing similarities increase, i.e., several similarities prove more than a single one.

Graebner reasoned that early man invented the basic of culture, such as language and tool making but soon formed a number of small bands that became isolated. Each of those developed their own distinctive cultures and they were the *Urkulturen* or 'Premeval culture', whose members, in course of time spread out in different directions, eventually populating all continents. It was the task and aim of culture historians to reconstruct the various Kreise or circle. He opined that the tracing of such relationship was the first and the most basic problem of ethnology (Graebner, 1911: 107). Graebner proposed this idea in his famous book, *Methodder Ethnology* (1911).

Realising that careful description must precede reconstruction. Graebner and all other pursuing this task, collected a truely impressive amount of data and described all items in detail. It is this part of research, that has remained valid and useful until the present day, but the reconstructions of possible Kreise and method employed have now largely been discarded.

Graebner and his followers were not satisfied with tracing connections, but were also interested in the reconstruction of chronology. On the basis of researches carried out in Oceania, Graebner reconstructed six successive layers of cultural development which are as follows:

(i) Tasmanian culture (the earliest one)
(ii) Australian boomerang culture
(iii) Totemic Hunter culture

(iv) Two-class horticulturist culture
(v) Melanesian bow culture
(vi) Polynesian Patrilineal culture (Recent one).

Each of these, alone or in combination with others, had counterparts in Africa and elsewhere. On the way of migration, blending with other culture had taken place, some traits had become lost completely, others added or elaborated and still other borrowed. To accommodate these and other complications, a very elaborate vocabulary was constructed. There were primary, secondary and tertiary Kreise or circles, each containing subcircles. Those that did not fit anywhere, were either marginal, peripheral or overlapping Kreise. In other words, the system did not work and all it proved was that culture spread and development did not take place in the ways posited by Kulture Kreise Scholars.

Graebner classified diffusion in two categories: Primary and Secondary. As referred earlier, Tasmanian culture being oldest one was example of primary diffusion. He was of opinion that Tasmania was the centre of Primary diffusion. Elements of complex culture developed all over Australia due to secondary diffusion.

Father Wilhelm Schmidt (1868-1954)

Schmidt was born in Australian in 1868. In 1906, Graebner, a museum curator of Berlin Ethnological Museum, went on to apply the culture circle and culture strata theory on a global level. Father Wilhelm Schmidt declared himself as a follower of Graebner. They both applied the rule of Criteria of Form or Quality and Criteria of Quantity to divide the culture of the world in to different strata and circles. By applying the superior culture-historical method to the known distribution of contemporary culture traits, they both claimed to be able to reconstruct a limited number of organised culture-circles. All of the world history was, thus, to be understood as the diffusion of these Kreise, out of the region, in which they were supposed to have evolved. About the Kreise of Graebner, a discussion has been already made. Father Schmidt's list of Kreise are the most influential example. Schmidt distinguished four major grades of culture circles which are as follows:

(i) Primitive culture circle
(ii) Primary culture circle
(iii) Secondary culture circle
(iv) Tertiary culture circle.

Within each of these grades of Kreise there were several sub-Kreise. Primitive Kreise was divided in to three sub-Kreise which were:

(a) Central or exogamous Kreise corresponding to pygmy people of Asia and Africa, distinguished by their exogamous hordes and their monogamous families.
(b) Arctic Kreise, corresponding to Samoyeds, Eskimo, Algonkians etc. distinguished by exogamous with sexual quality.
(c) The Antarctic Kreise (south eastern Australians, Bushmen, Tasmanian etc.), distinguished by exogamous with sex totems.

The next Primary stage was also divided into three Kreise which area:

(a) Patriarchal cattle-rearing nomads
(b) Exogamous patrilineal totemic higher hunters
(c) Exogamous matrilineal village dwelling horticulturists.

Secondary stage or grade was divided into two circle namely:

(a) A Free Patrilineal system (Polynesia, Sudan, India, Western Asia, Southern Europe, etc.)
(b) A Free Matrilineal system (southern China-Indo-China, Malenesia, north-eastern south America, etc.)

In tertiary state or grade, Schmidt placed earliest higher civilization of Asia, Europe and America.

The most striking feature of this scheme is its evolutionism. The succession of grades is nothing less than familiar sequences of grades leading from hunting and gathering types of socio-cultural systems through horticultural and pastoral types and to complex stratified civilizations. The evolutionary significance of the Kreise is further strengthened by the fact that Schmidt attempted to associate the sequence of grades with the main European archaeological divisions of prehistory.

Schmidt's evolutionism was by no means confined merely to the generalities of hunting, gathering, and civilization sequence. His notion of matrilineal horticultural Kreise was heavily in debt to the evolutionary logic of Bachofen and Morgan.

According to Schmidt, during the hunting and gathering stage, women were specialized in collection of wild plants. This led women to invent horticulture and, thus, to become the owner of products of the soil and land itself. On the basis of their economic ascendancy, women insisted on matrilocal residence and matrilineal descent. The supreme deity was given feminine attributes, girls puberty rights stressed and couvade instituted. He called this as a classical phase of mother right.

It is true that Schmidt made no attempt to arrange the three Kreise of primary stage in an evolutionary order. He did not propose that matrilineal Kreise had evolved before two patrilineal Kreise. All Kreise of primary stage evolved out of primitive stage apparently existed side by side. Schmidt's evolutionary sequence for matrilineal horticultural Kreise covered an extensive series of transformations. Property rights were supposed to have gone from equality in primitive stage, to female dominated in classic mother right to male dominated under masculine mother right. Thus, his sequence was very much similar to Morgan. The only difference was that Schmidt's sequence was supposed to have happened only once, whereas aspects of Morgan's sequence were supposed to have happened over and over again.

Thus, Schmidt as Kultur Kreise scholar, fitted cultures into his established sequences. He held a very living interest in chronology and development. He also used progress as an explanatory device, but he was also a great critique of evolutionism. He along with Graebner charged that Tylor and Spencer had looked upon culture as if it were one single entity that everywhere displayed the same tendencies towards progress and increasing complexities. According to them, neither of these were constant, and thus, could not be used as a device for explanations. Items of material culture sometimes became elaborated, but they were, often enough simplified, and degeneration was as much as fact of history as progress. Cultural institutions such as family organisation certainly did not increase in complexity. For example, European kinship systems were simpler than Australian aborigines. They were of opinion that evolutionists were at fault because they use their own culture as normative for all others and also because of their use of survivals as a tool of reconstruction.

Many of these criticism were telling ones, but Kultur Kreise scholar also sometimes fell into the same error. They also fitted culture into sequence and sometimes used progress as an explanatory device. For instance, Schmidt observed that pygmy burials were simpler than those of others and considered this evidence of their chronological priority. He also overlooked that his aim was different from evolutionists. The aims of Kultur Kreise school was to reconstruct whole cultures, while evolutionists attempted to reconstruct the development of descrete cultural institutions be family, marriage, kinship, law, religion etc. Kultur Kreise school could, thus, be more electic in their use of data and could select their evidence from ethnography as needed.

By and large, cultural historians were less interested in absolute origins than the evolutionists. But Father Schmidt was very much interested in establishing the origin of religion. For this purpose he reviewed many older theories and took specific issues with Tylor's theory that animism was the early form of religion. Backing his own contention with impressive ethnographic evidence, Schmidt showed that the most simple people often worshipped a high God as an All-father. Although there was no evidence of monotheism, he was convinced that this was the original form of religion. The later addition of other Gods and spirits was for him a clear-cut indication of the degenerative tendency of man thinking on this matter. Schmidt worked out this theory further in his book, *Der Ursprungder Gottesidea (The Origin of the Idea of God)* which was published in 12 volumes in-between 1926-1955).

Commentators have accused Schmidt of mysticism because of his religious commitments, but any unexplained mover of history is mystical in this sense, be it progress, degeneration, natural law or God. He was historical in the treatment of his data and honestly attempted to establish the age of the idea of high God. Of course, his conclusions about the origin of religion remained as speculative as those of Tylor, Spencer and Frazer.

Important books and papers of Father Schmidt are as follows:

1. *Der Ursprungder Gottesidea*, 12 volumes, Munster, 1926-1955. This book is also known as *The Origin of the Idea of God.*
2. *High Gods in North America,* Oxford, 1933.
3. *Primitive Man* in E. Eyread, European civilization, Oxford, 1934.
4. "The Position of Women with regards to property in Primitive Society", *American Anthropologist*, 37:244-56.
5. *Culture Historical Method of Ethnology*, New York, 1939.

German School of diffusion is also known as Vienna School of diffusion. Father Schmidt was elected as president of fourth ICAES (International Congress of Anthropological and Ethnological Sciences), which took place at the University of Vienna from 1st to 7th September, 1952. Thus, he made the anthropology discipline known at global level by hosting a grand ICAES and made the members of the Congress aware from the contributions of Australian anthropologists in the development of Anthropological theories in past as well as in present. He was the founder of Journal entitled *Anthropos*.

Weakness of Kultur Kreise School

The Kultur Kreise school is now practically defunct even in Europe, but some of its principles are used by art historians who attempt to establish relationship between art styles or motifs, but they do not deal with whole culture.

The theory has worked mainly to prove itself wrong, because in spite of monumental efforts, no circle could be established. The short coming of the theory rested both in its premises and its methods. As to the former, it was pure speculation to depict cultural differences, as having emanated from four or five early bands each with its own separate migrations. Even the scholarly-sounding criteria of quality and quantity did not yield always realistic result, because too many other influences interfere. It is beyond doubt that too many similarities in culture items witness historical contact of same kind. For example, if we find anyone having bottles of coca-cola in any remote area of the world, the conclusion will be certainly that they were not independently invented.

On the other hand, the mere facts that two or more cultures possess feathered arrows, matrilineality or myth about an all-father, does not necessarily prove historical relationship. Culture change may be divergent or covergent. The former means that similar forms may become dissimilar, while latter means that the dissimilar form may become similar in time. Diffusion of course plays havoc with the idea of pure culture circle.

The approach or methodology was barren because it did not attempt to reach about the dynamics of culture change. It was basically a descriptive or ideographic method that at best gave insight about spread of culture items, but over looked analysis of reasons behind their acceptance, rejection and modification. Thus, supporters of Kultur Kreise School tell us, in fact, about what is diffusion and migration, but they never explain why diffusion and migration takes place. This was the greatest weakness of the scheme.

The supporters of Kultur Kreise School are alleged that they took impetus from museum methodology and thus, were confined to typology of culture traits rather than explaining the causes of spread and diffusion.

American School of Diffusion

The founder of American School of diffusion was Franz Boas. Clark Wissler and A.L. Kroeber were his devout follower. As we have seen earlier, German diffusionists or followers of culture circle school or cultural historic school talked about complex form of diffusion of culture, but they failed to explain as to why diffusion took place. American diffusionists attempted to solve this question and to remove this shortcomings of culture historic school. On the basis of empirical researches, they discredited the universal sequences established by the classical evolutionists. They were of view that empirical researches were evidence to refer to that give and take of culture traits and culture complex had taken place through the medium of transport and communication. This process of give and take, of cultural traits and cultural complexes, was more prevalent among the cultural groups residing in close contact to each other. As culture is learnt, therefore, it becomes easy to imitate and adapt culture traits or complex among the groups residing in close proximity. Thus, diffusion of culture traits and culture complexes takes place, which is a continuous process.

American diffusionists did not held similar opinion on the question of degenerationism or loss of culture traits. European diffusionists, both British and German diffusionists stressed upon the degeneration theory which emphasised that one cultural groups progressed much than other. But American diffusionists were of opinion that every culture makes its own adaptation, therefore, the qucstion that one progressed more, thus, becomes futile.

The question about man's psychic unity also attained different dimensions in America. British and German diffusionists were not ready to accept psychic unity either as an ideology or an explanatory principles. Evolutionists had used psychic unity to explain cultural similarities that were not due to diffusion, but somewhat in circular fashion, they also held that such similarities proved men's mental unity. Franz Boas and other anthropologists led by him, embraced psychic unity as an ideology. It was not used as an explanatory principle, but as a tool to combat racism.

On the question as to why diffusion takes place, American diffusionists answers it in the ways: (i) the process of imitation causes diffusion of culture traits and complexes from one place to other or from one cultural group to another, and (ii) sometimes it looks easy to borrow some traits from other cultural groups instead of inventing separately. In the process of diffusion, the groups borrowing may adapt culture traits so that they might be useful for them. Thus, according to them, the diffused traits may or may not exist in original form. The similar diffused traits were more common in groups residing nearby geographically. They stressed that mountain, hill, river, desert, forest, lack of transport and means of communication, etc. were the great barrier in the diffusion of cultural traits or complexes.

In order to show the diffusion of cultural traits and complexes, American diffusionists devised a methodology which is known as culture area approach. They did not analyse cultural diffusion prevalent all over the world at the same time. Instead, they divided world into different cultural areas on the basis of geographical regions. They were of opinion that geographical aspects of culture can not be ignored in the study of culture area. They held view that dimensions of each culture can be studied on the basis of culture area study. If one passes through Europe, he or she may come across different cultural areas. If one compares those areas, he or she may arrive at conclusion that cultural groups residing in close geographical areas represent more uniformity than those residing in distant geographical region. Thus, according to them, the concept of culture area reveals geographical area of cultural similarities.

The concept of culture area was emphasised by Wissler and supported by A.L. Kroeber, Herskovite and Sapir. That's why American School of diffusion is also known as 'Culture Area School'. Methodological issues, followed in the study of culture area, were to divide world or a continent or a country into different culture areas. Then from each area, list of cultural elements or traits was prepared, which reached there in course of diffusion. They also emphasized upon the study of causes due to which the diffusion of cultural traits took place. In searching for the causes of diffusion, Boas was of opinion that we must not ignore the psychic bases of human beings. Clark Wissler, a follower of Franz Boas emphasised upon the changes that took place in diffused traits on account of which they could not persist in original form. This change can be seen especially in non-material aspects of culture. He also stressed upon the barriers of cultural diffusion like mountain, forest, hill, river, ocean etc. About culture area concept, a detail discussion will be made, while describing the contributions of Clark Wissler and A.L. Kroeber.

American diffusionists received inspiration from their German counterparts and museum methodology of Kultur Kreise or culture circle school. As Franz Boas was born at Germany and was students of three German Universities, it is generally argued that German school of diffusion and American school of diffusion were more or less similar and encouraged by museum methodology.

During 19th century, most museums displayed items arranged in evolutionary sequence under the influence of evolutionary schemes. For instance, all arrow heads were placed in series of increasing complexities, no matter where they had been found. Coinciding with the Boasian critique of evolution, both the American Museum of Natural history in New York and Field Museum in Chicago decided simultaneously to use geographical categories, instead of evolutionary trends, so that museum visitors might get better insight in to Indian cultures as a whole. When items of museum were arranged according to geographical areas, it was observed that cultural items of Indian tribes that lived close to another were more similar than those groups who lived further apart. The geographical regions that displayed such internal similarities, were called as "culture area", which also became the concept of culture area to be studied for showing diffusion of cultural items in American Anthropology. Isomorphism of cultural items was, thus, explained by diffusion. Now, let us discuss the contributions of individual American anthropologists, who deals with the theory or cultural diffusions.

Franz Boas (1858-1942)

Franz Boas was born in Westphalia, Germany, in 1858. It is often quoted that he was genius by birth. Even at the age of 13 years he had written a letter to his elder sister in which he had expressed his desire to study some unknown land of the world. This clearly indicates his curiosity by birth to understand mankind.

Boas was educated at three universities of Germany, namely Heidelberg, Bonn and Kiel. Under the encouraging and inspiring guidance of sixteen renowned teachers, he studied physics at Heidelberg, mathematics at Kiel and geography at Bonn. He wrote his forty-two page doctoral dessertation on the *Color of Sea Water* in 1881. The thesis was submitted to the University of Keil. His teachers were trained physicist, mathematicians and anthropo-geographer, from whom he learnt many theoretical concepts and applied them in the field of anthropological researches. He was also inspired by A. Bastian, a German evolutionist, who suggested him to undertake researches on culture complex.

Boas joined an artic expedition of Baffinland, North America, as a geographer in 1883-84. He first visited the Indians of north-west cost in 1886 and returned two years later at the request of Tylor. In 1893, he organised the anthropological collections for Chicago World's Fair. He joined as a staff of American Museum of National History at Clark University in 1888. He became Professor of Anthropology at Columbia University in 1986, where he remained till his death in 1942, though he was retired in 1937.

In addition, he was the centre of critical formative events, such as the modernising of the American Anthropologists in 1898, the founding of American Anthropological Association in 1900, the revitalization of American Ethnological society in the same year and the founding of American folklore Society in 1888.

Boas' accomplishments as a teacher, administrator, researcher, founder and president of societies, editor, lecturer and field worker are executing to behold. His academic activities were accompanied by seven hundred articles, several books and extensive myth collections. In American Anthropology, Boas occupied an image of father, hero and *Guru.*

When Boas received his first academic appointment at Clark University in 1888, Anthropology was firmly established in its four-field approach — linguistics, archaeology, physical anthropology, and ethnology. The first volume of American Anthropologist in 1888 dealt with articles on these four-field approaches. Anthropology was certainly empirical and emphasised upon fieldwork, and many good monograph had also been published. But in early part till his death Boas became an influential figure in America. He trained a great many anthrpologists, among them mention may be made of Alfred Kroeber, Alexander Golden Wieser, Frank Speek, Robert Lowie Paul Radim, Leslie Sapir, Herskovite, M.F. Ashley Montagu, Margaret Mead, and Ruth Benedict. These students in turn set forth the main lines of development of anthropological research and instructions at crucial installations throughout the country. For example, Kroeber and Lowie at Berkley, Cole and Sapir at Chicago, Herskovite at North-Western, while Boas himself was Chairman, division of Anthropology, Columbia University.

During the first half of twentieth century, Anthropology in United States was characterised by a programmatic avoidance of theoretical synthesis. The basic strategy for this period was formulated by Boas, one of the most influential figures in the history of social sciences. Boas was guided by a distinct sense of inductive purity, which he transmitted to generation of followers. It was a creed, however, which paradoxically dented its own existence. His students admitted not only that Boas had trained them to pursue their varied interests, mindful of data, free of prejudice, and distrustful of all schemes. They explicitly denied that Boas was a centre of school. His mission had been to free anthropology from its amateurs and armchair specialists, by making ethnographic research in the field, the central experience and minimum attributes of professional status. With the passage of time, a definite central them 'historical particularism' has come to be associated with Boasian period.

The perspective which we enjoy in these matter of historical particularism or 'cultural relativism', is in no way diminishing to the importance of Boas contribution in the development of anthropological theory. It is true that the strategy of historical particularism required an almost total suspension of normal dialetic between facts and theory. The causal processes, the trends, the long range parallels were buried by an avalanche of negative cases. It is true that the attempt to harden the fiber of ethnographic inquiry, with higher standards of proof, met with only limited success. Notable instances were witness in which Boas and his followers abused the facts as others before and after have done. But the standard he proposed, remained a permanent legacy.

Those who argue that Boas retarded the progress of Anthropology as a science make improper allowance for the cultural forces that lay behind the historical particularist reform. There were culturally determined ideological limits within which anthropological theory was largely constrained. Transgressors left no heritage within anthropology about which we are to-day aware. Boas and his first generation of students were obliged to build anthropology professional and university based practically from the ground up. Culturally prescribed limits were not so narrow and well defined that options did not exist. We have merely to consider the fate of anthropology within Soviet Union, Germany, and Italy during the same period, to realise that if historical particularism was essentially negative and theoretically sterile, it nonetheless avoided the worst pit falls of its times.

Boas touched all the aspects of man for the scientific study under the discipline anthropology. He made anthropology field based and stressed upon the need of studying ethnographic, linguistic, archaeological and physical aspects of man under the subject anthropology as a whole. Thus, with Boas anthropology had come of an age, when under his influence there was no singling out of any one method, psychologic, sociologic, functional or Kultur Kreise – as constituting superior to other. Thus, he does not belong to any particular school. As there was no school in physics, therefore, he believed that there should not be any school in anthropology.

Important books of Franz Boas are as follow:

1. 1888: *Central Eskimo*, University of Nebraska Press, Lincoln.
2. 1905: *Kawakiutl Text*, Publication of Jesup North Pacific Expedition.
3. 1911: *Mind of Primitive Man,* New York: The Free Press.
4. 1927: *Primitive Art,* Oslo: H. Aschelhoung and Company.
5. 1928: *Anthropology and Modern Life*, New York: W.W. Norton and Co.
6. 1940: *Race Language and Culture*, New York: Macmillan Company.

Besides these books, as stated above, he had contributed as many as 700 articles on different aspects of anthropology subject such as ethnology, folklore, linguistics, physical anthropology, museum ethnology, archaeology etc. In this way, he had left no branch of anthropology untouched on the basis of researches done among the primitive tribes of

America.

At the beginning of his anthropological career in America, Boas described the aims of ethnology as follows:

> The task of Anthropology is the study of the total range of phenomena of social life. Language, customs, migrations, bodily characteristics are subject of our study. Thus, first and most immediate object of ethnology is the study of history of mankind, not that of civilised nations alone, but that of whole mankind, from its earlier traces found in the deposits of ice-age, up to modern item (1940:627-28).

This formulation was not in contradiction to the aims of evolutionists, and like them, Boas felt that time that the search for laws of cultural evolution was a legitimate undertaking:

> A comparison of social life of different people proves that the foundation of their cultural development is remarkably uniform. It follows from this that there are laws to which this development is subjected. Their discovery is more important aims of our society (1940: 633-34).

His acceptance of the possibility of lawful sequence of events was reiterated in 1896, but now he attached importance to the comparative method, which evolutionists had used for the reconstruction of their universal stages. Boas had discussed this problem in his paper entitled, "The Limitation of Comparative Method" published in 1896. The paper highlighted the problem of separating instances of convergent from instances of parallel evolution. He did not doubt that there were many remarkable similarities of culture traits that could not be explained by diffusion. But the fact that such phenomena as shamanism, the concept of future life, use of bow, geometric design, use of mask and many other items, are widely distributed, which does not establish the uniformity of history. Conclusions, concerning whether evolutionary uniformities, i.e., parallel evolutionary sequences, have occurred or not, must be held in abeyance until data of certain sorts are collected. The data in question are the facts of historical sequences, by which, in particular local areas, the observed phenomena have come into existence.

> The facts that many fundamental features of culture are universal, or at least occurred in many isolated places, interpreted by the assumption that the same feature must always have developed from the same causes, leads to the conclusion that there is one grand system accord-

> ing to which mankind has developed everywhere. All the occurring variations are no more than minor details in this grand uniform evolution. It is clear that this theory has for its logical basis the assumption that the same phenomena are always due to similar cases (Boas: 1896).

This assumption is potently false in large number of concrete instances. For example, clans seem to have arisen among Navaho by fission of separate groups, but among North-west tribe, they resulted from village fission. Geometric design not necessarily results from gradual conventionalisation of realistic representations, as putforth by Haddon (1895), but from an infinite number of starting point. Similarly masks are used sometimes as disguises, to protect harmful effect of spirit, elsewhere they are worn to frighten off people and spirit, still in other context they are used to commemorate a deceased relative. On the basis of above examples, it seems unlikely that the same causal sequence can have decounted everywhere for the development of these phenomena.

Boas accused the evolutionists that they had never bothered to prove and to test their hypothesis. They had simply concluded that cultural similarities, no matter, where they found, indicated the existence of one grand system according to which human culture had evolved everywhere. Boas was of opinion that comparative method be replaced by historical method. He emphasised upon the importance of historical approach because, according to him, the culture of which social systems are part and parcel, is the product of historical process, emphasising the variety of history. Thus, historical method clearly reveals that like phenomena were not always due to same causes. He was of opinion that for every single instance a common cause must be empirically established. He was aware that this was a slow and laborious undertaking, but it would reconstruct the history of cultural development with great accuracy and for understanding social regularities.

Only one common cause for cultural similarities acceptable to Boas was common origin in history. He disagreed with the uniformity of the mind as an explanation, because man does not obey the same laws everywhere. Similarity of environment was equally ruled out on the basis of empirical researches, it could be shown that different forms of culture exist in similar environment and *vice versa*. Common historical origin first should be established in small and well defined geographical areas. The continuity of distribution was the major proof for historical connections. A break in this continuity should be presumed as similar traits had arisen independently.

Boas historical method denied the existence of general laws, because, similarities in phenomena were not on account of similar causes, except in very limited geographical areas. Thus, he arrived at a position known as historical particularism. He emphasised upon the need of explaining isolated parts of human history, but never its totality. Boas himself became increasingly pessimistic about the value of historical method. He discovered the role of individual in culture change. Once this was taken into account, search for laws became almost aphemeral.

By about 1910, Boas had given up the possibility that significant developmental uniformities involving whole congeries of institutions, would be found. However he continued to stress the probability that occurrence of similar institutions throughout the world reflected something inherent in human mind. In his book, *The Mind of Primitive Man* (1911), the absence of uniform developmental sequences is for the first time clearly and explicitly related to an absence of determinative order between the various parts of culture and between culture and natural environment. For example, he pointed out various forms of family which cannot be correlated with other institutional features.

Inventions, social order, intellectual and social life all may develop independently. For instance, Australians, whose material culture is quite poor, but have a highly complex social organisation. Similarly, the influence of environment is quite inpredictable. Proof of the spontaneous creative influence of mind, i.e. to be found in the grate diversity of culture among such pairs of adjacent people as Eskimo, chuckchee, the Hottentot and Bushman, Negrito and Malaya. The exploitation of food resources is itself, subject to the whim of culture. Even among Eskimo, who have so marvelously well succeeded in adapting themselves to their geographical environment, customs like the taboo, on the promiscuous use of carbon and seal prevent the fullest use of the opportunities offered by the countries. This appear to sundry ethnographic examples of alleged lack of correlation between the different parts of culture, and hence of the lack of parallel evolution.

By 1932, Boas had given up all hope for the discovery of any laws, general or particular. He held opinion that phenomena of our science are so individualised that no set of law could explain them. He was doubtful whether valid law could be found. But even then he was not tired of showing that the general sequences proposed by evolutionists were all wrong. Where most evolutionists had postulated the priority of matrilineality over other pattern of kinship, Boas went on to prove that in Kawakiutl society patrilineality had changed into matrilineality. When art historians quarreled about whether realism in art had proceeded geometric abstract design or *vice versa*, Boas proved both as wrong, emphasising that development may take place in either way.

When Boas became disillusioned in history and historical reconstruction, his interest in role of individual increased. While studying different cultural groups historically, Boas was aware of the fact that individual reacts to their cultures in different ways. Thus, culture and personality influences each other. These insights were more systematically analysed by latter anthropologist, Margaret Mead and Ruth Benedict, under culture personality School of anthropological thought.

Boas as an Ethnographer

Boas ethnographic researches were mainly directed toward the study of kinship organisation, art and myth. The last one was closely related to his interest in language, because he felt that best linguistic data could be obtained by the recording of people's oral literature. Keenly aware that much of this traditional material would soon be forgotten because Indian cultures were rapidly changing or disappearing, he collected myths, legends, folktales, prayers, folk medicine, and similar folkloric materials from many Indian groups, such as Eskimo (1888), Chinook (1894), Bellacoola (1898), Tsimshian (1902), and Kwakiutl (1905). His books *Central Skimo and Kawakiutl*, discuss in detail, the social, cultural, linguistic, religious, ceremonial and political aspects of both tribes. Full length monograph on this Indian tribe reveals clearly the interests of Boas in ethnographic study by self visiting the field area and staying with the group to be studied.

Boas as a Folklorist

It was Boas who introduced the study of folkloric traditions to understand the origin and historical development of primitive groups. He was of opinion that oral tradition was the unwritten historical account of tribal societies. He felt the urgency of need to preserve folklores for the academic benefit of many generations. He gathered a good amount of information on folk myths, legends, tales, riddles, art, magic, song, dance, idioms, tradition, custom, ceremonies etc. to explore and analyse the culture of American tribes. He was so interested in folklore that he founded a separate institutions to explore and analyse the folkloric traditions of the primitive in Columbia University. The Institute of American Folklore Society was founded in 1888. American anthropological association appointed him as an editor of *Journal of American Folklore* in 1908. He edited this journal till 1924. Boas, theoretical contributions to mythology and folklore are relatively small. He opposed the view that essential unity of human mind had produced similarities in folktales all over the world. He equally objected to the theory that myth had arisen from a universal tendency to anthropomorphise nature. He was of opinion that borrowing of myth was not an automatic process, but the themes of stories were commonly adapted to the culture of borrowers. Thus, myths were inpart culturally determined and inpart determined by human imaginations.

Boas as a Physical Anthrpologists

Boas as a physical anthropologist was more concerned with human growth, not on classification of racial type and racial affinity. His main emphasis was upon height and growth. He took measurement of 19,000 children of America in-between the age group of 13 to 19 and analysed these data from various angles. His study of tempo growth reveals that the tempo of an individual changes till his life meets an end. Thus, it is a continuous process in the life span of an individual.

Boas also devoted himself to the study of ecological impact upon the cephalic index. Boas also took somatometric measurement of Japanese children born in America. Thus, he was able to establish the cause of changing cephalic index owing to different environmental conditions.

Boas' Concept of Natural History and Social Philosophical Approach

From the very earliest period, the Boasian programme suffered the embarrassment of virtue which was at the same time its chief vice. It was inductive to the point of self-destruction. The proposal to substitute concrete historical data for speculative deductions about history needs no defence. On the other hand, to deprive science of speculation altogether is to deprive it of its very life blood. Yet in essence, this is what Boasian programme sought to accomplish. In view of fragmentary nature of ethnographic record and in view of the urgency of obtaining data from fast disappearing tribal group, all theory was deemed speculative. The need of the moment was fieldwork. The only corrective was to allow conclusions to follow from the data without the introduction of preconceived philosophical positions.

Boas emphasis on systematic fieldwork had to the collection of whatever data become available. If one found an informant to be particularly well versed in subject and concentrated on that subject, getting everything possible from him and following through with other informations, observations, and the like, even though the immediate usefulness of the material might not be apparent. This exhaustive collection of data which seems at the time to have little or no connection with particular problems, is peculiarity a feature of natural history approach. The masses of data may, therefore, be worked over with no clear knowledge of what is to be gained at the end.

Social philosophical approach is a part of natural history approach. History influences philosophy and philosophical laws are shaped according to growth of history.

Thus, several theoretical concepts and methods of anthropology emerged from the scholarly mind of Franz Boas, yet there is no Boasian school, nor are there any theories closely related to his name. But his influence is generally recognised by those who studied under him. He was able to communicate to them the urgency and importance of anthropological research, not by preachment, but by tempo, tone and gesture, and this urgency remained with them. His interests were so wide that no single individual could possibly pursue them all. Some followed up on his distribution and diffusion studies. Other concentrated on historical reconstructions or studied individual cultures in detail, still others began to examine the influence of personality on culture and *vice versa*, thus injecting psychological factors in anthropology.

Weakness of Boasian Scheme

In spite of his manifold contributions to the development of Anthropology, Boas was also criticized for his weaknesses.

It is alleged that his earlier monographs on Baffinland (1884 and 1885) were explained in largely in geographical terms. This attitude of geographical determinism was still recognizable in the monograph on 'The Central Eskimo (1888), although to a lesser degree. Harris (1968:267) opined that when he was writing these monographs, he was one of the aspirants for the post of geographer at the University of Berlin, Germany. Thus, he did not want to underout this discipline. After setting in America as an anthropologist in 1896, he never again stressed the geographical milieu as a factor influencing culture.

Lowie (1937: 142-44) observed in Boas' theories a strong functionalist component, but he ascribed this position to his teaches on slim evidence. According to him, Boas realised that cultures were not mere aggregates of separate elements, but integrated wholes. This insight is not necessarily related to functionalism, and Boas in fact criticised it because of its presumed antihistorical bias. But there is another important element in Lowie's statement that he himself over looks namely, the Boas used plural form of cultures. Thus, Boas shifted attention from general to the more specific fact that every society possesses its own culture, implying that each culture is an integrated way of life, valid and meaningful in its own right. This was the positive side of historical particularism. It followed logically from the rejection of earlier evolutionism division of mankind on an unequal basis, savagery and barbarism being lower than civilized man. Strongly popularising the idea, Boas opined that there was no fundamental difference in ways of thinking of primitive and civilized man. A close connection between race and personality had never been established. It is because of this facts, not surprising, that Boas' books were included in book burning ordered by Nazij in Germany in 1933.

Boas' recognition of the pluralities of cultures closely emphasises upon the fieldwork, but this has also been argued by Leslie White. White vindictively attempted to impugun Boas' competence as a field worker. He implied that he had inflated the amount of time actually spent in the field. He also alleged that Boas missed to deal with important aspects of social organisation of Kwakiutl. Nevertheless, Boas accomplished more in collecting vast amount of data than almost anyone else. He did not originate the practice of fieldwork, but he attempted to achieve higher standard by insisting that theory must be based upon objective empirical data. He advocated that fieldwork must be part of every anthropological training programme. He was of opinion that student must spend a year at least with the people under study.

Clerk Wissler (1870-1947)

Clark Wissler was a student of Franz Boas. He was very much influenced by the 'Natural History Approach' of Franz Boas. Dissatisfied with earlier writers as evolutionists, who had treated American Indian populations, as if they formed one uniform and undifferentiated whole. He was of opinion that steps should be taken to indicate and locate the varieties of their modes of life and to classify their social grouping according to their dominants traits and geographical locations.

Wissler like Franz Boas was of opinion that cultures of no two groups of people were identical. The customs of those who live close to one another tend to have greater similarities than do the customs of those groups who live farther apart. Some traits of culture, beyond doubt, will be more widespread than others, yet the setting of similar cultural items in total complexes of which they form parts, will differ in different regions.

The simple facts derive from the fundamental principle that since culture is learned, any element in it can be taken over by any individual or any groups of individuals exposed in different ways of doing and thinking. By the same token, it follows that the groups who live close together have greater opportunity to borrow from each other than those who are at distance. That's why when cultures are viewed objectively, they are seen to form cluster, so to speak, sufficiently homogeneous that the regions in which they occur can be delimited on the man. The area in which similar cultures are found is called a culture area.

The concept of culture area was propounded by American anthropologists, of whom Wissler was most important. The culture area concept had its origin in the practical exigencies of American ethnographic research, as a heuristic device for mapping and classifying the tribal groups of north and south America. The development of ethnographic collections at the American Museum of Natural History and the Chicago field museum in particular, coinciding with the trend against evolutionary typologies, fostered the development of geographical categories as display units implicit in name of sections or hall. It was Oils T. Mason, who employed the term 'Culture area' in an article entitled, "Influence of Environment upon Human Industries or Arts" published in *Annual Report of Smithonian Institution* in 1895. In this article, Mason identified eighteen American Indian environments or culture-areas which are as follows:

Arctic, Athabascan, Algonkian, Iroquoian, Muskhogean, Plains of Great West, North Pacific Coast, Columbia Drainage, Interior Basin, California-Oregon, Pueblo, Middle American, Andean, Andean Atlantic slope, Eastern Brazilian, Central Brazilian, Argentine-Petagonian, and Puagian.

In 1899, Mason produced a modified list which went as follows:

> Arctic, Canadian, Louisiana or Gulf, Plains, South-East Alaska, Columbian, Interior Basin, California, Pueblo, Middle American, Antillian, Cordilleran, Upper Amazon, Eastern Brazil, Matto Grosso, Argentine-Petagonian and Augian.

Mason's areas were subsequently refined and made basis of a landmark treatment of American Indian ethnology by Clark Wissler in 1917 and Kroeber in 1939. Though the credit of coining the term culture-area goes to Mason, but it was Clark Wissler, who first of all treated the culture area concept systematically in studying the American Indian cultures. His definition of culture area, though it has been sharpened, is still useful.

Wissler says,

> the natives of New World could be grouped according to culture traits, this would give us food areas, textile areas, ceramic areas etc. If, however, we take all traits into simultaneous consideration and

> shift our point of view to social or tribal units, we are able to form a fairly definite group. This will give us culture areas, or a classification of social groups according to their culture traits (Wissler 1922:218).

To classify whole cultures in this or any other way is, however, by no means as simple as it seems at first glance. The individual traits in to which a culture can be broken down for the purposes of objective analysis, may or may not have the same distributions. This becomes apparent if, for instance, we consider the distribution of certain elements in African culture. East Africa is to be delimited as culture area largely on the basis of the place of cattle in the lives of people there, the Cango because of its agricultural, political and artistic characteristics yet in both these areas, a wife is acquired, only after the passage of wealth from the groom to the father of the bride to ensure, among other things, that a woman will be adequately cared for her husband, while descent is counted on one side of the family rather than on both sides. The religions of Africa are customarily divided into two categories: one in which emphasis is laid on the ancestors, other where nature deities bulk large. Here we differentiate East Africa from Cango, but not the Cango from Guinea Coast or Western Sudan.

Nonetheless, such factors do not negate experience that the cultures of an area, considered as whole, do hang together. Boas has cautioned that since culture areas are commonly mapped on the basis of material culture traits, the Scholars interested in religion, social organisation and other aspects of non-material cultures would soon discover that the culture area based on material culture do not coincide with those that would naturally result from his studies. It is to be noted that Boas himself, in classifying North American Indian folktales, allocates several types of myth and dominant characters to the areas that do roughly correspond to conventional culture area scheme for the continent. In case of human tales were told, in all probability future study will show that its principle characteristics may well be defined by cultural areas of continent. Robert when studying the distribution of musical forms of aboriginal North America, found that musical areas, both instrumental and vocal, coincide with those based on other cultural traits.

Thus, culture area, for American historicists or diffusionists was a classificatory device, not in itself a very useful historical concept, but a necessary element in their reconstruction of past. It referred to groups of geographically contiguous tribes that contrast with other such groups. The similarity of culture was in part presumably the result of their communication with each other; so that a boundary enclosed a geographical area over which fairly intensive diffusion had taken place. It was thus a bounded system to study historical developments, usually the environment was relatively uniform throughout the area. This meant that one important variable accounting for inter-cultural differences was held more or less constant. And the area were not so large as to prevent detailed studies of many individual cultures within their boundaries to get an idea of the range of cultural variation.

The method, for determining the sequence in which traits spread across the area was suggested by Boas himself (1940:320) and developed by Clark Wissler in 1917, A.L. Kroeber (1923) and Sapir (1916).

Clark Wissler's map listed ten culture area for North America, four for South America, and a separate one for Caribbean. These are as follows:

A. North America	B. South America	C. Caribbean
1. Plains	1. Chibcha	1. Antilles
2. Plateau	2. Inca	
3. California	3. Gunaco	
4. North Pacific Coast	4. Amazon	
5. Eskimo		
6. Mackenzie		
7. Eastern wood land		
a) Iroqnian		
b) Central Algonkin		
c) Eastern Algonkin		
8. South East		
9. South West		
10. Nahua		

Seeking for a common denominator for each group, he took subsistence as the most basic factor, not only because it was necessarily related to environmental conditions. Reducing his original areas to eight food areas, his scheme was as follows:

Subsistence	*Area*
1. Caribon	Eskimo
2. Bison	Great Plains
3. Salmon	North Pacific Coast
4. Wild Seeds	California
5. Eastern Maize	South East and Eastern wood-land
6. Intensive Agriculture	South West, Mexico, Peru
7. Maniac	Amazon region, Caribbean
8. Guanaco	Guanaco

(Wissler 1917:370-74).

In order to indicate their internal coherences, and their differences from each other, Wissler began to list many of their cultural elements. Interested, also, in the prehistory of the Indians, he made maps based upon archaeology and other maps using ethnographic data. Finding a remarkable degree of coincidence between past and present, he concluded that Indian cultures were quite stable also. Trying to match his findings with linguistic and racial classifications, he found the correlation much weaker. Unable to explain these puzzling facts, he was satisfied that cultures themselves were relatively homogeneous. For instance, plain Indians typically depended upon the buffalo for food, clothing and tents. They did not fish, had no agriculture, possessed movable tepeetents, used dogs and travois for land transportation, had no property, no basketry, had highly developed leather works as well as circular shields, geometrical arts, men's societies, sweet lodges and scalp dances. They differed in their ways from North Pacific Coast tribes, who depended on Sea-food, made much use of barriers, cooked in baskets, built rectangular plan houses, had totem poles, dug out canoes, and weaven helmets, but no shield. Since it was unlikely that such typical trait complexes were invented independently, and since they appeared in groups living in close proximity, diffusion was the most logical explanation, and a separate setting of each area was implied.

Wissler found it necessary to posit a *Culture-centre* for each of his culture area. This centre was the place of early settlement from which the various traits had diffused. Unfortunately, it was unproven that all traits emanated from a single centre or even that a centre ever had existed. The centre was also the place where all traits typically appeared and they diminished in number with the increase of distance from the centre. Different elements became more numerous and eventually led to another culture centre in a different culture area. Firm boundary could, thus, not be established. His scheme resembled that of British diffusionists on a miniature scale. It appeared, as if only inhabitants of culture centres were innovators and all others were imitators. But he did not posit degeneration, like British diffusionists, because he was clearly aware that traits must be adapted to specific conditions, if they are to remain functional.

From the very beginning the concept of 'Culture-Centre' exhibited the full scale effects of basic dilemma: how to combine the environmental conditions with the apparently capricious freedom of culture. Wissler's vague references to ethnic factors and historic area are as follows:

The origin of culture centre seems due to ethnic factors more than to

> geographical ones. The location of these centres is largely a matter of historic accident, but once located and the adjustments made, the stability of the environment doubtless tends to hold each particular type of culture to its initial locality, even in the face of many changes in blood and language (Wissler 1926:372).

Elaborating further on the notion of culture centre, Wissler set forth "law of diffusion", to wit that anthropological traits tend to diffuse in all directions from their centres of origin. This law of diffusion constitutes the basis of *age-area* principle. Wissler called 'age-area' as a method for inferring the relative age of culture traits from their geographical distribution. It meant the most widely distributed traits around a centre would be the oldest one, if the directions of the diffusion were always from the centre outwards. The 'age-area' principle, thus, assumed a good deal about patterns of diffusions within and even between culture area: that traits tended to diffuse or spread outward in all directions from a point of origin in a pattern of concentric circles, i.e., the law of diffusion. The diffusion rate of traits tended to be uniform, and that as the traits diffused from their origin to peripheries of culture area, they tended to loose some of their complexity. Wissler recognised that these assumptions had to be heavily qualified in almost every specific case. So he was continually making rather grand statements followed by exceptions and explanations of why specific cases did not conform to the basic age area assumption.

Wissler observed, thus, two types of cultural diffusion: the natural diffusion and organised diffusion. In natural diffusion, culture traits of one group diffused in different parts of the same group or in different cultural groups by trial or error method and indigenous process, which is time taking. It is transmitted through natural agencies. Organised diffusions, on other hand, is very quick and transmitted through organised agencies like missionaries, invaders, contacts with inhabitants of alien culture etc.

Important Books of Clark Wissler are as follows:

1. 1917: *The American Indian : An Introduction to the Anthropology of the New World*. New York: D.C. McMurtrie.
2. 1922: *The American Indian.* New York: Oxford University Press.
3. 1923: *Man and Culture*. New York: Thomas Y. Crowell Company.
4. 1926: *The Relation of Nature to Man in Aboriginal America*. New York: Oxford University Press.
5. 1929: *An Introduction to Social Anthropology*. New York: Holt.

Alfred Lewis Kroeber (1876-1960)

A.L. Kroeber was the fist student of Boas to receive a doctoral degree at Columbia University. Unlike his mentor, Franz Boas, Kroeber did not possess a scientific background. He came to anthropology via humanities. His twenty-eight page doctoral dissertation entitled, "Decorative Symbols of the Arapaho", awarded in 1901, witnessed both his humanistic interests and Boas' influence. He showed, in this dissertation as to how in the arts of these Plain Indians realistic symbolism appeared together. Thus, he arrived at conclusion that a uniform development of art styles could not have occurred, because the origin of either styles could not be established. Eight years later, Boas made a similar point in his study of Alaskan needle cases.

He was born on 11th June, 1876 at Manhattan Island nearby New York. His grandfather Luis Kroeber and farther Florence Martin Kroeber had migrated to U.S.A. in the middle of 19th century from a village named 'Kroebern' near Leipzing in Germany. His father had established an European clock shop on Union Square in New York. A.L. Kroeber, during the childhood, used to assist his father in delivering clock packets to customers door.

By the time, Kroeber came under the influence of Boas, he had received his graduation and master degree in humanities (English) discipline and was teaching as lecturer in that subject. By that time, he was an assistant and used to teach 18th century literature and Fresh English composition.

When Franz Boas was appointed as lecturer in Anthropology at Columbia University in 1896, Kroeber came in contact with Franz Boas, whose able guidance and inspiring encouragement shaped his professional carrier as a leading anthropologists at U.S.A.

In 1897, Boas established a course in American Indian languages and Kroeber was enrolled in that course. In 1898, he was awarded a Fellowship in Anthropology from the Columbia University. In next summer, he was sent to conduct field researches among the Arapaho Indians. He submitted his Ph.D thesis in 1901 and awarded doctorate degree in the same year. In 1906, he became a full fledged assistant professor of Anthropology at Berkeley, California. Kroeber occupied the post of professor of Anthropology there till his death in 1960. He died on 4th October 1960 at Paris at the age of 84, when he along with his wife Theodora had gone there. During his life time as a professor of Anthropology, he organised many seminars, symposium special lecturers, etc. at Berkley, in which many leading anthropologist of different parts of world participated.

He was a successful research guide and many eminent anthropologists of America received doctorate degree under his supervision. Some of them were Margaret Mead, Coro-Du-Bois, Dorthy etc. R.H. Lowie and Clyde Kluckhohn were his distinguished colleagues.

Kroeber was authors of more than five hundred research articles and nearly a dozen of books covering all branches of anthropology subject.

His famous published books are as follows:

1. 1923: *Anthropology*. New York: Harcourt, Brace
2. 1925: *Handbook of the Indians of California*. Washington.
3. 1939: *Cultural and Natural Areas of Native North America*. University of California Press.
4. 1944: *Configuration of Culture Growth*. Berkeley: University of California Press.
5. 1952: *The Nature of Culture*. Chicago: University of Chicago Press.
6. 1957: *Style and Civilization*. Ithaca: Cornel University Press.
7. 1963: *Anthropologist Looks at History*. Berkeley: University of California Press.

After occupying the post of lecturer in Anthropology at California University, he followed the tradition of Franz Boas in developing theoretical concepts. He was of opinion, like Boas, that theory must result from fieldwork conducted as far as possible without theoretical preconceptions. Thus, he emphasized upon data collection. He himself admitted that he had not become interested in theoretical issues until he had reached middle age and he advised other to follow suit. Following publications concerned with the folklore of the Smith Sound Eskimo and of the Cheyenne, Kroeber submitted his doctoral thesis "Decorative Symbolism of Aparaho (1901), where he developed theory that both decorative and symbolic art forms could occur simultaneously. In this way, he defeated Alfred C. Haddon's (1895) notion that the art had developed in unilinear sequences: realistic, symbolic and geometric. This was Kroeber's conclusion to reach at the age of 25 years.

Kroeber's Attack on Morgan's Scheme of Kinship Terminology

Morgan, a classical evolutionist of America believed that classificatory terminologies were associated with evolutionary emergence of unilinear descent groups. They reflected the great way of kinship institution during most of human history. They were replaced by descriptive terminologies during the transition from kinship to state organised societies.

Kroeber in his paper, "Classificatory System of relationship" (1909) argued that the kinship terminologiės of all cultures, whether primitive or civilized, consisted of a mixture of classificatory and descriptive tendencies. There was no general rule by which one or other form could be correlated with social structure. One has to consider the classificatory nature of such english terms as 'uncle' and 'cousin' to realise that Morgan must have been carried away by his schemes to have supposed that such practices were confined to cultures on clan level organisation. Kroeber's attack on Morgan followed the strategy that has proved successful in his Ph.D. thesis that both forms of art developed side by side. Boas also concluded the same strategy in his book, "Mind of Primitive Man" emphasising that sequential elements could actually be found existing together in the same society.

Kroeber's attack on Morgan, unlike Lowie, did not arise out of a careful study of Morgan's contribution. It also looks possible that Kroeber's knowledge of Morgan was acquired second hand, or atleast he never seems to have taken Morgan seriously. By attacking Morgan, Kroeber missed a generation of anthropologist in to contempt for Morgan's most enduring contributions. It was Kroeber's view of the relationship between kinship terminology and social structure that subsequently proved to be incorrect and impoverished (Harris 1969: 321-322).

Kroeber's Concept of Cultural Climax and Cultural Intensity

Concentrating at California, Kroeber emphasized upon the traitlist approach in conviction that facts must proceed theory. He and his students amassed a wealth of detailed information. As a result of this; the subsequent book entitled, *Hand Book of the Indians of Kalifornia* (1925) came into existence. This thousand page book contained almost everything that was then known about these people. The same detailed description of most other North American Indians was present in his later work. *Cultural and Natural areas of Native North America* (1939).

Kroeber observed that inspite of their differences, culture areas often resembled each other in many ways. He proposed, therefore, that statistical correlations should be made in order to find the coincidence of typical traits, so that culture areas would become sharply delineated. Traits were minimum definable elements, but the question as to what constituted 'minimal' was not so easily answered. A canoe is a trait, but all its parts, its decorations, the materials used for it, and method of constructions could also be looked upon are traits, as well as such factors as who make canoes, which rituals are associated with their production and so forth. Impressed by Wissler's dictum that a culture is not to be comprehended until the list of its traits approaches completeness. Being eager to make the correct statistical correlations, fieldwork began to construct even more elaborate trait list.

In the first California trait list, published in 1935, Klimek included 430 items. Two year latter Gifford and Kroeber made list for the Pumpo and two other tribes, counting, 1,094 traits. Working with four tribal groups in Round Valley, Essence recorded 2,174 elements. In other parts of California, Stewart noted 4,662 elements for the Ute and Paiute. Voegelin listed 5,263 items for tribes of north-east California, while Ray increased the number to 7,633.

Recording of all these items was the most time consuming and difficult part for both researchers and informants. But however long the list were, they would never approach completeness. It was a barren exercise, because no insight was gained into dynamics of culture change. No analysis was made as to why some culture items were accepted and other rejected, nor of what their function might be. The dogmatic trait list was soon abandoned, but efforts to classify culture areas continued for at least another decade after the last trait list had appeared.

Kroeber revised Wissler's original division and eventually mapped seven 'grand areas', twentyone areas and sixtythree 'sub-areas' for North and Central America (1939). Stout recognised eleven areas in South America (1938), which were narrowed down to three by Bennett and Bird (1949), but increased again to twentyfour by Murdock in 1951. In other parts of the world. Elizabeth Bacon listed six areas and four blind areas for Asia in 1946, but revised them in 1953. Herskovits mapped nine culture areas in Africa, but he, too, changed his classification several times.

The mere fact that there was consensus about what constituted a culture area and the constant reworking and realising of existing classifications were indicative of the problem inherent in the concept of culture area. The approach appeared without historic depth. Migrations sometimes caused entirely different culture to appear side by side and interrelationships between traits and their functions within societies remained unexplained.

Kroeber felt that there could be no differing with his contention that mere description, which had been the objective of culture area concept, was no end in itself, and process must be analysed, if we were to understand the nature and functioning of culture. In achieving his ends, however, he added the concepts of *'Cultural intensity'* and *'Cultural Climax'* to that of area. Thus, he gave the concept greater historical depth by introducing the theories of 'cultural climax' and 'cultural intensity'. Nevertheless, the culture area trait list approach involved a mechanistic view of culture; that was not compatible with Kroeber's humanistic inclinations. He felt that culture could not be wholly understood even by most complete summation of observable elements, because every culture contained other elements that could not be caught by trait lists. Kroeber called these the *"sensitive indicators"* of culture. According to Kroeber, sensitive indicators of culture included art, music, religion, ethos, philosophy, and similar aspects of intellectual life; that do not easily land themselves to statistical treatment. He was convinced that the sensitive elements were more characteristic of culture than concrete elements, and thus, more diagnostic of cultural intensity. Intensity is reflected in the way in which cultures and areas achieved what is termed their level. A more intensive culture as compared with a less intensive culture normally contains not only more material peculiar to itself, as well as more precisely and articulately established interrelations between the materials. In accurate time reckoning, a religious hierarchy, a net of social classes, detailed property law, are illustrations of this.

'Culture Climax' is to be thought of as the dynamic equivalent of the descriptive term 'culture-centre'. It is the part of the area where the tribes have 'a larger contact of culture. In other words, more numerous elements and more sharply expressed and interrelated patterns. He regards 'above average developments' as 'centre' from which cultural stimuli have followed decreasing intensity, as the marginal regions are reached and the emanations from the next centre encountered. The idea of climax can be useful in solving that most vexing problem of the culture area, the setting of boundaries, is evident.

As it was obvious, traits do not spread at a uniform rate, some spread like wild fire, others such as property, law remained confined to a limited area for generations. The movement of traits could retrograte and thus, skew the assumptions about their relative age. There was the whole question of the point or points of origin of specific traits. Could these be multiple, and could they not shift from one culture to another in an area? Kroeber's answer to this last question was, "not necessary". He used the term culture climax to refer to that portion of a culture area from which most of the material in the area had spread. Kroeber believed that a culture climax tended to perpetuate itself. As it becomes more productive, it becomes more highly organised and, thus, better able to assimilate new ideas and techniques. With this greater input, culture's production become even greater. The process was a slow one, however, so, barring the introduction of a radically new subsistence mechanism, such as agriculture, may occasionally cause a rapid growth. It may be taken for granted that a climax in historic period was also a climax or atleast sub-climax, in the later prehistoric period, and probably at least of fairly high level of intensity before that.

Kroeber certainly gave no indication that he regarded the ecological aspects of cultural and natural areas as a central theoretical contribution. Instead, he chose to regard the refinement of culture areas by means of the concepts of cultural intensity and cultural climax is the most important basis for his future work. According to Kroeber, each of six major North American areas, with the exception of Eskimo, contained a climax sub-area which exhibited the highest intensity of the area's pattern. In addition, each of the areas relative to each other departed as possessing a particular level of intensity on a scale of one to seven.

Kroeber admitted that his identification of the climax areas and to their relative intensity was for the long time no more than personal estimate. It is a course symptomatic of Kroeber's inflexible theoretical contribution that he did not attempt to define intensity and climax interms of eminently measurable factors of population density, total population involved in a common production distribution net work, size and duration of armies and concentrated corvee labour or other factors related to general evolutionary processes.

The comparison of culture areas from the point of view of level of intensity can be achieved with greater objectivity by employing Julian Steward's concept of 'levels of socio-cultural integration'. Once again, there is shadow anticipation of approach Steward was to develop. But Kroeber was in reality travelling along a rapidly diverging track. He was off on the road to configurations, to the subleties of unique stylistic growth.

> Parallels with historic civilizations suggest themselves. Whatever one of these attained a clearly recognizable culmination, this seems to have corresponded essentially with a period of successful organisation of culture content inpart in to a conscious systems of ideas, but especially into integrated nexus of styles, standard and values (Kroeber 1939:255).

Culture Area and Configuration

After it became clear that territorial plotting of culture elements raised more problems than it could solve, Kroebar turned away from the study of minutise. He pursued his interests in more microscopic view of culture history, which resulted in publication of his monumental book entitled "Configurations of Culture Growth" (1944). In it, he dealt not only with Indian culture, but with civilizations of Egypt, Mesopotania, Greece, Rome, China and several European Nations. He had long been intrigued by the fact that these civilizations had known period of high achievement in art, music, drama, literature, science, philosophy, but later on declined again.

The relationship between Kroeber's treatment of culture areas and configurations has been correctly understood by Milton Singer (1963:VI). He opined that it was noteworthy that Kroeber developed the concept of 'climax', when he was finishing his book *Cultural and Natural Areas of Native North America*, but just before he returned to a serious study of civilizations. His theory of civilization was in continuation with his theory of preliterate cultures and his work on archaeology. The findings of Configuration of Culture growth, in any case, give the relations of growth culminations to a degree and intensity of civilization of culture content. Kroeber's finding shows that growth peak of a civilization tends to coincide with a period of successful organization of culture content i.e., the organisation of ideas, styles and standard. Kroeber sees cultural creativity and assimilation running behind, as the organization tends more and more to repetition and rigidity.

Kroeber's Version on Historical Particularism

Kroeber's article entitled, "The Eighteen Professions" published in 1915 in the Journal *American Anthropologists*, amounts to be the best available summary of Kroeber's version of historical particularism. These are as follows:

1. The aim of history is to know the relations of social facts to the whole civilization...... Relations is actual connection, not cause.
2. The material studied by history is not man, but his works, i.e., the result of his work.
3. Civilization, though carried by men and existing through them, is an entity in itself, and of another order from life ...... History is not concerned with the agencies producing civilization, but with civilization as such. The causes are the business of Psychologists.
4. A certain mental constitution must be assumed by the historian, but may not be used by him as a resolution of social phenomena.
5. True instincts lie at the bottom and origin of social phenomena, but cannot be considered or dealt with by history.
6. The personal or individual has no historical value save as illustration.
7. Geography or physical environment, is material made use of by civilization, not a factory shaping or explaining civilization.
8. The absolute equality and identity of all human races must be assumed by the historian.

9. Heredity cannot be allowed as a significant factor in history.
10. Heredity by acquirement is a monstrosity.
11. Selection and other facιors of organic evolution cannot be admitted as affecting civilization.
12. The so called savage is no transition between the animal and the scientifically educated man..... All men are totally civilized ..... There is no higher and no lower in civilization for the historian.
13. There are no special species or standard cultural type, or stages ..... A stage in civilization is merely a preconception made plansible by arbitrarily selected facts.
14. There is no ethnic mind but civilization.
15. There are no laws in history similar to the laws of physico-chemical science. All asserted civilizational laws are at most tendencies..... History does not deny them and may have to recognise them, but their formulation is not its end.
16. History deals with conditions, *sine qua non*, not with causes. The relation between civilizational phenomena are relations of sequence, not of effect.
17. The causality of history is teleological .... this does not suggest theology to those who are free from theology.
18. In fine, the determinations and methods of biological, psychological or natural science do not exist for history.

Kroeber's Concept of Culture as Superorganic and Super Individual

It was not Kroeber, who for the first time developed the concept of super organic. It was named by Spencer, defined by Tylor, applied by Summer and it was implicit in writings of Comte and Durkhiem. On its simplest level, it was nothing more than a recognition of culture as a leaned tradition and a realization that it cannot be explained totally by reference to biology or chemistry.

Kroeber's contemporary German philosopher Oswald Spengler (1880-1936) had advanced the explanation that the civilization can be equated with organism that are born, pass through childhood, maturity and old age, and finally to die. Kroeber felt strongly that this theory was not only false, but reductionistic to the almost. Culture and culture change could not be explained by reference to biology or psychology. In Kroeber's view, culture constituted a separate realm of phenomena, namely the super organic, and as such it could be explained only interms of its own laws. Kroeber, as superorganicist, developed concept that provided more dogmatic meaning, i.e., nothing in culture can be explained by reference to other disciplines. Neither biology, nor psychology, nor environment, nor even man himself could serve as an explanatory factor for culture and cultural developments. In this view, culture became endowed with dynamic inner force that determined its existence and regulated its own changes. Human volition or human genius had no decisive influence upon culture. superorganicists never tired of attacking "greatman" theory, which had precisely the opposite view.

Kroeber was already fully committed to the superorganic view, when he began to write his configurations, and it was meant to be a final defence of his position. Expressing his views on historical particularism, he convicted that personal or individual had no historical value save as illustration (1915: 183-284). Two years later, in his article entitled, "Superorganic", he produced a long list of western invention that had been made simultaneously by scholars working independently of each other. For example the telescope was invented by three people in 1968, Oxygen was discovered twice in 1774, the steal boat was developed by three different people in the same year, Neptune was discovered twice in the same year. Similarly inventions of photography, telephone, phonograph and the discovery of north and south poles, were made simultaneously. This principle of simultaneity was the best proof, for Kroeber, that invention or discovery was not due to some mysterious inherent faculty of individual mind, but not account of presence of majestic force or sequence pervading civilization. Kroeber called culture as superorganic and super individual and, thus, according to him, culture is both superorganic and super individual. It is true that individuals are carrier of culture and the existence of culture cannot be thought out in their absence. Even then culture is not the creation of any specific individual. Any culture is more than any individual human beings can grasp or manipulate. The stability or continuity of culture is not dependent upon any special individual, because culture is not behaviour of individual, rather it is integrity of the whole group habits or behaviour. The habit and behaviour of an individual meet an end with the death of the person, but group habits or behaviours continue generation after generation as traditions. As the creation and continuity of culture is not based on any individual, therefore, according to Kroeber, culture is super individual.

Kroeber was of opinion that culture is not only super-individual, rather it is superorganic as well. This cannot be meant that culture is inorganic and free from organic influence. According to Kroeber, superorganic means simply, when we consider culture, we are dealing with something that is organic, but which must also be viewed as something more than organic, if it is fully intelligible to us. If culture was only organic, it was not possible for it to be intelligible. Because culture is intelligible, it should, therefore, be accepted that it is not only organic but something more than that. In other words, culture is superorganic. As animal, plants, and vegetable, though they are organic, but may be called superorganic because some common principles are applicable to them. Similarly, culture develops in organic structure, but because it possesses such qualities as begin transferable, changeability, collectivity, value pattern, and ability to impress people, therefore, it should be called superorganic. According to Kroeber, these qualities of culture are not the products of organic individual man, rather they are the products of social behaviour.

Kroeber cited an example of English language. This language is a part of culture. It is not the creation of a single man. An individual adopts English language from tradition and learns it. His power of speaking, undoubtedly, depends upon organic principles, but the words and symbols, which he uses in speaking are not his own making, but are learnt. Therefore, English languages is super individual and super organic, because it is part of culture, and culture is super individual and super organic both.

Sapir's Reaction to Kroeber's Concept of Super Individual and Super Organic

Edward Sapir, who established the pattern of anthropological linguistics at Chicago and maintained life long interest in the field of personality and culture, reacted against the super individual and super organic views of Kroeber. He argued that the significance of individual in culture and cultural processes cannot be ignored. He pointed out that Kroeber had used only technological inventions that often depend upon previous ones (Neptune cannot be discovered before the invention of the telescope). He challenged Kroeber to occupy himself instead with man's religious, philosophical or aesthetic activities, which could never be abstracted from human beings. Although he admitted that the average historian tended to exaggerate the determining influence of specific personalities, this was no reason to eliminate the individual from all consideration as a cultural factor.

Kroeber's View on of Patterns

Kroeber spent rest of his career doing something very similar, what Sapir had said that it could not be done. He went on showing how patterns of art, religion, philosophy as well as technology and science, waxed and waved, required their characteristics content and kept rolling majestically along, quite independently of particular individuals. Among

American Indians as well as ancient Greeks, it is the cultural pattern which summons forth general uses in appropriate number.

As a matter of fact, it was Kroeber's special delight to pickout such aspects of culture, which seemed most vulnerable to the effect of individual fancy and to demonstrate the existence of patterns unknown to the culture carriers. His study of dress fashions was an impressive accomplishment along these lines. But 1919, he had measured enough changes in the styles of evening gowns to identify regular pulsations in the width and length of skirt. In 1940, he and Jane Richardson published a statistical study which covered three hundred fashion changes. The existence of unsuspected periodicities was confirmed, short run patterns of style distinguished from the long run pattern and the role of designer explicitly assimilated to that of genous in biology and physics.

Kroeber maintained this diachronic and superorganic orientation right through the period of anthropology's greatest retreat into psychological reductionism and synchronic functionalism.

Kroeber's explanations of superorganic and super individual cultural patterns, have not found general acceptance among anthropologists. Kroeber, himself, was attacked by his teacher, Franz Boas and his contemporaries. Boas (1928:245) and Ruth Benedict (1934:231) felt that it was mysticism to consider culture as existing outside of man and moving its own force. Bidney (1944:22) equally disapprovingly accused Kroeber of idealism because he reified culture. Morris Opler (1963:902) opined that superorganicism stripped anthropology of its warmth and purpose as well as its concern with humanity.

Kroeber's Concept of Style and Civilization

Kroeber's book *Style and Civilizations* reveals his inclination towards the growth of civilizations without bothering with the encyclopaedic inventories which had given configurations its saving claim as an inductive product. Instead, the free pay of intuition characteristic of more lucid judgements in configurations was now explicitly defended. Each civilization is to be characterised by a multiplicity of patterns, whose common denominators added upon its particular style or super style. Kroeber, himself, suggested the comparison between these super styles and the kind of patterns, portraits, which Ruth Benedict had achieved. The comparisons revealed the fundamental connectedness of Benedict and Kroeber within the historical particularistic tradition. Although Benedict's patterns are described in psychological idiom, this is a superficial difference. As far as Kroeber was concerned, the only distinction between his approach and Benedict's was that his portraits were to be dynamic, covering the early as well as nature phases of style growths. Thus, Kroeber favoured pluralistic and diachronic formulation. His styles are like organic growths, unfolding through time in an irreversible, but inexplicable, process.

Although Kroeber reaffirmed his belief that successful insight into the nature and history of human civilizations or cultures will be made via an empirical route, by means of something akin to natural history, his method for identifying super styles scarcely confirmed to empiricist model. The mental processes called for in dealing with styles are some what different from those ordinarily used by historians or scientists. What is needed is the kind of faculty we call on, when we identify individuals or identify organisms as members of this or that species. It is total immediate and final judgement, and it is neither inductive nor deductive. Artists and biologists seems to best represent the necessary qualities.

His wife Theodora explains, in the introduction to his 'post-humous' *An Anthropologists Looks at History* (1963), that after configurations Kroeber's substantive contributions became more frankly intutive and aesthetic. When configuration was at last behind him, Kroeber came out literacy on the sunny side of it, some how free at least as he had not felt before, to add his sensibility to form, styles, values and aesthetic truths to his other approaches to the always fascinating phenomena of culture. This sensibility should have been given fuller expression in a book on art (T. Kroeber 1963: xviii).

WEAKNESS OF CULTURE AREA SCHEME

Culture area scheme, as suggested by American anthropologists to deal with the process of cultural diffusion, has been subjected to many criticism. The main criticism levelled against this scheme are as follows:

1. An uncritical employment of this research tool can result in serious misconceptions. It is to understand that culture area is essentially a device that arises out of the need of the student to organise his data and depict, on a broad canvas, the range of cultures over a continent or an island region. This means that the area, such, as, exists in the mind of the student and has little meaning to those who inhabit it. The culture area is, thus,not an incipient nationality. It is a construct that those to whom it is applied, would usually be the first to reject. It calls for an overview that no people can have of the wider setting in which their ways of living lodge. It necessitates fixing the eye on the broad lines of

similarities and differences of cultures, not on detail seen by those who are too close to a culture. Where attention is concerned minutial the area vanishes into a mass of specific items. In this way, culture area scheme has to function within limitations, beyond which it cannot yield result.

2. A great caution has to do with the nature of the concept of cultural centres and marginal area. These are construct in the same way that the culture area itself is construct. Like it, they have the same ethnographic validity, the same lack of psychological reality. It is this negative point that gives rise to the need for a full limitations of these two ideas. Culture centre is the place where a cluster of traits is found, not where the richest life is led by the people. Marginal culture is one where traits from a neighbouring area are to be discerned. Difficulties arises in establishing cultural centre and cultural boundaries. Because migrations cause many cultural traits to appear side by side. It becomes difficult to trace the exact place from where traits appear. Thus, culture area concept appeared static and without historic depth.
3. The major difficulty has been experienced in applying the idea of culture areas to Euro-American groupings. Experience has shown that it is not adapted to use where the distribution of geographical differences between people is overridden by stratification resulting from the high degree of specialization of larger population aggregates. Area is only one of a number of criteria that can be usefully employed to distinguish cultures and most particularly subcultures. Industrial centres differ from agricultural regions. But all of them in United States, for instance, have such preponderant cultural similarities that it obscures rather than brings out the significance of differences between them to regard them as of order of cultural areas. The typical behaviour of social classes or occupational group is important here. Categories derived from distinctions drawn on the basis of local differences are obviously inapplicable to such cases and should be replaced by those are functionally relevant.
4. Cultural area approach is also criticized for the reason that its scope is narrow. It divides world or a nation into different regions or areas and, thus, fails to explain world wide diffusion of culture.
5. It is argued that cultural areaists emphasized too much on material aspects of culture, but they failed to explain clearly the non-material aspects of culture.
6. They emphasized, too much, on geographical areas and ignored other aspects that also marks the area feeling among the in-

habitants such as common language, common rituals, common food habits etc.

7. Culture areaists emphasized on culture centres which means only inhabitants of culture centres were the inventors of culture traits and complex and other inhabiting the same area were borrowers. But this does not have empirical reality.
8. They are also criticised because they could not explain the methods by which culture area boundary could be established with certainty, rather they made it vage. This disappointed to those who had expected otherwise.
9. Wissler's hypothesis that traits tend to diffuse in all directions from the centre of origin was declared as incorrect. Empirically, it was observed that the diffusion of trait from origin followed on line not in another and at various rates.
10. The trait listing approach was also confusing and time taking. It frustrated both researchers and informants. Again, there was no unanimity among the culture area anthropologists so far as the exact number of traits or element was concerned. Number sometimes increases or decreases in their own listing. This indicates clearly the problem concerning the trait listing and mapping scheme.

However, culture area scholars did not deny that independent invention took place and they were also well aware that migration could be a salient factor for explanation of culture change. They were also less dogmatic about their principle than their European colleagues. From early beginnings onward, they were aware of their shortcoming of their theories and tried to correct them in further application. Wissler realised that his mappings were static and could not explain or even indicate the changes that had taken place through time. Kroeber attempted to remedy this and suggested that several successive maps should be made and super imposed on each other so that distribution changes would be revealed. He also substituted the concept of cultural climax for Wissler's cultural centres, because the latter was static and revealed single point from where all other traits diffused.

COMPARISON BETWEEN BRITISH AND GERMAN SCHOOLS

British School of diffusion and German School of diffusion came into existence as a reaction against the evolutionary theories of classical evolutionists. They shared views in abolishing the universal stages, psychic unity, independent inventions, concept of survival as put forth by the evolutionists. Both were historically-oriented and attempted to reconstruct contacts between people, paths of diffusions and migration, and the spread of culture items. Both believed in degenerative theory and dealt in the direction of degenerationism. Inspite of all such similarities in their views, they also differ from each other. The main differences between British School of diffusion and German School of diffusion are as follows:

1. British diffusionists were so extreme in their approach that they went on popularising the concept that the people of ancient Egypt were the inventors of cultures and culture traits diffused in other parts of the world from a single origin, i.e., Egypt. But German diffusionists were of the views that culture traits developed at several places independently, but from there they diffused or migrated in other parts of the world. Thus, they were not in favour of single origin of culture at Egypt but in multiple origin of culture at several places for showing cultural diffusion.
2. German diffusionists talk about the criteria of form and criteria of quantity to show the process of cultural diffusions from one place to another. But British diffusionists do not talk about them.
3. British diffusionists emphasised, too much, on simple form of diffusion on the basis of culture traits, but German diffusionists talked about complex form of cultural diffusion.
4. British diffusionists stressed, too much, on material aspects of culture and ignored non-material aspects of culture. On the other hand, German diffusionists take into consideration both material and non-material aspects of culture, while dealing with the process of cultural diffusion.
5. British diffusionists never talk about the significance of evolutionary sequences, but German diffusionists while dealing with the phases or grades of cultural circles or Kultur Kreise, have taken into consideration the significance of evolutionary sequences.
6. British diffusionists have talked about only Egypt as cultural inventors, but in order to understand the cultural diffusion, German diffusionists developed the concept of cultural circles or districts. These cultural circles or districts were created in different places in different times.
7. British diffusionists have not mentioned any typology of diffusion, but German diffusionists have classified diffusion in two categories: Primary diffusion and Secondary diffusion.

COMPARISON BETWEEN BRITISH AND AMERICAN SCHOOLS

Both schools are anti-revolutionary and emphasise upon the history of cultural diffusion. They have similar opinion in discarding the inventiveness, universal sequences, and psychic unity as an explanatory principles. But they also differ in their opinions and approaches. The main points of differences between these two schools are as follows:

1. British diffusionists were of view that Egypt was the only cultural centre, where cultural traits appeared for the first time in history of the world and then diffused in its other parts. It is because of this fact that British diffusionists are also known as Egyptologist. But American diffusionists do not believe in Egypt as the only cultural centre of the world. It may be possible that some traits from the Egypt civilization would have diffused in other spheres of the universe, but not all.
2. British diffusionists never accept independent inventions at different places, other than Egypt. But American diffusionists believe in independent discoveries at several places and in continuity according to the need of cultural groups.
3. British diffusionists neither accept psychic unity as tool to combat racism, nor as an explanatory principle. But American diffusionist Franz Boas used psychic unity as a tool to combat racism.
4. British diffusionists talk about World cultural diffusion from the single origin, i.e., Egypt, but American diffusionists attempted to indicate the process of cultural diffusion by dividing world or nations into different cultural areas, not of entire world as a whole. For each cultural areas they emphasized upon one culture centre.
5. For British diffusionists Egypt was the only centre where all cultural traits originated, but for American diffusionists cultural centre of each cultural areas was originator of cultural traits and complexes.
6. British diffusionists stressed upon diffusion and migration both as a salient features for culture change but in each culture area, American diffusionists paid attention towards the traits that had diffused only from the culture centre.
7. British diffusionists talked about simple form of diffusion. They never took into consideration the complex form of diffusion, but American diffusionists, on the other hand, stressed on the diffusion of both culture traits and cultural complexes.
8. British diffusionists were degenerationists, because they attempted to show that one culture progresses more than other. On

the other hand, American diffusionists emphasized that every culture makes its own adaptations and, therefore, the question that one progressed more was futile.

9. British diffusionists did not make any typology of diffusion, but American diffusionist, Clark Wissler made classification of diffusion in two categories i.e. natural diffusion and organised diffusion.
10. British diffusionists did not talk about cultural intensity and cultural climax, but American diffusionist talked about them. The concept of cultural climax and cultural intensity was introduced by Kroeber to substitute Wissler's concept of culture area, because latter was static and unable to explain cultural dynamism.

COMPARISON BETWEEN GERMAN AND AMERICAN SCHOOLS

American school of diffusion and German school of diffusion both were anti-evolutionists. They shared views that similarities in cultures were not caused due to parallel inventions brought about by psychic unity. They were also critical of universal sequences of evolution of culture. They were of view that important inventions were made only once. They reached in other cultural groups or other parts of the world through the process of imitation, i.e., diffusion, or culture carriers broke away the original settlements and moved to other parts of the world, taking their cultural inventory with them, but adapting it to new environmental conditions, i.e., migration.

Both schools share common ideas also because of the facts that they were inspired by museum methodology. Being associated with museum, they were able to classify materials on the basis of geographical categories in order to show that those cultural groups, who lived close to one another had similar cultural items than those who lived farther apart. According to them, these similarities were likely due to diffusion. Inspite of having many similar views on cultural diffusion, they also differ on certain points and approaches which are as follows:

1. German diffusionists stressed upon degeneration theory by which they supported the degenerative tendency of man by which one culture progressed more than other. But American diffusionists were against the degeneration theory. According to them all culture adapts in its own way, therefore, it was futile to think that one culture progressed more than other.
2. German diffusionists have stressed, too much, on migration by

which culture traits and complex reached in other parts. American diffusionists stressed upon the process of diffusion from culture centres.

3. German diffusionists have not taken into consideration psychic unity either as an explanatory principle or as a tool to combat racism. American diffusionists have used it as a tool to combat racism.
4. German diffusionists talk about diffusion of culture through cultural circles or districts or Kreise, but American diffusionists stressed upon the culture areas and culture centres.
5. Cultural districts or circles indicate several layers or stages of cultural development, but culture-areas of American diffusionists were contrasted to culture circles. The culture area school of American diffusionists not only envisages geographical distribution of culture complex, but strive to dissect the history of cultural developments in various areas by studying a presumed stratification of these elements.
6. Circles have been used by German diffusionists as a dynamic device, in which different cultural traits and complexes are migrated and accumulated in different phases of time but in continuous process. American diffusionists used culture area and culture centre as static which could not explain the changes that had occured in time.
7. The major phases or grades of culture-circles or Kreise also indicated the evolutionary significance of the cultural circle. But culture areas of American diffusionists did not explain evolutionary significance, though they never deny the significance of independent inventions.
8. German diffusionists developed the criteria of form and criteria of quantity to explain the similarities and differences in cultural diffusion. American diffusionists stressed upon trait listing approach to indicate the process of cultural diffusion.
9. Both schools made typology of diffusion but not on the same line. Graebner talked about primary and secondary diffusion, whereas Wissler classified diffusion as natural and organised diffusions.

CULTURAL DIFFUSION IN INDIAN CONTEXT

Cultural diffusion is a process by which culture traits invented in one group or area reached in another group or area. They may reach by imitation or the migration of the group, who invented them into another area. When two cultural groups are taken into consideration, they may differ from each other in many respects, but on the other hand, they may possess some similarities, which throw light that cultural diffusion would have taken place.

DIFFUSION OF PREVEDIC AND VEDIC FAITHS

The cultural history of India reveals that tribals were the original inhabitants of the land of 'Bharat Varsha'. They had passed through the different stages of development and were the makers of Indus Valley Civilization. They happened to occupy the most fertile core of the country. They were driven back to hilly and forested areas during the time of Aryan invasion, which took place in the time when Indus Valley civilization was flourishing. Aryan invasion is also regarded as one of causes of down fall of Indus valley civilizations. Aryans had horses and iron made weapons, by which they could come out victorious easily over the indigenous races. Aryan culture developed for the first time in North-West regions and it gradually diffused in other parts of India. In the struggle of indigenous tribes and Aryans, at later stage, a policy of mutual give and take of cultural traits took place. Aryan sages played significant role in making the indigenous races Aryanised, by establishing marriages with latter's daughters and sisters. Thus, our present religious beliefs and practices reveal the fusion of Aryan and non-Aryan faiths.

After the Aryans gradually progressed eastward from the Punjab, they first sought to destroy everything that was non-Aryan. Gradually, there arose a tendency towards co-existence and the amalgamation of cultures. Authorities have tried to show the intermingling of prevedic and Vedic religion in the following context:

1. *Mahadeva* or *Shivalingam* worship was prevedic and gradually taken by Aryans.
2. Serpent worship was prevalent among prevedic non-Aryans and it also came in the religious beliefs of Aryans.
3. Tree worship was another feature of prevedic religion and in due course of time, Aryans also adapted it.
4. *Chaitya* worship was prevalent among prevedic inhabitants. *Chaitya* was a constructed place of worship usually associated with funeral remains.
5. *Yaksha* worship was another feature of prevedic religion. *Yakshas* are now regarded as semi divine being.

The gradual amalgamation and synthesis of Vedic and non-Aryan religions proceeded and the Vedic cult of sacrifice and *Brahmin* leadership was accepted by natives, and many native deities and modes of worship were accommodated in Aryan patheon.

Thus, tribals have lived in associations with non-tribal Hindus and have adopted many beliefs and practices of Hindu religion. They celebrate *Holi, Dashahara, Deepawali* and *Ramnawami*, and worship many Hindu Gods and Goddesses. Some of them also visit the Hindu shrines located in their areas to offer worship and making pilgrimage on the occasion of religious fairs.

DIFFUSION OF SUN-WORSHIP

Though sun-worship was prevalent among the inhabitants of Indus valley Indians, but we do not have any anthropomorphic representation of Sun-God of Indus valley patheon. Some representations on seals and pottery bear testimony that some kind of Sun-worship was prevalent in Indus valley. These representations are circular disc or wheel as representing the circular orbit of natural Sun-God. In ancient civilization of Egypt, Sun-God appears in anthropomorphic form. Historians have attempted to indicate that the process of anthropomorphization of Sun-God in India reveals that the anthropomorphic traits would have been borrowed from Egypt. In Egyptian civilization, which was contemporary to Indus valley civilization, Apollo, the Sun-God appeared as a ruler commanding the universe. The early representation of Sun-God in anthropomorphic form have been discovered from Patna on a pottery piece belonging to Mauryan period. This is the earliest image of Sun-God found so far in India. The Sun-God is depicted on a pottery piece in which Sun-God is standing with Aruna, his charioteer, on a chariot drawn by four horses. The Sun-God has a conical edged arrow in his hand. The lower portion of Sun-God is hidden by the chariot. Indian antiquarians have attempted to show the process of borrowing in the human representation of Sun-God, from Greeks. Chandra Gupta Maurya of Magadha had defeated Greek king Seleucus and liberated the north-western part of the country from Macedonian (Greek) yoke. He was married to the daughter of Seleucus. It seems probable that anthropomorphic traits of Sun-God reached in India from Greeks in his time.

However, it is a debatable point, whether the Solar images of early period were of purely indigenous tradition or they derived inspiration from foreign tradition? The great indologist, Cunningham suggested that the four horses and the general execution resemble to a great extent the Greek representation of Hellios — the Greek Sun-God. Some antiquarians opined that the anthropomorphic representation was purely indigenous, according to Vedic tradition.

Clearcut evidence of Sun-worship through Sun-temple came into existence during Saka-Kusana period (2nd B.C.-A.D. 2nd). The first temple dedicated to Sun-God was erected at Mulsthan, also known as Multan, now in Pakistan. Sakas or Magas of Iran had built the city of Multan and erected the Sun-temple. The image of Sun-God of Multan temple resembled with Kusana king. He wore cap and boot like Kusana ruler. Magas or *Sakaldwipi Brahmanas* gradually migrated in different parts of north-west India first and then in south-eastern parts of the country also. As a result of this, in the period between 4th to 12th century A.D., numerous Sun-shrines throughout the length and breadth of the country came into existence. In course of time, Greek and Iranian anthropomorphic images of Sun-God were also modified and by the time of Gupta age, they were completely indianised according to Vedic and Puranic traditions.

DIFFUSION OF BUDDHISM

Our country has played significant role in spread of Buddhism in different parts of Asia. Buddhism in India first came into existence during 6th century B.C. in Magadha region (at present roughly constitutes the old Gaya and Patna districts of Bihar State). It gradually spread in all parts of our country in general and countries like Sri Lanka, Myanmar, Malaya, Japan, China, etc. in particular. The early kings of Magadha became the followers of Lord Buddha and helped in the diffusion of Buddhist religion in different parts of the world.

Buddhism developed as a reaction against old Brahminism, which was full of inequality. All *Varnas* did not occupy equal place. Large number of animals were sacrificed in the name of *Yagya*. Lord Buddha criticised these activities in the name of religion. In the religious revolution, many kings became his followers, gave up non-vegetarian food and sacrifice of animals on different occasions, which can still be observed in life ways of majority of Hindus. The people of Magadha were treated as *Kikata* or *Vratya*, (impure) by Brahminas. Therefore, they all gladly became followers of Buddha against old Brahminism.

Lord Buddha had established an association of Buddhist monks. His ideas were democratic. The programmes of Buddhist association were also democratic. Buddhist association was a centre of kindness, sacrifice, humanity, virtue, non-violence, etc. Any person above *Varna* was allowed to become its member. Buddhist monks played significant role in spreading the ideologies of Buddhism to masses of the country and other parts of the world.

All contemporary kings of Buddha's time adopted Buddhism. The king Bimbisar and Ajatshatru of Magadha, Prasenjit of Kosal, Udayan of Avanti were true followers of Lord Buddha. After two hundred years of Buddha's death, Mauryan king Samrat Ashok followed Buddhism. His religious messengers reached in different parts of south-west and east Asia. He sent his son Mahendra, his daughter-in-law, Kanchan and daughter Sanghamitra in Sri Lanka for communicating the ideologies of Buddhism. In his time, Buddhism spread in Sri Lanka, Myanmar, Tibet, China, Japan, Thailand, etc. Initiatives taken by him made Buddhism a form of *Vishwa Dharma*. After Ashoka, Kusan king Kanishka, Thaneshwar king Harshavardhana and many kings of Pala dynasty helped the spread of Buddhist religion.

There were numerous Buddhist institutions, where students from foreign countries came to study books on Buddhism. Buddhist Vihar, Nalanda, Takshila and Vikramshila Universities, were the famous Buddhist institutions for learning the ideologies of Lord Buddha. These institutions were destroyed in Mediaeval times.

In diffusion of Buddhism, meetings also played significant role. Four great Buddhist meetings were held. In these meetings, Buddha's preachings were collected, corrected and published. The first meeting was held at Rajgir during the period of Bimbisar and Ajatshatru, in which Buddha's preachings were edited and named as *Tripitkaic*. Second meeting was organised at Vaishali in which books were modified. The third meeting was organised at Patliputra by Ashoka The Great, in which final edition of Buddhist literature were finalised. Fourth and last meeting was held during the period of Kusana King, Kanishka, in which annotations and ancient Buddhist books were written.

Though Buddhism was supplanted by Neo-Hinduism of Shankracharya, a great *Shaivite* reformer of 9th-10th century A.D., but even to-day, hundreds of foreigner Buddhists pay a visit at Bodh Gaya and Rajgir on the occasion of *Guru Purnima* (full moon-day of *Vaishak* month).

DIFFUSION OF CHHATH VRATA

Chhath Vrata is an important festival of Hindus of Bihar and Uttar Pradesh. This *vrata* is not performed in other States of the country, or if performed, they represent the people who have migrated from Bihar and Eastern U.P. to other parts of the country. This *vrata* is associated with Sun-worship. The *vrata* takes place twice in a year. Once, on 6th bright day of *Chait* month and second on 6th bright day of *Kartik* month. The duration of *vrata* is of four days. It begins from 4th bright day and ends on 7th bright day of both is *Chait* and *Kartik* months. In the evening of 6th day and again in the morning of 7th day, *Arghya* is offered to Sun-God on the bank of a river or pond. Why this *vrata* is so famous only in Bihar and in some parts of eastern U.P.? It means that the *vrata* had its origin in Bihar from where the performance of *vrata* had reached in parts of other States. According a mythological story, Chayaranashram Deokunda, an ancient famous place in Aurangabad district of Magahi region of Bihar is regarded as the originator of *Chhath Vrata*. The place has an ancient pond known as Deokunda with a hermitage of Rishichayavana. On this place, Shuknya, the wife of Chyavana had performed *Chhath Vrata* twice, i.e., in both months *Kartik* and *Chait*, to achieve eyes and good health of her blind and old husband. When she performed *Chhath Vrata*, on both occasions, according to an advice given by Ashwini Kumars, the sons of Sun-God and physician to Gods, her desires were fulfilled. Since then the place is regarded as the originator of *Chhath Vrata*, from where the traits of *Chhath Vrata* diffused in other parts of Bihar and eastern Uttar Pradesh.

DIFFERENT LAYERS OF RELIGION IN INDIA

German school of diffusion or Kultur Kreise or Culture circle or culture district school, lays emphasis not only upon a particular place like Egypt or British diffusionists, but according to them, culture originated at many places, and from there they diffused or migrated to other places. Thus, according to them, the development and diffusion of culture have taken place at and from different places. The diffusion of cultural traits and cultural complex follows a continuous trend. They are of view that if a culture is taken into observation, it reveals different layers of cultural traits. These cultural traits get accumulated in a particular culture through the medium of diffusion or migration. Thus, it reveals clearly that different circles of cultural traits or cultural elements arise at several places in different periods of time. These cultural circles then spread in other parts of the world. But it is not necessary that each cultural trait or complex may diffuse in all parts of the world. Each cultural trait or complex diffuses or migrates up to an extent of a circle or district. Though there is no clear-cut evidence that a trait or complex diffuse with a definite circle or district, but on the basis of historical evidence, it can be known that a particular trait or complex of a particular place has reached in another areas or places.

If one examines the religious life of inhabitants of India, it clearly reveals different layers arising out in different periods of time. The tribal religion is the earliest one, which is existing since pre-historic period.

Old Hinduism or Aryan religion came into existence after the destruction of Indus valley culture. The age of Indus valley culture, according to radio-carbon method, had been estimated as 2300 B.C. — 1750 B.C. and Vedic age has been accepted as flourishing between 1500 B.C. to 600 B.C.

In 600 B.C. the circle of Jainism and Buddhism arose in the Bihar and from here it reached in other parts of the country in general and different parts of Asia in particular. During the period of Shankracharya, in 9th century A.D., revival of old hinduism took place and, thus, a circle of neo-Hinduism developed in the land of India, which is still continuing. In Medieval time, a circle of Muslim religion appeared in India, with arrival of Afghan Muslims and Mughal emperors. In Medieval time, forcible conversion of Hindu into Islam also took place, particularly during the period of Aurangzeb.

A different religion, Sikhism developed in India to bridge up the gap between Hinduism and Muslim religions. It is because of this fact that the traits of Hinduism and Islam can be seen as fusing into religious ideologies of Sikhism.

Christian religion came in India during British period when conversion of Scheduled Tribes and Castes into Christianity took place. At present, some high caste Hindus have also become followers of Christianity.

Thus, it is evident that different circles of religions appeared in India in different historical periods.

CULTURE AREA CONCEPT

The concept of culture area as a tool of historical reconstruction developed against the evolutionary reconstruction. The comparative method of evolutionary reconstruction was based upon speculation and deduction. The historical reconstruction of evolutionists attempted to show that human culture had undergone progressive and accumulative growth, which was totally based upon speculation and deduction. Evolutionists relied too much upon ethnographic data supplied by travellers, missionaries, business men, etc. They never attempted to verify those facts on the basis of factual observation. They selected primitive people as representing the early condition of man kind and compared them with present civilized men. They, thus, attempted to establish evolutionary sequences by comparing and analysing certain aspects or institutions of primitive cultures and ordering them in a sequence from simple to complex. The equation of primitive with early was justified by the idea that primitives were conservative to an extreme degrees.

Franz Boas dealt a blow to revolutionary evolutionary theory and its comparative method. He proposed historical reconstruction in place of evolutionary reconstruction. His aim was to replace deductive approach of evolutionism with inductive method. It was to be accomplished by carefully working with many restricted cultural areas and then comparing the process of cultural growth in each area so as to arrive at sound inductive generalizations.

Thus, the concept of culture area was invented by American anthropologists in general, but it was Clark Wissler, who for the first time, used it as a tool for historical reconstructions. He thought that basic units of culture were cultural traits, which cluster together to form culture complexes, and which in their turn cluster together in an area giving rise to a culture area.

A culture area, therefore, is a geographical area occupied by people, whose culture exhibits a significance degree of similarities with culture of each other as well as significant degree of dissimilarity with cultures of other. The concept of culture area is like concept of geographical regions. This does not mean that culture areas do coincide with geographical regions in every detail, for man has control over his environment and its effect is not exclusive.

A culture area is also a short hand way of describing the way of life of thousands of people in a whole country or continent.

Culture areas are delineated by categorising cultures according to standard classification such as techniques, physical environment, religion, language, and saying that those that are similar and closely related belong to one culture area. In this way, a culture area is also a statistical concept since the important characteristics may be documented and plotted on a map.

As culture area is a geographical classification, based on similarities as well as differences, scholars have attempted to classify tribal India on the basis of geographical location into three groups:

1. *North-eastern Zone*: Tribal areas of eastern Kashmir, Punjab, Himachal Pradesh, North U.P., Assam and Sikkim fall in this category.
2. *Central Zone*: This tribal zone includes the tribes of Bengal, Bihar, Southern U.P., Southern Rajasthan, Madhya Pradesh, Bombay and Orissa.
3. *South-Western Zone*: This consists of old Mysore, Andhra Pradesh Nicobar and Andaman Islands.

Again tribal communities living in different regions have been divided by Roy Burman (1972) into the following five territorial groups, taking into considerations their historical, ethnic and socio-cultural relations:

(i) North-east India comprising Assam, Meghalaya, Nagaland, Manipur, Arunachal Pradesh, Mizoram and Tripura.
(ii) Sub-Himalayan region of north and north-west India comprising the northern submountain districts of Uttar Pradesh and Himachal Pradesh.
(iii) Central and East India comprising of West Bengal, Bihar, Orissa Madhya Pradesh and Andhra Pradesh.
(iv) South India comprising Tamil Nadu, Kerala and Karnataka.
(v) Western India comprising Rajasthan, Gujarat and Maharashtra.

Vidyarthi and Rai (1976: 66) have proposed a four-fold geographical region along with one distinct sub-region. These are:

(i) *Himalayan region*: This is further sub-divided in to three regions, viz. north-eastern Himalayan region, (b) Central Himalayan region and (c) north-western Himalayan region.
(ii) Assam, Meghalaya, Darjeeling, Arunachal Pradesh, Nagaland, Manipur, Mizoram and Tripura fall in north-eastern Himalayan region, whereas Tarai areas of Uttar Pradesh and Bihar come in central Himalayan region. Himachal Pradesh, Jammu and Kashmir constitute the north-western Himalayan region.
(ii) *Middle India region*: It comprises Bihar, Bengal, Orissa and Madhya Pradesh.
(iii) *Western India region*: It includes Rajasthan, Gujarat, Maharashtra, Goa, Dadara and Nagar Haweli.
(iv) *South India region*: It comprises Andhra Pradesh, Tamil Nadu, Karnataka and Kerala.
(v) *The Island region*: This comprises the islands of Andaman and Nicobar in Bay of Bengal and Lakshadweep in Arabian Sea.

CULTURAL-LINGUISTIC ZONES OF BIHAR

The State of Bihar, on the basis of languages spoken by the people, may be divided into four cultural linguistic zones, viz. Magahi cultural zone, Bhojpuri cultural zone, Maithili cultural zone and Tribal cultural zone. Magahi cultural zone roughly constitutes the present district of Gaya, Aurangabad, Jahanabad, Navada, Patna and Nalanda. Besides, Magahi is spoken in some parts of old Monghyr district, in northern-eastern Hazaribagh district and northern part of Palamau district. Bhojpuri cultural zone comprises the districts of Bhojpur and Rohtas in South Bihar and the districts of Siwan, Chhapra, Gopalganj, East and West Champaran in north Bihar. Maithili cultural zone comprises of the districts of Darbhanga, Madhubani, Samastipur, Muzaffarpur, Sitamarhi, Saharsha, Purnia, Begusarai and Bhagalpur. Tribal cultural linguistic zone consists of the districts coming under Chota Nagpur plateau and Santhal Parganas. However, minor variations in language, spoken by the people of adjoining areas can be seen, but these four are the broad cultural-linguistic zones of Bihar State.

CULTURE CENTRES

In India, some ancient places with ancient shrines or having confluences of rivers have acted as culture centres since time immemorial. From these places, the cultural traits of worship and making pilgrimages diffused in many parts of the country. According to Vedic and Puranic tradition, Gaya Vishnupada temples (Bihar), Ayodhya, Mathura, Dwarika, Badrinath (U.P.), Jaganathpuri (Orissa) are the famous cultural centres of Vaishnav cult. Baidyanath Dham (Deoghar, Bihar), Vishwanath (Kashi), Rameshwaram (South India), Pashupatinath (Nepal) are the important centres of Shaiv cult. Kamakshya (Assam) and Vindhyachal (U.P.) are the important cultural centres of Shakti cult.

Gaya attracts pilgrims and devotees from different parts of our country and Nepal to offer ancestral worship in the mouth of dark half of *Kartik* month, which is also termed as *Pitri-paksha Mela.* Thus, from the place Gaya the traits of offering *pinda,* in the name of ancestors for their salvation, diffused all over India and Nepal. The means of communication like buses, trains etc. has helped much in transmission of such religious faiths from the world famous sacred *Tirtha-Gaya*.

The place Rajgir of Bihar acts as a centre of cultural diffusion, because from the place the traits of making pilgrimage on the occasion of *Malmas* (which takes place after four years) are transmitted in different parts of the country. As a result of such cultural diffusion, on the occasion of *Malmas* fair, lakhs of devotees pay a visit to get religious advantage of making pilgrimage of this place.

The place Prayagraj or Allahabad having a confluence of Ganga, Yamuna and invisible Saraswati acts a cultural centre from where beliefs, related to making pilgrimage and having holy dip, are diffused among the Hindu folk. Each year, on the occasion of *Makarsakranti* and *Maghpurnima*, a religious fair is held in which lakhs of people assemble to make pilgrimage and take holy bath.

In India, Prayagraj, Hardwar, Nasik and Ujjain act as cultural centres during *Kumbha Mela*. *Mahakumbha* fair takes place after 36 years. *Kumbha* fair take place after twelve years and *Ardha Kumbha* fair is held every six years.

Ganga Sagar (confluence of Ganga and Sea in Bay of Bengal) acts as a cultural centre of *Makar Sakranti Mela* which takes place on 14th January each year, and where lakhs of devotees pay a visit for taking holy dip.

According to Hindu mythology, Kashi and Kurukshetra acts as a cultural centre of *Chandra Grahan* and *Surya Grahana Melas*. From these places, the motives and beliefs behind the performances of holy dip on these occasions, are transmitted among the Hindu folk of different parts of the country.

The boundaries of these cultural centres can not be limited in terms of geographical region, because the diffusion of cultural traits take place in all parts of India as a whole.

CULTURE CENTRES OF ART AND ARCHITECTURES

During Saka Kushana period (2 B.C.-2 century A.D.) Gandhara (Now in Afghanistan) and Mathura were the important cultural centres of art and architecture. These two schools sculptured many images of Lord Buddha, Hindu Gods and Goddesses. Gandhara school was under full influence of Greek art and architecture, but Mathura school was indianised. Beside Lord Buddha's images, Mathura school produced large number of images of Hindu Gods, Goddesses, trees, animals etc. The period of Kushana King Kanishka, Huviska and Vasudeva was a golden age for Mathura school of art. The artists of Mathura school introduced Indian traditions in image-making.

During Gupta period, the art of image-making and architecture reached its climax. By this time, numerous shrines were erected and images, sculptured according to Vedic and Puranic traditions, were enshrined. During Gupta period, Mathura (U.P.), Bharhut and Sanchi (Madhya Pradesh), Patliputra, Nalanda and Bodhgaya (Bihar) were important cultural centres of art and architecture.

The Orissan school of art and architecture came into existence, and ran from 8th to 13th century A.D. The Medieval North Indian architecture is best illustrated by three schools namely, Orissa, Bundelkhand, and Gujarat and South Rajasthan. There were other local developments, as well as the distinct style of Kashmir, but these three are certainly most important and their products are best preserved.

The chief monuments of Orissan school lie in and around the town of Bhubaneshwar. The finest Orissan temple is Lingaraja at Bhubaneshwar. Among the most important Orissan temples are the temples of Vishnu Jagannath at Puri and Black Pagoda of Konarka, built in 13th century A.D.

Under the Candella Kings of Bundelkhand, a great school of architecture flourished in 10th and 11th centuries A.D., the chief work of which is beautiful temples at Khajuraho, about 100 miles south-east of Jhansi.

Rajasthan and Gujarat have many Medieval temples, some of them have much architectural merits. We can mention here, the greatest of these western schools that arose under the patronage of Kandukya and Solanki kings of Gujarat, and flourished from 11th to 13th century A.D. This kingdom was wealthy from sea born trade with Arabs and Persians, and much of treasure of kings, ministers and merchants alike was spent on beautiful Jaina and Hindu temples. The most famous buildings of this school are the lovely Jaina Shrines of Mount Abu.

Considering the size of the land, Indian temple architecture is remarkable uniform, but authorities distinguish two chief styles and numerous schools. The Northern of Indo-Aryan style prefers a tower with rounded top and curvilinear outline, while the tower of southern or Dravidian style is usually in the shape of a rectangular truncated pyramid. The stages of stylistic development are clearer in south than in northern India, where many ancient temples, were destroyed by Muslim invaders.

In south India, temple building gained much from the patronage of Pallavas and Calukya kings in 6th-8th centuries A.D. The former dynasty are to be found at Mamallapuram and Kanchi, while the latter dynasty left temple remains at their capital Badami and at nearby site Aihols, both in Mysore. These styles show gradual emancipation of architect from the techniques of carpentry and cave architecture. The apogee of Pallava style was reached in shore temple at Mamallapuram and Kalisthans temple of Kanchi, built in early in the 8th century. The letter has a pyramidal tower formed of two corners of small barrel vaults, surmounted by a solid couple suggesting a *Buddhist Stupa*. The style of Pallavas was developed further under Cola dynasty (10th-12th centuries). Their finest products are the temple of Shiva at Tanjore, built by the Rajraja the great (985 century A.D.-1014 century A.D.).

In the next phase of Dravidian architecture the emphasis shifted from the tower above the chief shrine to the entrance gateway of surrounding wall. This new style is often called *Pandyan*, from the name of dynasty which supplanted the Colas in Tamil country. The culmination of *Padyan* style is to be seen in mighty temple complexes of Madurai, Sirirangam and elsewhere. While these developments were taking place in Tamil country, an other style developed in Deccan under the Chalukya, Rastrakutas and Hoysalas. The Hoysala features in South Indian temple architecture came into being in 11th to 14th century A.D. Now temples were not constructed on a rectangular plan, but were polygonal raised on tall solid platform.

The school, which flourished under Vijyanagara empire and reached its apogee in 6th century, shows both Pandyan and Hoysala features.

3

FUNCTIONAL SCHOOL

The late 19th century anthropological approach and early 20th century approach to the study of social systems have been named as evolutionism represented by Maine, McLennan, Tylor and Marret in England, Morgan in America and Bachofen and Bastian in Germany. These scholars are interested in origin and development of culture, or cultures, or cultural institutions. They are of views that historical explanations are sufficient to the understanding of varieties of culture. Their method is known as historical method, which means that human culture has undergone progressive and cumulative growth in course of history. Their historical reconstruction is based on assumption that human culture has evolved from simple to complex form. Not only human culture but cultural institutions like family, marriage, kinship, law, property etc. have also developed in evolutionary sequences i.e. from simple to complex, homogeneity to heterogeneity and indefinite to definite. They rely on comparative method and take into consideration primitive people as representing the early condition of man-kind. Thus, evolutionary sequences can be established by comparing and analysing certain aspects or institutions of primitive cultures and placing them in a sequence from simple to complex. When written record was not available, they take into consideration the concept of survivals, which means those customs which were functioning usefully in past, but have become functionless in present time, though some groups still practice them.

Diffusionists or pioneers of cultural historic school decried evolutionists approach, holding view that culture, of which social systems are part and parcel, is the product of historical process. Smith, Perry and Rivers in England, Ratzel, Graebner and Schmidt in Germany and Boas, Wissler and Kroeber in America, jointly as well as separately attacked on the concepts of psychic unity, parallel inventions and survivals of evolutionary reconstruction and their comparative method. They have levelled charges against evolutionists as arm-chair anthropologists, far away from the tradition of factual observation and fieldwork. They criticise their approach as deductive and speculative. They suggest historical reconstruction in place of evolutionary reconstruction and replacement of deductive approach with inductive approach, by carefully working in fields and comparing the processes of cultural growth so as to arrive at sound inductive generalization. They are of view that human culture or cultural institutions not necessarily follow evolutionary sequences. Similarities or differences in culture or cultural institutions are caused by the processes of cultural diffusion, by which culture traits developed at a particular place or in an area reached at another place or in another area either by imitation or by migration. Cultural groups that reside in close contact have many similarities in comparison to those reside far away.

Quite recently, Leslie White and Julian Steward in America and V.G. Childe in England, have advocated the revival of evolutionary approach. They took into consideration the severe criticism levelled against the classical evolutionism by diffusionists and on the basis of empirical evidence that particular cultures diverge significantly from one another and do not pass through unilinear stages. Since this basic fact of cultural history is no longer a major controversy, these neo-evolutionists, who sought to keep the tradition of 19th century evolution alive, have shifted their frame of reference from particular to general, i.e., a universal scheme into which all individual cultures may be fitted to a system of broad generalization about the nature of any culture. They conceded that particular cultures have distinguish features caused by divergent development in different areas as well as by the stage of development, but they now profess to be interested in the evolution of culture generically considered and not of cultures. Their reconstruction of world culture history is made in such a general terms as to be quite acceptable to every one. These neo-evolutionists argue that culture advances as the energy harnessed per capita per year increases or as the efficiency or economy or means of controlling energy is increased or both. Leslie White thinks that technological component of culture is the fundamental determinants of general evolution.

Sahlin, another advocate of the evolutionist approach in America, views it as a movement in the direction of increasing utilization of earth's resources. He thinks that evolutionary approach of the study of culture, complements the structural approach.

At the beginning of the this century, two British scholars forward what is generally called as the functional and structural approach to the analysis of culture. Malinowski is associated with functional approach, whereas Radcliffe-Brown is the pioneer of structural approach to the analysis of society, though he is also termed as structural-functionalist.

The notion of function itself was as old as recorded history. Herodotus, Plato, Aristotle, Augustine, Montsesquieu, Hoobes, Lock and most other social philosophers had recognised interrelationships between cultural institutions and used these in their explanations of society. They asserted and often demonstrated the necessary relations between social institutions, but they did not always seek for reasons behind them and did not construct a theory about functions. Even Saints Simon and August Comte, while using function as a major methodological tool, were more intent on creating their new science in image of positivism, and left function itself largely unexplained.

In the writing of Emile Durkheim, the concept of function got on greater methodological significance, and he is widely regarded as functionalist by sociologists and anthropologists alike. But, if a distinction is made between functionalism as a consistent theory and the use of function as a method of explaining certain social phenomena, Durkheim is not a functionalist in the first sense. While he used the notion of function quite extensively, his discussions about the meaning of function are relatively rare.

Clear-cut use of functional approach in the analysis of culture in anthropology appeared in the writings of Malinowski, first in his book entitled, *A Scientific Theory of Culture and other Essays* (1944) and then in another book entitled, *Dynamics of Culture Change* (1945).

He criticised the early evolutionary approach and diffusionary approach, which had emphasized upon the study of forms of culture or cultural institution. Though they talked about forms of culture or cultural institutions, but never explained their functions. He criticised the concept of survivals put forth by evolutionists and held opinion that no custom or institution in culture as a totality is functionless. Each and every institution or custom has some functional importance in culture. He criticised diffusionists who had treated cultures and cultural institutions in isolation. Malinowski's preoccupation was with the study of culture as a whole or totality. He introduced a new principle, now called as functionalism. He held opinions that it was useless to kill time in detail explanation of culture, but the need of the time was to examine, explain and analyse as to why and how culture functions, how different aspects of cultures are related into entire culture pattern? Malinowski opines that the answer of these questions can be given on the basis of functionalism.

According to Malinowski, functionalism attempts to explain the parts institutions play within the interrelated whole of a culture. Thus, according to functionalism, institutions of a culture operate to satisfy the needs of the individuals and that of society as a whole. Malinowski is of view that every aspects of culture has a function. They all are interdependent and interrelated. He cited an example of engine and said that different parts of an engine are interrelated and interdependent. Their main functions are to bring engine in motion. If one part of engine stops functioning, the movement of engine also gets stopped. This indicates that there remains a functional unity among the different parts of the engine. In the same way, though different cultural traits and cultural institutions contribute function in different way, but they are interdependent and interrelated. A functional unity among them can be seen in maintaining the existence of human beings on the earth. Thus, culture fulfils the needs of man through cultural institutions.

Malinowski opines that man has different kinds of need such as social, economic, religious, biological, physical and mental etc. In order to satisfy these needs, man has developed material and non-material aspects of culture. He has originated social, religious, economic and political institutions. The purpose of inventing language, literature, art technology etc. is the satisfaction of human needs. All human needs are interrelated to one another, because they are related to men as a whole. In the same way, culture traits appear externally as different, but they are integrated and united internally. The basis of this integration and unity is the satisfaction of human needs. Malinowski treats culture in the form of self-dependent and totality. He is view that change in one aspect of culture will bring change in culture as a whole.

Malinowski's chief argument behind the functionalism is that every aspect of culture has a function, i.e. the satisfaction of need. He distinguishes three levels of needs: (i) primary, (ii) instrumental, and (iii) integrative. By primary need, he means biological needs such as sex and feeding. By instrumental needs, he means those institutions such as economic, legal and educational, which help to achieve primary needs. By integrative needs, he means those that help the society to cohere such as religion, magic and play.

SALIENT FEATURES OF FUNCTIONALISM

Salient feature of functionalism are as follows:

1. Culture is a means for the satisfaction of human needs.
2. Each trait or element or aspect of culture performs certain function.
3. Clear form of these elements, or traits or aspects is social institutions, which are the means for the satisfaction of needs.
4. Though different elements or parts of culture perform different functions, but they are interdependent and interrelated in culture as a totality. In other words, culture is that interrelated or integrated arrangement in which interrelationship and interdepen-

dence among different parts are clearly observed.

5. Function is contribution of partial activity to total activity of which it is a part.

Between Malinowski and present day, the term function has been used in various ways to mean:

(i) The satisfaction of human needs
(ii) The modification of human needs
(iii) The elaboration of human needs
(iv) The moulding and training of human needs
(v) The integration of groups of human beings
(vi) The interdependence of cultural elements
(vii) The relationship between elements of culture
(viii) The principle of operation of partial system
(ix) The maintenance of statusquo
(x) The synchronic cause and effect within a culture
(xi) The diachronic cause and effect within a culture.

Malinowski's Publications

1. 1913(a) : *The Family Among the Australian Aborigines: A Sociological Study*, London: University of London Press.
2. 1913(b) : "Review of Durkheim's Las Formes Elementaries de la vie Religieus". *Folklore*, 24:525-31.
3. 1920 : "Kula: The Circulating Exchanges of valuables in Archipelagos of Eastern New Guinea", *Man*, 20:97-105.
4. 1922 : *Argonauts of the Western Pacific*, New York: Dutton.
5. 1912 : "Psychoanalyses and Anthropology" *Psyche*, 4:293-322.
6. 1926 : *Crime and Custom in Savage Society*. London: Kegan Paul, Trench, Trubnar.
7. 1927 : *Sex and Repression in Savage Society*, London: Routledge and Kegan Paul.
8. 1929 : *The Sexual Life of Savages in North Western Melenesis*. London: George Routledge.
9. 1935 : *Coral Gardens and their Magic*. London: Allen and Unwin in 2 volumes.
10. 1939 : "The Group and Individual in Functional Analysis". *American Journal of Sociology*, 44: 938-64.
11. 1944 : *Freedom and Civilization*. New York: Roy Publisher.
12. 1944 : *A Scientific Theory of Culture*. Chapel Hill: University of North Carolina Press.

13. 1945 : *Dynamics of Culture Change: An Enquiry into Race Relation in Africa*. P. Kaberi ed. New Haven; Yale University Press.
14. 1962 : *Sex Culture and Myth*. New York: Harcourt, Brace & World.
15. 1967 : *A Diary in the Strict Sense of the Term*. New York: Harcourt, Brace and World.

Bronislaw Kaspar Malinowski (1884-1942)

B.K. Malinowski was born on April 7, 1884 in Cracow, Poland (Germany) and died on May 16, 1942, at Yale in USA. His father was a noble man of landed gentry, but allowed an academic career as Professor of Slavic Philosophy at Jagiellon University in Cracow. Malinowski's early education was at the King Jan Sobieski Public School. From there, he entered the University at Cracow, the oldest university in Eastern Europe, where in 1908 he received Ph.D. degree in Physics and Mathematics. His degree was awarded with the highest honour in Australian Empire.

A promising career in physical sciences, which began with two years of study and research in Wilhelm Ostwald's laboratory of physical chemistry at Leipzig, was cancelled by Malinowski due to his illness. At the same time, he got opportunity to go through Frazer's book, *Golden Bough*. Before he put down the last volume of that work, his career in physical sciences had ended and he became dedicated to anthropology.

After a period at Leipzig Malinowski came to England in 1910. He became a post-graduate student at the London School of Economics. From here, he obtained D.Sc. Degree in 1916, with two printed works on Australian aborigines and on the Mailu. In 1913, he was one of the lecturers in special subjects at the London School of Economics. He taught in the Department of Sociology on primitive religion, social differentiation and social psychology. Unlike his idol and mentor, Sir James Frazer, Malinowski did not serve anthropology from library. After four years of research, study and writing at the London School of Economics, he set out on a field trip to Australia as Secretary to a field expedition sponsored by British Association for the Advancement of Science. He had been trained by the greater field worker of the day, C.G. Seligman, who thought so highly a Malinowski's potential as an anthropologist that he had offered to have his own salary cut so that Malinowski could be hired for the faculty of London School of Economics.

In 1914, largely through the help of C.G. Seligman, he was awarded Robert Mond Travelling studentship from the University of London and

Constance Hutchinson Scholarship of the London School of Economics. He went out to undertake researches in Guinea. Along with other anthropologists, going out for British Association meeting in Melbourne, he got opportunity to travel via Australia. It was at this time that he met first A.R. Radcliffe-Brown and received from him valuable hints about fieldwork. In September 1914, arriving in New Guinea, he spent about four weeks waiting for a boat to travel eastwards. He took advantage of this period to work with Ahuia Ova, Seligman's earlier informant. After some months with the Mailu, Malinowski returned to Australia in February 1915, making a call at Woodlark island on the way. A financial stringency having been overcome through Saligman's help, he returned to New Guinea in May 1915 with the assistance from Common Wealth Department of External Affairs, Dobu, as well as to Rossel island, which Seligman wanted him to investigate, but he stopped in the Trobriands because the people with whom he had made arrangements had moved elsewhere.

He returned from the Trobriand field in October 1918 and lived for a while in Melbourne. He married Elsis Masson, daughter of Sir David Orme Masson, Professor of Chemistry in Melbourne University. Threatened by tuberculosis on his return to Europe, Malinowski lived for a year or so with his wife on Tenerife, in Canary island, where in April 1921, the preface to his book, *Argonauts of the Western Pacific* was signed. He again took up a post as occasional lecturer at the London School of Economics in 1921-22, but this time in Ethnology. In this assignment, he gave eighteen lectures on 'Sociology and Economics of some island communities, i.e Trobriands'. He was appointed as lecturer in Social anthropology in 1922-23, in which he taught on early beliefs and social differentiation, social organisations of Australian Aborigines and Economics of Primitive People. In collaboration with Morris Ginsberg, he also led a seminar on 'Primitive mentality'.

From 1922, formerly twenty years, London was the academic home of Malinowski, though he travelled widely from here, especially during summer months. On the continent, he lectured at Geneva, Vienna, Rome, Oslo and other European capital cities. He also lived for a while at Tamaris in South of France.

In 1924, Malinowski was appointed as Reader in Anthropology in the University of London, tenable at the London School of Economics. In 1927, he occupied first chair in Anthropology in the University (Seligman held the chair in Ethnology). In May 1934, Malinowski went to South Africa to participate in New Education Fellowship Conference and from July till October, he toured in South and East Africa, visiting his students in the field and doing anthropological survey work among the Swazi,

Benuba, Chagga, Massai, Kikuyu and Maragoli people.

In 1926, he had visited United States for the first time at the invitation of the Laura Spelman Rockfeller memorial. This time, he got opportunities to visit some of Pueblo Indians, coming back with confession that at last he had found languages that were really difficult even for him to learn. He visited United States in 1933 to deliver the Messenger lectures at Cornell University and again in 1936 as a delegate of the University of London to the Harvard Tercentenary celebration, when he received honorary D.Sc. from Harvard. He went back again in 1938 on sabbatical leave and remained in north America for three and a half years until his death. He was appointed visiting professor at Yale, for the year, October 1939-June 1940. From September 1940, for a year, he was Bishop Museum Visiting Professor of Yale. This appointment was renewed for the following year. In the summer vacation of 1940-41, he carried out field trips to the Zapotee of Dexaca in Mexico and studied their peasant marketing system. At the beginning of 1942, he was appointed permanently as a professor at Yale from October 1942, but he died before this appointment became effective.

Besides C.G. Seligman and Sir James Frazer, Malinowski had studied with Westermarck, Rivers and Hobhouse in London.

Malinowski's Major Contributions in Anthropology

Malinowski's major contributions in the field of anthropology can be studied under the following headings:

1. Malinowski's criticism of the evolutionists, diffusionists and Patternists.
2. Malinowski's contribution to fieldwork Method and Writing Ethnography.
3. Malinowski's concept of culture.
4. malinowski's Theory of Functionalism.
5. Malinowski's Theory of Need.
6. Malinowski's Theories of Law.
7. Malinowski's Contribution to kinship.
8. Malinowski on Magic and Religion, Myth, Art and Science.
9. Malinowski on Economic Anthropology.
10. Malinowski on the study of Social Change.
11. Malinowski's Contribution to Anthropology as Public Service.

Malinowski's Criticism of Evolutionists, Diffusionists and Patternists

Although Malinowski defined anthropology as the 'comparative science of culture, but he was critical of comparative methods used by evolutionary anthropologists. He was especially critical of the concept of survival, which played such a crucial part in the evolutionary reconstruction. He could not accept the implication that an institution can outline its function and pointed out that so called survivals disappear as we learn more about the society and the specific cultural context of a given institution. In a typical polemic Malinowski suggests how survival can be misleading. For instance, marriage in past did not consist merely in the eating together in fish and hard boiled eggs, nor in the tossing of rice, not yet in wagging of rods or green trees. There is no reason, therefore, to assume that because in some tribes the marriage acts consist of a mimic capture, capture in dead earnest was the origin of marriage. Malinowski shared Tylor's concern that anthropology not become preoccupied with "Savage exocticism" and urged that anthropology emerged from its "Herodotage" (coined from Herodotus) and "Aneedotage". But contrary to Tylor, it was on reliance on survivals that Malinowski feared would help perpetuate a distorted view of primitive societies. Society, for Malinowski, consisted of a body of institutions related to current adaptive needs of man. It is the study of those institutions — economic, political system, law, education, religion, science, family organisation and individuals relation to them that must take precedence over historical reconstructions, whether in the hands of evolutionists or diffusionists.

While admitting that careful, sober and evolutionary reconstruction and diffusionists hypotheses could be profitable, if secondary enterprises, but he made no such allowance for so called "tribal genius" studies. He criticised Boas and his students, such as Ruth Benedict, for fostering the concept of culture, which was so general and vague as to defy any kind of scientific evaluation. Malinowski was uncompromising in his attack on this approach. He was of opinion that it is illegitimate to cover our inability to deal with certain facts by submystic labels as the 'genius of culture' or to describe this genius as Apollonian, Dionysian, Megalomaniac or hysterical.

Malinowski's criticism of evolutionists, diffusionists, patternists and others, must be seen against the background of his intense crusade for an individual functionalism in anthropology.

Malinowski's Contribution to Fieldwork Method and Writing Ethnography

Until the end of 19th century, most anthropologists wrote from the arm chair and relied for their raw data on material recorded by missionaries, explorers, travellers, government officials and settlers. They laid the foundation of cultural or social anthropology on the basis of information supplied by them.

The tradition of fieldwork in anthropology, for writing ethnography and developing theories on that basis, came into existence towards the late of 19th century. In 1883 Franz Boas visited Baffin land and there he did what may be called as the first systematic anthropological fieldwork. In 1898-99, Professor A.C. Haddon, of Cambridge University, who led a band of scholar to conduct field research in Torres Straits region of the Pacific in Malenesia. This expedition marked a turning point in history of social anthropology in Great Britain.

W.H.R. Rivers and Haddon came to India around 1905 and conducted field researches among the Todas of Nilgiri area and Veda tribe of Sri Lanka respectively. Monograph on Toda was published in 1906.

Professor, A.R. Radcliffe Brown, a pupil of Rivers and Hadden, visited India to study 'Onge' tribe of Andaman and Nicobar islands from 1906 to 1908. The monograph on 'Onge' was published in 1922.

Bronislaw Kaspar Malinowski, a pupil of Hobhouse, Westernmarck and Seligman carried field research a step further. If Professor Radcliffe-Brown has always had wider knowledge of general social anthropology and has proved himself the abler thinker, Malinowski was more thorough field worker. He not only spent a longer period than any anthropologists before and after him in a single study of primitive people, the Trobriand Islanders of Malenesia, but he was the first anthropologist to conduct study in Native's language.

Malinowski had stayed in Australia for six years and made three extensive field trips to New Guinea, one to Mailu (1914-15) and two to the Trobriand Island (1915-16 and 1917-18). This was a crucial experience for Malinowski's career. He lived like a native and with native experienced directly the demands and comforts of their culture.

Malinowski emphasised upon the participant observation, language of the native and writing ethnographic diary, for all researchers, while conducting field studies. Many later commentators became as critical as Radcliffe-Brown about Malinowski's brand of functionalism, but even the most severe critics have praised him for the excellence of his fieldwork, which set standard that are still adhered to. He stayed in Trobriand Islands for longer than any one before him had remained in field.

Malinowski, firstly used Pidgin English, in his first round of fieldwork. But as he was already familiar with the structure of Malenesian languages while working among the Mailu, so just after three months he was able to converse with the informants through native's language. He admitted that it was not until his second visit that he could easily follow conversations with the native and could talk rapidly in their dialect. Thus, Malinowski emphasised that a researcher should collect data through the medium of native language and researcher should learn their language before undertaking long intensive fieldwork among them. From the writing of Malinowski, informants emerged as living personalities rather than anonymous data providers.

Paying attention to all kinds of detail of everyday life, he described the routine of a man's working day, the care he took of his body, his personal ambitions, passing friendship as well as the tone of conversations, the laughing and weeping, and thus conveying to his readers a sense of the actually of Trobriand life. He also indicated that the first few weeks of fieldwork were most difficult, but that eventually he began. . .

> to take part in the village life, to look forward to the important or festive events, to take personal interest in group and the development of small village occurrences, to wake up every morning to a day, presenting itself to be more or less as it does to the native. With this and the capacity of enjoying their company and sharing some of their games and amusements, I began to feel that I was indeed in touch with the native, and this is certainly the preliminary condition of being able to carry on fieldwork. (Malinowski, 1961: 7-8).

In 1967, long after his death, Malinowski's widow decided to publish his personal diaries, kept in 1914-15 and 1917-18, which are the years spent mostly on Trobriand Islands. Written in Polish, Malinowski's native language, and never intended for publication, they gave a unique insight into Malinowski's own personality. His diary revealed the problem of fieldwork and adjustment to long periods of isolation in alien surroundings. Some sample statements in this regard are as follows:

(i) ".....The oldman began to lie about burials. I became enraged.
(ii) The stench, smoke, noise of people, dogs and bugs, greatly irritated me.
(iii) Sick, fever and a violent toothache.
(iv) With great effort .... I wormed out of him material relating to kinship.
(v) I often long for culture ..... Beethoven's melodies.
(vi) I was fed up with neggers and with my work.

Everyone who prepares to go into the field for the first time should read the diaries to achieve awareness that far from being romantic, fieldwork is often frustrating and strenuous, both physically and psychologically. Malinowski was perhaps more observed about his health than many other people are, and he was also perhaps overly preoccupied with his relations to his mother and his future wife, but culture shock and isolation will tend to magnify a field worker's personal worries. Malinowski, undoubtedly, used this diary as an emotional outlet, and it is unique record to personal honesty.

According to Malinowski, the goal of all fieldwork is to grasp the native's point of view, his relation to life, to realise his vision of this world or to get inside the native skin. While it is necessary to banish all preconceived ideas about how a culture must or should function, it is just as necessary that the workers have some positive theoretical framework with which to 'foreshadow' the problems. For Malinowski, this was functionalism.

Malinowski breaks scientific fieldwork down into three areas:

(i) The organisation of the tribe and the anatomy of its culture must be recorded in firm clear outline. The method of concrete statistical documentation is the means through which such an out line has to be given.

(ii) Within this frame, the imponderabilia of actual life and the type of behaviour have to be filled in. They have to be collected through minute, detailed observations, in the form of some sort of ethnographic diaries, made possible by close contact with native life.

(iii) A collection of ethnographic statements, characteristic narratives typical utterances, items of folk-lore and magical formulae has to be given as a corpus inscriptionum, as documents of native mentality.

These three categories correspond, in Malinowski's functional scheme, to

(i) the routine prescribed by custom and tradition,
(ii) the manner in which it is carried out, and
(iii) the commentary to the routine, as contained in native's mind.

Malinowski insisted upon "static documentation by concrete evidence" as the method for acquiring this information about a people, but not through the procedure of the fixed interview and the native interpreter. To get an integrated picture, a community worker must learn the language, live with the people, share their food and custom and learn, as far as possible to feel and think as they do. This is the doctrine of participant observation. For Malinowski, there was an intense personal satisfaction in studying a foreign culture which transcended the mere satisfaction of scientific curiosity. He states, to study the institutions, customs, codes or to study the behaviour and mentality without desire of feeling by what these people live, of realising the substance of their happiness, is to miss the greatest reward which can hope to obtain from the study of man.

In the study of Trobriand islanders, he used what he called static documentation of concrete evidence. This involved the collection of statements of norms and concrete cases, genealogies, village censuses, maps, and especially preparation of garden land, hunting and fishing privileges, the dovetailing of rituals and technical activities, the distribution of harvests, the pattern of gift exchange in association with its sociological, ceremonial and economic aspects. He regarded construction of such chart or table not only as an instrument in field to ensure the widest possible investigation of relevant facts, but as a part of writing the ethnography. They enable the reader to judge what is the result of direct and indirect observation, they constitute empirical charter for generalisation.

But Malinowski did not consider that the type of collection of data described above was sufficient. It provided the bare outlines of tribal constitution and anatomy of its culture. The ethnographer must also record imponderablia of actual life and this cannot be achieved by the method of question and answer. Here belongs such thing as the routine of man's working day, conventional and social life around the village fires, the existence of strong friendship or hospitalities and of passing sympathies and dislikes between people, the subtle, yet unmistakable, manner in which personal vanities and ambitions are reflected in the behaviour of the individual and the emotional reaction of those who surround him.

Malinowski recognised that this involved not only the superficial registration of details, but an effort to penetrate the mental attitude revealed in them. This in turn raised the problem of the personal equation of the observer. But he believed that it could in some measure be taken into account by keeping an ethnographic diary and by systematically noting the normal and typical, and the slight and more pronounced deviations from them over a prolonged period of fieldwork.

He also insisted that the adequate investigation of a culture demanded not only the documentation of aspects of social structure, the details of behaviour and emotional interaction, but also the native's commentaries on action, their beliefs and ideas. And here, it should be stressed that he was not concerned with the unique experiences and motives of individuals, but as members of community.

Such documents of native mentality, a corpus inscriptionum, entailed the native language of narrative, obvious, typical utterances, myths, folklore, magical formulae, and native explanations and interpretations of customs and beliefs.

Lastly, Malinowski, considered it the duty of anthropologist, to render a careful and sincere account of his credentials and his mistakes in the field. In Appendix II to his book, *Coral Gardens*, he recorded his confessions of Ignorance and Failure. In judging this method, he himself was his own most exactic critic. He admitted that a general source of inadequacies in all this material, whether photographic or linguistic or descriptive, consisted in fact that like every ethnographer, he was burred by the dramatic, exceptional and sensational. He castigated himself for not treating the drab, everyday, minor events with the same love and interest as sensational large scale happenings. But despite his strictures on his own work, he did accumulate a mass of detail on the drab and every day routine. And in spite of his impatience with the purely technological enthusiasm of museum ethnologist, he conscientiously recorded the technical processes of house building and canoe construction. In this sphere of research, he made his own contribution by emphasising the need to study a material object within the context of situation, i.e., in-terms of purposes for which it is made, the uses to which it is put, the rules of ownership, the native attitudes towards it. Conversely, he regarded as knowledge of technology as an indispensable means of approach to economic and sociological activities, what might be called native science.

Finally, he collected a certain amount of quantitative data, though he admitted that there were gaps in his assessment of some of the material aspects of grading. But he was of the opinion that the anthropologist should measure, weight and count every thing that could be legitimately measured, weight and counted.

Malinowski's Ethnographic Works: Between 1916 and 1935, Malinowski wrote a series of monographs and articles, which were concerned with the analysis of various aspects of Trobriand Economy, Social Control, marriage, family, ritual, belief, mythology etc. While each was focused on a particular institution or a set of closely related institutions, the treatment or exposition was fugal in the sense that a number of aspects were interwoven or counterpoised, whether the subject-matter permitted or not he presented his data in the form of a narrative of events, developing in process the implications of his generalisations for the theory in the fields of economics, law, kinship, magic and religions. Argonaut's of Western Pacific (1922) is a typical example of his method. In the Kula district, the landscape is recreated and, at each island, the physical characteristics of the native and main features of their social and economic organisation are indicated. Malinowski's own suspense and interest that we enter the community which is to be the centre of his fieldwork, a vivid picture of villages and garden emerges and were given an outline of Trobriand economy, kinship system, beliefs, ceremonies and especially, rank and chieftainship since he regarded a firm grasp of the main political institutions, as essential to the understanding of Kula. All aspects of tribal life, religion, magic, economics are interwoven, but the social organisation of the tribe lies at the foundation of everything else. In subsequent volumes, the sexual life of Savages and Coral garden, the reader is not only referred back to the preliminary account of structure in Argonauts, but further aspects are elucidated where relevant to the theme under discussion. If for Malinowski, social organisation or social structure, was merely one aspect of culture, he nevertheless regarded in analysis of 'Sociology of enactment', as an essential part of ethnographic writing.

On Kula system, Malinowski dealt with the types of valuable involved and the norms governing their exchange, the basis of partnership, the importance of secondary economic transactions, and the background of ritual and ideology. The rest of volume is devoted to a documentation of these generalization by an account of the links in the chain of Kula performance — from the building of a canoe, the departure of an expedition to Dobu, the ceremonial procedure which occurs at each stage of journey, to the return of Kitawa and Kiriwine. While the sequence of events provides the main thread of the argument, the themes of sociological mechanism underlying the activities and the system of ideas at work in regulating labour and magic are developed. But in demonstrating the inter-locking of structural, technological and ritual aspects, Malinowski does not stop short at integrative description, he used it as a basis for the enunciation and clarification of the sociological launching or a new canoe is made the occasion for an analysis of the rules governing the organisation of labour, and distribution of wealth, for the formulation of principle of reciprocity and its importance in kinship, political relations and law.

Many similar instances of this method can be taken from his ethnographic work, but particularly a good case takes place in *Coral Gardens*, where, while discussing the distribution of *Yam* harvest among affines, he points out that an understanding of the economic aspect of Urigubu involves a grasp of the laws of marriage, and native ideas of procreation and kinship. In the process of analysis, he elucidates the complex relations, with their personalities for tension and conflict between the genealogical unit of decent or unit of filiation on one hand, and patrilocal household or family on the other. He arrived at a hypothesis that 'Urigubu' is the outcome and economic expression of a compromise or adjustment between principles of patrilocal household and matrilineal filiation.

While passing from one dimension to another, from technological to structural or ideological, Malinowski has his own criteria of relevance and these are determined by the scientific rigour which he considers necessary for the documentation of his more abstract generalizations. Some of his colleagues have criticised Malinowski that he carries to excess his vivid presentation of detail and his wide contexualization of event, but he was never guilty of whipped postulates. As referred to earlier, he includes in his text linguistic statements made by informants, quantitative material on harvest and economic transactions, plans of villages and garden land, and chart which provides a synopsis of land tenure, exchanges, system of ownership, calendars of events and interlocking of magic with technical activities.

Lastly, in his vivid eye witness accounts of ceremonies, economic activities, domestic and village relations and guards, he records the imponderabilia of actual life. Some anthropologists have regarded it as impressionist and subjective. But to omit such vivid eye witness account as anthropologist is able to give often result in loss of something, which may be essential to an understanding of group's social life.

Malinowski's Concept of Culture

Malinowski's concept of culture, as he first developed it, was one of his most stimulating contributions to the anthropological thought of his day. The term culture stood for the set of ideas to which he himself attached the most importance and which enabled him to make some of his most original hypothesis. His scheme for analysing culture in to its different aspects formed a basis for the fieldwork methods, which he taught to his students. This contribution to anthropological theory seems to have been considerably undervalued since his death due to extreme intellectual and emotional reaction to his work which then took place. The later formulations of his view on culture as presented in posthumously published book entitled, *A Scientific Theory of Culture and other Essays*, published in 1944, are more confused and diffused than the earlier and give little idea of impact of his work on his students.

The term such as 'culture' or 'structure', as used in Sociological work, is inevitably a heuristic device or a way of looking at facts and hence its meaning can best be grasped by a study of its use in analysis of data.

Malinowski's own definition of culture given in 1931 states that, culture comprises inherited artifacts, goods, technical process, ideas, habits and values. He also included social organisation or social structure in analysis of culture because he was of opinion that this could not be understood except as part of culture. This was the main point of difference between Malinowski and most other British anthropologists of present time, in which Evans Pritchard and his followers occupy significant place. They have excluded social structure or social organisation from the analysis of culture.

Malinowski's definition of culture was different from the famous definition of culture given by E.B. Tylor in 1971 as, culture is that complex whole which includes knowledge, belief, art, law, morals, customs and all others capabilities and habit acquired by man as a member of society. Thus, Tylor spoke of culture as being a complex whole, but emphasis was rather on complexity than on wholeness.

In order to analyse Malinowski's use of the term culture more closely, it is necessary to distinguish between a number of different intellectual preoccupations, which were all subsumed for him under the one term culture. First, there is his concept of culture as a tribal macrocosm, the functioning whole, which as Fortes (1953) has pointed out, was a new and stimulating idea when it was propounded by Malinowski and Radcliffe-Brown in early twenties. Secondary, with this idea Malinowski went to emphasise on the need to study the 'use' or 'function' of the customs, institutions and beliefs which formed part of each culture. With all the different shades of meaning, he gave to the word 'use'. Thirdly, Malinowski, in common with other sociologists and psychologists of his day, was preoccupied with the difference between man's biological and sociological heritage and he identified the latter with the term culture right from the beginning. He also attempted from the first to analyse culture into a number of distinct aspects which could be used as a scheme for empirical research.

The concept of culture as a nicely balanced system of separate parts is found in both those famous books published in 1922: Radcliffe-Brown's *The Andaman Islanders and Malinowski's Agronauti's of the Western Pacific*. Radcliffe-Brown, then, used the term culture in somewhat the same way as Malinowski did. The later definition of Social structure as propounded by Radcliffe-Brown included much what Malinowski did under culture, except material culture, language, system of knowledge and education. Both worked in small islands where holistic conception of the culture seems more obvious than it does in an inland area with a great deal of movement of people and tribal admixture. Both were influenced by Durkhiem and Radcliffe-Brown permanently, and Malinowski temporarily. In the work of both, there is assumption that culture should continue to survive and they must be maintained.

Malinowski had recognised quite early (1929) that there were conflicts within cultures and it is to his credit that he did so. He observed in Trobriand society conflicting roles and rivalries expressed in reciprocal obligations, self-interest and fights for power, whereas Andaman Islanders were represented as being a united group, earnestly engaged in expressing their cohesion. In spite of these differences, both seems to have believed that culture had to be maintained as a whole. Malinowski's definitions of function of a custom or institution is in terms of part it plays in relation to the culture as a whole. He was of opinion that anthropological facts were to be explained by their function, by the part which they play in an integral system of culture. Some recent writers have categorically stated that Radcliffe-Brown viewed the function of an institution as the part it plays in the maintenance of tribal structure, whereas Malinowski examined its function only in relation to needs, mainly biological needs.

Many critics have pointed out that Malinowski never described a culture as a whole, but instead presented most of his work in the form of very detailed accounts of particular aspects. The wholeness in the treatment consisted of the study of one institution against the background of whole culture. It would be equally true to say that Radcliffe-Brown has often hinted to study and compare 'total social structure', but has never actually described one. Both 'culture' and 'Total Social Structure', were used as devices for the analysis of research data, and both were new and stimulating concepts in British anthropology when first introduced. They still remain valuable for teaching purpose.

Malinowski was of opinion that a culture characteristic or trait, which is functionless, would not survive and hence there was no cultural survival. Criticising the evolutionists and diffusionists, he argued that cultural trait should not be studied in isolation, because they are interconnected and interrelated to one another, hence they should be studied in integrated whole, which is also termed as Malinowski's theory of cultural integration

While studying culture, Malinowski was more interested in a people's own concept of their history than their actual history. There was little documentary history to be examined in case of Trobriand Society, but anthropological significance of their myths and legends in maintaining their system of clan structure, their land tenure, and their magic struck him forcibly. It was the basis of his formulation of the concept of charter of an institution which has since became an anthropological common place. There have been considerable developments in our knowledge of the sociological functions of current historical traditions since his days, and many anthropologists have described the significance of a people's own view of their past, the genealogies they invent, to account for their political institutions, or migration tales which act as charters for their rights of ownership. This functional concept of cultural history was first implanted in the mind of students by Malinowski's teaching on the function of primitive myth.

In his book, *Scientific Theory of Culture*, Malinowski defines culture as the integral whole consisting of implements and consumer's good, of constitutional charters for the various social groupings, of human ideas and craft, beliefs and customs, whether we consider a very simple or primitive culture or an extremely complex or civilized culture, we are confronted by a vast apparatus, partly material, partly human and partly spiritual, by which man is able to cope with the concrete specific problem that face him. These problems arise out of the fact that man has a body subject to various organic needs and that he lives in an environment which is his best friend, in that it provides the raw materials of man's handi work, and also his dangerous enemy, for that it harbors many hostile forces.

He was of opinion that the theory of culture must take its stand on biological fact. Human beings are an animal species. They are subject to elemental condition which have to be fulfilled so that individuals may survive, the race continue, organisms one and all be maintained in working order. From the above description, it appears that the satisfaction of organic or basic needs of man and of the race is a minimum set of conditions imposed on each culture. The problem set by main's nutritive, reproductive and hygienic needs must be solved. They are solved by the construction of a new, secondary or artificial environment. This environment, which is neither more nor less than culture itself, has to be permanently reproduced, maintained and managed. This creates a new standard of living, which depends upon the cultural level of the community, on the environment, and on the efficiency of the group. A cultural standard of living means that the new needs appear and new imperatives or determinants are imposed on human behaviour. Clearly, cultural tradition has to be transmitted from each generation to the next. Methods and mechanism of an educational must exist in every culture. Order and law has to be maintained, since cooperation is the essence of every cultural achievement. In every community, there must exist this arrangements for the sanctioning of customs, ethics, and law. The material substratum of culture has to be renewed and maintained in working order. Hence, some forms of economic organisation are indispensable, even in the most primitive culture.

Thus, man has, first and foremost, to satisfy all the needs of his organism. He has to create arrangements and carrying out activities for feeding, heating, housing, clothing or protection from cold, wind and weather. He has to protect himself and organise for such protection against external enemies and dangers, physical, animal or human. These primary problems of human beings are solved for the individual by artifacts, organisation in to co-operative groups, and also by the development of knowledge, a sense of value and ethics. Thus, a theory can be established in which basic needs and their cultural satisfaction can be linked up with derivation of new cultural needs, which impose upon man and society a secondary type of determinism. A distinction can also be made between instrumental imperatives, arising out of such type of activities as economic, normative, educational, and political, and integrative imperatives arising out of knowledge, religion and magic. Artistic and recreational activities are related directly to certain physiological characteristics of human organism and also to show their influence and dependence upon modes of concerted action, magical, industrial and religious belief.

The scientific analysis of culture, can point to another system of realities that also conforms to general laws and can thus, be used as a guide for fieldwork, as a means of identification of cultural realities and as the basis of social engineering. The relation between cultural performance and human need, basic or derived may be termed functional. For function cannot be defined in any other way than the satisfaction of a need by an activity in which human beings cooperate, use artifacts, and consume goods. The essential concept here is that of organization. In order to achieve any purpose, reach any end, human beings have to organise. Organisation implies a very definite scheme of structure, the main factors of which are universal in that they are applicable to all organised groups, which again, in their typical form, are universal throughout mankind. The unit of human organisation is institution. The concept of institution implies an agreement on a set of traditional values for which human beings come together. This also implies that these human beings stand together in definite relation to one another and to a specific physical part of their environment, natural and artificial under the charter of their purpose or traditional mandate, obeying the specific norms of their association, working through the material apparatus, which they manipulate, human beings act together and thus satisfy some of their desires, while also producing an impression on their environment. This preliminary definition of institution needs to be made more precise, more concrete, and more cogent. Unless the anthropologists and humanists agree on what is the definite isolate in concrete cultural reality, there will never be any science of civilization. On the basis of universally valid principles of institutional action, we may lay a scientific foundation for our empirical and theoretical pursuits.

Malinowski was of opinion that neither two cultures were identical, nor the student of culture must be more interested in identities or similarities, than in differences. In order to understand divergencies, a clear, common measure of comparison is indispensable. Most of the divergencies which are often attributed to specific national or tribal genius are the reason for institutions organised around some highly specialised need or value. Such phenomena as head hunting, extravagant death rituals and ways of burial and magical practices, can be best understood as the local elaboration of tendencies and ideas essentially human but especially hypertrophied.

Thus, our two types of analysis, functional and institutional, will allow us to define culture more concretely, precisely and exhaustively. He defines culture as that instrumental reality which has come into existence to satisfy the needs of man in a manner far surpassing any direct adaptation to the environment. A culture can be analysed into institutions, which are defined as group of people united in common task or tasks, bound to a determined portion of the environment, wielding together to some technical apparatus, and obeying a body of rules. Thus, he defines institution as concrete isolates of organisation. By studying institutions, workers get concrete picture of social organisation within a culture. It is institutions, not traits, forms, ideas or adventitious complexes of these elements which diffuse and evolve, while maintaining a basic integrity. The institutions exist to satisfy, directly or indirectly, the biological need of man and must be studied with the central idea in mind.

Thus, culture is an integral composed of partly autonomous, partly coordinated institutions. It is integrated on a series of principles such as the community of blood through procreation, the contiguity in space related to cooperation, the specialization in activities, and the use of power in political organization. Each culture owes its completeness and self sufficiency to the fact that it satisfies the whole range of basic, instrumental and integrative needs.

If we are to plot out all the manifestations of every culture in the world, we obviously would find such elements as cannibolism, head-hunting, couvade, potlatch, Kula, cremation, mummification, and a vast array of detailed peripheral eccentricities. From this point, no single culture covers all the itemised breaks and eccentricities of many others. But this approach is essentially unscientific. It fails to define, on the principle of relevancy, what can be regarded as the real and significant elements of culture. If fails to give any clue, in comparing some of these apparently exotic isolates to customs or culture arrangements in other societies. As a matter of fact, it can be shown that some realities cognate to very universal and fundamentally human cultural elements, and this very recognition will admit of explanation, i.e., the description in familiar terms of exotic customs.

It is also necessary, of course, to introduce the element of time, i.e., of change in the study of culture. It can be shown that all evolutionary or diffusionary processes happen, first and foremost, in the form of institutional change. Whether in the form of invention or as an act of diffusion, a new technical device becomes incorporated into an already established system of organised behaviour and produces gradually a complete remodelling of that institution. Again, interms of our functional analysis, it can be shown that no invention, no revolution, no social or intellectual change, ever occurs except when new needs are created. Thus, new devices, in technique, in knowledge or in belief are fitted into the cultural processes or institutions.

This brief, but fuller analysis of culture, reveals that scientific anthropology consists in a theory of institutions, i.e., the concrete analysis of type units of an organisation. As a theory of basic needs and derivation of instrumental and integrative imperatives, scientific anthropology gives us the functional analysis, which allows us to define the form, as well as the meaning, of a customary idea or contrivance. It can easily be seen that such scientific approach does not, by any means, override or deny the validity of evolutionary or historical pursuits, rather it simply supplies them with scientific basis.

Malinowski's Theory of Functionalism

Malinowski's early writings do not manifest a great detail of interest in function. In his first Trobriand monograph, he wrote that the final goal of fieldwork is "to grasp the native's point of view, of his relation to life, to realise his vision of his world", adding that "perhaps through realising human nature in a shape very distant and foreign to us, we shall have some light shed on our own". This can hardly be called a typical functionalist view, and it is not surprising that English reviews of Argonauts treated it simply as another ethnography. Malinowski achieved fame after writing a piece for the prestigious periodical *Nature* entitled, "Psychoanalysis and Anthropology" (1923). In it, he explained that Trobriand society is matrilineal and that in their family life the mother's brother takes on many authorative tasks and responsibilities which are assigned to father in western society. Having read Freud's theories about universality of the 'Oedipus complex', while he was in field, Malinowski found that much of the repressed hatred of father was, among the Trobriand, directed against the maternal uncle. The matrilineal inclination of this group provided the world with the first field examination of Freud's theories concerning the universality of Oedipus complex as well as many Freudian notions such as racial conscience and infant sexuality. Malinowski's conclusions were not unequivocal in this regard. But the net impression of Sex and Repression in Savage Society, is that of a substantial blow from which Freud's original doctrines were never able fully to recover. It was certain at least that relations between father and son in a matrilineal and avunculocal descent system were radically different from what Freud had been able to do in his Viennese Patriarchy. The Oedipus theory, thus, stood in need of re-examination, even more because Trobriand sex life was rather permissive and sexual frustrations were almost absent. His article on Psycho-analysis and anthropology became the subject of long series of published controversies, of which the English public is so fond of. Malinowski took advantage of the attention, he received, and wrote a number of books with sexy titles, among these are, *Sex and Repression in Savage Society* (1927) and the *Sexual Life of Savage* (1929). Undoubtedly to the disappointment of some readers, he dealt more with social organisation and family life than with sex.

However, gradually Malinowski developed his theory of function in part, because he, too, became imbued with the need to make his explanation more scientific. An erudite and well-read scholar, Malinowski was aware of the writings of French Sociologists, but he chose to ally his understanding of function to fieldwork research. In his thought, function was a specific way of understanding institutions and customs of Primitive life. In his famous book, *Magic, Science and Religion* (1929), he saw function as largely fulfilling the Psychological need. Magic was the standardisation of optimism serving to provide man with necessary confidence to carry out his important tasks, to maintain his poise and his mental integrity in fits of anger, in throes of hate, of unrequire love, of despair and anxiety. Religion also opened up escapes from emotional stress. A part from these function for the individual, religion also makes social contributions because it assists in maintenance of moral law and order and works towards the identification of whole tribe as a social unit. Eventually, Malinowski related psychological and social functions to biological ones. Optimism and confidence enabled Trobrianders to become better food providers and magic thus also contributed to physical survival. This notion of function as serving biological needs became the core of Malinowski's functional theory. In his posthumous methodological book, *A Scientific Theory of Culture* (1944), he reiterated his conviction that the functional method of investigation is best suited to give an accurate picture of the realities of culture. He warned that the aim of fieldwork was not to discover function, but that the function was a heuristic device, a method towards understanding, what culturally happens and what can be observed. He realised that even heuristic devices stood in need of explanation, and he began to spell out the basic biological needs of man and their specific cultural responses, about which we will discuss later on.

Malinowski had defined, in many places, the functional method in anthropology. One of the clearest general definition is as follows:

> The functional view of culture lays down the principle that in every type of civilization, every customs, material object, idea and belief fulfils some vital function, has some task to accomplish, represents an indispensable part within a working whole.

The functionalists present working of human culture, not with ambitions but questionable reconstructions of the past. Cultural laws, the relations that exist between individual needs and social institutions, can be discovered only through a comparative study of culture, where individuals are seen in his day to day adaptation, both physical and mental. Malinowski's creed and advice was, never to forget the living palpitating flesh and blood organism of man, which remains somewhere at the heart of every institution. The history of an institution, its form and distribution, its evolution and diffusion, all these problems are secondary importance. The important questions are how does an institution function now? How does it satisfy individual and cultural needs in the given society? And how it is related to other institution? Thus, his questions about the individual behaviour and cultural institutions were limited to: Does it work? How does it work? Why does it work? With these questions, he founded the functionalist school of anthropology.

Malinowski defines functionalism more specially as the theory of transformation of organic, that is, individual, needs into derived cultural necessities and imperatives. Society, by the collective wielding of the conditioning apparatus, molds the individual in to cultural personality.

The human individual has certain basic physiological needs, which require organised, collective responses from the members of society. These include the need for food, shelter, safety, relaxation, movements, growth and reproduction. The organised responses to these "basic imperatives", the commissariat for nutrition, shelter and dress for bodily comfort, protective devices and organisations for safety, marriage and family for reproduction, represent an other derived order of conditions by member of society. The acquisition of food require more or less complicated economic system; where the production, processing, exchange and distribution of food is regulated by certain social rules, proper shelter requires cooperative endeavour and communal consent regarding production. Maintenance and style, mating and parenthood must be regulated by social values, which define the rights and obligations of persons involved to each other; and to other members of the community and so on. Thus, the great institution of society, economic, political, legal, educational and social, are seen by Malinowski as responses to the problem of adaptation, posed by the more or less direct collective responses, to the basic physiological needs of man.

Then, there is third order of imperatives, the integrative or synthetic imperatives, which result in the creation of systems of sciences, magic, myth, religion and art: Although less directly of all living creatures, man alone can accumulate experiences, reflect on them, and use them to foretell the future. These capacities make man the tragic hero that he is. They reveal new possibilities and opportunities with each generation, but they also reveal man's relative importance and leave him striving for more than he can rationally expect to receive. Systems of knowledge, such as *Science*, serve to organise and integrate human activities, so that by the wise use of past experience, the present, and the future can be made to better serve the need of man. The gaps in man's knowledge and power create anxiety and hesitation, and here *magic* can be employed as a substitute for rational system and give man the courage to act even without perfect knowledge. *Myth* enhances social tradition by endowing it with a wisdom and glorified beginnings and thus promotes, sustains, and integrates appropriate social behaviour. *Religion* promotes individual security and social cohesion by sanctifying human life and making public, by dogma and ritual, the social contracts of cooperative existence. Malinowski sees *art* as satisfying the craving of human organism for combinations of blended sense impressions, whether in the rhythm of bodily movement or in the blending of tones.

Malinowski regarded his functionalism as differing from other social theories in its emphasis on the basic bodily needs. The intellectual, emotional and aesthetic aspects of man's behaviour — the higher side of man's activities and primary concern of most students, must also be seen as roofed in man's physicological need. Social or cultural commands, whether in the form of legal or moral codes, religious rites, economic regulation, customs or aesthetic taste, are the re-interpretation of organic drives and impulses. They must so shape individual motives that individual behaves in a manner which satisfies the conditions of cultural survival and harmony.

In functional approach, it is the job of researcher to discover the specific functions of the element of culture within the integrated scheme as outlined above. Functional analysis of culture reveals that it is the handi work of man and as the medium through which he achieves his end, a medium which allows him to live, to establish standard of safety comfort and prosperity; a medium which gives him power and allows him to create goods and values beyond his animal, organic endowment, that culture, in all this and through all this, must be understood as a means to an end, i.e., instrumentally or functionally.

In order to fulfil his various needs, man has established certain general type of organisation, found in every culture all over the universe. The list of universal institutional types as principle of integration, as suggested by Malinowski, is as follows:

Principle of Integration	*Types of Institution*
1. Reproduction (Bonds of blood defined by a legal contract of marriage and extended by a specifically defined principle of descent on the genealogical scheme)	Family, as the domestic group of parents and children. Courtship organisation. The legal definition and organisation of marriage as a contract-binding two individuals and relating two groups. The extended domestic group and its legal, economic and religious organisation. Groups of kindred united on the unilateral principle of descent. The clan, matrilineal or patrilineal. The system of related clans.
2. Territorial (Community of interests due to prompinquity, contiguity and possibility of cooperation)	The neighbourhood group of municipalities, such as the nomadic horde, the roaming local band, the village, the cluster of hamlets or homestead, the town, the city, the district, the province, the tribe.
3. Physiological (Distinctions due to sex, age and bodily stigmata or symptom)	Primitive sex totemic groups. Organisations based on physiological or anatomical sex distinction.

	Organisations due to sexual division of function and activities. Age groups and age-grades, in so far as they are organised. Organisation in primitive societies of abnormal, the mentally deranged, epileptics, (often connected with magical or religious ideas) at higher levels, in situations for sick, the insane, the congenitally defective.
4. Voluntary Associations	Primitive secret societies, clubs, recreational teams, artistic societies. At higher levels, the clubs, mutual aid and benefit societies, lodges, voluntary associations for recreation, uplift or the realisation of a common purpose.
5. Occupational and Professional (The organization of human beings by their specialized activities for the purpose of common interest and a fuller achievement of their special abilities)	At Primitive level, Primarily of magicians, sorcerers, shamans and priests, also guilds of craft man and economic team. As civilisation develops, the ennumerable workshops, guilds, and undertaking, economic interest groups, and association of professional workers in medicine, in law, in teaching, and in ministering to religious needs. Also specific units for the organised exercises of teaching (schools, colleges, universities), for research (laboratories, academics, institutes) for administration of justice (legislative bodies, courts, police force), for defence and aggression (army, navy, air force) for

	religion (Parish, Sects, churches).
6. Rank and Status	Estates and Orders of nobility, clergy, burghers, peasants, serfs, slaves, the caste system. Stratification by ethnics i.e. either racial or cultural distinctions at primitive and developed levels.
7. Comprehensive (The integration by community of culture or by political power)	The tribe as the cultural unit corresponding to nationality at more highly developed levels. The cultural sub group in the regional sense or in the sense of small enclaves (alien minorities, the ghetto, the gypsies). The political unit which may compromise part of the tribe or its totality or yet include several cultural subdivisions. The distinction between tribe-nation and tribe-state as a political organisation is fundamental.

Malinowski illustrated his functional scheme with the charter of an institution. He defined charter of an institution as the system of values for the pursuit of which human beings organise or inter into organisation already existing. He defined personnel of an institution as the group organised on different principles of authority, division of functions, and distribution of privileges and duties. The rules or norms of the institution are technical acquired skills, habits, legal norms, ethical commands, which are accepted by members or imposed upon them. Thus, it is obvious that both, the organisation of the personnel and the nature of rules followed, are definitely related to the charter. In a way, both the personnel and the rules are derived from and contingent upon the charter.

The first aim of every society, according to Malinowski, is survival. Thus, according to the charter, in every society, there are personnels who have norms or a set of values. These norms and value inspire personnel for material apparatus, which creates activities, and activities ultimately lead a function. This may be shown by a diagram as below:

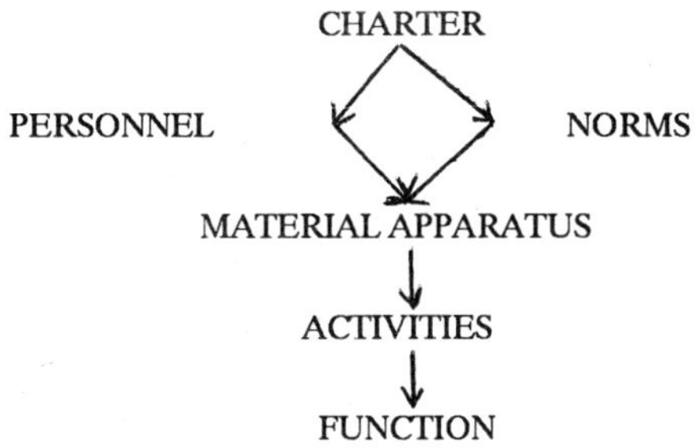

General Axioms of Functionalism: Malinowski's experience in field as well as the scrutiny of the really important manifestations of organised human behaviour demonstrate the validity of following axioms (self-evident truth) of functionalism:

(A) A culture is essentially an instrumental apparatus by which man is put in a position the better to cope with the concrete specific problems that face him in his environment in the course of the satisfaction of his needs.

(B) It is a system of objects, activities and attitudes in which every part exists as a means to an end.

(C) It is an integral in which various elements are interdependent.

(D) Such activities, attitudes and objects are organised to perform important and vital tasks in an institution such as family, clan, the whole community, tribe, and the organised team of cooperation, political, legal and educational activity.

(E) From the dynamic point of view, as regards the type of activity, culture can be analysed into a number of aspects such as education, social control, economic system of knowledge, belief and morality and also modes of creative and artistic expression.

Malinowski's Theory of Need

Malinowski developed a clearcut theory of need in his book, published after his death, entitled, *Scientific Theory of Culture and other Essays* (1944), though he was concerned with the functional interpretation of need since his return from the visits to Trobriand islanders in 1918. The views and explanations about this theory were incorporated in most of his research articles, books and seminar talks, but a scientific view on 'need theory' emerged in his posthumous publication.

In this book, he defines need as the system of conditions in human organism, in the cultural setting and in relation of both to the natural environment, which are sufficient and necessary for the survival of group and organism. A need, therefore, is limiting set of facts. According to functional approach of culture, institutions of a culture operate to satisfy the needs of individual and that of society as a whole. This reveals the biological foundation of culture. In this book, he distinguishes three levels of need which are as follows:

1. Primary or basic or biological need
2. Instrumental need or derived need
3. Integrative need.

By primary or basic needs, he means biological needs such as sex and feeding, by instrumental or derived need, he emphasizes upon those institutions such as economic, educational, legal and political which help to achieve the primary needs. By integrative needs, he means those that help the society to cohere such as knowledge, religion, magic and play. The theory of needs and their derivation gives us a more definitely functional analysis of the relation between biological, physiological, and cultural determinism. In the system of needs, primary or biological, derived or instrumental and integrative, Malinowski was able to link up functionally the various types of cultural responses, such as economic, legal, educational, scientific, magical and religious.

Taking first the system of condition in human organism, which involves the satisfaction of certain biologically determined impulses, in a series of vital sequences, Malinowski listed them as follows:

Permanent Vital Sequences Incorporated in All Cultures

(A) Impuse	*(B) Act*	*(C) Satisfaction*
Drive to breathe; gasping for air	Intake of oxygen	Elimination of CO_2 in tissues
Hunger	Ingestion of food	Satiation
Thirst	Absorption of liquid	Quenching
Sex appetite	Conjugation	Detumescence
Fatigue	Rest	Restoration of muscular and nervous energy
Restlessness	Activity	Satisfaction of fatigue
Somnolence	Sleep	Awakening with restored energy
Bladder pressure	Micturition	Removal of tension
Colon pressure	Defecation	Abdominal relaxation
Fright	Escape from danger	Relaxation
Pain	Avoidance by effective act	Return to normal state

The above table refers merely to the satisfaction of the impulses of an individual. It stresses the dynamic nature of 'human nature', conceived as pertaining to an individual organism. But this list of impulses corresponds only indirectly to the basic needs of man as an animal species, because at this level, the concept of individual and group survival is added to that of individual impulse. The two are, of course, interrelated, since individual impulses, on the whole conduce to survival. But it is possible, indeed necessary, to distinguish between them. An individual, under the stress of hunger or thirst may eat a poisonous plant or drink sea water and so die: the behaviour of individuals giving way to bright, as in a panic, may lead to decimation or extermination of group, not so long ago publicists talked of threat of 'race suicide' alleged tc be entailed in widespread practice of contraception, individual can and occasionally do neglect their children with fatal result for the latter, and it is possible to consider under the conditions of 'Social Pathology', such practices becoming so widespread that the group would become extinct. It was, therefore, necessary for Malinowski to construct a table of basic needs, which laid stress on the total conditions necessary to individual and group survival, and not merely on individual impulse. This table is as follows:

A *Basic Needs*	B *Cultural Responses*
1. Metabolism	1. Commissariat
2. Reproduction	2. Kinship
3. Body comforts	3. Shelter
4. Safety	4. Protection
5. Movement	5. Activities
6. Growth	6. Training
7. Health	7. Hygiene

What has been said about individual impulses and basic need would apply also to other animals, including sub-human primates. But man is a very particular kind of primate, and the special characteristic, which he has acquired in course of evolution, makes possible the development of that specifically human form of biological adjustment, which we call culture. Man is endowed with certain crucial physical characteristics — the upright posture, allowing for the emancipation of hands, and their specialization as organs of manipulation, the development of vision, muscular coordination and the association areas of the cerebral cortex, the nervous and muscular equipment which confers on man the power of articulate speech. To these anatomical and physiological characteristics can be related some of the universal and fundamental differential of human culture, such as technology, activities implying collective force thought and planning, the various forms of symbolism, particularly those which are concerned with normative behaviour and which make possible the emergence of values.

The entry *metabolism,* means that the process of food intake, digestion, collateral secretions, the absorption of nutritive substances, and the rejection of waste matter, are related in several ways to environmental factors and the interaction between the organism and the outside world, an interaction culturally framed. Thus, it has considered here several drives, which were separately stated in our previous table. The supply of solid foods or liquid, and of oxygen is all determined by the metabolic processes and so are the process of excretions, in which individual once more resorts to environment. In this context, it has not been referred to so much to drive of hunger, the impulse of air intake or the feeling of thrust. As regards the community as a whole, every organism in general requires certain conditions, which guarantee the supply of physical material, the conditions in which the digestive processes can be carried out, and the sanitary arrangements of end-process.

When we talk of *reproduction* as basic need, we are not concerned with individual drive or impulse of sex, and its realization in some particular case. Here we are stating simply that reproduction must go on in numerically sufficient extensive manner to replenish the numbers of the community. The need *bodily comfort* refers to the range of temperature, percentage of humidity and absence of noxious matter in contact with body, which allow such physiological processes as circulation, digestion, internal secretion, and metabolism to continue in purely physical sense. Perhaps, the range of temperature is the most significant element, since exposure to wind, weather, rain, snow, or continuous dampness, acts to a large extent through element of temperature upon an organism.

The basic need *safety* refers to prevention of bodily injuries by mechanical accident, attack from animals or other human beings. Here, we are interested interms of drive, in approximate individual types of behaviour reaction to danger or pain. We are interested in putting on record that under conditions, where most organism are not protected from bodily injury, the culture and its group will not survive.

The basic need *movement* predicts here that activity is as necessary to the organism as it is indispensable for culture. The difference between previous treatment of impulse and the definition of need is clear here. Our emphasis here is upon the general conditions, under which a group of people live and cooperate, and under which most members at any time, and all members at some time, have to obtain some scope for exercise and initiation.

The primary need *growth* which was discussed in list of impulses, but could not be placed there, has a legitimate position. It declares that since human beings are dependent in infancy, since maturation is a slow and gradual process, and since old age, in man more than any other animal species, leaves the individual defenceless. The facts of growing up, maturation and decay impose certain general but very definite conditions on culture. In other words, no group could survive, nor its culture endure, if the infants, immediately after birth, were left to its own devices, as is the case in many.

The biological need *health* refers to all other entries with the exclusion, perhaps, of second one. Even there, the protection of reproductive processes from possible external dangers is part of a hygienic procedure. Indeed, if we define health in general and positive terms, it would amount to the maintenance of the organism in normal conditions as regards its fitness for the indispensable output of energy. The only justification to making a separate entry would refer to health insofar as it is impaired and has to be regained. Since all our entries are positive, sickness would not be appropriate. Since sickness is not a need biologically determined by its overse. Our entry, if it reads, "relief or removal of sickness or of pathological conditions", it is probably justified, insofar as this imposes certain limiting conditions on human societies, and elicits certain organised responses.

Malinowski constructed basic needs and cultural responses in fairly elaborate manner, consisting of an outline in column that could be read vertically and horizontally. The vertical reading would give an overview of the major institutions of a specific group, while the horizontal readings would reveal how these institutions were connected to particular cultural aspects. Thus, the family, as one institution, based upon the need for reproduction, could be related to its material aspects, to its kinship usages, its religious orientation, its political affiliation, and so on. In other words, Malinowski devised a general frame-work very suitable for systematic collection and organisation of field data, lending itself also to cross-cultural comparisons.

Under the cultural response *commissariat*, which deals with the direct satisfaction of nutritive need, we would find that human beings eat and drink not by direct resort to nature, not yet in isolation, not yet in-terms of mere anatomical or physiological performance. If we were to look at to the lowest primitives, to an Australian aboriginal tribe, to a small group of fire-landers or to a highly sophisticated American or European community, we would come upon facts of commensalism. People often eat together on a common mat, or on a piece of ground or on a table or eat in bar. In all this, we would find that the food had already been prepared, i.e. selected, cooked, roasted, and seasoned. Some physical apparatus for eating is used, table manner observed, and the social conditions of the act carefully defined. It would be possible to show that in every human society and as regards any individual in society, the act of eating happens within a definite institutions it may be household or family, commercial eating establishment or a hotel. It always is a fixed place, with an organisation for the supply of food or its preparation, and for the opportunity of consuming it. At the times, the kitchen is run separately, even in primitive communities, as when the food is cooked at home and sent for consumption to men's house or women's club. At time, the place where food is stored in a commercial or communal establishment. But even the transferring of food already produced to the final consumer is invariably done by a series of more or less complicated organised system of activities, i.e., institutions. The process of production, distribution, storage, cooking, taking etc. are the organised behaviour system and form the part of the tribal or national communissariat. Thus, the every efficiency of cultural response, provides human beings with food for the survival of individual and culture both.

Kinship, as cultural response of reproduction as basic need, condensed the procreative processes which, in human cultures, correspond to the brief pairing and reproductive phases in animal life. The main distinction between human and animal mating is, no doubt, biologically determined, as is the need of reproduction itself. The human infant needs parental protection for much longer period than does the young of even the highest anthropoid apes. Hence, no culture could endure in which the act of reproduction, i.e., mating, pregnancy, child birth was not linked up with the fact of legally founded parenthood, that is, the relation in which father and mother have to look after the children for a long period and in turn derive certain benefits for the care and trouble taken. What ever the form of the institution of family or marriage may be, but it culturally responses to procreation of children and their maintenance.

Shelter culturally satisfies the bodily comforts of human being from severe heat, cold, wind, heavy rain, etc. For this purpose, human beings have made houses and used different kind of clothes. For providing better and better shelter to human beings, culture has produced several organised activities or has established institutions, according to which the needs of bodily comforts are satisfied.

Protection is cultural response of the basic need safety. The organisation of defence against natural danger or cataclysm against animal attack or human violence, involves such institutions as the household, municipality, the clan, the age grade and the tribe. These institutions provide human beings with safety into different groups.

Activities are the cultural response of the need movement. This is a very general imperative imposed by human nature upon civilization. The satisfaction of this need is, as one would, essentially determined by the fact that without different orientation of nervous system and muscular action, man achieves nothing. Thus, the system of bodily activities connected with economics, political organization, exploration of the environment, contact with other communities, one and all are related to individual muscular tension and their surplus of nervous energy. On the other hand, they are all instrumental, i.e., directed towards the other needs.

The entry of *growth* indicates that a full cultural analysis in descriptive terms as part of a scientific theory, must project the whole gamut of cultural processes and products on to the life history of representative individual, or where there is substantial difference as regards class, caste or status, of a member of representative individual. Most ethnographic records give a description of various phases such as infancy, childhood, maturity and old age. The scientific point of view, however would insist on dealing not so much with generalised description of each phase, but rather with the manner in which the individual is gradually trained in skill, taught to use language and other symbolic devices of his culture, made to enter ever-widening set of institution of which, he will become a full member, when he reaches full maturity and assumes his share of tribal citizenship. The whole set of problems, now elaborated under the heading 'culture and personality' obviously enter here.

The entry hygiene is linked up with all that refers to organic welfare, in other entries. Thus, sanitary arrangement, discussed earlier, might be analysed here from the point of view of native's beliefs as to health and magical dangers. Besides such considerations, the ethnographer would have to reigster here, the minimum of elementary common sense, rules about exposure, extreme fatigue, avoidance of dangers, of accidents, as well as limited but never absent range of household remedies. In most of primitive cultures, however, this aspect of cultural response is primarily dominated by beliefs in witchcraft or sorcery, i.e., the magical power of certain people or agencies to inflict bodily harm upon man. Thus, culture has biological survival value. Its adaptive character is in part, due to the fact that basic needs, shared with other animals, provide the primary determinism. The conditions of man's life as social animal impose a secondary determinism. Malinowski defines it interms of 'derived needs' or 'Imperatives'. Derived needs or imperatives relate to the requirements of maintenance of cultural apparatus, regulation of human behaviour, socialisation, and exercise of authority. The responses to them comprise those of economics, social control, educational and political organisation. Malinowski's list of derived needs or imperatives and cultural responses is as follows:

Derived needs or Imperatives	*Cultural Responses*
1. The cultural apparatus of implements and consumers' goods must be produced, used, maintained and replaced by new production.	1. Economics
2. Human behaviour, as regards its technical, customary, legal or moral prescription must be codified, regulated in action and sanction.	2. Social Control
3. The human material by which every institution is maintained, must be renewed, formed, drilled, and proved with full knowledge of tribal tradition.	3. Education
4. Authority within each institution must be defined, equipped with powers, and endowed with means of forceful execution of its orders.	4. Political Organisation

Integrative Needs or Integrative Imperatives: To the sphere of integrative imperatives, belong the phenomena subsumed under such term as tradition (including a culturally recognised and transmitted social structure), normative standard or values, religion, mythology, art, ceremonial, as well as language and other forms of symbolism. The comprehensiveness of Malinowski's scheme becomes apparent, since under it can be subsumed the views of those who hold that the essence of human culture is to be found in symbolism or in values, as well as the important concept of social structure. Contrast, for example the behaviour of groups of baboons, as described by Zuckerman, with that of any human group. The former is determined by adventitious acts of individual or collective behaviour in which the impulses of individual such as hunger, sexual desire, or protection of self or offspring, determine stability or change in the relation between organism, mainly on the basis of physical dominance. Corresponding behaviour in human group is determined by a fixed systems of values, which defines how individual should or should not behave. These values are crystallized in a system of symbols, which enable individuals to evaluate the behaviours of others, irrespective of whether they are or are not themselves affected or involved. Finally, the relations between individuals are given permanence through such structural principle as kinship, age and rank.

The rules of conduct are known and transmitted by tradition. In the concept of charter, which is crucial to institutional analysis, the codes of constitutional rules, mythological ideas, values, provide and integrate the behaviour of an organised group.

All this still somewhat remains in the air, so long as such phenomena as language, oral tradition, the nature of some dominant dogmatic concepts, the way in which subtle moral values are incorporated into human behaviour, interms of cultural analysis are not defined clearly. Every one knows that all this is based primarily on verbal instruction or linguistic texts. i.e, on the whole realm of symbolism. Symbolism is an essential ingredient of all organised behaviour, that it must have come into existence with the earliest appearance of cultural behaviour. It is a subject matter which can be submitted to observation and theoretical analysis interms of objective facts, to the same extent to which we can oversee material artifacts, collective movement of group or define the form of a custom. The central themes maintained, here, is that symbolism in its essential nature, is modification of the original organism, which allows the transformation of a physiological drive into a cultural value.

Instrumentally Implemented Vital Sequence: The functional analysis of culture from the concept of vital sequence refers to relation between drive, its physiological consumption, and the state of organic satisfaction. It will be useful to incorporate new analysis into previous diagram.

Diagram of Instrumental Sequence

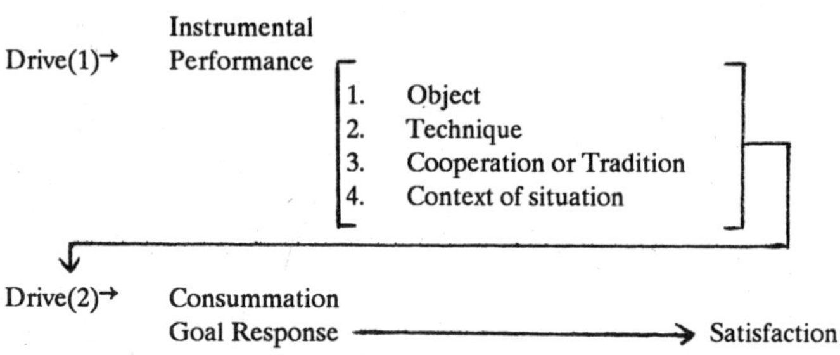

In the above diagram, the cultural equivalent of vital sequence has been represented. This represents the phase of human behaviour, which is typical of any and every activity connected with the satisfaction of need. The difference between this and previous diagram consists in the insertion of the instrumental performance, which becomes essential link in the pragmatic series. The entry drive has been duplicated and distinguished by numerical indices. This represents the fact that initial drive which sets in for all animal learning, in animal behaviour after the habit has been acquired and in all human cultural activities, leads not directly to the goal, but to the instrumentalities through which the goal can be reached.

Drive(2) represents the fact that after the instrumental phase had been adequately accomplished, of removal of pain or noxious bodily conditions, leads directly towards the physiological performance, whether it is positive or negative, the satisfaction of pleasure or removal of pain. It is also clear that reinforcement also refers to the situation, where the Drive (2) can be effectively satisfied. Since the instrumental performance is the integral part of the series, the reinforcement, or the psychologists call it as secondary reinforcement, becomes attached to the instrumental performance as a whole, and to all its component parts: the artifacts, the technique, the rules of cooperation, and the context of situation. All these elements become pervaded with the physiologically determined pleasurable tone. They become, in a derived or secondary manner, objects of desire. They become imbued with a pleasurable tone characteristics of successful execution of vital sequence. The organism, reacts to the instrumental-elements with the same appetitive force as it does to objects which reward it directly by physiological pleasure. This strong and inevitable attachment of the organism to certain objectives, norms or persons who are instrumental to the satisfaction of the organism's need, can be defined by the term value, in the widest sense of the word.

Symbolism means that something stands for something else. The sign or symbol contains in it an idea, an emotion or some other portion of the introspectively known substance of consciousness. Symbolism is founded not in a mysterious relation between the sign and the contents of human mind, but between an object, technical gesture, an action and its influence upon the receptive organism. Through the instrumental extension of vital sequence, an object, a technical gesture, the presence of another person, and his behaviour become calls or inducements to the performance of an instrumental activity. This diagram illustrates that the necessary implements or technique, or cooperative device, is gradually transformed into a pragmatic signal in the same way that food is a pragmatic symbol to hungry organism, or a female to male animal and *vice versa*, and water to thirsty or fire to cold. The inherent symbolism of instrumental performance is made public, adequate, permanent and transmissible.

Instrumental analysis of behaviour corresponds closely to the concept of institution and its component parts. The diagram, given above, contains as a definition of instrumental performance, the items, objects, techniques, the cooperation and transmission, as well as situation. In concrete sense, this means that human beings achieve their ends by using artifacts within definite environmental setting, by direct cooperation, which means re-enactment of establishment empirical processes and in all they followed the learned traditional techniques of their culture.

Comparing this with the diagram given in case of derived need or imperatives and cultural responses, we can see that material apparatus corresponds to environmental situation and object used directly. Techniques and rules of cooperations will be placed under the heading norms. The concept of cooperation refers to personnel, and so does that of traditional learning, because this can only be obtained through the fact of organisation.

The splitting of the drive into two components is necessary device of abstraction. It illustrates the fact that the drive is a necessary presupposition of the instrumental, as well as of any simple vital sequence. Drive is integral and it works right through the sequence, controlling all its phases, and invariably leading to the final stage, that is satisfaction. The device of splitting this concept, illustrates the fact that all elements in instrumental performance receive their value because initial stages of drive lead the conditioned organisms to the instrumental outfit, endowing it, thus, with the cultural value. Drive (2) which is directly based on organic impulse and reinforced by satisfaction, supplies the reinforcement to all the instrumental elements by being inseparably linked up with Drive(1).

The charter, which is traditionally established values, programmes and principle of organised behaviour, corresponds fully and directly to the concept of drive, in so far as this is culturally reinterpreted. This cultural reinterpretation, again means that drive operates in two fold manner, first by the establishment of value of the apparatus and instrumental quota in the performance, and then by reappearing as a culturally determined Drive (2), in leading to the culturally reinterpreted act of consummation.

To the entry activities, there corresponds clearly the instrumental series as a whole, in so far as it is observed in actual execution and not analysed into its constituent factors. The difference is that we observe in fieldwork, the constituent factors of the series in their ideal, traditionally defined form. In actual performance, we study them with all the inherent deviation, imperfections, and occasional failure. The concept of function, as appears in the diagram, refers not to a single performance, but to the same total of instrumentalities connected with all drives of a certain type. The function would mean here, the range of instrumentalities assessed with reference to the complex drives and manifold satisfaction of a need. This can be shown by the following diagram:

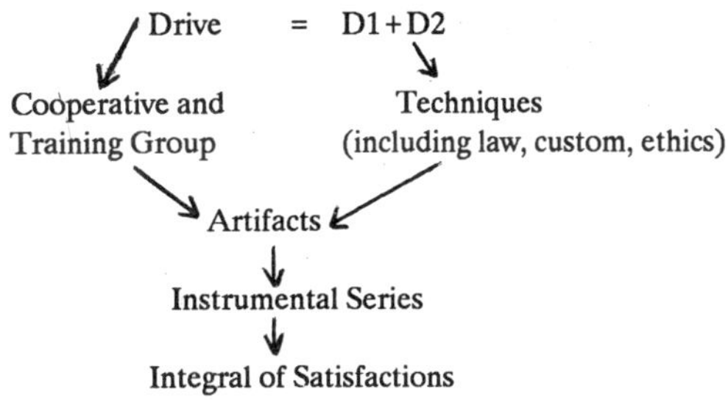

Some Contentious Points Related to Theory of Need: The theory of need as formulated by Malinowski, claims to provide a general basis for the understanding of human behaviour in all cultures, as well as conceptual instrument for the observation and recording of ethnographic data, but it would be surprising indeed if it were not open to question on several important points. The first of all is terminological. Malinowski was often inconsistent, even uncritical in his selection and use of terms. For the needs, which are called 'basic' in his posthumous work, he variously used in earlier expositions the term 'biological' and 'primary'. The last of these seems most satisfactory.

If Malinowski is correct in his contention that the 'derived' and 'integrative' imperatives, are just as necessary to the survival of human groups, as man's individual physiological requirements, then in a sense, the former, i.e., derived needs are just as 'basic needs'.

Malinowski is again inconsistent in the terms, which he applies in elaborating, three categories of needs, namely, 'basic needs' 'derived needs' or imperatives and integratives. Here, it seems better to use the term 'needs' throughout.

Another difficult question concerns the precise definition of different needs and minimum conditions necessary to their condition. But we must not become pessimistic about the future of definition of need. The need of the time is not to abandon the concept of need because of difficulty in definition, but to seek to define them with greater precision, which our present knowledge permits.

A more serious criticism concerns Malinowski's failure to state clearly the relation of certain needs to biological survival of individuals and groups.

Malinowski's theory of needs has also been criticised on the ground that it does not include human tendencies, which have been loosely subsumed under the term 'social appetite'. Perhaps this omission was part of Malinowski's protest against those vague even mystical, explanatory concepts, which have militated against searching for inquiry into complexities of human motivation. One recalls his structures on such concepts as social solidarity, group sentiment and Primitive Communism. One of the greatest contributions in this field was high insistence upon the empirical study of individualistic or egotistic elements in human motivation, and above all of social institutions through which they operate in specific cultures studied by field worker. But on this point, Malinowski may be accused of pouring out the baby with the bath water. In all cultures, human beings demonstrately seek association with their fellows, they strive for material and social rewards through that association. More so over, it is impossible to envisage the biological survival of a group from which such behaviour was absent.

This position has been argued by Ashley-Montague (1950-53) in presenting Malinowski's table of vital sequences in a slightly ammended form, adds the following basic needs:

				Satisfaction		
Physiological Tension	=	Urge of Need to	→	which leads To the Act of	→	Homeostatis
Feeling of non-dependency or aloneness	=	be with others	→	Physical contact, or association	→	Feeling of security of interdependency
General need or tension	=	express-ion	→	communication	→	Social recognition.

A point on which Malinowski has been extensively criticised is his contention that elements of culture do not survive unless they subserve some need, in other words, that there is no such thing as 'cultural lag'. The issue here really concerns the time span involved. Clearly, when a culture changes, as in contemporary culture contact, elements in it neither disappear over night nor change their function immediately to accord with new conditions. But Malinowski was thinking in term of a much longer time span. He was criticising the views of certain evolutionary school that elements of culture could survive through sheer inertia for century, long after they had ceased to serve any function. In this criticism, he was undoubtedly correct. But what is certain is that it would not survive indefinitely after it has ceased to satisfy any need, primary, derived or integrative. This should be obvious enough, and the real task is to define empirically, in terms of specific situations of social change, how long the elements of culture persists through cultural lag, how quickly they assume new function or soon they disappear?

In spite of these criticisms, the importance of Malinowski's theory of needs for contemporary anthropology rests on several bases. The first is operational and concerns the work of anthropological field workers.

Apart from few general surveys of cultures, modern ethnographers study culture as a wholes. They deal with the specific problems against the total cultural background. These problems are variable in their nature. An ethnographer may describe a particular system of activity such as Kula, or aspects of culture such as economics, religion, law, social organisation. Such studies are, in effect, concerned with the describing cultural responses to various derived and integrative needs. But the same can, and should be done with primary needs, particularly those for food and sex.

This aspect of Malinowski's theory has been naively criticised by Gluckman in the following terms:

> There appears to me to be little point in sending an anthropologist trained expensively and living at some cost in the field to Africa to find out that some Bantu tribe has a complex organisation to satisfy the need of its member for food, just as we have a complex organisation for this purpose (Gluckman, 1949:235).

This obvious comment is that there is no point in financing a field worker to discover that a Bantu tribe has a social structure. The task of field worker is always to describe in detail a defined system of human activities and interrelationship. The system connected with the satisfaction of primary needs is just as valuable a subject for the study as other and has been demonstrated in the work of Malinowski (1929) and Audrey Richards (1932). These studies reveal as to how different cultures not only satisfy, but also regulate and limit, the vital sequence underlying basic need. Apart from their purely anthropological importance as one way of arranging and analysing cultural data, they are of profound importance to psychologists, as demonstrating the different ways in which the raw material of human nature can be handled by different cultures.

Thus, it provides a basis for cooperations between psychologist and anthropologists. The concept of needs is identical with such psychological concepts as 'drives or instincts', which refer to individual motivation in particular situation or series of situations not to the total system of organisation of human groups. Human beings under their condition of culture wake up with morning appetite ready, and also with a breakfast waiting for them or ready to be prepared. From the psychological point of view, this situation is produced by a complex set of heterogeneous drives or motives of many individuals, such as the farmer, who produced food, the trader who sold it and the house-wife who cooked it. Broadly speaking, the psychologist is primarily concerned with the drives or motives of individuals, whether common to a group or idiosyncratic. To a large extent, he must take the context of institution within which these drives or motives operate as given. The social anthropologists, on the other hand, is primarily interested in the organisation of these institutions themselves, in the organised routine of satisfaction. The anthropological concept of needs is a biological as well as a psychological one, as pointed out earlier, needs are not coterminus with individual impulses.

To summarise, the theory of need is essential to a broad conception of biological and cultural determinants of human behaviour, to certain important phases of ethnographic research, and to the adequate development of social anthropology as a teaching subject. Furthermore, it provides one avenue by which some of the vital social problems facing humanity today may be approached. It attempts to answer some of the important questions, which people who are not anthropologists, insist on asking.

Malinowski's Theories of Law

Malinowski's conception of 'Law' has changed several times during the course of his career. Before conducting field research, he restricted the term 'Law' to social norms, which enjoy an organised, more or less, regulated and active social sanction. His basic premise was that all social organisation implies a series of norms, which extended over the whole social life and regulate more or less strictly all social relations. Different kinds of norms are enforced by different kinds of 'social' or 'collective' sanctions, and norms are classified according to their sanctions. For Australia, he distinguishes three main classes of norms:

(i) Religious rules or norms, the punishment of whose breach (sin) is supernaturally entailed by its very committal.
(ii) Customary rules or norms, whose breach (improper conduct) is punished by ridicule and social contempt.
(iii) Legal norms or rules, whose breach (crime) is punished by the decision of community, acting as a whole, or by its central organs or certain groups of it.

He emphasises that a given norm or rule is legal, if it is enforced by a direct, organised and definite social action. Without norms the social action would be mere violence. Without the social enforcement, the norm would be a moral or customary rule, so enforced, it may properly be called a law.

To make his definition plausible, he opines that Australian legal institutions correspond to what we call law and legal in higher societies. In his monograph on Mailu (1915), he is more cautious. He opines that, while describing native condition, it would be an obvious mistake to use such terms as law, legal, criminal, and civil law, in strict sense in which they are defined in jurisprudence. On the other hand, to use them loosely and without troubling as to their meaning would be essentially unscientific, because, in case of the field ethnologist, it would show that he has not been considering very carefully,, where to took for his facts and how to group them.

Following as closely as possible the conditions of native social life, he makes a distinction between civil law and criminal law. According to him, civil law comprises all rules governing social life. But elsewhere, he is more specific and narrow, when he opines that under civil law in a native society we can understand the set of rules regulating, all normal relations between persons, as kinship, marriage, economic co-operation and distribution, trading etc., and between persons and things and properly inheritance etc. These are the fundamental rules which must be observed. Their infraction in a lurking temptation and there are always individuals who succumb. As a preventative or reaction to this, there exist some measures of restriction and redness, broadly speaking some restraining forces. Thus, a distinction can be made between civil law and criminal law. *Civil law* is a set of rules regulating the social mechanism in its stationary normal course. Criminal law is the safety arrangements, putting things aright, whenever, there is any hitch in their normal course. The Mailu have no central authority, which would spontaneously and automatically deal with offenders, but there are various ways of reacting to murder, adultery, theft and evil magic, which he discusses under 'Rudimentary measures, corresponding to Criminal Law'.

In his writings on Trobriand Islanders, he discusses law in extensive detail and he returns to the fundamental rules of conduct. In his book Crime and Custom (1926), he refers loosely to *Primitive law* as the various forces which make for order, uniformity and cohesion in a savage tribe. Later on, he emphasizes that law is clearly distinguishable and distinguished by the natives from the other types of norms, whether moral, manner rules of art, or commands of religion, He holds view that in all societies, there must be a class of rules too practical to be backed up by religious sanctions, too burdensome to be left to mere good will, too personally vital to individuals to be enforced by any abstract agency. This is domain of legal rule. The rules of law standout from the rest in that they are left and regarded as the obligation of one person and the rightful claims of another.

In his book *Crime and Custom*, he defines civil law and criminal law comprehensively. According to him, civil law is class of binding rules, which controls most aspects of tribal life, which regulates personal relation between kinsmen and tribesmen, settles economic relations, the exercise of power and of magic, the status of husband, wife and their respective families. On the other hand, criminal law, is the fundamental rules safeguarding the life, property and personality. In this category, he also includes rules safeguarding such institutions as chieftainship, exogamy, rank and marriage. Civil law, in contrast to criminal law, is the law obeyed, not the law broken.

In his introduction to Hogbin's book entitled, *Law and Order in Polynesia* (1934), Malinowski stresses the importance of reciprocity, systematic incidence, publicity, and ambition, as the main factor in biding machinery in Primitive Law. Here, he discusses more fully the role of positive inducements, i.e., rewards of various kind in securing observance of the social norms, which was the most important aspects of functional theory of Primitive Law. It is very closely related to the fact that the most laws are the expression of some bound biological reality, of some important and functionally founded trend of culture.

He is no longer insistent upon establishing and maintaining a verbal distinction between law and other rules of conduct. He, sometimes uses law and custom interchangeable. He also emphasises upon the distinction between valid sanctioned customs and those that are neutral or indifferent. He refers law as one of the derived or instrumental needs, which in all societies have to be satisfied as urgently as biological requirements, if man is to survive. In his article on 'culture' (1931), he lists economic organisation and education among the instrumental imperatives or derived needs. In his book *Scientific Theory of Culture*, he stresses that training during childhood and youth, not merely compels general respect and obedience to tribal tradition, but also reveals to the individual, the consequences and penalties of deviation or breach.

In almost the last publication to appear during his life time (1942), Malinowski restated his view on law, in a manner superficially different from every thing before, but nevertheless repeating some earlier ideas. Asserting that in the study of law confusion has been created by the multiple meaning given to the main term. He seeks to introduce clearly by speaking of Law(1), Law(2) etc. He recognises four different meanings, which can be readily kept apart by contextual or adjectival distinction.

> *Law(1)* is, 'the law of cultural determinism'. Here the term law is used in the same sense as in phrase law of science, but with specific reference to natural laws of physical and biological process that effect human behaviour and determine the basic pattern of culture. Such

laws, the laws of science of culture can be formulated only by the scientific observer, although implicitly followed, are neither known nor stated by the native.

Law(2) is, 'the law or ruling native conduct'. It embraces rules of knowledge, technology, cooperation, common life and convention, all of which are standardized in behaviour or verbally formulated. They are automatically sanctioned by the coercion efficiency or by the conventions of conventionality. As they are not subject to tension and conflicts, they remain outside any socially organised enforcement.

Law(3) is, 'the law of order and maintenance'. It is also described as the law which is positively primed as baited, i.e., to which rewards for conformity are attached. It applies to rules of conduct which refers to relations between individuals and group, delimit divergent interests, and curtail disruptive physiological and sociological tendencies. It embraces most rules of property, contract, status, and authority as well as those protecting life and limb and defining sexual rights.

Law(4) is, 'the mechanisms of law when breach occurs'. It is defined as specific mechanism which is brought into existence, when a conflict of claims arises or a rule of social conduct is broken. It is also described as retributive and restitutive social action and as the more or less organised coercive reactions of a community, which are set in motion, when rule is broken definitely and conspicuously.

Law (1) is of no interest to jurisprudence. Law (2) corresponds to what he termed neutral or indifferent customs, Law (3) and Law (4) represent the two processes of maintenance of order and restitution or re-establishment, respectively. When we speak of law abiding community, we mean Law (3). When we say that Law has been brought in to action, we mean Law (4). Law (4) comes into being, when Law (3) ceases to work. As long as Law (3) reigns, there is no room for Law (4).

In the posthumously published book, *Freedom and Civilization* (1947), the four uses of the term is reduced to only two: Law(1) and Law(2), Law(1), intrinsic determinism of process or a phase of natural determinism, and Law(2), a promulgated command of authority sanctioned by force or human precept.

Malinowski's Contribution to Kinship Study

Kinship study has occupied significant place in anthropological theory and anthropologists were interested in it since the beginning of evolutional reconstruction. Evolutionists studied it to reconstruct the evolution of marriage, family, society, inheritance of property, state etc. In historical reconstructions of diffusionists, kinship also played significant role. Rivers books *History of Malenesian Society*, and *Kinship and Social Organisation* (both published in 1914), deal with the study of kinship. But these scholars were more interested in the study of kinship terminologies, what Malinowski called as *Kinship Algebra*. In the study of kinship terminology or kinship algebra, they emphasized too much on refinements and complexities of kinship terms. For Malinowski, the study of kinship terminologies, was nothing but the study of noun terms, denoting various kins. He was of opinion that we should not emphasize too much on language, but we should concern ourselves to those behaviour, rules, norms, usages which govern the kinship system functionally for the existence of the individual, culture and society.

In his biological foundation of culture, Malinowski puts kinship as a cultural response to reproduction as basic need. But it is also related to other derived need or instrumental imperatives. It deals with the study of such institutions as marriage, family, rules of property, rules of conduct, political authority, economic cooperation, etc. Thus, it should be studied, biologically, psychologically, culturally and socially. Many useful contributions in context of Malinowski's view on kinship systems have been discussed earlier, hence, it is useless to repeat them once again.

Malinowski's Contribution on Magic, Religion, Myth, Art and Science

Evolutionists have attempted to reconstruct the evolutionary sequence of religion. Tylor's evolutionary reconstruction of religion indicates what it has passed through the successive stages of animism, polytheism and monotheism. Belief in soul, animism, was the early form of religion from which belief in polytheism came into existence and monotheism was the present day form of religious belief. Sir James Frazer, in his book, *The Golden Bough* has supported Tylor's reconstruction of religion. He opined further that society has passed through three stages of development, i.e., magic, religion and science. The society in its early form was guided by magic, which gradually reached into next stage of development in which religion became the guiding force. With the enhancement of knowledge, the society reached in the scientific stage of development, which is present form of society. Haddon has attempted to trace the evolutionary sequence of art and opined that art as a whole, has passed through such developmental stages as realistic art, symbolic art and geometric art.

Contrary to these evolutionary views on evolution of science, art, magic and religion, Malinowski propounded a functional approach to the study of science, magic, myth, religion and art. He opined that they are the highest and most derived imperative of human culture. They are the third order of imperatives, i.e., integrative needs or synthetic imperatives. For him, magic, myth, religion, and art take their places along side of rational knowledge as the foundation of culture. Thus, they are instrumental for the existence of individual, man and society. Although less directly, these too can be traced to men's organic need. Of all living beings, man is the only animal, who can accumulate experiences, reflect on them, and use them to foretell the future. This capacities make man the tragic here that he is. They revel new possibilities and opportunities with each generation, but they also indicate his relative importance and leave him striving for more than he can rationally expect to obtain. *Science,* the system of knowledge, organises and integrates human activities, so that, the present and future can be made to better serve the needs of men, on the basis of past experiences. As man's knowledge is insufficient and subject of accumulation in each generation, the gaps between knowledge and power create anxiety and hesitation in him and he uses magic. Magic is employed as substitute for rational system, which gives him courage act, even without perfect knowledge. Myth enhances social tradition by endowing it with awesome and glorified beginning and thus, promotes, sustains and integrates appropriate social behaviour. Religion promotes individuals security and social cohesion by santifying human life and making public by dogma and ritual, the social contracts of cooperative existence. For Malinowski, art satisfies the carving of the human organisation for combinations of blended sense impressions, whether in the rhythm of bodily movements or in the blending of tones, colours, and forms. Major criticism levelled against the functional theory of science, magic, myth, religion, and art, was that his observations were mainly based on Trobriand islanders, but he made universal generalizations of these aspects of culture, strait from Trobrianders to Humanity.

Malinowski, defines magic as a body of purely practical acts, performed as means to an end. In this definition of magic, he has emphasized upon the practical or applied aspects of magic. Human beings attempt in many ways to fulfil their various needs related to daily life, on the basis of knowledge and skill. But sometimes, such a situation comes in to existence, when their knowledge, skill and attempt become failure to achieve the goal or desires. In this circumstance, they want to achieve desired goals with the aid of superhuman or supernatural powers, which governs the nature of man. It is in this very situation, that magic comes into being to achieve the end as a means. From this definition, it also appears that the magicians by magical acts try to please the superhuman power or supernatural powers to fulfil the needs of man kind.

Elements of Magical Acts: Malinowski has explained four elements of magical acts, which are: spell, material, technique or method and expression of emotions. *Spell* is very essential element for magical act. Without spell (*mantra*) a magician cannot achieve his end. On the basis of enchanting spell, a magician gets command over superhuman powers and compel them to fulfil the desired goal. Magical acts as spell have three characteristics: first, a magician in course of enchanting spell, follows some natural voices which create causes for the fulfilment of acts. This is based on the principle that 'like produces like'. Second, in spell some such words are used, which reveal the present situation and make order for the fulfilment of ends. In spell, the names of those ancestors are recited from whom a magician learns the magic.

Material: In order to perform magical acts some special kind of physical materials are used. For instance, flowers, dyes, turmeric, dub grass, kush grass, sun fried rice, ash, bone, water of sacred rivers or wells.

Technique: Magical acts are performed through following series of techniques or method one after the other. The magician has adequate knowledge by which act is performed first and in next following steps. If this technique is not followed, it will not yield the desired goal.

Expression of Emotion: In magical act, the magician expresses emotions in the same manner, following the objectives of the magical performance so that fulfilment of end may get strong force. For instance, if magical acts are performed to harm anyone, the magician has a sense of anger on his face.

Classification on Magic: Malinowski divides magic into two classes: white magic and black magic. *White magic* has social acceptance. It is used for the benefit of others or community as a whole. By white magic, magician obliges others, because white magic is guided by the sentiment of welfare. Malinowski divides white magic in two categories: first, those white magic, whose aims are to save human beings from the uncertainty of life and dangers, for instance, Trobriand Islanders, before making a departure for fishing, perform many magical acts so that they may be saved from the imagined dangers incourse of fishing. Second, those white magical acts by which a magician show such miracles as events, which are beyond the hope of common man. For instance, in the situation of starvation or spread of disease, a magician performs such magical acts to save the human beings from starvation or disease as miracles. His miraculous acts cause rain to fall and removing diseases.

Black magic, on the other hand, has no social acceptance, it is associated with harmful activities in which others are put to troubles of various kind including deaths. The magicians, who perform black magics, are looked down in the society with the vision of fear and doubts. Malinowski has included the acts of sorcery (*Mantra-Tantra*) and Witchcraft (*Bhut, Pret, Daine* etc.) under the heading black magic. Black magic or love magic comes from the natural human reactions to frustrated hate and important anger.

Malinowski opines that belief in magical power rests on inherited myths, which are full of description of magical feats. Equally, magic also creates and constantly replenishes its own running mythology of magical miracles, which relates all presumed magic success that can be remembered, and hence, in advance validates any future magical effort. Thus, if myths testify to the efficacy of magic, any contemporary act which seems to bear out such beliefs, in turn testifies to the authenticity of myth. The magic is a link between mythical tradition and the present day, while myth provides the foundation for a system of magic. Which ever way one looks at the circle, it justifies the assertion that whenever magic appears in institutionalised form, an appropriate mythology will also be present. But the nexus between the two is even closed. For the myth is said to crystallise into magical formulae, as the magical spell, in turn is always an occasion for mythological illusions.

Malinowski views religion from the all embracing perspective of human fate and destiny. On the basis of his observation among Trobriand Islanders, he defines religion as a means to free human mind from fears and emotions. He observed religion of Trobrianders contributing functionally to human beings or society in removing tensions and emotions, protecting norms and values, assisting in maintaining moral order, inserting the sense of unity, functioning as an agency of social control, inducing the sense of security and developing virtues such as love, pety, sympathy, honesty, truth, non-violence etc.

Similarities and Differences Between Magic and Religion: Malinowski makes a clear-cut opinion on similarities and differences between magic and religion. Magic and religion are alike in that both arise from emotional stress, from felt crisis of life, and from the realization that man's control of the universe, by reason and empirical skill, is tragically limited. They are alike also, in that both have their mythology, their miracles, and the taboos and observances separating the sacred from profane. Though they represent as escape from the impose of human importance, but they differ radically, in the nature of escape they afford.

Magic is characterised by limited technique and practical orientation, religion is a body of self-contained acts, complex and rich in content, and expressing itself in rituals and beliefs which have value not utility. Magic rests in simple trust in efficacious spells and rites, religion commands the whole supernatural world of faith, with a patheon of gods, spirit and, benevolent powers. While the mythology of magic only boasts of primeval achievements, religious mythology turns into cosmogony and opens vistas of a future life. Magic is in the hands of specialists-technicians as it were. Regarding the science, he opines that it is a logical coherent body of empirical knowledge, but merely technology and disconnected items of practical knowledge are not sufficient to sustain it. When he says, we know now that primitive humanity was aware of scientific laws of natural process, this is simply untrue. What primitive people are aware of are scattered facts about natural processes, which can be turned to practical use. They have not where reached the notion of scientific laws, or any other conception meriting the name of science. At least they have not done so in the stage of profane behaviour.

Similarities Between Magic and Science: However, he opines on the similarities and differences between science and magic in following ways:

1. Both magic and science are based on some definite laws. In other words, both follow systematically the laws to conduct their acts.
2. Both use special technique for their purpose.
3. Both accept the existence of natural laws.
4. Both accept, more or less, the difference of cause-effect and action of impersonal cause as mechanical.
5. Both assist in the fulfilment of human needs.
6. Both believe in law of contact and natural law and their unchangeability.
7. Both to some extent have the efficiency of making predictions.
8. Scientific and magical acts are performed by special persons, who are termed as scientist and magician respectively.

Differences Between Magic and Science: In spite of these common virtues, they also differ from each other to a great extent. The main differences between magic and science, according to Malinowski, are as follows:

1. Science even as represented by the primitive knowledge of Savage man, is based on the normal, universal experience of every day life, experience won in man's struggle with nature, for his subsistence and safety, founded on observation fixed by reason. Magic is based on specific experience of emotional states in which man not observes nature but himself, in which the trust is revealed not by reason, but by the play of emotions upon the human organism.

2. Science is founded on the conviction that experience, effort and reason are valid, Magic on the belief that hope cannot fail nor deceive.
3. Science is based on facts, whereas in magic, wonder, hope, despair, uncertainty prevail.
4. Magic is related to supernatural world while science deals with natural world.
5. Science accepts natural causes. In order to arrive at a particular conclusion, it takes help of observation, test. verification processes, which are done in laboratories, but magic images mysteriously divine causes and is performed in a mysterious environment. There is no laboratory to verify the inferences in magic, but they are the result of individual experiences. Sometimes magical usages and actions bring pre-expected result. In this situation, cause-effect relation is established and their result is true like science. Thus, magic becomes close to science and is termed as 'imitating science'.
6. Failure of science is due to inadequate knowledge which can be restored on the basis of further researches. The defeat in magic is caused either because magician does not observe taboos in established manner, or some other magician has made it unsuccessful by counter-magical acts.
7. In science, scientists follow some steps prescribed for scientific processes. They do not follow any taboo, while doing so. But in magic, magicians have to follow some taboos as essential part of magical performance.
8. Magic is related to primitive societies and science to modern or civilized societies.

Malinowski's Contribution on Economic Anthropology

According to Karl Marx, Man has three essential fundamental needs, namely, food, cloth and shelter, which are to be satisfied in order to maintain physical existence in the world. In order to satisfy these needs man performs various kind of activities. If they are not satisfied, the survival of man's and his social life will be in question. The activities carried out in course of fulfiling these needs, give rise to economy. He builds technology, uses it for production. Things produced are consumed. But he does not carry on the work of production alone, he takes help of his family members, his community members and his village members. Thus, production is dependent upon cooperation. In this way, things produced are to be distributed among other members, who participate in production. One individual family, or a group or a community can not produce all things. They are also dependent upon others, who produce other kinds of things. As a result of this, the system of exchange comes into being, by which things produced in one group reached in another group. Thus, the system of production, consumption, distribution and exchange makes economic life of man in action and gives birth to economy or economic organisation. Economic anthropology, studies the economic organisation of primitive societies, in which emphasis is laid on the activities and behaviour of individuals, groups, communities in the processes of production, consumption, distribution, exchange, property right, division of labour, reciprocity, trade etc. Now, let us see Malinowski's contribution on economic anthropology.

There is paradox in Malinowski's contribution to economic anthropology. At an early stage of his work, he wrote, "There is no other aspects of primitive life, where our knowledge is more scantly and our understanding more superficial than in Economics". This view is less true now and most of the credit for leading a way to a better appreciation of economic anthropology is due to Malinowski himself, though the knowledge of formal economics was always very limited. His approach to economic analysis began on a descriptive common sense level and for the most part continued to be unsophisticated. But we can value to his own work and stimulus, which he gave to the work of others in this field in terms of three things: (i) his first hand field investigations with their specific consciousness of economic implications, (ii) sincerity of his concrete exposition and (iii) his concern with the relations between economic and other aspects of the social system and with economic phenomena in themselves.

His concern with social context of economic phenomena, was due probably to the fact that his knowledge of economics and its emergence in economic anthropology was derived from the working sociologists, among whom mentioned may be made of Hahn, Schurtx, Cunow, Lewinski, Bucher, Thurnwald, Max Weber and Koppers. While Karl Bucher had a very considerable impact upon his presentation, from other writers he drew inspiration largely by reaction.

From this and analogous prepositions, Malinowski proceeded to the establishment of a number of positive analysis. Through such corrections of fallacies, he demonstrated the following points:

1. The assumption of primitive man as a being purely rational, utilitarian and logical in his economic affairs, was a grave error. Social convention, social restriction and the principle of social structure dictate much savage economic behaviour.

2. Among Australian aborigines, the Mailu, the Trobrianders, there was economic organisation. Hence, no pre-economic stage was likely among many modern primitive peoples.
3. So far from being indolent, individually self-seeking and irresponsible in his economic affairs, the Savage was capable of long and arduous work.
4. Contrary to common view, Savages had highly organised and systematic form of labour.
5. Trade and exchange among primitive communities were by no means necessarily rudimentary, but could be regular, elaborate, and complex, both in operation and as regards their stimuli.
6. Concepts of primitive ownership were not to be defined either by group attributions of communism, or by individual exclusive possession, but in terms of multiple rights of groups and individual.

His works dealing with the subject-matter of economic anthropology are as follows:

1. *The Economic Aspects of Intichuima Ceremonies* (1912).
2. *The Family among Australian Aborigines* (1913)
3. *The Natives of Mailu* (1915)
4. *Fishing in the Trobrian Islands* (1918)
5. *Kula: The Circulating Exchanges of Valuables in the Archipelagoess of Eastern New Guinea* (1920)
6. *The Primitive Economics of the Trobrian Islanders* (1921)
7. *Argonauts of Western pacific* (1922)
8. *Coral Gardens and Their Magic: A Study of the Methods of Tilling the Soil and of Agricultural Rites in Trobriand Islands* (1935)

In his essay for the Westermarck Festsskrift (1912), Malinowski deals with the study of labour cooperation, while describing the economic aspects of 'Intichuima Ceremony'. Here, the value of the treatment is three-fold. This essay provides us with material such as economics as theme in conjunction with ritual, anthropological concept of labour and the role of totemism as providing economic incentives. In a sense, the essay was contra-Frazer. Frazer had concluded that chief function of totemism lays in an elementary division of labour, this economic function was not of great importance. Malinowski, on other hand, argued that there was little or no real division of labour in totemic field but there were very important economic functions in the way in which intichuima ceremonies promoted economic ends, in particular arduous collective labour of an organised kind.

His next publication, *Australian Aborigines* (1913) deals with the economic analysis of the activities of the primitive people. He has examined the nature of property right, including those of land, and the division of labour on sex basis. He examines the economics of individual family and, thus, relates social structure and economic organisation. He observes that the division of labour within the household or family, which established the unity of social group from the economic point of view. He observes that sexual aspect of marriage should not be exaggerated and also brings out the fact that the role of women among the aborigines invites hard work to the maintenance of family as an economic unit. He opines that the division of labour between sexes in aboriginal society depends also upon sociological factors. He observes work done by aboriginal women as repulsive in that it differs most essentially from spot. He regards it as carried on only from strong compulsion by men and backs this up with the reference by the reference to the terrorism of women by the initiated males.

His field report on Mailu (1915), a strait forward ethnographic account, has some interesting data on economic material. Here, he examines Mailu's agrarian laws with some pertinent caution on the use of legal conceptions of ownership. He says that the correct course was to investigate all the rights enjoyed exclusively by individuals or groups with regard to particular portion of land. Such rights are not to be found concentrated in one and the same legal person. He has also given data on the use and ownership of canoes with details of price for hire, composition of crews, routes cargo, and handling of trading expeditions. He also gives some considerations to incentives for labour and its organisation in gardening, hunting and fishing.

Malinowski's article on fishing (1918) has only a few notes on the economics of ownership and distribution of catch. But by 1920, he is seen analysing his material on economic aspects of culture and crystalising his views. In the summer term of that year, he gave a lecture on Primitive Economics of Trobriand Islander's in London School of Economics and published a preliminary account of the 'Kula' as a special system of trade in (1920). He provided us a detailed account of 'Kula gift ceremonial exchange' in his book, *Argonauts of Western Pacific* (1922).

Kula Exchange: As referred to earlier, Malinowski conducted his field researches among the Trobriand Islanders, consisting of four major matrilineal tribes, namely, Papua, Mailu, Massiun and Pygmy of New Guinea. Among Trobriand Islanders, he observed the system of barter exchange termed as Kula. Kula barter exchange takes place through gifts, hospitality, and trade. This system of exchange is found among the aborigines of New Guinea, Trobriand Islands, Amplett Island, Loughlan

Island and Dobu. The culture of these aborigines are quite different from one another, but they are tied together by Kula gift exchange. Kula has not only economic function, but it is also significant from the ceremonial point of view. In fact, it is a complex whole of economic, social, political, cultural, magical, religious, recreational and communicational values.

Kula is a ceremonial exchange participated in by inhabitants of a close circle of islands as mentioned above. The objects concerned in this cycle of exchange are of no practical use or commercial value. The object concerned in the exchange are of two types which circulate in clock-wise and anti-clock-wise directions. These objects are: (i) Red shells necklaces termed as 'Soulawa' and (ii) white arm-shell bracelets called as 'Mwali'. These two types of valuable rotate in opposite directions, as gifts exchange between partners of Kula ring. Soulava always moves in clock wise direction, whereas Mwali moves always in anti-clock wise direction. Every participant has two kinds of partners, those from whom he receives Soulawa and to whom he give Mwali and those from whom he receives Mwali and to whom he gives Soulawa. This can be understood better from the diagram given below.

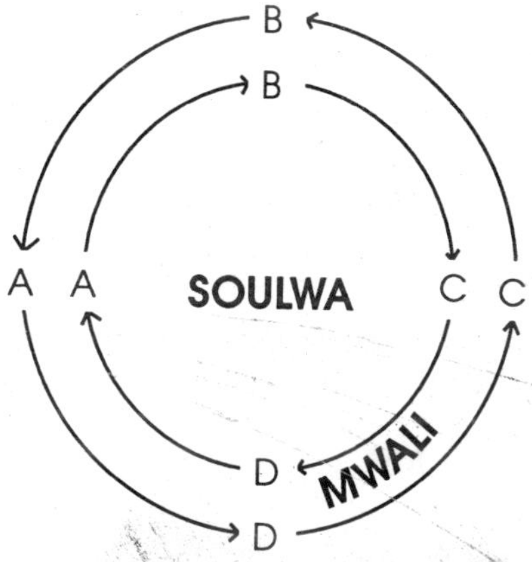

A gives Soulava to B and receives Mwali from him and again he gives Mwali to D and receives Soulawa from him. In this way, the objects of Kula circulates from one to other groups in a circular manner. Objects of Kula are not delayed in the process of exchange for a long time. Kula exchange may take place in four ways:

(i) between the individuals of the same community,
(ii) between inhabitants of two neighbouring islands,
(iii) between two neighbouring communities across of sea without organising ceremonies,

(iv) between communities across sea by organising ceremonies.

Though the ornaments of Kula exchange have no commercial value, they differ greatly in prestige value and its a matter of pride to have or dispose of a good piece. There is no bargaining or haggling about Kula gifts and a return for the gift may or may not be made at once, but after the laps of a year or two they are returned definitely. Kula relationship functions on the principle that 'once in Kula is always in Kula'.

Now question arises, if Kula system of institutionalised exchange is not economic, what functions it performs? Malinowski answers this by showing as to how Kula is bound up with a great many other social activities and values, which are as follow:

(i) Like all ceremonial activities, it has an expressive aspect, participation in Kula is an indication of social status: To possess many partners and to handle exceptionally valuable pieces, is to enhance one's social standing in community.

(ii) Kula involves such other activities as Canoe making, and these in turn, entail important cycles of economic and magical activity. When Trobriand islanders, making new canoes, proceed for meeting Kula relations, a grand scene can be observed, in which they perform various kinds of magical and religious acts. New canoes are constructed, and old ones are repaired. The journey may be more than hundred miles.

(iii) Although Kula valuables are themselves not traded, but there is trading on Kula expedition and Malinowski notes the contrast between the bargaining and haggling that takes place, when ordinary goods are bartered and exchanged in the formal ceremony of Kula exchanges.

(iv) The possession of Kula partner or partners in foreign countries provides protection from the dangers, which are to be expected, which are expected there from both human and the spirit inhabitants. This leads to the final point, as Mauss in his celebrated *Essai Sur Le dou*, states that the Kula is a means to social integration. It brings people into institutionalised relationship with other people, and so in some sense, makes them member of one society.

Every body cannot participate in Kula journey. Women are excluded completely, but they look after children and other properties in house. Thus, only male can proceed for Kula journey. These males may be inhabitants of a single village or some neighbouring villages, which are controlled by the same chief or *Mukhia*. It is chief, who takes courage to bear the expenses on Kula journey and provides guidance to Kulla-travellers. Every body will not be accepted as a member of Kula journey. Only those who have a recognised post in village with adequate magical knowledge can become member of Kula journey. Sister's sons become member of maternal uncle's Kula group. Sometimes, wife of chief or *Mukhia* also takes part in such Kula exchange, but generally women and children are excluded from it. As it involves long canoe voyages from one islands to another, Malinowski called his book *Argonauts* for they also set out on a long sea-voyage for economically useless objects.

Wasi: Malinowski has explained a similar system of exchange, like Kula, known as Wasi among the Trobriand islanders. In Trobriand Islands, inhabitants of villages situated on costal areas and inside the islands exchanged their things through the system of Wasi exchange. The inhabitants of costal villages are not permitted to carry out agriculture and the inhabitants of inside villages are not allowed for fishing. That's why both these groups exchange their things produced among each other. After harvest, inside villagers exchange their agricultural produce with costal villagers. The agricultural produce is termed as 'Yam'. For Yam they receive fishes. The fishing communities distribute Yam among their members and agricultural communities distribute fishes among their members. Wasi differs from Kula in the sense that in latter cultural materials are exchanged, which cannot be consumed, but in case of former consumable things like 'Yam' and 'fish' are exchanged. These two things are exchanged through barter system. The system of distributing fishes and Yam among the members is termed as 'Sagali'.

Urigubu System: The system of Urigubu reveals the processes of transfer of cultural materials obtained in Kula relation from one individual or group to other individual or group. Among Trobriand islanders, it is custom for brothers to send three-fourths portion of agricultural produce to their married sister's husband's once in a year. This is termed as the system of 'Urigubu'. This is a system of gift presented by brother's family to sister's family.

An another system of gift is *Pokala*. When a person presents something to the chief or *Mukhia* of the village, it is termed as *Pokala*. The chief, in turn, provides him political and religious services, which is termed as *Youla*. The objects presented in *Youla* are usually Kula valuables, which are not significant economically but are of great value socially.

In this way, gift, hospitality, trade, which comes under the exchange system of Trobriand islanders, reveal the principles of 'Reciprocity' and 'Allocation' of Trobrianders'.

Malinowski's book *Coral Gardens and Their Magic* (1935) deals with the methods of tilling soil and agricultural rights in Trobriand Islands. He has dealt with the economic role of magic in guiding gardening and agricultural activities of Trobrianders. The garden magicians give stimulus to production by their supervision of certain activities such as fencing, which were of general importance for the garden. They regulated the pace of work by inaugurating its successive stages. They set standard of quality by his control of certain key plots for magical purposes. By their imposition of taboos, they give specific sanction to work performance. Here, thus, he sees the relation of magic to economic activities.

In this way, Malinowski has given immense stimulus to parallel analyses to other primitive economic systems with a low technological content. He has opened up some of the basic problems such as problems of organisation of economic effort, of material incentives compared with those of social status and prestige, of relation of political and ritual leadership to entrepreneurship, in economic affairs, of the use of social symbols, of the subtle compounding of rights in ownership, or complexity of primitive market operations and the character of collective economic action in its social context.

Malinowski's Views on the Study of Social Change

Malinowski did not attempt to account for origin of institutions or other cultural items, not only because he felt that they could not be discovered, but also because they were unnecessary for the functional analysis and explanation. He was not interested in causality, but in utility. His concern was not with past, but with here and now. In his earlier years, he had followed the then fashionable trend of debunking historical explanations, but, later on, he admitted that history presented a different approach. History attempted to explain how cultures had become and what were they now. But Malinowski through his functional approach wanted to know why they existed in present form. It was not so much question of history, but of its relevance for the understanding of present day functioning of the societies. Thus, Malinowski, did not consider the two approaches — Diachronic and Synchronic — in compatible or mutually exclusive. They were, rather, complementary and inevitably correlated. Malinowski was, thus, not anti historical as is often maintained, but he was influenced by positivism and frowned upon speculations. It was true enough that evolutionists had been conjectural and their reconstructions about origins were not verifiable by scientific method.

Malinowski insisted on relegating the method of evolutionary anthropology to a minor role in the analysis of culture. Cultural processes are the subject to laws, but laws are to be found "in the function of real elements of culture", not in "survivals" upon which evolutionists reconstruct the stages and process of culture. Malinowski was convinced that 'there exists scientific law of culture' which can be verified and hypothesised by the fieldwork technique. The scientific laws of culture, or cultural laws are the relations that exist between individual needs and social institutions, which can be studied through comparative study of cultures in which individual is seen in his day to day adaptation, both physical and mental.

Diachronically-oriented schools of evolution and diffusion were also interested in the study of culture change through comparative methods. Malinowski's criticism of these theories was not concerned for their adequacy for the analysis of change, indeed, his insistence on the interpretation of institutions in terms of their contemporary significance, would logically have precluded an attack from this angle.

He emphasized upon the significance of time, i.e., of change for the analysis of culture. He held views that it could be shown that evolutionary or diffusional processes happen, first and foremost, in the form of institutional change. Whether in the form of invention or as an act of diffusion, a new technical device becomes incorporated into an already established system of organised behaviour, i.e. institution, and produces gradually a complete remodelling of that institution.

In terms of our functional analysis, we can show that no invention, no revolution, no social or intellectual change ever occurs except when new needs are created. In this way, new devices in technique, in knowledge, or in belief are fitted in to the cultural processes or institutions. Thus, culture is not static, but dynamic. From dynamic point of view, a culture can be analysed into a number of aspects such as education, social control, economics, system of knowledge, belief and morality and also mode of creative and artistic expression.

Malinowski defined culture as an integrated whole. Differences in traditions, customs, beliefs, ideas, institutions etc. were regarded as reducing conflict and tensions and, thus, contributed to the maintenance of whole, or else they had psychological function. Societies were viewed as if they were well-oiled machine, whose various parts were generally depicted as working well and contemporaneously. Though strange customs or institutions, such as canabolism, infanticide etc. were viewed as reducing tensions and conflicts, but why conflicts arose in the first place remained unexplained. This was lack of dynamism.

It could be asked, whether the posited functional integration of cultural whole, itself a verifiable hypotheses. If cultures are such well-functioning integrated wholes, why do they change. Malinowski was fully aware of this fact and he began to answer it in a variety of ways. In first place, he attributed change to diffusion, more particularly, the impact of a higher active culture upon a simpler more passive one. But this answer provided no answer as to why people should accept elements of the higher culture. Malinowski added that some small communities which so far had little contact with Western civilization were in temporary state of adjustment, and thus, could be considered as integral wholes. Moreover, even if, missionaries, traders, western administrators were present the society had also adjusted to them, and yet had remained a balance whole. In other words, Malinowski did not explain how change came about but proposed that once a simple non-western society was invaded, the interaction or contact between the two, especially the responses of the natives, could be studied and analysed under culture change or social change. Thus, he remained present oriented. It is because of this fact that his functionalism is also known as synchronic functionalism. The changes of the past were of little concerned, but the actuality of on going culture contacts and their results were valuable and important topic of research.

In his posthumous publication, *Dynamics of Culture Change: An Inquiry in to Race Relations in Africa* (1945), he prescribed a three-column approach to analyse the process of culture change, in which facts could be presented and connections could be brought out. In this three-column approach, the contributions of two cultures in contact-conceived always as those of an empirical power and its colonial subjects — were listed under separate headings, while between them stood the new cultural reality resulting from their interaction. Not only did he regard institutions as the significant cultural realities, but he saw the process of cultural change as an interaction of institutions. He held that organised system of European activities must be coordinated directly with corresponding phenomena of change.

Malinowski's theory of cultural change was a general one, but was concerned with the impact of industrialization on peasant societies. His illustrations were drawn from Africa and largely from the research carried out by his students. He remarked that culture change in Africa does not differ profoundly from that which is at present transforming the rural and backward communities of Europe from peasant communities into a new type closely akin to the proletariat found in industrial districts of United States, England and France.

Malinowski and other Anthropologists Views on Applied Anthropology

During 18th century, political philosophers had started studying the primitive societies. Many courageous travellers also provided informations on them. Due to industrial revolution, European countries in general and England in particular, began to contact people of other places to obtain raw material for their industries and to sell produced goods to them. They moved in Asia, Africa and distant places in eastwards. In order to protect business and trade interests politically, they attempted to establish imperialism and colonialism. New countries were searched for and made under their rule. It was necessary for these countries to know the customs, traditions, beliefs, values, language etc. of the people of those other countries, which were made under rule. Thus, many administrators incharge of the area under rule, produced a good amount of writing and publications on primitive people. Christian missionaries also became involved to study the socio-religious life of primitives from the point of view of attracting them towards Christian religion. Thus, the original source of knowledge about primitives came in to being with the attempts of travellers, traders, administrators and Christian missionaries.

In the middle of 19th century, evolutionary theory of anthropology came into being, whose pioneers were Tylor in Britain and Morgan in America. Tylor defined anthropology as a science of cultural history and reformists. He was definitely of opinion, while using it as a science of reformists, that anthropological knowledge should be utilised to bring reformation in the society. But applied aspects of anthropology was not taken into consideration till the period of 1920.

Applied anthropology was born in the year 1921, when third insurrection among Ashanti of West Africa took place. Before this event, both government and people were unaware of the fact that anthropological knowledge could be utilized for solving the problems of various kind. The king of Ashanti community used two stools at the time of sitting in his court. On one of the tools, he took up his seat, while on other he placed his hands. The second stool, upon which the king put his hands, was covered with gold. It was regarded as very sacred, common soul of entire community and divinely communicated. Thus, a great value was attached to that stool, for Ashanti community. In the year 1886, a struggle between British administrator and Ashanti took place. British administrators thought that they must possess the stool, which was status and power symbol of Ashanti community, with a view to make them under British control. Ashanti reacted against such British administrator's attitude. In 1921, a government anthropologist, Captain Pattray, was used to resolve the crisis between Britishers and administrators. He studied the value system of Ashanti and gave them full freedom to possess the stool, and persons found guilty of stealing gold of the stool were ordered for banishment. This incidence helped much in establishing the utility of applied anthropology.

Malinowski, on the basis of functional approach for the analysis of culture, attempted to broaden the scope of applied anthropology. He was of opinion that each custom performs certain function for the satisfaction of needs of individuals. Culture is instrument which helps in the fulfilment of needs, which may be basic, derived or integrative. It is culture, which makes man free from mere biological animal and it provides efficiency for the fulfilment of basic needs. It is because of culture that man becomes successful in a maintaining his physiological and social existence. From the functional view of culture, the utility of applied anthropology comes in being clearly. According to him, anthropology should be used for making the life of man and society easier, simpler and pleasant. Radcliffe-Brown also held the similar view regarding the scope of applied anthropology.

Wester Marck was of opinion that the scope of applied anthropology should cover the collection, analysis and interpretation of cultural facts.

Raymond Firth was of opinion that it is the work of applied anthropologist to bridge up the gap between primitive and civilized societies. Thus, applied anthropology should study the problems created by cultural or civilizational contacts among the aboriginals, and to suggest valuable means to save them before the situations become explosive. Firth has accepted applied anthropology as 'social Engineering', but he has admitted that anthropologists can not do the work of policy-making.

Kluckhohn held view that the scope of applied anthropology is like social medicine, not like social Engineering. Applied anthropologists should work like a social doctor, who makes proper treatment for removing social diseases. He was of opinion that policy decision and reconstruction was the work of administrators not of applied anthropologists.

Expressing his opinion on the scope of applied anthropology, Evans Pritchard held view that applied anthropology can not be regarded as practical science as applied medicine and Engineering. Those, who treat applied anthropology as applied medicine and Engineering, they treat applied anthropology as natural science, whose aim is to establish laws of social life, and once theoretical equation is established, the establishment of applied science is possible. Political philosophers of 18th century and ethnologists of 19th century, and many modern anthropologists have accepted natural science as their ideologies and have admitted that anthropology provides social control to social change through prediction.

Evans Pritchard held view that no science of society could be established like natural science. Till now, we do not have established any sociological laws, we can not use them as applied natural science. He opines further that this can not be meant that social anthropology can not become of applied value. His chief concern was that it can not be as practical science, as medical and engineering, from the applied point of view. Social anthropology is an ordered and arranged storage of knowledge about primitive societies. Anthropological theories and knowledge can be great value in solving social and political problems.

Nadel held view that anthropological studies are concerned not only with the studies of primitive cultures and their problems, but they can also be valuable for understanding our own present day problems, i.e., the problem of civilized societies. Anthropology can be of great help to administrators and showing relationship between different cultural groups. Nadel opines that anthropologists must take care of it that their anthropological knowledge should not be misutilized. African government had misutilized anthropological knowledge in supporting the policy of racial differences. He was of opinion that anthropologists should undertake researches of applied value, but not as a technician, but as simple individual who takes part in policy decision and social reconstruction. He has treated social engineering as area of study of applied anthropology.

In India too, applied anthropology is used in policy decision. Verrier Elwin was closely associated with Panchsheel Programme of late Prime Minister, Pandit Jawaharlal Nehru. Many eminent anthropologists are serving on different prestigious posts in ministry of welfare and scheduled castes and scheduled tribe commission. Many problem oriented studies are carried out by the anthropologists of our nation. Applied anthropology is being used in administration, resolving ethnic crisis, maintaining national integration, maintaining communal harmony, industrial field, medicine, tribal problems, backward class problems, criminal behaviour, etc.

Conclusions

Malinowski, the man of song, as Trobrianders called him, is no more with us. But after going through a good deal of discussion on his views on various areas of social anthropology and functional methodology, it appears that he was one of the founders of modern anthropology. It is the strength of functionalism that its generalizations are firmly rooted in direct observation of processes of interaction among the people. Function-oriented field researches have provided a great deal of penetrating ethnographic descriptions. The analysis of integration and interrelations between institutions have given many penetrating insights into the ways in which societies operate and maintain themselves.

Malinowski intended functionalism to be as heuristic device, and it certainly has proved to be a good method of studying societies in field. Its explanation requires empirical facts, and, thus, the conjectural and hypothetical reconstructions of the past have been superseded.

The major criticism launched at functional theory was its synchronic or ahistorical orientation and its alleged insight to explain change. It appears, however, that this failure was not so much a fault inherent in the theory itself as one due to idiosyncrasys of functionalist writers.

Radcliffe-Brown admitted that much when he said that he had a temporal preference for looking forward rather than looking over the past (Brown 1958:42). But nearly all important early functionalists included the possibility of dealing with change in their theoretical formulations. One of Durkheim's rules of sociological method was that the determining cause of social fact should be sought among the social fact preceeding it (Durkhiem 1958).

Radcliffe-Brown (1958:43) wrote that functional inconsistency exists whenever two aspects of social system produce a conflict. It can only be resolved by some change in system itself. While Malinowski, later in his life, wrote a book under the title, *The Dynamics of Culture Change* (1945).

It was the fact that Synchronic functional analysis was a seductive novelty that made several subsequent field workers prove to the neglect of history and change. They neglected and often explicitly rejected historical explanations of any kind, either because they were uninterested in change or unable to explain it. But it was rather a happy discovery that previously maligned savage customs such as witchcraft, canabolism, or infanticide had their own reasons for existence in culturers where they appeared. If no specific functions could be discovered, it was always possible to state that the existence of a ritual or of warfare contributed to the maintenance of the whole, or else they had psychological functions. It was, undoubtedly, true and logical and important enough to understand the working of the societies other than our own. But explanations were often facile and circular. Strange customs were viewed as reducing conflicts and tensions, b"t the question as to why conflicts arose for the first time remained unexplained.

In course of time, many field workers became dissatisfied with this lack of dynamism. The cultures, they studied often, displayed conflict and were by no means perfect balance. In other words, they rediscovered Radcliffe-Brown's distinction between functional and logical consistencies. They take into account both so that they could deal with change without abandoning the useful notions of structure and functions. Among them mention may be made of E.R. Leach, Raymond Firth, E.E. Evans Pritchard, Mayer Fortes, G.P. Murdock, Talcot Parsons, R.K. Merton, Lowie, Kluckhohn, etc. In their hands, functionalism became once more the dynamic and 'nomothetic' theory envisaged by its formulators.

RADCLIFFE-BROWN'S CONCEPT OF FUNCTION

Radcliffe-Brown of Britain, who established a separate school of anthropological thought known as, 'Structural School', about which we will discuss in detail in next coming chapter, was basically a functionalist. His understanding of function was in many ways similar to that of his predecessors. Most philosophers had realized that social phenomena are interrelated and together constitute the social whole. But no one had deemed it necessary to explain what function was. The concept was used electically and it was considered to be axiomatic as progress or natural law. Function as a principle of explanation that itself was not explained. To Radcliffe-Brown, function was more than a recognition of reality. It was to him, a very specific manner of analysis. It was one that could not be confused with any other methods and above all it was scientific. Function itself, thus, needed justification, and it is only when principles of explanation themselves are explained that one can identify a method. It is because of this fact that Radcliffe-Brown is known as functionalist, not simply as user of function, as his predecessors were. In fact, since the concept of structure became wedded to that of function, Radcliffe-Brown and his followers are known as 'Structural-functionalists', mainly to distinguish them from Malinowskian functionalists.

Radcliffe-Brown has taken the concept of function from biology. He has compared social life with biological life. Structure of an organism consists of many cells and parts. These cells and parts of body are interrelated and interdependent and perform various activities to maintain the body alive. The activities carried out by different cells and parts in the maintenance of body are their functions. The same matter can also be applied for the society. The structure of society also comprises network of status and roles which reveal status and functions of individuals. In order to maintain the continuity of entire social structure, the activities of different social elements or institutions, reveal their social function.

Defining function, Radcliffe-Brown (1952) holds view that function is the contribution, which a partial activity makes to the total activity of which it is a part.

COMPARISON BETWEEN MALINOWSKI'S AND RADCLIFFE-BROWN'S WORKS AND CONCEPTS OF FUNCTION

1. Both worked in small islands, (Malinowski among Trobriand islanders and Radcliffe-Brown among Andaman islanders), where the holistic conception of culture must seem more obvious than it does in an inland area with a great deal of movement of people and tribal admixture. Both books were published in the same year, i.e., 1922.
2. Both were influenced by Durkheim (Radcliffe-Brown permanently and Malinowski temporarily).
3. In the work of both, there is the tacit assumption, that it is essential that cultures should continue to exist or survive and that they must be maintained.
4. The concept of culture as nicely balanced system of parts is found in both those famous monographs published in 1922, Radcliffe-Brown's *The Andaman Islanders* and Malinowski's *Argonauts of the Western Pacific*. Then Radcliffe-Brown used the word culture in somewhat the same way as Malinowski did. Radcliffe-Brown's definition of social structure included much that Malinowski did under culture except material culture, language, system of knowledge, and education, the latter two which seem never to have interested Radcliffe-Brown particularly.
5. It is true that Malinowski recognised quite early (1929) that there were conflicts within cultures and it is to his credit that he did so. He distinguished in Trobriand society conflicting roles, rivalries expressed in reciprocal obligations, self-interests, and fights for power, whereas Andaman islanders were represented as being a united group earnestly engaged in expressing their cohesion. Yet Malinowski as well as Radcliffe-Brown seem to have believed that culture had to be maintained as a whole. Radcliffe-Brown's definition of function of a custom or institution in terms of part it plays in relation to culture as a whole. He held views that anthropological facts were to be explained by their function, by the part, which they play in an integral system of culture. The wholeness in the treatment of both consisted of the study of one institution against the background of whole culture.

Some recent writers have pointed out that Radcliffe-Brown viewed the function of an institution as part it plays in maintenance of the tribal structure, whereas Malinowski examined its function only in relation to needs and mainly biological needs. But in fact, the statements on function made by Malinowski and Radcliffe-Brown were almost identical.

6. Both were in opposition to the diachronic schools of evolutionary and diffusionist traditions and were supporter of synchronic functional traditions.
7. Both used function as heuristic devices for the analysis of culture and total social structure.
8. Both devoted their major efforts to intensive field experiences through participant observation method.
9. Both employed an organismic analogy as their main analytical crutch. As one of Malinowski's students has said,

> Both denied the value of speculative reconstruction of history, both emphasized the need to study existing social institutions, both conceived of cultures as wholes, and both developed the concept of functions interms of social effect of any custom or institution (Kaberry 1957:75).

But both had difference in their opinions as well, which are as follows:

1. In earlier writings both had used the term culture, but in later works, Radcliffe-Brown was confined to the concept of Social Structure. Malinowski had treated Social Structure or Social organisation as one of the aspects of culture. Thus, Malinowski deals with culture and Radcliffe-Brown with society.
2. Malinowski holds opinion that culture of a society operates to satisfy man's biological need. He has mentioned seven basic needs such as metabolism, reproductive, bodily comforts, safety, movement, growth and health. These are the fundamental or primary or basic needs of man for whose fulfilment he has made culture. Basic human needs, manifest in the cultural activities of men, in turn set up a series of derived needs, which means that culture supplies man with derived potentialities, abilities and powers. From the derived needs come a series of cultural imperatives, which give form to the institutions of culture that goes to make up those broadest divisions that we see interms of aspects or forms. He has listed economics. Social control, education and political organisations as cultural responses of derived needs. He has talked about a third level of need, the integrative needs in which he has put religion, system of knowledge, magic, artistic ex-

pressions etc. Integrative needs provide coherence in society. Thus, he has emphasized that cultural need is the body of conditions, which must be fulfilled, if the community is to survive and its culture to continue. He defines culture as essentially an instrumental apparatus, by which man is put in a position to better cope with concrete specific problems, that face him in his environment, in course of satisfaction of his needs. He looks customs, traditions, institutions contributing in maintenance of functional whole of culture. They are inseparable and interdependent as well as interconnected.

Malinowski was of opinion that functional whole of culture could be understood in its relationship to man's biology and his environment. It was this view that sets Malinowski apart from Radcliffe-Brown and other structural functionalist. He was not concerned so much with the discovery of law as Radcliffe-Brown was, but first and foremost with the understanding of observable realities of culture. He felt that this understanding must take into account the variables of physical environment and man's biology, since both interacted with one another and with culture. Malinowski, (1939) wrote:

> "Professor Radcliffe-Brown is still developing and deepering the views of the French Sociologists. He, thus has to neglect the individual and disregard biology. But functionalism differs from the other sociological theories more definitely, perhaps, in its conception and definition of the individual than in any other respect. The functionalist includes in his analysis not merely the emotional as well as the intellectual side of mental processes, but also insists that man in his full biological reality has to be drawn in our analysis of culture. The cultural relation to them, thus, have to be studied side by side".

Radcliffe-Brown, on the other hand, has criticised Malinowski's elaborate attempt to account for the universality of certain aspects of culture. Radcliffe-Brown (1949). states:

> "Malinowski has explained that he is the father and inventor of functionalism. His definition of it is clear. For him, functionalism, is a theory or doctrine that every feature of culture of any people past or present is to be explained by reference to seven biological needs of human beings. I cannot speak for the other writers to whom the label functionalist is

applied by the authors, though I very much doubt if Redfield or Linton accepts this doctrine. As for myself, I reject it entirely, regarding it as useless and worse. As a consistent opponent of Malinowski's functionalism, I may be called an antifunctionalist".

I have no wish to follow further the irresponsible extravagances of the authors. They certainly do not deserve to be taken seriously. I only ask to be permitted to register a personal protest against a procedure, for which they find no possible for me the label functionalists. They attribute to me, first Malinowskian theory of culture, which I reject. Second, the quite impossible view that all customs and institutions of any society are right and good, and I suppose that they may add that all socially accepted beliefs are true.

It is true that I make use of the concept of function, and I did so in my lectures at Cambridge and London School of Economics before the time Malinowski began to study anthropology. All physiologists make use of the same concept, but they are not called functionalists".

In this way, Radcliffe-Brown has labelled a severe criticism against Malinowski's theory of need and function. He holds view that the integration of culture is based upon the society. Each institution of society contributes functionally in the existence of society. They are certainly interrelated and interdependent as a whole. They perform function to maintain the unity and continuity of society, not that to fulfil physiological and psychological needs of man. According to Malinowski, the utility of culture is that it fulfils the physiological and mental needs of human beings. It is this very question on which they held dissimilar views.

3. Malinowski defined social anthropology as functionalism, but Radcliffe-Brown never defined social anthropology as functionalism.
4. Malinowski was concerned with relationship, whereas Radcliffe-Brown was concerned with arrangement of persons in institutionalised form.
5. Malinowski's cultural laws were the relations that exist between individual needs and social institutions, which can be discovered through a comparative study of cultures, where the individual is seen in his day to day adoptations, both physical and mental.

One of laws about social behaviour of Radcliffe-Brown was "there exists a certain degrees of functional consistency amongst the constituent parts of social system". His another law was that functional law was not same as logical consistencies. Radcliffe-Brown has attempted to formulate a universal law of synchronic functionalism, but he could not achieve that goal. Even after his death, his hopes for the discovery of generally valid predictive laws have not been realized.

Although Malinowski's concept of function developed along a trajectory, which removed it further and further from Radcliffe-Brown's formulation, there initially was a very strong resemblance between them. To outsiders, there appears paradoxes in the opinion of Malinowski and Radcliffe-Brown, but when one look deeply, he or she may find that they held similar views. Because, without individuals there is no society and without society individual cannot maintain their existence. Radcliffe-Brown has called himself as antifunctionalist, but this statement had less to do with the concept of function than with his relationship to Brownislaw Malinowski.

4

STRUCTURAL SCHOOL

In previous chapter we have discussed that Malinowski and Radcliffe-Brown both were functionalists by nature. So far as the question of concept of function was concerned, both held the similar views. Both were critical of diachronically-oriented evolutionary and diffusionists traditions of analysing culture. In their views, ethnological analysis of cultures about which written records were lacking, was not historical analysis but of psuedo-historical nature. Therefore, they developed the concept of synchronic functional analysis of culture which was concerned with present and now. They also attacked upon the historical and comparative methods of evolutionists and diffusionists, which attempted to show diachronic change by comparing historical stages (in case of former) and adaptation of borrowed traits (in case of latter). They gave a new dimension of comparative method. They opined that in older ethnological anthropology, comparative method was the reconstruction of the past by extrapolating from contemporary primitive societies. The things that were similar were generally accepted as indicating historical connections. In their views, in socio-cultural anthropology, the purpose of comparison was to explore socio-cultural institutions of present-day societies in terms of their structural functional similarities. Comparative studies, thus, could be carried out Synchronically (ahistorically) and Diachronically (historically). Synchronic study deals with description in which social life is taken as it is without references to change in its general features, and diachronic study deals with description which gives us an account of such changes. In a synchronic study, a culture is analysed at a given moment of its history so that its regularities and conditions of existence may be defined. A great many diverse type of cultures must then be compared in order to find the universal beneath the multitudinous differences. Diachronic studies seek to discover in which cultures or societies change and the general laws governing these processes of change. But in fact they did not make any diachronic studies. But the later structural functionist followed the diachronic approach to explain structure and function of societies, about which a detailed description has been made in previous chapter. But, later on, a difference in opinions of Radcliffe-Brown and Malinowski took place. Radcliffe-Brown, who had used the term function earlier than Malinowski, was not ready to accept Malinowski, who claimed himself as father of functionalism on the basis of theory of need for which culture, either in past or at present was functional instrument. Radcliffe-Brown placed great emphasis upon distinguishing the structural-function from the function of Brownis law Malinowski and others, who were associated with bio-psychological needs of individuals. According to Radcliffe-Brown, the only acceptable definition of function was, "the contribution an institution makes to the maintenance of social structure. He was of opinion that the theory of society in terms of structure, process, interconnected by function, has nothing in common with the theory of culture as derived from individual biological needs, with which Malinowskians were associated. It was this difference in views that compelled Radcliffe-Brown to comment upon Malinowski's functionalism as myth invented by Malinowski. The gap in opinions of Radcliffe-Brown and Malinowski became so wider that Radcliffe-Brown and his associates established a separate school of thought known as structural-functional school of anthropological thought. As the concept of structure became wedded with function, this school is also known as structural-functional school. The structural-functional theory also got acceptance in America by the sociologists and anthropologists, while in France, Emile Durkhiem and Lavi-Strauss developed structural-functional theory to a great extent.

Thus, for our study purpose, we may divide the structural-functional school of anthropological thought into three groups, namely, British School of Structural-functionalism, American School of Structural-functionalism and French School of Structuralism. The contributors of British School of structural-functionalism are Radcliffe-Brown, S.F. Nadel, E.R. Leach, R. Firth, Evans-Pritchard, Mayer Frotes, etc. The contributors of American School of structural-functionalism are Parsons and Merton (Sociologist) and Lowie, Kluckhohn, G.P. Mudrock (anthropologist). The contributors of French School of Structuralism are Emile Durkhiem and Levi-Strauss. This can be better understood by the chart given below :

STRUCTURAL-FUNCTIONAL SCHOOL OF ANTHROPOLOGY

British School of Structural-functionalism	*American School of Structural-functionalism*	*French School of Structuralism*
A.R. Radcliffe-Brown, S.F. Nadel, E.R. Leach, R. Firth, Mayer Fortes E.Evans-Pritchard	Parsons, Merton (Sociologist), R.H. Lowie, M.Kluck-hohn, G.P. Murdock, all anthropologists	Emile-Durkhiem and Levi-Strauss

But, before discussing their major contributions in the field of social anthropology, let us take into considerations some of the definitions of the term social structure as suggested by eminent sociologists and anthropologists. The analysis of these definitions will be helpful in understanding what social structure is ? What are its constituents? What are its salient features? etc. The concept of structure and function appeared for the first time in the writings of Herbert Spencer in his book, *Principles of Sociology* (1885, Vol. 1), where he has dealt with fundamental similarities between 'organism' and 'society'. He has treated society as integrated order of parts like an organism. As an organism's body is composed of different parts, which are interrelated and integrated to provide the structure of organism's body. Similarly, a society is composed of different parts or units, which are interrelated and integrated in an order to provide the structure of that society. Again, as different parts of organism's body performed different functions to make existence of body alive, in the same way, different units of society contribute valuable functions in integrated whole for the existence of society and maintenance of social order. This views of Spencer has made him structural-functionalist. But unlike later structural-functionlists, he was also a devout supporter of evolutionalism, because he was very much influenced by the work of Charles Darwin. He is of opinion that as the body of an organism has followed evolutionary process from simple to complex or homogeneity to heterogeneity, in the same way society has passed through the evolutionary processes of simple to complex forms. Thus, Spencer has shown structural-functionalism as 'Evolutionary Functional Process'.

The concept of structure and function also appeared in the writing of French anthropologist, Emile Durkhiem, in his books entitled, *Division of Labour* (1893) and *Rules of Sociological Method* (1895). He has also treated society like an organism. He holds opinion that as an organism needs, to make the body alive, the fulfilment of certain essential needs. In the same way, it is essential to fulfil certain needs for the existence of society. The activities by which essential needs of society are fulfilled, he calls them (activities) as function. He is of view that structural units of society such as family, religion, kinship, political and economic organisation contribute valuable function for maintaining the order of society. Durkhiem studied the Tribes of Australia and find out the function of religion is to establish unity in the society. He has also deal with normal and pathological functions of social institutions.

Later anthropologists and sociologists have provided us some precise definitions and meanings of the term social structure. Let us deal with those definitions one by one.

Karl Manheim in his famous book, *Ideology and Utopia* (1936: 45-46) has defined social structure as, "the web of interacting social forces from which have arisen the various modes of observing and thinking".

M. Ginsberg in his book *Reason and Unreason in Society* (1947:1-8) opined that "Social structure is concerned with the principal forms of social organisation, i.e. types of groups, associations and institutions and the complex of these which constitutes societies, a full account of social structure would involve a review of the whole field of comparative institutions".

R.M. Mac Iver and C.H. Page in their book, *Society* (1950:212) define it as, "the various modes of grouping together comprise the complex pattern of the social structure. . . . In the analysis of the social structure the role of diverse attitudes and the interests of social being is revealed".

They have also regarded the social structure as abstract which is composed of several groups like family, church, class, caste, state, community. They have given due consideration to those sources and power, which bind these groups in a chain to give them a definite form of social structure. Since society is organisation of social relationship and is also abstracts, so its structure is also abstract. They have also refer to stability and changeability of social structure. They held opinion that while social structure itself is unstable and changeful, it has a definite character at every stage and many of its major elements have greater persistence of type through change. In their study of social structure, they have included the study of institutions, associations, groups, functional system and institutional complex.

According to Talcott Parsons, "Social Structure is a term applied to the particular arrangement of interrelated institutions, agencies and social patterns as well as status and roles which each person assumes in the group" (1951:89).

Besides these Sociologists' views and definitions on Social Structure, some eminent anthropologists' definitions of social structure are as follows:

Radcliffe-Brown, the chief pioneer of British School of Structural-functionalism, opines that "components of social structure are human beings, the structure itself being an arrangement of persons in relationship institutionally defined and regulated" (1950:82).

In order to illustrate this definition of social structure, he cited examples of Australian and African natives of the system of marriage and kinship. He said that kinship system among them is the description of institutionalised relationships which binds the individuals together in a specialized way and, thus, ascribes to the particular positions. The kins occupying, the set of positions, creates a pattern, which is termed as kinship structure. He cited another examples from the Thonga and Bantu Tribes of South Africa. There is a custom of paying bride-price known as *Lokala*. This custom is related to the institution of marriage which binds the individuals together. For the payment of *Lokala*, not only the members of groom family, but kiths and kins of groom join their hands. This *Lokala* is given as economic aid to be used at the time of marriage of bride's brother or her near relative. Thus, the institution of marriage brings together not only family members, kiths and kins of the groom and bride families, but it also provides economic aid in their family. In this way, institutionally defined and regulated marital relations become a link between two families in socio-economic field, and thus their determined positions create pattern of marriage and kinship structure.

Later on, Radcliffe-Brown gave another definition of Social Structure in his famous book *Structure and Function in Primitive Society* (1952:190) as "Human beings are connected by a complex network of actually existing relations". The components of social structure are persons, and a person is not as an organism but as occupying position in a social structure. He considers social structure as real as are individual organisms. According to him, both the social structure and organism are prone to change yet they are stable. By change he means that organs of both the structure are liable to development and destruction. The capabilities of the human organisms first develop from infancy to maturity and then the down falls start in old age. Similarly in Social Structure new human beings take their birth and old go on dying. But in spite of this continuous change their basic features remain stable. In other words, we may say that the functional aspects of social structure are always under change, while outer framework is stable. He has used the term 'actual social structure' for the former and 'general social structure' for the latter. He made a distinction between 'Structural form' and 'Social Structure'. 'Social Structure' is abstract, its expression is possible only in the functions and roles of the parts or units of social structure. Therefore, we can understand social structures only interms of functions or roles of its components.

E.E. Evans-Pritchard, who made study on 'Nuer' of Africa (1940) binds social structure to the interrelations of groups, explicitly excluding "interpersonal relations". Among Nuer, he found a custom of bride-price in which 40 heads of cattle were paid by the group member of groom's family to the group member of bride's family. Thus in the payment of 40 heads of cattle, all kiths and kins of groom family extend their cooperation by giving at least one cattle each. Again, in bride's family all 40 cattle are given to maternal and paternal kins of bride. Thus, the institutions of marriage through bride-price among Nuer reveal the interrelationships of two groups and its family members, i.e. bride and her maternal and paternal kiths and kins and groom and his maternal and paternal kins.

F. Eggan in his book entitled, *Social Organisation of Western Pueblos* (1950) observed the components or units of social structure are the inter-personal relations, which become part of social structure in the form of status or positions occupied by individuals. Thus, status occupied by an individual among the Pueblos, indicate his or her role in the maintenance of social structure.

E.R. Leach in his book, *Political System of Highland Burma* (1934) held views that social structure of Highland Burma consists of a set of ideas about the distribution of power between persons or group of persons.

The book *Notes and Queries* in Anthropology provides us a catholic definition of the term social structure. According to it, social structure is the whole network of relationships in which are involved the members of a given community at a particular time.

Levi-Strauss, a French structural anthropologist, in his article 'Social Structure' in *Anthropology-Today* edited by A.L. Kroeber (1955) held opinions that, "Social Structure can by no means be reduced to the assemble of social relations to be described in a given community".

Mayer Fortes in his book, *The Web of Kinship Among the Tallency* (1949) opines that the elements of social structure are constant feature in the pattern of organization of all activities in which the relation is significant. He also maintains that social structure contains parts and relations of diverse nature and variability.

S.F. Nadel in his famous book, *The Theory of Social Structure* (1957:12) writes that we arrive at the structure of society through abstracting from the concrete population and its behaviour pattern of network of relations obtaining between actors and in their capacity of playing roles relative to one another. Thus, according to him, structure is property of empirical data, of objects, events or series of events, somethings they exhibit prove to possess an observation or analysis. The data are said to exhibit structure as they exhibit a definable articulation, an ordered arrangement of parts.

R. Firth in his book *Element of Social Organisation* (1963) has viewed social structure as an aspect of social organisation. He has made a distinction between social structure and social organisation. The former is arrangement of persons, and the latter is arrangement of activities of two or more persons of groups.

According to *Encyclopedia of Anthropology* (1976), the elements of social structure include among others, the patterns of kinship, descent and affiliation, the techno-economic system and political legal system.

From the above analysis of meanings and definitions as suggested by different scholars, the following conclusions may be drawn:

(i) Social structure is an abstract and intangible phenomenon.
(ii) As individuals are units of associations and institutions, so these institutions are the units of social structure.
(iii) These institutions and associations are interrelated in a particular arrangement and, thus, create the pattern of social structure.
(iv) It refers to external aspect of society which is relatively stable as compared to functional or internal aspect of society.

ELEMENTS OF SOCIAL STRUCTURE

In a social structure, the human beings organise themselves, into associations and institutions for the pursuit of some object or objects. The aim can be fulfilled only if the social structure is based upon certain principles. These principles set the elements of social structure in motion, which are as follows:

(i) *Normalitive System:* Normalitive system presents the society with the ideas and values. The people attach emotional importance to these norms. The institutions and associations are interrelated according to these norms. The individuals perform their roles in accordance with the accepted norms of the society.
(ii) *Position System:* Position system refers to status and roles of the individuals. The desires, aspirations, and expectations of individuals are varied, multiple and unlimited. So, these can be fulfilled only if the members of society are assigned different roles according to their capabilities and capacities. In fact, proper functioning of society depends upon proper assignment of roles and status.
(iii) *Sanction System:* For the proper enforcement of norms, every society has a sanction system. The integration and co-ordination of different parts of social structure depends upon conformity to social norms. The non-conformists are punished by the society according to nature of non-conformity. It, however, does not mean that there are no non-conformists in a well organised society. Non-conformity is also an essential feature of society, otherwise, there would be no progress. But it is, beyond doubt, that the number of non-conformists is smaller than the conformists. The stability of a structure depends upon the effectiveness

of its sanction system.

(iv) *A System of Anticipated Responses:* The anticipated response system calls upon the individuals to participate in the social system. His preparation sets the social structure in motion. The successful working of social structure depends upon the realization of his duties by the individual and his efforts to fulfil these duties.

(v) *Action System:* It is the object or goal to be arrived at by the social structure. The whole social structure revolves round it. The action is the root cause which weaves the web of social relationships and sets the social structure in motion.

The existence of social group, internal structure of group arrangement into social classes, social distinctions, arrangement of persons in dyadic relationship, and interactions between group and persons are the structural features of the social life. Family, horde, clan, tribe, kinship, moieties, social sanctions, totemic group, and social classes are constituent of social structure.

Now, let us discuss the contributors of anthropological school of structuralism in developing the concepts, meaning, definition, constituents and principles of social structure, one by one.

Alfred Reginald Radcliffe-Brown (1881-1955)

A.R. Radcliffe-Brown was born in 1881. From the very beginning of his career, he emphasized that the study of non-literate people constituted a separate branch of science, namely 'Social anthropology'. This branch of science was by no means to be confused with the already existing Tylorian anthropology. According to Radcliffe-Brown, Tylorian anthropology, was not a true science at all. In fact, it was not even anthropology but ethnology.

He started his career as a student of W.H.R. Rivers, a British diffusionists. He became Rivers first student in social anthropology in the year 1904. Rivers was always strongly interested in history, therefore, he sent Radcliffe-Brown out to Andaman Islands of India in 1906 with the task of reconstructing the cultural history of Andaman Islanders, who were non-literate. In the absence of written records, this was well-neigh impossible and the young field worker was averse to making hypothetical or conjectural reconstructions. He dutifully recorded Andamanese myths, ceremonies, and customs, but the publication of his findings was delayed for almost fifteen years. Meanwhile, he became acquainted with the writings and theories of Durkhiem and Mauss and arrived at conclusion that it was more important to study meanings and functions. When his book on Andaman Islanders appeared in 1922, it reflected the new insights developed from the books of Durkhiem and Mauss. Andamanese myths and customs were not only recorded but also interpreted, which meant, "discovery not of origins, but of meanings".

Radcliffe-Brown was a social anthropologist. He taught social anthropology at Chicago University, U.S.A., from 1931 to 1937. Thereafter, he continued at Oxford University, London, from 1937 to July 1946.

The challenge to 19th century evolutionism in England arose from two unequally endowed groups of scholars. On the one hand, there were diffusionists like Smith, Perry and Rivers, on the other hand, the foundations were being laid for another approach, which spurned both evolutionists and diffusionists. The leaders of this movement were Radcliffe-Brown and Malinowski. They equaled and in many cases surpassed the Boasians in their emphasis upon and actual exposure to fieldwork. Intensive field studies among a small number of aboriginal societies, and intensive analysis of data from such studies, were organized around the theme of synchronic functional relations. It was by means of synchronic functionalist framework that British Social anthropologists hoped to preserve the heritage of 19th century scientism, while riding themselves of the accumulated liabilities of the search for diachronic evolutionary regularities.

Before discussing the major contribution of Professor Radcliffe-Brown, it is necessary here to present his important publications, because their references will be cited, while dealing with Brown's contributions:

1. 1914: Review of Malinowski book, "The Family Among the Australian Aborigines". *Man*, 14:31-32.
2. 1922: *The Andaman Islanders*. Cambridge University Press.
3. 1924: 'Mother's Brother in South Africa', *South African Journal of Science*. 21: 542-55.
4. 1931: 'The Social Organisation of Australian Tribes', *Oscenaia.* 1: 426-56.
5. 1935: 'Concept of Function in Social Science'. *American Anthropologists*, 37: 394-402.
6. 1947: 'Evolution, Social or Cultural'. *American Anthropologists,* 49: 78-83.
7. 1948: *A Natural Science of Society*. New York.
8. 1949: 'Functionalism a Protest'. *American Anthropologists*, 51:320-23.
9. 1950: *An Introduction to African System of Marriage and Kinship*

(ed.) Oxford University Press.
10. 1952: *Structure and Function in Primitive Society*. London. Oxford University Press.
11. 1958: *Method in Social Anthropology*. Chicago. University of Chicago Press.

Radcliffe-Brown's Theory of Social Structure

Radcliffe-Brown used the concept of social structure, for the first time, as early as 1914, while delivering a lecture on 'Social Anthropology' in Birmingham. However, the concept of social structure was highlighted in detail in 1940, while delivering his presidential address to Royal Anthropological Institute of Great Britain. In this presidential address, he divided anthropologists into students of 'Society' and 'Culture'. According to him, social anthropologists are concerned with the study of society and its structural features.

In his book, *Structure and Function in Primitive Society* (1952), Radcliffe-Brown has elaborated his concept of Social Structure and its functional features. According to him, the concept of Structure refers to an arrangement of parts or components related to one another in some sort of larger unity. For instance, the structure of a house reveals the arrangement of walls, roofs, rooms, passage, windows etc. Similarly, the structure of music represents the arrangements of successive sounds. Likewise, there is structure of human body having different organs, cells, tissues, bones etc.

In social structure, the ultimate components are individual human beings or persons. Social structure consists of arrangement of persons in relation to each other. For instance, in a village we find an arrangement of persons into families or households, which is again a structural feature. In family, we find mother, brother, sister, uncle, aunt etc. Thus, in looking for the structural features of social life, we should look for the existence of social groups of all kinds and examine also the internal structural system of those groups.

STRUCTURAL FEATURES OF SOCIAL LIFE

According to Radcliffe-Brown, structural features of social life are as follows:

i) *Existence of Social Group:* Social Structure consists of all kinds of social groups such as family, horde, clan, tribe, kinship system, moieties, social sanction, totemic group, social classes. These groups are organised along territorial, kinship and political lines and inter-relations among them constitute the core of Social Structural phenomena.

ii) *Internal Structure of the Group:* These groups have a specific internal structure. For example, the family group consists of the relations of father, mother and children.

iii) *Arrangement into Social Classes:* These groups are arranged into social classes and categories such as the castes in Indian society and economic classes in Western society.

iv) *Social Distinctions:* There is again a system of social distinction between different classes based on sex, authority, economic distinctions, caste distinctions etc. One finds a system of social distance between them as can be seen between Brahmans and Shudras in India.

v) *Arrangement of Persons in Dyadic Relationship:* Dyadic relationships are person to person relationship such as those found between master and servant.

vi) *Interactions between Groups and Persons:* The most important feature of social life is interaction between persons and interaction between group. An example of interaction between groups is seen, when one nation goes to war with another. Interaction between persons can be seen in social processes involving cooperation, conflict, accommodation etc.

Importance of Social Institution in Social Structure

According to Radcliffe-Brown, Social Structure is continuing arrangement of persons defined or controlled by institutions. He defines institutions as socially established norms or pattern of behaviour. An example of institution is family which sets the patterns of behaviour of members in relation to each other. Thus, institutions provide status and roles which are guided by the norms and values of those institutions. Thus, according to Brown, social structure has to be described by the institutions, which define the proper or expected conduct of persons in their various relationships.

Structural Continuity

As referred to earlier, social structure is an arrangement of persons in institutionalized roles and relationships. The continuity of this arrangement, according to Radcliffe-Brown, is known as structural continuity. Since individual and group, constituting social structure, constantly change, one group or person being substituted by another group or person, the structural continuity is dynamic. In this continuity, while the matter change, the form remains the same. The matter of social structure are the individual human beings, who are born and who die. The form of social structure is supplied by social institutions. Radcliffe-Brown involves two important constituents, one, the human individuals and groups and the other their arrangements through social institutions. In other words, it is continuing arrangement of persons in relationships defined by social institutions, which is known as social structure.

Types of Social Structure

Radcliffe-Brown placed the model of studying social structure into two categories: (i) actual social structure and (ii) general social structure. According to Brown, in 'actual social structure' the relations of persons and group of persons change from time to time. New members come into being by birth or through immigrations, while others go out of it by death and migration. Besides this, there are marriages and divorces, whereby members change several times. Thus, while actual social structure changes many times, the general social structure may remain relatively constant for a long time. For instance, if one visits a stable community like village and again visits after ten years or so, he or she finds that many of its members have died and others have been enrolled. Those who survive, are now ten years older than previous visit. Their relation to one another may have changed in many respects. But the general structure remains more or less same and continuing. He held view that sometimes the structural form may change gradually or some time abruptly due to revolution or the military conquests, but even in sudden changes the continuity of structure is maintained to a considerable extent.

Distinction Between Individual and Person

While admitting that the concepts of social structure and social personality are closely related, but social personality of a village or community can be reflected through the study of social structure. He made a distinction between individual and person. An individual is a biological organism, consisting of bones, cells, tissues, veins, artery, organised into a complex structure of human body. In physiological structure of an individual, there occurs many actions and reactions as well as changes. These changes are mostly of physiological and psychological nature. It appears, therefore, that human beings as individuals are objects and subjects of study for physicologists and psychologists. But human being, as a person, is network of social relationship. A person may be a son, father, grandfather, brother, uncle etc. Again, he may be a religious leader, political leader etc. These varieties of relationships attached with a person are the subject-matter of social anthropology. Thus, social anthropologists are supposed to study, similarities, and differences of structural system on the basis comparative method of investigation.

SOCIAL MORPHOLOGY, SOCIAL PHYSIOLOGY, SOCIAL EVOLUTION AND SOCIAL CONDITION

Radcliffe-Brown has used the terms social morphology, social physiology, social evolution and social condition to reveal the function of social structure. When he talks about social morphology, he is referring to similarities and differences in structural system of societies. When he talks about social physiology, he means how social structure functions. According to him, social physiology includes the functional contribution of every social phenomenon in the maintenance of social structure. These phenomena are norms and values, moral, law, etiquette, religion, governmental education etc.

When he uses social evolution, he means how social structure changes or what are the processes which bring change in structural system. This change can be shown by studying complex or plural societies, which consist of classes of people with varied traditions, customs, languages, folkways, mores etc. He cited example oı composite societies from South African aborigines, where there is a one political structure, but the population is represented by various linguistic and racial groups. The changes are brought by two process — one by social evolution and other by contact with migration. He was of opinion that while studying the process of changes, in social structure, our emphasis should be laid on interaction between persons or group of persons. The complex form of societies, which is outcome of progress and change, can be studied with the help of interaction between persons or groups by comparing diverse type of structural forms.

Social Structure and History

Radcliffe-Brown was of opinion that the study of social structure can be done either diachronically or synchronically. Diachronic study of society means studying society in time and space, though it is doubtful, whether he means it cultural history of society? The synchronic study of society refer to how the society is at present. Here, great many divergent types of societies are compared to find out universal beneath multitudinous differences. However, he could not make any diachronic study, nor did he compare whole society. What he did was establishment of cross-cultural correlations between some institutions of society such as totemism, political system, kinship system etc.

Social Structure and Socio-cultural System

It is of greatest importance to specify how the notion of social structure is related to the other parts of socio-cultural system. According to Radcliffe-Brown, there are three heuristically separable adaptational aspects of the total social system. These are social structural, ecological and cultural. The social structure is the arrangement by which an orderly social life is maintained. Ecological is the way in which the system is adapted to the physical environment. Cultural is the mechanisms by which an individual acquires habits and mental characteristics that fit him for participation in social life.

Social Structure and Economic Institutions

What is the relationship between ecological economic adaptation and social cultural adaptation ? Is it the function of economic and ecological adaptations to sustain the social structure or is it rather the function of social structure to maintain the economic and ecological adaptation? According to Radcliffe-Brown, it is the social structure which always deserves priority of analysis. The economic machinery of society appears in quite a new light, if it is studied in relation to the social structure. The exchange of goods and services is dependent upon, is the result of, and at the same time is a means of maintaining a certain structure, a network of relations, between persons and collection of persons. For the economists and politicians of Canada, the potlatch of the Indians of North-West of American was simply wasteful foolishness and it was, therefore, forbidden. For the anthropologists, it was machinery maintaining a social structure of lineages, clans, moities, with which was combined an arrangement of rank defined by privileges.

During a particular period of time, the members of a social group may be seen busy in certain activities. The sum total of activities carried out by the members may be called as apportionments. These apportionments of activities are nothing but division of labour, which is an important feature of social structure. The apportionment of activities also reveals an apportionment of gratifications. Radcliffe-Brown helds view that economic institutions of society may be studied either as mechanisms by which different kinds of goods are produced, consumed and exchanged or relations between persons or groups involved in the production, consumption, distribution and exchange of economic system. Thus, economic machinery of society such as production, consumption, distribution and exchange is the subject-matter of economists, but arrangement and relationships between persons or groups involved in those economic activities are subject-matter of social anthropology.

Social Structure and Religion

Radcliffe-Brown was of opinion that the study of religion is an important aspect of social structure. It binds human beings in a group of persons. Human beings are guided by the norms and values of religion to which they belong. But while studying religion from structural point of view, we should lay emphasis upon rites, rituals and traditions. In performing these rites and rituals and following traditions, interactions between persons or groups of persons can be seen, which give us ample opportunity to view society from our structural-functional point of view.

Social Structure and Social Organisation

Radcliffe-Brown has made a clear-cut distinction between social structure and social organisation. According to him, social structure refers to arrangement of persons, whereas social organisation refers to arrangement of activities of two or more persons, which are adjusted to give a united combined activity. Social organisation can be explained by the examples of social groups, industrial groups, sport groups. An example is organisation of work in factory, where there are manager, foreman and other workers and they carry out different activities for the functioning of the factory as a whole. This arrangement of activities reveals the organisational aspect of the factory. Social structure can be explained by the examples of army and tribal groups, which reveal arrangement of persons in institutionalised form. Thus, an organisation is arrangement of relationship within the total activities of an institution. For example, activities of various members of household may be subject to some regular arrangement, and arrangement of these activities is its organisation. The arrangement of activities of one family may differ from another household, which is structurally of the same order. Radcliffe-Brown makes this distinction clear by stipulating that "when we are dealing with structural system, we are concerned with a system of social positions. While in an organisation, we deal with a system of roles". In the study of social structure, we deal with total network of social relationships, and not such relationship themselves.

Structure and Function

In order to illustrate the relationship between structure and function, Radcliffe-Brown turned, once again, to biology. The structure of an organism consists of ordered arrangements of its parts and the function of the part is to interrelate the structure of an organism. Similarly social structure is ordered arrangements of persons and groups. The function of persons and groups is to interrelate the structure of society or social organism. In fact, social function is the inter-connection between social structure and social life. Physiological phenomena are not simply the result of nature of cells, but cells are organised in specific ways, so that the various organs function to make continued existence possible. Likewise, social structure is not to be studied by considering the nature of individual members of group, but by examining the arrangement of functions that make society persistent. He further points out that the relationships of parts of an organism to one another are not static. The whole point abut an organism is that it is alive so that study of its structure — the relationship of parts — must be activated by a study of its functioning of processes by which its structure is maintained or changed (distinction between static and dynamics). In all organisms, other than dead ones structure and function are logically lined. Thus, structure and function are logically linked. Thus, structure and function support each other and are necessary for each other's continuity.

Like an organism, the social life of the community may be defined as the functioning of social structure. The function of any recurrent activity such as punishment of crime or a funeral ceremony, is the part it plays in social life as a whole and therefore, contribution it makes to the maintenance of the structural continuity.

The importance of the differentiation between structure and function is that it can be applied to the study of both of continuity in forms of social life and of processes of change. Moreover, it allows for more scientific comparative studies than could be made by Durkhiem, whose concept of function implied content as well as meaning. Radcliffe-Brown was very well aware that similar things may have different meanings in different cultures and also that different things may have similar functions. Comparisons, in order to have any value at all, should search for comparable structures, which meant that they must have comparable social functions also, although their individual meanings and functions may well be incomparable.

RADCLIFFE-BROWN'S VIEWS ON ETHNOLOGY, HISTORY AND SOCIAL ANTHROPOLOGY

Radcliffe-Brown makes a clear-cut distinction between ethnology, history and social anthropology. In past, no clear-cut distinction between ethnology and social anthropology was made before Radcliffe-Brown. According to Radcliffe-Brown, the task of ethnology is to classify people on the basis of their racial and cultural characteristics and then to explain their distribution in present or past time by movement and mixture of people and the diffusion of cultures. Thus, ethnologists attempt to reconstruct the history of primitive people, for whose past historical records are lacking. They are compelled to rely upon circumstantial evidences to reach their conclusions. Radcliffe-Brown helds views that history begins with written records. Therefore, ethnologists are not historians, rather pseudo-historians. History is reconstruction of past based upon written records, but since non-literate people by definition do not possess such documents, the ethnological studies have been anomalous. In contrast, social anthropology is based upon strictly scientific principles. According to Radcliffe-Brown, the two major criteria of science are: (i) verifiability and (ii) the establishment of universal law. Biology, in this sense is an exemplary science. Radcliffe-Brown applies its models to the explanation of the working of society in a very strong way:

> Every custom and belief of a primitive society plays some determinate part in the social life of the community, just as every organ of a living body plays some part in the general life of the organism. The mass of institutions, customs and beliefs forms a single whole or system that determines the life of the society. The life of society is not less real or less subject to natural laws, than the life of an organism (Radcliffe-Brown 1922:229-30).

There are other differences as well between social anthropology and ethnology. Ethnology is ideographic, can best tell that certain things has happened, which serves no practical purposes. On the other hand, social anthropology is nomothetic or explanatory. It can be of immense service, because it will discover universal laws of human behaviour. This practically is not conceived in terms of Durkhiemian moral philosophy, but rather within a framework of British colonial policy. Social anthropology may assist in the administration and education of backward people, or it can help the public servant engaged in dealing with practical problems of the adjustment of the native civilization to the new conditions that resulted from the occupation of the country or assist missionary to get rid of witchcraft. His faith in applied anthropology is the logical outcome of his admiration of the results of the natural sciences, which had also contributed to the welfare to man-kind.

Radcliffe-Brown's argument for the separation of ethnology and social anthropology resembles Durkhiem's differentiation between causal and functional studies. But while Durkhiem feels that both are legitimate and useful undertakings, Radcliffe-Brown has seen no need for a concern with causes. Social anthropology to him, is the sociology of non-literate people. In these simple societies, the general laws of social existence will be much easier to detect than in complex ones. He defines sociological law as a necessary condition of continued existence.

Radcliffe-Brown also accuses ethnologists of psychological reductionism, because they sometimes attempt to explain customs and beliefs in terms of mental processes of the individual. He does not object to psychology as its own right, but he feels that social phenomena cannot be explained in psychological terms. Further more, individual behaviour as studied by psychologists is not scientific in that psychologists neglect to note that seemingly individual notions and actions are conditioned by society. But Radcliffe-Brown has not subordinated the individual to society in the same manner as Durkhiem. He has recognised that members of society often consciously initiate social change, when they become aware or the inconsistencies of their social system. Particularly in his earlier writings, he has often presented what may be called socio-psychological explanations. The Andamanese weeping rite, for instance, demands that people who have been separated for sometime embrace each other and weep together upon meeting again. This obligatory social action serves to relieve emotional tensions. Similarly, dancing at peak making ceremonies functions to appease collective anger and, thus, the newly established peaceful relations become realized and internationalised.

STRUCTURAL-FUNCTIONAL LAW

Radcliffe-Brown claims that the structure provides the central set of variables for orienting social anthropology. According to him, by concentrating on social structure, anthropology can be cured of explanatory importance which had followed upon the demise of evolutionary schemes. This pretension to superior understanding or explanation is an explicit feature of the programme set forth by Radcliffe-Brown, and it was explicitly opposed to Boasıan conclusion that the search for socio-cultural laws was futile. Radcliffe-Brown's displeasure with dogma of no socio-cultural law was expressed as early as 1923.

> Now ethnology with its strictly historical method can only tell us that certain things have happened or have probably or possibly happened, social anthropology with its inductive generalizations can tell us how and why things happen etc. according to what Law (1958:28).

According to Radcliffe-Brown, law is a necessary condition of continued existence. Responding to his American critics, who insisted that "there were no discoverable significant laws such as the functionalist is seeking", Radcliffe-Brown opined that generalizations about any sort of subject-matter are of two types: (i) generalizations of common opinion and (ii) generalizations that have been verified or demonstrated by a systematic examination of evidence afforded by precise observations systematically made. The generalization of latter kind are called scientific laws. Those who hold that there are no laws of human society, cannot hold that there are no generalizations about human society, because they themselves hold such generalizations, and even make new ones of their own. They must, therefore, hold that in the field of social phenomena, in contradiction to physical and biological phenomena, any attempt at the systematic testing generalizations or towards the discovery and verifications of new ones, is, for some unexplained reason, futile. Argument against such a contention is unprofitable or indeed impossible (Brown 1952:187).

The structural-functional school, thus, can be judged on the basis of its explanations of socio-cultural differences and similarities according to the common standards of science. For Radcliffe-Brown, structural-functionalism was not to be valued merely for its stimulus to improve standard of fieldwork, or for its organising contribution to ethnographers in search of a theme to hang their data on. The tests of accuracy were to be the ability to generate lawful statements in terms of which explanations of socio-cultural phenomena could be achieved that were superior in accuracy, generality and economy to rival theories.

Another important outcome of Radcliffe-Brown's position was that the fieldwork was to be carried out by observers fully trained in the theory of anthropology as well as in methods of scientific observation. He demanded that his students should begin by making intensive studies of single cultures, observing the data, formulating hypotheses, and testing those in field. Once cultures had, thus, been examined, comparisons could be made, and hopefully, law would emerge.

However, it cannot be said that he discovered any startling new laws. One of this laws was that "there exists a certain degree of functional consistency amongst the constituent parts of social system. It may well be argued that this statement merely recognised the regularities of culture, and that it is far fetched to call this a law. Yet it is at this point that Radcliffe-Brown made a most profound observation, one that was overlooked or neglected by many of his followers, namely that functional consistency is not the same as logical consistency. Thus, the two often are in conflict. Social system never obtains a perfect functional consistency. It is for this reason that they undergo change. Radcliffe-Brown himself did not often deal with change. Because, he felt that the first order of business was to describe and order the social phenomena themselves and to discover their cross-cultural regularities. Later functionalists often emphasized social solidarity and functional integration so much that their analyses were static and precluded the explanation of change.

Radcliffe-Brown considered his specific kind of social analysis superior to all previous methods of explanation. It could relate how and why societies were organised in their specific manner. It could explain cultural similarities and differences and could generate laws about social behaviour. He was aware of the fact that his science was still far removed from achieving these goals. He felt that older field data were not useful and there were not yet enough scientific descriptions of cultures made by field workers trained in methods of social anthropology. But after his death his hopes for the discovery of universally and generally valid predictive laws have not been realized. Many variant interpretations of structure and function have since been advanced and enormous amount of fieldwork has been carried out that has greatly contributed towards our standing of structures and functions, but has not uncovered by unambiguous laws. Between time of Radcliffe-Brown and present day, the anthropologists have used the word structure to mean:

(i) Morphology of society and its Social Structure
(ii) The morphology of culture and its cultural structure
(iii) The model of social relations
(iv) Pattern of behaviour
(v) The pattern of culture.

Durkhiem and Structural-Functionalism

The fundamental theoretical premises of British social anthropology and structural-functionalism are based upon Emile Durkhiem's apotheosis of social solidarity. The theories of structural-functionalism have every thing in common with Durkhiem's approach to social-cultural phenomena via the conditions of social cohesiveness or social solidarity. The structural-functionalists basic assumption is that social system maintains themselves for significant intervals of time in a steady state, during which a high degree of cohesion and solidarity characterises the relationships among its members. The only difference between Radcliffe-Brown and Durkheim, in this regard, is that Radcliffe-Brown substituted the terms 'unit', 'harmony' or 'consistency' for Durkhiem's solidarity.

Criticism of Brown's Structural-Functionalism

The functional and structural approach of Radcliffe-Brown has been subjected to very strong criticism, some useful and some useless. The major criticisms are as follows:

(i) Some critics argue that it is wrong to look at society as a living organism because the structure of living organism does not change, but society does ?
(ii) The concept of social structure has led to the 'fallacy of misplaced concreteness', i.e. an error arising from assuming that one's abstraction of a social situation reflects social reality in all details.
(iii) In this approach, functions of units of society are determined. In absence of any concrete function, the analysis is done on the basis of imagination.
(iv) Structural-functional explanations are teleological explanations. The function has been used in terms of purpose.
(v) This approach does not deal with change. It believes in static, in place of dynamic.
(vi) This approach supports capitalism and the ruling class. In this way, it supports the exploitation of people to be ruled. This approach was followed more in capitalist countries.
(vii) This approach creates suspicion between cause and function. It does not reveal any difference between result of behaviour and their causes.
(viii) Structural-functionalists treat social order as an integrated whole. Sometimes, a situation arises in which a society can be seen in state of imbalance and disequilibrium for a long time.
(ix) Structural-functionalists are value-biased. They try to show as if purpose were kept in arrangement of order.

But in spite of all these criticism, the structural functional approach as laid down by Radcliffe-Brown and his supporters is significant from may point of view.

(i) It provides us such a foundation of knowledge and law by which we can control social behaviour.

(ii) It gives us such a conceptual frame work on the basis of which observation and explanation of social events is possible scientifically.

(iii) It builds such principles and theories by which social facts can be explained easily.

Nadel's Contribution to Structural-Functional School

Nadel was a close associate of Professor Radcliffe-Brown. He developed the theory of social structure in his book entitled, *Theory of Social Structure* (1957). In this book Nadel pointed out that the concept of society may be viewed from two angles: (i) action such as kinship and economics, and (ii) groupings such as family, clans. He also says that there are some social and cultural facts which fall outside the social and cultural scheme. These refers to an action autonomous.

Nadel helds view that the concept of social structure is still in a sense on trial. The variety of definitions lead us to fear that it is a concept the width of whose usages renders it analytically fruitless. Thus, there are two choices open to us. We may remove the concept of structure from the vocabulary of anthropology on account of its lack of precision or we can attempt to narrowly define it by giving a specific and limited connotation.

He opines that we are all surely agreed and there is no great difficulty involved in arriving at a general acceptable minimal definition of structure. Structure is the formal relation of parts such that a set of data may be said to exhibit structure in as much as they exhibit a definable articulation, an ordered arrangements of parts. The difficulties begin when we attempt to extrapolate this minimal definition from its purely formal sense to its supposed applications to sociological data. It is not difficult to see that technical problems which confront especially Radcliffe-Brown and Levi-Strauss, occur at this point in their analysis. The jump from definition to application, in other words, is crucial one.

According to Nadel, there are three dichotomies to resolve which are aspects of structure: (i) Structure as opposed to function, (ii) Structure as opposed to qualitative character and (iii) Structure as opposed to process. Unless we resolve these dichotomies, we are unable to give a satisfactory account of social structure.

Social behaviour, by definition, involves stereo-typed or relatively determinate ways of action within groups, between groups, and over periods of time, hence the continuity of group. Social behaviour, in other words, is institutionalised. The institutionalised behaviour is characterised by the consistency of the relationships of which it is composed.

But it must be made clear that what is constant is not concrete behaviour itself. It varies in detail according to occasion and circumstances, but its general character which allows it to be subsumed in an identical category of relationship, for example friendship, respect relationship, joking relationship etc. or within specific cultures or sub-cultures, for example, the child-parent relationship or avuncular relationships, which are clearly bound by the convention of particular society. We may note that all these cases contain an element of abstraction; they are all categories which we infer from a number of observed sequences of actions. Thus, we can not ignore the qualitative aspects of such relationship or their content in favour of their formal aspects. This is in fact, we cannot do, for distinguishing for example friendship from love or loyalty, or respect from servility. It is precisely this effective element, which is the criteria, by which we distinguish between the categories, even when we express these criteria in behavioural terms.

Therefore, the problem is to find a way of expressing the relationship between individuals acting as individuals and as their acting as part of a social network. The key to this is clearly that in most social contexts the actors behave in conscious or unconscious accord with some set of rules, beliefs, or expectations about the situations or conventions. We speak, that is to say, of individuals enacting roles. According to Nadel, it is through relationships in virtue of roles that society is arranged and ordered. Therefore, social structure lies not in mere presence and collection of relationships, but in the order in which they appear. According to him, there are two levels of order — one, within a particular relationship and which accounts for the constancy and identity of that relationship, and the other between all these various relationships.

Thus, according to Nadel, "we arrive at the structure of society through abstracting from the concrete population and its behaviour that pattern or network (or system) of relationships obtaining between actors in their capacity of playing roles relative to one another" (Nadel 1957:12).

Nadel has tried to explain in this definition that structure refers to a definable articulation, an ordered arrangement of parts. It is related to outer aspect of society and is totally unconcerned with the functional aspect of society. He has emphasized that social structure refers to the network of social relationship which is created among the human beings when they interact with each other, according to their status in accordance with the patterns of society. Nadel, therefore, says that structure indicates an transportable being relatively invariants, while the parts themselves are variable. According to him, there are three elements of society: (i) a group of people, (ii) institutionalised rules according to which members of the group interact, and (iii) an institutionalised pattern or expression of these interactions. The institutionalised rules or patterns do not change easily and this creates an orderliness in society. These rules determine the status and roles of the individuals. There is an order among these rules and status also which provide an ordered arrangement of human beings.

E.R. Leach's Views on Structural-Functionalism

E.R. Leach was a British social anthropologist, who disliked synchronic functionalism. He has dealt with change without abandoning the useful notions of structure and function.

In his book entitled, *Political System of Highland Burma* (1954), E.R. Leach proposed a creative solution by considering conflict itself as a form of structure. The social system in Highland Burma area was such that it presented individuals with inconsistencies in the schemes of values, by which they ordered their lives. They were, thus, faced with alternative mode of actions. Leach believed that such decisions were usually made in terms of gaining power to acquire accesses to office or of learning social esteem that would lead to increased power. He presented a wealth of evidence that this was, indeed, the primary mechanism of change among the Kachin and Shan populations of Burma. They consciously attempted to manipulate their myths and marriage choices in manner that would increase their status. Although, the cross-cultural validity of Leach's specific explanation has not been proven, his method is very important. He explained change not by preconceived causal factors, but from the reality of Kachin and Shan life. In his hands, functionalism became dynamic and diachronic.

Raymond Firth's Views on Structure-Function

R. Firth was an another British social anthropologists who disliked synchronic functionalism. He dealt with dynamic or diachronic functionalism like Leach. He equally proposed that variations of actual behaviour should be observed and recorded in order to discover the processes of change. Like Leach, he noted that individuals are often faced with a choice between alternative modes of behaviour. In Firth's view decisions are not made in terms of optimization of power, but according to personal evaluations of efficiency towards any given goal. These goals, themselves are not random, but formulated by the groups and sub-groups to which individuals belong. These sub-groups are both internally structured and interrelated with one another, so as to structure of society as a whole. Individuals belong to several sub-groups, determined by criteria of marriage, kinship, occupation, economics, status, class, religion and so forth. Since membership in these groups are overlapping, conflicts of choice of action will often arise. Because, what is efficient within the framework of the one may well be detrimental for membership in another. Firth hoped that intensive studies of these choices and conflicts would lead to the explanations of not only in single societies, but also on cross-cultural level so that the law of change may eventually be discovered (Firth 1956; 237-58).

E.E. Evans-Pritchard's Views on Structure-Function

The renewed interest in change and diachronic explanations moved several British anthropologists to return to considerations of history. Most explicit and most extreme among them is E.E. Evans-Pritchard. He, although declaring himself to be a functionalist and a follower in the foot steps of Radcliffe-Brown and Malinowski, nevertheless considered the search for laws a hopeless and even a rather wane undertaking:

> Up to the present, nothing even remotely resembling, what are called laws, in natural sciences has been adduced — only rather native deterministic, teleological and pragmatic assertions. The generalizations which have so far been attempted, have, moreover, been so vague and general as to be, even if true, of little use and they have rather easily tended to become mere tautologies and plastitudes on the level of common sense deduction (Evans-Pritchard 1964:57).

He diagnosed this failure as resulting from the insistence that social anthropology was a science in par with all other sciences. This he called 'doctrinaire positivism at its worst'. Legal systems were not comparable to planetary or biological ones because social systems were not natural but moral or symbolic systems, and thus by their very nature incomparable. If there were any laws or regularities at all, they were to be sought in history, which would reveal that these are sequences of development in time. History alone provides a satisfactory experimental situation in which the hypotheses of functional anthropology can be tested. He defined social anthropology as:

> . . . Social anthropology studies societies as moral or symbolic systems and not as natural systems. It is less interested in design and, therefore, seeks pattern, not laws. It demonstrates consistency not necessary relations between social activities. It interprets rather than

explains (1964:62).

According to him, social anthropology is best regarded as an art and not as a science (1964:85). He fully expected that most of his colleagues would be in disagreement with his statement. Indeed, many rose, to the defence of scientific status of their discipline.

Mayer Fortes' Views on Functionalism

Mayer Fortes (1953:28) stated that the functionalist point of view has always been concise and consistent. It had its goal to search for general laws that could be discovered without the aid of history. Significant social analysis, thus, could be made regardless of past. He was convinced that social laws must exist because social life is not random. At the same time, he was forced to admit that the combination of factors present on any particular occasion can never be predicted. Social laws, thus, refer to ideally isolated features of social life and can be stated only interms of probabilities. In fact, they would not have much reference to social reality at all.

AMERICAN SCHOOL OF STRUCTURAL-FUNCTIONALISM

American Sociologist and Their Views on Structural-Functionalism

Functionalism was accepted not only in Britain but in America as well. However, it is true that functionalism in America was first accepted by sociologists than anthropologists. Anthropologists in America first had to overcome the influence of Boas, who was anti-evolutionism and anti-functionalism, although he himself did not lack functionalism. The two most influential leaders of American Sociological functionalism are Talcott Parsons and Robert K. Merton. Both were critical of certain presuppositions of classical functionalism, and sought to refine its methods. Let us discuss their views on functionalism.

Talcott Parsons' Views on Functionalism

Talcott Parsons used the concept of function uncritically in his earlier writings, but he began to scrutinize it later on in his book entitled, *The Social System* (1951). Like his British counterparts, he became conscious about the problem of how to relate the static concept of structure to the dynamic aspects of social change. He, too, formulated his conclusions in terms of conflicting values. Every society has certain necessary preconditions, without such functional imperatives societies are unable to operate. But these imperatives are different for different social institutions. Kinship systems have different requirements than economic or political systems and situations will arise where individuals will have to decide their course of action in terms of one or other. In Parsons' Social system, such decisions are not guided by a desire for power or by any other personal advantage, but by moral standards of society. The conflicts are, therefore, not between institutions, but between them and social morality. Human action is, thus, both functional and symbolic and the tension between the two will lead to continuous change in both, always 'Straining' towards greater balance. According to Talcott Parsons, social structure is a term applied to the particular arrangement of the interrelated institutions, agencies and social patterns as well as the status and roles, which each person assumes in the group.

Talcott Parsons has tried to explain the concept of social structure in abstract form. All the units of social structure i.e. institutions, agencies, social patterns, status, and roles are invisible and intangible and hence are abstract. He has emphasised that the status and roles of individuals are determined by customs, traditions and conventions of society. These status give birth to different institutions, agencies and patterns. All these when interrelated and organised in particular manner, build the social structure of society. Social structure is concerned with forms of interrelationships between these units rather than with the units. These units constitute the society. The ordered arrangement seen between these units is social structure.

He, in his book *Social System* (1951) has described four principal types of Social Structure. His classification is based on four social values: universalistic social values, particularistic social values, achieved social values and ascribed social values.

Universalistic social values are those which are found almost in every society and are applicable to every body. For example, every society values the expert craftmen as in that case the production is cheaper and superior. Thus, efficient craftmen are selected in every society all over the universe.

Particularistic social values are the feature of particular society and these differ from society to society. If for example, selection is made on the basis of caste, religion, state etc., it means that in such societies particularistic social values are considered important.

When status are achieved on the basis of efforts, it means societies attach importance to achieved social value. When the status are hereditary, then society gives consideration to ascribed social values. A man on the basis of his efforts can change his ascribed social status. He may be born in a lower caste families but he may become minister, P.M., Governor or President.

Robert K. Merton's Views on Functionalism

Robert K. Merton, particularly opposed Malinowski's postulates of indispensability, of universality and of functional integration, in his famous book, *Social Theory and Social Structure* (1957), citing Malinowski's statement that "Magic fulfils an indispensable function within culture. It satisfies a definite need which cannot be satisfied by any other factors of primitive civilization. Merton objects this in following words:

> This twin concept of the indispensable function and the irreplaceable belief and action pattern, flatly excludes the concept of functional alternatives (Merton 1957:34).

Merton meant that social needs can be answered in many different ways, a point that Malinowski and other functionalists would not deny. But Malinowski did not consider magic irreplaceable in overall sense. Rather, he insisted that in certain primitive civilizations functional alternatives for magic were absent and unavailable. Therefore, in those societies magic fulfilled an indispensable function. It was Malinowski's theory that magic was used primarily in precarious situations. The Trobriand Islanders carried out a great deal of open-sea magic, because their canoes were relatively fragile and unequipped with modern safety appliances. It was for this reason that magic was indispensable to them, but it could be replaced by scientific inventions to which Trobrianders had not been introduced.

The difficulty may perhaps be related to the fact that Merton, a sociologist, used to deal with complex societies where functional alternatives are abundantly present in almost every situation, while Malinowski's conceptual framework was that of relatively simple cultures, where functional alternatives, are much scarce. Merton's own convincing analysis of functional alternatives and their consequences for change, deals largely with the political machinery in American political structure, a situation hardly comparable to Trobriand fishing practices.

In his book, *Social Theory and Social Structure*, he defines function as, "Functions are those observed consequences which make for the adaptation or adjustment of a given system" (1957:51).

In the same book he opines that the English term 'Function' has been used in five different ways, which are as follows:

(i) To designate socio-ceremonial occasions
(ii) To denote different kind of trades
(iii) To reveal the social status of a person
(iv) To show interrelationship between two variables (in case of mathematics)
(v) To indicate the activities of different parts in the maintenance of body as a whole (in case of Biology).

According to Merton, the term function is not only used in various ways, having different meanings, but various words are used to designate function such as utility, purpose, motive, aim, consequences, etc. Merton has presented a paradigm for functional analysis. In the area of functionalism, he has developed many theoretical concepts such as 'Function and dysfunction', and 'Manifest and Latent functions'. Let us discuss them what they mean.

Function and Dysfunction

The term function has been used in varieties of sense. But in sociology the terms function and dysfunction carry different connotations. Merton has defined function and dysfunction in following words:

> Functions are those observed consequences which make for the adaptation or adjustment of a given system, whereas dysfunctions are those observed consequences which lessen the adaptation or adjustment of the system (1957:51).

From the above definition, it is clear that if any elements or units of social structure fulfils the need of that structure and contributes in its adaptation or adjustment, we will call them the function of that unit or institution of social structure. But if that unit, institution or custom creates obstacles in adaptation or adjustment, we call the function of that unit as dysfunction. The distinction between function and dysfunction can be better understood by following examples:

(i) In India we have joint family system. In this, girls after marriage leave parents house and become members of in-law's family. But boys after marriage bring wives in the house. Sometimes more than 3 generations live in the same house, eat food cooked by same person and on same hearth. They have property in common. They have equal share in produce. The head of the household looks after each family member. Each family member provides full cooperation to head of the family. These are the functions of our joint family system. But if head of the family makes distinction in treating his family members unequally, or if he destroys the property of the family without taking permission of his members, it brings disintegration of the joint family system. The functions of head or any member in disorganising the joint family system, may be termed as dysfunction.

(ii) Similarly function and dysfunction can be explained in bureaucracy. Administrators in bureaucracy are promoted on the basis of seniority. This incentive given to bureaucrats has many functions. It compels them to work sincerely and devotedly to achieve the promotion. Efficient working brings prestige in organisation.

But this principle of promotion has also some dysfunction. After achieving promotion, the person concerned is found working not so efficiently as at the time of appointment. As they feel security in service, some of them do not work efficiently and with dedication, because they do not have fear of demotion. The function and dysfunction can also be seen in many unions.

Manifest and Latent Functions

Defining manifest and latent functions, Merton says, "Manifest functions are those objective subsequences controlling to the adjustment or adaptation of the system, which are intended and recognised by participants in the system. Latent functions, on the other hand, being those which are neither intended nor recognised" (Merton 1957:63). In other words, manifest functions are consciously recognised by member of a culture, whereas latent functions are neither intended nor recognised by the participants in the system.

Merton used this distinction to account for the persistence of certain practices despite the fact that their manifest functions are not always successful. He cited example of Hopi rain dances. Hopi rain dances are overtly carried out in order to produce rain. But rain does not always follow the ritual. Nevertheless ceremony has not disappeared. Because, although unrecognised by the performers, it has the latent function of promoting group solidarity. If rain ceremonies do not produce rain and the Hopi are unaware of its solidarity prompting properties, the continuation of these practices appears to be a rather irrational affairs. As Kalpan and Manners (1972:51) pointed out, there must be other manifest functions to account for their persistence. First of all, rain often follows afterward, and the Hopi may continue the ceremonies because they believe that it works. Moreover, they may well enjoy the getting together and colourful ritual itself. The fact that performances may indeed promote group solidarity in an accidental consequences, which cannot account for the origin or persistence of rain dance.

The difference between manifest and latent functions may be understood clearly by one more example. In all societies incest taboos are found. According to this, sex relations between incests, such as brother-sister, father-daughter, son-mother, are strictly prohibited. This principle of society reveals its manifest function, because if they are permitted to have sex relations, offsprings produced might be disabled and ugly. Some held view that it was the basic tendency of man that he could not establish such relationship. Its latent function reveals that incest marriages might brought conflicts and tensions among father-son, mother-son, brother-brother and family system was bound to be destroyed and disorganised. Marriage between two groups brings solidarity in family and cooperation between them.

American Anthropologists' Views on Structure-Functionalism

As referred to earlier that in America functionalism was accepted earlier by sociologists than anthropologists. It was because of the fact that American anthropologists had to overcome the influence of Boas, who was anti-functionalists, although he did not lack functionalist perspective.

American anthropologists were fully aware of the importance of the function long before the theories of Radcliffe-Brown and Malinowski became widely known here, Morgan had already eruciated one of its principles. When he wrote, "every institution of mankind, which attained permanence will be found linked with a perpetual want (Morgan 1963:98) and his whole evolutionary scheme was predicted on an understanding of functional relationships between such social institutions as family structure and kinship or between family interaction and house types. Boas repeatedly demonstrated how several aspects of culture influence one another. His criticism of British functionalism was directed at its lack of historical insights and its futile search for laws. Kroeber explained the integration of Mohare culture by tracing the interrelationships between its myths, songs and dreams, while Cora-Du-Bois showed that the prestige of wealth could serve as an independent variable. That went a long way to explain tribal ideology and other cultural elements in North-West Indian culture. Their view, that functional analysis is an approach that can meaningfully be combined with others, has remained present in most subsequent anthropological writings.

Fred Eggan and the Resumption of Diachronic Research

It must be made clear that the end of Synchronic obsession has been brought about less by this kind of attack than by a gradual drift among the younger generation of British Social anthropologists towards combining diachronic and synchronic interests. This reconciliation may actually have been stimulated by Radcliffe-Brown himself, upon his return to Oxford in 1937 as a result of his American experience.

Certainly, the most profound effect of his sojourn at Chicago, was the development of a point of view, most impressively represented in the work of Fred Eggan. In the work of Fred Eggan, the structural functionalists principles were combined with the Americanists concern with historical documents. By the time of Radcliffe-Brown's departure, Eggan (1937) had already achieved a brilliant synthesis of structural functional and the historical particularist approaches. Using the method of controlled comparison, Eggan (1954) attempted to explain puzzling variations in Crow terminologies among the Choctaw, Creek,Chickasaw, and Cherokee, a group of Southern United States tribe, which had been exposed to a similar set of acculturative pressures. Eggan demonstrated that length of time and degree of exposure matched the amount of departure in the terminological systems from a matrilineal Crow type to something more closely resembling patrilineal Omaha type.

George Peter Murdock's Views on Structure-Function

G.P. Murdock's book, *Social Structure* (1949) was most explicit on the point of functionalism. In this book, historical, functional, psychological and statistical methods are brought together to form a harmonious synthesis of cross-cultural comparisons. The statistical elements entered because of his participation in the Yale University Institute in Human Relations Area Files (HRAF), which he later on directed. The HRAF consist a classification system of ethnographic data in all culture areas of the world. Vast bodies of material, taken from both published and unpublished sources, are coded and cross-fed, so that researchers have easy access to data that otherwise would take them a life time to accumulate. At the time, when Murdock wrote his book on 'Social Structure', he used data from some 250 different societies about which the coded material was already available.

Murdock's approach may be illustrated by his analysis of incest taboos. Prohibitions of sexual intercourse within the nuclear family are universal, but in every known societies these taboos are extended beyond the father-daughter, mother-son and brother-sister relationship. These extensions are not the same everywhere. Sometimes, they include maternal cousions only or parental ones only. Many scholars attempted to account for this seemingly strange phenomenon. Some held that the horror of incest was instinctive, but in that case taboos would not need to be stated and the extensions remained unexplained. Other fell that people living in close proximity for long periods of time lost all sexual interest in one another, which is simply untrue. Murdock grasped the complexity of the problems and showed that it could not be explained by the anthropology alone. He credited Sigmund Freud with the explanation of the universality of incest taboos, because he had shown that nuclear family was constituted in such a way that it generated 'Oedipus complex', so that rather than having instinctive aversions, a boy desired his mother sexually. Social training strongly repressed his desire, which accounted for the emotional quality of the prohibition of incest and often very severe punishments for breaking the rules. Sociology, which Murdock equated with functionalism, had shown that without incest taboos, sexual competition within the family would weaken its important institution, thus, endangering the whole society. It remained to be explained why the prohibition extended beyond the nuclear family.

Using data from HRAF, Murdock demonstrated the extension in the direction of maternal relatives is most common in matrilineal societies, in the patrilineal directions in patrilineal societies and in both directions, in case of double descent. These and many other findings of cross-cultural regularities are in turn functionally interrelated with other cultural rules such as exogamy, preferential marriage, family organisation, and residence rules.

There is perhaps no other aspects of social structure that has fascinated anthropologists quite as much as the analysis of kinship. Murdock's book on Social Structure, although giving new dimensions to this subject, is but one in a very long list of publications emphasizing kinship. Some of these studies are quite abstract, written in a kind of kinship algebra that can be deciphered only by other specialists in this field.

On the whole, American anthropologists have been more critical in their acceptance of pure functionalism, i.e., synchronic functionalism than some of their British colleagues. Lowie (1937:230-49) already argued in favour of a tempered functionalism.

Kluckhohn's Views on Structure-Functionalism

Kluckhohn made a functional study of Navaho Witchcraft (1967). He defined function in following words:

.... a given bit of culture is functional in so far as it defines a mode of response, which is adaptive from the stand point of the individual.

But, later on, he became dissatisfied with functional theory because it dealt with structure but not with process. He wrote that historical and functional approaches were not mutually exclusive alternative, but necessary supplements of one another. He made no specific recommendations how their integration could be achieved.

FRENCH SCHOOL OF STRUCTURAL-FUNCTIONALISM

In France, Emile Durkheim led French Social Science to its emancipation from biological reductionism. Like Boas in the United States, Durkheim founded a school of anthropology to which the great majority of French Professional anthropologists still owe their origin. But because of rigidities and conservatism inherent in the structure of French Higher education, it was not until the 1920's that academic curricula resembling the English and American reformulations of anthropology began to appear. To this day, anthropology means physical anthropology to the educated Frenchman. Yet Durkheim's sociological school grow the outset concerned itself as much with the data of primitive ethnography as with Euro-American sociology. Moreover, as Durkheim's interests matured, he became increasingly involved with the study of ethnographic data.

The rejection of Spencerism in France was not related to a vigorous expansion of fieldwork. Indeed, one set of intensive field studies by French anthropologists began in the 1930s with pupil sent out by Marcel Mauss, himself a pupil of Durkheim. Nonetheless, there was much in common between trajectories of French and American schools. Both moved away from an evolutionary perspective. Both tended to encourage emic approaches on the model of linguistic analysis. Both produced a steady erosion of the strategy which would have sought the lawful principles of socio-cultural phenomenon in the material condition of human life. For Durkheim, social facts were entities suigeneries, but from the beginning, they resembled mind more than pattern. Durkheim's progressive commitment had returned almost to the rationalism in the work of Claude Levi-Strauss.

Durkheim's influence abroad was perhaps even more important than it was in France. His monumental work, such as *The Division of Labour in the Society* (1893), and the *Rules of Sociological Method* (1895), provided the basic orientation for the British School of Structure-functionalism, the central movement in modern British Social Anthropology.

Emile Durkheim (1858-1917)

Durkheim was born on April 15, 1858 at Epinal (Vosges) in Lorraine province of France. He was the descendant of a long line of rabbi. At an early age, he began to prepare for the rabbinate and studied the old Testament, the Tamud, and the Hebrew language and history. He abandoned these interests early in his life, but in latter part of his career as a social anthropologist and sociologist, religion became the subject of one of his most interesting topics during studies. He would often remind the people that he was, after all, the son of a rabbi.

He was always a brilliant student. At his first school, the College d'Epinal, he was put ahead of his class several times and won academic contests with ease. He was sensitive, delicate, and very keen, the traits which persisted throughout his life. He decided to become a teacher and went to Paris to study at Lyc'ee Luis-le-Grand in order to prepare for admission to the Ecole Normale Supérieure. After three years of preparation, he got chance to enter in that institution in 1879. He was now quite mature and of twenty-one years. He was extremely entense and serious, even solemn. These traits, along with a bushy beard and mustache, earned him the name of the Metaphysician.

He found the Ecole Normale Supérieur stimulating, but uncongenial. The strong emphasis there on a rhetorical humanism conflicted with Durkheim tough minded concern for what he considered to be serious, pressing problems. The solutions to these problems did not, Durkheim was convinced, lie in pretty words or metaphysical ecstasy. According to him, the methods of science and practical co-operative endeavor in empirical enterprises must form the basis for any kind of diagnosis and treatment of society and these remained unshakable tenets all his life. Three thinkers whose works especially influenced Durkheim at time were Denouvier, Kant and Comte. Towards the end of his studies there, Durkheim decided (around 1882) to become a sociologist. His aim was to study social phenomenon with all the rigorous objectivity of the scientific disciplines.

He was appointed as professor of Philosophy at Lyc'ee of Sens in 1882. He served this post till 1887. In 1885, he made a formal entry into the field as a collaborator on Rebot's Revue Philosophique. By 1886, he had made the first formulation of his theory of social solidarity and social evolution. By 1887, he was recognised as an eminent sociologist. At the University of Bordeaux a course in social sciences was created for him — the first recognition of social sciences in France.

In 1887, he organised the Anne'e Sociologique. Immediately many consider this successful project as his greatest service to sociology. Its twelve volumes eventually covered the years from 1898 to 1914. It presented specialised monographs, many on cultures of non-literate people and made annual surveys of the work and literature of social sciences. Durkheim gathered a group of brilliant men around him for this project, and they made a detailed and critical analysis of much of the sociological and anthropological literature. The Anne'e Sociologique became an important source for original, empirical investigation and also served as a lively forum for current theoretical discussion. Its moto became 'The Unity of Social Sciences and Specificity of Research'. It was always a collective enterprise. The major headings of its great range of subjects were: General Sociology, Juridicial and moral Sociology, Religious Sociology, and Social Conditions of Thought.

Durkheim was an outstanding and popular teacher. His students called him as one of the great heroes of human thought. He brought to his students a great wealth of subject-matter, and a profound, critical acumen in the treatment of data. Durkheim was intensely patriotic. At the outset of First World War, he devoted himself to education and propaganda related to war effort. As a lecturer and writer, he engaged in what he called 'moral refreshment' both for the troops and the people at home. He accepted an official position with the government during this time and was known for his motto: Patience, Effort, Confidence.

Though as brave as he tried to be in practical world, his essential delicacy could not withstand personal tragedy. His son Andre, a promising student in sociology, was wounded twice in the war and died in 1915. He could not bear the shock and became seriously ill in December 1916. He made one last effort to complete a large work in the field of ethics, but died on November 15, 1917, with much of his contemplated work unfinished.

In the writings of Emile Durkheim, the concept of function took on greater methodological significance and he is widely regarded as a functionalist by sociologist and social anthropologists. But if a distinction is made between functionalism as a consistent theory and the use of function as a method of explaining certain social phenomenon, Durkheim is not functionalist in case of former. Although he had used the notion of function quite extensively, his discussions about the meaning of function are relatively rare.

One of Durkheim's concerns was to establish sociology as an autonomous discipline. Although Comte had baptised the new science and enunciated some of its principles, sociology was not recognised in France until 1887, at which time Durkheim was appointed to a lecturership in social science at the University of Bordeaux. To many of his contemporaries, sociology appeared to be a dangerous innovation. When

Durkheim was called to the University of Paris, in 1902, he occupied a chair of ethics and philosophy of education, because sociology was so far non-existence in French capital.

In Durkheim's view, sociology had to be both autonomous and scientific, if the subject was to have any future. Autonomous meant that its data and explanations must be independent from biology, psychology or from any other science. Social data were to be explained by their own principles, but sociology must be on the same scientific footing as the natural sciences. Positivism dictated that science must deal with concrete and observable things. Durkheim found such things in the social realm, what he called 'Social facts'. These facts were marked off from all other phenomena by their 'exteriority' and their 'constraint'. Exteriority meant that they were given to an individual. Social beliefs, duties, practices, were waiting for him ready-made at the birth. Social facts were also constraining, because they were endowed with coercive powers imposed themselves upon people, regardless of their personal wills or desires.

These formulations create the impression that Durkheim was superorganicist, conceiving society a reitied entity residing in a separate realm and binding people to its will. In fact, this was just the opposite of what he had in mind. In his view, society was completely inseparable from people not merely because, obviously, society cannot exist without its carriers, but more important because society makes man social.

This view of Durkheim differed sharply from Enlightenment rationalism, which had depicted man as the sole master of his fate, capable of freely selecting better ways of life, to liquidate the past, and to shed the constraints of religion. Durkheim felt strongly that social facts could not be manipulated, but that there was a continuous interaction between man and society, and a necessary interrelationships between the two. Man was not the sole manager of society, but neither was he a robot. In fact, it was individualism that had caused society to change. Individualism, however, itself was not of a completely personal nature, but was itself some how a social fact that had progressed and evolved through its interaction with other social institutions.

Durkheim's Organistic View of Society

The basis of Durkheim's work in sociology was laid down during the five years (1882-1887), when he served as professor at the Lycee of Sens. It was during this time that he adopted what is called organistic view of society. Here, he was indebted to Spencer and Espinas, who conceived of society as some kind of 'living whole', Durkheim's view of the 'organic nature of society'; is different, however, from the scholars mentioned above. Suffice it here to say that Durkheim would use such phrases as social body, social brain, social protoplasm and cerebro-spinal system of social organism, i.e., society.

With Durkheim, as with Spencer, a necessary implication of the organic view of society was that, being a reality, society must be studied, described and explained in a separate realm. Although obviously related to psychological phenomenon, 'social facts' cannot be explained by psychology, the whole what is more than some of its parts and must be studied on a separate level. Durkheim has been criticised for this view as imputing a metaphysical reality to society, but while his language supports this change, it seems clear that he simply wanted to consider social facts as things so that social phenomena could be treated with the scientific method.

Durkheim's Contribution to Methodology in Social Sciences

Durkheim's contributions to methodology in Social Sciences are of great importance. His general aim was to make society an empirical study and he endeavoured in his work to practise the 'crucial experiment' used so successfully in physical sciences. This was in sharp contrast to philosophers, like Hobbes and Hegels, who attempted to construct systems which would embrace the entire field of human activity, and to the anthropologists, like Spencer, Tylor, and Frazer, who made great comparative survey from the point of view of evolutionary sequences. Talcott Parsons, a Sociologist of America, calls Durkheim as "one of the greatest empirical scientists of his days" and goes on to say that "Durkheim was a scientific theorist in best sense of one who never theorized in air, never indulged in idle speculation, but was always seeking the solution of crucially important empirical problems".

In the preface to the *Division of Labour* (1893) Durkheim writes, "This book is above all an attempt to treat the facts of moral life by method of positive sciences". According to Parsons, Durkheim is faithful to the true positivist position.

Durkheim insisted that for an empirical treatment of social data it is necessary to treat 'social facts' as 'things'. This important postulate, the basic to all his works, has caused much confusion, a condition which can be traced to his use of language. Durkheim's insistence on considering social facts as things grew out of his determination to avoid the deductive, rationalistic approach which characterized so much of the work of Comte and Spencer, among others. As an empiricist, Durkheim had to work with data which could be observed, described, classified and explained, not merely deduced form a few arbitrary postulates, such as psychic unity of mankind and unilinear evolution. For Durkheim, to say that a social fact is a thing, is simply to identify social data. All that is given, all that is subject to observation, has thereby, the character of thing. To treat phenomena as things is to treat them as data, and these constitute the departure of science.

In his zeal to emulate the methods exact sciences, Durkheim probably over-dramatised the reality of the social realm and left himself open to the charge of attributing a metaphysical reality to social phenomena. But all he seems to be saying is that since social institution are exterior to individual and exert a power of constant over him, they can be considered as a part of individual's world. They can be studied as such: "A social fact is to be recognised by the power of external coercion which it exercises, or is capable of exercising over individuals, and the presence of this power may be recognised in its turn either by the existence of some specific sanction or by the resistance offered against every individual efforts that tend to violate it.

Although they originate in collection of individual minds, social facts come to any given individual from a realm outside himself (society) and must, therefore, be explained in terms of other social facts, not interms of facts of a different order, such as biological or psychological. Durkheim was of opinion that social phenomena could not be explained by psychic phenomena. Social facts, though they come to each individual from an external reality, do become internalised in the individual consciousness and represent what the individual has in common with the group. They are, so to speak, society within the individual and can be distinguished from the biological consciousness which defines a unique individual. In the social category, Durkheim included such concepts as time, space, force, causation, legal and moral codes and the like.

The implications of methodology outlined above, earned for Durkheim, the title of 'Father of Functionalism in Social Sciences'. Radcliffe-Brown and Malinowski were influenced by Durkheim's concept of functionalism. Radcliffe-Brown cites Durkheim's definition of function as, "the function of social institution is correspondence between it and the needs of the social organism". The needs of a society are related to, but are on a different level from, the needs of individuals who constitute that society. The individual is born into social world as he is born into physical world. It existed before him and will exist after him. The conditions of the existence of the social world are not necessarily the conditions of the existence of the individual and must be studied separately.

Radcliffe-Brown states that Durkheim was first to make a systematic formulation of the analogy between society and organic life, and that his basic assumption was functionalism. As the life of an organism is considered to be the functioning of its organic structure, therefore, social life is conceived by Durkheim to be the functioning of social structure.

Durkheim's Contribution to the Development of General Sociological Theory

Talcott Parsons has listed four stages in the development of Durkheim's general sociological theory. These stages are:

1. Early Formative Period: Division of Labour (1893)
2. Early Synthesis: Rules of Sociological Method (1895) and Suicide (1897).
3. Transition: Individual Representation and Collective Representation (1899), Moral Education (1902-3), Determination of Moral Facts (1907).
4. New General Position: Elementary Forms of Religious Life (1912).

His book, *The Division of Labour* (1893) takes up as its central problem the nature of social solidarity and evolution. On the assumption that the hostile forces in man require some kind of enforced cooperation for survival, Durkheim takes examination of social rules of conduct, both legal and moral, in order to discover the conditions of social solidarity and evolution. He was of opinion that variations in society would serve as reliable clues to the enternal structure and function of the society. He found these variations in moral and legal codes, social statistics (suicide rates) and religious practices. The division of labour concentrates on the legal and moral codes, which are seen as expressing the social needs of a society.

Emile Durkheim was of opinion that early societies were small and homogeneous. People had similar tasks, and thus, possessed similar values and emotions. This totality of social similitudes led to what Durkheim called a collective or common conscience or a set of social rules held in common and experienced in common. In such a situation, individualism could not find expression and was weakly developed. The integration of this type of society was one of 'mechanical solidarity' based upon the common values, in the absence of a division of labour. Those who attempted to express their individualism and broke social rules were severely punished by repressive law', not so much for the purpose of correction, but because anti-social behaviour threatened the solidarity without which these primitive societies could not persist.

Thus, Durkheim turned to a study of legal and moral codes as the place to look for the true sources of social cohesion. He was of opinion that the characteristics of moral rules was that they enunciated the fundamental condition of social solidarity. He finds there a distinction between two types of law: (i) Repressive and (ii) Restitutive. Repressive law, according to Durkheim, is an expression of traditional customs, beliefs and sanctions of a society and is blindly adhered to under threats of punishment. He calls social solidarity based on repressive law as mechanical solidarity. Mechanical solidarity, maintained largely by hereditary right, is found in primitive, undifferentiated societies, which are organised on totality of beliefs and sentiments common to all members of the group. He calls this as collective type.

Restitutive law, on the other hand, stresses restitution instead of punishment and affects only certain segments of the group at any one time. Its function is to preceive the *status quo*, not to enflict punishment for crimes against the communities. Restitutive law is an indication of organic solidarity. According to him, organic solidarity is based on the cooperation of specialized individuals.

Where the restitutive law predominates, the society is organised on the basis of specialized difference, in which solidarity rests on a system of different, special functions with definite unity. Since mechanical solidarity rests on the absorption of individuals into a totality of common beliefs and sentiments, it is achieved at the price of individual personality. Organic solidarity, on the other hand, rests on the assertion of that which is personal and distinct in the individuals, but it must not be supposed that in case of organic solidarity an individual comes to depend less upon society. The exact opposite is the case, for increased specialization (assertion of individual differences) results in need for greater interdependence, and society supplies rules for regulating the necessary relations between individuals. This type of social solidarity, like the unity of the organism, is as great as the individualism of the parts is moire marked. Hence, he phrases organic solidarity.

As the society increased in size and complexity, the social tasks could no longer be the same for every one. In other words, a division of labour came into being and the differentiation of social tasks also caused diversification of values and emotions. It was then that individualism could begin to assert itself. Certain personality broke away from tradition and mechanical solidarity, and became the first political leader.

> Chiefs are, in fact, the first personalities to emerge from the social mass. Their exceptional situation, putting them beyond the level of others, gives them a distinct physiognomy and accordingly confers in-

> dividuality upon them. In dominating societies, they are no longer forced to follow all of its movement. A source of initiative is, thus, opened, which had not existed before them. There is, there after, some one who can produce new things and even, in certain measure, deny collective usages. Equilibrium has been broken (Durkheim 1893:195).

Mechanical integration or solidarity could no longer be operative, when this trend further developed. A new form of solidarity had to come into being, because people were no longer of one mind and presumed different goals. These ambitions themselves were socially organised in and through division of labour. Division of labour reduced competition and assigned different tasks to different people, who thus became increasingly mutually dependent. The new form of solidarity was called as organic solidarity, by Durkheim. Organic solidarity meant that the division of labour itself had integrative power. The term organic was borrowed from biology. However, Durkheim noted that there was an important difference between the biological and social realm. In the organism, each cell had a defined role and was unable to change it, while men, even in rigid social systems, were not so predetermined and always possessed a certain degree of liberty. As division of labour increased, liberty also increased.

The change from homogeneous to heterogeneous was, thus, explained as an interaction between social and individual factors. Individualism, in Durkheim's view, was not a personal pursuit of happiness or a decision to banish religion, but an almost necessary development in the growth of society. The ultimate cause of change was the natural increase in population that brought about an increased moral density. This was not merely a matter of large numbers, but also related to degree of communication. If communication increases, people will also have to cooperate more. If populations also increase in number, the communicating and cooperating segments will differentiate from other such segments.

Perhaps not overly satisfied with this explanation, Durkheim appealed to Darwinian theory to explain as to how differentiation may arise. Since organism, everywhere, struggled with one another, such competition would evolve in human societies, too. Thus, Durkheim did not take social change for granted, but searched for the explanation as to how transition from mechanical to organic types of society could have taken place. While the social change had been progressive one in as far as social personalities could better express themselves, individuals were not necessarily happier in modern societies than in traditional ones.

Durkheim felt that 'anomi' — absence of norm — had entered, threatening society with disintegration. Individualism was desirable in itself, but contained inherent danger because it might divorce people from Society. Thus, Durkheim when talked about primitive to civilized societies, he held evolutionary views. In this connection, he agreed with Spencer that increased specialization among the individuals of a group led to the cooperative interdependence which has characterised the evolution from primitive to civilized societies. But where Spencer, a prominent of utilitarian individualist theory in economics, attributed this cooperation to contractual relations between individuals for their mutual advantage, Durkheim, on the other hand, insisted that such regulations are given by society and are not created by individuals, while pursuing their own immediate interests. Thus, the happiness or self-interest principle, which according to utilitarian view, was supposed to lead men to social cooperation was entirely discounted by Durkheim.

Durkheim's famous study on Suicide (1897), represents an extension of the basic idea found in his first book, *The Division of Labour* (1893) to another empirical field. These are important theoretical refinements and modifications in this study. In this book, he continued the analysis of pathological aspects of modern society. He selected the topic suicide for study, because it demonstrated the coercion of social facts even in these seemingly most personal decisions. More over, the occurrence of suicide illustrated in the most striking manner the interrelationship between the individual and collectively.

In division of labour, Durkheim had cited the increased suicide rate in nineteenth century as an argument against the happiness principle of utilitarians. Using statistical tabulations, Durkheim showed how there were no consistent correlations between rates of suicide and organic or psychic dispositions such as race, poverty, insanity, personal unhappiness, similar personal factors, and heredity. There may be psychological and biological predispositions, but since frequencies of suicide remained fairly constant in given societies or regions, they must be due mainly to social determinants. On the basis of statistical and theoretical construct, he distinguished three factors operating in suicide rate, altruistic, egoistic and anomic. Each one was related to existing degrees of mechanical or organic solidarity.

The altruistic suicide is associated with the idea of extreme mechanical solidarity, where the collective attachments and pressures are so strong that the individual life becomes relatively unimportant. An example of the altruistic suicide in Indian context is *Sati Pratha*, in which a Hindu widow throws herself on the funeral pyre of her husband and is cremated with him. She, thus, follows the command of the society without asserting her individualism.

The egoistic suicide was committed most often in transient types of society, where mechanical solidarity had diminished and organic solidarity was not yet in full force with the progressive emphasis on value of individuality (a characteristic of social evolution and the growth of civilization). The individual tends to become exalted over all other objects and ideas, such as God, society, country and all other repositories of collective sentiments. When, in the extreme, the individual becomes so detached from social institutions that he cannot recognise or feel the power of an authority beyond himself, he is faced with a desolation which can make life unbearable. In course of dislocation, the stress and anxiety he finds himself without group support and is likely to take his own life out of desperation.

To illustrate the egoistic suicide, Durkheim cities statistics from political, religious and family life. He shows that suicide rate has significant relationship to family status: married persons have lower rate than unmarried and parents have lower rate than childless couple. The parents of large families have the lowest rate of all. In the field of religion, he finds that free-thinkers have the highest rate of suicide followed by protestants, catholics and Jews respectively. The suicide rate is lower in the measure that the assertion of authority in religious group is higher. Durkheim opines that the distinction between the protestant and catholic is not that one is free of group pressure and other is not. The protestant, too, is under group pressure.

Anomic Suicide was the type that predominated in societies with organic solidarity. It is increased in terms of social stress and unrest. This type of suicide was related to the presence of strong individualism which often gave rise to social expectations that could not be realised. The increase in anomic suicide rates revealed the pathological aspects of modern society, which in turn were related to lack of integration of the individual with his society. Durkheim attempted to demonstrate that neither family, nor religion, nor State or government could provide a context of integration in modern societies. He felt that only corporations or professional organisations could reintegrate society. This was the Durkheim's version of socialism. It was also his moral philosophy, namely that social facts must be constraining by their authority and that man should live willingly and even happily by these commands. According to Durkheim, anomic is simply the weakening or disruption of conscience collective — that system of social norms which reflects a commonality of beliefs, sentiments and feeling. It is a disastrous freedom from social constraint, where individual can find no direction or meaning to life. Anomic is not to be confused with egoistic freedom, which is really a special kind of constraint and a positive expression of the conscience collective.

According to Durkheim, Suicide cannot be regarded as abnormal because it is a phenomenon invariably associated with all societies. In deed, he points out that suicide is a close kin to genuine virtues, which it simply exaggerates. He means, here, the virtues of social solidarity (attruism), individuality (egoism) and flexibility (anomee). But Suicide can become abnormal when it passes beyond certain limits, the limits being relative to any given society. The great increase rates in suicide during the 19th century, according to Durkheim, be classified as abnormal and pathological in origin. Then the question is, what are the sources of increased rate and how can it be reduced?

Durkheim finds that the altruistic current in suicide has not increased, in fact, it has diminished. The egoistic and anomic currents have shown a great increase and can alone be considered morbid. In both cases, the underlying cause is a weakening of social solidarity due to rapid expansion and differentiation of a revolutionised economic structure. The old institutions, family, political state, religion, are not meeting the needs of individuals. The modern state is too far removed from individual and, too complex to permit a day to day personal identification and assimilation.

Like Comte, Durkheim turned to the analysis of religion towards the end of his life, coming from a family, with a long lineage of rabbi, he had broken away from its tradition and become agnostic. But throughout his life, he remained convinced that religion was a social fact acting as a moral force. Unlike Comte, Durkheim did not repudiate any of his previous theories, when he began to write about religion, but he considered his last book, *The Elementary Forms of Religious Life* (1912), a summing up of his whole sociology. In this book, he wanted to demonstrate that religion was a social fact par excellence and said that Comte was wrong, when he believed that one individual could create a new religion. He also attacked Tylor, Frazer, Spencer, and all others, who had explained religion in individualistic and cognitive terms as a belief in supernatural powers. To him, religion was not an illusion, not an idle fantasy, but an identifiable social fact with important social meanings and functions. The study of religion, according to him, is a study of social reality that it expresses.

His book, *Elementary Forms of Religions Life* (1912), is based on secondary sources for its data, primarily on the anthropological material from Australia. It is important not only as a treatise on primitive religion, but also as a major contribution to sociological theory and general epistemology. When he finally applied himself to a full-scale study of religion, instead of making a comprehensive survey of the field (like Tylor, Spencer, Frazer), he selected a specific case for intensive study, namely Australian totemism. He undertook this study with familiar assumption that religion, like any social institution, must be regarded as a response to specific social needs and that as a social phenomenon, religion is a product of collective thought. Durkheim makes two distinctions which are basic to his entire study of religion. These are: the distinction between belief and rites and the distinction between sacred and profane. The first distinction separates the elements of thought and action in religion, whereas the second separates religious attitudes from other human attitudes. It is the origin of sacred ideas that receives most attention. According to Durkheim, sacred is a set of rituals and objects set apart from the profane by special prohibitions, dispensations, and prescriptions that do not pertain to every day life. Religion is, then, a united system of beliefs and practices relative to sacred things., which unite into one single moral community, all those who adhere to them. The question was as to how sacred could have arisen. In order to solve this question, Durkheim turned towards most primitive religion, namely the totemism of Australian aborigines.

Among Australian aborigines, society was perfectly homogeneous, with most rudimentary civilization and most simple social organisation. They lived in small nomadic groups. Several nomadic groups were related among themselves by bonds of kinship, which gave birth to clan. The members of clans gathered together at specific times when food was plentiful. Clans had their own names, most often, taken from a species of plants or animals, which was called as totem. Each object of totem had its visual representation in an emblem, serving as proof of identity with the clan. The collective label was often engraved on objects of stone or wood, tattooed or drawn on the body or carved on shields and ornaments.

On the basis of these ethnographic data, taken from secondary sources, Durkheim reconstructed what might have been the origin of religion. He opined that nomadic groups were normally busy with food-gathering, hunting, fishing etc. Thus, their life was uniform and dull. When annual meetings of clans took place, the things began to change. Members met their kinsmen and heard the latest news. Now there was plenty of food and exchange of wives also took place. Young men, thus, underwent initiation rites and everyone wore his or her most beautiful decorations. When clans were united, conditions became very far removed from those, when simple nomadic groups used to wander in isolation from each other. The clan gatherings were festive and exciting, and primitive aborigines almost lost control over themselves and their emotions.

According to Durkheim, there is nothing inherent in an object, such as the totem, which evokes a sacred attitude. Rather, it is projection of belief upon an object that makes it sacred. In other words, a sacred object is a symbol. It stands for some reality and our search should be not for the origin of sacred ideas and object, but for the realities which are being symbolized. According to Durkheim, the positivist, such realities must be observable. He holds views that reality is society, because only society can be observed to exercise moral authority. Religion is a society symbolized and elevated to a position of unassailable moral authority. Society as the expression of collective sentiments of people, is above all moral reality. Religion is complete representation of that reality. It is better to say that for Durkheim, society is a religious phenomenon. All the great social institutions have been born in religion. If religion has given birth to all that is essential in society, it is because the idea of society is the soul of religion.

Thus, the world of sacred things came into existence through the unification of clan. The clan itself was symbolised and made visible through the totemic emblems that were all around during these festive meetings. Thus, the objects of totem became the sacred entity. Religious power — religion itself thus, was nothing other than the collective power of the clan. The objects of totem representing it became the God of primitive societies. It was towards this impersonal power that worship was directed, since totemic societies are permanent than any one individual. Totems or societies based on them are external to man and superior to him. Religion is, thus, social reality that develops moral forces in man. Because morals are those of society itself, they must be obeyed.

In this way, Durkheim explained and analysed the totemism in different way than 19th century evolutionists, who attempted to establish absolute origin of religion as a historical fact. In other words, evolutionists attempted to discover how it happened. Durkheim, on the other hand, wanted to discover as to why it happened. He took into consideration the religion of simple society for discovering the essential social characteristics of religion in general. According to him, these social characteristics of religion remained the same throughout the history. Aboriginal religion, i.e., totemism, was not different from the most advanced religions, but only the appearances differed. God may be personal or impersonal, ritual may be simple or complex, but everywhere, religion distinguishes between profanes and sacred realms. Everywhere, religion is essentially social and it symbolizes moral and social interests. In this way, the function of religion is that it reaffirms society and also reaffirms man as a social being.

From the above descriptions, it is evident that the concept of function is inseparable from his basic concept of society, namely that it is suigeneris, representing a reality of its own. Thus, function was not the serving of needs of individuals, but the needs of society as a whole. It is this concept that separates Durkheim most sharply from British functionalists. The latter often transferred Durkheim's social functions to an individual level and discussed them in terms of biological, psychological, or personal human needs.

Considering the above contributions of Durkheim, it can be said that Durkheim was an inspiring force for later anthropologists and sociologists. Anthropologists, for the most part, have emphasised his contributions to ethnological literature, specially as the editor of Anee's, his study of totemism and his functional method. The sociologists have paid less attention to his specific contributions to the study of primitive people and have emphasized upon the importance of his general sociological theories, especially as they appear in Division of Labour and Suicide. They have also hailed him as the founder of modern sociological method. He has been called the First of the Moderns in Sociology and the Father of Functionalism in Anthropology. Both of these titles he earned by his particular methodology. His idea of applying the methods of physical sciences to sociological data was insisted upon to a remarkable degree.

Durkheim is criticized for his neglect of psychology. In stressing the importance of studying society as a reality suigeneris, Durkheim refused to acknowledge the relevance of individual psychology for sociology. According to him, a collection of human individuals create phenomena far beyond the expectancy of any one individual. In this situation, how can we explain these phenomena by making the individual the central problem. In fact, since man is primarily a social product, therefore, it is the study of society, which must precide the study of individual behaviour.

Although often considered as averse to psychology, he emerges in this area as a Social Psychologists of the first order. This is especially clear when he makes functional analysis of ritual and ceremonies in primitive societies, where he insists on relating these symbolic activities to what people actually do in their everyday social life.

Claude Levi-Strauss

Levi-Strauss was born in 1908 in Belgium. From 1914-1918, he lived with his parents near Versailles. From 1927-1932, he was a student in the University of Paris, where he took a degree in law, with aggregation in philosophy. His reading included works by the masters of the French School of Sociology — presumably Saint Simon, Comte, Durkheim, Mauss. From 1932-34, he worked as a teacher in Lyc'ee. He was professor of Sociology at the University of Sao Paulo Brazil from 1934-1937. During this period he seems to have returned to France on several occasions. He also made several brief visits to interior of Brazil to engage in ethnographic investigations by the end of the period, he had about five months of actual field experience. In 1938-39, having resigns from the service of the University of Sao Paulo, he obtained French Government financial support for a more extensive expedition to central Brazil. The details of expedition are hard to determine. Everything Levi-Strauss has written about the Nambikwara and Tupi-kawahib Indians seems to be based on this experience. From 1939-40, he was in France on military service. In 1941, he was invited at New York to take up a post at the New School of Social Research Engineered for him by Robert Lowie, E. Metraux, and Max Ascole. From 1946-47, he served as the French Cultural Attache in U.S.A. He came back to France in 1950 to occupy the post of Director in the Laboratory of Social Anthropology, University of Paris. In 1959, he was appointed as Professor of Social anthropology at the College de France. At present, in addition to the chair of social anthropology, he occupies the chair of comparative religion of non-literate people. He has been an editor of Scientific Research journal in France since its inception in January 1961.

Claude Levi-Strauss, Professor of Social Anthropology at College de France, is by common consent, the most distinguished exponent of his particular academic trade to be found anywhere outside the English speaking world. The scholars who call themselves social anthropologists, are of two kinds: the prototype of the first was the late Sir James Frazer, the author of *Golden Bough*. He was a man of monumental learning, who had no first hand acquaintance with the lives of primitive people about whom he wrote. He hoped to discover the fundamental truths about the nature of human psychology by comparing the details of human culture on a world-wide scale. The prototype of the second was Bronislaw Malinowski, born in Poland, but naturalised English man, who spent most of his academic life analysing the results of research, which he had himself personally conducted over a period of four years fieldwork, in a single small village, far off Malenesia. His aim was to show how this exotic community functioned as a social system and how its individual members passed through their lives from cradle to the grave. He was more interested in differences between human cultures than their overall similarity.

Most of those, who call themselves social anthropologists, either in

Britain or in United States, claim themselves as functionalists. In other words, they are anthropologists in style and tradition of Malinowski. In contrast, Claude Levi-Strauss is a social anthropologist in the tradition not in the style of Frazer. His ultimate concern is to establish facts which are true about the human mind, rather than about the organisation of any particular society or class of society. The difference is fundamental. Levi-Strauss record has been quite different. From the very beginning, he has been a strait scholar intellectual. By Malinowski standard, Levi-Strauss field research is of only moderate quality. The outstanding quality of his writing, whether in French of in English, is that it is difficult to understand. His sociological theories combine baffling complexity with overwhelming erudition. Some readers even suspect that they are being treated to a confidence trick. Even now, despite his immense prestige, the critics among his professional colleagues still greatly out number the disciples. Yet his academic importance is unquestioned. He is admired not so much for the novelty of his ideas, as for the bold originality with which he seeks to apply them. He has suggested new ways of looking familiar facts. It is the method that is interesting, rather than the practical consequences of the use, to which it has been put. His method is as much linguistic as anthropological. It has aroused excitement among many different brand of intellectuals, students of literature, politics, ancient philosophy, theology and art.

Levi-Strauss' structural approach is partly based on Sapir's and partly on Troubetzkoy's linguistic approach. Troubetzkoy says that structural linguistics is based on four operations. These are: (i) the study of unconscious linguistic structure, (ii) the treatment of terms not as isolate, but as a set of relations, (iii) the study of structure of a system, and (iv) discovering the general laws. Levi-Strauss, following the approach, considers that social structure is distinct from empirical reality. Social relations consist of raw materials, out of which models making up the social structure are built. Before dealing with the theoretical contributions, it will be the fitness of the thing to present the publications of Levi-Strauss. His major publications are:

1. *The Elementary Structure of Kinship* (1949)
2. *Tristes Tropeques* (1961)
3. *Structural Anthropology* (1963)
4. *Totemism* (1963)
5. *Mythologiques* in four volumes (1964, 1966, 1968 and 1972)
6. *Savage Mind* (1966).

Levi-Strauss Contribution to Models and Reality of Social Structure

To Levi-Strauss, the most fundamental problem is the understanding of modes of human thought, for cross-cultural comparisons. He is of opinion that the principles of cognition or of thought may be comparable for cross-cultural analysis. His particular approach is known as structuralism, but his concept, nature and analysis of social structure are very different from Radcliffe-Brown. Levi-Strauss agrees with Radcliffe-Brown that structure is an ordered arrangement of parts or components, but Radcliffe-Brown took interpersonal social relationships as his point of departure. Radcliffe-Brown examined social structure in order to discover social functions. These functions always possessed an utility, minimum serving to maintain the coherence of the social whole. Levi-Strauss is not concerned with such functions and considers them self-understood. Function is to produce the consequences, which it does produce. He is concerned with the structure not from the aspect of interpersonal relationships, but he wants, first and foremost, to discover the structure of human thought process.

While Radcliffe-Brown conceives of the concept of social structure as a kind of model, he nevertheless considers it to be an actual aspects of reality, especially insofar as it has descriptive as well as analytical use. Levi-Strauss rejects this position from the out set:

> The term social structure has nothing to do with empirical reality but with the models which are built up after it. This should help to know clearly the difference between the two concepts which have often been confused, namely, social structure and social relations. It will be enough to state at this time that the social relationship consists of raw materials out of which the models making up the social structure are built, but while social structure, by no means, be reduced to the ensemble of social relations to be described in a given society. Therefore, social structure cannot claim a field of its own among others in social studies. It is rather a method to be applied to any kind of social studies, similar to the structural analysis current in other disciplines.

Thus, a structure is model which fulfils certain specified criteria, it must exhibit the characteristics of a system, i.e, the behaviour of any one part modifies all other parts. It must be possible to order a series of transformations on the basis of any given model, which will result in the generation of a group of models of the same type. It must be possible, in the light of foregoing properties, to predict how the model will react, its parts are replaced or modified and the model must be such that it immediately renders all the observed facts in illegible.

Levi-Strauss' Mechanical and Statistical Models

According to Levi-Strauss, there is relationship between the scale of the phenomena to be analysed and the scale of appropriate model. Mechanical model is a model, the elements of which are on the same scale as the phenomena. Statistical model is a model, the elements of which are on different scales as the phenomena. An example of mechanical model is the model of law or kinship in primitive society in which prescribed and prohibited unions can be generated from a knowledge of certain defined principles of affinity. Kinship in our own society would have to be interpreted according to a statistical model, on the other hand, because permitted and prescribed marriages are not governed by a set of generative rules, but by factors as diverse as chance, social mobility, social class, and even the pure emotional desires of those involved. However, Levi-Strauss does not make clear what he means by scale ? In this regard, an attempt has been made by Leach to clarify this problem. He draws a distinction between Jural rules (mechanical model) and statistical norms (statistical model). But this distinction of Leach does nothing to resolve the problem, because the relationship between them is still left problematical. The formers are qualitative rules of behaviour supported by social sanctions, while the latter are simply statistical averages of individual behaviour. Further more, as both Leach and Levi-Strauss deny the empirical reality of their model, we are left to explore by ourselves the implications of the employment of "ideal types" as our models and clearly the relationships between two classes of abstracts is even more obscure than the relationship between those abstract and reality.

Thus, what makes social structural studies valuable, is that structures are models, the formal properties of which can be compared independently of their elements. The Structuralist's task is, thus, to recognise and isolate levels of reality which have strategic value from this point of view, namely, which admit of representation as models whatever their type. Structural studies aim at isolating strategic levels and this can be achieved only by carving out a certain constellation of phenomena. From that point of view, each type of structural study appears autonomous, entirely independent of all others and even of different methodological approaches to same field. On the other hand, the essential value of these studies is to construct models, the formal properties of which can be compared with, and explained by, the same properties an in models corresponding to other levels. Thus, it may be said that their ultimate end is to override traditional boundaries between different disciplines and to promote a true-interdisciplinary approach.

Distinction Between Social Anthropology, Sociology and History

According to Levi-Strauss, anthropology uses and devotes itself to the construction of mechanical models and exists in context of reversible and non-accumulative time. In other words, it is timeless. Sociology and history, on the other hand, deal in time, that is an oriented and non-reversible process and its constructions are statistical.

Levi-Strauss' Notion of Communication Structure

Levi-Strauss notion of communication structure forms a bridge between Radcliffe-Brown's recognition, i.e., the functioning of structure and the notion of transaction. The processes which activate social structure, can, be seen as communication of people, goods, services, ideas or whatever. Furthermore, communication, by definition is not arbitrary, but operates according to rules. The activities which constitute social communication are, thus, structured. In this way, structural anthropology becomes a contributor to a much wider discipline —that of communication, and this underlines the formalism of the method, which we have been expounding:

> The next advantage of this increasing consolidation of social anthropology, economics and linguistics into one great field of communication, is to make clear that they consist exclusively of the study of rules and have little concern with the nature of pattern (either individual or groups) whose pay is being patterned after these rules.

This seems to be a quite remarkable thing for a social anthropologist, for it describes a subject with form, but no content. But it is a natural consequent of arguing that models are constructs, not empirical entities or processes. Levi-Strauss' constant preoccupation with mathematics is to be seen as both a cause and an effect of his wider structuralist doctrine. We also see here notion that the function or recurrent activity is to maintain the structural continuity of the group. Kinship system, marriage rules, and descent groups constitute a coordinated whole, the function of which is to ensure the permanency of social group by means of intertwining consanguineous and affinalities. They may be considered as the blue-print of a mechanism which pumps women out of their consanguineous family to redistribute them in affinal groups, the results of this process being to create new consanguineous group, and so on. As

Levi-Strauss recognises, that structures are not static, but are subject to out side pressures and internal developments, so we must introduce a diachronic elements into our model to allow for this. Furthermore, there is more to social structure than to kinship structure. These two factors must be absorbed into the working of our model.

We may do this by three means. Firstly, we may regroup the facts relevant to the simplest possible model which will explain the situation. It is the first step in structural analysis.

Secondly, when we have ascertained these facts, we may attempt to correlate the phenomena belonging to new order but showing a direct connection with the former. Thirdly and finally, our problem is purely formal. It consists in a *priori* deduction of the types of structure likely to result from relations of dominance or dependency as they might appears at random.

With the aid of certain quantifiable concepts such as transitivity, order and cycle, it becomes or could become, when the appropriate mathematical techniques become available, possible to study formally the generalised types of social structure when both the communication and sub-ordination aspects are fully integrated. It is also possible to enlarge the field of inquiry and to integrate, for a given society, actual and potential types of order.

The anthropological conception of society is, thus, a network of orders, such as the kinship system, social organisations, and orders of stratification. An order of orders or analytical hierarchy can be constructed by showing the relationship which exists between the various sub-order within the total network. The legitimacy or integration of such a network may, further more, need to be explained by ideological or supra-rational orders such as myth and religion. These orders are not themselves real in the sense applying objectively verifiable existent entities, but are never the less part of the social structure in so far as they contribute to its functioning and its explanation by those who belong to it. Levi-Strauss is of view that social anthropology can only become rigorous, when a methodology appropriate to the level of complexity of the material is found and applied. The details of this methodology as conceived by Levi-Strauss are to be seen in it, application to concrete cases of sub-orders of the social structure. For example, myth, totemic organisation and kinship prescription and prohibition. In his paper entitled, "Social Structure" (1953), Levi-Strauss is concerned with abstract and general principle upon which such analyses are based. But for this, he has been criticized because he is of opinion that prerequisites of structural analysis, are to collect facts and to order them. But he does not refer to criteria by which we may collect such facts. Unless there are independent criteria for selecting the facts, how does one decide which to include or which to exclude?

Levi-Strauss attempts to counter this criticism by making a distinction between observation and experimentation. According to him, to observe facts and construct model out of them, is not the same as experimentation on those models on the observational level. The rule is that the facts should be carefully observed and described, without allowing any theoretical preconception. This rule implies that the facts should be studied in relation to themselves and in relation to the whole. Experimentation includes what happens when we investigate, what happens when a given model is subjected to change or when we compare models.

There is direct relationship between the detail and concreteness of ethnographic description and the validity and generality of the model which is construct after it. Though many models may be used as convenient devices to describe and explain the phenomena, it is obvious that the best model will always be that which is true. The simplest possible model which, while being derived exclusively from the facts under consideration, also makes it possible to account for all of them.

Levi-Strauss makes a clear-cut distinction between conscious and unconscious models as the latter is fundamental and the former is derivative. One is, thus,faced, with the formidable task of clearing away the conscious models formulated by people to explain their culture or society to themselves in order to get underlying basic structures. Levi-Strauss notion is that social structures may be conceived of communication structures, which are partly concerned with structural linguistics and partly on structural relationships.

Levi-Strauss' Views on Structural Linguistics

According to Levi-Strauss, linguistics itself is a social science, but it is only one among all the social studies, to have attained the status of a full science. The more affinity a subject has with linguistics, the more closely should it seek to collaborate with it. He is of view that ever since the distinction between kinship terminology and kinship structures cleared, social anthropologists interested in the study of kinship organisation have been unable to pay considerable attention towards the structural aspects of language. Therefore, in order to deal with kinship structure, the structure of language is also necessary from the study point of view. Similarly, there are areas of historical and socio-linguistics in which linguist cannot make progress without utilising anthropological data. According to Levi-Strauss, the piecemeal and unsystematic collaboration between anthropology and linguistics has been revolutionized by the appearance of structural linguistics.

Method of Structural Linguistics

According of Levi-Strauss, the methods of structural linguistic may be reduced to four basic operations. Firstly, it shifts its attention from the study of conscious linguistic phenomena to the study of their infrastructure, which is unconscious. Secondly, it does not concern itself with linguistics terms as distinct or isolated entries, but rather with the relations between terms. Thirdly, it employs the concept of systems and fourthly, or finally, it aims at discovering general laws.

Levi-Strauss held opinions that in the study of kinship or other problems as well, the anthropologist finds himself in a situation, which formally resembles that of the structural linguist. Like phonemes, kinship terms are elements of meaning. Like phonemes, they acquire meaning, only if they are integrated into systems. Kinship systems, like phonemic systems, are built by the mind on the level of unconscious thought. Finally, the recurrence of kinship patterns, marriage rules, prescribed attitudes between certain types of relatives and so forth, either in scattered regions of globe or in fundamentally different societies, lead us to believe that in case of both, kinship as well as linguistics, the observable phenomena result from the action of laws, which are general but implicit. Thus, although belong to another order of reality, kinship phenomena are of same type as linguistic phenomena. Thus, according to Levi-Strauss, the relationship between methods of anthropology and linguistics is one of the analogy, but there are also some limitations. For example, if we are to study kinship terms as phonemenas, i.e., breaking them down into their components, the result in practice will be more abstract than principle. In other words, the resulting system will be more complex than empirical data on which it is based.

According to Levi-Strauss, bearing in mind distinctive characteristics of kinship terminology, we can overcome the above difficulty. The kinship terms by definition are also parts of speech and must be treated directly by method of linguistics. The linguistic structuralism is not applicable directly and just as there is no necessary relationship at its vocabulary level. In other words, kinship terms, as vocabulary elements, are not themselves amendable to structural treatment. The kinship system of terminology, is also a system of attitudes comprising of elements such as respect or familiarity, rights or obligations, and affection or hostility. The system of terminology and system of attitude need not necessarily be coterminus, and in practice they frequently are not, although they are functionally, related. Levi-Strauss believes that the application of formal method of structural linguistics in the theory of attitudes may provide the means of elevating such a theory to a generalizable and analytically valuable level. His illustration about this may be found in his notable discussion of structural principles governing the avuncular relationship.

Several quasi-linguistic points do emerge from the analysis of avunculate. The first of these is proposition that a kinship is a language. Just as language is semantic system par excellence, so kinship, art and other aspects of culture may also claims to be systems with semantic functions, even though such functions may be fragmentary or subjective. In other words, like language they are symbolic systems. The second point is that the structural principles or grammars of such systems are largely unconscious, although this does not prevent them from being elucidated by correct method. The corollary of this is that we may be able to show that all forms of social life are substantially of same nature. As the projection on the level of conscious and civilized thought, they provide illustration of the universal laws, which regulate the unconscious activities of the mind. They apparently may be subject to universal but unperceived laws, stateable interms of abstract and measurable relationship, which constitute the basic nature of phenomena under study.

Levi-Strauss Views on Language and Culture

Levi-Strauss is of opinion that: (i) language and culture are homologous, or (ii) language and culture are formerly similar, or (iii) language and culture are analogous to one another, or (iv) language and culture are correlates. The bases for this belief are that (i) they both admit of structural treatment, and (ii) they are both products of activities which are basically similar. The consequences of this are that (i) the principles of their working must be sought at unconscious level, and (ii) each is governed by universalizable rule. The whole argument is underpinned by the generalization that like language, kinship, art and other manifestations of culture are communication system. Levi-Strauss says:

> Without reducing society or culture to language, we can interpret society as a whole in terms of theory of communication. This endeavour is possible on three levels — (i) kinship and marriage rules serve to ensure the circulation of women between groups, just as (ii) economic rules serve to ensure the circulation of goods and services, and (iii) the linguistic rules ensure the circulation of messages. Thus, art, religion, myth, ritual are also example of such languages.

The difficulties appear to be two-fold: First if we use the term communication to describe all systems in which something is transferred from one actor or group of actors to another, it is clearly the danger that any process, by virtue of its being a process, has some communicative function in natural sense. But it is equally clear that 'semantic communication', i.e., transfer and sharing of meaning, is something other than the mechanism of transfer themselves. They need not always accompany those mechanics, as when a language user fails to communicate, even when he is employing the medium of his own language.

Secondly, we may ask question, is kinship, or art, or religion, etc. a language? To solve this question, we need three things: (i) which cultural processes are language and how do we distinguish them from non-language aspect of culture? (ii) In what respects do these cultural language differ from language itself? And (iii) if all these manifestations are the product of the same innate structuring capacity, how do we account for these differences in its specialised product? These questions are obviously very closely related.

On these questions, Levi-Strauss says,

> I think all problems are linguistic ones. Languages seems to me the cultural phenomena par excellence for several reasons. First of all because, language is part of culture, one of the skills or habits we acquire from external tradition. Secondly, because language is essential instrument, the special means by which we assimilate group culture. Thirdly and lastly, important of all, because language is the most perfect of all those cultural manifestations which, in one respect or another, constitute systems. If we want to understand art, religion, law, even cooking or rules of politeness, we must imagine them as being codes formed by articulated signs, following the pattern of linguistic communications.

Thus, we see that Levi-Strauss borrows his most important methodological tool from linguistics with particular reference to phonemics. Thus, so-called Prague School of Linguistics, led by N. Troubetzkoy and Roman Jacoban, demonstrated that the structure of language cannot be found by a mere inventory of its sounds, but it is the relationship between sounds that provides significance. These relationships are not normally conscious in the minds of speakers, but they from the basis for discovering cross-culturally valid invariant rules.

Levi-Strauss Contribution to Kinship Study

Turning first to the study of kinship organisation and marriage rules,

Levi-Strauss examined the structural relationships of their constituent elements, rather than considering them in isolation. Before Levi-Strauss, kinship system had been studied in the manner of prestructural linguistics. The sets were broken down into their smallest units and the nature of these elements was discussed in terms of interpersonal relationships or related to other social meanings and functions. Levi-Strauss attempts to solve the unconscious logic behind kinship classification and marriage rules by considering the relationship between their constituent units. These relationships consist of opposition and correlation, interchanges and transformations. Thus, correspondences are not explained in terms of mechanical casualty but in terms of logic. Since this logic is universal, both intra- and inter-cultural comparison become possible.

In his book entitled, *Elementary Structure of Kinship* (1949), Levi-Strauss took incest taboo as his point of departure. Incest taboo is not *a priori* category, because it has been empirically established that it appears in every society, though specific rule differs from society to society or culture to culture. It is fact that incest taboos possess social functions, these cannot account for their origin. It is so because, it is impossible to believe that early men who instituted these rules, could have known their possible social advantages. Instead, incest taboos ultimately depend upon the property of human mind to think in opposites. The most fundamental dichotomy to be recognised for man to become human and to develop culture, is that between self and others. Only when this distinction is made, a true symbolic communication is possible. The communication is reciprocal exchange that takes place on three fundamental levels: (i) exchange of messages, (ii) exchange of goods, and (iii) exchange of women.

According to Levi-Strauss, incest taboos are concerned with exchange of women. Among animals, mating is random and promiscuous, but incest taboo, by its very nature, dictates an ordered exchange of women, and, thus, also institutes marriage rules. This reciprocity sets in motion a cycle of reciprocal exchange on the other levels. Incest taboo, thus, marks the differences between animal and man, which is also between nature and culture. This most basic dichotomy is present in many cultural systems, such as totemism, myth, art, ritual and the ways in which people name their pet animals.

Levi-Strauss View on Totemism

In his book *Totemism* (1962), he attempts to show that animals and natural objects are chosen as symbols of clans or families, because they are useful as linguistic and classificatory devices to order social relationship between groups. Totemism also reveals the relationship between nature and culture. Criticising the old pattern of studying a totemic group, Levi-Strauss points out that a strong tradition connects totemic institutions with the strict rule of exogamy. He is of opinion that when we speak of totemism, we actually confuse two problems. The first problem is that posed by the frequent identification of human beings with plants or animals, which has to do with general views of relations between man and nature. The second problem is that of designation of group based on kinship, which may be done with the aid of animal or vegetable terms, but also in many other ways. The term totemism covers only cases in which there is coincidence of two orders.

There are two questions related to this. Firstly, why it is that animal and vegetable species should be chosen to provide a nomenclature of a social system? Secondly, there is the question of what kinds of relationship exist between animal/plant species and social system ? The answers of these questions by that animal world and plant life are utilized not merely because they are present in natural environment, but because they suggest the mode of thought of human mind. The relation of man to nature and the characterisation of social groups, only seem so because the real link between the two orders is indirect, passing through the mind.

The nature of the factors involved can be elucidated by the application of the structural method which will enable us to define objectively and in most general aspects the semantic field within which are found the phenomena commonly grouped under the name of totemism. This is to be done by recourse to three operations:

1. We may define the phenomena under study as a relation between two or more terms, real or supposed.
2. We must construct a table of possible permulations between these terms.
3. The resulting table is to be taken as the general object of analysis, because at this level only it can yield the necessary connections, the empirical phenomena being contingent.

Thus, the concept of totemism covers relations, posed ideologically, between two series, one natural and the other cultural. The natural series comprises, on one hand, categories, and on the other, particulars. The cultural series comprises groups and persons. These terms may be associated in four ways:

	1	2	3	4
Nature -	Category	Category	Particular	Particular
Culture-	Group	Person	Person	Group

Each of these four combinations has its empirical counterparts. The first combination may be noted in social and sexual totems of some Australian tribes, where there is a relationship between a natural category of animal and a cultural group — moiety, section, sub-section, cult-group or corporate group of members of same sex. An example of second combination is North-American Indian individual totemism, in which an individual seeks to identify himself with some natural category by means of physical traits. The third combination may be represented by the case of totemism in Mota (Bands Islands) in which a child is believed to be the incarnation of an animal or plant discovered and consumed by the mother at the time, when she becomes aware of her as an expectant mother. The fourth combination is the familiar example of a natural species being accorded protection by a social group as among Maoris. According to Levi-Strauss, only first two instances have been included in sphere of totemism. The rest two, the totemic illusions are the result of distortion of semantic field, which results from a mistaken division of reality. According to Levi-Strauss, the earlier totemists had committed two mistakes. Firstly, they assumed the relationship between the totem and man as a direct one, based on contiguity, whereas, in fact it is always masked or metaphorical. Secondly, they ignored the opposition between personal and collective relation with the totem.

In this double sense, the totemic relationship is implicitly distinguished from guardian spirit, which involves a direct native theory itself. This invites us to separate stress, the mediating and metaphorical character of the relationship between man and the eponym of his clan. It puts us on our guard against the temptation to construct a totemic system by accumulating relationship taken one by one and utilising in each case one group of men to one animal species. The primitive relation is between two systems: one based on distinction groups, and other on distinction between species, in such a fashion that a plurality of groups on the one hand, and a plurality of species on the other, are placed directly in correlation and opposition.

There are many situations in which to represent the world of animal life in terms of human social relations and in which the resemblances and differences of animal species are translated into terms of friendship, conflict, solidarity and opposition by grouping them in pairs of opposites, which have at least one characteristic in common, and which allows them to be compared. In other words, we can see at work, a general structural principle consisting of the union of opposites.

The alleged totemism is no more than a particular expression, by means of a social nomenclature formed of animal and plant names, which is its sole distinctive characteristic, of correlations and oppositions. In totemism, natural species are chosen not because they are good to eat but because they are good to think. Their perceptile reality permits the embodiment of ideas and relations conceived by speculative thought on the basis of empirical observation. Thus, Levi-Strauss has not dissolved the problem of totemism. He has merely lifted it to the plane of logic, rather than of fact. His is a mental totemism, not a non-totemism.

Levi-Strauss, Views on Savage Mind

In his book entitled, *Savage Mind* (1962), Levi-Strauss tries to reach into human mind at the structural aspects of unconscious. His approach is through linguistics rather than through psychology. He is of view that the basic property of human mind is to think, the resulting systems are by no means simple. The dualism itself is often sub-divided. Its element may be unequal or asymmetrical and triadic divisions may intertwin with all others. It is evident that dualism is not a mere catchword. The dichotomising of human mind is of a structural nature. While it is not necessarily conscious, it gives a specific shape to the arrangement of social phenomena. Any dualism evokes new arrangement and new complications. Thus, it does not lead to identical social organisations, but produces every new forms. The most important activity of human mind is to organise the raw materials of experience provided by history and environment, but the laws of organisation are common to all human beings. Thus, when he talks about Savage Mind, he is not concerned with primitive mind, but with universal mind of human beings.

His starting point is that human mind has a language. At one level, this allows man to communicate and form social relations, and another level, it is essential element in mysterious process we call thinking in that we must first categorize our environment and then represent these categories by symbols (elements of language, words), before we can think about them. The process of thinking by means of word and symbols entails a highly complex interplay between the individual, who is doing the thinking and the environment about which he is their king.

Levi-strauss holds view that human mind has a logical mind of thought, which is found in all societies whether primitive or civilized. He points out that each culture has its own system of concepts and categories derived from experience and imposed by the surrounding natural world. Through the order in naming of plants and animals, concepts of space and time, myths and rituals, how do primitive societies engage in high level of abstract reasoning different from but not necessarily inferior to that evolved in cultivated systematic thought.

Levi-Strauss' Contribution to Structural Analysis of Myth

Since the time of Frazer, the study of myth has been a major area of anthropological investigation. But also since Frazer, confusion has flourished as to how myth should be approached, interpreted, and explained. The competing views are that myth represent archetypal and fundamental human feelings, they are explanations of natural phenomena, and they are disguised description of social relationships within the society. These views carry with them little evidence on the basis of which we might decide between their claims. The problem, which perhaps, first springs to mind in dealing with myth, is its apparent contradictions. On the one hand, everything goes, there seems to be no logic, little formal continuity, and the attributes of people, animals, and objects can change at a moment's notice in most fantastic manner. On the other hand, many mythic themes are universal and constant. How can we explain this basic antinomy ? According to Levi-Strauss, this problem can be solved only by recourse to the insights of structural anthropology.

But before dealing with Levi-Strauss' structural analysis of myth, let us discuss some peculiar characteristics to myth. The first of these is the notion that myth is a language or code at one level, and at another that myth is a language, in its original form, it does not exist except as a speech act, an oral phenomena. We may, thus employ, both Saussure's distinction in that myth, like language, is both *langue* (the structural and reversible aspect) and *Parole* (the statistic and non-reversible aspects). Myth may also be distinguished by a third characteristic, that the pattern of events or attitudes described is timeless and that explains or applies to present, past and future equally. In other words, myth is linguistic and that, it possesses the characteristics of langue and parole, but is distinct from language in that it is a historical. Secondly, Levi-Strauss is of view that we must place myth at the opposite end of spectrum of linguistic expression from poetry. Poetry is a kind of speech which cannot be translated, expect at the cost of serious distortion, whereas the mythical value of the myth is preserved, even through the worst translation. The substance of myth does not lie in its style, its original music or its syntax, bu in the story which it tells.

Finally, Levi-Strauss sums up his views on myth in series of propositions, which are as follows:

1. If there is a meaning to be found in mythology, it cannot reside in the isolated elements, which enter into the composition of myth, but only in the way those elements are combined.
2. Although myth belongs to the same category as language, being a part of it, language, in its mythic usages, has certain specific properties.
3. These properties are more complex than those found in any other kind of linguistic expression, i.e., they exist above the ordinary linguistic level.
4. Myth, like rest of language, is constituted out of units.
5. The units, while they presupposes the constituent units of language (phonemes etc.), differ from these that the mythic units are of higher and more complex level.

Levi-Strauss search for nature of unconscious mind led him almost inevitably to the study of myth. Of all activities of human mind, myth making is least ruled by functional necessities and nearest to the unconscious. Kinship system, marriage rules, and village organisation are at least particularly influenced by the contingencies of social life as it has to be lived, but myth stands apart from such considerations. The myth-making mind is constrained mainly by its own inherent principles and not by social utility. Mythology has no obvious practical function. If then, the human mind proves to be structured in the function free realm of myth: It must also be so determined in all other spheres of mental activity.

Describing his basic method in an article entitled, "The Structural Study of Myth" (1963:206-31), Levi-Strauss took various versions of Oedipus myth as his example. Levi-Strauss opines that for studying myth, we must have some way of identifying the units of myth, i.e., mythemes and of distinguishing them from the lower level linguistic units. We must look for these mythemes at sentence level. Thus, we may proceed to analyse myth by breaking down its story into shortest possible sentences and each sentence will generally show that each function is linked with a given subject. Each units will consist of a relation. The next step is to recognise that the true constituent units of a myth are not the isolated relations, but bundles of such relation. It is only as bundles that these relations can be put to use and combined so as to produce a meaning. Thus, the first task is to note down each function-sentence in the myth and them to arrange these sentences in bundle. Thus, myth is not to be read as story, but must be broken down into its basic constituent elements or mythemes and the relationship between them must be examined. They represent the nature-culture dichotomy, hinging on the incest taboo.

In his subsequent four-volume *Mythologiques* (1964, 1966, 1968, 1972) Levi-Strauss shows the full strength of his method. In the Raw and the Cooked (1969), he explores 187 South American myths and in subsequent volumes, a further six hundred Indian myths are examined and analysed. While they are often very different in content, Levi-Strauss endeavours to demonstrate that their underlying structures display significant similarities. Together, they are like an orchestral score, where each instrument says something different, but what it says is part of a structural whole.

The differences between myths are brought into harmony by analysing them in terms of relatively simple oppositions, among which one between nature and culture figures quite prominently. This implies that it must be shown that unlike mythical elements possess the same structural significance. It is at this level that great difficulty arises. Although Levi-Strauss stresses again and again that overt meaning are not important, it is nevertheless necessary to deal with semantic meanings in order to show that myth are structurally equivalent. Mythemes are, thus, translated, transposed and transformed to indicate their common ground. Though Levi-Strauss does this with great elegance and eloquence, the transformation often appears arbitrary and far-fetched. Thus, since honey is always consumed raw, it represents nature. But honey is also enticing and seductive. Hence, all myths dealing with seduction stand in same structural position as honey. Ashes are produced by fire. Fire is one of man's earliest inventions, and both fire and ashes signify culture. Tobacco needs fire for its consumption, and wild Pig's meal is never eaten uncooked. Myths dealing with tobacco or with the origin of wild pig are, thus, related to those dealing with fire, ashes, cooking, smoke and burning.

Although, Levi-Strauss holds that the unconscious logic of mind is of much greater importance than the analysis of the content of the myth, and thus he seemingly attempts to remove myth or kinship or totemic beliefs away from concrete empirical reality. But he did not remain satisfied with structure devoid of social meaning. He well realises that incest taboos, once they are instituted, possess certain social advantages, and that art of myth reflects other things than the unconscious structure of mind. In pursuing those aspects, Levi-Strauss is more closer to, what anthropologists consider, the core of their discipline and here he is most brilliant and creative. Where Boas did not really know what to do with the Indian myths, that he so painstakingly collected, Levi-Strauss shows how each myth reflects and interests with features of environment, and is meaningful and concrete at social level also. Particularly when he analyses song myths and when he places them within their own ecological and socio-cultural matrix, he shows that they can have explanatory functions that had not been previously realised and that they are much more systematic than as they had been supposed. But for these kinds of explanations, it is not necessary to invoke the unconscious structure of mind.

Although with different emphasis, this aspect of Levi-Strauss cultural analysis is not unrelated to the work of cognitive ethno-scientists, who also elicit the rationality of folk-classifications and relate them to other social facts.

5

CULTURE AND PERSONALITY SCHOOL

In previous chapters, we have seen that evolutionary theories of culture came into being by the efforts of classical evolutionists, who believed in progress of culture or cultural institutions in unilinear sequence, i.e. from simple to complex form. On the basis of empirical studies, diffusionists discredited the evolutionary sequences of cultural growth They opined that culture not always progresses, but some traits also disappcar. This doctrine of diffusionists was known as 'degeneration theory'. Diffusionists attempted to show that culture traits diffuse and migrate and are borrowed from one place to another or form one cultural group to another. Both schools of anthropological thought, evolution and diffusion, were historically-oriented. In the middle of present century, neo-evolutionary school of anthropological thought came into being, which revived the theory of cultural evolution with some modifications. The pioneers of neo-evolutionary school proposed such universal and multilinear sequence of cultural evolution, which was accepted to all.

British anthropologists, namely, Malinowski and Radcliffe-Brown, discredited both the historically-oriented schools of evolution and diffusion. They held view that historical reconstructions of evolutionists and diffusionists, based on ethnological and ethnographical accounts, were not historical in strict sense, because history begins with writing. Therefore, to show evolutionary sequences, and cultural borrowing, diffusion and migration, on the basis of unwritten account, was not historical rather pseudo-historical. Therefore, attempts should be made to emphasise upon present and now, rather than past and then.

Malinowski developed a methodology for the scientific analysis of culture by which the existing cultures could be compared, analysed and interpreted. This methodology of Malinowski was known as functionalism. According to Malinowski, the functional analysis of culture aims at explaining that culture is an instrument for the satisfaction of needs of human beings, which may be basic, derived and integrative. It is the satisfaction of these needs, upon which the survival of human beings and culture is dependent.

This view of Malinowski was not accepted to his colleague, A.R. Radcliffe-Brown who emphasized upon the need of studying society in place of culture from the structural-functional point of view. He preferred to include the study of society or societies under a separate branch of anthropology, known as social anthropology. He was of opinion that a society is composed of different structural units such as social institutions (family, marriage, kinship etc.). The study of these social institutions reveals interrelated and interpersonal relationships between their members in an ordered arrangement, like the ordered arrangement of parts of an organism, house, music, etc. He was of opinion that structural-functional methodology for studying, explaining, interpreting and analysing a single society or for making comparisons between different societies, was the most useful tool in social anthropological studies. However, the functionalism of Malinowski and structural-functionalism of Radcliffe-Brown was criticised because they were lacking historical explanations or diachronic description. Their theories were based on ahistorical explanation or synchronic description. Later on, followers of Malinowski and Brown admitted the significance of diachronic or historical or change-oriented studies. They started dealing with change and dynamism of culture or society.

In British anthropology, the followers of Radcliffe-Brown began to emphasise the importance of social anthropology in place of cultural anthropology, as the subject-matter of the latter included more than the study of social institutions, which form the subject-matter of the former. British School of Structural-functionalism was influenced by the French anthropologist and sociologist, Emile Durkheim, who stressed upon the study of social facts or things in order to show the social solidarity. While in France, Durkheim emphasized upon the study of social facts consisting of social solidarity, Levi-Strauss, another French anthropologist, emphasized upon the study of structure of unconscious mind of human beings. His approach is known as Structural-linguistic, because he stressed upon the need of analysing unconscious structure of human thought through the study of language.

During 1920s, some students of Boas and Kroeber, namely Ruth Benedict, Margaret Mead, Linton, Cora-Du-Boris, etc. became critical of the theories of evolution, borrowing, diffusion, migration, function, social structure, and other traditional approaches of anthropology. They held views in common that these anthropological theories of culture and society could not lead any basic understanding of cultural practices. According to them, cultural practices were nothing but the character, or temperament or personality of members of a particular group. The cultural practices were different for different groups. In other words, they began to deal with such question as to why there is similarity in personality or character traits of members of a particular group, though examples of individual variations were not exception. Again, why the personality type of one group differes from other? They arrived at conclusion that differences in cultural practices or personality traits, or pattern of behaviour, etc. among different groups, were due to differences in cultures. In their views, it was culture, which influenced the practices, character, temperament or personality of group members. All members of a particular group are reared in the same cultural environment, according to which their character traits or personality types are shaped. In other words, culture plays significant role in personality formation.

These scholars felt the necessity of studying inter-action between culture and personality or *vice versa* on the basis of psycho-analysis. In their views the two subject, anthropology and psychology, should come at the same platform for studying the influence of culture on personalty or *vice versa* or both. Their methodology or approach is known as anthropo-psychological approach or culture and personality approach. Their methodology, views, and contributions, formed the culture and personality school of anthropological thought. This school is also known as school of psychological anthropology.

The pioneers of psychological school of anthropology were influenced by 'Gestalt psychology'. Gestalt psychology deals with total perception of behavioural pattern of human beings. They were also influenced by theory of cultural integration as putforth by Malinowski. They perceived integration of culture as configuration of cultural traits and complexes. These traits or complexes were interrelated and interdependent, but their accumulation in integrated whole, provided a special design or pattern of a culture. It is on this basis of pattern or design, that similarities and differences in character or personality between two or more groups can be revealed on the basis of cross-cultural comparisons.

The primary aim of culture and personality school of anthropology is to examine the interrelationships between culture and personality. Instead of seeking to analyse culture as it is manifested in material items or non-material items, like social institutions, the scholars of culture and personality school of anthropology or psychological anthropologists, study culture as it is embodied in the character of its member. In other words, they deal with the study of role of culture in formation of character or personality. According to them, as culture is acquired, imitated and learnt, it gives rise to character formation or development of personality traits before the period of adolescence.

MEANING AND CHARACTERISTICS OF PERSONALITY

Before discussing the theoretical contributions of each scholar of culture and personality school, it will be fitness of the thing to present here, in brief, the meaning of personality and its characteristics.

The term personality has been used in several senses, both popularly and psychologically, but the comprehensive and satisfactory being the integrated and dynamic organisation of the physical, mental and social qualities of the individual as that manifests itself to the other people, in the give and take of social life.

We may define personality as the more or less integrated body of habits, attitudes, traits, ideas of an individual as these are organised externally into specific and general roles and statuses, and internally around self-consciousness and the concept of self, ideas, values and purposes which are related to motives, roles and statuses.

To sum-up, the following characteristics of personality may be listed:

(i) Personality is not related to bodily structure alone.
(ii) Personality is an indivisible unit.
(iii) Personality is neither good nor bad.
(iv) Personality is not a mysterious phenomenon.
(v) Every personalty is unique.
(vi) Personality refers to persistent qualities of the individual.
(vii) Personality is acquired.
(viii) Personality is influenced by social interaction.

DETERMINANTS OF PERSONALITY

The factors or determinants, which affect the personality formation are as follows:

1. *Environment:* The geographical or physical environment sometimes determines the variation in personality construction of members of a group. The personality of two cultural groups, residing in two geographical areas is found different, because of the fact that both groups have different geographical environments. For example, Eskimos have different cultural personality than American Indians because of the fact that former have a geography different to the latter. The culture and personality of people residing in hills and plain areas of India are different, as they belong to different geographical area. The cultural practices, characters, personalities of tribals inhabiting the hilly and forested area are quite different from the inhabitants of plain area. Thus, to the extent

that the physical environment determines cultural development and to the extent that culture in turn determines personality, a relationship between personality and environment becomes clear. Nearly two thousand years ago, Aristotle claimed that the inhabitants of Northern Europe were full of spirit, but lack in intelligence and skill, owing to a cold climate. On the other hand, natives of Asia are intelligent and inventive, but lack in spirit, and are, therefore, slaves. Thus above-cited examples reveal clearly that climate and topography determine, to a great extent, the physical and mental traits of the people, but they alone do not determine personality.

2. *Heredity:* Heredity is another factor which determines the traits of human personality. Some of the similarities in man's personality are said to be due to common heredity. Every human group inherits the same general set of biological needs and capacities. These common needs and capacities explain some of our similarities in personalities. Thus, personalities of Hindu, Muslim, Sikh, Christian are different. Again among Hindu, personalities of different castes are different.

As an infant inherits biological characteristics from parents, they resemble parents in physical appearance and intelligence. It is due to this factor that the children of white-skinned and intelligent parents are found white and intelligent. A man with good physical structure and health generally possesses an attractive personality. A man of poor health, pigmy size, and ugly physical features develops inferiority complex. The growth of his personality is checked, rejected and hated by society. He may turn out to be a thief, dacoit or drunkard. It is also probable that he may become a leader or a genius like Socrates and Napoleon. It is important to mention here that heredity alone is not solely determinant of personality, but other factors as well such as environment, and culture etc.

3. *Culture:* Besides, heredity and environment, it is culture which largely determines the types of personality that predominate in particular group. It is the culture, as an important factor in shaping personality of a group, which has attracted the attention of the scholars of culture and personality school of thought, who are also designated as psychological anthropologists. According to them, personality is subjective aspect of culture. They also regard culture and personality as two sides of the same coin.

Ruth Benedict's study (1934) reveals that the cultural pattern or personalities of Zuni and Kawakiultl, of south-western and north-west cost of United States respectively, differ because they are reared in two different cultures. Mead's study on Sex and Temperament in Three Primitive Society (1935) of New Guinea, reveals that the personalities of

Arapesh, Mundugumor and Tschambuli, the three primitive groups of same geographical region of New Guinea, are different from each other because they differ significantly in their cultural background and behaviour.

In India, the influence of culture on personality formation can be seen in different groups. The personality and status of male and female among Toda, Garo and Khasi, who are matrilineal societies, are different from Munda, Oraon etc., who are patrilineal, because both societies have different cultural patterns according to which personalities of their members are shaped. The character and personality of different tribal communities are different due to different cultural processes and practices. The personalities of Tribal, Hindu, Muslim and Sikh communities differ because they have acquired traits and complexes of their own cultural-religious beliefs and practices. It is because of differences in cultures that different Hindu castes possess different character and personality.

From the above examples it is clear that culture plays a valuable part in personality-construction. However, there are other factors as well, which also reveal their considerable influence upon the development of personality.

4. *Peculiar Experiences:* Personality is also determined by another factor, namely, the particular and unique experiences. There are two types of experiences, one those that stem from continuous association of one's own group, and second, those that arise suddenly and are not likely to recur. The type of people, who meet the child daily, has a major influence upon his or her personality. The personality of parents does more to affect a child's personality. If the parents are kind, tolerant, interested in athletics, and anxious to encourage their child's separate interests, the child will have a different experience, and there shall be different influence on his personality, than one whose parents are unkind, quick tempered and arbitrary. In the home, the style of personality is fashioned that will, by and large, characterise the individual throughout his life. Social rituals, ranging from table manners to getting along with others, are consciously inculcated in the child by the parents. The child picks up the language of his parents. Problems of psychological and emotional adjustment arise and are solved appropriately by each child in terms of cultural values and the standards of the family. The family set up tends to bring the child into contact with the play-mates and teachers. Who are his play-game members, or his school teachers etc., this also determines his personality development. Group influences are relatively greater in early childhood. This is the period when the relationship of child with his mother, father and siblings affects profoundly the organisa-

tion of his drives and emotions, the deeper and unconscious aspects of his personality. A certain degree of maturation is needed before the child can understand the adult norms. The basic personality structure, that is, formed during this period, is difficult to change. Whether a person becomes a leader, a coward, an imitator, whether he feels inferior or superior, whether he becomes attruistic or egoistic, depends upon the kind of interaction he has with others. Thus, group interaction moulds his personality.

Sometime, a sudden experience leaves an abiding influence upon the personality of an individual. Thus, a small child may get frightened to see a bloody accident, and even after the accident, he may be obsessed by the horror and fear. Sometimes a girl's experiences with a rapist may condemn her to a life of sexual maladjustment. A book may not often change a man to renounce the world and seek God. If a man meets an accident which cripples or weakers him, he may come to entertain the feeling of inadequacy. Lord Buddha is said to have been led to renunciation by the sight of a funeral procession. Thus, experience also determines one's personality.

Thus, it appears clearly that the personality is a result of the combination of four factors, namely, physical environment, heredity, culture and particular experience. These are the factors responsible for personality — its formation, development and maintenance. However, there is one difficulty that there is no way yet known to measure the effect of each factor or to state how the factor combine to produce a given result. The behaviour of juvenile delinquent is affected by his heredity and by his home life. But how much is contributed by each factor cannot be measured in exact terms. It also appears that personality is a biological, social, cultural and psychological phenomenon.

The terms personality, character, and temperament have been used by the scholars synonymously. In the study of personality, sciences like biology, psychology, sociology and anthropology have taken keen interest. It is because of this fact that the term personality has been used to denote various meanings. A total study of personality can be done by interdisciplinary approaches in which biologist, psychologist, sociologist and anthropologist must joint their hands and extend cooperation. Biologists deal with physicological characteristics of personality of individuals. Sociologists attempt to know the influence of social environment on personality. Psychologists concern is with nature and mental aspects of personality, while anthropologists are concerned with the relationship between culture and personality.

Personality formation is related to mainly three aspects, such as physical, social-cultural and psychological. It will become clear from the diagram given below.

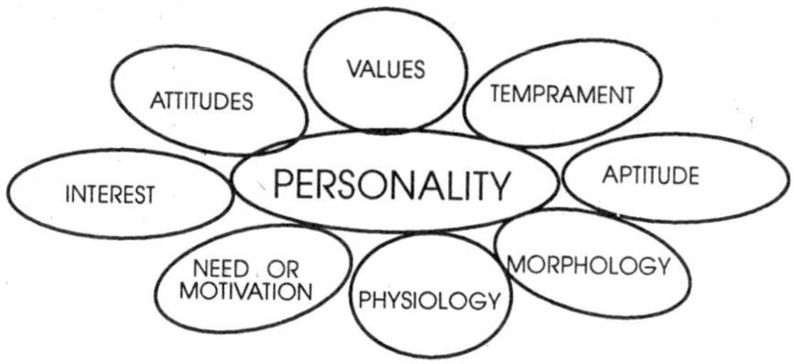

Physical aspect of personality reveals differences in physical construction, form stature, height, weight of individual. Seeing the physical appearance of an individual, we say that his or her personality is very attractive.

In socio-cultural aspects of personality, we study and discuss the socio-cultural behaviour of an individual. In this form, each individual represents culture of a special society. The culture and society, in which an individual is born influence his or her personality through tradition, customs, mores, values, religion, art, literature and language. Thus, personality is an expression of culture of the society.

The third aspect of personality is psychological. In this we can include interest, sentiment, attitudes, values, temperament, impulse, aptitude, motivation etc.

Influence of Psychodynamics on the Study of Culture

Paradoxically, it is Freud's early work in the field of individual psychology, and not his later sociological studies, that contains something of value for the social scientists. He described a psychodynamic system in which the reactions of the individuals to the problems of adaptation can be recorded. It becomes possible, therefore, to relate the conditions under which ontogenesis takes place to the end product, i.e, to the character of the individual or his neurosis.

Instead of making use of this verifiable procedure, most sociologically minded followers of Freud have attempted to some part or combination of Freud's instinct theories. It may come as a surprise to some to learn that there are several major schools in modern psychodynamics, with widely divergent points of view. Even the social scientists often overlook these differences and group the different approaches under the single headings of Freudian or Psychoanalytic. Psychodynamics is not a united theory and method, any more than is cultural anthropology or social psychology. Since there is no uniformity of theory and method, there can be no uniformity of result in its application to the study of culture. It is necessary, therefore, to distinguish several psychodynamic procedures that have been employed in this field.

First, there is Freudian concept that employs Lamarkian idea that acquired characteristics of the individual can be genetically transmitted to offspring. The general assumption that what is unconscious in contemporary man, was conscious in primitive man, is derived from this concept. It led to the theory that the Oedipus complex originated with primal parricide, that the latency period in the individual is a recapitulation of the ice-age, that Eucharist is a repetition of primitive totemic feast, and that infantile phobias are repetitions of totemism.

Freud's thesis about the origin of totems, incest taboo, exogamy and the Oedipus complex is well known. He posited the existence of a primal horde, the leader of which was the oldest male, who assumed exclusive sexual rights over all females in the group. Frustrated, the sons murdered and ate their father; but overcome by guilt afterwards, they decided to obey his commands and abstain from sexual intercourse with their mothers and sisters. Selecting a totem animal as a symbolic father substitute, they declared that it must be protected during the year and consumed only on ritual occasions. These ritual totem meals, thus, reenacted their original deed and reinforced their self-imposed incest prohibitions. According to Freud, all cultures originated from this sacrificial meal.

Freud's concept of evolution was perhaps most unacceptable of all. It represented a mixture of biological determinism and strict unilinealism. He was much more dogmatic than any or all the early anthropological evolutionists. According to Freud, mankind had developed along the same lines as infants growing into adult. Contemporary savages represented an arrested stage of the childhood of man, while Western man had attained mental maturity. As adulthood could not be reached without passing through infancy and childhood, so culture must go through predetermined biological stages of mental and social development. Not only did savages resemble children, but their fears, compulsions, lack of motivation, and attraction to what is forbidden, were traits that Freud had frequently encountered in his neurotic patients. Then, it followed that savages habits could be profitably studied by psychoanalytic method.

Another line of psychodynamic thought has Freud's libido theory as a central idea. Attempt has been made to employ this theory as scheme of social evolution. The energetic aspect of libido theory has also been applied to the explanation of social phenomena. As clinical phenomena were seen as transformations of sexual energies, so were social phenomena, such as friendship, cooperation. In this scheme, friendship was seen as a manifestation of desexualized libido. Freud's Libido theory advocates that human nature contained bio-psychological components, such as libido and its complexes, which express themselves in definite behavioural stages, independently of the specific socio-cultural environment. In other words, Freud, in the nature-nurture controversy, leans heavily towards the side of psychologists, biologists, instinct psychologists and Spencerian anthropologists. Freud and his disciples were convinced that cultural differences were superficial, and that in most significant psychological sense, all human beings were led along similar developmental routs by their common heredity endowment.

From the morphology of the ego and superego to the interpretation of dreams, to the origin of civilization, Freud's scheme depended upon the existence of a well defined universal human instinctual endowment and a definite universal ontogenetic progress through maturational stages (oral, anal, genital). Freud originally gave the name libido to instincutal source of human behaviour. Later, with the publication of *Civilization and Its Discountants* (1939), he spoke of and opposed this life force to a death instinct, from which he derived such phenomena as masochism, suicide and war.

Freud's theory regarding the universality of Oedipus complex has been criticised by Malinowski. Boas also criticized Freud's concept of origin of Oedipus complex by saying that his method was one sided and could be nothing to advance understanding of cultural development. Kroeber also held similar views. Margaret Mead's approach weighed against such compulsory psychic fright. It was her mission, set for her by Boas, to defeat the notion of narrowly fixed racial or pan human hereditary nature, and it was for this reason that he tirelessly stressed the absence of maturational regularities: Aldolescence is not always a time of stress, children are not necessarily more imaginative than adults, women are not necessarily more passive than men.

The Freudian psychology was subjected to a new synthesis by a number of American Anthropologists like Ruth-Benedict, Margaret Mead, Linton, Kardiner, a psychoanalyst and Cura-Du-Bois. This new synthesis emphasized the adaptational, rather than the istinctual, aspect of Freudian theory. They laid stress on the use of adaptational psychodynamics in the social sciences. Subsequent anthropological fieldwork was carried out in order to demonstrate the relationship between culture and personality. These scholars form a school of anthropological thought known as culture and personality school of thought. The scholars of this school have suggested three approaches to study and examine the interrelationship between culture and personality. These approaches are as follows:

(i) Culture determines the formation of personality.
(ii) Personality builds culture.
(iii) Culture and personality, both are inseparable and influence each other.

Margaret Mead, through her studies, has attempted to show the impact of culture on personality formation. It is a fact that an individual is born in a particular culture, and he or she enters into a pre-formed cultural environment, which plays significant role in his or her personality formation. An individual adopts not only the material aspects of a culture, i.e., house, tool, furniture, art, etc., but he or she also adopts non-material aspects of culture, such as religion, tradition, custom, rituals, beliefs, norms, values, ideals, etc. It is culture which teaches an individual to behave in society in a systematic way. An individual adopts culture by the processes of enculturation and assimilation. Mead studied the impact of culture on personality formation among three primitive groups of New Guinea, namely, Mundugumor, Arapesh and Tschambuli. Though these tribes were living in same geographical region, but had different characters and personalities, because of differences in their cultures. About this, we will discuss in detail, while describing the contributions of Margaret Mead.

Ruth Benedict, another lady anthropologist of America, has dealt with the impact of personality on culture. According to her, culture is personality *writ at large*. This reveals clearly that she was deeply interested in examining and exploring the impact of personality on culture. It is also a fact that culture is not self-created, but it has been created by man for the fulfilment of various kind of needs. Thus, it is individual or man, who is creator of culture. Thus, man has developed culture as a means, since time immemorial, in order to fulfil his various kinds of need. It is individual who plays significant role in handling down the culture from one generation to another. Invention, innovation, acculturation etc. form the growth of culture. In this sense, culture is a gift of personality.

There are scholars like Linton, Kardiner, Cora-Du-Bois, who believe that culture and personality are assistant to and influenced by each other. They are interdependent and inseparable. Now, let us discuss the contributions of each scholars of culture and personality school one by one.

Ruth Fulton Benedict (1887-1948)

Ruth Fulton Benedict was born in New York City on June 5, 1887. Her parents were Frederick Samuel and Bertrice-Fulton. Her father, a promising young man in surgery and medical research, died before Ruth Benedict was two years old, leaving his wife to support their two daughters. When Ruth Benedict was seven years old, her mother left the family farm and moved to the middle-west. Here, her mother was able to get a teaching profession. Four years later, they returned to New York and settled in Buffalo. Here, her mother got a post as librarian at the Buffalo Public Library.

Despite the years of financial struggle and hardship, Benedict was able to take a college degree at Vassar. She graduated in 1909 with honours. She was married to Stanley Rossiter Benedict in 1914. In this way, after marriage, she was known as Ruth Fulton Benedict. A brief career as an English teacher at a girl's school in California was followed by her marriage. Her husband was a professor of Chemistry at the Cornell University Medical School in New York City.

In 1919, Ruth Benedict, was invited to attend lectures at New School for Social Research. Here, she met Alexander Golden Wieser, a famous American anthropologist, who inspired her to join Columbia University under Professor Franz Boas. In the year 1921, she came to Columbia University. In 1922, at the age of thirty five, Benedict conducted her first field study among the Serrano Indians of California under the supervision of A.L. Kroeber. In 1923, she was awarded a doctorate degree in Anthropology from the University of Columbia. Her topic of Ph.D. thesis was, 'The Concept of the Guardian Spirit in North America'. In her thesis, she attempted to show that among North American contemporary societies, people have in mind a concept of guardian spirit. This guardian spirit commands every kind of respect and is held responsible for joys and sorrows. Thus, guardian spirit moulds the behaviour pattern of the group members. Such patterns can be seen in performances of rites, rituals, ceremonies, festivals etc., which form the part of cultural practices of a particular group. According to her, guardian spirit plays significant role in character and personality formation.

In the same year, in which she got Ph.D. degree (1923), she was appointed as a lecturer in Anthropology at Columbia University. Her field studies among the Zuni (1924, 1925), the Cochiti (1925) and the Pima (1926) followed. She also made extensive use of the field studies of Franz Boas (Kwakiutl), Ruth Bunzel (Zuni) and Rao F. Fortune (Dobu). The studies of Zuni, Dobu, Kwakiutl were presented as documentation for the central idea: the almost limitless variation of cultural pattern.

Benedict's field experience with Pima was crucial, because here she tried out the idea of studying and understanding through an analysis of their characteristic "culture pattern". This concept of culture pattern was first formulated in her paper entitled, "Psychological Types in the Culture of South-West" (1928). The concept of patterns of culture was elaborated in her famous book, *Patterns of Culture* (1934).

In addition to her fieldwork with Indians of South-West in the twenties, she studied in the forties, Asiatic and European culture patterns by using acculturated informants in the urban areas of the United States. Her book on Japanese culture, *The Chrysanthemum and the Sword*, (1946) is her best known work in this field. This book reveals the pattern of Japanese national character.

At Columbia, she carried heavy teaching and administrative responsibilities. During World War II, she made valuable contributions to government as social science analyst with the office of war information.

In the summer of 1948, Ruth Benedict attended a UNESCO Seminar in Czechoslovakia. She died in the fall of that year on her return to New York, at the age of sixty-one. Though she is no more with us, but her theories of pattern of culture and her study on Japanese national character provided feed back to many social scientists to undertake more and more researches in those areas.

Benedict's Concept of Culture-Pattern

Though the concept of culture pattern was already known among the anthropologists, but prior to Benedict, attempt was not made to show universal pattern of culture. A culture pattern is formed when traits and complexes become related to each other in functional roles. Culture traits are the smallest or single element of a culture. These units or elements when organise about some nuclear point of reference, they form culture complex. When many traits and complexes of culture become integrated into functional whole, they form culture pattern. Thus, it is clear that culture pattern of a society consists of a number of cultural traits and cultural complexes. Our Indian cultural pattern consists of Gandhism, Spiritualism, joint family system, *Jajmani* system, caste system, and ruralism. Each of these is a culture complex consisting of numerous culture traits, which give rise to culture pattern universally applicable. These are: (i) Speech and language, (ii) Material traits such as food habits, shelter, transportation, dress, tools and utensils, weapons, occupations and industries, (iii) Art, (iv) Mythology and Scientific knowledge, (v) Religious practices, (vi) Family and Social System, (vii) Property, (viii) Government, and (ix) War.

Malinowski, while dealing with the theory of need, has also formulated universal patterns of culture for the fulfilment of seven basic need. Thus, from the above description, it is quite clear that the concept of culture pattern was in vogue among the anthropologists, but they had attempted to study the universal pattern of culture, which was applicable to all existing cultures of the world.

It was Ruth Benedict who, for the first time, attempted to study the culture pattern of a particular group. The culture pattern of two societies or groups appeared dissimilar. It means that culture pattern of a group is contrasted to other group's culture pattern.

Benedict's instinct for integration and generalization prompted her to take a comprehensive view of culture. A listing and analysis of discrete culture traits seemed to her to offer little help in attempt to explain culture. With the functionalist, such as Malinowski, she insisted on studying cultures as more or less integrated wholes. But where Malinowski started with the individual, and saw cultural phenomena as derivative of individual needs, Benedict, on the other hand, started with 'cultural configurations" and saw individual behaviour as a largely conformance to given cultural imperatives.

According to Benedict, most societies have a dominant drive which tends to elaborate recurring human situations, birth, death and the quest for food and shelter, according to its own bent. For example, death among the Indians of western plains is an occasion for violent,uninhabited and extended grief among the mourners, whereas among the Pueblo of South West, the cultural injunction is to forget the departed ones as quickly and quietly as possible. The two cultures have opposite drives, which Benedict summarised under Nietzsche's terms as Dionysian (plains) and Appollonian (South-West). The former is characterized by frenzy and excess, the latter by measure and order. The exercise of religion, warfare, sex in both culture is fashioned so as to serve as occasions for the indulgence of the respective cultural drives. Thus, meaning and function of these and other institutions will be different in two cultures. The variability in any cultural trait, according to Benedict, is almost infinite.

For Benedict, there can be a functional interpretation of cultures, but never of culture. In fact, according to Benedict, there can never be a science of culture. For, if there is almost infinite variation, there can be no scientific explanation. This is the outstanding implications of Benedict's radical cultural relativity, and it can be traced directly to her teacher, Boas.

In her famous book, *Patterns of Culture* (1934), she has developed the concept of culture pattern. While clarifying the concept of culture patterns, she has talked about the configuration of culture. The culture described in Patterns of culture, illustrates Benedict's idea that a culture can be viewed as consisting of cultural configurations integrated under the domination of one general master pattern. A culture, therefore, is analogous to an individual being, in that it is a more or less consistent pattern of thought and action. Psychological terms could be used to analyse and summarise cultural characteristics. She states that cultures are individual psychology, thrown large upon the screen, given gigantic proportions and a long time span. It is this use of psychology that places Benedict among the modern anthropologists, who have attempted an inter disciplinary approach to the study of man and society.

According to Benedict, culture can be divided into big segments or sections. Again each big segment or section can be divided into sub-segments or sub-sections. The sub-segments when united themselves in a special manner, they give rise to a big segment. When these big segments, coming together in a functional whole, they form a special design of a whole culture. This special design of whole culture is known as configuration of that culture. In other words, when more traits and complexes become integrated in functional whole, they build a culture pattern and many patterns together form the culture as a whole.

According to Benedict, integration in any culture is due to the arrangements of its content in a temporary or permanent style or design. This arrangement is called pattern by Benedict. There is a particular style or design in every parts of a culture. These separate designs combine together present a grand design of culture as a whole. This is the configuration of culture. The production of this re-union in culture is due to the common tendency seen in all aspects of culture. This main tendency is called a 'special genius' of culture by Ruth-Benedict. It is this 'genius of culture' that brings about its integration. This alone is the basis of integration of form.

According to Benedict, there are two kinds of this 'genius' found in human society. One is Appollonian and the other is Dionysian. The world Appollonian is made of a Greek word *Appollo*, which means peaceful sun-deity. Lord Sun is regarded as God of peace, discipline, kind, and humanity by Greek people. Thus, in Appollonian pattern of culture, one finds the existence of peace, discipline and kindness. Benedict has cited example of Pueblo of New Mexico as representative of Appollonian culture. Pueblo are peace-loving and disciplined. They extend help and cooperation to each other. Not only in Pueblo, but Appollonian genius is found in those societies, which have peace and tranquility as their main qualities and this is the cause of their integration.

The word *Dionysian* is derived from the name of a Greek God

Dionysius, who appears to be connected with drinking and a luxurious life. In this way, Dionysian genius is found in a culture, in which great deal of storm and changes are experienced. Benedict cited examples of Dobu and Kwakiutl cultures of North-West coast of America as representatives of Dionysian genius. Thus, Benedict has accepted patterns or genius as an ideal or an induced theory, which determines the behaviour of human beings. In each culture, we come across some basic impetus, ideal of theory, which are different from other culture.These ideals or theories are accepted by all members, by which integration in behaviour pattern of people comes in to being.

Impact of Personality on Culture

As referred to earlier, besides theorising the concept of culture pattern, Benedict was also concerned with showing influence of personality on culture. She selected Appollonian and Dionysian genius as integration of personalities of two culture groups, quite opposite in their behaviour pattern. She successfully shows that how these two genius mold the personality of members of their cultural groups. The Appollonian personality compels the member of the group to behave peacefully and in disciplined way, which ultimately form special cultural characteristics for the group concerned. In the same way, Dionysian personality also shows its impact upon the characteristics of culture of that group. In this way, personality influences culture. Ruth Benedict, in order to show the influence of personality on culture, has cited examples of three cultures, namely Pueblo Zuni, Dobu and Kwakiutl. The first (Puleblo Zuni) is an example of Appollonian type of personality and the other two (Dobu and Kwakiutl) are representatives of Dionysian personality.

Pueblo Zuni of New Mexico are peace-loving, cooperative, helpful, kind and never quarrelsome. They are less inventive and respect their traditions with great enthusiasm. They have common ownership and individualism is quite absent. They work to fulfil the needs of group members, not for self. The integration of such traits and complexes in the character of Pueblo, reveals their character or personalities which determines their course of cultural behaviour. They use rituals and magic to fulfil their aims and purposes. Their religious practices show complex traits. Ritualistic activities take major part of their time. They have a keen memory regarding the details of rituals. Benedict found imitative magic among them. For example, they rolled big stones down the slopes in order to bring rains, on the faith that thunderous sound made by the stones will make the clouds thunder and rain. Thus, among them the religion is mixed with magic. Religious and magical performances are held for common welfare in the group. Competition and conflict is absent. They are non-violent and do not like change in their traditional life.

The Dobu of Malenesia are exactly in contrast to Pueblo Zuni in their temperament and character. Among them, one finds abundance of conflict, competition, combat and violence. Among Dobu also, religion is mixed with magic, but this magic is used to bring harm to others or to defend oneself against other. They are deceivers. They scarcely care for promises and compromises. In their society, promises are normally broken.

The Kwakiutl of North-West Coast of America, do not believe in religious practices. They are materialists. In their culture, wealth determines the status and prestige. Hence everyone is seen busy in earning money by hook or crook. Those, who have less money, feel ashamed on account of it. The tendency of self-assertion is fairly clear. Self-assertion is exhibited in a strange custom known as Potlatch, in which a rich person destroys even more than he has.

Above studies clearly reveal the influence of personality on culture. The culture of these groups differ because their members have different characters and personality, according to which they behave in their cultural group.

Benedict's study on National Character

During World War II, Ruth Benedict turned towards the study of national character. In the war period, anthropologists were not allowed to conduct field researches among the natives. Ruth Benedict was associated with U.S.A. Government as social science analyst with the office of War Information. During this period, she made a significant contribution in developing and applying content analysis method to the study of culture at a distance. She had been asked, by the U.S. Office of War Information to undertake research on occupied or enemy nation. Ruth Benedict selected Japanese kept prisoned in concentration camp of America for studying national character of Japan. In absence of intensive fieldwork,it was a difficult task for an anthropologist like Benedict to conduct study on Japanese national character. But she got success by examining historical documents, Japanese literature, and art form. She took interviews of Japanese imprisoned in America, went through their diaries, took life histories and case studies. She also interviewed Japanese immigrants in U.S.A. and met many reliable government officials and others, who had some first hand knowledge of Japan.

Content analysis of data was made and informations were arranged in scientific manner. As a result of all these research procedures adopted by Ruth Benedict, her book entitled, *Chrysanthemum and the Sword* appeared in 1946. The book deals with Japanese national character. Japanese culture has two methods of rearing the individual, when he or she reaches in the stage of adolescence. During childhood, an individual in Japanese culture, is given full love, freedom, care and cooperation. But as soon as he or she reaches in the period of adolescence, a strict discipline is imposed. He or she is asked to behave in manner which will be pleasant and appealing to elders. An individual as adolescent is not expected to break cultural traditions. In fact, he or she has to work according to guide-lines provided by family traditions. This paradox in personality traits of a Japanese appears due to different cultural traditions of rearing in two periods, i.e. childhood and adolescence. The title of the book is *Chrysanthemum and the Sword*. Chrysanthemum is national flower of Japan. It symbolises the socialization process of Japanese during childhood. In childhood, Japanese parents take every care of their children to make them blossomed like a Chrysanthemum flower. When the children are fully blossomed like adolescents, they have to face a situation of uttar strain. Parents leave them to earn something and lead independent life. As a result of this, they become aggressive and violent. A sword always hangs on their neck, because they do not seek cooperation from the elders. Thus, the title of the book, *Chrysanthemum and the Sword* is justified.

Though in this book, she used adaptational psychology to account for the continuities in culture, his approach is still based on the idea of genius. The personality of childhood period of Japanese is like Appollonian genius, whereas the personality of adulthood is like Dionysian genius.

Criticism of Benedict's Theory of Culture Pattern

Ruth Benedict's theory of culture pattern interms of Appollonian and Dionysian, has been criticised by another American Anthropologist, Morris E. Opler. He in his book entitled, *An Apache Life-way : The Economic, Social and Religious Institutions of Chiricahua Indians* (1941) presented a theory of themes in order to define integration of culture. He criticised the cultural configuration theory of Benedict, in which she had emphasized upon only two bases of cultural integration, namely, Appollonian and Dionysian. He was of opinion that there were not only two bases of cultural integration as putforth by Benedict, but there were many. Therefore, theory of cultural configuration propounded by Benedict was narrow, because it limited the genius of people's attempt of self-fulfilment in a culture.

Thus, Morris E. Opler begins his theory of cultural themes with the criticism of Benedict's theory of cultural pattern. According to him, themes mean those common inspirations, which create various types of behaviours in a culture. In Benedict's theory of cultural patterns, cultural integration is tied down to two special kind of behaviours viz. Appollonian and Dionysian, but in Opler's theory of themes, the integration of culture is not tied down to any special kind of behaviour. According to him, in each culture there are differences in behaviour of man. It is because each culture has its own characteristics, which are different from other. The differences in cultures are due to existence of different themes. Themes are like a kind of motivation, which provides a special form or design of both material and non-material cultures. Defining themes, he writes, "themes are proclaimed self-proved theory or situation, which controls or activates behaviour. According to him, a theme has many characteristics. In each culture, there may be many themes. In order to clarify culture themes, he has cited example of Chiricahua-appache Indians. Among them a male enjoys high status in comparison to female. The importance of male in their culture can be seen in all spheres of culture. They perform all religious rites and rituals. On the occasion of ceremonies and feast, males are given prime importance. Females are not allowed to participate in social ceremonial occasions and plays. Thus, importance of male is prevalent in culture of Appache. It is male who is maintaining integration and organisation of Appache Indian's culture.

Margaret Mead (1901-1978)

Margaret Mead was one of the two leading lady anthropologists of Columbia University. She was also a student of Franz Boas, like another lady anthropologist Ruth Benedict. It is significant to mention here that Margaret Mead was also a student of Ruth Benedict at Columbia University. Besides being a serious student of Ruth Benedict, Margaret Mead was also Benedict's close colleague. She shared with Benedict not only anthropological researches of psychological orientation, but also her (Ruth Benedict's) poetry, which she composed. Margaret Mead was influenced by Edward Sapir, another anthropologist of America and a student of Franz Boas.

Configurationalism, the identification of salient-cultural characteristics, representing the patterns of a culture, and their presentation in a familiar psychological idiom, was the fore-runner of rapprochement between historical particularism of Boas and psychoanalysis of scholars of culture personality school. We can see this quite clearly in the case of

Margaret Mead, who as a student of both Franz Boas and Ruth Benedict, made extensive use of configurationalist frame-work during her formative period. Indeed, without minimizing Benedict's contribution, Mead claims to have been an active participant in all important events leading upto the publication of Patterns of Culture by Benedict in 1934.

When Mead entered in Columbia University as a student, it was the time when British anthropologists, Radcliffe-Brown and his followers, were attempting to discredit the historical study of culture and emphasising to establish a special branch of anthropology known as social anthropology, whose prime aim was to study social structure or social organisation of communities with the help studying social institutions. In fact, Radcliffe-Brownians were attempting to establish social anthropology as a separate branch from cultural anthropology. But in America, the study of culture and its historical depth never lost its importance. Ruth Benedict and Margaret Mead's attention towards the psychoanalysis of culture brought a turning point in the study of culture in anthropology discipline. It was the time when cultural anthropologists in America began to deal with configuration of culture as integration of its patterns. The patterns of culture began to be viewed as temperament, character and personality. The influence of psychodynamics on the study of culture, led the anthropologists to form a separate school of thought under the title, "Culture and Personality School of Thought". Margaret Mead was one of the leaders of this school. Before describing the various contribution of Margaret Mead, it will be the fitness of thing to present here her publication:

1. 1928 : *Coming of Age in Samoa*. New York: Morrow.
2. 1930 : *Growing Up in New Guinea*, New York: Blue Ribbon.
3. 1935 : *Sex and Temperament in Three Primitive Societies*. New York : Morrow
4. 1937 : *Cooperation and Competition among Primitive People*. New York : McGraw-Hill.
5. 1939 : *From the South Seas*. New York: Morrow.
6. 1942 : *And Keep Your Powder Dry: An Anthropologists Looks at America*. New York: Morrow.
7. 1949 : *Male and Female*. New York: Morrow.
8. 1951 : *Growth of Culture: A Photographic Study of Balinese Childhood*. New York: Putnam. (Co-authorship with F.M.C. MacGreger).
9. 1953 : *The Study of Culture at a Distance*. Chicago: University of Chicago Press. (co-authorship with R. Metraux).

10. 1955 : *Cultural Patterns and Technical Changes*. New York, New American Library, Mentor Book (ed.).
11. 1956 : *New Lives for Old: A Study in Culture Transformation*. New York: Morrow.
12. 1964 : *Continuities in Cultural Evolution*. New Haven: Yale University Press.

Her first book entitled, *Coming of Age in Samoa* (1928) dealt with the question of whether the rebellion, that marked adolescent personality in western cultures, was a product of biological changes occurring at puberty or a result of cultural circumstances. In course of study, she found that the whole cultural mood in Samoa was much less emotional than that in America. Facts of birth, death and sex were not hidden from Samoan children. Premarital sex was considered natural and did not demand strong emotional involvements and adolescents were not confronted with the necessity of selecting from a variety of often conflicting standards of ethics and values. Adolescence was, thus, not marked by storm and stress in Samoa, but was simply a part of the gradual development of life. The major point of the study was, in Mead's own word, "the documentation, over and over, of the fact that human nature is not rigid and unyielding.

The book *Coming of Age in Samoa* bore sub-title, 'A Psychological Study of Primitive Youth for Western Civilization'. As the title and sub-title of the book reveal that Mead's mission was to emphasise the existence of bio-psychological plasticity in human affairs sufficient to permit the cultural conditioning of adolescent behavioural patterns along the lines which contrast with the stereotype of adolescence in Middle class Euro-American culture. The use of the phrase for Western civilization, in the sub-title and the inclusion of two chapters concerned with the comparison of the Samoan adolescent girl with her counterpart in the United States, indicate the importance, which Boas and Mead attached to the simple demonstration of power of cultural conditioning in this area of life. The fact that Samoan sex patterns, turned out to strikingly less inhibited than their Western analogues, could not have been unanticipated. The Adolescence, not necessarily a stormy and awkward biological epoch, was additional support for Boas emphasis upon the influence of culture as opposed to biology. It also corresponded well with contemporary interest in Freudian psychology and the role of sex in pathological personalities. The Samoan's relative freedom from sexually inspired frustrations was largely incorporated into the social foundation, while sexual revelation with the American middle class was the process of experiencing. There was also a strong feminist moral in coming of

Age in Samoa, highlighted by the description of a carefree premarital sex life for adolescent girls. But the most important moral proposed by Mead was very similar to that which Benedict, was to urge in Patterns of Culture (1934). Like Benedict, Mead found an antidote for cultural determinism in the prospect that once acknowledge of alternative determinism becomes widespread, significant changes in Euro-American way of life would necessarily ensue.

Coming of Age in Samoa did not attempt the configurationist synthesis of the sort on which Benedict was working. But there are many points of similarities between Mead's and Benedict's early writings, especially from methodological perspective, and these resemblances increased as the time wore on. Mead, as much as Benedict, succumbed to the temptation to exaggerate the decisiveness with which both individual and cultural personality types can be identified and contrasted. Although, the proposal to find out what is going on inside of people's heads, to find out how they think and feel, is perfectly respectable, it must be admitted that other forms of cultural investigation are decidedly less risky. The problems associated with developing verifiable statement about how a man feels towards his mother or his wife are more numerous and much more exposed to observer's moods and fancies. Thus, in the absence of operationally acceptable research techniques, it might very well be argued that the entire configurationist approach was premature and that the attempt to sketch the typical Samoan girl's feeling and emotions during the transition from puberty to marriage was an entirely too ambitious undertaking.

Mead has argued that the adherence to a physicalist model of science in anthropology is premature. Arguing against the relevance of statistics for the type of study that requires complex, situational and emotional of context, she compared her role to that of insightful medical diagnostician.

Mead's next major book, *Growing Up in New Guinea* (1930) is essentially a repeat performance in a new locale of her Samoan study. This book is concerned with the kind of enculturation processes by which Manus of New Guinea brought their children up from infancy to childhood and childhood to adulthood. In fact, the book deals with educative role of culture in development of personality of a child through different ages of life such as infancy, childhood and adulthood etc. In the introductory remarks of the book, Mead admits that she made the study of educational and socializational processes of Manus of New Guinea to prove no thesis and to support no preconceived theory. But in the appendix of the book, she described as to how she had originally intended to test the belief propounded by Levi Bruhol, a French anthropologist, that the animistic ingredients in primitive mentality were similar to childish thought ways, and that they would, therefore, be more pronounced among primitive children than among their parents. This hypothesis is interesting for its continuation of main Boasian thrust again biological determinism. Mead found that Manus child turned out to be less animistic than his parents and even less animistic than American children. Largely left to their own devices, Manus children remained stunted and they manifested a conspicuously dull unimaginative play life. It is a fact from which Mead drew not the altogether shattering conclusion that the movement in American education to give more freedom would produce no desirable results, unless they were given something upon which to exercise their imagination.

Mead's third important book is entitled *Sex and Temperament in Three Primitive Societies* (1935). In this psycho-cultural study, Mead deals with the impact of culture on personality formation. She has also turned to the question of degree of malleability of sexes with respect of culturally assigned sex-linked behaviour. In this book, the parallelism in method between Mead and Benedict is clearly visible. Both have dealt with pattern of cultures. Only difference is that Mead's research data are largely drawn from her own field research, whereas Benedict used data from the fieldwork of Boas and others. Like Benedict, Mead compared three different cultures, namely Arapesh, Mundugumor and Tschambuli, to test the range of variation of cultural patterns. Instead of psychologistic portrait of entire culture, Mead restricts herself largely to the problem of typing the varieties of sexually assigned behavioural roles.

As referred to earlier, Mead selected three societies of New-Guinea, namely Arapesh, Mundugumor and Tschambuli, residing in same geographical region. Though they were residents of same geographical area, New Guinea, but their culture patterns were quite different from each other. Mead became interested to study as to why societies living in same area differ in their character, personality and temperament? Again, as to why in the same society, temperaments of male and female differ. Having these questions in mind, Mead's study reveals that differences in personality types of male and female in the same society or in different societies are due to cultural processes, which differ from one cultural group to another or from one society to another. Thus, it was culture which moulds the character, temperament and personality of members of the group. Mead's conclusion, about the influence of culture on character and personality formation, on the basis of comparative study of three cultural groups of New Guinea, are as follows:

Arapesh live in such a naturally protected area of New Guinea, where they do not have fear of attack of enemy from out side. Due to this geographical location, a sense of security develops in the personality of Arapesh. Their population is also low and the yield obtained from land is also sufficient to meet food of every member. Thus, in economic field, they do not have conflict, struggle and competition. Because of these facts, their traits of personality can be identified as Arapesh are cooperative, sympathetics, peace-loving, non-quarrelsome, and kind. In Arapesh, cultural environments are such that both males and females have submissive temperament. In their culture, such personality traits are a matter of great praise, and all members of Arapesh group follow these cultural traditions with great enthusiasm. In their society, great cultural values are attached towards the observance of these traditions, which are reflected in the personality traits of Arapesh.

In the same New Guinea, there is an another cultural group, known as Mundugumor. The character and temperament of members of Mundugumor tribe are contrasted to Arapesh. In Mundugumor society, the personality traits of its members are reflected by such characters as suspicious, competitive, quarrelsome, egoistic, jealous and unkind. Among Mundugumor, both males and females are aggressive. Children are the worst sufferers on account of aggressiveness character of parents, as a result of which they also turn in to aggressive temperament. In this society, the status of male is measured on the basis of number of wives he has. Greater is number of wives, his status is regarded higher. In order to acquire more and more wives, they are found struggling among themselves. The plurality of wives disturbs the peace of family atmosphere. Females are found quarreling among themselves as well as with husband. Marriage by exchange is also prevalent in culture of Mundugumor. According to this rule, a husband is entitled to exchange his daughter for his new wife. It is because of this fact that infanticide is prevalent among Mundugumor. A mother does not like to rear his female child properly, because she believes that when she (daughter) will grow up, she will be exchanged for co-wife. Sometimes, situations become so strenuous that the mother kills the daughter. Marriage by exchange also brings conflict between father and son. Father wants to exchange daughter for his own marriage. The son, on the other hand, feels that if father goes on exchanging all daughters for himself, no daughter will be left to be exchanged at the time of his (son) marriage. Thus, a conflict between father and son becomes visible on this issue. From the above description, it is clear that the entire cultural environment of Mundugumor is such that every member is found in struggle, conflict, competition etc. with other. These cultural practices have direct bearing upon the personality formation of members of Mundugumor. It is because of this cultural factor that aggressiveness dominated in the personality formation of Mundugumor.

The third cultural group of New Guinea, on which Margaret Mead made study, is Tschambuli. The cultural traditions of Tschambuli are such that males acquire submissive temperament and females possess aggressive character. Females are all in all in the family. They are prime authority and all members never dare to disobey her. In this society, a female is free to select her husband, and males are dependent upon females. It is male who cooks, cleans houses, provides food to children. Females are found making fun with companions and providing administration in the family. It is because of this cultural facts that Tschambuli males have developed a kind, peaceful and submissive personality and females have possessed aggressive character.

Mead's Use of Photographic Technique

Right from coming of *Age in Samoa to Sex and Temperament of three Primitive Societies*, Margaret Mead conducted her researches on the basis of traditional techniques adopted by many anthropologists. She went in field, observed phenomena, interviewed male and female informants, made household census and took selected case studies. In other words, she relied too much on qualitative data. She has been often criticized for not using statistics, while making cross-cultural comparisons of personality types.

By 1936, she herself had become convinced that the method, she had been using to describe the ethos of Samoans and New Guineans, was unsatisfactory from many points: (i) it transgressed the canons of precise and operational scientific exposition proper to science, (ii) it was, too, dependent upon idiosyncratic factors of style and literary skill, (iii) it was difficult to duplicate, and (iv) it was difficult to evaluate.

One of the ways, in which Mead has attempted to overcome this difficulty, is strictly methodological. She has sought to improve the demonstrative power of her observations by employing camera and tape recorders to capture characteristically significant behavioural events in their situational context and to publish and display these records along with world descriptions. The latter are in turn based on phenomenally skilled facility for note-taking. Mead's turning to photography, both still and movie, was a direct response to the criticism to which her three books were subjected.

In 1936, Mead along with Gregory Basteson visited among the Balinese of Indonesia. She took along an unprecedented array of photographic equipment and film. Altogether, during the fieldwork period, some 25,000 Leica stills and over 22,000 ft. of 16 mm film were exposed. These pioneering experiments, in the use of mechanical aids to give ethnography an unimpeachable documentary foundation, may very well constitute Mead's most enduring contribution to the development of anthropology as a discipline. Now-a-days, visual anthropology a branch of anthropology, has emerged, whose main aim is to study the cultural behaviour and practices with the help of camera and tape recorder. She published her book on Bali of Indonesia in 1951 under the title, *Growth of Culture: A Photographic Study of Balinese Childhood*.

Her book, *Cooperation and Competition' among Primitive People*, was published in 1937. In this book, Mead has attempted to show that cooperation and competition both were present in primitive societies and were dependent on cultural and environmental factors. She selected 13 cultural groups for study. Some of them belong to food gathering and hunting, some from agricultural stage, some from industrial stage, and some from acculturative stage. She attempted to show as to why certain groups are cooperative, certain individualistic and some competitive. She found cooperation among those groups, where there was common ownership of property. She found non-cooperation among the members in societies having individual or private ownership. Competition came into being when the greed for acquiring more and more individual property went on increasing.

She also made a detail study of cooperative and competitive habit of man. She also found cooperation and competition based on age, sex, status, role, economic and political activities. On the basis of studying cooperative and competitive habits of primitive societies, she arrived at following conclusions:

(i) The competitive and cooperative behaviour are primarily the part of human organism to a situation which is set up by the natural environment itself. This is based upon a hypothesis that cooperative and competitive tendencies develop in man in struggle of survival with other organisms.

(ii) The competitive and cooperative habits are developed in the members of any group on the basis of technology.

(iii) The Social Structure of the society is the most dynamic factor in inculcating the tendencies of cooperation and competition. The social forms or institutions, which govern the interrelations of individuals in the group, and the resulting presence or absence of individual or group goals, mould the cooperative and competitive behaviour of the members.

(iv) The process of socialization and educational system play significant role in developing cooperative and competitive behaviour of members of a group.

Thus, by comparing 13 primitive cultures, she brought the point to the light that competition and cooperation habits cannot be explained in-terms of process of civilization. This can be explained in terms of variations in culture. Among the food-gathering, hunting and fishing communities, one also finds the existence of cooperation and competition. For example, Dakota, an American-Indian tribe, are cooperative, Manus of New Guinea are competitive, and Eskimo are individualistic. At the agricultural stages, competition and cooperation exist among the agricultural tribes. For instance, Arunta of middle Asia are cooperative, Ojibwa are individualistic and Ifugeo of Philippines are competitive. Thus, Mead attempted to show that the hypothesis, that primitives were cooperative, was wrong on the basis of empirical evidences. Primitives were both cooperative and competitive.

Mead's Contribution to the Study of National Character

Thereafter, Margaret Mead did not confine herself to the study of character, temperament and personality of different cultural groups. She began to study the character of a nation as embodied in its inhabitants. It was her sincere interests, that she started looking at a nation, not merely having a population, geographical boundary and stable government to rule, but as having people with cultural traditions. Cultural traditions inculcate the characters in the mind of the people, whose common behaviour, ideals, sentiment interest, ultimately form the character of a nation. Before discussing, Mead's approaches to the study of national character, it will be proper to present here the meaning of nation, the constituent elements of the nation, and the meaning of national character.

A nation can be defined as a human group, which inhabits a country determined by geographical limit, is tied by common traditions, common interests and common sentiments, and in which are found common political ambitions and the desire to be tied in a knot of unity.

A national character may be defined as the totality of traditions, interests and ideals (aspirations), which are so wide-spread and influential in a nation that they mould its image, both in mind of nations concerned and in that of other. The objective elements of nationhood are: geographical unity, unity of language, community, race and religion, and political unity and independence. The subjective elements of nationhood are: community of history and traditions, community of political aspiration, and community of sentiment.

Thus, studying national character means the study of character formation of civilizations of national territory or place. Many things come into mind, when one thinks to study national character. For instance, if one has to study the national character of India, he or she will have to go through the history of cultural traditions of India through the ages — Indus valley civilization, Vedic age, Epic age, Puranic age, Muslim period, British period and Independent India. Again he will have to go through ethnic, cultural, social, religious, communal, regional and linguistic composition of Indian population. He will also have to look at the number of states, territories, formation of government, etc. On this basis, the characters, which India possess, are a big territory, occupied by 24 States and 5 union territories, having democratic constitution and parliamentary system of Government, based on election, etc. On historical side, its character reveals that India is a country of multi-ethnic and multicultural groups, having a historical traditions, from the period of Indus valley civilization, which its inhabitants have shared and transferred to generations since time immemorial. When one considers language as a variable of national characters, he finds that India is a country of multi cultural-linguistic zones. When one considers religion as an aspect of national character, he finds India is an abode of numerous religious groups having countless number of Gods and Goddesses. Similarly, domination of villages, joint family system, *jajmani* system, socio-economic stratification, etc. reveal the characteristic features of India. These are the variables or factors to be taken in to considerations, while making a study of national character of a country. These are the characters which reveal unity as well as diversity of our country. In spite of being a nation of multi-ethnic, multi-cultural, multi-religional, multi-regional, multilinguistic groups, all inhabitants are tied together by a sentiment of we-feeling and a democratic government to look after them. This reveals the character of India as to phrase 'Unity in diversity'.

Long before the culture and personality school of Anthropology was established and systematized, it was generally recognised that human groups could be characterised by overall personality traits. Often enough, this resulted in formation of unanalysed stereotypes, depicting whole nation as brave, proud, cruel, sentimental, aggressive or weak.

Several pre-Freudian scholars were well aware of the fact that personalities were formed largely through cultural training. John Loke in his book, *An Essay Concerning Human Understanding* (1963), wrote that little or almost insensible impressions on our tender infancies have very important and lasting consequences.

David Hume in his essay entitled, "Of National Character" (1942) made the same point, when he said that men acquire manner through their relations with one another.

The German philosopher, Immanuel Kant in his book, *Anthropology* (1789) dealt with the character of people and related them to historical factors as well as to consciously directed cultivation or enculturation. His description of German National character remains of interest even today and it was based on observation of many behavioural data. The German is home-loving, solid but not brilliant, industrious, thrifty, cleanly without much flash of genius, intelligent, capable but lacking in wit or taste, over methodological, pedantic, without impulse towards equality, but addicted to a painstaking hierarchical grading of society that sets title and rank above natural talent, docile under government, accepting depotism rather than resisting the established order of authority.

The Swiss historian Jacob Burckhardt in his book, *The Civilization of the Renaissance in Italy* (1860) was even more modern in his approach to cultural personality. He compared the over all character of Medieval people in Italy with that of Renaissance. In Middle ages, men tended to identify themselves closely with collective social entities such as their ethnic or national groups, corporations, and extended families. The Renaissance was marked by rise of individualism. Italians became less dependent upon their social affiliations, and were, thus, enabled to view their government with greater objectivity. He has demonstrated these characters by analysing various cultural manifestations, including art, literature, folk-festivals, forms of dress, etiquette, humour, and similar factors which, later on, received much attention in the study of national character.

Although culture and personality approach to the study of national character have their roots in earlier thought, but it was during the period of Second World War, when anthropologists paid their attention towards the study of national character. A more sophisticated attempt to reconstruct the cultural personality of a nation was developed by the Columbia University Research in Contemporary Cultures Project, inaugurated by Ruth Benedict shortly after the out break of World War II. Its participant included Margaret Mead, Rodha Metraus, Gregory Basteson, Jane Bele, Geoffery Gorer. This approach became known as 'The Study of Culture at a Distance'. The war had curtailed travel and field research, yet there was a demand to arrive at a better understanding of both enemies and allies. Culture-at-a-distance studies concentrated on film analysis, and participants scanned news papers, letters, propaganda, humour, and similar documents. They supplemented their findings by interviews with immigrants, asking them to write life histories, and to take psychological tests. A model was, thus, provided for analysis of cultural regularities in the character of nation in accessible to direct observation.

Margaret Mead and Rodha Metraus edited a book entitled, *The Study of Culture-at-a-Distance* (1953). This book deals with the methodology of studying national character as reflected in the personality of inhabitants of a nation, even without making direct observation. Following culture and personality approach, Ruth Benedict and Mead studied the national character of Japan and America respectively. Their books dealing with the characters of those nations are, *Crysthanthemum and Sword* (1946), and *Keep Your Powder Dry: An Anthropologist Looks at America* (1942) respectively. In her book, Margaret Mead deals with the national character of America. She did not find differences in the personality of baby in America to that of Japan and Russia. Thus, the early personality was similar. They gradually start differing as the growth follows and family education and school education come into being. In this way, culture and personality develop in them, which also reflect their national character.

Margaret Mead was of opinion that the study of national character can be had by culture and personality approach. Culture has been developed by human beings and is successively learned by each generation. The learned behaviour is reflected in the character of the group or nation. Thus, the study of national character has historical depth of traditions, continuity and change as various dimensions.

Mead's Re-study Approach

Mead went a step further among the scholars of culture and personality school by applying a re-study approach to see continuity and change in formation of characters and personality. She considered her study of *Manus of New-Guinea* (1930) as the base line and visited them again after 25 years. She recorded the changes that had taken place among Manus during this period, and especially after World War II. She published her findings dealing with changes in Manus Society in her book, entitled, *New Lives for the Old: A Study in Culture Transformation* (1956).

Mead's View on Continuity in Cultural Evolution

While Mead was propagating the importance of culture and personality, Steward, White, Sahlin and Service, were dealing with evolutionary theory under new perspective. Stewards multilineal approach differs from earlier ones, but does not necessarily discredit them. White stressed the general, Steward the particular, and the debates between evolutionists with different prediction were nothing more than semantic squabbles. White maintained that Steward confused history with evolution, because history, according to White, is concerned with particulars, while evolution seeks to generalise. Steward, on the other hand, felt that White's generalizations were barren. Sahlin and Service pointed out that White and Steward simply dealt with evaluation in two different ways. White observed the overall directional advance of culture in absolute terms, Steward dealt with related historical sequences.

Mead (1964:23) added that a third approach is possible for dealing with continuity in cultural evolution. This is the study of actual processes of change, as they occur in our generation or between adjacent generations. Her book, *Continuities in Cultural Evolution* (1964) is of great significance in this regard.

Death of Margaret Mead

Mead died suddenly in November 1978, when she was to come to Ranchi (India) to preside over the post plenary session of Xth ICAES (International Congress of Anthropological and Ethnological Sciences). She was also awarded Jawaharlal Nehru Award for Scientific Understanding of Man in 1973. This award was presented to her by, the then Prime Minister of India, Smt. Indira Gandhi at New Delhi.

Ralph Linton (1893-1853)

Linton was an internationally renowned anthropologist of America. He belonged to culture and personality school of anthropological thought. He started his career as an archaeologist. He was sent to Marquesa Island in 1920-22, by the Bishop Museum in Hawaii. While visiting there, Linton became interested in culture of Marquesa Islanders and, thus, he turned towards cultural anthropology.

As referred to earlier, there are three sub-schools of culture and personality school. One sub-school deals with the influence of culture on personality. Margaret Mead was leader of this sub-school. Another sub-school, led by Ruth Benedict, is concerned with the influence of personality on culture. The third sub-school, whose leaders are Linton, Kardiner, Cora-Du-Bois, attempt to study the influence of culture on personality and vice-versa. The scholars of this sub-school regard culture and personality as interdependent and complementary to each other.

The important books of Linton are as follows:

1. *The Study of Man*, New York, 1936.
2. *The Culture Background of Personality*, New York, 1937.

As referred to earlier, Linton was basically an archaeologist. Archaeological influence on his writing can be seen in his book, *The Study of Man* (1936). In this book, he has clearly shown the adaptation of culture traits in American culture. For instance, the bed which American leaves in the morning was invented in near east and was reformed in Europe. The curtain which he removes are made of cotton, which was first grown in India. If curtains are made of silk, they were invented in near east, and if linen, they were discovered in China. The soft leather shoes, which he puts on, were made by Red Indians of North America. The bath-room he uses was the result of European and American inventions. The soap, he uses, was made by the people of ancient Gal first of all. The razor, he uses was made in Sumer of Egypt. The necktie used by him is residual of shawl used by croatatian people on their shoulder in 17th century. The felt of his cap is the invention of Asian Steppes. Umbrella is discovery of south-east Asia and the rubber is invention of primitive inhabitants of America. Utensils and plates, he uses, is invention of China, whereas steel knife is an invention of South India and the fork is invention of Italy in middle period. The spoon is invention of Ancient Rome. Among the articles of food, orange is discovery of Mediterranean countries, Coffee of Abysinia, tea of China and sugar of India. The pipe which he smokes, has been taken from native of Virginia and the cigarette has come from Mexico. The tobacco was first grown in Brazil. If he uses cigar, it is the origin of Antelese of Western India archipelago. If he reads newspaper, it is the product of printing system invented in Germany. Thus, being an archaeologist, he attempted to trace the Origin of material traits of culture and their borrowing, diffusion, migration and adaptation in American context.

But he was not satisfied by the study of only material aspects of culture. In the same book, he began to deal with status and role, which an individual acquires and plays in his culture. According him, role means rules of behaviour attached with a given status or social position. He has divided roles into two categories, viz., ascribed roles and achieved roles. Ascribed roles are determined by birth. The roles of an individual based on birth in a particular caste, community, kinship, sex, etc., are ascribed roles. Achieved roles are determined by achieved status such as leader, teacher, doctor, engineer, lawyer, etc. He has also talked about role conflict, when different members occupying different positions have some more expectations.

Linton's interest in culture and personality approach was developed, when he participated in an interdisciplinary seminar organised by Columbia University. The participants of the seminar were Abram Kardiner, a practicing analyst, Linton, an anthropologist and Cora-Du-Bois, an anthropologist. The seminar discussed in detail the importance of interdisciplinary approach in studying the role of culture in personality formation, and the influence of personality on culture. It was felt that the greater cooperation in at least there disciplines, namely psychology, sociology and anthropology, was needed to understand the basic features of culture and personality. Individual, man and society, are the subject of study for psychology, anthropology and sociology respectively. While studying culture, personality and society, the cooperation of each discipline is a must, because they all are interdependent and interrelated in the whole of the same phenomena.

Linton's most famous book is, *Cultural Background of Personality* (1945). In this book, he has attempted to define culture and to classify culture on the basis of behaviour. He has also defined personality and attempted to show as to how personality is formed in a given cultural situation. He has emphasised also as to how personality influences cultural behaviour.

According to Linton, culture may be defined as the sum total of knowledge, attitudes and natural behaviour pattern, shared and transmitted by the members of a particular society.

He divides culture into three groups on the behaviour of the member. These are: (i) Real culture (actual behaviour), (ii) Ideal culture (philosophical and traditional culture), and (iii) Culture-construct (what is written about culture). Real culture is some total of behaviour of the members of society, which are learned and shared in particular situation. It is the ways of life of community member. The ways of life differ from culture to culture. Ideal culture pattern is formed by philosophical traditions. In this, some traits of culture are regarded as ideals. When a culture is studied, it also reflects our understanding of that culture, which is to be written. This is known as culture-construct.

Linton has also made a distinction among cultural universals, cultural alternatives and cultural specialities. He is of opinion that some culture traits are necessary to all members of the society, while the other traits are shared only by some members. The traits, which are followed by all members, are called universals of culture. For instance, man must clothe certain parts of body, we must condemn free love and infanticide, these are the universals of Indian culture. On the other hand, a person may choose among a number of religious beliefs, or even adopt none. One may travel on foot, rickshaw, bullockcart, *Tanga*, Bus, train, aeroplane, eat at home or in hotels, are alternatives. It may be mentioned that alternative in one society may be universals elsewhere or universals may be alternatives.

Specialities are elements of culture, which are shared by some, but not all, groups within a society. Baby nursing is obviously a female speciality not shared by men. Nearly every cultural group in society, based on age, sex, occupation, religion, language etc., has certain traits not shared by other groups.

A general cultural pattern has also sub-cultural patterns. They are the cultural traits a of particular group. They are, of course, related to general cultural pattern, but are distinguishable from it. Thus, the cultural pattern of age, sex, religious, linguistic and occupational groups are sub-cultural patterns of general cultural pattern of India. Similarly, Hindu culture is sub-culture of Indian culture.

Linton used the tern contra-culture pattern to designate those groups, which not only differ from the prevailing pattern, but sharply challenge them. For instance, a group of dacoits has its own norms and standards, which are compelling for all members of the group, but these norms and standard sharply differ from the conventional prevailing patterns.

Thus, Linton points out that above-mentioned backgrounds of culture play significant role in personality formation. When personality is formed, it also has effect on the culture.

In this book, Linton has also attempted successfully to define personality. According to him, personality is the organised aggregate of psychological processes and states pertaining to the individual. He is of opinion that the organised aggregates of habits, which have been established in the individual, constitute the bulk of personality and give it form, structure and continuity.

In this way, Linton has attempted to define personality in relation to habits and tried to explain it from the functional point of view. He is of view that culture is a product of need. It is the satisfaction of needs which maintains survival of man and culture. The needs are of two types: (i) Biological or physiological needs and (ii) Psychic needs. He holds views that satisfaction of psychic need is also a must, from the very beginning. For example, a baby does not need mother only for the survival, but he or she also requires her affection and love. In absence of affection and love, he or she may not survive or may turn into abnormal.

According to him, physic need can be satisfied by three kinds of responses. These are:

(i) *Emotional Response:* The satisfaction of emotional needs is essential for the survival of individual. If they are not satisfied, he may turn out to be abnormal, mad and frustrated.

(ii) *Security for Long Term:* The satisfaction of this psychic need is also essential. A man cannot live in isolation. He can not feel himself safe, unless he gets some help from other. In other words, he needs society to help him for long-term.

(iii) *Novelty of Experience:* Change in life is a natural law. It provides new experiences and satisfaction of needs in changed situation. The society on the basis of previous experiences tries to satisfy the needs of individuals.

Linton suggests that in order to satisfy the varieties of needs in society, an individual makes responses in simultaneous ways. This is known as 'simultaneous response principle'. Linton points out that responses can be made by individual in three ways: (i) by imitation, (ii) by trial and error method, and (iii) by intellectual method. An individual has capacity to imitate things. He can makes corrections in committing mistakes by trial and error methods. He can also satisfy his needs on the basis of his intellectual background.

Linton is of view that each society has a basic culture by which all its members undergo similar process of socialization, and share similar custom, belief and traditions. As a result of it, a common pattern in the behaviour of member of that group is evident. This common characteristics reveal the basic culture of that society. In basic culture of a society, one also finds status personality. Status personality reveals special position occupied by a member with some privileges. Again in basic culture type, one also finds individual as social inventors, who bring changes by discovering new traits or substituting the old ones with new inventions.

Linton also developed the concept of 'basic personality' along with Kardiner, about which we will discuss, while describing Kardiner's contribution in culture and personality school.

Abram Kardiner

Abram Kardiner was a psychiatrist or psycho-analyst by profession. He was attached to Psychoanalytic Institute of New York. He was also a student of Sigmund Freud. Kardiner was a neo-Freudian. The term neo-Freudian was applied to those who accepted some of Freud's theories, but rejected or modified others. Kardiner believed that the early years of life were most crucial in formation of personality. Thus, he dropped Freud's theories of Oedipus Complex and sexual determinants of culture. In other words, he emphasised upon the adoptational, rather than instinctual, aspect of Freudian theory.

Kardiner's use of psychodynamics in the anthropology can be distinguished from other psychodynamic procedures by following tenets :

(1) Social evolution has not followed a unilinear course. Hence, each society must be studied as an entity in itself. In this, he agrees with Malinowski and the functionalist.
(2) In order to understand the institution of society, an attempt must be made to reconstruct the problems of adaptation the society has faced. It is recognised that there are many ways of solving the same social problems. In some communities, where there is starvation the population must be limited. The problem is solved by female infanticide, and in others, by eating children.
(3) The social institutions are the patterned relationship which accommodate the individual to the human and natural environment.
(4) The success or failure of social patterning is a matter of consequence. The extreme relativists, who hold that in social patterning anything goes, are in error. There is penalty for bad social patterning: the effects on human unit are disastrous and the entire culture is put in jeopardy sooner or later.
(5) Freud's method of investigation can be used to relate social institutions to individual and his genetic inheritance. The result of this interaction is not stereotyped, but falls within a fixed ambit of variation, known as personal character. The individuals of society in their interaction create new institution, which promotes cooperation and others which stimulate anxiety and rage. The success or failure of a society depends upon a balance in favour of the former.

The important publications of Kardiner are as follows:

1. *The Individual and His Society*, New York, 1939 (ed.).
2. *Psychological Frontiers of Society*, New York, 1945 (Co-authorship with Linton).
3. *They Studied Man*, 1961 (co-authorship with E. Preble).

As we have seen earlier, the neo-Freudian approach, which came closest to achieving a theory of psycho-cultural analysis, was that of Abram Kardiner. In 1936, Kardiner, a practising analyst, organised a seminar. Sapir, Benedict and Bunzel were participants. In 1937, the seminar moved to Columbia University in which Ralph Linton, Cora-Du-Bois and Karl Withers contributed papers, based on ethnographic data. The papers of the seminar were edited by Kardiner in book form under the title, *Individual and his Society* (1939). In this book, the techniques, that were developed in this new application of psycho-dynamics to anthropological data, resulted in the acquisition of three related bodies of knowledge. These are:

1. A description of the homeostatic processes that operate in society.
2. A description of basic personality type that results from the particular homeostatic patterns of society.
3. A description of culture change.

Kardiner, together with Linton, developed the concept of 'basic personality type' in his book, *Psychological Frontiers of Society* (1945). Well aware of the fact that degree of individual variation in character exists in every society, Kardiner and Linton developed the concept of 'basic personality type', to indicate their common ground. The concept of 'basic personality type' means that in every culture, there is common characteristics of personality among all members of a group, which is the basic personality type of the group. The basic personality type is outcome of cultural influences on the individual.

Kardiner observes that the techniques of child rearing, duration of breast feeding, methods of weaning, sexual training and similar conditioning factors are roughly similar in given group. The adults, thus, have had certain important common experiences that give rise to a common basic personality type. While postulating the existence of a basic personality type or structure, Kardiner, divided the institutional aspect of culture in to two categories: (i) Primary and (ii) Secondary. Primary institutions are those responsible for forming the basic personality structure. An analogy with Freudian doctrine, these institutions were ones most directly concerned with disciplining, gratifying and inhibiting the infant and young child. However, he does not mention a fixed list of primary institutions. He opines that the relevant disciplines were administered in different institutional forms from one culture to another. In general, the intended aim of Kardiner is at family organisation, in group formation, feeding, weaning, care or neglect of children, sexual training and subsistence patterns. Thus, a primary institution is one which is older, more stable, less likely to be integrated with by vicissitudes of climate or economy.

Secondary institutions are those which satisfy the needs and tensions created by the primary or fixed institutions. Among the secondary institutions, Kardiner gives greatest prominence to taboo system, religion, rituals, folk tales and method of thinking. Between primary and secondary institutions, Kardiner poses the basic personality structure. Fashioned by the childhood disciplines, the basic personality in turn expresses itself in the group's indeologies, in emotional and cognitive orientation to life and death.

Kardiner's concept of 'Basic personality type' can be understood better by going through the example of Marquesas, a Polynesian Island culture. Among Marquesa islanders, periodic starvation due to severe draught, constitutes the chief problem in social adaptation. Marquesans deal with the problem of limited food supply by the expedient of female infanticide. They do not kill the female infants themselves, the children are simply exposed to Marauding tribes, who do the jobs of killing for them. The destruction of these potential child bearers served as an effective control over population growth, keeping the population within the limits of available food supply, In this simple solution to a basic survival problem, one sees a gross illustration of social homeostasis or adaptation.

In any homeostatic or adaptational process, the solution of one problem poses derivative problems. In Marquesas, the control of population by female infanticide creates an excess of men over women in the ratio of about five to two. This discrepancy in male-female ratio creates an unequal distribution of sexual opportunity. The obvious solution to this problem is polyandry, an institution of marriage, which permits a women to have more than one husband. This is not an ideal situation, but under the circumstances, this is probably the best solution by compromise.

This necessary compromise has important effects on the attitudes and behaviour of the Marquesans, beginning in infancy. Even in a monogamous set-up, the women has the problem of equitably devoting her time and attention between her husband and children. With several husbands to satisfy, the problem is greatly magnified. Specially the children suffer directly from this deprivation. Since their needs are more pressing an unalterable, frustration, despair, fear and anxiety among children are inevitable consequences in Marquesas. There mother spends most of her time with her several husbands, and when not with them, at the local version of beauty shop, maintaining the conditions of here status and prestige. This maternal neglect is partially compensated in Marquesas by the attention shown to the children by chief husband, secondary husbands, aunts and uncles. This attention is enough to give the children minimum protection against physical dangers and to indoctrinate him in the simple social conventions and taboos. However, it can provide the emotional security and affection that is associated with a devoted mother child relationship.

In Marquesas, the husband, too, suffer from female neglect. However, for them this is a condition to which they have been forced to adapt since childhood, the destructive manifestations of this neglect are better disguised. Jealousy among men is suppressed in the interest of socially productive cooperation. It emerges only when men are drunk. The men turn to each other for a sense of social solidarity and identification. They join at times in a united front against the women in the form of certain ceremonial taboos. Beneath the formality of this taboos lay a common shared hatred for women.

The most convincing evidence of the animosity towards women in this society is found in Marquesan legends and folk tales. In these tales, women are commonly represented as wicked, heartless, exploiters. They are portrayed as cannibals, seductress of innocent youngmen and robbers of children's food. In the fantasies of their folk lore, Marquesans express a fear and hatred for women.

Viewed as isolated traits, some of the products of parental difference in Marquesas have a positive connotation. Lack of care implies lack of restriction, and in the area of sexual behaviour, the absence of childhood restrictions contribute to an enviable degree of sexual impotency. The Marquesan men can be said to have made the most of their limited opportunities. Marquesas culture also fosters a high degree of independence and precocity, due to the absence of dependency ties and restrictive injunctions.

Thus, in Marquesas, the food scarcity, the institution of polyandry and the relative absence of basic discipline in childhood, constitutes the main primary influences in the development of individual members of that society. The effects of these social influences can be observed in the general personality make-up of the Marquesans, as described by ethnographer. In addition, the entire institutionalised fabric of this society can be as reflecting, complementing and expressing the basic personality type or structure. In this frame of reference, the social institutions of Marquesans do not appear as fortuitous, or evolved, or borrowed pattern of cultural behaviour, but rather as specific implements of human adaptation within a unique homeostatic pattern.

Thus, Marquesan study suggests a methodology and a frame of reference with which the study of the effects of specific social institutions on the individual members of a society can be done. It opens up the possibility of creating a useful critique of the structure and dynamics of human social organisation. Thus, from the start, the application of adaptational psychodynamics to cultural data is devoted to a practical and, social survival and human happiness.

Kardiner has presented a dynamic model for the study of basic personality type, which also serves to explain culture change. He is of opinion that if primary institutions change, the resultant changes in basic personality structure will also alter the secondary institutions. For instance, if the economy of certain group demands that mother should spend much time away from home, older siblings or others will be charged with carrying for the infants. In these circumstances, many tension may develop and a child may feel ambiguous towards the mother, which in turn will become reflected in myths and folk tales, beliefs etc. Should there be a shift in economic patterns allowing mothers to become more nurturant, the basic personality will change, and with it also the secondary institutions.

This logic of Kardiner's scheme is certainly an important improvement over some previous efforts that labelled religious practices or myths as irrational, or resulting from a kind of infantile neurosis, as Freud would have it. Even the anthropologists, who have not given psychological interpretations, can point out that Kardiner's theory plausibly explains the existence of certain cultural institutions, but can account for them only in psychological terms. Thus, if neglecting mothers give rise to a concept of threatening female deity, all that can be said is that this is possibly a projection of hostile feelings or an outlet for them, reflecting insecurity and so on. Cultural functions are, thus, neglected and it appears as if primary institutions have no other function than to form the personality, while the secondary institutions serve mainly to cope with frustrations of that personality. Moreover, Kardiner's theory cannot account for the existing differences among primary institutions and provide no answer as to why some societies are patrilineal, others matrilineal, or why some practice cross cousin marriage and others not, why some societies prefer polyandry, some polygeny and others monogamy.

It follows, however, from Kardiner's theory that the contents of secondary institutions can be examined for possible clues about basic personality and primary institutions, even in those societies where myth and folk-lore are the only available documents left of an extinct group.

Examples of Basic Personality Type in Indian Context

Kardiner's theory of basic personality type refers to that the members of each society or culture possess similar personality traits which reveal the basic personality structure or type of that society. However, individual variations are no exception, but the members of a group are characterized by some common characters. This commonness in personality or character of entire members of group, is outcome of common influence of primary and secondary institutions upon the members of a group. The basic personality type is formed in childhood, because all infants are socialized and reared in common manner in a group. The childhood disciplines play significant role in formation of basic personality structure.

Thus, the basic personality type expresses itself in group's ideologies, in emotional and cognitive orientation to life and death.

From the above description, it appears that each society or culture has its own basic personality type. Thus, the basic personality type of Toda of Nilgiri area, South India, is different from Munda and Oraon of Central India. In case of former, the basic personality structure is shaped by the socialization processes observing the norms and value of the institution of matriarchal family. In case of latters, the socialization of infants is followed according the rules of the institution of patriarchal family. Even in patriarchal or matriarchal cultural groups, the basic personality type of one group varies from the other. For instance, the basic personality types of Munda, Oraon, Ho, Santal, Kharia etc. are different, though they all are patriarchal. In the same way, the basic personality type of Muslim, Christian, Hindu, Sikh is different from each other. In Hindu culture, the basic personality type is shaped by the institutions of joint family, monogamy, caste system and hierarchical position, *jajmani* relationship, beliefs in thirty three crores of Gods and Goddesses, but Parmeshwar as the supreme deity, the worship of cow and land as mother. The basic personality of different castes also varies. The Brahmans are supposed as learned, Rajput as warrior, Gwala as robust and Harijan as submissive and hardy.

Cora-Du-Bois

Cora-Du-Bois, a lady cultural anthropologist of America became a close associate of Abram Kardiner, a psychoanalyst. She was an active participant of interdisciplinary seminar, organised by Kardiner at New York and at Columbia University in the year 1936 and 1939 respectively. Thus, a thorough and systematic attempt to use psychodynamic techniques in anthropology began in 1936, with the participation of Cora-Du-Bois. After a preliminary attempt to work with existing ethnographic data on Trobriand Islands, and Chuchechee Zuni, it became clear that these data would not yield the information necessary for a systematic psychodynamic analysis. It was decided, therefore, to initiate a field expedition designed to meet the methodological specifications of an approach that would furnish information about social adaptation, as effected through the lives of the individual members of society.

In 1937, Cora-Du-Bois departed for the island of Alor in the East Indies. She proceeded for fieldwork with the following general aims in mind:

(i) To determine and describe the institutional constellations of Alor culture.

(ii) To participate actively in the life of the culture.

(iii) To document the biographies of individual members of the culture, using such psycho-analytic criteria as dreams and fantasies.

(iv) To administer Roscharch and intelligence tests to selected individuals.

With these aims in mind, she collected not only a rich material on traditional ethnographic facts, but also collected eight lengthy biographies on dreams and children's drawing. She also administered a number of projective tests.

Upon her return, she submitted the life histories to Kardiner for his analysis. The test results were given to Dr. Emile Oberholzer, while she asked the assistance of Trude Schmidt for the interpretation of the Alorese drawings. Each of these specialists worked "blind", i.e., without knowledge of ethnographic data and without consulting one another. The results of specialists showed a great deal of correspondence. All noted the shallowness of Alorese emotional life, insecurity, apathy and suspiciousness. The conclusions were made by pooling all individual responses to the various tests and averaging them, so that the resulting psychogram described the most prevalent personality feature of the group. Cora-Du-Bois called this the 'modal personality', because it was directly derived from the testing, while Kardener's concept of 'basic personality' was inferred from cultural data.

Cora-Du-Bois published the findings of her research on Alore in book form under the title *The People of Alora : A Social Psychological Study of East Indian Island* (1944). In this book, she has shown that among Alor, the vegetable food supply is controlled by the woman, while the meat supply is controlled by the men. On the face of it, this may not appear to be a critical or even particularly significant feature of this culture. Then a question arises, what happens to kids, while the mother is in the field of the vegetable crop? The answer is that they are left back in the village usually in the care of a reluctant older sibling. This particular division of labour in this culture has a persistent influence during the critical and formative years of Alorese children. Further observations, such as feeding and frustrations, continue throughout childhood. The direct training of children is unsystematic and sporadic, even in such basic activities as walking and talking. Conformity to parental demands does not guarantee rewards. Punishment for misbehaviour is inconsistent and capricious, a behaviour which brings approval on one occasion may bring punishment on the other.

The overall treatment of children in Alor can be characterized as one of neglect and inconsistency. From studies in our own society, one would suspect that those conditions would produce serious integrative disorders in the individual. The biographics and psychological tests of individual Alorese confirm this suspicion. The Alore are suspicious, mistrustful, and anxious. They lack confidence and self esteem. They are fearful and unaggressive, but prey on their neighbours by means of lies, deceptions and chicanary. They are unable to sustain a love relationship or a friendship based on voluntary interest. They have a limited capacity to master or enjoy the over world. The appearance of these traits as the common inheritance of Alorese does not surprise us, knowing what we do about the early experiences of these people with parents and the environment. What is more interesting or what constitutes a real addition to our knowledge of cultural process, is the observation, that these traits are reflected throughout the entire social structure of the culture.

In folklore and religion of Alor, we note theme and motifs directly related to the life experiences and character traits of the Alorese. In their folklore, the most common motif is parental frustration and hatred. In their religion, there is no idealization of the deity. The deity has no great power for beneficence and is, therefore, not placated in the experience in the expectations of rewards and benefits. The sacrifices to the deity are offered reluctantly and grudgingly, and then only in emergencies. There is no concept of forgiveness, no storing up of virtue as a form of insurance. The only conforming theme that appears in Alorese religion, myth and folklore concerns supernatural Good Being, who beshows favours capriciously and without solicitation. They are, significantly enough, always total strangers to those whom they help. The underlying tone in Alore religion and folklore is one of severely constricted affectivity. Considerations concerning the formal structure of these institutions, their origin, evolution, diffusion, are of secondary importance in our efforts to find out how this culture functions. The correlation between the early strangulation of affectivity in the individual and impoverished nature of institutionalised religion and folk lore should lay to rest, once and for all, the idea that institutions interact with each other on a super organic level.

Once, when we have reached these central insights about Alor, many seemingly idiosyncratic features of this culture take on meaningful and significant relationship. This applies to individual traits, such as the tendency to collapse and wait for death in event of any kind of illness, and it applies to social institutions, such as, socio-economic system, which greatly exaggerated the importance of status and wealth. In the first example, we recognise the Alorese conviction that one can expect only the worst from life and in second we recognise a frantic desperate effort to bolster self-esteem.

When all the individual traits, which Alorese share in common, are put together, we have a record of specific imprint of a given set of social institutions. It must be noted, however, that there are no two Alorese, who will show exactly the same traits. Each individual has a specific and unique combination of traits, which we call individual character. But all these individual traits are selection from the general ambit of potentialities offered by Alorese culture. This wider ambit of trait can be called 'basic personality' structure, or 'national character' or 'modal personality'.

The study of personality as illustrated by the Alor study, is important because the personality structure of the individual is a critical factor in social homeostasis. The society is not an organism, so the term homeostasis is used metaphorically here to suggest the balance that is maintained in society by the capacities of individuals to co-operate and share common interests. Social homeostasis is vested in the kind of human beings it creates, hence the study of personality in culture is the only guide available to indicate how effectively a society is functioning.

The agreement among the specialists, who had blindly interpreted the Alorese material inspired confidence in projective testing, and a large amount of test material was brought back by subsequent field workers. It was felt that the testing was a scientific method that reduced the impressionistic qualities of earlier studies and the 'modal personality' was a true reflection of the personality feature of a majority of people in a culture. Among the various tests available, the 'Rorschach' was particularly favoured. Named after the inventor, Rorshach Test consists of presenting the subject with ten non-pictorial "inkblot" cards and inviting him to describe what he sees in them. The test is neither difficult to administer, nor culture-bound, nor measure intelligence, but thoughts, feelings and views. The answers are counted, scored and interpreted in terms of degree of originality, imagination, repression, conformity, aggression, emotional control and similar underlying characteristics of the personality. Other psychological tests often used are Murry's Thematic Apperception Test, Bender's Gestall Test, Immanent Judgement Test. These tests are supplemented by data derived from doll play, free drawing, autobiographics and dreams.

Once the modal personality, the characteristics of personality derived from tests, is established, it becomes relatively easy to relate its feature to dominant social patterns. The frequency of Warfare, belief in sorcery, or harsh initiation rites can be explained by such modal personality features as aggression, insecurity or guilt feeling.

Criticism

1. Although results obtained from the modal personality are very neat, but they are not very satisfactory. They are not predictive in any sense and at best, they stress the great diversity of modal personalities between cultural groups. Thus, they represent a version of Boasian historical particularism on a psychological level. Most anthropologists became dissatisfied with this dead end approach and began to reappraise their theories and methods.
2. This particular approach to culture personality investigation in anthropology has ground to a halt. One of the main reasons is that approach requires an expert knowledge of psychodynamics. This imposes a severe restriction on the recruitment of workers and collaborators. Another reason is that this work constitutes an invasion by psychodynamics of another discipline (anthropology). Academic restriction can be powerful deterrent. Sooner or later, however, we are confident that these obstacles will be overcome, for simple reason that if man is to survive in modern world, he must learn how society works. Man was probably reached the stage, where organic evolution is not longer a factor in adaptation. Man is now in a position, where he can practically remark the natural environment according to his bodily needs. It is now social evolution which will determine man's fate. Unfortunately, patterns of social cooperation carry no guarantees of success. One pattern will be successful under one set of conditions and fail under another. No society has a permanent tenure, especially those that are subject to constant change. Man must be given every opportunity to direct social evolution.
3. It is not necessary that adult personality, which reveals 'basic personality' or 'modal personality' or 'group character', is total outcome of early childhood experiences. Margaret Mead, among others, has directed attention towards the importance of totality of expectations and pressures communicated to individuals sharing the same culture. The explanation of personality, must then, take into account the cultural conditions under which attitudes and feelings are learned and experienced during the individual life time, and should include adult interpersonal relationships and adult interactions. In fact, the study of personality development must consider the whole range of social interactions.

6

THEORIES OF SOCIETY, CULTURE, CIVILIZATION AND CIVILIZATION STUDY

THEORIES OF CULTURE AND SOCIETY

The social anthropologists, formerly the students of small scale societies, generally use different techniques of study from the sociologists, formerly the students of large scale society. But it is possible for each to use the technique of other or to say, what has been the traditional field of other.

In the 19th century, the anthropologists built their theory from the incomplete reports of early traveller, colonial administrators and the missionaries. In 1883, Franz Boas, a German born American anthropologist of diffusion or historical particularism school, visited Baffin land and there he did, what may be considered to be the first systematic anthropological fieldwork. In 1898, Professor A.C. Haddon conducted a survey among the islanders living in the Torres Strait in Melanesia. He stayed their for a period of six months with his team, studying their culture, physique and mental capabilities.

Thus, fieldwork technique was initiated in late 19th century. By the beginning of 20th century, when Brownislaw Kaspar Malinowski and Radcliffe-Brown, both British anthropologists, studied Trobriand Islanders of Melanesia and Andaman Islanders of India respectively, the technique of living in a society and studying it extensively began.

It is now traditionally accepted method that an anthropologist should spend at least a year in the field, studying the culture of the people. Each study helps us to add to our knowledge of human society by contributing something to existing theories about culture and society.

Three theories about culture and society have been put forward by both scholars of anthropology and sociology. These are: (i) Evolutionary theory (ii) Diffusional theory and (iii) Sociological theory.

The evolutionary theory assumes that complex society developed out of simple ones. Some evolutionists argue that the so-called primitive societies, that still exists to-day, are survivals from the past. Max-Muller and McLennan were the earliest classical evolutionists and Sir James Frazer was the latest classical evolutionist.

By the end of 19th century, a number of scholars have began to attack on the evolutionists. They argue that evolution alone cannot account for all the differences between primitive or small-scale societies. They became interested in the distribution of cultural traits and elements. It means that they hoped to find out as to how cultural traits or elements had diffused, migrated, borrowed and adopted from a common origin. These diffusionists were condemned for mainly atomising culture into elements.

In the 19th century, Emile Durkheim, a French sociologists and social anthropologist, began to study society as a unit whose different parts are interrelated. He is now regarded as the father of Sociological approach.

CONCEPT OF CULTURE AND SOCIETY

Three main groups of anthropologists have come to establish 'culture' and 'society' as concepts in the study of social science. These consists of :

(i) Anthropologists, who define culture as all embracing including society. One of the chief proponents of this view was Malinowski.

(ii) Anthropologists, who dichotomise between society and culture. For example Radcliffe-Brown, Evans-Pritchard, Leach and most British anthropologists.

(iii) Anthropologists, who steer a middle course by accepting the society and culture as two aspect of social realities, viewed from different dimensions, that of relationship and grouping and that of action and behaviour. The chief advocate of this approach is Levi-Strauss, a French anthropologist.

Levi-Strauss' statement reveals that society appeared before culture, because it obliquely refers to evolutionary development of culture and society and also because its implication has very significant bearing on the reason, why different views are held by anthropologists.

Kroeber, an American diffusionist, was one of the earliest anthropologists to say that society do exist without culture and that culture makes human society different from other animal society. He holds that men's culture directs the kind of life they can lead. The cultural determinism of Kroeber has rightly been challenged. Kroeber pointed out that culture and society are arbitrary concept and as actual phenomena are interwoven and difficult to disentangle. He postulated a truism in the study of man: No society no culture, no culture no society. By this, he was emphasising upon the uniqueness of human society as opposed to that of animal species.

Leslie White, in his neo-evolutionary approach to culture, holds that man is the only living species that has culture. Culture, he says, depends upon symboling. He defines symboling as the ability to originate and bestow meaning upon a thing and ability to grasp and appreciate such meaning, Man, he says, is the only animal that can distinguish water from holy water. This is due to man's ability to symbol, which is fully expressed in articulate speech. The transition from anthropoid society to human social organisation was made possible by the emergence of faculty of symboling.

Symboling made the development of culture possible. It also made human society unique and different from other types of animal societies. It is clear from this reasoning that human society is different from that of ants, birds or anthropoid apes. Thus, culture is a society based, an ability to use symbol.

The civilizationists or Redfieldians have used the term culture and society as synonymic. They have regarded both as interrelated and inseparable.

General Meaning of Culture

The English term 'culture' has been used in various concepts. Kroeber and Kluckhohn in their paper entitled, "Culture: A Critical Review of Concepts and Definitions", have collected the concepts and definitions of culture. According to them, the term 'culture' has been defined as having 108 different meanings. Literaturists have used the term culture for social charm and intellectual excellence. A great critique and poet, Maithu Arnold has termed light and softness of life as culture. Some sociologists have accepted intellectual leaders as cultural elite or leaders of society. According to Sorokin and Maclver, both sociologists, culture stands for moral, spiritual and intellectual attainments of man.

In Hindi, the term *Sanskriti* (culture) has been taken from Sanskrit language. Both terms *Sanskriti* and *Sanskrit* have been composed from the term *Sanskar*. The meaning of *Sanskar* is satisfaction of total rituals. In Hindu Society, an individual has to go through various ritual performances from the very day of his or her birth. Though there are 16 *Sanskar*, important among them are birth, *Mundan, Janew,* marriage and death. In this sense, culture means fulfilment of aims of social life through different *Sanskars*. It is a process of integration. By performing *Sanskar*, a man becomes social being.

Anthropological Meaning of Culture

In anthropology, the term culture has been used in a different senses. Tylor was the first anthropologist to provide a scientific definition of culture. He, in his book entitled, *Primitive Culture*, (1871), defines culture as that complex whole which includes knowledge, belief, art, morals, laws, customs and any other capabilities and habits acquired by man as a member of society. According to this definition, culture is a social heritage which is given by society to its individual.

Explaining the definition of culture as suggested by Tylor, Malinowski opines that we can divide social heritage in into material and non-material or shape and shapeless. Thus, according to Malinowski, culture is total way of life and it includes all the mental, social and physical means which make life run its course. In other words, according to Malinowski, culture may be defined as a system of derived needs and an organized system of purposeful activities.

Bidney has presented this fact in detail in his book, *Theoretical Anthropology* (1952:3-4). He holds view that culture of a people may be defined as the some total of material and intellectual equipment, whereby they satisfy their biological and social needs and adopt themselves to their environment.

In the definitions of culture by Malinowski, Bidney and Piddington, two aspects of culture — material and non-material — come into existence. In material culture, we can take into consideration, house, means of communication (cycle, bullock-cart, camel-cart, *tanga*, bus, train, plane etc.), dress, industries, weapons, etc. In non-material culture we can deal with knowledge, belief, value, customs, traditions, law, war, etc. But these two aspects of culture are complementary to each other.

E.A. Hoebel in his book, *Man in Primitive World* (1958:7), has defined culture as the sum total of integrated behaviour pattern, which are characteristics of the members of a society, and which are, therefore, not the result of biological inheritance. Thus, according to him culture is not determined by heredity, but it is a result of total social inventions. In other words, culture is invention of man for the fulfilment of social needs. It is transferred from one generation to another through socialization process and exchange of ideas.

Herskovits, an American anthropologists, in his book, *Man and His Work* (1956:17), has defined culture as the man-made part of environment. According to him, environment is of two type: (i) natural environment, and (ii) Social environment. The total social environment of man is his culture, because it is made by man himself. The natural things which are shaped into different forms represent the work of the man.

Thus, all material and non-material things made by man represent culture.

Leslie White, a neo-evolutionist of America, has emphasized upon the symbolic view of culture. According to him, culture is a symbolic, continuous, cumulative and progressive process. Leslie White has expressed this view in his paper entitled, "Culturological is Psychological Interpretations of Human Behaviour", in *American Sociological Review* (December 1947:693).

Robert Redfield, a cultural civilizationist of America, has also laid emphasis on symbolic view of culture. According to him, culture is an organised body of conventional understandings manifest in art and artifacts which, persisting through tradition, characterizes a human group. Thus, for him, culture is sum total of conventional meaning embodied in artifacts, social structure and symbols. (Quoted from Ogburn's book, *A Handbook of Sociology*, p.15).

Ruth Benedict, a lady anthropologist of culture and personality school of anthropology, in her book, *Patterns of Culture* (1936:46), has defined culture from personality point of view. According to her, "A culture, like an individual, is more or less consistent pattern of thought and action. Thus, she has defined culture with a formal and aesthetic view point".

Most of modern anthropologists adopt the functional mode of culture. Malinowski and Radcliffe-Brown have given an instrumental and humanistic definition of culture. According to Malinowski, culture is an instrument for the satisfaction of needs of man. On the other hand, Radcliffe-Brown, regards culture as a social heritage which perpetuates social life. The structural-functionalists have regarded the whole of culture as unit of study. They take a holistic view of culture.

Some other anthropologists have regarded culture to be subjective. According to Linton, the life of people is one thing and what we study and write is another thing. The first is reality and the second is our understanding of that reality. The first is culture and the second is culture construct. Thus, according to him culture may be defined as the sum total of knowledge, attitudes, and natural behaviour pattern, shared and transmitted by the members of a particular society (Cultural Back Ground of Personality, 1945). This definition reveals that culture is a dynamic concept. Its forms are not similar in different periods or ages. They change according to time.

According to R.H. Lowie, culture is nothing but total or whole of social tradition (Lowie, *Primitive Society*, 1920).

Kluckhohn, an American anthropologists in his article, 'Concept of Culture' in R.Linton's (ed) book, *The Science of Man in World Crisis*

(1945:97), has defined culture as all those historically created designs for living, explicit and implicit, rational, irrational, non-rational, which exist at any given time as potential guides for behaviour of men.

From the above analyses of definitions of culture, it is clear that there is no unanimity among the anthropologists so far as the question of one definition of culture is concerned. This reveals its merits and demerits both. Beals and Hoijer in their book, *An Introduction to Anthropology*, (1955:228-229), have attempted to summarise the definitions of culture as suggested by anthropologists. According to them, the term culture, as used by anthropologists, may be applied as follows:

(i) To the ways of life or designs for living common at any one time to all mankind, or
(ii) To the ways of living peculiar to a group of societies between which there is greater or lesser degree of interaction, or
(iii) To the patterns of behaviour peculiar to a given society, or
(iv) To special ways of behaving characteristic of the segments of a large and complex organised society.

NATURE OR CHARACTERISTICS OR ATTRIBUTES OF CULTURE

From the definitions as given by the anthropologists for the term culture, the following nature or characteristics or attributes of culture may be noted:

(1) Culture is man-made.
(2) Culture is learned.
(3) Culture is transmitted.
(4) Every society has got its own culture.
(5) Culture is social, not individualistic.
(6) Culture is ideal for the group.
(7) Culture satisfies human need.
(8) Culture has adaptability.
(9) Culture has integrative quality.
(10) Culture shapes human personality.
(11) Culture is both super-individual and super-organic (see Kroeber's contribution on culture as super organic and super individual).

Components of Culture

In each culture, we come across a structure and organisation. This structure of culture comes into existence due to organisation of different small units or traits or elements or section or sub-sections. They are interrelated to and interdependent on each other, and maintain order and equilibrium in culture. Thus, culture is integrated whole of elements, traits or parts. The parts or components of culture are following:

(i) *Culture trait or element*: Culture traits or elements are the smallest and indivisible unit of the culture. They cannot be divided further. This does not mean that they are not subject of further division, but their further division becomes meaningless. As culture is material and non-material both, therefore, culture traits are also material and non-material. For instance, material traits of culture are radio, watch, television, house, furniture, dress, ornament etc. Non-material traits of culture are symbol, word, view, custom, tradition, etc. Any culture can be seen as to include thousands of such traits. Thus, shaking hand, touching the feet, tipping hats, the kiss on the checks as gesture of affection, giving seats to ladies first, saluting the flag, wearing white *Sari* at mourning, eating vegetarian food, walking bare-footed, sprinkling water on idols, carrying kirpans, growing beard and hair, eating in brass utensil, etc. are cultural traits. These traits are elemental units of a culture. It is these traits, which distinguish one culture from another. A trait found in one culture may not have significance in another culture. Thus, offering water to sun may have significance in Hindu culture, but not in the western culture.

(ii) *Culture-Complex*: As a part of body is composed of organization of different cells, a community is composed of organisation of different families, in the same way organisation of different cultural traits gives rise to cultural complex. The importance of a single trait is indicated, when it fits into a cluster of traits, each one of which performs a significant role in the total complex. Thus, kneeling before idol, sprinkling sacred water over it, putting some food in its mouth, folding hands, singing *Arati* or *Kirtan*, performing the ritual of *Hawan*, taking *Prasad* from the priest and distributing *Prasad* among the others, etc., form a religious complex.

(iii) *Culture-Pattern:* A cultural pattern is formed when traits and complexes become related to each other in functional roles. Each culture complex has to pay a role in society. The culture pattern of society consists of a number of cultural complexes. Thus, the Indian cultural pattern consists of Gandhism, spiritualism, joint family system, caste system, jajmani system and ruralism. Each of these is a culture complex consisting of numerous culture traits.

(iv) *Culture Area:* In the study of culture, its geographical aspect cannot be ignored. Each culture develops in its own geographical boundary. If we travel in a country, we come across different cultural areas. If we compare different cultural areas, we find that the culture areas, which are geographically close, possess greater similarities in comparison to those situated far away. This reveals that the diffusion of culture traits, culture complexes or culture patterns, takes place in a definite geographical area. This geographical area is termed as cultural area. (For detail see Clark Wissler's contribution under the chapter School of Diffusion).

(v) *Edos and Ethos:* An attempt has been made by Kroeber to give the universal characteristics of culture, while defining it. According to Kroeber, culture has two aspects, namely, edos and ethos. The first includes the formal appearance of culture derived from its constituents or elements. Ethos, on the other hand, is aggregate of those elements which determine the qualities, interests and patterns of culture.

(vi) *Implicit and Explicit:* Kluckhohn has classified cultural elements into two: explicit and implicit. According to him, we cannot know everything about people's life merely through sense organ by focusing observation. Those items of culture which are known through sense organs like eye and ear, are only explicit. Besides these, there are some other items of culture, which can be perceived only by those who are specially trained to look for them. These are the motivations and impulses underlying human actions of which the actors themselves may not be conscious. These are the implicit item of culture. Both these items must be included in the study of culture of any society.

Theories of Culture Growth

Anthropologists have developed various theories to deal with the growth that takes place in culture. These are:

(i) Evolutionary Theory
(ii) Diffusional Theory
(iii) Acculturation Theory.

About the evolutionary and diffusional theory, we have discussed in detail in first two chapters. Let us discuss here, acculturation theory of cultural growth. We are aware of the facts that evolutionists attempted to explain the growth of culture in a sequence, in which the direction was from simple to complex. They dealt with parallel discoveries or inventions all over world. Diffusionists attempted to show the growth of culture by means of diffusion. According to diffusional doctrine, culture traits were discovered or invented at a particular place, from where they reached at other places by diffusion or migration or borrowing.

Acculturation

Some anthropologists have attempted to explain the process of development in culture through acculturation. When culture traits or complexes discovered or invented at one place reach at another place, it is called diffusion. But when whole system of life in a culture begins to change under the influence of any other culture, it is called as the process of 'acculturation'.

The concept of 'acculturation' was first developed by Redfield, Linton and Herskovits in their joint paper entitled, "Memorandum on The Study of Acculturation", in *Journal of American Anthropologist*, (Vol. XXXVIII, 1936:149). According to them, acculturation comprehends those phenomena, which result when groups of individuals having different cultures come into first hand contact, with subsequent changes in the original cultural patterns of either on both groups.

Acculturation results either due to self-interest or under pressure. Acculturation takes place due to many causes such as pressure of ruler, adoption of modernity, rise in status, advantage for the group etc. Acculturation is not always advantageous. Sometimes it brings adverse effect. This happens when a common agreement is not reached between the cultural norms and values of each group. Acculturation under pressure also has devastating effect and in this situation split is evident. When one group develops hate, jealous, rivalry, enemity etc. against the other groups, the process is known as contra-culturation.

While dealing with the concept of acculturation, the knowledge of some more concepts in this regard is also essential. Redfield, Linton and Herskovits are of opinion that when a child learns his or her own culture, the process is known as *enculturation*. When two cultures make exchange of their cultural traits among themselves, it is known as *transculturation*. When a culture adopts other culture, losing its own original form, in such a way that it becomes difficult to make a distinction between the two, it is known as *assimilation*. When a group losses its own culture under the influence of other, the process is termed as *deculturation*. To adopt new traits in its own culture, is called as *neo-culturation*.

Some conditions are essential for the process of acculturation. These are: (i) both groups must have close and continuous contact, (ii) both groups should have some similarity in their culture pattern, and (iii) both groups should have similarity in their objective.

Theories of Integration of Culture

Various theories have been presented to define integration of culture in modern anthropology. These are:

1. Theory of functionalism
2. Theory of pattern of culture or cultural configuration
3. Theory of themes
4. Theory of style of life.

The theory of functionalism has been explained in Chapter 3 and theories of pattern of culture and themes have been described in Chapter 5. Let us discuss here theory of style of life.

Theory of Style of Life

The latest theory to define culture integration is the theory 'style of life'. The style of life does not include only culture, but also includes the most fundamental and permanent elements. It includes the means of livelihood only to the extent to which they can be helpful in giving a practical shape to the conception of good life. Style of life includes explicit and implicit judgements about right conduct. It also includes comparatively less important elements which explain the individual character of some group.

It was Redfield, who presented the Theory of the Style of Life. He regards the style of life like the concepts of manners. According to him, each culture has its own ways of living and thinking, which reveal the especial style of life of that group. This style of life influences each aspects of culture due to which integration in culture comes in to existence. Therefore, it is necessary to understand the style of life in order to understand a culture.

Paradoxes of Culture

Herskovits in his book, *Man and His Work* (1956:18-21) has explained some paradoxes in relation to culture, which clarify more the nature or characteristics of culture. These paradoxes are:

1. Culture is universal in man's experience, yet each local or regional manifestation of it is unique.

   Man is the creator of culture, this phrase of Herskovits attracts our attention towards the same. Wherever men reside, there is existence of culture. Being heir of culture is a special feature of man, whether he lives in hilly-forested area or plain, or islands or lands, in urban or rural areas. Not only this, each culture has some such characteristics and aspects, which are common to all cultures. For instance, each culture has some kind of means of livelihood, all societies have institution of family, kinship and some kind of arrangement for political control. In the same way, in each society there is religious order in one form or the other. In spite of being all these similarities, if we focus our attention towards the detail analysis of these aspects of culture, we will find clearly that no two customs, traditions, religious orders and means of political control are identical. In other words, different aspects of culture in a society get their expressions differently. In this sense, no two cultures are identical or similar. This dis-similarities in cultures are responded in local environment and historical processes. It is, therefore, said that a culture cannot be understood, unless one possesses the knowledge of local environment and its past.

2. Culture is stable, yet culture is also dynamic, and manifests continuous and constant change.

If one collects the probable historical proof, it will reveal clearly beyond doubt that culture is dynamic. It is not stable or static. Total stability or staticity symbolizes dead culture. As has been referred to earlier, the aspects of culture are influenced by physical, mental and social needs of man. If man's needs change, they bring change in culture as well. These needs change in different periods of time. The processes of change is so slow that we cannot know them without making a comparison of present prevailing situation with past. In fact, these changes in culture are not so rapid that they produce disorder in total cultural system. Amidst the scene of changes, there is organisation and equilibrium in cultural traits or complexes or patterns, which provide staticity or stability in culture. For instance, if one compares the cultural remains discovered at Indus valley civilizations with present day Indian culture, he or she finds that main traits of Indian culture are still static, though in the periods of Indus valley and present day many thousands of years have passed. Some traits of Indus valley culture are certainly different from present day Indian culture. This example reveals clearly that a culture is static as well as dynamics. If an old individual is shown his photo of childhood, he cannot deny that it is not his or her photograph. At the same time, he or she cannot deny the change that has taken place from childhood to oldhood. It reveals clearly that the study of cultural change is possible in the context of cultural staticity. The term culture staticity does not reveal that culture is not changing, but it simply admits that with the changeability in cultural traits, there is also stability in culture.

3. Culture fulfils and largely determines the course of our lives, yet rarely intrudes into conscious thought.

   An individual is born in a culture, and he leads his entire life in it. Thus, culture determines our ways of life. Our life-ways are determined, guided and controlled by the culture. But in fact, an individual learns culture in unconscious form. He or she never knows, about the learning of many things. It means we learn many things unconsciously in culture. Our many behaviours are found working unconsciously in accordance with our culture about which we hardly attempt consciously. Thus, it appears that though culture determines our life-ways, but if rarely intrudes into our conscious thought.

Man as Creator of Culture

Man is a man among other animals because he has culture. A man cannot be regarded as superior to other animal in absence of culture. If culture is snatched from men, he will represent like other animal. Now question arises as to why man developed culture and other animals not ? Leslie White, a neo-evolutionist of America, solves this question in his book, *Evolution of Culture* (1959:3). In this book he had dealt with those five characteristics of man, due to which the creation of culture became possible. These are:

1. *Erect gesture:* Man is the only animal who has efficiency to stand vertically followed by bipedal walk. The other animals follow quadrupedal walk. On account of this special characteristic, man uses his hands in performing other works, where as other animals are not in this position.
2. *Freely Opposable Thumb:* Human beings have the efficiency to move his hands in any direction freely. His thumbs are opposable by which he can catch any thing easily. His efficiency of freely movable hands makes him competent to easily handle tools, implements, machines, etc. and to possess control over them. If this efficiency in man was lacking, the creation of tools, implements, machines, art, architecture, paintings, drawings, etc. was

certainly beyond possibility.

3. *Stereo-scopic and Chromatic Vision:* Man possesses stereo-scopic and chromatic vision by virtue of which he makes observation on natural and other events and also makes invention related to them.
4. *Intelligent Brain:* The greatest efficiency of man is reflected through the possession of intelligent brain. His brain is certainly more logical, thoughtful and active in comparison to other animals. It is because of possession of intelligent brain that he can think, plan, express ideas and find out cause-effect relationship. All discoveries and inventions for better and better living are the product of intelligent brain, which human beings possess. Some scholars are of opinion that human brain differs from animal brain in degree not in kind. Charles Darwin holds view that there is not fundamental difference between man and the higher mammals in their mental faculties, the difference between them consists of solely in man's almost infinitely larger power of associating together the most diversified sounds and ideas. The mental powers of higher mammals do not differ in kind, though greatly in degree, from corresponding powers of men (Charles Darwin, *Descent of Man*, 1871:18). Ralph Linton, a cultural patternist of America, opines that there are many differences in behaviour patterns of man and animals, but these differences are of quality, but not of quantity.

   But the views of Darwin and Linton are not acceptable by majority of scholars, because it is not difficult to prove that the difference between human brain and animal brain is of kind as well. For example, it is man who can make difference between holy water and common water, other animals cannot do so. It is man who makes difference between sister and wife and it is man who can make borrowing to aeroplane. Can any animal do these works ? Only man knows the importance of magic, religion and science, the significance of heaven and hell, and the reality of mortality and immortality. These differences between human and animal brains clearly reveal that the two differ both in degree as well as in kind. Thus, it is the existence of intelligent brain in man which is responsible for the existence of man as a human being.
5. *Creation of Symbol:* The efficiency of making symbols is unique characteristic of man, which other animals certainly lack. Between man or groups, exchanges of ideas take place through the medium of language and symbols. It is true, as supported by Darwin, that animals, too, understand words and sentence of their

language, but it is man who gives birth to symbols, not animals. Again, it is man who makes the symbols meaningful. These meaningful symbols are expressed through language by which, ultimately, exchange of ideas between man or groups becomes possible. This unique characteristic of man is definitely beyond the efficiency of even higher mammals. Animals cannot transfer their experiences and ideas to the next generation, but men, by using language and culture, transmit their experiences and ideas from one generation to next and so on. This signifies clearly the role of language and symbols in creation and development of culture.

Theories of Civilization

The term civilization has been defined in different ways by the scholars. The classical evolutionists, who believe in ordered development or progress of culture of man-kind, mean civilization as a developed form of culture. According to them, culture or society of man-kind has passed through the successive stages of development in sequence, namely, savagery, barbarism and civilization. Savagery was the earliest form of culture or society in which appropriation of natural products, ready for use, predominated. The things produced by man were mainly the instruments that facilitated this appropriation. These instruments were related to food gathering hunting and fishing. The stage of savagery was followed by another stage of development in culture known as barbarism. It was a period in which the knowledge of cattle-breeding and land-cultivation was acquired and in which the methods of increasing the productivity of nature through human activities were learnt. Civilization was the most developed form of culture or society. This was a period in which knowledges of further working up of natural products with implements of metals, industry proper, art, phonetic alphabet and writing were acquired. The advent of writing in stage of civilization marks the beginning of historical era. Before the development of writing, men belonged to the period of prehistory. There was also a stage of protohistory in which some kind of writings were certainly developed, but they have not been read successfully by our archaeologists. For example, writings of Indus valley civilization have not been understood till now. It is because of this fact that the Indus valley culture is also known as protohistoric civilization of India. Attempts have been made by the archaeologists to reconstruct the history of Indus valley culture on the basis of studying protohistoric objects such as seals, sealing, pottery, coins, architecture, images, etc. The above views of evolutionists clearly reveal that civilization is evolved or developed form of culture.

The diffusionists, who believe in migration, diffusion of borrowing of culture traits or complexes, from one place to another, mean civilization as a developed stage of mankind in history which was marked by the introduction of agriculture, irrigation, facilities, writing, art, architecture and monument making, plus use of developed technology.

Historians regard writing as beginning of historical era. As writing was developed in the stage of civilization, so civilization also marks the beginning of history.

All the historically-oriented scholars like evolutionists, diffusionists and cultural historians regard civilization as a changed or developed stage of culture. The stage of civilization was marked by the organisation of the complexities, heterogeneities and certainties.

The sociologists like Ogburn and Nimkoff conceived civilization as the latter phase of superorganic culture. Some sociologists have viewed civilization and civil organisation as contrasted to clan or kinship organization. Since civil organisation was found more commonly in large towns, so people living these towns were called civilized. A.A. Goldenwieser, an American anthropologist, used the word civilization as synonymous to culture and applied the term even for non-literate peoples.

Some scholars reserve the word civilization for some selected part of culture. Brooks Adam thinks of civilization as being essentially a highly developed organization. His concept of civilization implies order maintained over an area by governmental power. To Arnold Toynbee, a civilization is essentially a religious and ethnical system, holding away over an area often longer than a state or nation. Such a system is unified by customs, institutions and ideologies.

The Sociologists, John Lewis Gillin and John Phillip Gillin employed the term culture to designate the ideas and techniques behind the concrete objects, and cultural equipment to describe the objects themselves. According to them, civilization is more complex and evolved form of culture.

Maclver and Page in their book, *Society* used the word civilization to denote utalitarian things, the whole mechanism and social organism, techniques and material instruments, which have been devised by man in his endeavour to control the conditions of life. These things operate as means to ends.

A.W. Green holds that a culture becomes civilization, only when it possesses written language, science, philosophy, a specialized division of labour and complex technology and political system.

Leslie White, an American neo-evolutionists, believes that culture advances as the energy harnessed per capita per year increases, or the efficiency or economy of the means of controlling energy is increased. He is of opinion that early man was dependent on nature because his technology was poor to control energy. As his efficiency of controlling energy grew up, he reached in to a developed and civilized stage.

Robert Redfield, and American anthropologists, brought a turning point in the history of anthropology by providing a more logical and scientific definition of the term civilization. It was he who initiated the study of dimensions of civilization in anthropology. It is because of this reason that he is known as founder of civilizational school of anthropological thought. His followers like Marriot, Singer, Lewis, etc. are also known as Redfieldians or civilizationists. Robert Redfield was well aware of the fact that civilization began with writing, urban life, and civil government to control the area. But he observed that the history of world was witness that man had achieved the stage of civilization nearly five thousand years before to-day, then why certain cultural groups are in the stage of primitive, some in the stage of advanced and some in between the two. Observing these facts, he came to the conclusion that civilizations has many dimensions such as folk and urban, on the basis of residence, and great traditions and little traditions, on the basis of written and oral traditions. In India, the dimensions of civilization are tribal, rural and urban, Redfield is of opinion that both folk and urban civilizations are not in isolation, rather they are interdependent and interactive. It is on this idea that he developed the concept of folk-urban continuum in order to understand the processes of interaction between folk and urban, the two aspects of the civilization. In order to understand the interaction between folk and urban civilization, he divides the traditions into two parts, oral and written. The oral tradition is the property of folk people, whereas written tradition is property of urban people. The folk-people with oral traditions are termed as little traditions and the urban people with written tradition have been designated as Great traditions by Robert Redfield. We will discuss the contribution of Redfield and other Redfieldians, later on, in this chapter. But let us now discuss the differences between culture and civilization. According to famous sociologists, MacIver and Page,the important points of differences between culture and civilization may be described as follows:

I. *Civilization has a precise standard of measurement, but not culture.*

Civilization is susceptible of being quantitatively measured on the grounds of efficiency. On comparing the products of civilization, we can prove which is superior and which is inferior. There efficiency can be estimated and in fact be measured. For example, lorry runs faster than a bullockcart, an aeroplane runs faster than a lorry, a powerloom produces more than a handloom, tractor is superior to hand plough, modern currency system is superior to barter exchange, etc. These examples reveal clearly that one is superior to other. On the other hand, there is no measuring rod by which we can assess the cultural objects. Different ages and groups have their own standards of judgements. To some, paintings of Ellora cave appear as an abomination, while to others they are invaluable models of art. To some Bernard Shaw is a better dramatist than Shakespeare. Some like folk songs, other prefer film songs.

II. *Civilization is always advancing, but not culture.*

Civilization not only marches, it marches always, provided there is no catastrophic break of social continuity in the same direction. Civilization shows a persistent upward trend. It is unilinear and cumulative and tends to advance indefinitely. The various constituents of civilization, for example, machines, means of transportation and communication, etc. are constantly progressing. But concerning culture, it cannot be asserted that art, literature, thoughts or ideas of to-day are superior to those of past.

III. *Civilization is passed on without effort, but not culture.*

Culture is transmitted on a different principle from that of civilization. The former can only be assimilated by the like minded. It can be had only by those who are worthy of it. No one without the quality of artist can appreciate art, nor classical music can be judged by those who do not have an ear for it. Civilization in general makes no such demand. We can enjoy its products without sharing the capacity which creates them. Every one can use breeze from the ceiling fan, whether he knows the mechanism of fan or not.

IV. *The works of civilization can be improved by any body, but that is not possible in the case of culture.*

Lesser minds can improve the work of the great inventors, but lesser artists instead of improving may rather spoil the poems of Milton or Tagore. The accomplishments of culture can be perfected only by the persons who produced them. Again, the product of the artist is more revealatory of his personality than that of the technician. Culture, being the immediate expression of human spirit, can advance only if that spirit is capable of finer efforts, has itself something more to express.

V. *Civilization is external and mechanical, while culture is internal and organic.*

Civilization is inclusive of external things, culture is related to internal thoughts, feelings, ideas, values etc. Civilization is that we have and culture is what we are. Thus, civilization is the means for the expression and manifestation of culture. It is body and culture is soul.

VI. *Civilization is borrowed without change or loss, but not culture.*

The transfer of civilization from one generation to another or from one place to another is quick and easy. Given adequate means of communication, things of civilization can quickly spread to the whole world. Radio, television, printing machine, automobiles, and aeroplane are no longer monopoly of any one country. The corporate form of industry has increased everywhere on older forms. The factories have replaced the domestic system of production. Peasant societies have started using tractors in place of plough and oxen. The new techniques of constructing buildings and building roads have everywhere been adopted. On the other hand, culture has an intrinsic quality and can only be imbibed. It will have a limited appeal. In India, we have borrowed much western civilization, but not western culture. Though, there are some cultural borrowings, but they are insignificant compared to borrowing of civilization. It is only a few aspects of culture which are borrowed and even in this act of borrowing, borrowed culture is largely modified by the personality of the borrowers. Thus, it is clear that expansion of civilization follows different principles from those which determine cultural development. Civilization proceeds more rapidly, more simply, less selectively, always spreading outward from the foci of technological advance.

Thus, Maclver and Page have emphasized upon the developed material objects of culture as symbolizing civilization. According to them, civilization includes all those things by means of which some other objective is attained, such as type-writers, press, lathe, motor, etc. In civilization are included both, basic technology, which means the authority of man over natural phenomena, as well as social technology or model, which controls man's behaviour. On the other hand, culture comprehends such elements as religion, art, philosophy, literature, music etc., which bring satisfaction and pleasure to man. Culture is expression of our nature in our modes of living, thinking, everyday life, art, literature, recreation and enjoyment.

Difference Between Simple or Primitive Society and Complex or Advanced Society

In anthropological literature, various terms have been used to designate the tribal communities or backward people of the world. These terms are: native, naive, primitive, aboriginal, savage, barbarous, simple society, small-scale society, uncivilized society, pre-literate or non-literate society, homogeneous society, traditional society, pre-industrial or non-industrial society, stateless society, folk-society, little community etc. These terms used for them clearly reveal that they differ certainly from present day advanced or civilized societies. The main points of difference between simple and complex or primitive and advanced societies are as follows:

Simple Society or Primitive Society	*Complex or Advanced Society*
1. No developed technique of writing	1. Developed technique of writing
2. Rudimentary technology	2. Developed technology
3. Low output	3. High output
4. Little scope of specialization	4. High scope of specialization
5. Low density of population	5. High density of population
6. Homogeneous production	6. Diversified production
7. Low ratio of capital to consumer good	7. High ratio of capital to consumer good
8. The distribution is chiefly non-market and monetary sector is undeveloped.	8. The distribution is chiefly by market and monetary sector is chiefly developed.
9. Mainly multi-interest social organisation in which status holding and wealth holding are conguent	9. Mainly single-interest social organization
10. Kinship tie is stronger	10. Kinship tie is weaker
11. Unspecialized political and legal institution	11. Specialized political and legal institution

CIVILIZATIONAL STUDY IN ANTHROPOLOGY

As referred earlier, the term civilization was known to anthropologists since the postulation of evolutionary theory, but it was the pioneering work of Robert Redfield of Chicago University, America, who brought a movement in the history and development of anthropology by introducing the study of civilization. He viewed civilization as having folk and urban dimension. He made study of folk-villages and urban centres and attempted to understand the patterns and processes of interaction between them. Thus, he developed the concept of folk society, urban society and folk-urban continuum. Since then the study of village as a unit of rural civilization and urban-centre as a unit of urban civilization came into existence.

In order to understand the role of religion in development of civilization, Redfield developed the concepts of Great and Little tradition and he defined civilizations as a complex whole of great and little traditions. Great traditions refers to the formal literate tradition of a civilization, which is maintained by the elite of the society. The concept of little tradition refers to formal illiterate tradition of rural people living within a civilization. He also introduced the term cultural specialists, who mediate between great and little traditions. Some Indian anthropologists have used the term *Shastriya* or written tradition to designate great tradition and the term *Laukik* or worldly or oral tradition in place of little tradition used by Redfield.

Redfield's approaches to select a village or a religious centre as representative unit of civilization of an area or region or nation, got more popularity among the anthropologists all over the world. Many anthropologists of America namely, Oscar Lewis, Marriot, Milton Singer, Mandel Baum added some new concepts in the study of civilization as proposed by Robert Redfield. These scholars are also known as Redfieldians or civilizationists. It is important to mention here that Redfield and these civilizationists of America paid a visit to India and studied Indian villages with a view to throw light on Indian civilization. Let us now discuss their contribution one by one.

Robert Redfield (1897-1958)

Robert Redfield was born in Chicago, Illinois, on December 4, 1897. His father Bertha Dreier Redfield, was an eminent attorney at Chicago. His education was held at School System of Chicago University, U.S.A. He graduated from this University High School in 1915. He received a degree of law in 1920 from the same University. He was married to Margaret Lucy Park, the daughter of Robert, E. Park, an eminent professor of Sociology at Chicago University.

As his degree was in Law, he practised as a lawyer for a brief period, but in 1923 he got a chance to visit Mexico. He observed Mexican Indians and attempted to understand their society and culture in brief. Thus, his interest towards anthropology developed. Coming back, he undertook graduate course in anthropology in 1924. After receiving this degree, he was appointed as an instructor in the Department of Sociology and Anthropology, University of Chicago, U.S.A. In 1928, he was awarded with Ph.D. degree from this University and his position was upgraded to an assistant professor in Sociology and Social Anthropology.

In 1930, the separation of Anthropology from sociology was made. Robert Redfield's position was again upgraded to the post of Associate Professor in Anthropology. In 1934, he achieved the post of professor and Dean in Social Science Division. He occupied this post till he resigned in 1946 to become chairman of the Department of Anthropology, University of Chicago, U.S.A.

Redfield's major publications are as follows:

1. 1930: *Tepoztlan: A Mexican Village*
2. 1934: *Chankom*
3. 1941: *Folk Culture of Yukatan*
4. 1953: *The Primitive World and its Transformations*, New York
5. 1955: *The Little Community: Viewpoint for the study of Human Whole*, Chicago
6. 1955: *Thinking About Civilization*
7. 1956: *Peasant Society and Culture.*

During 1927-28, Robert Redfield made a trip to Mexican traditional village known as Tepoztlan. He published a book on folk-society of this traditional village of Mexico in 1930. He found this village an ideal type of folk-society, which is the polar opposite of the urban society. According to him, ideal type is mental construct and no known society corresponds to it.

According to Redfield, folk type of society is characterized, as such a society is small, isolated, non-literate and homogeneous with a strong sense of group solidarity. The ways of living are conventionalized into that coherent system, which we call 'a culture'. Behaviour is traditional, spontaneous, uncritical and personal. There is no legislation, habit of experiment and reflection for intellectual ends. Kinship, its relationship and institutions are the type of categories of experience and the familial group is the unit of action. The sacred prevails over the secular and the economy is one of status, rather than of market.

So, we can summarise the characteristics of folk societies, as follows:

1. *Isolated:* Folk Society is isolated. It is physically immobile. It has its own territory to which it is limited.
2. *Small in size:* Folk society is small society in reference to the number of members. Members have direct contact with each other, but its numerical strength cannot be fixed.
3. *Feeling of 'We' and 'They':* Folk society has community sentiment. Members know that who is a member of the society to whom they include in 'we' and who is from outside, who is considered as 'they'. In fact, folk society has group consciousness.
4. *Personal relation:* In folk society, there is personal relation among members. They know each other not only by name, but by face.
5. *Common interest:* Folk society has common interest. Their common interest is to lead a good life. They collect or produce food commonly and all members of the group share them.
6. *Simple division of labour:* In folk society, there is no division of labour on the basis of specialization. The division of labour is on the basis of age and sex. Within the same age and sex group, activities are the same.
7. *Homogeneity:* Members of the folk society show similarity on the basis of dress, custom, culture, way of life etc.
8. *Tradition have a big role:* The ways of life in folk society is guided by customs and traditions. Their behaviour is spontaneous and uncritical.
9. *Simple technology:* Folk society is characterized by simple technology. Their technological implements or tools are simple and traditional. They are usually got from natural resources.
10. *Independent:* In relationship with production and consumption, they produce for subsistence and they are independent in that.
11. *Importance of kinship system:* In folk society familial relationships are established from birth. Range of kinship system is larger. Matrilineal and patrilineal, both type of kinship can be seen in folk society.
12. *Magic:* Magic has a great importance in folk society. From some specific emotional experiences, people try to increase the emotion of the group and reveal the truth.
13. *Sacred prevails over Secular:* In folk society, certain objects are considered as sacred. They offer worship to their implements, food items, hearths, or any other objects, which help in satisfaction of their needs.
14. *Economy is for status:* The economy of folk society is status-oriented, not market-oriented. They consume whatever they produce. The concept of market and saving is not developed in

them. Barter exchange is prevalent, but this exchange is also consumption-oriented.

In 1930, Redfield along with his associate, Alfousa Villa Rojas, conducted a study of peasant village Chankom, which was published in 1934. In this book, Robert Redfield with his associate, has attempted to show the characteristics of a peasant village. He opined that a peasant society is characterized by excessive love for the land. For them, land is not merely a piece of earth, but like a mother, which nurtures them and fulfils their requirement. Their entire economy is dependent on land, by which they subsist on.

According to Redfield, peasant society differs from folk society in that it has developed a market system. So, they are in contact with the traders of urban centre. In other characteristics, such as 'we' feeling, personal relation, common interest, homogeneity, observance of traditions, simple technology, simple division of labour, kinship system, magical and religious beliefs, a peasant society characterizes, more or less, like a folk society. As peasant society is in contact with urban centres, its members possess some cultural traits of urban society and some traits of folk society. Thus, peasant society, is, in between the two societies folk and urban.

Redfield's Concept of Folk-urban Continuum

In 1941, Robert Redfield published a book entitled, *The Folk Culture of Yukatan*. This book is based on comparative study of four communities, namely, a city society, a town society, a peasant society and folk or simple society. He selected these four communities or societies in the Mexican province of Yukatan, where he had visited many times for his fieldwork. The four places in the Mexican province of Yukatan, representing he habitation of four communities were: Marida (city society), Diztas (a town society), Chankom (a village of peasant's society) and Tuski (a village of folk society or simple society).

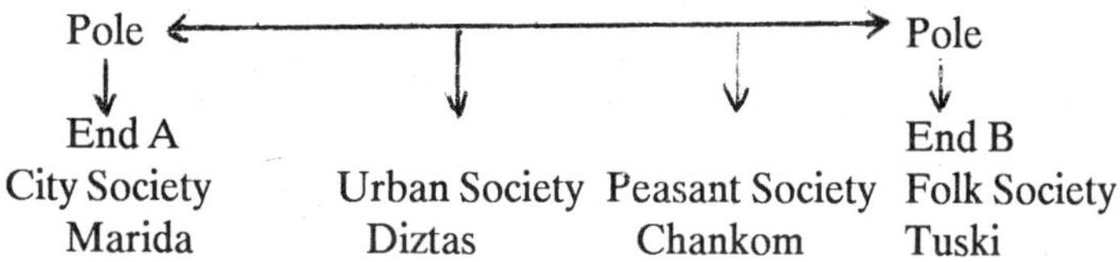

Robert Redfield placed Tuski at one end of the pole and Marida at the opposite end of the pole. He observed the characteristics of Tuski (a folk society) quite different from Marida (a city or a developed urban society). He observed the characteristics of Chankom (a peasant society) as resembling more with the Tuski (folk society). Redfield also observed great similarities between the characteristics of Diztas (urban community) and Marida (a city community), such as both possess market economy and civil administration to rule them. In Diztas (a urban society), he observed similarities in some traits of Chankom (a peasant society) such as presence of market, middlemen, shops and daily going and coming. As city community was resembling more with town community, and peasant community more with folk, therefore, he termed Marida and Diztas as urban community and Chankom and Tuski (as folk society). He then proposed the concept of *Folk-urban continuum*. Folk-urban continuum, is a polar-ideal type of construction, which implied that no known society precisely corresponds to the description of the extreme ends, but fall near one or the other of the two, and of the same poles or in between.

After establishing a concept of folk-urban continuum, Redfield begin to sum up the typical characteristics of 'folk' and 'urban', and used their dominant outlooks on life as his main criteria of distinction. He observes moral order as typical characteristics of folk society. The moral order, typical of folk society, signifies all the biding together of men through implicit conviction as to what is right, and through implicit ideals, which means, in turn, that member of folk-society persued their own ideals of the *"good life"*. The technical order of urban life is composed of opposite attributes. The bonds that hold urban societies together do not rest on convictions of "good life". They are not characterized by a foundation in human sentiments. They result instead from mutual usefulness, deliberate coercion, and from necessity and expediency. According to Redfield, in folk-urban continuum or folk-urban dichotomy, folk society comes in contact with urban society and inherits certain characteristics, so a folk society has certain characteristics of urban. It is between illiterate and literate, between undeveloped and developed, between simple and complex societies. Folk society is loosing its characteristics because of contact with urban society. Isolation, kinship system, group feeling, homogeneity, are no more there.

Increase in contract, bringing about heterogeneity, is sufficient cause of secularization and individualization. Thus, contacts result in change and disorganization of chief traits of folk-society as well. It may become more heterogeneous, develop a market economy, and thus, indication of disorganization appears. It is not only true with folk-urban societies, but contact among any two dissimilar societies results in change.

Evidence of disorganization and of secularization and impersonal behaviour, is more evident in relationship between member of different ethnic groups of a community. Redfield's methodological approaches reveal that any attempt to characterize the whole society and to compare it with others indedicates that it will come under the polar characteristics of one end or the other or in between. This will tend to show that the folk-urban continuum study deals with the problem of the relative presence or absence of polar characteristics. In Yucatan study, Redfield treats isolation and homogeneity of community as independent variables, where as he regards organisation or disorganisation of culture, secularisation and individualization as dependent variables.

Redfield is of opinion that if a society looses its isolation or homogeneity, it becomes secularized and its members work more for their own interest, rather in the interest of group.

When Redfield makes a comparison of Yukatan study with the study of Guatemala by Sol Tax, another American anthropologist, he arrives at conclusion that there is no single necessary cause for secularization and individualization.

Sol Tax study of Guatemala societies reveals that they are small and homogeneous in beliefs and practices, but possess impersonal relation, weak familial organisation, and secular life, with individuals acting more from economic or other advantages, than from any deep thought of social good.

However, it is beyond doubt that Redfield has used the concept of folk-urban continuum as a device to explain the changes in society and the interaction between the two polar ends, folk and urban. He has suggested a great many ways in which the relationship between simple culture or folk society and complex culture or urban society can be conceptualized, such as by looking at a community as an ecological system, a social structure, a typical biography, a kind of person, outlook on life, and so forth.

Criticism of Folk-urban Continuum

Oscar Lewis, an American colleague of Redfield made a study of Pedro Martinze, a Mexican peasant society. His book on, *Pedro Martinze: A Mexican Peasant and His Family* was published in 1967. He has pointed out some points against the study of Redfield. These are:

1. The folk-urban conceptualization of social change focuses attention primarily on the city as a source of change, and neglects or other factors of an internal or external nature. For example, great heterogeneity in the division of labour requires a large popula-

tion, while a large population may exist as an elaborate division of labour.

2. Culture change may not be a matter of folk-urban progression, but rather an increasing or decreasing heterogeneity of cultural elements.
3. Some of the criteria used in definition of folk-society are treated by Redfield as linked or interdependent variables, but might better be treated as independent variables.
4. The question posed by Redfield, namely, what happens to an isolated homogeneous society, when it comes in contact with an urbanized society, can not possibly be answered in a scientific way, because the question is for general and the terms used do not give us necessary data in this regard.
5. The emphasis upon essentially formal aspect of culture leads to neglect of psychological data.
6. The folk-urban dichotomy as used by Redfield is a system of value judgement.
7. World view can bring change in dependent characteristics of folk-society without having any change in independent characteristics.
8. The quantity of contact of folk with urban cannot be measured. The whole criticism can be summarized as follows:

(i) The problem of lack of fitness in empirical evidence.
(ii) The problem of definition of the characteristics of ideal type.
(iii) The limited theoretical applicability.

In spite of these criticism levelled against Redfield, Redfield's methodological approach to treat a community as a whole, whether urban, peasant or folk, and to reveal an interaction and change among them, has received wider popularity all over the world. Now anthropologists select a community as an ideal representative of folk or peasant or urban societies and attempts to make a comparison among them with special reference to change and interaction. Thus, we can proceed from a larger or complex or urban culture towards small or simple or folk culture in order to perceive change and interaction pattern or vice versa. In other words, we can proceed from mega culture to micro culture or micro culture to mega culture.

Redfield's Concept of Little Community

Robert Redfield in his book entitled, *Little Community: View points for the Study of Human Whole* (1955), develops the concept of Little Community with a view to study human whole. According to him, Little Community is a small group of individuals living together, in whom all characteristics of a communal living are found. There is mass participation by its members in various communal activities. The Little Community, according to Redfield, is a kind of human whole. This whole is the smallest unity to the humanity. He has opined that little communities have been the most predominant form of human living throughout the history of man kind. From the holistic point of view, anthropologists have done most of their fieldwork in little communities. Little communities have also been called as small communities by Robert Redfield. He has mentioned the following characteristics of a Little Community:

1. *Distinctiveness:* A Little Community has its own individuality or distinctiveness. According to Redfield, in a sense it is distinct, where the community begins and where it ends. The distinctiveness is expressed in the group consciousness of the people of the community. It is known, who is a community member and who is outsider.
2. *Smallness:* Little Community is a small group of individuals having mutual relationship. However, it is not possible to determine the numerical strength. But the number of members in a little community should not exceed beyond a point where a direct and first hand contact among members become difficult. Therefore, little community is a unit of personal observation fully representative of human whole.
3. *Homogeneity:* In a little community, activities and states of mind of all persons, belonging to a sex and age, are alike. Similarly each generation repeats activities of the preceding generation. Therefore, little community is slow changing. The members of community show similarity in matter of dress, ways of life, language and cultural outlook, ethos or world view.
4. *Self-Sufficiency:* Little Community is characterized by Self-sufficiency. It satisfies all needs of its members from birth to death. It is because of this fact that Redfield has called little community as a cradle to the grave arrangements.

On account of these characteristics, only those community can be considered as little communities, which are having their own culture and to a great extent away from large complex culture. Redfield opines that in present context, little communities are coming in contact with urban civilization. Now, they only satisfy two characteristics — smallness and distinctiveness, but are no more homogeneous and self-sufficient.

Importance of the Study of Little Community

According to Redfield, since the little community is the smallest unit, representative of the whole society, its scientific study gives us knowledge of whole society. Analytic and atomistic studies of the little community have been attempted by many social anthropologists. Some others have studied social groups within the community. According to Redfield, communities cannot be completely described. The phrases such as Ecological System, Social Structure, Human Career, Personality type, and World-view, comprehend the community more or less as a whole.

From the period of Redfield, when he proposed the concept of little community as a human whole, many anthropologists adopted this methodological approach of Redfield in the study of tribal village, rural communities and urban communities. They, like Redfield, treat a community or a village as representative unit of whole social order. Thus, they treat their micro-cosmic studies of communities/villages as representative of whole area, or state or nation. Following Redfield's methodological approach of little community, a good number of village studies have also been a carried out, about which we will discuss later.

Redfield's Concept of Peasant Society

Redfield makes an important contribution in the study of Peasant Society by publishing a book entitled, *Peasant Society and Culture* (1956). As referred to earlier, Redfield made study of Chankom village, a peasant society in 1930 and published a book on Chankom in 1934. He again visited Chankom and made a restudy of the same peasant society. He also studied Maya people, a peasant society of England. He compared the peasant society of Chankom with Maya and arrived at a conclusion that peasant society of the world has some common characteristics. He observed that peasant society was in-between folk and urban societies. In a sense also of an ideal construct, peasantry was nevertheless an explaining and observable form of social life. Peasants raise crops like post-neo-lithic groups. They use their surpluses not for the discharge of rituals and kinship obligation, but for trading with cities. Peasants are also to be distinguished from farmers, who are businessmen in industrial setting, cultivating their crops for selling and profit only. Peasant societies are relatively self-contained and possess their own indigenous culture, structure and values, but they stand in a subordinate relationship to the city, which often controls their land and labour and determines the prices of their agricultural products. They are, thus, structurally related to more complex cities. Not only do they trade with them, but they also consider the city as the primary source of innovations because of prestige of city life. The recognition of peasantry as a social type has led to many important studies contributing to increased knowledge about economic, ecology and culture change.

Redfield opines that peasants of different parts of the world have certain similarities of value, while they have dissimilarity of values as well. He calls this similarity as 'Imperturbable sameness'. Good life as peasants think, according to him, is the integrated patterns of dominant attitudes and ways of thinking, which are considered as ideals. Redfield, in his anthropological studies of peasant culture, seems to find a cluster of three related attitudes. These are:

1. A reverent attitude towards the land
2. The idea that agriculture is good and business bad
3. Industrious nature.

1. *A reverent attitude towards the land:* Peasant society has a reverent or intimate attitude towards the land. They consider land as *Bhumaiya* or *Dharatimaiya* (Mother land). They honour land as mother because it is mother land, which nourishes them from the childhood to the end of the life. They do not prefer to sell land, except on emergent situation. They offer worship to land before starting any cultivation work. They take help of the priest to know the correct time for carrying out agriculture. They never touch the crop with their feet. Robert Redfield observed that when a Yucatan people or Maya people see a piece of grain lying in the way, they take up and offer salutation. Such grains found are termed as lost child in peasant parlance. Thus, land is a status symbol in their culture and provides security in life.
2. *The idea that agriculture good and business bad:* Peasants consider land as mother and because of it they do not like to sell land. They do not like to sell land for business or service. They like to do agriculture, because in their culture, agriculture is regarded as superior to business and service. An Indian proverb, which Indian peasant societies use frequently in this regard, is as follows:

Uttam Kheti, Madhyam Ban
Nich Naukari, Narak Saman.

This proverb reveals clearly the attitudes of peasant towards agriculture as superior and business and services as inferior.

3. *Industrious nature:* Peasants consider hard working the value of life. They cultivate the land of their own and they also work as labourers in the field of others. A lazy man is considered bad for peasant community. An Indian folk proverb in this regard is as follows:

Askat Put·Kisan Nase, Chor Ke Nase Khanshi.

This proverb indicates that as coughing is bad for a thief, in the same way, idleness is bad for peasantry.

Finally, Redfield takes two values as the general index of peasantry. These are:

(i) *Practical disposition:* Peasants approaches to marriage, family, etc. are generally practical. There is little room for bravado.
(ii) Premarital relations are allowed but adultery is criticized.

Redfield's Concept of Great and Little Traditions

While conducting researches among peasant society, Robert Redfield observed two kinds of tradition, though separate in origin but inter-dependent and interactive with one another. One was formal, written, literate and reflective few. On the other hand another is informal, oral, illiterate and unreflective many. Redfield called the former as Great tradition and the latter as little traditions. He observed Great tradition being cultivated in school and temples located at different places. These places were visited by peasants. He also observed teachers and priest mediating between the two tradition. Thus, great tradition is cultivated in schools and temples with the help of teachers and priest to mediate, whereas little tradition works itself out and keeps itself going in the lives of unlettered village communities.

For example, in India many religious centres such as Prayag, Gaya, Varanasi, Ayodhya etc. have great traditions. These places have traditional temples and schools, where offering of worship and teaching of Sanskrit by head priest or *Mahantha* take place. *Mahantha* or his disciples move village to village among peasant communities to raise subscription in cash or in kind, to maintain Sanskrit teaching in the school and worship in the shrine. These sacred specialists also popularize the myths and legends associated with the place and shrine which form deep spiritual belief in the mind of peasants. This continues one after another generation through oral tradition. They also teach the peasants about the spiritual importance of paying a visit to these places in course of making a *Tirtha* (pilgrimage). Thus, religious attitudes develop in the mind peasants and as a result of which several rituals and offerings come in to being, which are performed by Hindu folk on different occasion. Thus, the two traditions, great and little, are brought in interaction by cultural specialists. The term cultural specialists has been used by Redfield to designate those organised group of people, who mediate between great and little traditions.

Redfield's Concept of Civilization

After formulating the concepts of great tradition, little tradition, and cultural specialists, Redfield proposed a concept of civilization — as a complex structure of great and little traditions. Thus, civilization has many dimensions such as great and little traditions, as well as tribal, rural and urban culture.

Redfield has also conceived of civilization as an organization of specialists in functional relation to folk societies. He also views civilization as world view, ethods, temperament, value system, cultural personality etc. (*Redfield, 1955:95*).

Redfield's concept of style of life as reviewing cultural integration has been described earlier. His concept of accumulation is also explained there. Therefore, it is not necessary to repeat them again.

Redfield became an anthropologist of international fame, when he developed such concepts as folk society, little community, peasant society, urban community, folk-urban continuum, peasant ethos, great and little traditions and interaction between them, civilization as a complex whole of great and little, written and oral, literate and illiterate, formal and informal traditions, etc. All his concepts have been used as a methodology to study communities and civilization.

When Redfield became internationally known, he was invited by many universities of the globe either to deliver lecture or to participate in research programme. In the year 1952-1953, he delivered messenger lectures at Cornell University, U.S.A. He was also a visiting professor at the University of Perish and at the Upsala University, Sweden. He delivered lectures for Adult Education Fund at the University of California. He was also a consultant to the Social Science Centre at the University of Puerto Rico and Cooper Foundation lecturer at Swarthmore. He was awarded by Vinking Fund Medal by his colleagues in America in the 1954. In the year 1955, he was awarded Huxley Memorial Medal from the Royal Anthropological Institute of Great Britain.

A growing interest in the comparative study of civilization led him to set up a Special Programme of Discussion and Research on civilizational study in 1951, with the financial assistance of Ford Foundation. He directed this research programme with the cooperation extended by Milton Singer, an American anthropologist as well as a colleague of Robert Redfield.

In the spring of 1955, Redfield paid a visit to India to participate in a conference of Dimensions of Indian Civilization, such as tribal, rural or peasant and urban communities. He also wanted to make a study of these communities as reflecting the various dimensions of Indian civilization. But he could not accomplish this task due to serious illness and returned back to Chicago. In the spring of 1958, Redfield participated in a seminar on the comparative study of civilization, organised by Centre for Advanced Study in Behavioural sciences. He fell seriously ill and was admitted to Billing Memorial Hospital, where he died on October 16th, 1958.

Oscar Lewis

Oscar Lewis was an American anthropologist at the University of Illinois, U.S.A. He is known among the anthropologists of the world for contributing such concept as *'culture of poverty'* in anthropological study. He also paid a visit to India and made a study of Rampur village in Western U.P. in 1951. While studying an Indian village, he developed the concept of *Rural Cosmopolitan.* His major publications are:

1. 1959: *Five Families: Mexican Case Studies in Culture of Poverty,* New York.
2. 1963: *The Children of Sanchez: Auto biography of a Mexican Family*, New York.
3. 1965: *Lavida : A Puerto Rican Family in the Culture of Poverty*, New York.
4. 1967: *Pedro Martines: A Mexican Peasant and His Family*, New York.

Lewis' Concept of Culture of Poverty

Oscar Lewis in his Mexican studies, (1959, 1963, 1965, 1967) has demonstrated as to how poor economic conditions give rise to similar behaviour and expectations. Mexicans belonging to same socio-economic status can be marked by the development of despair, fear, non-involvement in modern games, shy natured, etc. In their personality type, he observes this so pervasive cross-culturally, that he coins the phrase *'culture of poverty'* to indicate the regularities of personality among people living under deprived social conditions.

Lewis' Concept of Rural Cosmopolitan

As referred to earlier, Oscar Lawis visited India in 1951 and studied a village named Rampur in Western U.P. Highlighting the reality of Indian village as a whole, Lewis opines that members of Indian village have a deep ownness. Such feeling is not confined only to relation of an individual to another individual, but such relationship is also extended upto individual and nature, such as men and land, house, cattle, bird, tree plants and other natural objects. All these natural phenomena are related to internal environment of an Indian village. He further holds view that land relation, martial relation, religious order, political organisation and business build an extended relationship in Indian village system. He calls this extended relationship of Indian village order as *'Rural Cosmopolitan'*. His monograph on Rampur was published in 1958.

McKim Marriot

McKim Marriot was a disciple of Robert Redfield, Chicago University, U.S.A. He visited India and studied a village named Kishangarhi in U.P. Marriot, while examining the religious content, he has contributed two useful concept to the study of Indian civilization. These concepts are: (i) Universalization, and (ii) Parochialization.

Universalization is process by which cultural traits of a little tradition are absorbed into a great tradition. Thus, by this, a local phenomenon becomes universalized.

Parochialization is opposite process to universalization by which some written or literate or *Shastriya* or *Sanskritic* elements of great traditions are learnt about, and reformed or modified by the folk people or villagers to become a part of their cult.

Thus, Marriot has modified the concept of great and little traditions as developed by Robert Redfield. Marriot is of opinion that the twin concepts of universalization and parochialization are operating in continuity in the socio-religious system of Indian villages. Thus, Indian civilization can be understood with the help of universalization and parochialization processes. These two processes are complementary to each other. The study of one in isolation of another is not possible to understand the Indian civilization as a whole. Marriot's concepts of universalisation of little traditions and localization of great traditions are not applicable only to Hindu culture, but also other cultural dimensions of great and little traditions. Marriot edited a book entitled, 'Village India' in 1955. Marriot has also made study of Wai town near Poona with a view to show cultural roles of a city in Indian civilization.

Milton Singer

Milton Singer was an another disciple of Robert Redfield of Chicago University, U.S.A., who visited to India in 1954-55. He made a study of Madras City. His important publications are:

1. 1958: *Structure and Change in Indian Society*, (ed.).
2. 1972: *When a Great Tradition Modernizes: An Anthropological Approach to Indian Civilization.*
3. 1975: *Traditional India: Structure and Change.*

His edited book, *Structure and Change In Indian Society* (1958) has great relevance to the contemporary study of religious traditions in India. This volume, unlike the other two (1972, 1975), includes papers dealing with both textual and contextual analysis of recorded and oral traditions. Though the theme of the book is to understand the image of 'new India' in the light of his rich and deep-rooted heritage, almost all papers have some bearing on religions traditions, which obviously have been the common idioms of Indian history.

Singer also studied the cultural role of a traditional city Madras, South India and attempted to show as to how great traditions are modernised in sphere of little traditions.

In his book, *Traditional India: Structure and Change* (1975), Singer has developed the concepts of cultural geography, cultural performances, cultural specialists, cultural media such as song, dance, *Bhajan, Kirtan*, prayer, *Geet*, etc. All these aspects of cultural complex form the parts of interaction between great and little traditions of Indian civilization. Later on, Professor L.P. Vidyarthi, (former Director and Head, U.G.C. Centre of Advance Study, Department of Anthropology, Ranchi University, Ranchi), following Redfield's and Singer's theories and methodological frame work, made a full-length study of the Sacred City of Gaya. His book, entitled, *Sacred Complex in Hindu Gaya* (1961) deals with sacred geography, sacred performances and sacred specialists as different religious traits. They together constitute the complex whole of the same phenomenon, sacred complex of Hindus, making Gaya as a centre of Indian civilization.

Morris E. Opler

Morris E. Opler was an anthropologist from Cornel University, who came to India in 1951 to make a systematic and scientific study of an Indian village. He, together with an Indian R.D. (Rudra Dutta) Singh, selected a village Senapur in U.P. They developed the concepts of Unity and Extension (1948, 1952) of Indian village, which became a popular methodology in study of Indian villages for the analysis of the factors which contribute to unity in Indian villages. R.D. Singh (1948) highlights that deep sense of we-feeling, participation in each other's joys and sorrows, fighting unitedly to meet the threats created by another village or antisocial elements, such as thieves, dacoits, etc.. reveal unity as a cultural aspect of Indian village. Indian villages maintain exogamy, a rule by which members of a village are married in another village, but never in the same village. As a result of exogamic rules, matrimonial relations at distant places are found. This reveals extension of and interaction between villages through marriage. Villagers in order to sell their produce and purchase various kinds of things visit market centres. This reveals extension of village upto different market places. Establishment of urban and industrial towns has brought non-agricultural occupations. Villagers are being benefitted by opportunities of employment. These villagers move, time to time, in their respective villages from the place of working. Thus, establishment of industries and urban towns has contributed to the extension of Indian village.

Facility of education, medical facilities, opportunities of serving on a post at different places, have also extended the interaction of village with urban centres. Distribution of loans through banks situated in different areas, distribution of seed, fertilizer, etc. through block headquarters also reveal extensional aspect of Indian village.

India is an agricultural country. Agriculture is carried with the help of oxen. Cows and buffaloes are 'reared to get milk. In order to sell and purchase cattle, villagers go to different places where cattle fairs take place, which reveals extension of a village upto those places of fair.

Again, India is a religious country. There are many pilgrim-centres located in different parts of the country, where religious fairs takes place each year on various occasions from *Chait* to *Phalgun* months of our national calendar year. Small religious fairs also take place in local areas on the various religious occasions in a year. These places of pilgrimage and fairs are visited by villagers. This also reveals extension of an Indian village to various places of local, or regional or national level. Thus, studying an Indian village from unity and extension as methodology, throws much light on Indian traditions. It also reveals folk-urban continuum and interaction between great and little tradition. By this methodological approach, study of Indian civilization can also be done.

Morris E. Opler, also published a book entitled, *An Apache Life-Way: The Economic, Social and Religious Institutions of Chirikahua Indians* (1941). In this book, he developed the concept of cultural theme, which has been discussed in detail in chapter on Culture and Personality School

7

NEW ANTHROPOLOGY

In post-World War II period, specialists in several sub-fields of anthropology, such as physical, archaeological, cultural and linguistic anthropology, critically evaluated their methodological approaches. Conscious efforts were made to create new approaches. W. Taylor (1948) emphasized upon the foundation of a new archaeology, S. Washburn (1951) laid emphasis for a new physical anthropology. Similarly linguistic and cultural anthropologists equally sought new directions.

In mid-20th century, there arose a movement dedicated to the improvement of standards of ethnographic descriptions and analysis within cultural anthropology, having the techniques of linguistics as its source and inspiration. This movement, for which the name 'New Ethnography' has been proposed, originated at Yale University, U.S.A. It has spread rapidly throughout the United States, known variously as 'ethnolinguistics', 'ethno-science' or 'ethno-sementics'. Its manifest appeal lies in its promise to achieve the precise and highly operationalised paradigmatic rendering of cultural phenomena, which have come to be associated with linguists description of phonology and grammar. Its covert appeal, however, is that it carries forward the tradition of cultural idealism in anthropology while supplying that tradition with impressive new scientific credentials.

To a significant degree, these efforts led to a closer cooperation, tending to reaffirm and strengthen the four-field approach, folklore, prehistoric archaeology, physical anthropology, and linguistic anthropology, which, for a while, stood under the threat of dissolution. New archaeologists view their findings as representative of cultural systems, and attempt to grasp the meanings of archaeological remains, not as an ends in themselves, but as a means to understanding the human beings, who made them, and the societies in which they lived.

The new trend in physical anthropology is to project human evolution against the background of culture and ecology, while field studies of living primates search for the interrelationships between animal and human social behaviour.

Many present-day linguists concern themselves with cultural and psychological elements of language, while cultural anthropologists often take linguistic methodology as a model for their own studies.

Anthropological efforts to revise and refine older concepts have gone in many different directions, but over all concern is the attempt to discover units of explanation that can be used cross-culturally in an objective and unbiased manner. Dissatisfied with historical particularism, anthropologists now feel that meaningful cross-cultural comparisons cannot rest upon often undefined categories that were used earlier, such as trait, pattern, theme, custom, folk-ways etc.

The interest in cross-cultural analysis attracted the scholars towards the attempt to discover universals in culture. They realised that human behaviour is flexible but not ultimately so and that culture varies but also possesses common grounds of existence. These developments were not unrelated to the increasing concern for bringing the study of primitive societies into greater relationship with complex one. For a long period, anthropologists had described primitive cultures as if they were timeless and unchanging isolates, but such a romantic outlook could no longer be maintained. Tremendous changes, going on in the world after World War II, touched primitives, peasants, townsmen and industrialized city dwellers. Thus, the study of acculturation began to show how primitives become members of modern society, how migrants adjust to new surroundings, how peasants become industrialized farmers.

The community study method was perhaps the first conscious attempt to extend the insights gained from the study of homogeneous societies to more complex ones. The method signaled a breaking away from particularized concerns with tribal groups, and demonstrated that cultures were functionally dependent parts of larger wholes. In itself, however, the method contained no directions as to how various larger wholes could be brought into relationship with each other in a meaningful way. Searching for a wider framework, one in which the finding of archaeology, linguistics and physical anthropology also could be encompassed, anthropologists rediscovered evolution, known as neo-evolutionary theory.

Although Boas and his followers were not quite as anti-evolutionist as they are sometimes called to be, but they made few efforts to discover possible regularities of development and change. Nevertheless, the evolutionary concerns that had marked the beginning of anthropology as an independent discipline, were never completely lost from the sight. V. Gordon Childe and Leslie White kept this tradition alive in England and America, respectively.

Childe described evolution interms of three major events: invention of food production, urbanization and industrialisation. Analysing the transitions that took place under the impact of these revolutions, Childe presented an overall view of the evolutionary process and delineated its common factors.

Leslie White went a step further. Though he was a student of Franz Boas, but he was a great admirer of Tylor and Morgan. Like them, White believed in progressive course of evolution, but he tried to explain what caused progress itself and how it worked. Searching for a universal principles of explanation, he found it in energy. He reasoned that culture is basically a survival mechanism and that energy is required to provide man with the necessities for his continued existence. In the earliest stage of human development, man used his own body as the major source of energy, but soon he began to capture other natural resource of energy and utilized fire, water, wind, etc. for his purpose. Tools became increasingly efficient, animals were domesticated, engines constructed and so forth, so that amount of energy harnessed per cepita and the efficiency of technology increased as culture evolved. Each type of technology, moreover, conditioned a specific type of social organisation. Pastoralism, agriculture, metallurgy, industry, and militarism, each found a corresponding expression in a social system.

In the latter proposal that is somewhat dubious, one to one correlation between technology and social organisation has not been supported by ethnographic evidence. For instance, agricultural societies are widely divergent in their forms of social organizations, and further more, technological types are widely overlapping. Pastoralism, agriculture, metallurgy, and industry, often, occur side by side. But White's greater relevance is that he continued the work began by Tylor and Morgan. Rather than repudiating the concept of universal evolution, he improved it by using observable material factors as parameters of change, rather than referring to abstract notions of progress.

It is beyond doubt, White's over all view of evolution did not account for particular event. He has dealt with advance, not with divergent, and with general process not with adaptation. He takes the position that evolution does occur on a planetary scale, and that it is worthy object of study.

It is obvious enough that overall view of evolution has shown negligence towards the significance of particular events. It is on this ground that White's concept of universal evolution has been subjected to a great deal of criticism, due to its inability to account for short-time development.

Julian Steward has opined that, both, 19th century classical unilinear evolution and White's universal or general evolution, deal with culture of man-kind, as a whole, not with cultures that originate in short time development. Instead of dealing with evolution of culture as a whole through certain stages and following sequences in historical perspective, Julian Steward proposes a theory of multilinear evolution, dealing with particular events, which takes place in comparatively short period: His theory of multilinear evolution indicates that evolution in cultures of man has followed a multilinear development and change. In other words, Stewards' multilinear approach to study evolution of cultures is to establish sequences of parallel development that can be investigated in empirical reality. It is Steward's thesis that societies with a similar technology will parallel one another also in their forms of social and political organisation. It appears to him that hunter-gatherers tended to form patrilineal band, and that widely scattered Indian societies that has accepted the horse after its introduction into America, are comparable in their socio-political organisation. Such argument of Julian Steward, was strengthened by a research of Karl Wittfogel, (1957) who shows that societies located near undulating rivers, which carried out hydraulic (irrigation) agriculture, had originated state organisation. Thus, it indicates interaction between environment, technology and political organization.

We have seen earlier, Steward's multilinear approach to study cultural evolution differs from earlier ones, but does not necessarily discredit them. White has stressed upon the general evolution, while Steward has emphasised upon particular. The debate between evolutionists on these issues are nothing more than sementic squabbles. White accuses Steward for confusing evolution with history, because dealing with particular events as indicating evolution, is the subject-matter of history. Steward has labelled charges against White by calling his general evolutionary scheme as barren. Sahlin and service opine that evolution of culture can be studied both from the particular and general point of view. Margaret Mead has suggested a third approach to study of evolution. According to her, evolution of culture can be shown by studying the actual processes of change as they occur in one generation or between adjacent generations.

Subsequent neo-evolutionists have not brought these approaches into harmony. White's followers tend to stress material factors and technology as determinants of social organisation. But theirs approach is also often a functional. Multi-evolutionists have generally acknowledged the inter-relationship between environment and technology, so the latter (technology) became viewed as a variable, rather than as ultimate cause of evolution. Others became interested in the study of different parameters of change such as occupational specialization and urbanization as basic indicators of cultural advance. Some suggested 'scale-analysis' for studying, qualitatively different cultural features, which would also reveal the functional interrelationships between traits. Others examined innovative processes. Service (1971) published an ethnographic compendium in various cultures in ascending orders of political complexity, bands, tribes, chiefdoms, primitive states and modern folk societies. Mead's suggestions for short-time study are not generally termed evolutionary, but are more often considered as instances of culture change.

Thus, various new approaches to the study of evolution called attention to the question of how to combine the particular with general, or how the study of individual cultures could yield meaningful information about culture writ large.

NEW ETHNOGRAPHY

The question, how the study of individual cultures could yield meaningful information about culture writ large, was sharpened by Marvin Harris, who drew the attention to Radcliffe-Brown's earlier distinction between nomothetic or law-giving and ideographic or descriptive, in particular terms. As nomothetic is law giving, nomothetic researches attempt to discover general social laws. Ideography, on the other hand, means description in particular terms, is thus not necessarily analytical. In new ethnography, Harris favours nomothetic approach. However, he does not advocate the abandonment of detailed description, but indicates that data must be collected in such a way that they may become cross-culturally comparable, and thus, can lead to valid cross-cultural comparisons. Earlier attempts to do so has been done by impressionism and vague categorizations, while in reality, there has been no consensus about what constitutes a trait, an institution, or a role.

In his book, *The Nature of Cultural Things* (1964), Harris takes the movement of body as incontrovertible unit of observation. Body motions constitute non-verbal behaviour, which is indeed, an important aspect of all cultural descriptions. Non-verbal behaviour is generally explained by seeking verbal information about its meanings or by taking note of the words that regularly accompany it. Here, Harris wants to take an unambiguous and depersonalised view of culture, and since language is often ambiguous, he leaves out linguistic verification or explanation given by informations.

Where Kluckhohn (1949: 300) maintains that the first responsibility of an anthropologist is to record events as seen by the people themselves, Harris denies this explicitly (1964:93). He is of view that this actor oriented approach leads to a great confusion, not only because language is ambiguous, but also because the actors themselves do not generally know the social purposes or meanings of their behaviour. In Harris' observation-oriented approach, it is first responsibility of the anthropologists to set down events as seen by him or her.

As the older terminology (trait, customs, and so forth) is considered redundant, Harris develops a new vocabulary to express classes of behaviour. The smallest items of behaviour are actones, just visible behaviour. The actones that are recurrent are termed as actonemes. Two of twenty-two examples of actonemes are as follows:

Actoneme	*Body Part*	*Body Motion*	*Environmental Effect*
Pick up	hand	hand elevates, while fingers grasp	object is raised
drink	mouth	mouth opens	liquid disappears inside mouth

(Harris 1964:49)

From these basic units more complex classes of behaviour are constructed, such as, actonemes following each other in sequence are actone chains, and in order of complexity follow episodes, nodes, nodal chains, scenes, serials, nomoclones, permaclones, paragroups, nomoclonic types, permaclonic types, permaclonic systems, and permaclonic supper system. If acts of those are operationally described, we have culture (1964:168).

Harris is aware of the fact that in practice, such detailed analysis of cultural behaviour is wellnigh impossible, and cites budgetary limitations and lack of manpower as the main reasons for the dubious future of atomic research. The significance of his position is, however, a theoretical one. He demonstrates that a consistent scientific approach to cultural taxonomy is indeed possible, but at a cost that is more than financial, namely, that of the subjective meaning of culture.

EMIC AND ETIC

In his book, *The Nature of Cultural Things*, but more explicitly in his later books, *Rise of Anthropological Theory* (1968), Harris deals with the contrast between emic and etic approaches. The terms etic and emic are coined by linguist Kenneth Pike (1954), utilizing the last part of the word phonetic and phonemic. In linguistics, phonetics is the description of all speech sounds as they are produced by the human speech organs, while phonemics is the Sorting out of these sounds in order to arrive at their distinctive differences. Phonetic systems are universally applied, because human organs of speech are similar everywhere, but phonemic systems differ from language to language, because sound combinations and distinctive differences are unique for every linguistic groups. In terms of cultural behaviour, etics would provide a set of criteria capable of classifying all data into single system, while emics would attempt to discover the meaningful structure of specific cultures. To Pike, etics is the handmaiden of emics. Etics is classificatory and non-structural, emics reflect the internal structural relationships found in specific cultural systems (Pike 1954:8-9).

Here, Harris' opinion is quite different and opposite. He favours etics over emics. According to him, phonetic and etic analysis can proceed purely by observation and meaning does not enter the picture. This is very similar to Harris' atomic approach, while phonemics and emics are particularistic. Pike has explicitly stated that emic units relate to actors purposes and meanings. It is absolutely essential, if one is to study the behaviour as it actually functions, that the analyst can detect the presence and, to some degree, the nature and meaning of purpose (Pike 1954:80).

But of course, as soon as meaning and purposes enter the picture, individual actors become involved and scientific purity fades away. Emic studies, according to Harris, deal with inner psychological states, and assume that an actor knows his own inner state better than observer does, and that it is also essential for the observer to know the actor's inner states. But this is an impossibility, because, the actors meaning will not generally coincide with social meanings, and the essential structural features of a culture are generally unknown to informants.

Moreover, human thought is sometimes rational and logical, sometimes, irrational and illogical, again human thought occurs on conscious, unconscious, and preconscious levels. Inner psychological states, are, poor and unreliable guides. Thus, emic research will lead to unscientific results which are ideographic, idealistic and particularistic. Etic is nomothetic, materialistic, general and scientific.

The whole status of anthropological research is, thus, put in doubt. Etic research is, too cumbersome and too expensive, whereas emic research is useless. Harris himself retreats from this uncompromising position by stating that both emic and etic from the part of adaptive process of cultural system, but warns that emic and etic aspects of behaviour must never be confused, because each will lead to an entirely different type of analysis.

Harris' Definition of Emic and Etic

According to Harris, emic statements refer to logico-empirical systems, whose phenomenal distinctions or things are built up out of contrasts and discriminations significant, meaningful, real accurate, or in some other fashion regarded as appropriate by actors themselves. As emic statement can be falsified, if it can be shown that it contradicts the cognitive calculus by which relevant actors judge that entities are similar or different, real, meaningful, significant, or in some other case appropriate or acceptable.

Etic statements depend upon phenomenal distinctions judged appropriate by the community of specific observers. Etic statements cannot be falsified if they do not confirm to actor's notion of what is significant, real, meaningful, or appropriate. Etic statements are verified when independent observers using similar operations agree that a given event has occurred. An ethnography, carried out according to etic principles, is, thus, a corpus of predictions about the behaviour of classes of people. Predictive failures in that corpus require the reformulation of the probabilities or the description as a whole.

The definitions setforth here will be best clarified by viewing them in the context of some of the major misconceptions which have attached themselves to the etic/emic distinction.

Emic not Necessarily Less Empirical than Etic

In theory, an emic ethnography needs to be neither more nor less empirical, scientific, or inter-subjective than an etic ethnography. Historically, of course, emic imponderables have been more prevalent than etic ones, if for no reason than that, almost all traditional ethnography is heavily biased in favour of emic approach. There is no reason, however, why emic statements can not be operationalised to the point of achieving high standards of inter-subjectivity, verifiability, and standards. The current concern with rigorous paradigmatic treatments is emic phenomenon.

Informants may Supply both Emic and Etic Information

The relationship between an etic perspective, and the traditional dependency upon native informants for ethnographic information, deserves special comment. An ethnography of etic statements is not incompatible with operations involving recourse to the information to which an informant has access by means of verbal exchanges with him. The critical issue here is, whether information in question is etic or emic. It is emic, if the informants native distinctions, significances and meanings provide the semantic ground for communication between him and the ethnographer. An example of the use of an informant to maximise the emic content of ethnography is Duana Metzger and Gerald Williams (1963). Their method is known as 'eliciting heuristics'. These methods involve a prolonged educational exposure, during which an ethnographer teaches the informant how to teach the ethnographer to think in appropriate emic terms. An equivalent amount of effort can be devoted to teaching the informant to think in ethnographer's term, as for example, when native assistants learn to measure field, weigh harvest, take censuses, describe past and present events, in conformity with the categories of significance which the ethnographer has brought to the task. When an informant is used etically, he joins the community of observers. He becomes ethnographer's assistant, part of a team, which can produce more information in less time than one man working alone.

Emic cannot be Transmuted into Etic

One of the categories of etic, non-structrual classifications foreseen by Pike (1954), allows for a mixture of etic and emic operations:

> The units of behaviour, though classified without reference as such to the individual systems from which they were abstracted, may nevertheless be classified in reference to the fact that they were in fact abstracted from purposive human behaviour, so that elements of meaning or purpose, constitute one of the sets of criteria for such etic classification.

This type of etic description is an anomaly for which there can be no epistemological justification. By admitting units which are simultaneously emic and etic, we reduce the distinction to an emic status. It is this misconception which led Sturtevant (1964) to make a historically misleading claim that Kroeber's (1909) treatment of the semantic dimensions of kinship was the basic paper on the statics of kinship. But the whole point of Kroeber's famous article was to replace Morgan's treatment of kinship with a linguistic treatment. The eight principles or categories of relationship, proposed by Kroeber, are categories alleged to underly the hundreds or thousands of slightly varying relationship that can be expressed by various languages of man (Kroeber 1952:176).

If a semantic distinction is found in more than one culture, this does not mean that such distinctions cease to be semantic in nature. Concepts such as filiation, agration, territoriality, ownership, affinity, religion, unilineal descent group, etc. are applied in a wide variety of cross-cultural contexts. The test of whether these are emic or etic concepts resides in their logico-empirical relationship to cognititive processes. If the verifiability of an ethnographic statement involves a confrontation with cognitive adequacy of appropriateness, then we are dealing with emic categories, no matter how many cultures contribute to that confrontation. Identification of similar emic categories merely establishes such categories as cross-culturally valid logico-empirical abstraction. It does not transform them into etically derived phenomena. As we have seen, the data language of cultural and social anthropologists derives from a melange of emic and etic operations, which it will undoubtedly take several generation to unscramble.

Kinship as Mixed Domain of Emic and Etic

The domain of kinship has not escaped this confusion between etic and emic phenomena. Floyd Lounsbury's (1965:191) assertion that kin types are composite of the semantic discrimination made in many societies is historically inaccurate. Genealogical reckoning was not invented by anthropology. The apparent success of a mating, reproduction, and genealogy frame from eliciting categorization, which are amenable to contrastive analysis, has an etic basis. Mating, reproduction, and genealogical relationships have a rather precise biological meaning. The enthnographic mating, reproduction, and genealogy frame, however, is a lethal mixture of emic and etic categories. For a biologist, all fertile matings are equally relevant of tracing genealogical connections, but for ethno-semantics of kinship, only those matings and geneaological connections which occur, through marriage are relevant.

In order to elicit questions about kinship, the ethnographer must first discover an inter-cultural gloss for the particular kind of mating, which in English goes by the term the marriage or in Hindu by the term *Shadi* or *Vivah*. Incidentally, in the search for native equivalent, it must be remembered that the informant has not already fallen victim to a standardized equivalence, is also straining to find the proper gloss for the ethnographer's concept. Murdock (1949:1) defines family in such a way as to commit us to a consideration of whether there is a socially approved sexual relationship between mated pair. Having children and feeding and housing them is an etic phenomenon, but doing it in a socially approved manner puts the whole matter in an eminently emic frame.

Lounsbury's kintypes are, thus, etic and emic composites,

Godenough's (1964:10-11) claims that analogue of phonetic notion has already been developed for kinship studies, is true only for biological frame, which does no. apply to emic aspect of kinship. A recent exchange between David Schneider and John Beattie (1964:1965) rests on the conviction that there must be a cross culturally valid emic definition of kinship, distinct from a biological genealogy, but they are unable to agree on what it might be. Beattie solves the problem in a highly instructive fashion.

> "What kinship as an anthropological concern is all about are those social relationship, whatever, their social and cultural content, which the people who have them think about and talk about in the idom of kinship (1965:123).

A side from the biological reproduction fame, the content of kinship types is emic and must always remain emic until the observers decide, what bits of behaviour (analogous to phones) will constitute the minimum etic definition of marriage and descent. It is an error of capital importance to suppose that the scrambling of the emic and etic components in the study of kinship will convert one into the other. In deed, as far as American cultural anthropology is concerned, there is strong presumption of cause and effect between this misconception, and the fact that no consistent etic treatment of marriage and kinship has been attempted.

An etic approach by definition, avoids the premises of the emic approach. From an etic point of view, the universes of meaning, purposes, goals, motivations, etc. is, thus, unapproachable. But to insist upon the separateness of emic and etic phenomena and research strategies is not to affirm a greater or lesser reality of higher or lower scientific status for either of them.

Both Emic and Etic Data can be Studied Cross-culturally

It should be obvious that emic phenomenon can be studied cross-culturally. The question of whether patrilineal descent rule of Omaha kinship terminology, recurs in different societies, has nothing to do with the emic/etic distinction. What is involved is the setting of intersubjective standards of similarity and difference. Both emic and etic phenomena may be defined with an abundance of detail sufficient to confound an attempt to find replicative instances anywhere in the behaviour stream. However, there is conscious and overt commitment to the study of inner meaning, and psychic complexities have usually been associated with a considerable amount of indifference towards the quest for the scientific explanation of socio-cultural differences and similarities. In the case of new ethnography, the prevailing research strategy frequently seems to be unconcerned with whether new insights in to diachronic and synchronic regularities will result from the higher standards of emic descriptions that are being developed in research and publication. Harold Conklin (1964:26) has listed three criteria by which ethnographic statements must be evaluated. These are:

1. Appropriateness of anticipation
2. Replicability of testibility
3. Economy.

A number of other ethno-scientists have concerned themselves al-length with the question of whether their models represent as closely as possible the way in which the natives actually think. But few ethnographers have considered the question of how to distinguish the important from unimportant ethnographic descriptions. With all due regard to the need for the widest latitude of interest in common scientific endeavour, it can be said that an important ethnographic description is one which is merely accurate, elegant and economical. Scientific ethnographic models pave their way to the extent that they link up with the theories, which explain diachronic and synchronic differences and similarities. Admittedly, it is not always possible to know in advance, when and how such a link-up will be achieved, but in case of ethno-restudies, there are a number of historically demonstrated adverse considerations, of which the practitioners seem unaware.

Emic/Etic versus Ideal/Actual

On superficial inspection, the contrastive research strategies suggested by the well worn, phrases 'ideal versus actual behaviour' or 'ideal versus actual culture', would seem to be aimed at the same distinction as that which is involved in emics versus etics. But the two sets of strategies do not share much in common. Indeed, they derive from very different epistemological positions. The ideal/actual distinction is not grounded in the consideration of how one can know, that the cultural things are what they are said to be, by the ethnographer. Instead, it merely assumes that there is one set of patterned regularities consisting of what people say or believe about what they do or should do. Another set of patterned regularities are concerned with what they actually do. In the ideal/actual contrast, the problem of specifying the operations by which one gets to know what people actually do, is not even broached, whereas, in the emic/etic contrast, this problem is fundamental. The entire weight of the latter dichotomy rests upon the epistemological significance of describing cultural things through categories and relations, which are necessarily isomorphic with those appropriate or meaningful to the actors, as opposed to categories and relations which arise independently in the ethnographer's data language. Thus, actual behaviour can be treated in both an emic and an etic fashion. An informant's description of what is actually happening during a work scene or inside a household, need not correspond to what the ethnographer sees or would seen in the same situation.

Cultural anthropology will not easily overcome its heritage of ethnographics, an actual behaviour carried out in a manner, which permits slipping back and forth from an emic to an etic frame in an unconscious and unpredictable fashion. The effect of the lack of attention to emics and etics distinctions has been specially deliterious in the ethnography of primitive and peasant economic systems, where descriptions of essential economic processes have been obscured and disorted by emic descriptions of actual behaviour. Malinowski's description of the Kula is a classic instance in this regard.

AMBIGUITY AND LINGUISTIC MODEL

While Harris has stressed the difficulties of entering in side the heads of informants, many modern investigators are attempting to do precisely that. For instance, Frake (1964:133) has stressed upon the importance of emic approach. These ethno-scientists as they are sometimes called, also take their clues from language. They are not examining the inter-psychological states, focus on cognition as it is expressed in linguistic categories. In kinship analysis, for instance, they searched to identify cognitively contrasting components of specific kinship systems. The most successful method is known as componential analysis (Goodenough 1956). This method avoids the use of ethnocentric kinship terms, such as "uncle" or the "cousin", because those relatives, whom we call uncle, may be classified quite differently elsewhere. All kinship terms are classified in terms of distinctions such as sex, age, generation, lineality, collaterality, affinity, and other culturally appropriate criteria, resulting in a diagram that shows the formal cognitive rules in a kinship system, as it is utilized by members of the group. In this way, a researcher discovers, what goes on inside someone's head, whether or not this process is conscious.

Componential analysis goes further than that because it does not merely point the way to recognise the relatives, but systematically describes the structural relationship between relatives in total kinship system.

Ethno-science, thus, accounts for cultural items and cultural relationship in terms of information used by members of a culture in their linguistic categories. This information, itself, is related to culturally significant behaviour, which demands delineation of the conditions under which such behaviour occurs. Among the best known example of such research domains, other than kinship, is Harold Conklin's (1955) study of colour categories among the Hanunoo in Philippines. He found significant differences in ways in which the Hanunoo classified colours as compared to western categorizations. The latter depend on hue, brightness, and saturation, but Hanunoo use moisture, surface texture and lightness as the critical attributes for naming colours. Their classification is associated with other cultural phenomena, particularly in plant life and its desirability interms of consumption.

In a similar Vein, Franke (1961), working among the Subanum of Mindaneo in the Southern Philippines, showed how these people diagnosed disease according to a specific set of cultural criteria expressed in terms of mutually exclusive linguistic categories and indicated how their system of diagnosis was related also to treatment and therapy.

Many other studies demonstrated that different cultures structure their fields of cognition in entirely different manners. Art, food taste, plant and animal classification, supernatural entities, mental illness, deviancy, crime and many other cultural categorizations are conceptualized in different cultures by different criteria. Several anthropological sub-fields have developed based on this insight, each stressing a separate and specific cultural aspect and all using the prefix 'ethno' to indicate their alliance with ethno-science, ethno-musicology, ethno-botany, ethno-zoology, ethno-medicine, ethno-psychology, ethno-ecology, ethno-folklore and so forth.

The greater advantage over the previous ethnographic research is that the procedures of discovery can be precisely described, so that subsequent field workers can replicate and verify the analysis, build upon it, and note changes if and when they occur. Although complete ethnoscientific ethnographics are scare, it should be possible to correlate all cultural cognitions with one another and, thus, to achieve a meaningful cultural analysis.

The new ethnologists have been relatively silent, however, about the possibilities of cross-cultural comparisons. If each culture is described in its own terms, how cultures be compared. One possible answer is that if the descriptive techniques are universal, the resulting system should be comparable. Another answer is that the principle of cognition of thought may be comparable. It is in this field that Claude-Levi Strauss has made his contributions, which have been described in detail while dealing with Levi-Strauss' contributions in Chapter 4.

The fundamental error of new ethnography is that it is based upon a potently false analogy between vernacular codes on the levels of phoneme, morpheme and syntax on the one hand, and on the other, the higher order codes, which are, in some way, related to semantics of everyday speech behaviour, and historical unfolding of non-verbal behaviour. In linguistic analysis, it is assumed in theory and followed in practice that the phonemic, morphemic and syntactic descriptions of a language can be achieved by working with a small group of informants. This procedure is justified by the empirically established fact of uniformity of the sound discriminations, which constitute the basis for verbal communication. Whatever else a speaker must accomplish, he must be able to convince his fellows that he has something to say that they could understand if they wanted to. The actor, who speaks gibberish, who mumbles or garbles his words, who uses deviant pronunciations or otherwise fails to demonstrate that he is in a condition to deliver an intelligible message, is seldom accorded a serious audience, except for ceremonial or ritual performances, in which paralinguistic codes bear the burden of the message. The lack of tolerance of such deviations emanates from the most primordial functional conditions underlying the evolution of language, whereby viable ratios of signal to noise have become established. These linguistic features evidently enjoy selective advantage of the highest magnitude.

8

INDIAN ANTHROPOLOGISTS

SARAT CHANDRA ROY: THE FATHER OF INDIAN ETHNOGRAPHY 1871-1942)

Sarat Chandra Roy has been adorned with many great titles by Indian and world anthropologists such as the father of Indian ethnology, the first Indian ethnographer, the first Indian anthropologist, etc. These great titles for Sarat Chandra Roy throw sufficient light upon the contributions made by S.C. Roy in the field of Indian anthropology. Before discussing his major contribution in the field of anthropology, it will be the fitness of the thing to present here the life history of S.C. Roy.

S.C. Roy was born on 4th November, 1871 in a well known and prestigious Kayastha family in a village named Karapara of Khulna district, now in Bangladesh. One of his ancestors, Parmanand Roy, was regarded as one of the 12 big landlords in East Bengal. His family was closely related to Raja Basant Roy, a big landlord of that area. His father, Purna Chandra Roy, was a member of Bengal Judicial Service. Young Sarat Chandra Roy moved with his father wherever he was posted. When his father was posted at Purulia, S.C. Roy came in contact with tribal people of that area for the first time. His father died in 1885, when S.C. Roy was only 14 years old. For the next few years, his life was one of adversity as family was involved in litigation relating to property. However, S.C. Roy continued his studies under the guardianship of his maternal uncle at Calcutta. He passed his matriculation examination in 1888 and graduated with honours in English in 1892 from General Assembly Institute, now Scottish Church College, in Calcutta. He passed his M.A. Examination in English from the same college and took his law degree in 1895 from the Ripon College, Calcutta. He worked as headmaster of the Mymensingh High School and was later invited to work as Principal of GEL Mission High School, Ranchi. It was during this sojourn at Ranchi that he was intimately drawn towards the sad plight of the tribals. He left teaching to set up practice as a lawyer. He became pleader in the District Court of 24-Pargana at Alipur, Calcutta in 1897. The call of tribals proved irresistible for him and in 1898 he transferred his practice to

Ranchi. In a short period, he built up a lucrative practice in the Court of Judicial Commissioner, Ranchi.

As a lawyer, S.C. Roy used to visit the interior areas of Chota Nagpur on commission from courts and could observe the tribals from close quarters. He was moved by the oppressions and hardships of Munda and other tribal communities through the ignorance and apathy of the government authorities. He was distressed by the way tribals were treated in the court of law. He saw that the courts of law could not provide them justice as their cases were not pursued with sympathy by the lawyers dealing with them. This could not be done as the lawyer had no knowledge of tribal languages, culture, customary law etc. He, therefore, made it a point to study tribal culture in depth and also to master their language. His deep interest in tribals resulted in publication of a book entitled, *Munda and Their Country* (1912). This book is first monograph written on Indian tribe by an Indian writer. It is because of this fact that he is regarded as the first Indian ethnologist or ethnographer or Indian anthropologist. His publication of monograph on Munda attracted the attention of Sir Edward Gait, who was then the Lieutenant-Governor of Bihar. He saw Roy's work and gave him financial assistance for his further research on the Oraon. His book on the Oraon entitled, *The Oraon of Chota Nagpur* was published in 1915 from Ranchi. Thus, he was launched as an anthropologist and in course of time produced a number of monographs on different tribes such as the Birhor (1925), Hill Bhuiya of Orissa (1935). The Kharia (2 volumes) in 1937. His another book on Oraon, entitled, *Oraon Religion and Customs,* was published in 1928.

Since S.C. Roy was devoted to Indological researches, he took keen interest in the activities of the Bihar and Orissa Research Society, which was started in January 1915 and of which he became general secretary. Anthropology and folklore were included in the scope of research for this organisation and Roy was placed as incharge of Anthropology and Folklore section, with Sir Edward Gait and Mahamahopadhyay Har Prasad Shastri as members. He regularly contributed to the journal of the society and also enriched the Anthropology and Prehistoric Gallery of Patna Museum with his personal collections.

His deep concern for the poor and the down-trodden tribals of Chota Nagpur and devoted labour for their upliftment led to the election of Sarat Chandra Roy as a member of Bihar Legislative Council for several terms from 1921 to 1937. He was also elected as a member of the Provincial Committee that sat with Simon Commission in 1928. He also served as a member of the Indian Franchise Committee headed by Lord Lothian. His interest in anthropological studies began to take most of his time and he gave up his legal practice in 1933. From then till his death, he devoted himself entirely to his own researches and to editing of *Man in India*, the first anthropological journal in the country, which he founded in 1921.

S.C. Roy was also deeply interested in social work. He served the Ranchi District Board as a Vice-Chairman for many years. He was the president of the Governing Body of the Bengali Boy's School and also of the Bengali Girl's School at Ranchi. He was, at the same time, President of the Harijan Sewak Samiti, Anti-Drink Society, the Oraon-Munda Siksha Sabha and Brahmacharya Sangh. These wise ranging interest kept him extremely busy and one wonders how he could combine his professional work as a lawyer and scholarly interest as an anthropologist along with the huge burden of social work.

In fullness of time, the services of S.C. Roy in the field of Anthropology and in that of social service received due recognition. He was awarded a *Kaiser-i-Hindi* Silver Medal in 1913 and the title of 'Rai Bahadur' in 1919, besides two more certificates of honour and two other medals. In 1920, he was elected honorary member of the Folklore Society of London, the only Indian to be honoured with this distinction. The same year, he was elected president of the Anthropological Section in Indian Science Congress. In two successive years, 1932 and 1933, he was elected president of the Anthropology and Folklore Section of the All India Oriental Conference. Later, he was elected as a member of the Council d'Honour of the International Congress of Ethnological Sciences. He was a Foundation Fellow of the National Institute of Sciences in India and also of the Patna University. In 1941, on the occasion of his Seventieth birthday, the Indian Science Congress decided to present him with commemorative volume, 'Essays in Anthropology' written in his honour by some eminent Anthropologists of the day. Unfortunately, his volume was published one week after his death. The list of contributors to this volume shows the high esteem in which S.C. Roy was held by his colleagues at home and abroad.

Sarat Chandra Roy breathed his last on the morning of the Buddha *Purnima*, 30th April, 1942, after a prolonged illness of several months. His death was widely mourned not only at Ranchi, but by anthropologists in different parts of India. The eminent scientific journal *Nature* in an editorial observed, "The dry light of pure science and the disinterested research was kept afflame (in India) by a small band of devoted enthusiasts among whom the veteran anthropologist Sarat Chandra Roy will ever be held in honour".

Although anthropology was more a labour of love than a profession for Sarat Chandra Roy, his devotion to the subject was unbounded and he left no stone unturned to stress its importance and usefulness in quarters, where it mattered most. He was the first person to deliver a University Readership lecture in Anthropology at Patna University in 1920 on topic, "The Principles and Methods of Physical Anthropology". This was one year before the first fullfledged university department of Anthropology was started at Calcutta University through the efforts of Sir Asutosh Mukherjee. From time to time, he delivered lecture in new department at Calcutta and enthused its members to make it an important centre of anthropological research in the country. In the different presidential addresses, he delivered to the Indian Science Congress, Oriental Conference, and other learned bodies, he dwelt upon the current status of research in various branches of anthropology, and thus raised the status of the subject at national scientific gathering. He also demanded opening of departments of anthropology in different universities of the country. It is furtherance of his aim to promote anthropological research that Sarat Chandra Roy started the research journal entitled, *Man in India* in 1921. This journal attracted important contributions from scholars at home and abroad. Besides original paper, this journal carried book reviews, notes and quaries and also notices of anthropological interest in current Indian literature. It continues to be published even now.

S.C. Roy was a source of inspiration and a tower of strength to many budding anthropologists. N.K. Bose and D.N. Majumdar received active encouragement and guidance from him in their early years. It was at his best that S.S. Sarkar studied Maler of Rajmahal Hills in 1935. He also encouraged Charulal, an advocate like him at Dumka, to undertake researches on the Santhal of Mayurbhanj in Orissa. The study was later published as a monograph. In this way, Roy not only helped train and guide professional anthropologists, but builtup and nourished a vigorous tradition of anthropological research in the country. His major contributions in the field of anthropology can be understood in terms of five broad headings, which are as follows:

1. Contribution on Tribal Cultures
2. Studies in Physical Anthropology and Prehistoric Archaeology
3. Anthropology of Caste
4. Study of Folklore
5. Applied Anthropology and Tribal Policy.

Studies in Tribal Culture

As referred to earlier, the miserable conditions of tribals of Chota Nagpur, attracted S.C. Roy, an eminent lawyer by profession, to undertake studies on their customs, beliefs, traditions, life-ways, cultures etc. He was first drawn to the study of the Munda of Chota Nagpur, and wrote some articles in journals on some aspects of their life before his first monograph appeared in 1912. It was the time when most of the anthropologists, even in West, were still engaged in evolutionary and diffusional studies. They were of views that anthropology was a branch of history dealing with tribals. This history was partly valid and partly conjectural or its reconstruction was based on scanty evidence drawn from myths, legends and folklore. Roy believed that the knowledge of history of a tribe would help us appreciate its culture better. It is thus, no surprise that Roy's monograph on the Munda contains only one chapter on ethnography against five chapters on history. In the earlier chapters, Roy tries to trace the origin of the tribe from clues drawn from folklore, linguistics, and prehistoric evidences. He then proceeds to reconstruct the long history of the tribe from the time of *Vedas* to the beginning of Christian era. It is only in early medieval and modern period that some historical evidence on tribe is available. In the modern period, he brings the narrative down to the Birsa revolt. In this chapter of modern history of the Munda, he traces in detail the various socio-economic movements that raged in the Munda in the nineteenth century. The section on ethnography deals with physical appearance, dress, ornaments, weapons, material culture, the description of a Munda village, the detail of tribal agricultural operations, social and political organisation of the Munda, religion, superstition, festivals etc. The book gives a short and generalised account of Munda life and culture. He also gives some details about the Mundari language, folktales, proverbs, folksongs etc. But the book does not deal with regional differences of customs and practices among the Munda.

His next book deals with the Oraon (1915), another major tribe of Chota Nagpur. In this book, he makes amends for the earlier excessive obsession with history. Out of six chapters, only one has been devoted to history and migrations of the tribe, while the rest are devoted to detailed ethnographic description of Oraon life and culture. The material collected on the Oraon was so voluminous that the bulk of data on religion was left to be dealt with in another volume (1928). Roy throws a flood of light on the social organisation of the Oraon community. He was the first person to draw our attention to the existence of *Dhumkuria* or the Youth dormitory. He detailed its functions and explained its role in the socio-economic life of the Oraon. He also gives a detailed description of the village organisation, the village Panchayat and the *Paraha* system. In the study of culture change among the Oraon, the greatest difficulty that the present writer faced was in regard to the regional variations. It is, therefore, difficult to treat Sarat Chandra Roy's first book on Oraon as a bench-mark data for future comparison. Since pioneers have to labour under limitations and as at that time anthropology had not developed the sophistication, precision or objectivity as now, the book was ranked among the very best monographs of an Indian tribe published by that time. Sir James Frazer, congratulated Roy for collecting so rich anthropological information and setting forth facts carefully distinguished than from the inferences which Roy drew from them. A.C. Haddon, who wrote the introduction to this first book on Oraon, tried to relate some of Roy's findings to the current thinking in British ethnography.

The second book on Oraon (1928) is devoted to description of religious and magical beliefs, the cycle of socio-religious rites and ceremonies, feast and festivals, and the magical practices of the Oraon. This is the first monograph in India which is completely devoted to a study of one particular aspect of a tribal culture. Roy does not only deal with a description of rituals, but shows how some of these feasts, and festivals intensify the feeling of social solidarity in the village. Towards the end of the book we find a detailed description of the various nativistic and reform movements among the Oraon. All this reflected the impact of Hinduism. Not only have the origin and growth of Tana Bhagat movement been traced, but some of their important hymns have been translated into English in this book. Roy came to the conclusion that these puritanical movements among the Oraon were not just religious in character but had strong social and economic undertones. The movement offered them as escape from the general dissatisfaction with their current economic condition and social status. He believed that the movements were more or less based on the Oraon's traditional way of thought and belief. Roy, however, did not elaborate the political implications of the Tana Bhagat movement and he also underplayed the very important role played by the Oraon in the national non-cooperation movement in 1921 as well as in national freedom in the years that followed.

S.C. Roy did not confine his attention to study of the larger tribes alone. One of his monographs is on the Birhor (1925), a small tribe which only numbered two thousand in his time. The study of this nomadic tribe took more than fifteen years. He took help of an intelligent Birhor, who acted as the primary informant and guided Roy to the Uthulu Tanda (temporary settlement) spread throughout Chota Nagpur. The arrangement of data follows the traditional pattern of a tribal monograph. He has succeeded in giving a description of Birhor life from which 'nomadism' emerges as a style of life. He makes an occasional distinction between the patterns of living of settled (*Jaghi*) and nomadic (*Uthulu*) Birhors. At the end of the book, he appended sixteen folk-tales and gives details of games, proverbs, riddles, and other means of recreation of the Birhor.

His other book was on Hill Bhuiya of Orissa (1935). In this study his son, Ramesh Chandra Roy, a trained anthropologist, helped him in the collection and analysis of anthropometric data. This book gives a comparative description of plain and Hill Bhuiyas. Roy does not tell us the name of villages where data were gathered, although he takes care to describe the regional and local variations in the culture of the Bhuiyas.

The last monograph which Roy wrote in collaboration with his son was on Kharia published in two volumes in 1937. The Kharia live in South Western corner of the Ranchi district. Researches on Kharia were carried out for 12 years. It was possible for Roy to give a comparative description of all the three divisions of the Kharia. The Dudh Kharia, the Dhelki Kharia and the Hill Kharia, Roy held that the three sections of the tribe represent three successive layers in the development of a primitive culture. Since the bulk of this tribe has been converted to christianity, it was possible for Roy to take help of some educated informants. He was helped in his efforts by Christian missionaries. The monograph was published in two volumes and may be ranked as the most scientific and elaborate among the books written by Roy. In this book, Roy does not attempt any reconstruction of the history of the Kharia. He takes into consideration the history of migration as well as the origin of the tribe as revealed by its myth. Roy describes the various aspects of the social, economic, political, and religious life of the community. Anthropometric measurement taken from each of the sub-tribes have also been given.

Besides monographs that he wrote, S.C. Roy contributed a number of papers in research journals on some aspects of the life and culture of other tribes and communities both in and out of Bihar. He wrote on totemism among the Asur, the Ho of Singhbhum, and Pahira of Chota Nagpur. He also published articles on the Lepcha funeral, kinship among the people of Sikkim, the Khasi kinship terms, the Khond human sacrifice, the Korku memorial tablets, the black Bhils of Jaisamand lake in Rajputana and on the people of Burma.

Studies in Physical Anthropology and Prehistoric Archaeology

Although Sarat Chandra Roy was essentially a cultural anthropologist, he did not neglect other branches of anthropology like physical anthropology, prehistory, folklore etc. In fact, his Patna University lectures were exclusively devoted to physical anthropology. In this, he dealt at length with the scope, divisions, methods of physical anthropology, man's place in nature, the antiquity of man detailing characteristics of fossil man, human evolution, in the background of general theory of evolution, controversies regarding the first home of man, racial migration, and finally the classification of human races, racial taxonomy etc. He also noted details of various anthropometric measurements.

In his various tribal monographs, he tried to give, as far as possible, details about the physical characteristics. For the Munda, he observed,

> "The head inclines to be long (Dolicocephalic), the nose is thick and broad and sometimes depressed at the root, the lips thick, the facial angle comparatively low, the face wide and flashy, the features irregular, the figure squat, limbs sturdy and well formed and the stature rather short (Roy 1912:209).

He also took care to mention the anthropometric measurement of one hundred Mundas from the specimens provided by Sir Herbert Risley in the 'Tribes and Caste of Bengal'. He gave details about length, breadth, as well as the cephalic index, nasal index, naso-maler index, frontozygomatic index, vertico-cephalic index, vertico-bimalar index, vertico-frontal index, vertico-bizygomatic index, facial angle, nasal height, nasal breadth, bimalar breadth, naso-malar breadth, cephalic length, cephalic breadth and minimum frontal breath. He also writes about their skin colour and breath.

In his last two monographs, on the Hill Bhuiya and the Kharia, Roy did not depend upon any earlier references but used his own resources to get the measurements done. In taking these measurements, he was helped by his son, Ramesh Chandra Roy, a trained anthropologist. P.C. Mahalanobis, who was at that time at the Presidency College, Calcutta, assisted him in the analysis of the anthropometric data and the statistical calculations in the form of an appendix in his book on the Kharia. The measurements were taken from one hundred individuals from each of the three sections of the Kharia tribe.

S.C. Roy felt that many problem of Indian ethnology could be solved by an exploration of prehistoric evidences. He was the third person to study prehistoric sites in Ranchi district, the first two were Valentive Ball and WHP Driver. Ball discovered a beautifully made stone celt at the foot near village Barua-dih in Tamar, while driver found a few small stone arrow-heads at Ranchi. Both of these were briefly described in archaeological report. Sarat Chandra's attention was drawn towards a triangular stone axe-head presented to him by one of his clients in 1914. He then started collecting stone implements. In a couple of years, his collections went up to a hundred. In all, about 46 sites were reported by him. Most of them were located in Ranchi district. In Jurdag, he found a Paleolithic implement. Later, some flakes, scrapers, knives, and burins were collected from a site near Chakradharpur. They were found mostly between gravel and alluvial deposits at approximately 18 ft below the existing soil level along the banks of Binjai and Sanjai rivers. The polished stone implements were made of gniess, schist, slate, quartzite, basalt etc. Most of the celts were polished over the whole surface, some were chipped and not ground except on the edges and a smaller number of them were merely chipped in to shape and not ground even at the edge.

Sarat Chandra's main contribution in the field of prehistoric archaeology is digging up of Asura site. The traditions about Ancient Asura are still widespread in Ranchi district and the implements and ornaments of copper, bronze and iron dug up are invariably attributed to these pre-Munda inhabitants of Chota Nagpur. He made exploratory investigation and found here and there villages containing remains of very ancient brick-buildings, stone temples and sculptures, cinerary urns and huge slabs, columns of sculptural stones, large tanks, mostly silted up, which were locally attributed to an ancient people called the Asura. He discovered stone implements, stone sculptures, stone beads, potsherds, copper implements and ornaments, bronze tools, iron implements from the Asur sites. His contention was that the Asur belonged to the same age as that of the Indus valley culture. On many points, he finds that the two areas resemble to a surprising degree. In Asur culture of Chhotanagpur, Roy finds an earlier stage of (1) organisation of society into cities, (2) the continued but sparing use of stone, side by side with copper and bronze for the manufacture of weapons, tools and vessels, (3) the invention of the potters wheel, and production with its help of improved kinds of pottery, (4) invention of wheeled vehicles, construction of buildings with kiln and sun-burnt bricks, (5) use of maces of stone, and (6) fashioning of ornaments out of faience, shell and stone. The absence of some features in these finds, namely pictograph, artifacts of gold, silver and human figure in different forms, does not preclude the possibility of these finds in the unexplored and partially explored tracts of Chota Nagpur. The sites discovered by Sarat Chandra Roy afforded evidence of chalcolithic culture in Ranchi district. Although relics of Paleolithic period are not well marked in Chota Nagpur, there appeared to be abandoned relics of the neolithic period, particularly in northern and north-eastern part of Ranchi district, and from the association of some stone objects with the reputed sites of Ausuras. The presence of stone tools and copper tools and implements bears evidences of a period of transition from later neolithic to copper age. The presence of iron implements in Asura sites reveals an another phase of prehistoric development i.e. iron-age. Roy also came across a number of Asur burial sites locally called Asur Khutty. The excavations of burial sites revealed earthen jars which were found placed one over the other upto a maximum of four at a time. Placed in the jars were copper ornaments and also beads together with the bones of the dead. The Asur civilization in Chota Nagpur, according to Roy, continued at least up to the Kushan period as indicated by the find of three Kushan gold coins.

The Asur problem has been a bone of contention between the archaeologists and the anthropologists. While Sarat Chandra Roy believed that Asur sites he discovered could be connected with the ancient civilized people called Asura, the archaeologists do not agree. They do not see any connection between the Asur sites in Chota Nagpur and the Asur tribe which was supposed to have preceded the Munda in the south eastern parts of the Ranchi district. Even now the Asur living, on the Netarhat plateau, are known for their iron smelting. Roy felt that these are the same people who were the creators of the civilization, which is revealed in the Asur sites.

Anthropology of Caste

Sarat Chandra Roy was of the opinion that our ancient books, namely the *Puranas, Samhitas, Dharmashastras*, and *Griha Shutras* as well as the great Epics held a rich treasure house of data for social anthropology. The *Puranas* attempt to present a crude picture of the origin of man and of the gradual development of society and culture from very early time. The *Puranas* and the *Shastras* form the store house of the social customs, usages, rites, and ceremonies, ethics, politics and laws. They furnish picture of contemporary Indian societies with its ideals and different types and levels of culture. According to Roy, the *Puranas* combine in them history, cultural anthropology and ethics. The *Samhitas* and *Griha Shutras* describe the various social regulations and customs prevalent in various localities and communities in India and by arranging, classifying and correlating them, delineated contemporaneous Hindu society as it was governed by a system of socio-religious and religio-legal rules suited to different levels of culture in the land. Of the eight kinds of Hindu marriage, enumerated in *Samhitas,* we find many which are prevalent in tribal areas, of these only the first four were considered good, while others were tolerated, but not recommended.

The *Puranic* literature has been styled on *Itihasa, Puranas* or history and tradition. The tradition is in itself an important subject matter for anthropologists and as such it could not be neglected by them. Since history in Roy's days dealt with the activities of kings and courts, he believed that it could not reveal a complete picture of life of the society. The style of daily life of men and women organised in society and their economic and social aspirations and activities from the real life of community which the anthropologist seek to understand. This could easily be accomplished by a study of the *Puranas* and the *Samahitas*. It is for this reason that Roy commended to anthropologists the study of our ancient books. He realised that anthropology is not only a study of the quaint and exotic manners and customs of the primitive tribes. Anthropology did not only study primitive man, the broad subject matter of Anthropology is the entire life of mankind. The only reason why much attention is devoted to "Primitive society" by anthropologists is that primitive society exhibits the ground plan on which the more complex structure, which we call civilization, has been built up.

According to S.C. Roy, in India the task of anthropologists must necessarily include the study of complex civilizations. It is in this context that he made a detailed study of caste, race, and religion in India. He tried to explore the origin of caste system and for this reason, included in his sweep, not only ancient Hindu literature, but also the vast amount of ethnographic literature on castes and tribes in the various parts of the country. He began with a detailed critique of the different theories put forward by scholars for the origin of caste system. This was followed up by an assessment of the contributions of the various ethnic elements to the evolution of Indian culture with special reference to the caste system. Caste system, as it operates in India, is unique, and although certain elements of caste may be seen outside the Indian sub-continent, the complexity is a peculiarly Indian phenomenon. The constant interaction between people belonging to diverse ethnic elements and culture areas must have had a bearing on the making of the caste system in India. Sarat Chandra Roy took care to make fine distinctions between different areas in India with regard to the rigidity of the caste system and the way it effected the life of the people.

Study of Folklore

In his presidential address to the Anthropological Section of the Sixth Oriental Congress held at Patna in 1930, Sarat Chandra Roy made a strong plea for the study of folklore by anthropologists. It is not difficult to observe, record and study the traditional customs, rites and beliefs, stories and myths. Such customs, rites, beliefs, may belong either to individuals or to families, clans, or other groups. They may stand on a lower intellectual level and are often inconsistent with orthodox or officially recognised customs, rites, and belief of people wherever they occur. The term folklore is no longer restricted to traditional customs, rites and beliefs of the past lingering among backward people in complex civilizations, but now extended to include folkarts, folkabuse, folkproverbs, riddles, idioms etc. both among people of civilization and among primitive civilizations. Roy believed that folklore throws a flood of light on the early intellectual evolution of human society and for this reason he regarded folklore as "pre-history of human mind".

Roy held that Indian students are in most advantageous position to collect and study folklore, although many folkloric traditions have already disappeared due to various reasons. He emphasized upon the need to collect and preserve folkloric traditions, because they are the treasury of our past handed down from generation to generation. According to him, in the study of folklore of India, a systematic collection of these folklore material can be done on the basis of districts, taluks, cultural regions and smaller territorial segments. He held that the study of folklore should include, folksongs, ballad, folkrites, folktraditions, folkbeliefs associated with dreams, superstition, omen, folktales, folkproverbs, folkriddles, folkmagic and *Totaka,* folkabuse, folkrecreations etc.

To know exclusively about the origin of any item of folklore, the student will have to make a deep analysis and distributional study of such folklore items by plotting it out on a map, determining its focal centre and tracing its diffusion to marginal areas. Roy did not refute the possibility of independent origin of a custom of different places. He, however, advised the students to study different items in the context of the culture complex in which they figures. The search for origin of folkcustoms was referred to by Roy as tracing the genealogy of folklore. To engage in this task, the student must not only acquire full knowledge of the present culture and mentality and the past history of the people whose folklore he studies, but also equip himself with the knowledge of life and culture of the neighbouring communities with whom they have been in contact. The folklorist must draw upon the resources of comparative ethnology, social psychology, prehistory, philosophy, as well as literature.

Applied Anthropology and Tribal Policy

S.C. Roy was a highly respected public man known for his deep scholarship, understanding, and sympathy for tribal life and culture. As such, the Government sought his advice whenever it was faced with any administrative problem in dealing with the tribals. A few such cases may be cited in which Roy assumed the role of a trouble shooter. He showed how timely intervention by an anthropologist can lead to ending a condition of stress and strain in society.

During the days of the non-cooperation agitation in 1921, a police officer came across a notice circulated in the name of the Raja of some Munda *Parha* (inter-village council). In this notice, the police officer scented a plot to subvert the British government in Chota Nagpur and to set up a Munda Raj. The Deputy Commissioner felt concerned at this and called Sarat Chandra Roy for consultation. Roy at once saw that it was just a notice for the meeting of the *Parha* in which there was nothing wrong. He advised against sending police officers to observe the proceedings of the meeting. Since the authorities were still worried, Roy was sent to attend this meeting along with some police-men in plain clothes. In the meeting, Munda ventilated a number of agrarian grievances and discuss their educational and other needs. Roy promised to represent their troubles to the authorities and secure such redress as was feasible. Thus, through proper handling of the situation, a violent demonstration was prevented.

In the Oraon areas, during inter-tribal dancing meets, known as *Jatra*, each village carries a flag of its own. No village can use the standards of another village. Once a Railway bridge was being constructed over a river near Lohardaga. The bridge repeatedly gave way and it was believed that this was because the supernatural spirits of the two villages on either side were displeased with the idea of the bridge. It was only when the contractor offered to repair an old dilapidated temple of a Hindu village which was on one side of the stream and to present the Oraon village located on the other side, with a new flag that the bridge was satisfactorily completed. The new flag contained the replica of a railway train. Another village also made the same kind of flag for itself and this led to trouble at the *Jatra* held at *Bhasko*. At this time, the Subdivisional Magistrate thought of consulting Roy. Roy knew that Oraon believed that the emblem of the flag endowed the village with an extraordinary power. He, therefore, got a large flag made with a symbol of an aeroplane on it and easily persuaded the other village to adopt it. They easily did so on account of the superiority of an aeroplane to a railway train.

In his various speeches, addresses, and memoranda, Roy made a strong plea for giving anthropological training not only to administrative and judicial officers, but to forest and excise officers also who were posted in tribal areas. He thought that such training would not only improve the quality of judicial and executive work, but also help the cause of science through the observation and investigation of aboriginal customs that might be recorded in the field by such trained officers. He strongly felt that anthropology could be applied to solve certain carrying problems of our national life. He felt that the study by man of races, customs, religious and manners of one another might help in mutual amity and knitting even more closely the bonds of unity between them and, thus, eventually help to banish much of the communal animosity, which is the bane of Indian national life at the present day.

Throughout his public life and also as a member of the Bihar and Orissa Legislative Council for more than fifteen years, S.C. Roy was solicitous of the welfare of the tribal people of Chota Nagpur. He was cautious and conservativist in matters relating to the political advance of the tribals.

In 1935, the Bihar Legislative Council passed a resolution recommending to the government to take steps to see that no part of Chota Nagpur is made excluded or partially excluded area. The resolution was stoutly opposed by the government which declared that such a move was not desirable. Four reasons were advanced for the government's view:

1. The tribals had not attained the same standard of civilization as other minority communities, nor were the tribals equal in wealth and position,
2. They were extremely backward in literacy and education,
3. They were not strongly organised politically, and
4. It was necessary to include tribal areas in excluded or partially excluded category.

S.C. Roy rebutted all the four points enumerated above and added that the immediate need of the tribal people was to promulgate a well considered tenancy law, as also a law against usury, greater employment to tribal people in public services, promotion of education and culture, gradual step leading to temperance among them, and pasting of such areas of qualified and sympathetic officers conversant with their language and customs. These interests could be safeguarded by the Governor under his special responsibilities for minority communities. It was, therefore, not necessary to include Chota Nagpur in the excluded and partially excluded category.

S.C. Roy saw that when it comes to the question of poverty or social inequality, there is little difference between how advanced sections of the population treated rural cultivators and artisans and the tribals. He, therefore, held that the problems of development of the peasant and handicraft workers is just the same, whether the person speaks a tribal language or one belongs to Indo-Aryan or Dravidian language family. It is the problem of poverty, lack of education, prevailing in sanitary conditions and belief in superstition. It is these that have to be removed without making any distinction between tribal and non-tribal communities.

NIRMAL KUMAR BOSE (1901-1972)

N.K. Bose was born in Calcutta on 22 January, 1901. He received his early education in four schools situated at four distinguished places of three States of the country. In this way, he was educated at Anglo-Sanskrit School, Patna (Bihar), Sagar Dutta Free High School, Kamarhati, 24-Pargana (West Bengal), Ranchi Zilla School, Ranchi (Bihar), and Puri Zilla School, Puri (Orissa). He was admitted to Scottish Church College, Presidency College and University College of Science, Calcutta. He had passed his Matriculation, Intermediate Science, Bachelor of Science with honours in Geology, and Master of Science Anthropology examination with First Division in the year 1917, 1919, 1921 and 1925 respectively.

He was appointed as Research fellow in Anthropology, Calcutta University in 1929-30. He left this post to join *Salt Satyagraha*. Again, he was recalled by Syama Prasad Mookherjee, the then Vice-Chancellor of Calcutta University in 1938 and appointed as Assistant Lecturer in Anthropology. He served this post till 1942, when he was arrested by the British. He returned in 1945 as Lecturer in Human Geography and then became Reader in Geography in the Science College, Calcutta.

He was invited as Visiting Scholar (with the status of visiting professor, but with no teaching assignment) in the University of California, Berkeley in the Department of South-Asian Studies in 1958 and continued on the same position in the University of Chicago, Department of Anthropology in 1959. He was also invited to lecture on Social and Cultural Change in India at the Universities of Wisconsin and Michigan. On return, he was appointed as Director of Anthropological Survey of India. He served this post for a period of nearly five years (1959-64), until and unless he got retirement in 1964. During this period, he also worked as Advisor to the Government of India on Tribal Affairs.

In post-retirement period, he served as special invitee of study team for Hill Districts of Assam under the chairmanship of Mr. Tarlok Singh in 1965. He was invited by the Administration of NEFA to report on educational problems in 1966. In 1965, he was again invited to the U.S.A. to represent India at the annual conference of the Association for Asian

Studies in New York. He lectured on Social and Political Changes in India and on the Political Philosophy of Mahatma Gandhi in Columbia University, New York, University of California, Berkeley, University of Michigan, Ann Arbor, Duke University, North Carolina, University of the State of New York, and Harvard University, Washington.

In recognition of his excellent work in anthropology, Professor N.K. Bose, was awarded Annandale Gold Medal of the Asiatic Society of Bengal in 1948. He was elected as the President of Anthropology and Archaeology Section of Indian Science Congress in 1949. He was elected as Fellow of the National Institute of Science of India in 1955. In course of his career, he became life member of a large number of professional organisations. He was also invited by a number of organisations to deliver special lectures.

Professor Bose was a devoted social worker and served in various capacities in many philanthropic organisations. He served as a volunteer in the famine relief organised by Sadharan Brahma Samaj in Bankura district in 1917, as an honorary director in the Goa Bagan working men's institution in 1919, as chairman of Pali Seva Niketan. He organised Khadi Sangh in Bolpur in 1930. In 1946, he was invited by Mahatma Gandhi to act as his interpreter and secretary during his march in Bihar and Bengal. He received President's award of *Padmashri* in 1966. His major publications are as follows:

1. 1929: *Cultural Anthropology*. Bombay: Asia Publishing House.
2. 1932: *Canous of Orissan Architecture.* Calcutta: Ramananda Chatterji.
3. 1948: *Excavations in Mayurbhanj*. University of Calcutta.
4. 1967: *Culture and Society in India*. Bombay. Asia Publishing House.
5. 1959: *Modern Bengal*. Vidyodya Library, Calcutta.
6. 1963: *Fifty Years of Science in India: Progress of Anthropology and Archaeology.* Calcutta: Indian Science Congress Association.
7. 1957: *Problems of National Integration*. Simla, Indian Institute of Advanced Study.
8. 1934, 1952, 1968: *Selections from Gandhi*. Bombay: Nawjiwan Publishing House.
9. 1959, 1962: *Studies in Gandhism*. Calcutta, Merit Publishers.
10. 1953: *My Days With Gandhi*. Calcutta: Merit Publishers.
11. 1969: *Problems of Nationalism*. Calcutta: Allied Publishers.

Bengali Books

Professor N.K. Bose had written a good number of books in his regional language, Bengali. These are as Follows:

1. 1926: *Konaraker Bibran*. Calcutta.
2. 1949: *Hindu Samajer Gdan* (Structure of Hindu Society) Calcutta: Vishwabharati Granthalaya.
3. 1956: *Nabin O Prachin* (Collection of Essays), Calcutta: Bengal Publishers.
4. 1969: (Reprinted and also translated into Oriya and Marathi): *Gandhi Charit*. Calcutta: Merit Publishers.
5. 1969: (Reprinted and translated into Hindi as 'Gandhiji Kya Chahate Hain?'): *Gandhi Ki Chau*. Calcutta: Merit Publishers.
6. 1954: *Swaraj O Gandhivad*. Calcutta: B.S., IAP Co.Ltd.
7. 1954: *Parivrajakar Dacri* (Book of Travells), Calcutta.
8. 1961: *Bharatar Gram Jeevan* (Peasant Life in India). Calcutta. *Banjeya Sahitya Parishad*. Also translated into Japanese by Hiroshima University.
9. 1967: *Ganatantrer Sankat* (Democracy in Danger), Calcutta: Merit Publishers.

Besides these books in English, Hindi and Bengali languages, Professor Bose contributed more than 700 articles in the eminent journals of the country and abroad. He was also the editor of the first Anthropological journal, *Man in India* since 1951.

Franz-Boas and Bose

Professor Bose was greatly influenced by the 'Inductive Natural History Approach' of Professor Franz-Boas, an American diffusionist and historical particularist. According to Bose, Franz Boas started with observations and then moved towards classification and generalization, rather than starting with a deductive hypothetical model like evolutionists. Professor Bose read Boas' position that language, race and culture are independent and yet historically linked variables.

Kroeber and Bose

Professor Bose read Kroeber's (an American anthropologist) article on, 'Super Organic' (1917) with great deal of interest and reacted that the over-riding role of culture on the lives of men does not cover the full story of man's behaviour. At critical point of history, creative deviant individuals may be the starting point of change. There is no doubt that most men generally play a passive role, but they can behave in a different way also. There have been moments in history when the active element has asserted itself in individuals, as well as in large masses of mankind and given culture, including the course of economic events, an unexpected turn. Such occasions have been rare, due to the fact that men like to avoid the sufferings consequent upon every change, and thus, conserve their nervous energy. And it is this inner acquiescence, born out of conservatism, which gives culture its apparent power of rule over the lives of men (Bose, 1940: 6).

Bose as a Diffusionist

Bose was fascinated by Kroeber and Wissler's trait distribution studies and by the chronological implication of the distribution of cultural traits. He applied this approach in the study of diffusion of *Spring Festival Culture Complex* (1927), *Elements of Temple Architecture* (1949) and *Basic Material Traits in Rural India* (1961). The imprint of American Diffusionists School is also very much there in his famous book, *Cultural Anthropology* (1929). This little book, from an unknown young Indian scholar, attracted the attention of Kroeber, who reviewed it favourably in the journal of American Anthropologist (Kroeber 1929). Later on, Kroeber and Kluckhohn in their compendium 'Culture: A Critical Review of Concepts and Definitions (1952)', included as many as ten citations from Bose's Cultural Anthropology.

Freud and Bose

Among the masters in Social Science, Freud left a deep impression on Bose. Although he did not expressedly utilize Freudian theories in most of his writings, Freud's ideas stimulated in him a great deal of interest on the behaviour of individuals under a situation of cultural stress. He felt that Freudian concept of sublimation helped him to understand the apparently paradoxical behaviour of Mahatma Gandhi in the critical situation of Naokhali pilgrimage in 1946-47.

Marx and Bose

Bose went through the Marxist literature with great interest and reacted to them in the same manner as he did to Kroeber's theory of Superorganic. He takes the position that human behaviour is much more random, individualistic and purposive than theory of economic determinism. (Bose, 1940: 4-7). Yet he accepted from Marx, the critical significance of social organisation of production in the study of persistence and change in the caste system in India (Bose, 1951).

Bose as Functionalist

Bose responded very favourably to Malinowski's functional approach to anthropology. In his book on *Cultural Anthropology* (1929) he has independently taken a functional approach in defining the nature of culture as an adaptive device organised around what Bose figuratively calls 'the Soul of Culture'. But he rejected the historicism of functionalists and has taken a consistent position that the proper domain of cultural anthropology is a functional study of the process of cultural change. In Bose's book, however, one finds a clear expression of the 'Adaptive function of Culture' and of the 'Soul of Culture'.

According to Bose, beneath the outer frame of culture, there lies a body of beliefs and sentiments which are responsible for the particular manifestation of culture. Such a body of ideas and sentiments grow out of life's philosophy and is consequently conditioned by the needs and aspirations of each particular age. Historical developments bring in number of unresolved problems and if the cultural heritage of an age does not serve those needs, it is sure to undergo modifications by those who inherit it. Thus, culture is a perpetually unstable equilibrium with the experiences of men (Bose 1929: Chapter II).

Bose has suggested that Hindu textual categories such as *Satva, Raja, Tamas* and *Dharma, Artha, Kama* and *Moksha* may be utilized in the classification of cultures. According to Bose, four distinct categories of behaviour may be identified in any culture. They are: (1) *Vastu* (Material object), (2) *Kriya* (Habitual action), (3) *Samhati* (Social grouping), and (4) *Tattwa* (Knowledge). The last one again may be divided into two, according as the knowledge is *Vicharamulaka* (based on experiments or criticism), or *Visvasamulaka* (based on faith).

Bose as a Social Worker

Although Professor Bose readily admits his intellectual indebtedness to a wide range of scholars and writers, but he also insists that his main learning in social sciences has been through involvement in the problems of regeneration of tired ancient society, groaning under the shackles of colonial rule.

At the young age of 17 years, Bose participated in a famine relief operation in Benkura District, organised by Sadharan Brahma Samaj in 1917. He used this opportunity to conduct a systematic survey of economic conditions of a large number of rural families. This was his self-styled initiation to field studies before he had any knowledge of the disciplines of anthropology and sociology.

In 1921, following the suggestion of C.F. Andrews, Bose and two of his associates organised the repatriation of indentured Indian labourers from Fiji. Here again, his passion for rigorous survey of social facts found expression in the collection of detailed census on social background of 1050 persons belonging to about 450 families. This survey report provides plenty of information on how Indian Rural Society placed numerous obstacles in the process of reabsorption and rehabilitation of indentured labourers, who had migrated to the other countries from the Indian main-land and wanted to come their home back.

In 1922, Bose left Presidency College of Calcutta in response to the non-cooperation movement under the leadership of Mahatma Gandhi. From then onward Gandhi's ideas and action programmes have been the major subjects of his intellectual interest. During 1930–36, he was engaged in a Gandhian village reconstruction programme with his centre in a slum in the outskirts of Bolpur town. Many of his co-workers were untouchables belonging to Harijan, Mochi and Baurin castes. It is generally stated that Bose's interest in Indian caste system developed with his active participation in organising social reconstruction programme.

Learning from the Silpis of Orissa

Bose received his formal training in anthropology as an M.Sc. student in Calcutta University during 1923-24. He came to the discipline of anthropology by an accident. In 1921, after obtaining his B.Sc. (Hons) degree in Geology, he was preparing himself for a career as a geologist. In geology, his special interests were Palaeontology and Petrology. When the non-cooperation movement was launched, he decided to leave the Government college for ever. He left Calcutta and settled down at Puri.

In Puri, he came across a master Silpi (temple architect) named Ram Maharana, who initiated Bose to the traditional canons of Orissan architecture. He edited an Oriya manuscript on Silpa Sastra, which was later published in 1932. Thus, he learnt from the field that a student of civilization will have to integrate information from various levels: the text, the material products and the learned specialists' interpretation of the text, as well as the products of arts. The elegance of ancient Orissan temples fascinated Bose so much that he started giving lectures on these temples to the visitors to Puri. It was in this connection that he came in contact with Sir Ashutosh Mukherjee, the then Vice-Chancellor of Calcutta University. He persuaded Bose to joint the new department of

Anthropology as an M.Sc. student. He passed his M.Sc. examination with brilliant records. His M.Sc. dissertation was a diffusionist study of 'Spring Festival in India'. Since 1923, Bose has published 37 books, 23 in English and 14 in Bengali. He has written more than 700 articles. Of these half belong to the domain of anthropology proper, while the rest cover a wide range of interests like politics, travelogues, art, architecture, literature, social work etc. Many of his important articles have been written in Bengali. As editor of Man-in-India since 1951, he has played a very constructive role in encouraging young scholars to publish the result of their research.

Phases of Research in Anthropological Survey of India

During the period 1959-1964, when Bose was the Director of Anthropological Survey of India, he divided the researches to be carried out by this India-level anthropological institution into five phases. They were:

Phase I : Study of distribution of material traits all over India and mapping out the pattern of their distribution *vis-a-vis* linguistic areas.

Phase II : Study of a few important ancient craft techniques — pottery and metal craft.

Phase III : Study of social organisations of crafts and of caste organisation in different regions of India.

Phase IV : The study of the Superstructure of Indian Society — through the study of temples, Mathas and the kinghips.

Phase V : Study of the process of modernisation in castes, occupation, urbanization, tribal movements and social movements in different regions of India.

Bose's Contribution on the Study of Caste System

As referred to earlier, Bose's interest in the study of caste system in India appeared in his mind, when he was working among the slums with untouchables of Bolpur town under the Gandhian Reconstruction Programme. He rejected the myth of divine origin, reincarnation and notion of purity and pollution. In a series of brilliant articles — 'Hindu Method of Tribal Absorption' (1941), 'Caste in India' (1951), 'Some Aspects of Caste in Bengal' (1958) — Bose proposes that the root of persistence of the caste system is to be found in the economic and cultural security provided by the non-competitive, hereditary, vocation based productive organisation, which operated in isolated village communities and were guided by a general norm of inter-ethnic cultural tolerance. Further, the institutions of *Sanyas* (asceticism) provided at least a limited avenue of freedom and prestige to the individuals, who were, otherwise, bound to the rigid hierarchy of the system. Bose has been quick to point out that such an ideal pattern of caste based rural society could thrive adequately, only when there was adequate ecological and demographic space to setup new villages. A demographic base, for the caste system was, thus, clearly hinted in a recent article, 'Competing Productive System in India' (1968).

On the basis of above logic, Bose proposed that fundamental structural change and even breakdown of caste system would be possible only when the economic base of the system was qualitatively transformed. It was this consideration that prompted him to initiate a series of research on change in traditional occupation in different regions of India, particularly West Bengal. His general proposition has been that caste, as an economic system and as a regulator of social life, is disintegrating at different rate in different regions of India. Bose was particularly curious about what has happened to the caste system in a city like Calcutta, which has been exposed to nearly two hundred years of modern commercial, industrial and urban development.

On the basis of a rapid survey during 1962-63, he has arrived at a conclusion that the diverse ethnic groups, in the population of the city, have come to bear the same relation to one another as do the castes in India as a whole. Actually, the superstructure that coheres the caste under the old order seems instead to be re-establishing itself in a new form. Calcutta today, is far from being a melting pot on the model of cities in the U.S.A. In Calcutta, the economy is an economy of scarcity. Because, there are not enough jobs to go around. Every one clings, as closely as possible, to the occupation with which his ethnic group is identified and relies for economic support on those who speak his language, or his coreligionists, or members of his own caste and or fellow migrants from the village or district from which he has come. By a backwash,reliance on earlier modes of group identification reinforce and perpetuate differences between ethnic groups (Bose, 1965: 90-105).

Bose has emphasised upon the consciousness or ideal model of caste as a normative system, while studying change. For example, the recent proliferation of politically competitive caste associations are not considered by him as indication of strengthening the caste system. He is of opinion that these recent developments rather indicate deviations from the non-competitive ascribed traditional system towards a competitive one. In other words, the old structures being used in various new combinations in new social meaning.

Although Bose has utilized traditional textual categories such as *Satva, Raja, Tamas* and *Dharma, Artha, Kama* and *Moksha* in the classification of cultures, he is very critical about simplistic extrapolation of textual notions in the study of Indian civilization, without taking full note of historical and social context. For instance, Bose is critical of Weber for assuming that the Indian theory of *Karma* carries only a social message of *status quo*. Bose observes that the notion of *Karma* has been used as a doctrine of moral endeavour by Buddha at a certain turning point of history, whereas it was utilised by the latter day Brahmans and other upper castes for the perpetuation of *status quo*.

Besides interest in the change-oriented study of Indian caste system, Prof. Bose developed interest in the study of castes as self regulating corporate groups, guiding the social life of their members. A number of studies on operation of caste association in different regions of India were initiated by him. In some of these the roles of kings, temples, *Mathas,* etc. were also brought into focus in the regulation of caste norms.

Contribution on Tribal Studies

Bose wanted to begin his professional career with an intensive field research on the Juang of Orissa, but after a brief spell of fieldwork in 1928, he had to leave the state of Keonjhar by the order of the police. The data gathered, during the short period of fieldwork among the Juang, resulted in publication of three short papers (Bose, 1928, 1929, 1930). The brief field study among the Juang provided him the basic insight on how tribes following a relatively primitive productive technology like swidden cultivation, were being absorbed into agriculture and craft-based Hindu society. In this various insightful papers on tribals, he attempted to highlight the tribal economy, absorption of tribes into the Hindu caste system, and the root of tribal separatist movement. In his book *Tribal Life in India* (1970), Bose has observed that barring a very small fraction, there is little difference in economic life of tribals and peasant and artisan communities. The difference between our rural folk and urban classes is undoubtedly greater than that between peasants and the tribal communities, so far as their occupations are concerned.

Contribution on Structure of Indian Civilization: Unity and Diversities

From the writings of Bose, it appears that as early as 1929, he had decided to study not only tribes and the caste system of villages, but the structure of Indian civilization as a whole. During 1942-45, as a political prisoner under British Government, he gave a series of lectures on the structure on Hindu society to the fellow political prisoner. These lectures formed the basis of his Bengali book, *Hindu Samajer Gadan* (Structure of Hindu Society, 1949). This book was published few years before 'comparision of civilization' became a proper subject of study by the American anthropologist, Robert Redfield. In this book, Bose has highlighted many dimensions of Indian Social Structure and Social processes, such as tribal enclaves and their absorption, the dual themes of self-sufficiency of village communities and their boarder links with kinghip, fairs, pilgrimage-centres, norms of sacred and secular life in ancient texts, social movements in the Medieval period in relation to Islam, the impact of British rule and the emerging economy of Indian Society, particularly of caste system. From this book, it appears that anthropological study of Indian civilization involves a combination of many perspectives such an analysis of classical and Medieval texts, administrative records, particularly of land tenure, and study of villages, individual caste association, and the wider social net work of the civilizations in kingships, fairs, pilgrim centres, and so on. The persistent focus of this study has been on a study of the fate of the *Varna-Jati* systems at different phases of Indian History.

Bose has observed that the historical situation in which the classical *Varna Jati* system of social order came into being, will not be repeated in modern times. It will not suit our times, for the population of India has increased manifold and land per capita has diminished considerably. Yet if we discover some values and social designs in the traditional system, which has relevance for the modern times, it will be unwise not to utilize them in solving our contemporary problems. Because in the ultimate analysis, the human kind cannot be set apart by time and space. However, the cultural history of Indian civilization presents an example of unity in diversities. Although the inhabitants of India present diversified scenes on the basis of region, religion, language, community, race, occupation and material possessions, but they share many traits, customs, traditions, beliefs, etc., in common which are handed down generations after generations. The diversified groups are tied together by Indian system of Jajmani, in which each caste serves for another according to hereditary positions and occupations. The inter-regional and inter-ethnic unity can be seen at the time of making pilgrimage at *Dhams* located in different parts of India. Fairs also present examples of inter-communal unity. Thus, India is excellent example of unity in diversity.

Cultural Zones and Pattern on Unity

To the students of Indian society and history, the great cultural division of India has always been the Aryan North *vis-a-vis* the Dravidian South. This has also been indicated by Iravati Karve's extensive study on kinship system (1953). As an acute observers of cultural facts and an indefatigable traveller (Bose, *Diary of a Wanderer*, 1940), Bose observed that the division of Indian population on the basis of language was oberlain on a different set of cultural divide in terms of items of material culture — North-West continuous with West Central Asia, and East, continuous with Southern Asia. This proposition was later on elaborately worked out on the basis of an extensive survey of the distribution of a set of material traits and forms and techniques of potters all over India. Apart from the intrinsic theoretical interests of unravelling archaic and persistent culture-historic processes through distribution studies, Bose's special interest in bringing the archaic links into relief was to indicate how regions or states of India, which are today separated by difference of language, share many elements of material culture in common.

In his book, *Peasant Life in India: A Study in Indian Unity and Diversity*, Bose proposes a pyramidal imagery of the unity of Indian civilization. According to him, if the regionalisation is in evidence to a certain extent in relation to the material arts of life, it is apparent already that the degree of differentiation is less in respect of the country's social organisation. What is more reassuring is that if one rises to higher reaches of life confined to ideals, or faith or arts, the differences which one noticed at the material level of life gradually become feebler and feebler. They are eventually replaced by a unity of beliefs and aspirations which gives to Indian civilization, a character of its own. The structure of Indian unity can be compared to a pyramid. There is more differentiation at the material base of life and progressively less as one mounts higher and higher.

In another article, 'The Geographical Background of Indian Culture' (1950), Bose discusses as to how a kind of uniformity grew up between geographically and even ecologically distinguishable regions of India, through economic tradition of caste system. He also discusses about the various traditional cultural media which provided a mechanism through which the unifying thoughts and feeling of thinkers, artists, and saints of India were brought to the door of most distant communities and enabled them to share some common intellectual and emotional elements of civilization.

In his Jagdish Bose Memorial Lecture of 1971, Bose stated that Indian civilization was in contrast to the civilization of Europe. The civilization of Europe was essentially based on repeated experience of war leading to the spirit of nationalism. The civilization of India, on the other hand, developed a pattern of cultural pluralism under relatively peaceful conditions sheltered by the geographical barriers along its frontiers. According to him, Indian civilization encouraged diversity of culture, but in its economic organization, it tried to weave all communities into a network of interdependent, but distinct entities.

Civilization at a Phase of Confidence

According to Bose, the creative potentialities of the traditional structure of Indian civilization cannot be properly assessed, if the observations are only limited to the post-Medieval and recent phase of recession of the civilization. The civilization has to be studied in a phase of expansion and confidence. In his Bengali article 'The Temple of Konark', Bose refers to the expansive and confidence phase of Indian civilization in a vivid manner. According to him, the temple of Konark was built in a glorious period of Orissan history. The king Narsinghdev of Ganga dynasty had just defeated the Sultan of Gaura with his powerful army. The state was prosperous and people were infused with a passionate mood to enjoy life and to assert independence. The architects were brought up in this atmosphere and tried to give shape to this confident and livelihood in their work. The sculptures are full of light. The sculptors mind were not laden with any false shame. Even-to-day, partly buried under a debris of broken stone pieces, withstanding the ravages of time, the temple of Konarka preserves a vivid picture of a by-gone confident past.

Bose has also tried to capture the expressive modern thrust of Indian civilization through a number of critical character sketches of a few outstanding personalities. In Bengali Book, *Nabin-O-Prachin* (New and Old), he writes about Gandhi's *Satyagraha* and search of truth, Tagore's creative pursuits and paintings, Jamini Roy's views on art and Ramkinkar Baij's paintings. Although Bose has been a persistent student of Indian civilization, but he has not made any conscious efforts to distinguish the concept of civilization from that of culture. He has, however, thrown some interesting hints on the general characteristics of a civilization.

In the particular case of encounter of East and West in Bengal, Bose is of opinion that the civilization of Bengal cannot be defined in terms of spatial and temporal continuity of tradition. According to him, in the formidable and venture of cultural recognization, Bengali culture has always been in the process of becoming, instead of merely being. This tradition to become something is the characteristic of any civilization.

Thus, the study of civilization is essentially a study of the inner moods, i.e., matters of the mind, responding to the changing life experiences of a people.

Contribution on Problems of National Integration and Modernisation

At the Indian Institute of Advanced Study, Simla, Bose delivered a series of lectures on the problem of national integration in the year 1966. The main theme of these lectures is that development of the post-independence spurt of subnationalist movement is due to the fact that the different states and communities living within each state have been subjected to unequal forces of economic, social and political changes. Under such circumstances the rising middle class tended to create boundaries around narrow parochial lines in order to consolidate their secretarian advantage.

Professor Bose has taken a consistent plea against a communal basis for administrative categorization of backwardness. His suggestion is that modern India should set her primary task as dispersal of political power to the toilers irrespective of castes and communities. Being the Commissioner for Scheduled Castes and Scheduled Tribes during 1967-69, he emphasized upon the same points in his various reports.

On Gandhism

Professor Bose was greatly influenced by the ideologies of Mahatma Gandhi or Bapu. Ever since responding to the non-cooperation movement in 1921, Bose has been an ardent student of Gandhi's ideas and activities. What impressed Professor Bose towards Gandhi was his (Gandhi's) experiment on endeavour for truth with ordinary people. Instead of depending upon the middle class intelligentsia to spearhead political movement, Gandhi's focus was on involving the common people to bring about institutional change. His intellectual involvement with Gandhism has passed through three phases: (i) classification of the whole range of Gandhi's ideas in terms of clusters of themes, (ii) critical analysis of Gandhi's economic action programmes, and (iii) explanation of political ideas of Gandhi. He has published a number of books on Gandhian ideas and thoughts. They are: *Selections from Gandhi* (1934, 1952, 1968), *My Days with Gandhi* (1953), *Gandhi Charit* (1969), *Gandhi Ki Chau* (1969).

Contributions in Prehistoric Archaeology

Professor Bose carried out pioneering field research in Palaeolithic archaeology of Mayurbhanj in collaboration with Dharani Sen. The work was designed to establish stratigraphic sequence between different types of tools recovered by excavations. Hitherto different types of Palaeolithic tools in Peninsular India have been almost used as index 'fossils', without taking the stratigraphic context in to consideration. Bose was completely against this practice. He tried to establish, purely on the basis of stratigraphy and correlated techtonic movements, a regional scale which might later on be used for dating in nearby areas, instead of using the pluvial and glacial cycle sequences established in far away places like Narmada Valley and Soan Valley. Another attempt was to correlate the finding of prehistory with contemporary ethnographic information on ancient crafts like pottery and casting of nonferrous metals etc.

Contributions in Methodology

Bose was influenced to a great extent by American School of Diffusions, as revealed by his book, *Cultural Anthropology* (1926). In the study of distribution of elements of temple architecture, he attempted to date the temple by combining the distributional techniques with epigraphical information. One of his major conclusions was that different elements of architecture travelled at different rates in space. As a director of Anthropological Survey of India, he encouraged researchers to collect information on the distribution of selected material traits from all over India and of some major ancient craft techniques.

DHIRENDRA NATH MAJUMDAR (1903-1960)

D.N. Majumdar was born on June 3, 1903 at Patna (Bihar). He was the second son of the couple Mrs. Kushum Kumari and Mr. Rebati Mohan Majumdar. Mr. Rebati Mohan Majumdar was a Zamindar of Kushumhaty estate (Dacca in East Bengal). Kusum Kumari had come to her brother, Sri Jogesh Chandra Dutta, who was magistrate at that time in Patna. She delivered her second child at Patna who was named as Dhirendra Nath Majumdar.

D.N. Majumdar was educated at Dacca Government College, University College, Calcutta, Cambridge University and Dalton Laboratory London. He passed his Matriculation and Intermediate Science examinations with first divisions from Dacca Government College. He was admitted to Faculty of Arts of the University College, Calcutta for graduate study. He graduated from this institution with distinction in Bachelor examination in 1922. In 1924, he received his M.A. degree in Anthropology from the University of Calcutta. He toped the list among the first class candidates. The same year, he made his first trip to Chota Nagpur (Bihar), where he was initiated into anthropological fieldwork by veteran ethnographer Sarat Chandra Roy, the father of Indian ethnography. In 1926, he was awarded the much coveted Prem Chand Roy Chand Scholarship of the University of Calcutta in recognition of the research work already done by him. The scholarship enabled him to continue his study of the Ho tribe of Kolhan (Bihar). Three years later (1929) he was awarded the 'Mout Gold Medal' by the Calcutta University.

In 1928, Majumdar was appointed as a Lecturer in Primitive Economics in the Department of Economics and Sociology at the University of Lucknow. After a period of five years (in 1933), he went to Cambridge to study Social Anthropology with Professor T.C. Hadon and Physical Anthropology with Professor G.M. Morant. While at London, he also attended Malinowski's Seminar at the London School of Economics and he was greatly influenced by Malinowski's functional theory of culture. He received his Ph.D. degree from Cambridge University in 1935 and was elected a fellow of Royal Anthropological Institute of Great Britain and Ireland (in 1936). While in Cambridge he gave a series of lectures on Indian culture after having his doctoral degree, he also visited Vienna, where he also delivered a series of lectures on Tribal Culture in India.

He returned to India in 1938 and again joined his old post in Lucknow University. In 1936, he presided over the Anthropology and Archaeology Section of Indian Science Congress held at Lahore. In 1941 he was elected a fellow of National Institute of Sciences. He was also elected a fellow of American Association of Physical Anthropology. He was awarded Research Medal by Gujarat Research Society, Bombay in 1950 and Anandale Gold Medal by the Asiatic Society of Bengal in 1958 for his contribution to Asian Anthropology.

He was invited by a number of National and International organizations to deliver lectures and undertake *ad hoc* researches. He delivered the Rathodkar Memorial Researchship lectures at the Nagpur University in 1946 and was visiting Professor at Cornell University U.S.A. (1952-53), and in School of Oriental and African studies in 1957-58. He attended several International Congresses such as Anthropology organised by Wenner Gren Foundation in New York (1952), the World Conference on Population held in Rome (1954), and the International Sociological Congress in Paris (1954).

He founded the Ethnographic and Folk Culture Society in 1945 and started the publication of the quarterly journal, the Eastern Anthropologist in 1947. He was member of a number of national bodies like the Research Programmes Committee of the Planning Commission (1955-60), Member of the Central Advisory Board for Anthropology (1958), Indian Council of Medical Research (1958). He also presided over a number of national conferences as Indian sociological conference and convention of Indian anthropologist.

In 1946, the University of Lucknow promoted him to the post of Reader in Anthropology in the Department of Economics and Sociology and as Professor in Anthropology in the same institution in 1950. In 1951, the University of Lucknow created an independent Department of Anthropology, the third University of India to do so. (The first Calcutta University in 1920 and the second the University of Delhi in 1947). Thus, in 1951, he was made University Professor and Head of the Department of Anthropology, Lucknow University (U.P.). He collaborated with Professor M.E. Opler of Cornell University in a research project on Village Studies near Lucknow started in 1953. This was followed by another village study near Dudhi in Mirzapur district of U.P. An ambitious city survey was undertaken by him in collaboration with Dr. N.S. Reddy (formerly Head of the Department of Anthropology, Madras University) at Kanpur. The Research Programmes Committee had financed this project and the report came out a few weeks before Majumdar's death. A third major project, on the Process and Problems of physical growth among children in U.P., financed by Indian Council of Medical Research was in progress at the time of his death.

On April 1, 1960 he took over as Dean of the Faculty of Arts at the University of Lucknow. Two months later, on May 31, 1960 he breathed his last at Lucknow on account of cerebral haemorrhage.

His important published books are as follows:

1. 1937: *A Tribe in Transition: A Study in Culture Pattern*. Longmans Green & Co., Calcutta and London.
2. 1944(a): *A Fortune of Primitive Tribes*. Universal Publishers Ltd., Lucknow.
3. 1944(b): *Races and Cultures of India*. Kitabistan, Allahabad.
4. 1950: *The Affairs of a Tribe: A Study in Tribal Dynamics*. The Universal Publishes Ltd., Lucknow.
5. 1956 (With T.N. Madan): *An Introduction to Social Anthropology*. Asia Publishing House, Bombay.
6. 1958a: *Caste and Communication in an Indian Village*. Asia Publishing House, Bombay.
7. 1958b: *Bhartiya Sanskriti Ke Upadan* (Hindi). Asia Publishing House, Bombay.
8. 1960: *Social Contours of an Industrial City*. Asia Publishing

House, Bombay.

Posthumous Publications

1. 1962: *Himalayan Polyandry*. Asia Publishing House, Bombay.
2. N.D.: *A Village on the Fringe*. Asia Publishing House, Bombay.
3. N.D.: *Chhor Ka Ek Gaon* (Hindi). Asia Publishing House, Bombay.
4. N.D.: *Pragithas* (Hindi, co-author: Gopala Sarana). Asia Publishing House, Bombay.

Besides these books, he contributed a good number of articles on socio-cultural and physical aspects of tribes of Bihar, Madhya Pradesh, Uttar Pradesh and Gujarat. etc., which were published in the journals of national and international repute.

Contributions in Cultural Anthropology

The major part of Majumdar's published work was in the area of ethnography. As a student of the behavioural aspect of man, his approach was that of a cultural anthropologists rather than that of a social anthropologist. He regarded the works of man or the products of human activity – language, magic, religion, art, groups, institutions, goods and services etc. as the subject matter of anthropology. In his opinion, social anthropology was a subdiscipline within cultural anthropology and not an alternative frame of reference for the study of human behaviour.

His approach, to the study of human culture, was that of functionalists. He regarded functionalism as the best method for the collection and interpretation of data concerning human behaviour. Majumdar studied culture rather than problems. In nearly all his ethnographic works whether monographs or articles, he included a discussion of cultural dynamics. He maintained and followed Malinowski's teaching that, although changes are ever occurring in a culture, yet it retains its character of being an integrated whole. But he never made a clear distinction in his work between cultural integration in terms of content and function as Malinowski did. He was also influenced by Benedict's concept of cultural pattern study. His Ph.D. thesis published in book form entitled, *A Tribe in Transion: A Study in Culture Pattern* (1937), bears testimony in this regard. This book is regarded as the first scientific study of impact of modern civilization on an Indian tribal people.

His another book, *The Fortunes of Primitive Tribes* (1944) deals with ethnographic essays on various tribes of Uttar Pradesh. He also underscored the importance of studying the psychological dimension of human behaviour, particularly in the study of culture change. His book, *The Affairs of Tribe: A Study in Tribal Dynamics* (1950) deals with changes taking place in tribal cultures in India.

Thus, his contributions in the field of cultural anthropology consisted of ethnographic accounts of the Ho (Bihar), the Khasa, the Korwa, the Tharu and the so called criminal tribes (all of U.P.), the Gond of Bastar (M.P.), and the Bhil of Gujarat. He published his books on the Ho and the Khasa, whom he knew best and published many papers on the above mentioned tribes. He was a true field worker. He was in the habit of spreading fieldwork in a tribe or village over several years, either conducting fieldwork himself or in a company of his students. He spent nearly 22 summers with Khasas, totalling five years of fieldwork among them, (see his book Himalayan Polyandry, 1962). All fieldwork was done through the local dialects. In the presentation of his data, he followed the method of covering all the major aspects of culture — economics, kinship, religion, etc.

He was the first Indian anthropologist to study and write about the impact of non-tribal culture on the ways of life of Indian tribes. His early interest in the study of culture change led him in 1950 to welcome the emergence of rural studies in India by anthropologists. He played valuable part in this new field of research and produced one of the first full-length village studies in India entitled, *Caste and Communication in an Indian Village* (1958). He also pleaded for the application of the findings of anthropology to the task of national development. As a member of Research Programmes Committee of the National Planning Commission, he emphasised upon the role played by anthropologists and sociologists in helping the administration and the Government by studying and exploring the problems of backward areas and its people, and by assessing the impact of Government sponsored programmes of the national reconstruction of the people at village level. His posthumous book, *Khasa, Himalayan Polyandry*, (1962) also contains a detailed discussion of the Community Development Programmes in Jaunsar Bawar (U.P.).

It was Majumdar's conviction in the utility of applied anthropological sociological research which made him undertake in 1954 a survey of the industrial city of Kanpur (1960). It can be pointed out here that such research was an orthodox undertaking for an anthropologists at that time.

It is generally argued that Majumdar's work often lacked theoretical sophistication, but that was probably inevitable because he broke much new ground and engaged in research in such fields where there were few or no precursors.

Almost all of his work, either in physical anthropology or in cultural anthropology, is of a pioneering nature. He endeavoured, more than many other individual of his generation, to place anthropological studies in India on a scientific footing. The success he achieved was huge, considering the circumstances.

Contribution to Physical Anthropology

Majumdar conducted an extensive anthropometric and serological surveys in Uttar Pradesh, Bengal and Gujarat. He also collected similar data among Ho of Singhbhum (Bihar) and Gond of Bastar (M.P.).

In the field of methodology, he realized quite early the importance of refined statistical treatment of data. His collaboration with Mahalanobis and Rao resulted in the formation of D^2 or the 'generalised distance statistics', which is regarded as an advanced and highly favoured statistico-taxonomic method in biometrical anthropology.

On the basis of serological studies, he demonstrated the genetic relationship of the population of Uttar Pradesh with those of Bengal in East and Punjab in the West. In Uttar Pradesh itself, he showed that the caste hierarchy has a biometric basis. The castes which constitute clusters, being close to each other in hierarchical organisation, were shown to be also within a close range of biometric variation. It was H.H. Risley, the author of *The People of India* (1908) and *Tribes and Castes of Bengal* (4 vols.) (1891), who suggested a link between tribe, caste and race. Majumdar also got his idea from Risley, but he took it further and confirmed it by his own investigations.

In his book, *Races and Culture of India* (1944), he defined race as if a group of people who by their possession of number of common physical traits can be distinguished from others, even if the numbers of this biological groups are widely scattered, they form a race.

Majumdar did not confine his attention to distribution studies of racial characters, but he was also interested in the ontogenetic development of Indian children. His study of school children in the city of Lucknow (1951) is an important landmark in the physical anthropological studies in India. At the time of his death, he was the supervisor of a research project on a cross-cultural study of growth among children in Uttar Pradesh. Data on about 30,000 cases had been already obtained by a team of investigators including doctors, physical anthropologists, social workers and statisticians. He was keen on determining the purely physical as well as the cultural determinants of growth.

At the time of his death, he was also engaged in a study of the A BO and Rh blood groups among the criminal tribes of Uttar Pradesh. A.E.

Mourant regarded Majumdar as pioneer in the application of blood group testing to anthropology in India.

SHYAMA CHARAN DUBE (1922-)

S.C. Dube received his master degree in political science from Nagpur University with Social Anthropology as a special group. He did his Ph.D. from Nagpur University. His doctoral dissertation was on 'Kamar', a tribe of Madhya Pradesh. He was awarded K.E.M. Scholarship and Moris Memorial Fellowship of Nagpur University.

Dr. Dube was lecturer at Nagpur, Lucknow and Osmania Universities. For sometime, he was visiting professor at London and Cornell Universities. He also served for sometime in Anthropological Survey of India and National Institute of Community Development, Government of India, where he was Director of Research and Principal of the Institute.

He conducted field researches in Chhatisgarh (M.P.), Telangana (A.P.), West Orissa and North Andhra Pradesh. His chief theoretical interest is in social structure and change as well as sociology of economic development.

He attended the World Congress of Anthropological and Ethnological Sciences at Vienna and the UNESCO working group on human progress and technological change held at Paris in 1953. He has been invited to several major international conferences and seminars to each of which he contributed substantial papers. He attended conferences and seminars at London, Paris, Burg, Watenstein and Moscow. In 1962 he went to Pakistan as a UNESCO Consultant to advise on a major study of rural leadership in that country. In 1963, he attended a UNESCO Expert Working Group Meeting in Cyprus on 'Social Prerequisites of Economic Growth'. In the same year, he attended a seminar in Manila (the Philippines) on, 'Religion and Economic Progress', and contributed a substantial papers to the Rehoboth (Israel) conference on comprehensive planning of agriculture. In 1964, he attended a six week International Development Workshop at the East-West Centre, Hawaii. In August-September 1965, he directed the International Development Seminar on 'Community Development and Local Government' at the East-West Centre, Hawaii. He has also served as Director of Indian Institute of Advanced Study, Simla and as Vice-Chancellor of Sagar University. Now he is leading a retired life.

Some of his publications are as follows:

Books in English

1. 1954: *The Kamar*. Lucknow: Universal Publisher.
2. 1955: *Indian Village*. London: Routledge & Kegan Paul, Ithaca, Cornell University Press.
3. 1958: *India's Changing Villages: Human Factors in Community Development*. London: Routledge & Kegan Paul, Ithaca, Cornell University Press.
4. — *Power and Conflict in Village India*. London: Routledge & Kegan Paul, Ithaca, Cornell University Press.
5. 1968: *Institution Building for Community Development* (ed.). Hawaii: East-West Centre Press.
6. —*Sociology of Economic Development.*

Books in Hindi

1. 1960: *Manav Aur Sanskriti*. Delhi: Rajmahal Prakashan.
2. 1962: *General Editor of Bhartiya Samaj Parichay Mala*. Delhi: Rajmahal Prakashan.

Besides these books, Professor Dube contributed nearly two dozen papers in several books, edited by national and international anthropologists, and several research articles in renowned journals of the country and abroad.

Contribution in Tribal Study

Dube's first book, *The Kamar* (1951), deals with a total study of this tribe of Madhya Pradesh. This book is a full length monograph on this tribe of middle India. The book is published version of his Ph.D. thesis.

Contribution in Village Study

Dube's another book, *Indian Village* (1955) deals with a total study of village Shamirpet in the region of Telangana of Andhra Pradesh State. The book is based on data collected from the village Shamirpet by five research investigators. The author was further assisted by five other faculty units which did social work within their special areas of interests and technical competence. This interdisciplinary collaboration was sponsored and financed by the Social Service Extension Project of Osmania University in 1951-52 which Dube directed.

The village Shamirpet located at a distance of nearly 25 miles from

Hyderabad had a population of 2494 including 340 Muslims and 19 ethnic groups belonging to Hindus. In the light of the field data, an integrated picture of the village has been presented. In the book, historical, geographical and sociological perspectives have been adequately taken care of, Morris E. Opler, the writer of foreward of the book, introduced it as a solid study which would doubtlessly take its place among the standard community studies made in various parts of the world. He further observes that in a number of ways this volume is specially valuable and challenging and is tonic to the present day research into Indian village life.

This book is the first to provide convincing and reasonably adequate introduction to the historical, geographical and political setting as well as to the social, economic, religious practices of a village in India. If Robert Redfield is credited for making the first village study in 1930 in Mexico, it was for Dube to describe a Deccan village in India more or less on the same lines in 1955. Many of his conclusions could provide the first insight in the complex web of Indian village life. He observes:

> No village in India is completely autonomous and independent, for it is always one unit in a wider social system and is a part of an organised political society. An individual is not the member of a village community alone, he also belongs to a caste, religious group or a tribe with a wider territorial spread and comprises several villages. These units have their own organisation, authority and sanctions.

Although it is one of the earliest monographs on a village, it presents a comprehensive picture of the functioning of village institutions. Dube notes that the economic system of rural India is founded mainly on caste's functional specialization, interdependence and occupational mobility. He also notes that the elements of classical Hinduism of an all India spread are mingled with the regional religious beliefs and practices of Hindus of Deccan plateau. Three major types of religious services and festivals are observed in the village. They are: (1) family ceremonies, (2) village ceremonies, and (3) caste ceremonies. The Muslims have their own familial and communal festivals. The Muslims and Hindus interact with each other during festivals.

In this book Dube also gives a short account of world view, intergroup relations, inter caste attitudes and stereotype and he also goes on to discuss the three most significant stages of life, namely, childhood, youth and old age in a generalised biography.

Contribution in Political Anthropology

In addition to this full-length book, Dube has written a few papers on the village studies among whom mention may be made of one of the ranking of castes in Telangana village published in the book, *Rural Profiles of India* edited by late professor D.N. Majumdar (1955). To Dube, the fundamental principles of caste-ranking is a concept of ritual purity and pollution. The caste ranking in Shamirpet is also determined by traditions and myths since caste is based on an ascribed system of status. He also established that the observance of prescribed daily rituals, hierarchy of food eaten, occupations allowed and practised and observance of rules connected with life cycle rituals also determined ranks. Dube makes repeated emphasis that the main criterion used for caste ranking in village are rituals and not economic. However, in certain cases, for example Coorgs of South India studied by M.N. Srinivas, the economic dominance of a group leads to ritual rationalization of its high status. Marriot also suggests that the caste are ranked on the basis of interaction among them, instead of attributes.

Dube in his paper entitled, 'Dominant Caste and Village Leadership' read at a seminar on 'Trends of Change in Villages India', organised by Central Institute of Study and Research in Community Development, Mussoorie in 1961, has added to the concepts and methods of study of pattern of rural leadership in India. Srinivas in his study of Rampura village has added to the concept of 'dominant caste' as crucial for understanding of power relation in rural social life in most part of the country. Dube in this paper has expressed his disagreement with Srinivas. He finds the political power concentrated in few individuals rather than diffused in caste. In each village, there are some dominant individuals, who have decisive say in political participation of the members of a village. They play significant role in settling dispute, guiding the youth force for maintaining unity in the village, organising the villagers for common celebration of festivals. Their roles at the time of election of Gram Panchayat, M.L.A. and M.P. can also be observed.

Dube in his paper, 'The Restive Students: Strands and Themes in Contemporary Youth Culture' (*Akasvani,* Vol. 35, No. 32, 1972), objects to the use of the term Indian students or Contemporary Youth as an undifferentiated mass. In the light of the differences in their background, orientation, and outlook, he identifies four subcultures of the contemporary youths. These are: (1) the Indian counterpart of the Hippies, (2) the models coming from the Westernized and alienated families, (3) youths of the medium to low privileged strata of society, and (4) by far the largest group consists of first generation of literates and those whose parents had not had the benefit of higher education. Professor Dube is of opinion that school system fails to mould them to the requirements of the universities, and the universities themselves have done little to adopt to the needs of the new entrants. In the view of this, some of the students are distracted by glittering non-academic environment and they find in the inflexible and sterile university system, very little to inspire or stimulate them. Some become indifferent and stay indifferent, others learn to articulate their resentment. Some graduate into open definance and revolt. The unorganised minority crystallizes dissent and spearheads the revolt.

Contribution in Family Planning Research

The Central Family Planning Research Institute, Delhi, has published a series of monographs written by sociologists and other experts on Family Planning. Monograph series No. 6 (1968) and No. 8 (1969) deal with Dube's study on Family Planning. In the monograph No. 6, Dube studies the diffusion of IUCD (intra-uterian contraceptive devices) which is relatively a new method of family planning in India. As the study was done in the initial phase of the IUCD Programme and as the cases of acceptance were limited, he studied the whole universe of users to ensure reasonable number of respondents. The study also brings out the need for improvements in the research tools, and it was suggested to develop a scale to measure variables related to general background variables indicating life orientation and life style of the respondents. Dube also suggested that as diffusion studies are concerned with the element of time in the processes of acceptance of innovations, i.e., diffusion period and acceptance period, these items deserve special studies.

In another monograph No. 8 (1969), Dube makes a review of findings and implications of studies on communication. The monograph is based on more than 60 family planning studies, conducted in different parts of the country since the inception of the family planning programme. Some of these studies deal with the communicational aspects of the programme as their major areas of concern. While others include communication as a part of their other research interests in family planning. Dube has made an attempt to put together the widely scattered findings and has systematised them in some frame-work to enhance their usefulness to the programme. He has also evolved some future tentative strategy for a more need-oriented family planning communication research programmes.

Contribution in Community Development Programme Research

Dube's book, *India's Changing Villages: Human Factors in Community Development* (1958) deals with changes brought about in Indian villages by the initiation of Community Development Schemes in all parts of the country. The book discusses at length the human factors responsible for bringing changes in villages of India through community development. The study is based on fieldwork in two villages of Western U.P., one Rajput and the other Tyagi. His another edited book, *Institution building for Community Development*, contains articles of eminent anthropologists of the world. The papers attempt to show the importance of institution building for the development of community.

M.N. SRINIVAS (1916-)

Mysore Narasimbachar Srinivas was born on 6th November, 1916. He graduated with Hons. in Social Philosophy in year 1936 from the University of Mysore. He obtained M.A. degree in Sociology (1939), LLB (1940) and Ph.D. (Sociology in 1945) from Bombay University. In 1945, he went to Oxford University, where he received D.Phil in Social Anthropology in 1947.

He was research fellow (1940-42) and research assistant (1942-44) in Sociology in Bombay University. While at Oxford, he was awarded carriage grant (1945-47). He was also awarded Simon Senior Research Fellowship to visit Manchester University (1953-54), Rocke feller Fellowship to stay in American Universities (1956-57).

Srinivas held many appointments such as University lecturer in Indian Sociology at Oxford University (1948-51), Professor, M.S. University Baroda (1952-59), Professor, University of Delhi (1959-72), Joint Director, Institute of Social and Economic Change, Bangalore (1972-73), Simon Visiting Professor, University of Manchester (June 1963), and Fellow, Centre for Advanced Study in the Behavioural Sciences, Standford, California (1964-65 and 1970-71). He was appointed as Andrew D. White Professor at Large, Correl University, U.S.A. (September 1970 to November 1976).

He was awarded D.Sc. (Hons.) by the University of Chicago (1971), D.Litt (Hon.) by the University of Mysore (1972), Doctorate Honoris Causa, University of Nice, France (1972), Foreign Honorary Member, American Academy of Arts and Sciences, Baston (1973), Honorary Member, American Philosophical Society, Philadelphia.

He has received several awards such as Rivers Memorial Medal (1955), S.C. Roy Memorial Medal (1958), Honorary Fellow of the Royal

Anthropological Society of Great Britain and Ireland (since 1964). He also received Dadabhai Naoroji Memorial Prize for social sciences other than economics (1971), T.H. Huxley Memorial Medal for 1976 from the Royal Anthropological Institute of Great Britain and Ireland, London (1976), Honorary Life Member of South Asian Association, Australia and Padma Bhushan, Government of India (1977). He delivered lectures in several foreign universities including the Tagore Memorial lectures in the universities of California, Berkeley (1963). He was the president of Anthropology and Archaeology Section of 44th Indian Science Congress in 1957 and was president of the Indian Sociological Society (1966-69).

He has done fieldwork in Coorg for two years (1940-42), in Tamilnadu for three months (1943), Andhra for three months (1944), Rampura in Mysore for 13 months (1948 and 1952). His chief interests lie in the study of regional culture of South India, religion and social change.

His authored and edited books are as follows:

Books

1. 1942: *Marriage and Family in Mysore*, New York Co., Bombay.
2. 1952: *Religion and Society among the Coorgs of South India*, Clarendon Press, Oxford, Asia Publishing House, Bombay, 1965 (Reprint).
3. 1962: *Caste in Modern India*, University of California Press, Berkeley.
4. 1962: *Caste in Modern India and Other Essays*, Asia Publishing House, Bombay, 1964 (Reprint).
5. 1966: *Social Change in Modern India*, University of California Press, California.
6. 1966: *The Remembered Village*, University of California Press, Berkeley and Oxford University Press, Delhi.
7. 1976: *Nation-Building in Independent India*, Oxford University Press, Delhi.

Edited Books

1. 1955: *India's Villages,* West Bengal Government Press, Calcutta, Asia Publishing House, Bombay, 1960, 1963 (Reprints).
2. 1959: *Method in Social Anthropology*, by A.R. Radcliffe-Brown, University of Chicago Press, Chicago, Asia Publishing House, Bombay, 1961 (Indian edition).
3. 1977: *Dimensions of Social Change in India*, Allied Publishers, Delhi (co-author).

Besides these books, Professor M.N. Srinivas has contributed more than five dozen research articles in journal of national and international repute.

Mysore has been veritable laboratory of social anthropological research for M.N. Srinivas. He wrote his first doctoral dissertation on 'Social Organisation of Mysore Families', which was published under the title "Marriage and Family in Mysore" (1942). He then submitted his doctoral dissertation on 'Religion and Society Among the Coorgs of South India' to Oxford University. This dissertation was published in book form under the same title, in 1952. In course of his field inquiry, he stayed in village Rampura for 10 months in 1948 and for two months in 1952. He paid several visits to the Coorgs village Rampura from time to time. The village is located at a distance of 25 miles south-east of Mysore city. In several research papers, the social system of Rampura has been explained. Under the influence of Radcliffe-Brown, he made structural study of relationship of roles and statuses of castes and their occupations.

Srinivas emphasized upon the unity of the village and observes that the village is a vertical entity made up of several horizontal layers each of which is a caste. The unity of the village is expressed by village officials supervising the rituals, village elders and dominant caste.

Concept of Sanskritization

Srinivas in his book, *Religion and Society among Coorgs of South India* (1952) developed the concept of Sanskritization to understand the process of Social Change taking place among the low caste Hindus/tribals and other groups in upward direction. According to him, Sanskritization is the process by which a low Hindu caste, or tribal, or other groups having lower status, changes its customs, rituals, ideology and way of life in the direction of a high and frequently twice-born caste (*Dwij-Jati*). Generally such changes are followed by a claim to a higher position in the caste hierarchy than that traditionally conceded to the claimant caste by the local community. The claim is usually made over a period of time, in fact, a generation or two, before arrival is conceded. Occasionally, a caste claims a position which its neighbours are not willing to concede. This type of disagreement between claimed and conceded status may be not only in the realm of opinion, but also in the more important realm of institutional practice. Thus, Harijan caste in Mysore do not accept cooked food and drinking water from the Smiths, who are certainly one of the touchable castes and, therefore, superior to Harijans. Even their claim to be Vishwakarma Brahmins is not accepted.

Similarly peasants (*Okkaligas*) and others such as shepherds (*Kurubas*) do not accept cooked food and water from Marka Brahmins, who are certainly included among Brahmins. Similarly, Coorgs are referred to as Jungle people (*Kadujana*), but Coorgs themselves contradict this reference and they claim themselves as true Kshatriyas and even Aryans. Srinivas has cited these examples all from Mysore state, but parallels can be cited from every part of India, because everywhere the tradition of caste hierarchy and associated statuses and roles come in to being.

Nowadays, the effect of Sanskritization can be seen in almost all villages of India. In Bihar, Rajwars, a scheduled caste, claim themselves as Rajvanshi Kshatriya. Similarly, Koyeris, a backward caste, claim themselves as Kushwaha Kshatriya and Dusadh, an another scheduled caste, claim themselves as Gahlout Kshatriya. Some of their members use titles like 'Singh' and 'Thakur' like Rajputs of the area. Previously, Koyeris did not wear sacred thread, but now they have started wearing it. Not only this, many lower Hindu castes have started a Brahminical way of life. They have given up non-vegetarian food items and unclean traditional occupations. They take food after performing bath and making prayers. They read *Ramayana* and *Hanuman Chalisa* daily as a part of religious duty like a Brahmins. Many of them have long beard and put *Tilak*-mark on their forehead. By claiming themselves as Kshatriya and observing the rituals like Brahmins, they claim their statuses like Brahmins and Kshatriyas of traditional India.

Sanskritization is generally accompanied by, and often results in, upward mobility for the caste in question, but mobility may also occur without Sanskritization and vice-versa. However, the mobility associated with Sanskritization results only in positional changes in the system and does not lead to any structural change. That is, a caste moves up, above its neighbours, and another comes down, but all this takes place in an essentially stable hierarchical order. The system itself does not change.

Sanskritization is not confined to Hindu castes, but also occurs among tribal and semitribal groups like Gonds, Oraons, Cheros of Central India and the Pahadis of the Himalayas. This usually results in the tribe undergoing Sanskritization claiming to be a caste and therefore, Hindu. In the traditional system, the only way to become a Hindu was to belong to a caste and the unit of mobility was usually a group, not an individual or a family.

However, Srinivas has emphasized upon the Brahminical model of Sanskritization and ignored the other models like Kshatriya, Vaishya and Sudra. Even the Brahminical model was derived from the Kannada, Tamil and Telugu Brahmins and not from Brahmin castes in other regions.

Concept of Westernization

Srinivas in his book, *Social Change in Modern India* (1966) has attempted to understand caste mobility and change in Indian society in-terms of concepts like Sanskritization, westernization, dominant caste and secularization.

Of two processes, Sanskritization and westernization, Sanskritization seems to have occurred throughout Indian history and still continues to exist. Westernization, on the other hand, refers to changes introduced into Indian Society during British rule and which continue in some cases with added momentum in independent India. Westernization, unlike Sanskritization, is not confined to any particular section of Indian population, and its importance, both in the number of people it affects and the ways in which it affects them, is steadily increasing. The achievement of independence has in some ways quickened the process of westernization, and it is not unlikely that independence was a necessary precondition of such acceleration.

It is beyond doubt that British rule produced radical and lasting changes in Indian society and culture. It was unlike any previous period in Indian history as the British brought with them new technology, institutions, knowledge, beliefs and values. The new technology and the revolution in communications enabled the British to integrate the country as never before in its history. During the 19th century, the British slowly laid the foundations of modern state by surveying land, settling the revenue, creating a modern bureaucracy, army, police, courts, schools, colleges, universities, railways, posts and telegraphs, roads and canals and printing press. The profound and many sided changes brought about by them in Indian society and culture deserve a volume in itself. One obvious result was that books and journals with schools made possible the transmission of modern as well as traditional knowledge to large number of Indians. Knowledge was now no longer the privilege of a few hereditary groups. The news papers made the people, dwelling in different parts of the world, aware of each other.

Christian missionaries from Europe knew India long before the arrival of British. However, during the early days of the East India Company, the entry of European missionaries into India was banned, which was lifted in 1813 when British parliament permitted them to enter the country under a new system of licensing. This eventually threw the entire subcontinent open to missionary activity.

In the first half of 19th century, the British, with the support of enlightened Indian opinion, abolished such institutions as *Suttee* or *Sati* (1829), female infanticide and human sacrifice and slavery (1833). The

Indo-British impact was profound, many sided and fruitful.

Srinivas has used the term westernization to characterize the changes brought about in Indian society and culture as a result of over 150 years of British rule. The term also subsumes at different levels — technology, institutions, ideology and values.

Westernization, Urbanization And Industrialisation

Srinivas has distinguished conceptually between the westernization and the two other processes usually concomitant with it — urbanization and industrialization.

There is common consensus among the scholars that industrial revolution resulted in an increase in the rate of urbanization and highly industrialized areas are treated as highly urbanized, but urbanization is not a simple function of industrialization. We have references about urbanities of Indus valley culture and places dealing with ancient civilizations of India like Gaya, Prayag, Varanasi etc. Thus, urban cities were existing even in preindustrial world.

While the most westernised groups are generally found in big cities, a caution must be uttered against equating westernization with urbanization. Even in a country such as India, it is possible to come across groups inhabiting rural areas which are more westernized in their style of life than many urban groups. The former are to be found in areas where plantation or commercial crops are grown or which have a tradition of supplying recruits to the Indian army.

Westernization results not only in the introduction of new institutions (for example, news papers, elections, christian missions etc.), but also in fundamental changes in old institutions. Thus, while India had schools long before the arrival of the British, they were different from British introduced schools in that they had been restricted to upper caste children and transmitted mostly traditional knowledge. Other institutions such as army, civil service, law, courts etc. were similarly affected.

Westernization and Modernization

A popular term for the changes brought about in a non-western country by contact, direct or indirect with a western country is 'modernization'. Daniel Lerner in his book, *The Passing of Traditional Society* (1958: 45-49), has opted modernization over westernization after considering the suitability of both. According to him, modernization includes a disquieting positivist spirit touching public institutions as well as private aspirations. But positivist spirit is not enough, a revolution in communication is essential. Modernization is also marked by increasing urbanization which has, in turn, resulted in the spread of literacy. The urbanization has tended to enhance media exposure and finally enhanced media exposure is associated with wider economic participation (per capita income) and political participation (voting). Modernization also implies social mobility. A mobile society has to encourage rationality for the calculus of choice. It shapes individual behaviour and conditions its rewards. People come to see the social future as manipulable rather than ordained and their personal prospects in terms of achievement rather than heritage.

Modernization means only an increased effectiveness in goal attainment with no increase in the rationalization of the goal setting process. Modernization, thus, involves the rationalization of ends, which means that the goals chosen by a society should be rational and the subject of discussion. It needs to be pointed out here the social goals are, in the final analysis, the expression of value preferences and therefore, non-rational. The public discussion of goals can in no way guarantee their rationality. Rationality can only be predicted of the means but not of the ends of social action.

The term westernization, unlike modernization, is ethically neutral. It does not carry the implication that it is good or bad, whereas modernization is normally used in the sense that it is good.

Concept of Secularization

Srinivas is of opinion that British rule brought with it a process of secularization of Indian social life and culture, a tendency that gradually became stranger with the development of communications, growth of towns, cities, increased spatial mobility and spread of education. The two World Wars and Mahatma Gandhi's civil disobedience campaigns, both socially and politically mobilized the masses, also contributed to increased secularization. After independence, there began a deepening as well as broadening of the secularization process, as witnessed in such measures as the declaration of India as a secular state, the constitutional recognition of equality of all citizens before law, the introduction of universal adult suffrage, and the undertaking of a programme of planned development.

As mentioned earlier, that Sanskritization is also spreading and it seems paradoxical that both sanskritization and secularization are gaining ground in modern India. Of the two, secularization is more general process affecting all Indians, while Sanskritization affects only Hindus and tribal groups. Broadly, it would be true to say that secularization is more marked among the urban and educated groups, and Sanskritization among the lower Hindu castes and tribes. It is necessary, however,to reiterate that one of the results of a country of westernization — secularization is subsumed under westernization — is a reinterpreted Hinduism in which Sanskritic elements are predominant.

The term secularization implies that what was previously regarded as religious is now ceasing to be such. It also implies a process of differentiation which results in various aspects of a society, economic, political, legal and moral, becoming increasingly discrete in relation to each other. The distinction between church and state, and the Indian concept of secular state, both assume the existence of such differentiation.

Another essential element in secularization is rationalism, a comprehensive expression applied to various theoretical and practical tendencies which aim to interpret the universe purely in terms of thought or which aim to regulate individual and social life in accordance with the principles of reason and to eliminate as far as possible or to relegate to the background everything irrational. Rationalism involves, among many other things, the replacement of traditional beliefs and ideas by modern knowledge.

Hindus were more affected by the secularization process than any other religious groups in India. The concepts of pollution and purity of Hinduism were greatly weakened as a result of variety of factors. Different sections of Hindus are affected in different degrees. The effect of secularization can be seen in daily life, rituals, ceremonies, occupations etc.

Concept of Dominant Caste

M.N. Srinivas developed the concept of dominant caste on the basis of his long and continued study in Rampura village in his paper entitled, 'Dominant Caste in Rampura' (*American Anthropologist*, Vol.61, No.1, pp. 1-16). According to him, a feature of rural life in many parts of India is the existence of dominant land owning caste. For a caste to be dominant, it should own a sizable amount of the arable land locally available, have strength of numbers and occupy a high place in local hierarchy. When a caste has all the attributes of dominance, it may be said to enjoy decisive dominance. Occasionally there may be one dominant caste in a village. Thus, according to him, a caste may be said to be dominant when it preponderates numerically over the other castes and when it also wields preponderant economic and political power. A large and powerful caste group can be most easily dominant if its position in local caste hierarchy is not too low.

Srinivas, in the light of caste ethnography in Rampura, suggests that the peasants in Rampura enjoy all the elements of dominance. The identification of the dominant caste gives a better understanding of the features of rural social organisation, as the council of the dominant tries to create a structure of authority within each group it has to deal with. The dominant caste plays a very important role in the settlement of disputes, which are settled by the traditional village and caste council and not by modern statutory Panchayat. A caste council usually has jurisdiction over all the castes living in a village. The leaders of dominant caste not only settle disputes between members of different caste but are also frequently approached by non-dominant castes for settlement of their inter-caste and even domestic disputes.

According to Srinivas, there are four factors related to dominant caste. They are: numerical strength, control of resources, i.e. land, possession of political power, and socio-religious status. New factors affecting dominance have emerged in the last eighty years or so. Western education, jobs in the administration, and urban sources of income are all significant in contributing to the prestige and power of particular caste groups in the village. The introduction of adult franchise and Panchayatiraj (local self government at village, tehsil, and district level) since independence has resulted in giving a new sense of self respect and power to low castes particularly Harijans, who enjoy reservation of seats in all elected bodies from village to union parliament. The long term implications of these changes are probably even more important, especially in those villages where there are enough Harijans to sway the local balance of power one way or the other. In the traditional system, it was possible for a small number of people belonging to a high caste to wield authority over the entire village, when they owned a large quantity of arable land and had a high ritual position. Now, however, in many parts of rural India, power has passed into hands of numerically large land owning peasant castes. It is likely to remain there for some time, except in villages where Harijans are numerically strong and are also taking advantages of the new educational and other opportunities available to them. Endemic factionalism in the dominant caste is also another threat to its continued enjoyment of power.

No longer is dominance a purely local matter in rural India. A caste group which has only a family or two in particular village, but which enjoys decisive dominance in the wider region, will still count locally, because of the net work of ties binding it to its dominant relatives. What is equally important is that others in the village will be aware of the existence of this net work. Countrywise, a caste, which enjoys dominance in only one village, will find that it has to reckon with the caste which enjoys regional dominance.

S.C. Dubey (1961) and B.K. Roy Burman (1978) have disagreed with Srinivas over his concept of dominant caste. S.C. Dube holds that instead of any caste group, an individual dominates in the society. He is of opinion that power remains concentrated in a few individuals rather than diffused in the caste. Roy Burman has used the concept of dominant communities in place of Srinivas' concept of dominant caste. According to him, the dominant communities have several dimensions, such as control over resources, social status, maintenance of law etc.

Concept of Spread

In order to understand the Hinduism of India, M.N. Srinivas developed the concept of spread in his book, *Religion and Society among Coorgs of South India* (1952). According to him, Hinduism has a long history in course of which it has spread over the whole India. Buddhism, in origin a Hindu schism, is now religion of great part of Asia. While explaining the concept of spread, Srinivas has talked about four types of Hinduism. They are: (i) local Hinduism, (ii) regional Hinduism, (iii) all India or national Hinduism and (iv) peninsular Hinduism.

According to Srinivas, local Hinduism has a local spread, in which Hindus inhabiting in a local areas share common beliefs, rituals and performances. Regional Hinduism has a more restricted spread over a particular regions in terms of common cultural, linguistic and geographical boundary within a country. According to him, in Malabar, Coorg proper is a smaller area within it. All India Hinduism is common Hindu beliefs, rituals and festivals shared by all Hindu inhabitants of the nation. For instance, places like Gaya, Ganga Sagar, Kurukshetra Rameshwaram, etc. attract Hindus of all parts of the country on different religious occasions. The great Hindu festivals like Holi, Dashara, Dipawali, etc. are celebrated by Hindus inhabiting in all parts of the country. Peninsular Hinduism spreads over the entire part of Indian peninsula.

Concept of Vertical and Horizontal Caste Solidarity

M.N. Srinivas in his books, *Caste in Modern India* (1962) and *Caste in Modern India and Other Essays* (1962), opines that *Varna* model has produced a wrong and distorted image of caste. He considers it necessary for the sociologists to free himself from the hold of *Varna* model, if he wishes to understand the caste system, specially in the middle regions which are missed under the influence of *Varna* model. Although he avoids giving a clearcut definition of caste, he does believe that the structural basis of Hindu society is caste. He examines the interrelationship between various facets of castes and subcastes in common unity and regionwise setting.

Observing the diversities of castes in India, M.N. Srinivas propounds the concept of 'vertical' and 'horizontal' solidarity of Indian caste system. He observes some common elements of local culture shared by all castes living in a region from the highest to the lowest. Thus, the Brahmin and Harijan of a region speak common language, observe some common festivals, and share some common deities and beliefs. Srinivas calls this unity of castes as 'Vertical solidarity'. Horizontal solidarity is contrary to vertical solidarity. In horizontal solidarity, members of a single caste share common rituals, beliefs, traditions etc. irrespective of their regions and languages. Thus, Brahmins of south, north and central India share more or less common Sanskritic traditions and rituals. Srinivas calls this solidarity among the members of a caste as horizontal solidarity.

Contribution on Village Study

The year 1955 was a landmark in the history of social anthropological researches on village in India, because in this year three books namely *Indian Village* by S.C. Dube, *Village India* (ed) by McLim Marriot, an American anthropologists and *India's Village* (ed) by Srinivas came into existence. Srinivas (ed), book, *India's Village* (1955) consists of thirteen articles, contributed by 5 American, 5 British and 3 Indian anthropologists. American anthropologists were: Beals, Mandelbaum, Gough, Marriot and Martin. British anthropologists as contributor of articles in the book were: Bailey, Collin, Carstairs, Miller and Newell. Indian anthropologists were: Dube, Sharma and Srinivas. Except one paper by Mandelbaum, all papers were based on fieldwork conducted by them in different village of India. These papers reveal several important concepts as well as preliminary methodological and theoretical leads concerning rural sociology. The concepts of Sanskritization, dominant caste, universalization, parochialization, unity and extension, caste ties, intercaste ties etc. are among the major leads which found fuller treatment in latter works on village studies.

LALITA PRASAD VIDYARTHI (1931-1985)

L.P. Vidyarthi was born on 28th February, 1931 in a village of Patna District. He matriculated from City High School, now known as Rajendra Vidyalaya, Gaya in 1946 with first division. He passed his inter examination from Patna College with high Second division in 1948. He passed Bachelor of Arts Examination (Geography Hons) with first class from the same institution in 1950. He was admitted to Patna University for his Master of Arts courses in Geography and passed M.A. Part I Examination of Patna University with first class in 1951. He could not accomplish courses in M.A. Part II of Patna University, because he was awarded Government of Bihar Scholarship in Anthropology in 1951 to be admitted at Lucknow University in Anthropology. He did M.A. in Anthropology from Lucknow University in 1953 with High Second Class, but had topped the list among all successful candidates and was awarded by Indrajit Singh Gold Medal of Lucknow University.

He was awarded the Ford Foundation Fellowship and University of Chicago fellowship in 1957-58 to conduct field researches among Sauria Paharia of Rajmahal hill of Santhal Pargana (now in Shahebganj district) for his Doctoral dissertation, under the supervision of Robert Redfield. His doctoral degree was awarded in 1958 from Chicago University.

Dr. Vidyarthi was appointed as Lecturer in anthropology at Ranchi, then under the University of Bihar in 1953 and served this post till 1956. From 1957 to 1958, he was Doctoral Fellow at Chicago university. Coming back, he again joined the Department of Anthropology (Ranchi) Bihar University as Lecturer and Head in 1958 and in the same year he became Reader and Head of the same institution. In 1968, Dr. Vidyarthi became University Professor and Head, Department of Anthropology, Ranchi University, Ranchi.

Professor Vidyarthi's successful efforts raised the status of Department of Anthropology, Ranchi University, Ranchi as U.G.C.'s Department of Special Assistance (DSA) in 1978 and he became the Director of this centre. The status of DSA was raised by the establishment of Centre of Advanced Study (CAS) in Anthropology, Ranchi University, Ranchi, on 2nd October, 1985. This was the highest status achieved by a post-graduate department and Professor Vidyarthi's conscious and continuous efforts could achieve this success easily. This was the only department in the subject anthropology in India which could got opportunity to wear the crown of 'Centre of Advanced Study'. In this way, Professor Vidyarthi was the luckiest and most successful person in his attempts. His sound footing in research methodology and theories compelled the reviewers to plead U.G.C., Government of India, to provide the highest status to the Department of Anthropology, Ranchi University.

When U.G.C., Government of India, declared this Department as C.A.S. on 2nd October 1985, this was the happiest moment in the life of Professor Vidyarthi over his grand success. But he could not direct C.A.S. in the Department for a period more than two months. When

U.G.C.'s letter declared Centre of Advanced Study, Professor Vidyarthi was not well at that time, but he came to the Department to communicate this happy news among his colleagues, teachers, researchers and students of the department. During *Durga Puja* vacation of 1985, his condition became more and more worst. He was advised by doctors of RMCH to take rest and to go to AIIMS, Delhi for his treatment, but he could not follow their advice. Even in the period of serious illness, he could not stop visiting the department, guiding the researchers and replying the letters to colleagues of India and abroad. Professor Vidyarthi was admitted at RMCH in unconscious state, where he breathed his last in the morning of 1st December 1985. His death was mourned over the whole country by the social scientists as well as anthropologists of abroad. Sorrowful news of his death was broadcasted by All India Radio and B.B.C. London in which his contributions and services in the development of Indian anthropology and world anthropology were highlighted in brief.

Professor Vidyarthi was a good teacher and he used to teach anthropological theory to the students very clearly.

He was winner of several fellowships and awards such as Government of Bihar scholarship in anthropology (1950), Indrajit Singh Gold Medal, University of Lucknow (1953), Fullbright and Smithmundt Scholarship (1956-57), Ford Foundation Fellowship (1957), University of Chicago Fellowship (1957), Foreign Fellow, American Anthropological Association (1958), Indo-G.D.R. Cultural Exchange Fellowship (1959), Indo-USSR Cultural Exchange Fellowship (1959), Rome Civic Reception Bronze Medal (1976).

He was president of Folklore Section, All India Folk Culture Conference, Bombay (1959), Anthropology and Archaeology Section, Indian Science Congress, Varanasi (1968), Indian Social Science Association (1959-74), Indian Anthropological Association (1970-till death), International Union of Anthropological and Ethnological Sciences (1973-78), and International Congress of Anthropological and Ethnological Sciences (1978).

He was Chairman of All India Social Science Congress, USEFI, New Delhi (1960), Study Team on Tribal Labour, Indian Commission on Labour (1968), Standing Committee on Anthropology, Indian Council of Social Science Research (1966-75), Task Force on the Development of Tribal Areas, Planning Commission, Government of India (1972), and Committee on the Identification of Primitive Tribes of India, Ministry of Home Affairs (1974).

He was member of Panel on Backward Classes, Planning Commission, Government of India (1964), Founder member of Indian Council of

Social Science Research, New Delhi (1974), Advisory Committee, Anthropological Survey of India (1968-71), Steering Committee on the Backward Classes, Planning Commission, Government of India (1972), Central Tribal Research Institute Advisory Committee (1973), Committee for the Development of Primitive Tribes of Andaman and Nicobar Islands, Government of India (1976), Panel on Scheduled Castes, Ministry of Home, Government of India (1978).

He was editor of *Journal of Social Research* (Ranchi) since 1958, *Indian Anthropologist* (Delhi) 1971, *Research Journal of Ranchi University* (Ranchi) 1964, *Sociological Bulletin* (Ghaziabad) 1966, *Folklore* (Calcutta) 1966, etc.

He directed many large scale Research Projects like the Urban Pattern of Ranchi (1960), From Simple Economy to Industrialisation: A Techno-cultural Implication of Change of India (1958), Tribal Indebtedness in Two Oraon Villages (1962), The Birhor Action Research Project (1966), Monographic Study of Munda Village: Ghaghra (1965), Changes in Leadership Pattern in Tribal Society in India (1966-68), Student Unrest in Chota Nagpur (1969-70), Sacred Complex in Kashi (1972-76), Restudy of Kharia (1975-77), the Cultural Linguistic Zones of Bihar (1976), Revival of Indigenous Nutritive Dietary Habits and Recipes in four Cultural Linguistic Zones of Bihar (1975-77), From Cradle to Playground Socialization Process in Tribal Bihar (1982-84) and Techno-cultural Implication of Industrialization in Central India (1982-84).

His important books are:

1. *Sacred Complex in Hindu Gaya,* Asia Publishing House, New York, 1961.
2. *The Maler: Nature-Man-Spirit Complex in Hill Tribe of Bihar*, Bookland Private Ltd., Calcutta, 1963.
3. *Manava Shastra Ki Rup Rekha* (with K.S. Mathur and I. Singh), Kedarnath Ramnath, Meerut City, 1963.
4. *Cultural Contours of Tribal Bihar,* Punthi Pustak, Calcutta, 1964.
5. *Ghaghra: A Village in Chota Nagpur,* Census of India, Ministry of Home Affairs, New Delhi, 1966.
6. *Bhartiya Nagar,* Rajmahal Prakashan, New Delhi, 1966.
7. *Cultural Configuration of Ranchi*, Planning Commission Publication, 1969.
8. *Socio-Cultural Implications of Industrialization in India: A Case Study of Tribal Bihar*, Planning Commission Publication, 1970.
9. *Dynamics of Tribal Leadership in Bihar,* Kitabmahal Allahabad, 1976.
10. *Student's Unrest in Chota Nagpur*, Punthi Pustak, Calcutta, 1976.

11. *Bhartiya Adivasi: Unaki Samajik Aur Sanskritic Prishtha Bhumi,* Hindi Samiti, U.P. Government, Lucknow, 1976.
12. *Tribal Culture of India* (with B.K. Roi), Concept Publishing Co., New Delhi, 1976.
13. *Peasant Organisation in India: A Study of Voluntary Organisation in Tribal Bihar* (IL & FAD Report), Council of Social and Cultural Research, Bihar, Ranchi, 1977.
14. *Rise of Anthropology in India: A Social Science Orientation* (two volumes), Concept Publishing Co., New Delhi, 1977.
15. *Harijan To-Day* (with N. Mishra), Classical Publishers, New Delhi, 1977.
16. *Sacred Complex in Kashi* (with B.N. Saraswati & M. Jha), Concept Publishing Company, New Delhi, 1978.
17. *The Kharia – Then and Now* (with V.S. Upadhyay), Concept Publishing Company, New Delhi, 1979.
18. *Trends in World Anthropology*, Concept Publishing Company, New Delhi, 1980.
19. *Rise of World Anthropology*, Concept Publishing Co., New Delhi 1980.

Edited Books

1. *Anthropology and Tribal Welfare in India*, Council of Social and Cultural Research, Bihar, 1960.
2. *Indian Anthropology in Action, Council of Social and Cultural Research*, Bihar, 1960.
3. *Bihar Ke Adivasi,* College Centre, Patna, 1961.
4. *Aspects of Religion in Indian Society*, Kedarnath Ramnath, Meerut City, 1961.
5. *Leadership in India*, Asia Publishing House, Bombay, 1967.
6. *Applied Anthropology in India*, Kitab Mahal, Allahabad, 1968.
7. *Tension, Conflict and Social Change in India*, Punthi Pustak, Calcutta, 1968.
8. *Tribal Labour: Agriculture and Industrial, National Commission on Labour*, Manager of Publications, New Delhi, 1968.
9. *Gandhi and Social Science in India* (with B.N. Sahay and B.K. Srivastava), Book and Hive, New Delhi, 1970.
10. *Bihar in Folklore Study* (with G. Choubay), Indian Publication, Calcutta, 1971.
11. *Researches in Complex Societies in India* (with B.C. Agarwal) Indian Academy of Social Science, New Delhi, 1973.
12. *Essays in Indian Folklore*, Indian Publications, Calcutta, 1973.

13. *Applied Anthropology and Development in India* (with B.N. Sahay) National Publication, New Delhi, 1979.
14. *Research in Prehistory and Physical Anthropology in India* (with B.B Lal and I.P. Singh) in three volumes, Classical Publications, New Delhi, 1978.
15. *Growth and Development of Anthropology in Bihar*, Classical Publications, New Delhi, 1978.

Besides these books, Professor Vidyarthi contributed nearly 150 research articles in different journals of India and abroad. Throughout his life, he struggled to establish anthropology as integrated discipline, of Social-Cultural anthropology, Prehistoric archaeology and Physical anthropology, Folk-lore and Applied and Action anthropology. His major contributions have been discussed under several sub-headings in the coming pages.

Contribution on Sacred Complex Study

Vidyarthi in his book, *Sacred Complex in Hindu Gaya* (1961) describes in detail three analytical concepts: a sacred geography, a set of sacred performances, and a corps of sacred specialists. These three concepts conceived collectively are termed as sacred complex, the application of which methodologically has been done in relation to the study of sacred city Gaya. In the study of sacred city of Gaya as a part of Hindu civilization, certain broad based concepts propounded by Redfield (great and little traditions, folk urban continuum) and Milton Singer (cultural centres, cultural performances, cultural specialists, cultural-media etc.) are tested. His hypotheses had been:

(i) That the sacred complex – a happy synthesis of sacred geography, sacred performances, and sacred specialists – of a Hindu place of pilgrimage reflected a level of continuity, compromise and combination between great and little traditions.
(ii) That the sacred specialists of a place with their distinctive style of life transmit certain elements of great tradition to the rural population of India, and
(iii) That the sacred complex has been in the process of modification and transformation.

In the study of sacred complex of Gaya, Vidyarthi is clear in his stand with certain necessary specifications. Firstly, for him the reference has been made to the Hindu civilization, and not to the Indian civilization.

Secondly, in place of culture, he applies the term sacred to evolve the analytical concepts of sacred geography, sacred performances and sacred specialists. Thirdly, he introduces the term sacred complex to indicate the integrative pattern, envisaging all the sacred elements.

The period of author's visit was from 1948 to 1956. The sacred complex of Gaya is predominantly great traditional. The author finds out a peculiar process of combination and compromise in the past leading to the development of Hinduism. In the same way, the sacred complex provided a meeting place for different kinds of people, traditions, castes, sects, class and status and nourished a sense of Indian unity, even at a time, when the spirit of nationalism was lacking. And finally, the sacred complex was observed to be undergoing secondary urbanisation, which remains to be studied in future. A number of rich and valuable appendices are attached at length, which further enhances the utility of the book.

Apart from intensive study of Gaya, Vidyarthi undertook short trip to sacred places like Banaras, Bhubaneshwar, Puri, Deoghar, Dwarika, Rishikesh, Haridwar, Rameshwaram, etc. and paid visits to many rural temples and bathing centres. He also organised a seminar on sacred complex in India in the Department of Anthropology, Ranchi University, with the collaboration of ICSSR in 1973. The findings of the seminar has been published by the Department of Anthropology, Ranchi University.

Contribution on Nature-Man-Spirit Complex Study

Professor Vidyarthi in his book, *The Maler: Nature-Man-Spirit Complex in a Hill Tribe of Bihar* (1963) developed a methodological frame- work to conduct analytical study of complex phenomenon of Nature-Man-Spirit in the life of tribals residing in hilly and forested area. He studied the Sauria Paharia tribe of Rajmahal Hill of present Sahebganj district. Sauria Paharia are also termed as Maler. Professor Vidyarth in course of his several visits to the Malers observed that their life was revolving round phenomenon of nature-man-spirit complex.

Under the sub-heading 'Nature', Vidyarthi explored the interaction between the Malers and their habitat, i.e., ecological setting of hill and forest. He observed that Malers were dependent upon the hill and forest for their livelihood and survival. They practised shifting or Jhum or Kallu cultivation in the forest. They collected fruits, fuels, roots, herbal medicine etc. from the forest. Forest also provided hunting animals to be hunted or trapped. Not only this, different spirits of the Malers also took abode in and around the forest. In this way, the life of Malers was dependent upon forest for manifold purposes. According to Vidyarthi,

Kallu cultivation of Malers is marked by a series of processes. They were: (i) selection of the field and cutting of forest, (ii) burning and removing of wood, (iii) sowing, (iv) weeding, (v) watching, (vi) harvesting, (vii) worshipping, and (viii) merry-making.

Under the sub-heading 'Man', Vidyarthi describes the social institutions of Sauria Paharis such as marriage and family. They lack clan organisation, but he has attempted, in brief, the social structure and kinship system of the Malers. He also explains the process of socialization, courses of life and personality formation of the Malers.

Under the sub-heading 'Spirit', Vidyarthi deals with the concept of spirit and supernatural world, which every Maler has in his mind. The different types of spirits are termed by the common term Gossaiyan among the Malers. The Maler children are instructed about the Gossaiyan form the very beginning. The term Gossaiyan is a household word and is used to denote a group of spirits that are believed to guide their destiny.

Vidyarthi observes the prevalence of ancestor worship among the Malers. They have faith that the spirits of dead ancestors have powers to decide their destiny. Malers are very cautious in performing the rites and observing ceremonies carefully. The newly dead persons are believed to have joined the earlier dead ancestors. The spirits of ancestors are called and worshipped annually, or occasionally, or when one is economically able to perform it. They believe that unless the spirit of newly dead ancestors is worshipped, it continues to exist and appears in dream and harasses family members to expedite the preparation for worship, mortuary, sacrifice and feast.

Malers have too many *Gossaiyans* like *Beru Gossaiyan* (Sun-God), *Belpu Gossaiyan* (Moon-God), *Bindke Gossaiyan* (stars) etc.

With the methodological approach of sacred complex study, as developed by him in 1961 on Hindu Gaya, he describes the religious activities of the Maler. As referred to earlier, the sacred complex is a happy synthesis of sacred geography, sacred specialists and sacred performances. Sacred geography of the Maler envisages two things: (i) sacred area and (ii) sacred centre. The sacred area of the Maler includes the whole village and its vicinity. The household deity, who is generally their ancestral spirit, resides in the kitchen, or part of the hut or gods of village reside in the village or on the outskirts of the village. The god of forest lives in nearby jungle, whereas every stream, river, ditch, hill, and old tree are the abodes of numerous other deities.

Sacred centres are sacred spots where varieties of rituals and religious activities are carried on. A Maler values three village deities very much. They are: *Chal Gossain, Raksi Gossain,* and *Kando Gossain.*

Chal Gossain resides in the *Jaherthan* or sacred grove. On every occasion, sacrifices are offered to him for the well-being and prosperity of the village. *Raksi Gossain* resides in *Raksithan*, somewhat away from the village. He wards off any evil influences likely to enter the village. Sacrifices are offered to him by village priest on the occasion of annual worship. *Kando Gossain* is the presiding deity of the village. His abode is a wooden seat placed in the house of *Kando-Manjhi* or placed centrally in the village under some thatched structure.

Among the Malers, other sacred centres are *Manjhi-than*, where the village deity, *Jhanda Gossain*, resides; *Singpate Nadu*, who is worshipped at the *Bandana* festival, is represented by two black stones; *Chalnadu* is located on a hill top, *Maler Gossain* is represented by 11 cylindrical stones; *Kanhaiya Nadu* is stream spirit and *Tudu Nadu* is the spirit of tiger.

Among Maler, there are three sacredotal functionaries at the village level. They are: *Kando Manjhi, Kotwar* and *Chalwe*. The *Kando Manjhi* controls and directs the ritualistic life of the people. He is supposed to be chosen by the God. For his selection, villagers gather in the middle of the village in front of the house of secular headman. Incense is burnt there and the *Kotwar* prays and worships to invoke the deities for the selection of the *Kando-Majhi*. If everything goes well, it is believed that the *Gossain* has accepted him. He is then formally declared *Kando-Manjhi* or the head priest of the village.

Kotwar is assistant to *Kando Manjhi* or head priest. He performs the actual worship including offering of sacrifices to the deity. A Kotwar has life tenure and is selected in the same manner as his chief. At the time of his selection *Kando-Manjhi* invokes the help of *Gossaiyan*. *Chalwe* is the assistant of the *Kotwar*. He is also selected in the same manner as the other two religious dignitaries.

Sacred performances of the Maler include worships offered to *Gossaiyan* on different occasions and rituals observed in those connection. The Malers take help of the sacred specialists at the time of performing rituals and offering worships. The objects of sacrifice vary from egg to buffaloes. The other articles of *Puja* are vermilion, sun-fried rice, flowers, wild-fruits, new cereals, liquor etc.

Thus, Vidyarthi evolved a methodological approach (Nature-Man-Spirit complex) to analyse the tribal way of life in terms of their ecological setting, social institutions and spirit world.

Other Contributions on Tribal Studies

Vidyarthi studied a tribal village named Ghaghra under the auspices of

Census operation in 1961. The study of this Munda village reflects as to how *Manjhi*, a section of Munda tribe, has adopted the Hindu style of life and has become a caste.

Vidyarthi edited a book under the title, *Aspects of Religion in Indian Society* (1961). In this book Vidyarthi contributed a paper on sacred complex of a tribal village. The other contributors were Gopala Sarana, McKim Marriot, Aiyappan, K.N. Sharma, R.S. Srivastava, Carstairs, Mathur, I.P. Singh, T.N. Madan, Yogesh Atal, Chattopadhyay, T.R. Singh, Surjit Sinha, K.N. Sahay. This book covers a wide range, from the way religion is practised by folk in different parts of India to an analysis of certain complex beliefs present among tribal people and which have become modified on account of contact with Hinduism.

His book, *Cultural Contours of Tribal Bihar* (1966) explains the historical, geographical, and social background of the tribes of Chota Nagpur. Some concepts like unity and extension, sanskritization and desanskritisation, tribalisation and detribalisation have also been attempted in the context of tribal Bihar. The book also explains the factors responsible for bringing changes in tribal societies of Bihar.

His paper, 'Cultural Types in Tribal India with Special Reference to Tribal Bihar' (1966), deals with the classification of Bihar's tribes into four cultural types. In evolving the cultural type, significant factors are: (i) economy, (ii) ecology, (iii) socio-cultural adaptation to ecology and economy, (iv) religious beliefs, and (v) emerging contemporary situations. The four cultural types of tribal Bihar are:

(1) Hunting and gathering type: Birhors
(2) Cultivation type: Hill – Sauria Pahariya or Maler, Plain – Munda, Oraon, Ho, Santhal
(3) Artisan type: Lohera, Mahalis, Karmalis, Chickbraik
(4) Industrial and urban labour type.

Professor Vidyarthi made a field visit of Andaman and Nicobar Islands with his post-graduate students in 1970. He published two papers on Andamanese and Nicobarese in the *Journal of Social Research* and each in vol. 1 and 2 of 1971. His first paper, entitled, 'Cultural Diversities in Andaman and Nicobar Islands', explains the diverse-cultural groups of the Islands and makes a comparison of their social, cultural, religious, political, and linguistics aspects of way of life. His another paper, 'Ranchi Tribals in Andaman and Nicobar' describes the migration of Oraon and Munda tribes of Chota Nagpur in the Islands of Andamans and Nicobar in search of livelihood. They have settled there since generations and have played significant role in making of modern Andaman.

Professor Vidyarthi and Dr. B.K. Roy, wrote a famous book under the title, *Tribal Culture of India* (1976). Taking data through secondary sources at India level, the authors have successfully attempted to present a comparative and comprehensive views on social, economic, political and religious life of Indian tribes. The book also presents a good amount of informations on folklore, art, craft, courses of life, personality structure etc. in the context of tribal India. The book highlights the characteristics of tribal village, matriliny in and polyandry in tribal India, approaches, planning and programmes for tribal development and culture change in tribes of India. This book is regarded as base book for I.A.S. examination.

On History of Indian Anthropology and Trends of Anthropological Researches

Professor Vidyarthi in his paper on, 'Social Anthropological Researches in India', published in *Journal of Social Research,* Vol. IX, No. 1, 1966, has reviewed the rise of social anthropological researches in Indian context. According to him, the formative phase of Indian history was from 1774 to 1919. Another constructive phase was from 1920–1949. The third phase known as analytical began in 1950 and is going on. Vidyarthi's classifications of history of Indian anthropology differ from earlier classification made by Dr. D.N. Majumdar, who treated the three main phases of development of anthropology in India as:

1. Formative period	1774-1911
2. Constructive phase	1912-1937
3. Critical phase	1938 onward.

Vidyarthi held that Dr. Majumdar treated the publication of monograph on Munda by S.C. Roy (1912) as beginning of constructive period, but this was not a major change in anthropological study. The constructive phase began in 1920 with the establishment of teaching of anthropology in Calcutta University. However, both agreed that formative phase began in 1774 with the establishment of Royal Asiatic Society of Bengal, under the chairmanship of Sir William Jones to explore man and his society. The beginning of the third phase, the critical phase, has been conceived by Majumdar from 1938, when Indian and British anthropologists met on the occasion of Silver Jubilee of Indian Science Congress in Lahore and took stock of anthropological developments in India. Incidentally, that year also witnessed the publication of his problem oriented monograph on Ho tribe (1937), which was submitted as doctoral thesis to the Cambridge University. Vidyarthi viewed beginning of analytical period in 1950, when Indian anthropologists under the influence of American anthropologists started the tradition of village studies and analysis of data in terms of certain proposed concepts like great and little traditions, universalisation and parochialisation, unity and extensions, sanskritization, dominant caste, vertical and horizontal solidarity etc.

In his second paper on 'Researches in Social Sciences in India' published in the *Journal of Social Science Information,* International Social Science Council, Paris, Vol. V, No. 1, 1966, Vidyarthi referred to the recent trends in social anthropology and pointed out the approaches of anthropologists to integrate the knowledge of various disciplines for a proper understanding of men and his society. He made special mention of the various efforts of the social scientists to study the problems of tribal and rural societies in India.

In another paper entitled, 'Social anthropology in India since Independence' in *Man and Society* (1972), Vidyarthi examined the rise and growth of social anthropology in India and concluded that anthropological researches in India, organised and developed under the British influence, were flourishing under the influence of, and stimulus from America and the other countries of the west. The administrative anthropology of colonial pattern was getting an orientation of academic interest and with this, a new quest for interdisciplinary approach to understand the various dimensions of complex Indian societies had become evident.

In his trend report submitted to ICSSR on the Tribal Studies in India (1972), Vidyarthi elaborately viewed researches in different tribal zones of India. As regards anthropological researches in the north-eastern Himalayas, he found that the area had relatively been better explored, as a series of ethnographic publications had been made by the British administrators, missionaries, and anthropologists. Ethnographic works in the central and north-western Himalayas revealed that very little ethnographic work was done in this area till independence. In post independence era, the ethnography of these regions received attention from scholars of the universities of Lucknow, Chandigarh and Delhi, Census Operations and the Anthropological Survey of India. The tribal belt of central India had been exposed to anthropological researches and extensive ethnographic work had been done. About the tribal studies in western India, he felt that the research tradition in Gujarat had been quite strong. Regarding the tribal studies in South India, he viewed that they had an early beginning, but anthropology at analytical level could not flourish there due to lack of academic recognition till recently. While reviewing the existing material, Vidyarthi had pointed out the gaps in tribal studies and priority of tribal research to be conducted in different zones.

In his book, *Rise of Anthropology in India: A Social Science Orientation*, Vol. I (1977), Vidyarthi had given a critical appraisal of the Indian social scientists in general and social anthropologists in particular. The book aims at highlighting some of the basic factors in genesis and development in social-cultural researches in India. An attempt was made to record and examine the researches that had been conducted by Indian Social Scientists on Indian tribal society and culture. Besides reviewing the ethnographic researches on the tribal culture of different parts of India, the Vol. I of the book included a theoretical and methodological appraisal of the study of social changes in the tribes of India.

The book, *Rise of Anthropology in India: A Social Science Orientation* (Vol. 2) (1977) is dedicated to evaluate the researches on rural, or village, urban, industrial, caste, psycho-social, applied and action as well as folklore studies in India. The book fills the long felt gap in the knowledge of social anthropological researches in India.

Contribution on Urban and Industrial Anthropology

Urbanisation has been an old process in the human history. Recent researches done in the field of prehistoric India bear sufficient testimony of the origin of urban centres in the Indus valley as early as 5000 years ago. The prehistoric urban centres of Mohenjodaro, Harappa, Chanhudaro, Lothal, Kalibangan etc. were followed by the ancient cities of Kashi, Prayag, Ayodhya, Mathura, Gaya, Patliputra, Rajgir and others, which emerged, in ancient times, either as religious or religio-administrative towns. These towns were greatly integrated with the respective regions, and in several cases with the whole of India, as religious or religio-administrative, or religio-commercial centres. These ancient urban centres in Redfieldian terminology were of 'ortho genetic origin and represented the phase of primary urbanisation in the civilizational frame of India.

During Muslim periods, specially during the reigns of Akabar, Shershah and few other city builders, several towns such as Agra, Delhi, Jodhpur, Firojpur, Daulatabad, Fatehpur Sikri, Farukhabad and several others were established.

When British came to India with the advanced technology, scientific knowledge and commercial motivations and the process of urbanisation, India took a definite turn, which according to Professor Vidyarthi, marked the beginning of urbanisation based on industrialization. This phase of urbanisation was characterised by the exploitation of mineral resources, establishment of mineral based industries, investment of foreign capital and employment of foreign technicians, which eventually led to the emergence of mining, industrial, commercial, transportational and administrative centres of large magnitudes. Along with expansion of the pre-existing traditional cities of India, located on the banks of major rivers and their fertile valleys, a number of mining and industrial centres came into existence in hilly and forested areas. All these led to secondary process of urbanisation, which continues on an accelerated speed after India's independence.

Under the influence of Chicago School of Cultural Anthropology, the need was felt to study the cultural roles of city and their contribution to the development of India's civilization. Such an anthropological approach, to study Indian civilization in terms of various dimensions, including traditional and industrial urban centres provided stimulus and directions to several researchers interested in the study of complex societies (see Vidyarthi's paper 'Thinking About Sacred City', *Eastern Anthropologist*, Vol. XIII, No. 4, 1960). His book on *Sacred Complex in Hindu Gaya* (1961) is a study of traditionally emerged urban centre, with a view to throw light on interaction between folk and urban communities and between the great community having great traditions and the little communities having little traditions in terms of Sacred Complex of Sacred Geography, Sacred Specialists and Sacred Performances. Thus traditional Gaya was revealing dimensions of Hindu civilizations. Vidyarthi's concepts and methodological approaches were followed by many scholars to study the other traditional centres like Kashi, Janakpur, Rajgir, Deoghar, Puri, Rameshwaram, Dwarika, Prayag, etc.

Professor Vidyarthi in his paper, 'Historical Factors of Urbanisation in Ranchi' (*Journal of Social Research,* Vol. VII, No. II, 1964) and in his book, *Cultural Configuration of Ranchi* (1969), has attempted to highlight the origin, morphology, function and influence of Ranchi as a city as a link between the interaction of two distinct cultures, folk and urban or the tribal and the non-tribal. He also attempted to show Ranchi as a tribal city acting as centre of transformations of various tribal societies in the midst of which it is located. In fact, he attempted to present a monographic study of the city, bringing out the geographical, historical, demographic, socio-economic, and religio-political characteristics of the city as a whole.

Considering the importance of industrial urbanisation and the consequent implications, Professor Vidyarthi took up the study of industrial complexes of Chota Nagpur, with a view to develop a new branch of Industrial Anthropology. His book, *Socio-Cultural Implications of In-*

dustrialization in India: A Case Study of Tribal Bihar (1970) deals with the study of Hatia-Industrial Complex, which is an excellent case study for the understanding of form and process of culture change, caused by the emergence of factories in an underdeveloped areas. The study, of this industrial complex, provided a case for a longitudinal analysis of the various phases of industrialisation such as formulatory, constructive, productive and elaborative phases. The formulatory phase of industrialization included the uprooting of folk and peasant societies having social and cultural base, their rehabilitation and reactions. The constructive phase included the establishment of factory, the township and communicational net work, etc. In the productive and elaborative phase, the full-fledged development of the industrial means of production and the industrial style of living came into existence.

Taking the special expansion of the industrial complex and its radiating influence, Professor Vidyarthi noted that the industrial core had undergone geographical expansion. Even at the second phase of development, three concentric regions of expansion and influence can be established. These three regions are:

(i) The core of the industrial complex;
(ii) The fringe of the industrial complex; and
(iii) The margin of the industrial complex.

The first circle with a radius of five miles covers all the factories, township, dam, railway station, official building, the eight uprooted villages, and also the village Hatia, which is even now standing in the core of industrial complex.

The second concentric circle extends beyond this circle but upto a radius of ten miles from the industrial core and includes about 150 villages. Four villages, belonging to this fringe industrial complex, were selected for intensive study. The impact of successive phases of industrialization on these villages were recorded to provide a comparative analysis of demography, economy, socio-religious customs of the pre-industrial and the industrial periods.

The third concentric circle, which extends upto 20 miles from the industrial core, covers more than 200 villages and constitutes the industrial marginal circles. This belt seems to be less affected by the industrial core, and its impact has been recorded again by an intensive study of four villages selected at different distances within the margin of the industrial complex.

Vidyarthi's book, *Bhartiya Nagar* in Hindi (1966), reviews the historical growth of urban centres in India, classifies them from several angles, examines the cultural life of urban centres with two illustrative account of the sacred city of Gaya and the emerging industrial city of Ranchi. The book based on both literary and field-work, has proved useful in giving a picture of urbanisation in India and in view of its utility. It has been translated in Gujarati by two eminent sociologists of Bombay University, A.R. Desai and Meera Desai.

Contribution in Political Anthropology

Vidyarthi's edited book, *Leadership in India* (1967) is a result of all India seminar on tribal and rural leadership in India, held at Ranchi in 1962, under the joint auspices of the Council of Social and Cultural Research, Bihar, and Ranchi University, Ranchi. As the volume stands, it makes a valuable contribution to the leadership studies in terms of substantive reporting from the tribal and rural villages. Moreover, the book taken as a whole, provides certain theoretical and methodological leads relevant to leadership studies.

The first part of the book includes ten chapters in which the problem of leadership in India has been discussed at the theoretical and methodological levels. The second part, which includes thirteen chapters, explores the authority and leadership pattern of tribal India.

Vidyarthi in his book, *Dynamics of Tribal Leadership in Bihar* (1976) has attempted to explore the dynamics of tribal leadership in the context of tribal Bihar. He discusses the genesis and development of tribal leadership, Jharkhand movement in post independence period, ecological, economic and social-structural background of tribal typology, biographical analysis of tribal leaders, preelection study of tribal voters, tribal leadership as reflected in the elections, village level leaders' attitude towards modernity, urban leaders in comparison to village and subregional level leaders and followers attitude towards leadership, modernity and political consciousness.

In his book, *Student Unrest in Chota Nagpur* (1976) Vidyarthi has also attempted to explore certain political issues related to student leaders and the functioning of their unions.

Contribution in Psychological Anthropology

Vidyarthi in his book, *Sacred Complex in Hindu Gaya* (1961) has analysed the detailed biographies to highlight the process of personality formation among the Gayawals, priestly community associated with Gaya pilgrimage and performance of offering Pinda for the salvation and peace of ancestors. The children of Gayawal are dependent upon their family for everything, but they, later on, find that their community is dependent upon pilgrims coming from different parts of India for their livelihood and for the meaningfulness of their profession. In the light of biographic materials, Vidyarthi extracts the 'style of life' of the Gayawal, which is characterised by caste-consciousness, conservatism and ritualism.

The use of biographies to understand the process of personality formation as well as personality type has also been made by Vidyarthi in the study of *Nature-Man-Spirit Complex* of Sauria Paharia tribe of Rajmahal Hills (1963). He has devoted a chapter in this book on the personality type of the Maler. In many of his later writings, he found the use of biographies useful in understanding the ethos and world-view of a particular cultural situation at the axis of self.

Contribution on Folklore Study

Professor Vidyarthi was the President of Folklore Section, All India Folkculture Conference, Bombay (1959) and the editor of the journal *Folklore* (1966). He always thought for the integrated development of the subject anthropology. He was of opinion that the teaching and research of the subject anthropology must include such fields together as social-culture anthropology, prehistoric archaeology and physical anthropology, folklore, applied and action anthropology. As folklore deals with our traditional heritage, continuing generation after generation, since time immemorial, Professor Vidyarthi initiated the teaching of folklore as special paper having 200 marks in Ranchi University.

Vidyarthi attempted to collect rich materials on folklore and folkloric traditions in different parts of India with the help of students in course of 45 days fieldwork for each post-graduate session, since late fifties. He was also deeply interested in collecting folklore of Magahi, Bhojpuri, Maithal and tribal cultural-linguistic zones of Bihar. In his book on Maler (1963), he also attempted to collect and analyse folklore of the Maler dealing with their habitat, family, economics, religion, festivals, fairs and cultural history. He edited a book under the title, *Folklore Researches in India* (1973). This book is collection of essays on Indian folklore written by eminent anthropologists on the basis of fieldwork.

On Scheduled Caste Study

Professor Vidyarthi made a study of scheduled castes of Bihar with N. Mishra, now Professor in the Department of Anthropology, Ranchi University. The results were published in the form of a book under the title, *Harijan-Today* (1977). The book explores and analyses the socio-cultural, religious, economic and political aspects of life of scheduled castes of Bihar, who were termed by Gandhiji as Harijans. It also highlights changes taking place among them due to several schemes for their social, economic, educational and political upliftment.

On Applied and Action Anthropology

As referred to earlier, Professor Vidyarthi was chairman of several committees set up by the Government of India for the upliftment of scheduled tribes, scheduled castes, backward classes, primitive tribes and rehabilitation schemes meant for them. As an anthropologist, he made several suggestions, on the basis of studying their cultural institutions and traditions, which were of applied value. He also evaluated the rehabilitation scheme of Birhors and stressed upon the importance of the Action Anthropology.

Professor Vidyarthi organised a series of nine all India seminars on the practical problems of the tribals and had published their proceedings and several papers during the period under review, and also brought out several full-length publications which helped other universities to initiate and/or strengthen the teaching of Applied and Action Anthropology. His edited book, *Applied Anthropology in India* (1968) includes 38 valuable and highly thought provoking papers covering a wide spectrum of research. It has been divided into four parts: (i) general concepts, principles, problems and postulates of applied and action anthropology, (ii) problem of tribal welfare, (iii) case-studies drawn from specific tribes, and (iv) few problems of applied physical anthropology.

In another edited volume, *Conflict, Tension and Cultural Trends in India* (1968), 24 papers, on the various themes of conflict and tension as well as on social and economic changes in the tribal and rural societies of India, have been published.

9

FIELDWORK TRADITION IN ANTHROPOLOGY

Fieldwork is the soul of the subject anthropology. In fieldwork, an anthropologist goes to the field and stays with the people whom he wants to study. He observes the phenomena under study and records them systematically. It is true that all events taking place in society cannot be studied at the same time. It is also true that all phenomena are not visible to sense organ. In these circumstances, an anthropologist takes help of other techniques of data collection such as interview, case study, schedule, questionnaire, etc. All techniques of data collection have some advantages and disadvantages. Therefore, an anthropologist takes help of more than one technique, when he or she goes to collect data from the field. It is also true that an individual anthropologist cannot conduct a large research project independently in a limited time schedule. In this situation, he takes help of some young anthropologists, who are employed as research investigators, research assistants and research associates. They are selected for a particular research project and trained in the art of data collection and report writing. They are sent in the field from time to time to observe the phenomena and record them. The are also sent with interview-schedule to record data with the help of informant and to take case-studies to provide information in depth. These research personnel are supervised by some well-trained and experienced anthropologists. Thus, fieldwork is an important means for the anthropologists to explore and analyse the data and to develop a theory on that basis.

Now question arises, when fieldwork tradition appeared in the field of anthropology. The foundation of evolutionary theory in the field of cultural anthropology is regarded as the theoretical beginning in anthropology. But cultural evolutionists are generally criticized as armchair anthropologists, because they were not field workers. They relied too much upon data gathered by travellers, businessmen, administrators and missionaries, who were not anthropologists and lacked anthropological knowledge of data collection. However, their informations played significant role in the study of classical cultural evolutionists, who attempted to reconstruct the evolutionary developmental stages of culture or cultural institutions like family, marriage, kinship, law, property, society, art, religion, etc. in a unilinear sequence. It is true that accounts and publications of travellers, missionaries, adventurers, administrators, colonists, sailors and like, were largely fragmentary, uncritical, biased and generally unreliable. The facile use of this kind of material resulted in confusion and contradictions.

Tylor was very much aware of the problem. He was not uncritical of these data and often attempted to test their accuracy by comparative method. His main tool was "the test of recurrence" or "undersigned coincidence", by which statements were evaluated according to their frequency in other accounts. The most unique statements being assigned the highest probability. Although Tylor had spent an year in United States, six months in Mexico, and a shorter period in Cuba, he himself was not basically a field worker, and he relied upon secondary sources for his own reconstruction. Tylor was not a field worker, but as Lowie has insisted that he was not a strict arm-chair anthropologists. He studied culture, wherever he happened to be, in a junk store of a big city, at a school for the deaf and dumb, at a knitting mill, a butcher shop, and at festivals and religious ceremonies. After he had established anthropology as a separate discipline, he was able to send his students all over the world, as the field naturalist of human nature. They went into the field with precise instructions and techniques for gathering data and for organising the material so that it would yield useful relationships and generalizations. Tylor had also employed social arithmetic to disclose the course of social history. Tylor gathered data from over 282 societies, from savage hordes to cultured nations, to know the cultural laws of marriage and descent. He classified and tabulated all customs related to the subject. Correlating the post-marital residence pattern with the custom of in law avoidance, Tylor concluded that matrilineality and matrilocality had preceeded patrilineality and patrilocality.

L.H. Morgan, an American classical cultural anthropologists and a contemporary of E.B. Tylor, had attempted to collect data from the field using some research techniques, though not very scientifically and systematically. Morgan, by profession, was a lawyer at Rochester. All his life, he was in close proximity to Iroquois Indians. Morgan met a young Seneca Indian, whose non-Indian name was Ely Parker. It was Ely Parker, who brought Morgan in contact with Indian chiefs and later on, introduced him in several Indian communities. Hearing the story of exploitation and oppression of Iroquois Indians from Ely Parker, Morgan took the side of Seneca and assisted them in legal struggle with the government over land right. Morgan also felt need of recording the customs and traditions of Iroquois, though they were vanishing rapidly. With Ely Parker, as assistant and translator, Morgan visited and interviewed many Indians with note-book in hand and collected data on games, dance, religious beliefs, customs and traditions, language, material culture, form of government and family organisation of Iroquois. He published them in the form of a book, *League of Iroquois* (1951). Here Morgan also used genealogical technique to study kinship organisation. Since then genealogical technique became an important tool to study kinship system of a society and associated behaviour patterns like duties, privileges, status, roles, etc. This method was successfully applied by W.H.R. Rivers in his study on Toda of Nilgiri area, which was studied in 1904 and published in 1906.

Morgan used an another technique of data collection known as 'Questionnaire technique'. In order to establish data on evolution of kinship terminologies and origin of American Indians in Asia, Morgan constructed a seven-page questionnaire with more than two hundred questions with the financial aid from Smithonian Institution. The questionnaires were mailed to foreign missions and diplomatic representatives in the United States and all over the world. Although rate of return of questionnaires was very low, but the question that trickled intended to show that other American groups used similar 'classificatory' kinship terminology, contrasting the 'descriptive system' of advanced societies. When information was received that Tamil in India used classificatory system, Morgan was happily convinced that Indians were Asiatic in origin.

In America, the systematic field survey began with the work of Franz-Boas in Baffin land and British Columbia. Franz Boas had gone to Baffin land in 1883 primarily as a geographer, looking for the cultural effect of people of their physical environment. But as he lived and travelled with the Eskimos, he became concerned with the importance of social tradition as a determinant of culture and personality. His realization of the social traditions of shaping human lives turned his interests from geography to ethnology, and marked the beginning of his career as an anthropologist. In 1888, he began his serious fieldwork with the tribes of North-Western Canada. He became especially interested in their folklore, noting its marked dissimilarity from European folklore, and started what became one of the greatest collections of folklore in anthropology. His field visit to British Columbia was sponsored by the British Association Committees on the North-Western Tribes of Canada, whose chairman was E.B. Tylor. Boas' field expedition brought a turning point in the history of American anthropology. All anthropologists of America trained under his able guidance, followed this tradition in one way or the other.

The field expeditions was followed by A.C. Haddon of Cambridge shortly afterwards in England. Haddon led a band of scholars to conduct field research in Torres straits region of the pacific in 1898 and 1899. The famous 'Torres Strait Expedition' became a turning point in the history of Social Anthropology in Great Britain. This expedition was the first interdisciplinary anthropological expedition meant to cover all sides of primitive life by trained anthropologists.

W.H.R. Rivers and his students C.S. Meyers and William McDougall had examined the psychological abilities of the native, more especially their sensory capacities, in the Torres Strait Expedition. Rivers, a medical doctor by profession, concluded that there were no racial differences in pure sense. A more important result for Rivers based on Torres Strait Expedition was his article, 'A Genealogical Method of Collecting Social and Vital Statistics' (1900), which has become a standard work in the study of kinship organisation. Like Morgan, he recorded genealogies and kinship terms, observing specific behaviour patterns associated with them, including duties, privileges, status, roles and thus, placing such studies in meaningful contexts.

Rivers came to India in 1904 and studied Toda Tribes of Nilgiri area. The monograph on Toda was published in 1906. Seligmen, another British anthropologist, conducted fieldwork among the Vedas of Sri Lanka, which was published in 1911.

Professor A.R. Radcliffe-Brown, a student of Rivers and Haddon, came to India to conduct fieldwork among tribes of Andaman Island. He stayed among them from 1906 to 1908. He dutifully recorded Andamanese myths, ceremonies, customs etc. with a view to reconstruct the cultural history of these non-literate people of Indian Island. The publication of his findings was delayed for fifteen years. During this period, he became acquainted with the writing of Durkhiem and Mauss, and he turned towards functionalism. When the book on Andaman appeared in 1922, it reflected new-insights. Andamanese myths and customs were not only recorded but also interpreted, which meant the discovery, not of origin, but of meaning.

Brownislaw Kaspar Malinowski, a pupil of Hobhouse, Westermarck and Seligmen, carried field research a step further. If professor Radcliffe-Brown has always had a wider knowledge of general social Anthropology and has proved himself the abler thinker, Malinowski was more through fieldwork. He not only spent a longer period than any other anthropologists before him and after him also, in a single study of primitive people, 'The Trobriand Islanders of Malenesia', between 1914 to 1918, but he was also the first anthropologist to conduct fieldwork through native language. He was the first to live through his work in centre of native life and introduced the method of participant observation in anthropological research. In these favourable circumstances, Malinowski came to know the Trobriand Islanders well and he was describing their social life in a number of bulky and some shorter monographs up to the time of his death. Being a participant observer and having a knowledge of native language, whom he was studying (Trobriand Islanders), he was successful in gathering, vast informations on social, religious, economic and political life of Trobriand Islanders of Melanesia. All the social anthropologists, who now hold chair in Great Britain and Dominions, were taught by him. It can be fairly said that comprehensive field studies in modern Anthropology, directly or indirectly, are derived from his teaching. Throughout his life, he insisted that social life of primitive people can only be understood, if it is studied intensively.

Up to the time of Malinowski, studies were carried out among very small political communities, Australian hordes, Andamanese camps, and Malenesian villages etc. In which certain aspects of social life, such as kinship and rituals, were studied in detail to neglect others, such as political structure, which was not given attention till African societies began to be studied. Many later structural-functionalists began to study tribes of Africa to understand the political structure and change. Leach studied the political systems of Highland Burma (now Myanmar), which was published in 1954. Firth carried out fieldwork among the Tallancy, which was published in 1949. Firth studied the primitive economics of the New Zealand Maori, which appeared in 1949. Evance Pritchard studies the Azande and the Nuer, which were published in 1937 and 1940 respectively.

While British anthropologists conducted researches on different tribal groups, following structural functional approaches, in the third decade of 20th century, American anthropologist started fieldwork with a view to know the impact of culture on personality or influence of personality on culture or both. They formed a separate school of anthropological thought, which is known as 'Culture and Personality School'.

Margaret Mead conducted fieldwork among Samoa with a view to record whether the rebellion that marked adolescent personality in western cultures was a product of biological changes occurring at puberty or a result of cultural circumstances. She found that the whole cultural mood on Samoa was much less emotional than that in America. Samoa adolescence was not marked by storm and stress, but was simply a part of the gradual development of life. Her study on Samoa was published in 1928. Her book *Growing Up in New Guinea* (1930) was based on fieldwork carried among Manus tribe of New Guinea. It was concerned with the kind of enculturation process by which the Manus brought their children to adulthood. Her book, *Sex and Temperament in Three Primitive Societies* (1935) was based on material gathered from three primitive societies, namely, Mundugumor, Arapes and Tschambuli. She compared three different cultures to test the range of variation of cultural patterns. In conducting her researches, she recorded the socialization process, took interview of individual or group of individuals, collected case studies, etc. to demonstrate the impact of culture on personality formation. Mead brought another improvement in the study of culture personality by employing camera and tape recorders to capture characteristically significant behavioural events in their situational context and to publish or display these records along with word descriptions. Mead's turning to photography was a direct responses to the criticism to which her first three configurational books were subjected. In preparation for her fieldwork in Bali (1936) with Gregory Basteson, Mead took along an unprecedented array of photographic equipment and film. Altogether, during the fieldwork period some 25,000 Leica St'lls and over 22,000 ft. of 16 mm film were exposed. These pioneering experiments used for data collection were important contribution in fieldwork tradition in anthropology. Her books, *Male and Female* (1949) and *Keeps Your Powder Dry* (1942) are based on some fieldwork in America with a view to study national character. The use of small number of informants, as the basis for generalisation about the intimate psychic constellations of great masses of people, is the most troublesome aspects of the study. Mead has responded to such criticism by insisting that a single informant, provided that his social and cultural position is carefully specified, can be satisfactory source of information about widely distributed pattern. Another improvement in fieldwork tradition by Mead is use of 'Re-Study method' to show changes taking place in a society. She had studied Manus in 1928 and again visited among them in late forties to record changes in Manus society. Her book *Cultural Patterns and Technical Change* (1955) deals with changing aspects of Manus life.

Ruth Benedict, an another pioneer and patternist of culture personality school, conducted her first fieldwork among the Sarrano Indians in California under the supervision of A.L. Kroeber in 1922 at the age of 35 years. Her field studies followed of the Zuni (1924, 1925), the Cochiti (1925), and the Pima (1926). Benedict's field experience with Pima was crucial, because here she tried out idea of studying and understanding people through an analysis of their characteristic 'culture patterns'. This was the concept first formulated in her paper, 'Psychological Types in the Cultures of South-West' (1928), and later on in her famous book, *Pattern of Culture* (1934). In this book, she has also made extensive use of the field studies of Franz Boas (Kwakiutl), Ruth Bunzel (Zuni), R.F. Fortuno (Dobu). In addition to her fieldwork with Indians of South West in twenties, she studied the Asiatic and European Culture Patterns by using acculturated informants in the urban areas of this country. Her book, *The Chrysanethemum and the Sword* (1946) deals with Japanese National Character on the basis of fieldwork conducted in a small group of Japanese informants imprisoned in concentrated camp at America during World War II.

Another pioneer of culture personality was Linton, who was basically an archaeologist, but turned into cultural anthropologist in 1922, when he was sent to Marquesa Island by the Bishop Museum. Thus, he got opportunity to live with the people of Marquesa Island and centred his interest on personality structure, social and cultural traditions and material cultures. He, with Kardiner, developed the concept of 'basic personality type'. However, he was not a true field worker in strict sense. He took data from other studies also.

Kora-Du-Bois, another lady anthropologist, besides Margaret Mead and Ruth Benedict, conducted fieldwork in village on the Indonesian Islands of Alor, and recorded not only the more traditional ethnographic facts, but also collected eight lengthy biographies, dreams, and children's games and administered a number of projective tests. Her book on Alor was published in 1944. She developed the concept of 'Modal Personality'.

A very important development in the fieldwork tradition came into being when an American anthropologist, Robert Redfield, conducted fieldwork among folk and urban villages in America, with a view to know the dimensions of civilization and folk-urban continuum. In 1927-28, Redfield made two trips to traditional Mexican village which resulted in publication of his book, *Tepoztlan* (1930). In 1930, he took ethnological and sociological investigation on Yucatan, which was published under title, *Chankom* (1934). In the Mexican Province of Yukatan, Redfield selected four communities in four settings for his study around 1930 to 1936. These settings and communities were: The city of Marida, the town of Diztas, the Peasant village (Chankom) and a Tribal village Tuski. The study in these villages and urban town and city resulted in publication of his book, *Folk- Culture of Yukatan* in 1941. This study illustrates the empirical application of the concept of folk-urban continuum. Redfield also conducted fieldwork on little communities, characterised, by distinctiveness, smallness, homogeneity and self-sufficiency. He called the village, Tepoztlan, Chankom, Tuski as the villages of little communities. On the basis of his fieldwork in a peasant village Chankom in America and Maya village in England, Redfield published his book on, *Peasant Society and Culture* (1956). Since then the study of peasant communities got momentum in fieldwork tradition of anthropology. In France, Levi-Strauss, though basically an arm-chair anthropologist, has made some field expeditions on tribes of central Brazil, namely, Boganda and Arande in forties.

FIELDWORK TRADITION IN INDIAN CONTEXT

In India the study of man and his society was started from the period of Manu in one way or the other. The *Manusmriti* gives an exhaustive social and structural account of the people of India. The main principle of social structure presented by Manu are many, but important ones are: (i) Origin of the Universe, (ii) Principle of *Varna*, (iii) Principle of *Ashram*, (iv) Division of labour, (v) Religious duty and responsibility, and (vi) Inheritance of property.

Tradition of Tribals Studies

The systematic study of Indian society is recent in origin. During 18th century A.D., the British Government felt the necessity to have an ethnographic account on different tribes and castes of India with a view to rule them easily. Thus, fieldwork and researchers of anthropological interest were started in India in 18th century A.D. by colonial administrators, missionaries and some orientalists, who wanted to know the cultural history of India. They were not anthropologists by training and profession, but their accounts provide detail information on various castes, tribes and cultural history of India as a whole. Their accounts were published not only as books, but also as papers in *Journal of Asiatic Society of Bengal* (1784). The Asiatic Society of Bengal was formed in 1774 with Sir William Jones as its Chairman. But here we are not concerned with the fieldwork and studies of scholarly-oriented British administrators, but our concern is with the fieldwork tradition in India by anthropologists, whether Indians or abroad.

As referred to a earlier, some British anthropologists like W.H.R. Rivers and Radcliffe-Brown came to India to record the customs and traditions of Indian tribes. Rivers came in India in 1904 and studied the Toda tribe of South India, which was published in 1906. Another British anthropologist, Radcliffe-Brown came to India to study 'Onge' tribe of Andaman Island in 1906 to 1908. Monograph on 'Onge' was published in 1922 under the title, *Andaman Islands* from London.

Among Indian scholars S.C. Roy is regarded as 'The Father of Indian Ethnography'. He is also regarded as the first Indian anthropologist. Roy was a lawyer by profession. When he settled at Ranchi to establish his practice as a pleader, he came in contact with the tribal people of Chota Nagpur. He gradually developed interest in life and culture of Chota Nagpur. He moved in different tribal villages to record their traditions. Besides, as he was a lawyer of Chota Nagpur tribals, he got opportunities to take group and individual interviews of tribal informants, who used to come to him in connection with cases. As a result, he published his book on 'Munda' (1912), Oraon (1915, 1928), Birhor (1925), Kharia (1937). He also conducted fieldwork among Bhuiyas of Orissa and published book in 1935. He not only made field expeditions in connection with social cultural anthropology, but his expeditions in the field of physical anthropology and prehistoric archaeology are also of equal significance. In his various monographs on tribals, he tried to give physical characterises, as far as possible. In the field of prehistoric archaeology, his important contribution is digging up of Asura sites. According to him, from material obtained during excavations, Asuras were the pre-Munda inhabitants of Chota Nagpur.

In 1920, the teaching of anthropology was started in Calcutta University by Ashutosh Mukherjee, the then Vice-Chancellor of Calcutta University. The teaching of sociology was started in Bombay University in 1919. Now, Indian anthropologists and sociologists were produced and trained in the art of field expedition. To publish the research work of anthropologists, S.C. Roy started an anthropological journal, *Man in India* in 1921. The two universities acted as centre for sociological anthropological researches very soon, subjects like kinship studies and social organisations among different tribes and castes were taken up for the purpose of field expeditions. D.N. Majumdar conducted fieldwork among Ho tribe of Kolhan Bihar (Singhbhum), which appeared as book in 1937. M.N. Srinivas conducted fieldwork in Coorg for one year (1940-41) and gathered data on marriage and family, which was published in 1942.

Varrier Elwin, basically a missionary, but turned to be an anthropologist, conducted field researches among tribes of Madhya Pradesh and Orissa. He published a series of problem-oriented studies conducted on them. His important publications are: The Baiga (1939), the Agaria (1943), the Maria (1943), the Murias Gothul (1947) and Saora of Orissa (1955). Furer-Haimendorf, an anthropologist of Vienna, conducted fieldwork among tribes of Andhra Pradesh and published books and papers on them. His important book is on Chenchus (1943).

Tradition of Village Study

Thus, before independence, Indian anthropologists were influenced by British anthropologists and attempted to conduct fieldwork among tribes in different parts of India with a view to record their culture and social organization. After independence, Indian anthropologists came in contact with American anthropologists and fieldwork on villages and castes of Indian began. Now field data were not only collected and described, but they were also analysed to develop certain theories. Some American anthropologists like Morris Opler of Cornell University, Oscar Lewis of the University of Illinois, David Mandelbaum of University of California, and many their students in a team came to India and created an atmosphere of village study with certain hypotheses and methodological frame work and to assist the community development programmes in the Indian villages.

In Punjab-Delhi cultural linguistic zone, Oscar Lewis conducted field research in Rampur village in Delhi State for a period of 8 months (October 1952 to June 1953). The result of the researches in Rampur, which shared the general cultural traits of the most of villages of Punjab, was published in two books, *Group Dynamics in a North Indian Village* (1954) and *Life in a North Indian Village* (1958). His first book highlights the nature, number, size, age composition, economic and social characteristics and internal factors of faction of a Jat village having 12 ethnic groups. The second book examines the *Jajmani* system, intercaste conflict and cooperation and celebration of festivals.

Moris Opler, as early as 1947, undertook researches on Uttar Pradesh villages, namely Madhepura and Rampur in Eastern Uttar Pradesh. Opler's repeated effort and continued training programmes in Uttar Pradesh drew number of graduate students from Cornell University as a strong hold of village studies. He with R.D. Singh, a resident of village in Eastern Uttar Pradesh, attempted to study intercaste relationship and Jajmani system, unity and extension of village.

W.A. Rowe did fieldwork in Shenapur between August 1955 to July 1958 for his doctoral thesis at Cornell University, which was awarded in 1960, but remained unpublished. M.S. Luschinsky, another scholar of the same research team of Cornell University, conducted fieldwork in Senapur in 1954-57, and wrote an article on problems of culture change in Indian village.

Under the collaboration of Cornell-Lucknow University on village study in U.P., D.N. Majumdar studied a village Mohna near Lucknow in between the end of 1953 to the end of 1955. The findings of the research were published as book entitled, *Castes and Communication in an*

Indian Village (1958). His another book, *Chor Ka Ek Gaon* in Hindi (1960) is based on fieldwork carried out in Village Chittora in Mirzapur district in 1955. This village was inhabited by 12 castes and 5 tribal groups, namely, Manjhi, Kherwar, Bhuiya, Chero and Panikar. The book claims to describe all aspects of village life.

S.C. Dube studied two villages of western Uttar Pradesh — one of Rajputs and other of Tyagi, a Muslim group. The study was published in 1958 under the title, *India's Changing Village: Human Factors in Community Development* (1958). The study attempts to discover the cultural change experienced by a technologically underdeveloped Indian village under the influence of externally induced community development programme.

McKim Marriot, a disciple of Redfield of Chicago University, studied a village 'Kishangarhi' in western Uttar Pradesh from March 1951 to 1952. This was a Hindu village inhabited by 24 castes, the most populous being Brahmans. He developed the concept of 'Universalization' and 'Parochialization' in order to understand the universalisation of little traditions and Parochialization of great traditions. Both processes are opposite to each other. Marriot applied Redfield's concepts of great and little traditions and established that both, little traditions and great traditions of little communities and great communities respectively, were mutually necessary conditions of each other's existence.

John T. Hitchock, one of the scholars of Cornell University, conducted fieldwork in a village Kalapur of Rajput community located in Saharanpur district of U.P. in the period October 1953 to July 1955. The study was conducted for doctoral dissertation, which was submitted in 1956 to Cornell University. The findings revealed that the 2000 Rajputs of Kalapur trace their descent from illustrious ancestors and hence believe in their innate capacity as warriors and rulers.

The same village Kalapur was studied by P.M. Mahar and J.J. Gumperz during the same period. Mahar in her study carried an extensive research in inter-group relationship with special reference to Harijans. She brought out the dominant nature of Rajput and pointed out changes occurring in caste relationship, which have occurred due to internal factors of stress and strain and external factors of modernization such as education, political parties, Government institutions.

Gumperz conducted fieldwork on socio-linguistics of the village Kalapur. He identified social stratification in terms of linguistic differentiation. He also devoted his attention on mass communication and media of cultural transmission.

Another scholar Kolenda worked as a post-doctoral fellow on the same village Kalapur with special reference to sweepers to test the concept of *Karma* and *Punarjanma*. She found that sweeper caste of Kalapur village observed simpler, localised and parochialized form of religion. They believed that God and fate were not absolute, and supernatural events existed independent of them.

Ralph H. Retztaff, conduced field inquiry on village Government of Kalapur during the same period with a view to analysing its functioning in historical perspective. In his book, *Village Government in India* (1962), he described the traditional Panchayat of various types and traced their evolution in and around village Kalapur. He also examined the functioning of official Grampanchayat, which came into existence from July 1949.

Harold A. Gould, another American scholar conducted fieldwork in a village Sherpur in Faizabad district of Western U.P. in 1959-60 and again in 1960-62, as Post-doctoral fellow with special reference to *Jajmani* system and peasantry. The village had 12 castes distributed in 91 families. They maintained service type relationship with their clients in washing clothes, carpentry, barbering, pottery and blacksmithy. Gould also found payment of grains biannually to this service castes. He suggested that Indian village was both centripetal and centrifugal. Peasantry were self-contained as autonomous. He also found the village dependent on urban centres and on the numerous processes of national culture. He called the first set of characteristics as centripetal and second set of characteristics as centrifugal.

In the State of Bihar, L.P. Vidyarthi in his book *Ghaghara* (1966) and Sachchidananda in his book, *The Tribal Village* (1968) had made village study in tribal areas, to test the concepts like unity, extension, sanskritization, desanskritization, tribalisation and detribalization and to study social economic and political institutions.

In Orissa, F.G. Bailey, a noted British social anthropologist, conducted field researches at Bisipara, an Oriya village located in Phulbani district. The fieldwork was carried out in 1952-1954. The full length monograph on Bisipara was published in 1957 under the title, *Caste and the Economic Frontier*. The book analyses the changes, that have taken place in the internal organization of Bisipara village, as a result of the extensions of its economic and administrative frontiers. It is a study of change in a peasant economy, which has come into prolonged contact with traders, frontiers, which is caused by caste system, Government policies and other external factors. In his next book, *Tribe Caste and Nation* (1960), Bailey makes study of political activities and changes in highland Orissa. The book based on field researchers in Bisipara (1952-54) was supplemented by fieldwork in village Bederi in 1955. Though the materials for the analysis are drawn from two villages, the study attempts to explore the interaction between tribals and non-tribals through political organisations, Bailey's third book, *Political and Social Change: Orissa* (1959) is based on informations gathered from Mohanpur village in close contacts with an urban centre. Bailey observed that the village Mohanpur had unity of its own with traditional village council, school, common village festivals and common observance of rituals and ceremonies.

In Madhya Pradesh, A.C. Mayer of London School of Economics, conducted fieldwork in a village Ramkheri, located at a distance of 7 miles from a small town of Dewas on the plateau of Malwa and 30 miles from Ujjain in the period 1954-56. The findings were published in a book under the title, *Caste and Kinship System in Middle India*. Here Mayer makes observation that it is sub-caste which is really endogamous, and the caste has no mechanism of settling dispute for adjusting the status of members etc. Here he agrees with G.S. Ghurye that though caste is recognised by the society at large, but it is sub-caste which is regarded by the particular caste and the individual. He also makes the analysis of the distinction between internal and external aspects of caste. The external relation exists mostly within the village, whereas the internal order of caste group is based on the large extent on kinship relations within the population of a number of adjacent village caste groupings. Here, he seems to be influenced by Srinivas' distinction of vertical ties within a village settlement and horizontal ties between villages.

K.S. Mathur, an eminent Indian anthropologist, conducted fieldwork in a village Potlod in the period April 1955-April 1956, under the guidance of S.F. Nadel. The findings were published in a book under the title, *Caste and Ritual in a Malwa Village* (1964). In the light of Potlod materials, Mathur establishes the fundamental feature of the Hindu social organisation, i.e. the caste, and observes the entire caste system bound up with the notion of purity and pollution in the intra-caste and intercaste relationship.

In Rajasthan, Carstairs undertook fieldwork in a village Deoli, near Udaipur in 1951-52 under the financial support of Rockfeller Foundation. The village had 36 communities including Sikhs, Muslims, Bhils and others. The findings were published in 1957 under the title, *The Twice-born: A Study of High Caste Hindus*. In course of fieldwork, G.M. Carstairs used certain psychological experiments like Raven's profession matrices tests and Rorschach test. In addition to depth interviews, case histories from different communities were also collected.

B.R. Chauhan, an Indian social anthropologist, conducted intensive fieldwork on a village Sadri located in Chittorgarh district of Rajasthan. Here, he criticises the concept of peasant society, which limits to agriculturists, but he prefers to use 'little community', a term coined by Redfield, in village study because of the wholistic implication of the community.

Under the guidance of B.R. Chauhan, Yogesh Atal made a valuable study of caste system in Rajasthan and studied the importance of Bheru deities of a Mewar village with reference to their specialized function and mode of worship. He also attempted to compare the Bheru worship in Malwa village reported by A.C. Mayer. Unlike in Malawa, the Surini of Bheru in Mewar is a centre of corporate worship. In Malawa, it is lineage deity, but in Mewar it is a village deity and has inter-village significance. Since the cult of Bheru has both, Brahminic and non-Brahminic attributes and rituals, it is difficult to apprehend whether *Bhairav* of great tradition is universalised version of *Bheru* or *Bheru* is parochealised form of *Bhairava*. He considers it as parochially universalised form and modes of worship are more significant than the universalised traits.

In Gujarat, Geital P. Steed of Columbia University, studied a village Kasandra in Ahmedabad district with the help of four American and three Indian collaborators. The fieldwork was conducted between November 1949 to January 1951. The study attempts to formulate an approach to the study of personality formation in a Hindu village.

In Maharashtra, Henry Orensteen made study of a village named Gaon in Poona district in 1954-55 and Summer of 1961. The village is situated nearby the market town of Mot and has 14 castes with Dhangar as dominant. The Dhangar were traditionally shepherds, but claimed as Rajput. He published a full length monograph on *Gaon: Conflict and Cohesion* (1965). In general, he tried to establish that the nature of caste system is undergoing change in India and particular castes, and their customs are changing due to processes of sanskritization, westernization and secularization.

G.S. Ghurye, an Indian sociologist and social anthropologist, did field researches in village Haweli Taluka in four seasons between 1954-1958, and published a book *After a Century and a Quarter* (1960). The study was undertaken with two-fold purpose. Firstly, to test the concept of folk-urban continuum and secondly, to plot out the socio-economic changes which have occurred in the village life since 1819. His next book on village life was published in 1963 under the title, *Anatomy of a Rural-Urban Community*, which embodies the result of the pilot study of whole Haweli Taluka in Maharashtra in-between 1954-60. He covered 117 villages including 8 agricultural towns, 15 super villages, 34 big villages, 39 standard villages, and 21 small villages.

In Andhra Pradesh, S.C. Dube carried on fieldwork in Shamirpet village situated between the twin cities of Hyderabad and Sikandarabad, in 1951-52 and published a full length monograph under the title, *Indian Village* (1955). Here Dube has attempted to present an integrated picture of the village taking proper care of geographical, historical and sociological perspectives adequately.

Y.V. Lakshmana Rao has conducted field researches on two villages of Andhra Pradesh. One of them is called as Kathuru meaning new in Telugu, on account of being progressive, developed and industrialised than another village termed as Pothru meaning old due to having more traditional character. The results of field visits have been published in book form under the title, *Communication and Development: A Study of Two Indian Villages* (1955). He has attempted to analyse the relationship between communication and development. As communicational facilities were available to Kothru, therefore, its members were developed. Pothru was not developed due to lack of communication.

In Karnataka, Dhillon studied village named Harpura in Malvali Taluka in Mandya district of Mysore State. The study's results were published under the title, *Leadership and Groups of a Mysore Village* (1955). The study attempts to delineate factions and leadership patterns in the village.

Mysore has been known for anthropological researches by M.N. Srinivas. He first wrote his doctoral dissertation on social organisation of Mysore and then on religion and society among Coorgs of South India. Here, he postulated the idea that Sanskritization spread vertically and horizontally indicating the unity in village India. In course of field inquiry, he stayed in village Rampura for 10 months in 1948 and for 2 months in 1952. He also paid several visits to the village from time to time. Besides studying the relationship of roles and statuses of castes and their occupation, he developed the concept of dominant caste. Here, he established numerical preponderance, economic and political power, high ritual status, western education, and occupation as criteria related to dominant caste.

A.R. Beals carried on field researchers in two villages of Mysore namely Namhali and Gopalpur. He studied the village Namhali for 15 months in 1952-53 to explore the social structure and change in the village since 1800. He studied the village Gopalpur with his wife in 1959-60. On the basis of fieldwork in Namhali, Beals submitted his doctoral dissertation to California University on 'Cultural Change and Social Conflict in a South Indian Village'. He also wrote several papers on leadership patterns, political institutions, factors of cultural change etc.

Scarlett Epstein, a British economist as well as social anthropologist, carried on field inquiry in two villages — Wangala, an irrigated and Donela, an unirrigated for two years during 1954-55. The results were published in book under the title, *Economic Development and Social Change in South India* (1962).

E.B. Harper, an American scholar conducted fieldwork in the village Totagadal in Malnad of Mysore State in 1954-56, on pattern of *Jajmani* system. He discovered two types of economic transactions — (1) the *Jajmani* system of traditional nature and (2) *Malnad* which occurs between the *Jajmani* and the artisans, characterised by cash payment. He observed that *Jajmani* was disintegrating into the Malnad type of economic relation in Indian village.

K. Ishwaran made an intensive field enquiry in a village Sherapura near Dharwar and gathered informations on economic activities of the villagers in relation to their social activities. Informations were published in two books under the titles, *Tradition and Economy in Village India* (1966) and *Shivapura: A South Indian Village* (1968). His first book, besides describing village economy and associated traditions, explores the exchange system of the village termed as *Aya*. According to him, the *Aya* is the unmeasured and unconditional gift and reflects the motive of sharing one's possessions with the others. In the legal sphere, traditional Aya system, recognises rights of individuals, groups, and of the community in the sphere of politics. The *Jajmani*, whether of street, village or community, get leadership and headship automatically. He finds a close correspondence of 'Aya' system with the potlatch institution of polynesia and kula exchange of Trobriand Islanders. The next book of Ishwaran explores the style of life of various caste groups of village Shivapura such as Lingayats, Marathas and Muslims. He also explains inter-caste and inter-village relationship.

In Kerala and Tamil Nadu, the village studies have remained neglected, though the study of tribes of Travancore and Cochin was initiated by the noted scholar Ananta Krishna Iyer in twenties, which was followed by communities study of Andre Mayer and Kathleen Gough. In coursc of conducting studies on the cult of dead of Nayer and Nambudris, Gough conducted fieldwork in three villages of Kerala during 1947-49 and published few papers on village life in Kerala. She also worked in the village of Tanjore of Tamil Nadu and wrote about the social structure, kinship system, caste organisation and caste-ranking.

A.C. Mayer studied a village in Malabar and wrote a book on *Land and Society in Malabar* (1952). Andre Beteille, an Indian sociologist studied a village Shivapuram in Tanjore district. It was a multi-caste village (92 Brahmin, 118 non-Brahmin and 89 Adi-Dravida families) situated on the bank of river Kaveri.

Tradition of Researches on Religion

An objective study of primitive religion in India was initiated by Majumdar on the basis of his fieldwork done among the Ho tribe of Singhbhum of Bihar State. His concept of Bongaism developed in its final form in his books, *Affairs of a Tribe* (1950). This was modern anthropological trend in the study of religion in Indian context. The full-length study of tribal religion was published by Elwin (1955), on Savara tribe of Orissa, in which he supports the concept of spiriticism as suggested by S.C. Roy in his book, *Oraon Religion and Customs* (1928). The study on religion in the context of Indian villages, was initiated by M.N. Srinivas in his book *Religion and Society Among Coorgs of South India* (1952). He developed the concept of Sanskritization to explain the Brahminical process of change in Hindu villages.

Two anthropologists attempted to edit books on *Aspects of Religion in Indian Society* and *Religion in South Asia*. They were Professor L.P. Vidyarthi (1961) and Harper (1964). Vidyarthi's edited book, *Aspects of Religion in Indian Society* (1961) is in memory of late Professor D.N. Majumdar. This book contains several papers written by several anthropologists on the basis of field researches. Anthropologists like Gopala Sarana, Marriot, Aiyappan, Sharma, Srivastava, Carstairs, Mathur, Singh, Vidyarthi, Madan, Atal, Chattopadhyay, Sahay, Sinha and Bose contributed papers in this edited volume. Harper's book *Religion in South Asia* (1964) originated from a conference on Religion in South Asia held in August 1961. It consists of 9 papers by nine eminent foreign anthropologists like Mandelbaum, Ames, Breman, Kolenda, Opler, Gumperz, Beals, Yelman, and Harper. All papers were based on village studies in different parts of India.

Another volume, *Traditional India:Structure and Change* (1956) also has great relevance to the contemporary study of religious traditions in India. This volume, unlike previous ones, contains papers dealing with textual and contextual analysis of recorded and oral traditions. The papers deal with the various dimensions of Indian civilization, and analyse some aspects of cultural media and cultural performances, including religious ones. A full-length study of the Sacred City of Gaya is attempted by Vidyarthi in his book, *Sacred Complex in Hindu Gaya* (1961). The study focuses the city of Gaya as a dimensions of Indian civilization in the framework of Redfield and Milton Singer's theories of civilization.

Tradition of Urban Studies

The researchers of Robert Redfield, Milton Singer, McKim Marriot of Chicago University (U.S.A.), in Indian context, gave further theoretical methodological leads for the study of the folk, peasant, and urban communities in India as dimensions of Indian civilization. Indian anthropologists, under the influence of Chicago University, started studying traditional and modern cities of India to understand them as dimensions of Indian civilizations, and also to analyse the folk-urban continuum and interactions. Processes of urbanization and industrialization have also been taken up by social scientists because such researches were financed by the National Planning Commission. Among the important researches conducted in this line are by Singer on Madras, Marriot on Wai, Oraon on Jamshedpur. These studies on cultural roles of cities attracted Indian anthropologists to broaden the scope of anthropology, from isolated tribal communities to folk-communities, and then to urban and industrial centres. The study of Calcutta by Bose (1958), Kanpur by Majumdar (1961), Lucknow by Mukherjee and Singh (1961) and of Gaya and Ranchi by Vidyarthi (1961, 1969) bear sufficient testimony in this regard.

Tradition on Studies on Power Structure and Leadership

The attempt to analyse the power structure and decision-making in Indian rural society was taken up by American anthropologists and Indian anthropologists in course of studying different villages. Credit goes to Oscar Lewis and his Indian collaborator, who initiated the study of faction and leadership with their two volumes on North and South Indian villages respectively. These two volumes, published under the auspicious of Planning Commission, brought to the light the varied roles of kinship and caste-oriented factions in the decision-making in rural India. These researches inspired a number of scholars to take up the study of rural leadership in different parts of India. Professor Vidyarthi wrote a book on *Dynamics of Tribal Leadership in Bihar* (1973). He made extensive and intensive study of the pattern of tribal leadership in context of Bihar, both in diachronic and synchronic terms. This large scale study highlights the dynamics of traditional, modern as well as transitional leadership among the tribes of various cultural types.

Tradition on Action Research

The tribal and rural development programmes of Government of India have further given a fillip to the Indian anthropologists to study and evaluate the process of change in tribal and rural India. In such developmental programmes, the concept of Action Anthropology formulated by Sol Tax, for the first time, partially replaced the principles of 'Applied Anthropology' developed during British colonial administration. In the writings of Majumdar 'The Changing Convas of Tribal Life', *Eastern Anthropologist*, (Vol. 14, No. 1, 1949); Elwin (Philosophy of NEPHA, 1958), Vidyarthi (1957, 1960, 1968, 1972), Jay (Anthropologist and Tribal Welfare', *Journal of Social Research*, Vol. II, No. 2, 1959), the importance of action-oriented researches has been highlighted. Now-a-days greater significance is being attached by the anthropologists on problem-oriented researches. The problems related to urbanisation, industrialization, women, children, deprived ecological settings, bonded labour, health, education, etc. are being explored, and impact of development schemes are being assessed and evaluated. Some useful suggestions are also being made to solve the problems and to make the programmes successful.

Tradition of Folklore Researches

Folk-lore is regarded as prehistory of a society. The folklore researches, which were at the level of sporadic collection of tribal songs and taken to be included in the monograph, received a systematic treatment with Verrier Elwin to begin with, under the influence of F. Boas and E.B. Tylor. With the passage of time social elements hidden in folklore were unearthed by few anthropologists, and also by several scholars of different literature, specially Bhojpuri, Assamese and Marathi. Now-a-days, anthropologists are attempting to collect informations on folksongs, balled, folk tales, folk belief, folk tradition, folk magic and *Totaka*, folk medicine, folk plays, games and sports, folk riddles, folk proverbs, etc. under the topic folklore to explore folk-culture of an area or region.

Tradition of Studies on Tribe-Caste Continuum

The term continuum was used for the first time by Robert Redfield in his book, *The Folk Culture of Yucatan* (1941), to understand the interaction between tribal, folk, semi-urban and urban communities. The study of caste dynamics, in terms of tribe caste continuum, also attracted the Indian ethnographers and anthropologists to understand the process of caste formation among the tribals of India. The concepts like tribe-caste continuum, Tribe-Rajput continuum, Hinduisation, Aryanisation and Sanskritization etc., refer to the same or similar process of 'caste formation' from the tribal matrix under the impact of caste dominated major regional societies.

Since the bulk of tribal communities have existed for centuries in close interaction with Hindu social order, the process of Hinduisation is very long standing. Ghurye in his book, *The Scheduled Tribe* (1959) characterised the tribals as backward Hindus. B.K. Roy Burman in his paper entitled, 'Tribal Demography: A Preliminary Appraisal' in K.S. Singh (ed.) *Tribal Situation in India* (1972), has attempted a classification of Indian tribes in terms of their orientation towards Hindu social order. Some tribes like Bhumij, Bhil, Gond in some parts of Bihar and Raba, Moch and Rajong in Assam, have been fully incorporated into the Hindu social order. They have almost turned into castes and can hardly be differentiated from the neighbouring Hindu peasantry. Then there are tribes like Santal, Oraon, Munda and Gond, who are positively oriented towards Hindu social order. Though the bulk of their population have not been included in the caste frame, they have largely accepted the symbols, ethos and world-view of their Hindu neighbours. Hinduisation has been a gradual process and, except in certain cases, does not involve any conversion.

Sanskritization is the part of the same process and starts with the simple claim of the group as being members of the greater Hindu society. This varies in direct proportion with their giving up of unclean, non-Hindu habits such as beef eating, rearing of pigs and fowls, and eating of pork and fowls. Abstraining from beef is an indication that the group in question wants acceptance in the Hindu society. Those, who give up beef eating or pork rearing, look down upon those who do not do so. The second step in sanskritization is the suspension in belief in tribal Gods and deities, and gradual adoption of the deities of Hindu patheon along with their traditional rituals. They also begin to celebrate Hindu festivals. In the third and final stage, same tribals seek to give up their clan organisation and also in some cases give up matrilineal inheritance and adoption of the patrilineal complex. In many cases, tribal language is also given up.

Majumdar's study of the Khasa (1952) and S.K. Srivastavas study of Tharus of Cis-Himalayan region (1958) lead us to infer that though they have a tribal matrix and continue to practise certain distinctive tribal customs, but they have been accepted as Kshatriyas. The Tharus have greatly succeeded in getting themselves accepted as Thakurs by wearing thread, established marriages with already established Thakurs, and modelling the *rites-de-passage* in accordance with the Hindu models. The culture of the Khasa of Cis-Himalayan region has been greatly modelled on the ways of living of Rajputs and Brahmins in the neighbouring plain area. With their fast adoption of the Hindu surnames and social connections with Rajputs and Brahmins of the plains, they claim themselves as Rajputs, and along with Brahmins of the area, they constitute the apex of the social order.

The most significant work to establish this process of caste formation out of the tribal matrix is reflected in the historical and ethnographic studies of the Bhumij by Surjit Sinha in his paper, 'State Formation and Rajput Myth in Tribal Central India (*Man-in-India*, Vol.42, No.1, 1962). On the basis of studies among he Bhumij, he speaks of the tribal-Rajput continuum. The process of state formation among the Bhumij followed the diffusion of the Rajput-model, both on the sacred and secular levels. The Rajput model was built up with the help of Brahmin priests in search of clients in the growing aristocratic strata in the tribal frontier.

In Palamau district of Chota Nagpur plateau, Chero and Kharwar have been assimilated as Rajput Castes in regional caste hierarchy. The Parahiyas, now, prefer to call themselves as Hindus of Chero brand.

It was N.K. Bose, who first drew attention to the Hindu mode of tribal absorption. In recent decades, some studies have clearly brought this out through the concept of cultural approximation and of the tribe-caste continuum. K.C. Sasmal in his doctoral thesis on 'A Study of Eight Bauri-village' has established that the Bauri of West Bengal claim to be Brahmin, owing to their observance of mourning period of eleven days, putting sacred thread, accepting *vaishnavism*, going on pilgrimage, and onducting the worship of two popular village deities — *Sitala* and *Mansa*.

In another doctoral dissertation on Mahalis of Midnapur in West Bengal, Sen Gupta has established that the Mahalis of Bengal have accepted the Hindu caste system along with the doctrine of *Karma*, the concept of purity and pollution, fast and festivals, worship of Hindu patheon and adoption of caste surnames.

Vidyarthi's study on Ghaghara (1961) records the emergence of Manjhi as a caste, who in course of time have adopted Hindu style of life and have distinguished themselves from their Munda counterparts.

Sachchidananda's paper on 'Tribe-caste Continuum: A Study of the Gond in Bihar' (*Anthropos*, Vol. 65, 1970), reveals that the Gonds of North Bihar have accepted Hindu Gods, festivals and rituals as well as social norms. They are now regarded as backward Hindu castes. They have given up polygyny, widow-remarriage, eating of beaf etc. However, they maintain marital links with the Gonds in Chota Nagpur, who are still regarded as tribal.

The study of Bhagat movement establishes that a number of plural groups, like Vishnu Bhagat, Mahadeo Bhagat, Kabirpanthi Bhagat, Tana Bhagat etc. among the major tribes of Chota Nagpur, and Safa Hor among the Santhals of Santhal Parganas, have been formed within the respective tribal groups under the influence of Bhagat movement. Among these Bhagat sects, Tana Bhagat movement is said to have been initiated by Jatra Bhagat in 1914.

BIBLIOGRAPHY

Bachofen, J.J., 1961: Das Mutterecht. Basel: Beno Schwabe.

Bastian, A., 1860: Der Mensch in der Geschichte. Leipzeg: O Wigand.

Bastian, A., 1895: Ethnische Elementargedanken in der Lehre vom Menschen. Berlin: Weidmann'sche Buchhandlung.

Benedict, R., 1934: Patterns of Culture. New York: Houghton Mifflin.

Benedict, R., 1945: Race Science and Politics: New York: Viking Press.

Benedict, R., 1946: The Chrysanthemum and The Sword. Boston: Houghton Mifflin.

Boas, F., 1888: The Central Eskimo. Washington: Smithsonian Institute.

Boas, F., 1897: The Social Organisation and the Secret Societies of the Kwakiutl Indians. Washington.

Boas, F., 1911: Mind of Primitive Man. New York: Macmillan.

Boas, F., 1927: Primitive Art. Oslo: H.Aschelhoung and Company.

Boas, F., 1928: Anthropology and Modern Life. New York: W.W. Norton and Co.

Boas, F., 1940: Race, Language and Culture. New York: MacMillan and Company

Bose, N.K., 1929: Cultural Anthropology. Bombay: Asia Publishing House.

Bose, N.K., 1932: Canons of Orissan Architecture. Calcutta: Ramananda Chatterji.

Bose, N.K., 1948: Excavations in Mayurbhanj. University of Calcutta.

Bose, N.K., 1967: Culture and Society in India. Bombay: Asia Publishing House.

Child, V.G., 1925, The Dawn of Western Civilization. New York: Knopf.

Child, V.G., 1946: What Happened in History. New York: Pelican.

Child, V.G., 1951(a): Social Evolution. New York: Henry Schuman.

Child, V.G., 1951(b): Man Makes Himself. New York: New American Library, Mentor.

Child, V.G., 1953: What is History. New York: Henry Schuman.

Child, V.G., 1958: The Dawn of European Civilization. New York: Knopf.

Darwin, C., 1859: Origin of Species. New York: New American Library, Mentor.

Darwin, C., 1871: The Descent of Man and Selection in Relation to Sex. New York: D. Appleton.

Dube, S.C., 1954: The Kamar. Lucknow: Universal Publisher.

Dube, S.C., 1955: Indian Village. London: Cornell University Press.

Dube, S.C., 1958: India's Changing Villages: Human Factors in Community Development. London: Cornell University Press.

Dube, S.C., 1958: Power and Conflict in Village India. London: Cornell University Press.

Dube, S.C., 1960: Manav Aur Sanskriti. Delhi: Raj Mahal Prakashan.

Dube, S.C., 1968: Institution Building for Community Development (ed.). Hawai: East-West Centre Press.

Du-Bois, C., 1944: The People of Alor: A Social-Psychological Study of an East Indian Island. Minneapolis: University of Minnesota Press.

Durkheim, E., 1893: Division of Labour in Society. New York: Macmillan.

Durkheim, E., 1895: The Rules of Sociological Method. New York: Free Press.

Durkheim, E., 1897: Suicide. New York: Free Press.

Durkheim, E., 1912: The Elementary Forms of Religious Life. London: Allen and Unwin.

Evans-Pritchard, E.E., 1949: The Sansui Cyrenaica. London: Oxford University Press.

Evans-Pritchard, E.E., 1951: Social Anthropology. New York: Free Press.

Firth, R., 1921: Primitive Economics of the New Zealand Maori. London: George Routledge.

Firth, R., 1957: Man and Culture: An Evaluation of the Work of Brownislaw Malinowski. London: Routledge and Kegan Paul.

Firth, R., 1963: We the Tikopia. Boston: Beacon Press.

Firth, R., 1964: Essays on Social Organisation and Value.

Fortes, M., 1945: The Dynamics of Clanship among the Tallensy. London: Oxford University Press.

Fortes, M., 1949: The Web of Kinship among the Tallensy. London: Oxford University Press.

Fortes, M. and E.E. Evans-Pritchard (Eds.), 1940: African Political System, London: Oxford University Press.

Frazer, J.C., 1887: Totemism. Edinburgh: Adams and Charles.

Frazer, J.C., 1911-15: The Golden Bough, 3rd ed. London: Macmillan.

Freud, S., 1913: Totem and Taboo. London: Penguin Books.

Freud, S., 1928: The Future of an Illusion. London: Institute of Psychoanalysis.

Freud, S., 1930: Civilization and its Discontents. New York: Jonathan Cape and Harrison Smith.

Frobenius, L., 1898: Dieweltanschaung der Naturevolker. Weimar: E. Felber.

Gluckman, M., 1949: Malinowski's Sociological Theory. New York: Oxford University Press.

Gluckman, M., 1955(a): Custom and Conflict in Africa. Oxford: Bosil Blackwell.

Gluckman, M., 1955(b): Judicial Process among the Barotse of Northern Nigeria. Manchester: Manchester University Press.

Gluckman, M., 1962: Essays on the Rituals of Social Relations. Manchester: Manchester University Press.

Gluckman, M., 1963: Order and Rebellion in Tribal Africa. New York: Free Press.

Goldenweiser, A., 1933: History, Psychology and Culture. New York: Knopf.

Goldenweiser, A., 1937: Anthropology: An Introduction to Primitive Culture. New York: Appleton-Century-Crofts.

Haddon, A.C., 1895: Evolution in Art. London: W. Scot.

Haddon, A.C., 1908: The Study of Man. London: J. Murray.

Haddon, A.C., 1910: A History of Anthropology. New York: Putnam.

Haddon, A.C., 1927: The Wanderings of Peoples. Cambridge: Cambridge University Press.

Haddon, A.C., 1934: History of Anthropology. London: Warrs.

Harris, M., 1964(a): The Nature of Cultural Things. New York: Random House.

Harris, M., 1964(b): Patterns of Race in the Americas. New York: Walker.

Harris, M., 1968: Rise of Anthropological Theory. New York:

Herskovits, M., 1948: Man and His Works. New York: Knopf.

Herskovits, M., 1953: FRANZ BOAS. New York: Sribner-

Hobhouse, L.T. et al., 1915: The Material Culture and Social Institutions of the Simpler Peoples: An Essay in Correlation. London: Champman-Hall.

Hoebel, E.A., 1949: Man in Primitive World. New York: McGraw-Hill.

Honigmann, J.J., 1954: Culture and Personality. New York: Harper and Row.

Honigmann, J.J., 1963: Understanding Culture. New York: Harper and Row.

Kalpan, B., 1954: A Study of Rorschach Responses in Four Cultures. Harvard University.

Kalpan, B., 1961: Studying Personality Cross Culturally. Evanston: Raw, Peterson.

Kardiner, A., 1939(ed.): The Individual and his Society. New York: Columbia University Press.

Kardiner, A., 1945: The Psychological Frontiers of Society (co-author). New York: Columbia University Press.

Kardiner, A. and Prevel, E., 1961: They Studied Men. Cleveland: World Publishing Company.

Kluckhohn, C., 1949· The Mirror for Man. New York: McGraw-Hill.

Krober, A., 1923: Anthropology. New York: Harcourt, Brace.

Krober, A., 1925(ed.): Handbook of the Indians of California. New York: Harcourt, Brace.

Krober, A., 1939: Cultural and Natural Areas of Native North America. University of California, Press.

Krober, A., 1944: Configurations of Culture Growth. Berkeley: University of California Press.

Krober, A., 1952: The Nature of Culture. Chicago, University of Chicago Press.

Krober, A., 1957: Style and Civilization. Ithaca: Cornell University.

Krober, A., 1963: An Anthropologist Looks at America. Berkeley: University of California Press.

Leach, E., 1954: Political Systems of Highland Burma. Boston: Beacon Press.

Leach, E., 1961(a): Rethinking Anthropology. London: Athlone Press.

Leach, E., 1961(b): Pul Eliya, A Village in Ceylone. New York: Cambridge University Press.

Levi-Strauss, C., 1949: Elementary Structure of Kinship. Paris.

Levi-Strauss, C., 1963(a): Structural Anthropology. New York: Basic Book.

Levi-Strauss, C., 1963(b): Totemism. Boston: Beacon Press.

Levi-Strauss, C., 1964: Mythologiques. Paris: Plon.

Levy-Bruhl, L., 1966: The Soul of the Primitive. New York: Praeger.

Lewis, O., 1951: Life in an Mexican Village. Urbane: University of Illinois Press.

Lewis, O., 1961: The Children of Sanchez, New York: Random House.

Lewis, O., 1966(a): The Culture of Poverty. Scientific American.

Lewis, O., 1966(b): Lavida. New York: Random House.
Linton, R., 1936: The Study of Man. New York: Appleton Century.
Linton, R., 1945: The Cultural Background of Personality. New York: Appleton.
Lowie, R., 1917: Culture and Ethnology. New York: D.C.Mc.Murtrie.
Lowie, R., 1920: Primitive Culture. New York: Bone and Liveright.
Lowie, R., 1927: The Origin of State. New York: Harcourt, Brace.
Lowie, R., 1937: History of Ethnological Theory. New York: Farrer & Rinehart.
McLennan, J.F., 1865: Primitive Marriage. Edinburgh: Adem and Charles Black.
McLennan, J.F., 1876: Studies in Ancient History. London: Macmillan.
Maine, H.S., 1861: Ancient Law, London: J. Murray.
Maine, H.S., 1871: Village Communities in East and West. London: J. Murray.
Maine, H.S., 1883: Early Law and Customs. London: J. Murray
Maine, H.S., 1888: Early History of Institutions. New York: Holt.
Majumdar, D.N., 1936: A Tribe in Transition: A Study in Culture Pattern. London: Longmans Green and Company.
Majumdar, D.N., 1944: Fortunes of Primitive Tribes. Lucknow: Universal Publisher.
Majumdar, D.N., 1946: Races and Cultures of India. Allahabad: Kitabistan.
Majumdar, D.N., 1950: The Affairs of a Tribe: A Study in Tribal Dynamics. Lucknow: Universal Publisher.
Majumdar, D.N., 1958: Caste and Communication in an Indian Village. Bombay: Asia Publishing House.
Majumdar, D.N., 1960: Social Contours of an Industrial City. Bombay: Asia Publishing House.
Malinowski, B., 1913: The Family among the Australian Aborigines: A Sociological Study. London: University of London Press.
Malinowski, B., 1922: Argonauts of Western Pacific. New York: Duttan.
Malinowski, B., 1926: Crime and Custom in Savage Society. London: Kegan Paul.
Malinowski, B., 1927: Sex and Repression in Savage Society. London: Routledge and Kegan Paul.
Marret, R.R., 1909: The Threshold of Religion. London: Methuen.
Marret, R.R., 1927: The Diffusion of Culture. Cambridge: Cambridge University Press.
Mead, M., 1928: Coming of Age in Samoa. New York: Morrow.

Mead, M., 1930: Growing up in New Guinea. New York: Blue Ribbon.

Mead, M., 1935: Sex and Temperament in Three Primitive Societies. New York: Morrow.

Mead, M., 1937: Cooperation and Competition among Primitive People New York: McGraw-Hill.

Mead, M., 1939: From South Sea. New York: Morrow.

Mead, M., 1942: And keep your Powder Dry: An Anthropologist looks at America. New York: Morrow.

Mead, M., 1949: Male and Female. New York: Morrow.

Mead, M., 1955: Cultural Patterns and Technical Change. New York: Mentor.

Mead, M., 1964: Continuities in Cultural Evolution. New Haven: Yale University Press.

Mead, M. and R. Bunzel (ed.) 1960: The Golden Age of Anthropology: New York: George Braziler.

Mead, M. and F.M.C. MAC Gregor, 1951: Growth and Culture: A Photographic Study of Balanese Childhood. New York: Putnam.

Mead, M. and R. Metraux, 1953: The Study of Culture at a Distance: Chicago: University of Chicago Press.

Morgan, L.H., 1851: League of the Iroquis. Rochester: Sage and Bora.

Morgan, L.H., 1870: Systems of Consanguinity and Affinity of Human Family. Washington: Smithsonian Institute.

Morgan, L.H., 1877: Ancient Society. New York: World Publishing.

Morgan, L.H., 1881: Houses and Houselife of the American Aborigines. Washington: U.S. Geological Survey.

Murdock, G.P., 1937: Statistical Correlations in the Science of Society. New Haven: Yale University Press.

Nadel, S.F., 1951: The Foundation of Social Anthropology: New York: Free Press.

Nadel, S.F., 1957: The Theory of Social Structure. New York: Free Press.

Opler, M., 1951: Village Life in North India. Chicago: Delphian Society.

Opler, M., 1952: "Extension of an Indian Village", Journal of Asian Study, 1952.

Parsons, T., 1937: The Structure of Social Action. New York: Free Press.

Pike, K., 1954: Language in Relation to a Unified Theory of the Structure of Human Behaviour. Glendale: Summer Institute of Linguistics.

Radcliffe-Brown, A.R., 1922: The Andaman Islanders. Cambridge: Cambridge University Press.

Radcliffe-Brown, A.R., 1948: A Natural Science of the Society. New York: Free Press.

Radcliffe-Brown, A.R., 1950: African System of Marriage and Family (ed.). London: Oxford University Press.

Radcliffe-Brown, A.R., 1958: Method in Social Anthropology (co-author). Chicago: University of Chicago Press.

Ratzel, F., 1882: Anthropo Geographic. Stuttgart: J. Engelhorn.

Ratzel, F., 1896: The History of Man Kind. London: Macmillan.

Redfield, R., 1930: Tepoztlan. Chicago University Press.

Redfield, R., 1934: Chankom. Chicago: Chicago University Press.

Redfield, R., 1941: Folk Culture of Yukatam. Chicago: Chicago University Press.

Redfield, R., 1953: Primitive World and its Transformation. New York.

Redfield, R., 1955: The Little Community: View Point for the Study of Human Whole. Chicago: Chicago University Press.

Redfield, R., 1956: Peasant Society and Culture. Chicago: Chicago University Press.

Rivers, W.H.R., 1906: The Tode. New York: Macmillan.

Rivers, W.H.R., 1914(a): The History of Melanesian Society. Cambridge: Cambridge University Press.

Rivers, W.H.R., 1914(b): Kinship and Social Organisation. London: Constable.

Rivers, W.H.R., 1922: History and Ethnology. New York: Macmillan.

Rivers, W.H.R., 1923: Conflict and Dream. New York: Harcourt, Brace.

Roy, S.C., 1912: Munda and Their Country. Calcutta.

Roy, S.C., 1915: The Oraon of Chotanagpur. Ranchi.

Roy, S.C., 1925: The Birhor. Ranchi.

Roy, S.C., 1935: The Hill Bhuiyas of Orissa. Ranchi.

Roy, S.C., 1937: The Kharias in Two Volumes. Ranchi.

Sahlins, M. and E. Service, 1960: Evolution and Culture. Ann. Arbor: University of Michigan Press.

Sapir, E., Language, New York: Harcourt, Brace.

Schapera, I., 1947: Migrant Labour and Tribal Life. London: Oxford University Press.

Schmidt, W., 1933: High Gods in North America. Oxford: Clarendon Press.

Schmidt, W., 1939: The Culture Historical Method of Ethnology. New York: Fortunys.

Seligman, C.C. and B. Seligman, 1911: The Veddas. Cambridge: Cambridge University Press.

Singer, M., 1972: When a Great Tradition Modernises. Chicago.

Singer, M., 1975: Traditional India: Structure and Change. Chicago.

Srinivas, M.N., 1942: Marriage and Family in Mysore. Bombay: Asia Publishing House.

Srinivas, M.N., 1952: Religion and Society among Coorgs of South India. Bombay: Asia Publishing House.

Srinivas, M.N., 1962(a): Caste in Modern India. Berkeley: University of California.

Srinivas, M.N., 1962(b): Caste in Modern India and other Essays. Bombay: Asia Publishing House.

Srinivas, M.N., 1966: Social Change in Modern India. California: University of California Press.

Srinivas, M.N., 1976(a): The Remembered Villages. Berkeley: University of California.

Srinivas, M.N., 1976(b): Nation building in Independent India. Delhi: Oxford University Press.

Steward, J., 1955: Theory of Culture Change. Urbana: University of Illinois Press.

Tax, S., 1964(eds.): Horizons of Anthropology. Chicago: Aldine.

Taylor, S., 1956: Conceptions and the Theory of Knowledge. New Haven: Bookman Associate.

Teggart, F., 1941: Theory and Processes of History. Berkeley: University of California Press.

Tylor, E.B., 1861: Anahuac or Mexico and the Mexicans: Ancient and Modern. London: Longmans, Green, Longman and Roberts.

Tylor, E.B., 1865: Researches into Early History of Mankind and the Development of the Civilization. London: J. Murray.

Tylor, E.B., 1871: Primitive Culture: Researches into the Development of Mythology, Philosophy, Religion, Language, Art and Customs. London: J. Murray.

Tylor, E.B., 1881: Anthropology: An Introduction to the Study of Man and Civilization. New York: D. Appleton.

Vidyarthi, L.P., 1961: Sacred Complex in Hindu Gaya. Bombay: Asia Publishing House.

Vidyarthi, L.P., 1963: The Maler: Nature-Man-Spirit Complex in a Hill Tribe of Bihar. Calcutta: Bookland Private Limited.

Vidyarthi, L.P., 1964: Cultural Contour of Tribal Bihar. Calcutta: Punthi Pustak.

Vidyarthi, L.P., 1976: Tribal Culture of India. New Delhi: Concept Publishing Company.

Vidyarthi, L.P., 1977: Rise of Anthropology in India (Two Volumes). New Delhi: Concept Publishing Company.

Vidyarthi, L.P., 1980: Trends in World Anthropology. New Delhi: Concept Publishing Company.

Westermarck, E., 1891: The History of Human Marriage. New York: Macmillan.

White, Leslie, 1949: The Science of Culture: New York: Grove Press.

White, Leslie, 1959: The Evolution of Culture. New York: McGraw-Hill.

Wissler, C., 1917: The American Indian. An Introduction to the Anthropology of New World. New York: D.C. McMurtrie.

Wissler, C., 1926: The Relation of Nature to Man in Aboriginal America. New York: Oxford University Press.

Wissler, C., 1929: An Introduction to Social Anthropology. New York: Holt.

Wittfogel, K., 1931: Wirstchaft and Gasellschaft Chinas. Leipzeg.

Wittfogel, K., 1957: Oriental Despotism. New Haven: Yale University.

INDEX